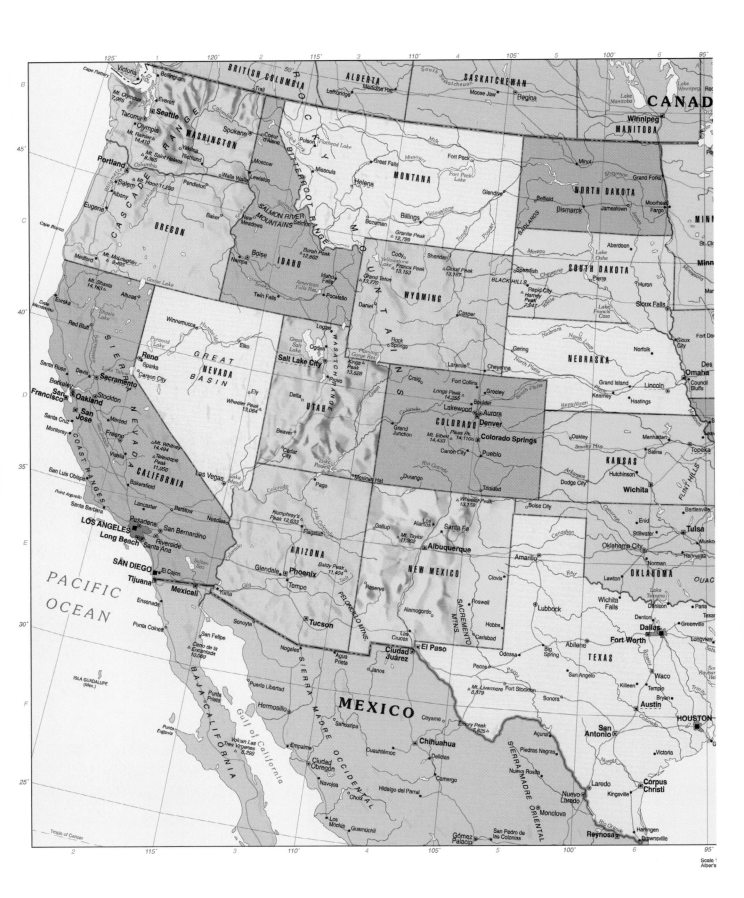

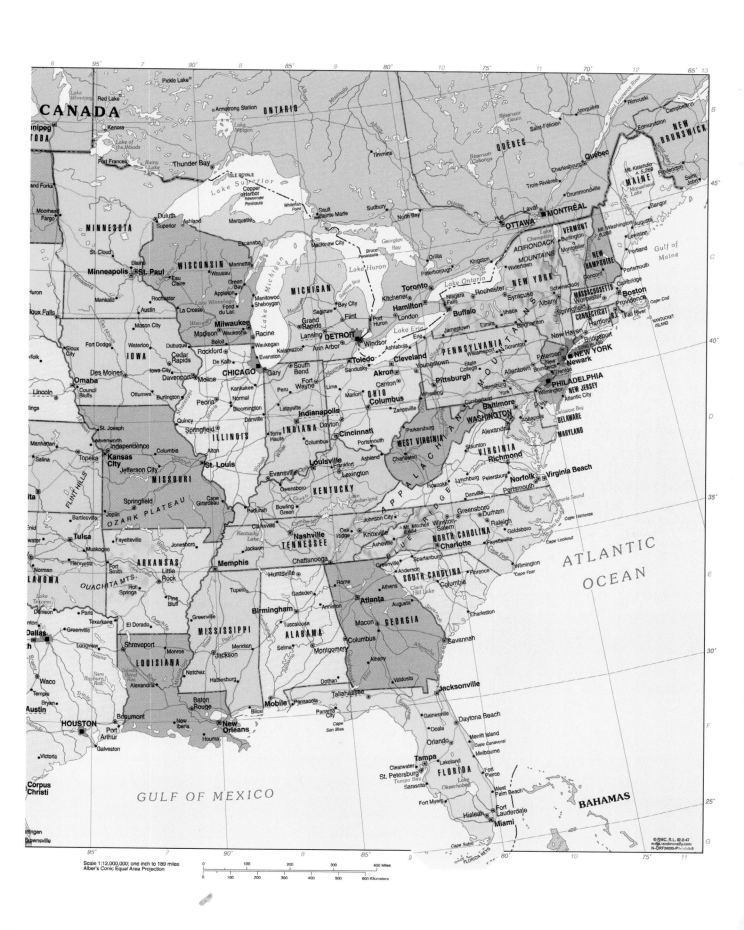

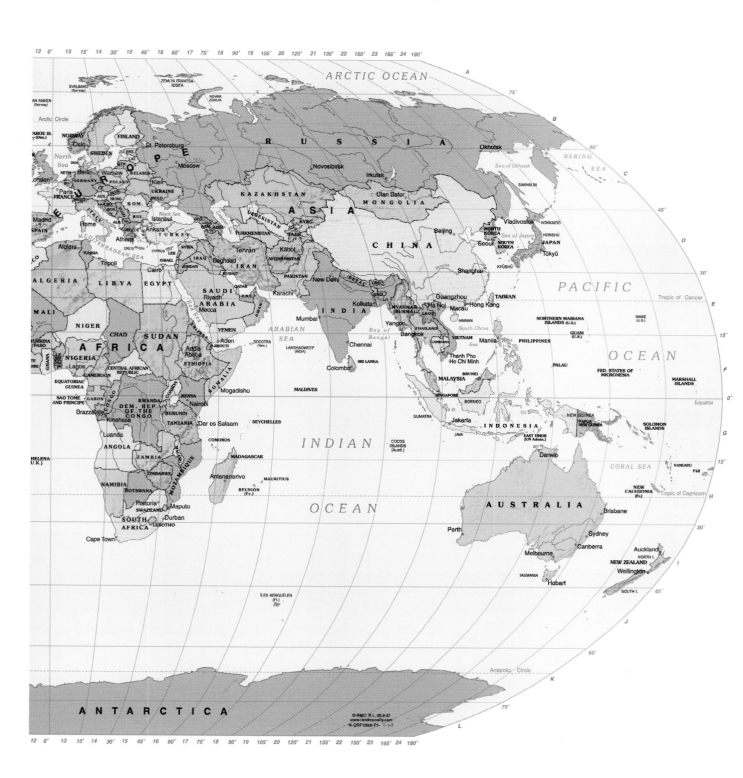

THIS LAND
A HISTORY OF THE UNITED STATES

THIS LAND

Brandywine Press • Maplecrest, New York

A History of the United States

PHILIP J. DELORIA
PATRICIA NELSON LIMERICK
JACK N. RAKOVE
DAVID BURNER

FIRST EDITION
VOLUME 2

Cover Illustration: Thomas Moran, *Cliffs of the Upper Colorado, Wyoming Territory*, 1882. (Courtesy, Smithsonian American Art Museum. Bequest of Henry Ward Ranger through the National Academy of Design)

Library of Congress Cataloguing in Publication Data

Main entry under title:

This Land

Includes bibliographical references and index.
1. United States—History. I. Burner, David,
1937–   II. Burner, David, 1937–   .
vol. 1, ISBN 1-881089-70-3
vol. 2, ISBN 1-881089-71-1
Combined edition, ISBN 1-881089-89-X

Telephone Orders: **1-800-345-1776**

PRINTED IN THE UNITED STATES OF AMERICA

First Printing 2003

Dedicated to
Thomas R. West

About the Authors...

PHIL DELORIA, an associate professor of history at the University of Michigan, earned his doctorate at Yale. A cultural historian of the nineteenth and twentieth centuries, he is a specialist in Native American history. His Yale University Press book, *Playing Indian*, won an outstanding book award from the Gustavus Myers Center for the Study of Human Rights. Phil is on the editorial board of the *Journal of American History* and won a National Endowment for the Humanities Fellowship. He has edited with Neal Salisbury *The Blackwell Companion to American Indian History.* One of his current projects is the Leonid meteor storm of 1833, which evoked a variety of responses: from slaves, Plains Indians, millennialists, Mormons, Philadelphia scientists, and peoples of the Mexican Southwest.

PATRICIA NELSON LIMERICK, the recipient of a MacArthur Award, was born in the West that she has observed for many years. She earned her doctorate at Yale. After teaching for several years at Harvard, she moved to the University of Colorado at Boulder. There she serves as chair of the Center of the American West, besides teaching a summer class on writing for entering freshmen of color. Ms Limerick is a past president of the Western History Association and the American Studies Association. Her books include *The Legacy of Conquest, Desert Passages,* and *Something in the Soil*; her current research project is entitled *The Atomic West.* She has held a fellowship from the American Council of Learned Societies.

JACK N. RAKOVE is Coe Professor of American Studies at Stanford. He earned his doctorate at Harvard, where he studied under Bernard Bailyn. His 1996 Knopf book, *Original Meanings,* won the Pulitzer Prize. His present research agenda is to complete a history of American polity from the late 1770s carrying through to the debates over the Constitution in the 1780s and culminating in the partisan conflicts of the 1790s. He has also published on James Madison, the Continental Congress, and the election of 2000.

DAVID BURNER, a professor of history at SUNY at Stony Brook, received his doctorate at Columbia, where he studied under Richard Hofstadter. He has held a Guggenheim Fellowship and was a Ford Fellow at Harvard. His early books, published by Knopf, are *The Politics of Provincialism* and *Herbert Hoover: A Public Life.* In 1996 he wrote *Making Peace with the Sixties* for Princeton University Press, and his *John F. Kennedy and a New Generation*, a Library of American Biography book, entered its second edition in 2003. He is currently writing a history of West Point.

About This Land...

Whatever else a history text may be, it ought to be a good story. The tale of European, African, Hispanic, and Asian Americans who have made their experimental way toward building something new on this generous land, often with terrible consequences for the continent's Native Americans, is rich material for many good stories.

In telling them, a history book should avoid biases that will distort, belittle, demonize, or bestow easy sainthood; and clarify, so far as that is possible, complex or bewildering forces. Yet bias of some kind is inevitable, and coming to terms with it gives history writing much of its energy. Even in deciding what is a major event or actor, a historian of necessity brings some degree of personal conviction. Should a text spend most of its time on elite figures, the George Washingtons and the Theodore Roosevelts who in their day and afterwards won the most public visibility, or should it stress ordinary workers and the unnamed poor? American historians have debated that question, and their debates reveal ideological commitments. This textbook goes on the assumption that good coverage requires a large inclusion of both the elite and the unnamed, and more particularly a full range of social history.

The authors have striven for the standard virtues and tried to avoid the predictable vices. They have their biases, but these they have attempted to control by examining carefully the claims of historical figures, political movements, and social forces with which they are not quickly sympathetic. However closely they have aimed for balance and judgment, though, they have brought to their subjects a full measure of passion. They feel passion enough toward the injustices that mark American history, from slavery through the government's support of repressive regimes abroad. Above all, they have enjoyed telling a story of the stumblings, the failures, the successes, the sweep and grandeur of the American past. The nation's story demands many tellings. Here is ours.

*   *   *

The authors have decided to repeat for Volume II not only the chapter on Reconstruction but that on the Civil War. The reason for this break with the usual practice for texts in American history is in part thematic. No period in history, of course, can be described as though it had no past. The story of Reconstruction, however, is especially truncated if presented in isolation from the great war that directly determined its detail and introduced many of the major actors: free slaves, white soldiers of both armies, black soldiers of the Union. Another purpose for repeating the chapter on the Civil War is to make a volume of use to instructors who will teach only the more recent part of American history and want to begin with the Civil War. It is even more critical to accommodate students who take only the second semester of the survey course. In an increasing number of states, all students in public institutions are required to take at least one course in American history, and on most campuses that is more likely to be the second semester. Including the Civil War gives that course a good beginning.

Philip J. Deloria
Patricia Nelson Limerick
Jack N. Rakove
David Burner

Contents

16 Raiding the Continent / 481

17 The Search for New Frontiers / 513

21 Hitting Bottom and Coming Back Up / 637

22 World War II and Its Prelude / 677

28 The End of Nature? / 861

Civil War Drum. *(Courtesy, Library of Congress)*

The Civil War

★

SOUTHERN HONOR: A CAUSE OF THE CIVIL WAR?

In 1861 a few months after the Civil War began, the passionate Mississippi secessionist L. Q. C. Lamar wrote to his friend Mary Chesnut about what he believed to have been a defining moment in the clash between North and South: the caning of Charles Sumner in 1856 on the Senate floor by Representative Preston Brooks of South Carolina. Had Sumner "stood on his manhood" and fought back, Lamar declared, the incident would not have been the "opening skirmish" of the war to come.

In sneering at Sumner's failure to return the blows, no consideration was given to his having been stunned and physically unable to strike back. But Lamar expressed a view common in the South: that northerners were weaklings, unfit to be fellow citizens with the proud and gallant southerners. The spirit of the South, according to rebels, lay in dash and boldness. In September 1861 the *Richmond Examiner* pronounced "altogether unsuited to the genius of our people" a defensive strategy of merely waiting for northern assault and meeting northern attacks; the true way of the South was to go on the offensive.

Nations at the beginning of a war customarily bluster. But the comments of Lamar and the *Examiner* cannot be dismissed as normal bragging. They conform, rather, to what one historian has identified as a southern concept of honor. Honor is an ethos going back countless centuries that seeks not private, interior virtues but public approval. That approval is sought in visible acts inspiring admiration, such as dueling or valor in war: actions that uphold community values and traditions. The man or woman of honor fears shame, which amounts to looking bad in the sight of neighbors. "It was threat of honor lost, no less than slavery, that led [the

South] to secession and war," explains Bertram Wyatt-Brown in his examination of the concept of southern honor.

From the point of view of a more inward morality, the quest for honor and the shrinking from shame can appear cowardly. A southern seeker after honor may, for example, go with a lynch mob rather than stand against it, for the mob is enacting the tradition and the collective judgment of the community, and the dissenter will seem a traitor to these. Southern documents of the years before the Civil War reveal an obsession with reputation, with how the individual will look to others. (Sumner, lying defenseless and half-conscious on the floor of the Senate, looked bad.)

In the North, meanwhile, religion and morality combined to produce a different kind of character, more inward turning, more given to self-questioning. The Civil War displayed plenty of aggressive gallantry on both sides, of the kind that southerners thought belonged to them alone. But in the end, qualities of quiet endurance, patience with a seemingly unending war, a willingness to accept one defeat after another and plod on to the next engagement probably counted more toward defining the outcome of the conflict.

HISTORICAL EVENTS

1859
John Brown's raid at Harpers Ferry

1860
Lincoln's speech at Cooper Union • Abraham Lincoln elected president

1861
Eleven southern states secede from the Union • Jefferson Davis becomes president of the Confederacy • Charleston, South Carolina, batteries fire on Fort Sumter • first battle of Bull Run (Manassas) • *Trent* Affair

1862
Homestead Act • Morrill Land Grant Act • Peninsular Campaign • battles of Shiloh, Second Bull Run, Antietam, and Fredericksburg • Lincoln suspends writ of *habeas corpus*

• Emancipation Proclamation issued to take effect January 1, 1863

1863
Battles of Chancellorsville, Gettysburg, Fort Wagner and Chickamauga • anti-black draft riots in New York City

1864
Ulysses Grant given command of all Union armies • battles of Fort Pillow, Cold Harbor, and Petersburg

1864–1865
General Sherman's march through Georgia and the Carolinas

1865
Grant takes Richmond • General Lee surrenders at Appomattox Courthouse

THE LAST DAYS OF PEACE

In 1857, four years before secession, proud southerners had cause to think that the future was theirs. What especially gave them such confidence was the Supreme Court's ruling that year in the *Dred Scott* case, in which the Court rejected the claim of Scott, a slave, that his residence with his master in a free territory had freed him from slavery. Earlier in that decade the Kansas-Nebraska Act, which adopted Stephen A. Douglas's doctrine of popular sovereignty, had served the South by opening up to the possibility of slavery a great stretch of land north of the old Missouri Compromise line. All that slaveholders needed was for the voters of Kansas territory to choose slavery. But now the slave power had in *Dred Scott* something even better, much better. As entities under federal control, territories had to permit slavery, regardless of what the voters there wanted. Southerners could now brush aside their one-time friend Douglas. Even more pleasing in their view, surely, was the Court's absolute identification of slavery with property. Slavery was not merely a social system that could be defended, attacked, or modified on the basis of its practical effects. No, slaves were property; slaveholders had fundamental rights of ownership in them exempt from federal interference. The implications loomed particularly large, angering Republicans and delighting proslavery Democrats: that *Dred Scott* might point the way toward requiring even the northern free states to allow slavery within their boundaries. The Court did not explicitly say so—it relied in the ruling on the Fifth Amendment, which restricts only federal as opposed to state seizures of property. But in fixing firmly on slaves the condition of property, Chief Justice Taney's Court made it look as though from the instant the free states forbade slavery, they had violated venerable and perhaps legally binding traditions of private ownership. And to their ideological victory, southern cotton growers added what they perceived as an economic triumph. A severe depression in the North in 1857 spared the cotton states. That, defenders of slavery claimed, proved the superior health of southern institutions.

A Prophet at Harpers Ferry

The year 1857 brought southerners gratification in *Dred Scott*. In 1858, however, came a danger they could not yet recognize, the elevation of Abraham Lincoln to national prominence through his debates with Stephen Douglas in their Illinois senatorial campaign. Another danger was more readily apparent: Republican midterm victories that took the lower House out of the control of the proslavery Democratic administration of President James Buchanan. And the following year gave the slave power additional reason to believe that it faced in abolitionism an enemy that would never accept peaceable relations with it.

John Brown, the fiery abolitionist who in Kansas had executed five proslavery men, has been captured particularly well in a daguerreotype taken in that year of 1859: a craggy, humorless face, eyes for which the adjective "piercing" is not a cliché. Utterly committed to a religion rooted in the prophetic grimness of the Old Testament, Brown continued to seek in violence the answer to slavery. With support from six prominent northern aboli-

Daguerreotype of John Brown taken by Augustus Washington. (Courtesy, National Portrait Gallery, Smithsonian Institution)

tionists, the "Secret Six," he devised the plan of sparking a slave rebellion in the southern Appalachian Mountains. On October 16, 1859, he and twenty companions, five of them black, carrying rifles, seized the lightly defended federal arsenal at Harpers Ferry, now in West Virginia but then a Virginia town, and took several hostages. In fighting the next day with Virginia and Maryland militia along with residents of the town, ten of the revolutionary band died, two of Brown's sons among them. Then a force of federal marines led by Colonel Robert E. Lee stormed the fire-engine house that had become a fortress for the insurrectionists. Two more of the defenders were killed and seven captured, including Brown.

The state of Virginia sentenced Brown and the other six to be hanged. Brown's turn came on December 2. Sitting atop his own coffin, he was driven in a wagon to his place of execution, the parade grounds on the outskirts of Richmond. Throughout his imprisonment, he had conducted himself with such firm conviction in the rightness of his cause that the governor of Virginia called him "the gamest man I ever saw." His memory became an object of southern rage, while northern abolitionists sang:

John Brown's body lies a-mould'ring in
  the grave,
But his soul goes marching on.

The music the song was set to would soon carry the words of the great *Battle Hymn of the Republic.* John Brown, in death, had provided the abolitionists with an anthem. And in his last hour, as he fearlessly neared the gallows, he handed a note to one of the soldiers escorting him. It read: "I, John Brown, am now convinced that the sins of this guilty land shall never be purged but by blood." Ralph Waldo Emerson predicted that Brown would "make the gallows as glorious as the cross."

The Last Year of the Old Union

The rapidity with which opinions had hardened on all sides of the slavery issue is well illustrated by a set of resolutions that Jefferson Davis of Mississippi introduced in the Senate in early February 1860. They declared, among other things, that neither Congress nor a territorial administration could interfere with slaveholding, which must be pro-

tected by the federal government. Only when a territory was moving formally toward statehood could it decide whether to exclude slavery. In May, the Senate adopted the Davis resolutions, a propaganda victory for the South. Southerners now saw Stephen Douglas as the enemy. The Supreme Court had declared slaveholding to be a fundamental property right; to allow a majority in a territory, therefore, to vote against that right, as Douglas's doctrine of popular sovereignty ordained, amounted to war against the South. The Republicans, like southerners, dismissed the concept of popular sovereignty but for entirely different reasons. While the South in the wake of *Dred Scott* insisted that no new territorial government could ban slavery, the Republicans with equal insistence demanded that no such territory be allowed to permit it. And there remained a substantial body of voters and leaders who simply wanted the whole slavery controversy somehow to go away. These divisions now determined party alignments in a turbulent and badly fractured political system.

Meeting in Chicago that year to select its presidential candidate, the robust young Republican Party sifted among various aspirants. At first William H. Seward of New York had the largest backing. But after two inconclusive ballots, the delegates turned to Abraham Lincoln of Illinois, famous for the Lincoln-Douglas debates of 1858, and since then a dynamic Republican orator. Lincoln firmly supported the party's stand against slavery in the territories. But on the larger questions of human bondage and race relations, he remained cautious and elusive, making his presidential candidacy less threatening to voters hostile to pressing antislavery militancy any further. The party platform concentrated on economic questions only obliquely related to the issue of slavery but more pleasing to the North than to the South. It called for a homestead law inviting settlement by farmers in lands owned by the federal government. That would mean, though the platform did not say so, that the trans-Mississippi West was to be populated by small farmers rather than large planters. The Republicans also proposed federal aid for constructing a transcontinental railroad and improving rivers and harbors. The platform hinted as well at a protective tariff, which would be against the economic interest of much of the South that preferred to trade its cotton internationally in return for cheaper manufactures from abroad. The Republicans, in sum, had

Abraham Lincoln and Stephen Douglas dominated the 1860 election. Douglas toured the South in 1861, trying to prevent the outbreak of war. (Courtesy, Museum of American Political Life)

adopted an essentially northern program, looking to northern settlement of the West, protection of northern industry, and a railroad that could transport goods back and forth between northern industry and western agriculture. The platform's combination of economic and social programs even allowed Republican speakers to play on northern race prejudice, to envision a West settled by white homesteaders and free of the presence of both planters and their legions of slaves. And at the same time the Republicans suggested enough genuine moral opposition to slavery that abolitionists looking for the best party available to them could be attracted to the Republicans.

The Democrats were hopelessly split between Douglas and his followers, who stuck to the principle of popular sovereignty, and partisans of slavery who now despised the Douglas program nearly as much as they hated the Republicans. The party leaders might have chosen to hold their early spring national convention on relatively neutral ground. Instead they picked Charleston, South Carolina, the leading city in a militantly proslavery state. Southern delegates demanded that the party affirm the property rights of slaveowners throughout the territories. When the convention instead seemed to be heading toward Douglas's position, the delegates from eight slave states withdrew. The convention puttered on for a time, then adjourned. In June the Douglas Democrats held their own convention in Baltimore, nominating their leader. Democrats who wanted slavery protected throughout the territories met in the same city later that same month and nominated John C. Breckinridge of Kentucky.

A few national leaders attempted to restore some semblance of normality to politics. The Whig Party, which had once stretched across both North and South, still had adherents. Together with members of the anti-immigrant American Party, they met in Baltimore to form the Constitutional Union Party, on a platform that urged nothing much more specific than support of the Constitution and the Union. Its presidential nominee was John Bell of Tennessee. The age of the party's leaders earned it the label of "Silver Grays."

The results of the presidential vote in November fell cleanly along sectional lines. Lincoln won 1,866,000 popular votes, fewer than forty percent of the total, yet carried eighteen free states for a huge majority in the Electoral College. Douglas came second in the popular ballot, gaining under thirty percent, but taking only Missouri and three

The Political Quadrille. This cartoon portrays the four presidential candidates from 1860. Clockwise: John C. Breckinridge, Abraham Lincoln, John Bell, and Stephen A. Douglas. All dance to a tune played by Dred Scott, indicating the importance of slavery in the election. (Courtesy, Library of Congress)

electoral seats from New Jersey. Breckinridge won just eighteen percent of the vote at the polls, but his victory in eleven slave states gave him over five times the number of electors garnered by Douglas. Bell's appeal lay chiefly in the border states that supported slavery but not the fire-eating militancy so widespread in the Deep South. In this bizarre election, Bell earned the smallest share of the popular vote but took more seats in the Electoral College than Douglas. The Republicans, besides gaining the presidency, won commanding majorities in both the Senate and the House of Representatives.

Right after the election, South Carolina decided that the North, the region that was sending Lincoln to the Executive Mansion, had become the irreconcilable foe of southern slavery. In December a convention called by the state legislature declared South Carolina's secession from the Union. And whatever turn events might take thereafter, it was clear that the United States would no longer be the nation that had now existed under the Constitution for over seven decades.

POLITICS YIELDS TO WAR

For the first half of the nineteenth century, it was customary to refer to "the United States" in the plural, indicating a collection of separate states ("the

United States *are* prospering; *they* have a thriving agriculture"). People debated whether the country constituted a single republic or a league of sovereign states, each free to withdraw from the arrangement. And even among Americans convinced that the United States made up one indivisible nation, the question remained of what the Constitution permitted the federal government to do if the people of a state decided to secede.

Secession Spreads

One after another, southern states followed South Carolina's example and announced their withdrawal from the Union. The lame-duck Democratic president, James Buchanan, was stuck with the problem until early March 1861, when Lincoln would take over. Buchanan denied that states had any right of secession, but also contended that he could find no way of stopping it. This position, said the leading Republican politician William Seward, amounted to announcing that the president had the duty to enforce the laws unless anyone objected. But Buchanan faced a real dilemma. Not since President Andrew Jackson faced down South Carolina's attempt in the early 1830s to nullify federal law had there been any situation remotely like the crisis of 1861. And that earlier confrontation had involved only marginally the threat of secession.

By February 1, 1861, a band of seven states in

The American eagle screams "ANNIHILATION TO TRAITORS" as it hovers over slimy secessionist states being hatched while a copperhead snake prepares to strike at the national symbol. (Courtesy, Library of Congress)

the lower South, stretching from Florida and South Carolina through Texas, considered themselves out of the Union. Later that month a convention of the seceded states meeting in Montgomery, Alabama, came together in a new union, the Confederate States of America, with a constitution modeled in great part on that of 1787. As its provisional president, the Confederacy chose Jefferson Davis, a lean, fair-haired pragmatic southerner who had been trained at West Point. For the moment, the slave states of North Carolina, Virginia, Tennessee, and Arkansas chose to stay within the old Union, but

they also opposed any federal effort to subdue the states that had seceded.

First Days of a President

Lincoln's journey to Washington for his inauguration fell under a shadow. In response to rumors of a plan to assassinate him, he was hustled secretly by bodyguards into the nation's capital at night by train from Baltimore. That humiliating entrance of the president-elect into the city that housed the government he would soon head added one more

Jefferson Davis. The president of the Confederacy was a graduate of West Point and had served as secretary of war under President Franklin Pierce. (Courtesy, Library of Congress)

indication that the old Union no longer had much force or presence.

The new president inherited Buchanan's dilemma: how to preserve the Union by use of the resources at the government's disposal. The difference between the two was that Lincoln showed less interest in the formal constitutional question of what the federal government had the authority to do. Shortly after his assumption of the presidency, he would demonstrate a willingness to employ whatever forces he could muster. His more practical problem was to determine just what those forces were. And he had to move carefully: as of the day of his inauguration, March 4, 1861, eight slave states remained in the Union, and anything looking like coercion of the already seceded states might well drive others to join the Confederacy.

Could an understanding be reached with the seceded and the wavering states? Lincoln's inaugural address expressed the hope that "the sacred chords of memory, stretching from every battle-

field, and patriot grave . . . will yet swell the chorus of the Union. . . ." As a gesture of conciliation, the address promised no interference with slavery where it already existed. But that mild concession to the South did not address the demand of the southern militants that the territories be opened to slavery. The previous December, while still only president-elect, Lincoln had rejected the proposal of John J. Crittenden of Kentucky to recognize slavery in the territories south of the old Missouri Compromise line of 36°30'.

William Seward, Lincoln's newly-appointed secretary of state, made certainly the most bizarre proposal yet to come from a holder of that office. To reunify the country, he suggested, the new administration should go the length of threatening war on Spain and France over their apparent designs in the West Indies. Lincoln ignored the idea. The device he himself hit upon, in anticipation of the possible use of armed force, was to put the secessionists in the position of being the aggressors. That way he might be able to convince the slave states still in the Union that the federal government had not chosen to make war. Essentially, his plan was not to send troops south to attack the Confederacy directly but rather to secure the federal installations that be-

The unannounced arrival of president-elect Lincoln. (Courtesy, Library of Congress)

longed to the Union. What this amounted to was to say to the secessionists, in effect though not in words: fly what flags you want, give yourselves what official titles you wish, but do not take yourselves seriously enough to interfere with the real business and holdings of the Union.

Actually, even this approach was already compromised. In the last months of the Buchanan administration, secessionists had seized a number of federal arsenals. Lincoln, however, could ignore that; part of his political genius was an ability to decide what was essential and what could be overlooked. One important military post did remain: Fort Sumter, in the harbor of Charleston, South Carolina. Its commander, Major Robert Anderson, came from Kentucky, a southern state in which a majority of the people was to remain with the Union. Anderson ranked among the prominent southern officers in the Union military. On April 6, 1861, Lincoln informed the South Carolina authorities that he was sending provisions to Sumter, which was running out of supplies. He thereby forced on the secessionists a critical choice: either accept the continuance of a federal post on territory that they claimed as their own, or go to war. South Carolina chose war. On April 12 state artillerymen began shelling Sumter from the shore. After nearly a day and a half of pounding during which the fort's garrison had no means of retaliation, Anderson surrendered. Lincoln, hoping that the rebellion could be disposed of quickly, called upon the states to provide seventy-five thousand militiamen for ninety days of federal service to put down what he described as a major insurrection against the Union. These would supplement the small regular army already in existence.

The War Begins

The immediate result of the federal government's new determination was disastrous. Four slave states that had remained tentatively in the Union so long as Washington took no action against their fellow southerners joined the Confederacy: Virginia, Arkansas, Tennessee, and North Carolina. In May the rebels moved their capital from Montgomery, Alabama, to Richmond, Virginia, which meant that for the duration of the war much of the fighting was to be on the terrain less than two hundred miles long between Richmond and Washington, D.C. Only four slave states remained in the Union. Of

the four, Delaware had only vestiges of slavery within its borders. In Maryland, Kentucky, and Missouri, the other three, strong secessionist sentiment confronted Unionists.

In Maryland late in April, this persuasion took the form of a riot in Baltimore against Massachusetts troops on their way to join the forces that were gathering in Washington. Four soldiers and twelve civilians died and many times that number suffered wounds. The song in use today as Maryland's official anthem contains references torn from their original meaning:

> The despot's heel is on thy shore,
> Maryland, my Maryland!
> His torch is at thy temple door,
> Maryland, my Maryland!
> Avenge the patriotic gore
> That flecked the streets of Baltimore,
> And be the battle queen of yore,
> Maryland, my Maryland!

"Patriotic gore" refers to the blood of the rioters shed that April day; the "despot" is the Union or Lincoln himself, and the song was asking Maryland to join the Confederacy.

In the national memory of the Civil War, battlefield fighting is customarily thought of as beginning with the first Battle of Bull Run in eastern Virginia on July 21, 1861, when the rebels won an important victory against federal troops. But much serious shooting preceded Bull Run, on the whole to the advantage of the Union.

Early in 1861, Missouri's governor attempted to lead that state into the Confederacy. But by the end of spring, a little over two months before Bull Run, federal troops and Missouri Unionists had for the moment bested the secessionists. That summer, Confederate forces temporarily took over much of the state. But they did not keep together as a coherent army, and over the course of the war, most Missourians in uniform supported the state's makeshift Unionist administration. At the same time there existed a rival secessionist government in Missouri, and rebel guerrillas conducted raids against the Unionists. Numbered among these Confederate partisans were Jesse and Frank James and the Younger brothers, now better known by far for their criminal exploits after the war.

In Kentucky too, secession failed. During the first months of the war, Kentuckians organized themselves into both Unionist and secessionist militias but without fighting of the kind that bloodied Missouri. Most Kentuckians stayed loyal to the Union, though like Missouri the state would have an alternative shadow government as well. The stunningly impressive Confederate battle flag—a red field setting off a white-trimmed blue cross with white stars—contained thirteen stars instead of eleven, for on the basis of the secessionist minority factions in Missouri and Kentucky, the rebels had ranked both these states as Confederate.

The secessionist states bordering the Union had their own problems of dissent. In the mountains of eastern Tennessee and western North Carolina, loyalty to the Union abounded. One explanation is that hill folk had long looked on the affluent planters of the lowlands as monopolizing power and privilege. And while slavery existed also in the hills, it was not a strong enough part of the economy to make its defense appear urgent. In mountainous western Virginia, feeling ran strong for a reverse secession—a separation from the rest of the state. Midwestern militia called into federal service and commanded by George B. McClellan, William S. Rosecrans, and Jacob D. Cox moved into the region to join with local Unionists. Before the end of June, the outnumbered Confederate forces were on the defensive; and by mid-July, Union troops had chased them out of much of northwestern Virginia. In 1863 West Virginia become a separate state mandating an early end to slavery.

First Battle of Bull Run

With the secession of the four additional slave states, the first months of armed confrontation between the Union and the Confederacy after Fort Sumter brought a grave political and strategic reversal to the federal cause. Then on July 21, Washington received one of the worst shocks of the war.

On his authority he wielded as commander-in-chief, Lincoln had called the various state militias into federal service. From Minnesota came soldiers clad in black trousers and red shirts; from Wisconsin, Iowa, and Vermont, varieties of gray. New York militia, calling themselves Zouaves, sported uniforms fashioned after the military clothing of the original Zouaves, Algerian soldiers under French command: red fezzes and billowing trousers. Added to the regular career army, these made up the troops that Abraham Lincoln had on hand: units of volunteers who had perhaps expected nothing from militia service but fellowship, drilling, and uniforms.

Full of confidence, a Union army under General Irvin McDowell set out to attack Confederate troops commanded by Generals P. T. G. Beauregard and Joseph E. Johnston at Manassas Junction in Virginia. In the course of the day, something like eighteen thousand soldiers in each army entered the battle at Bull Run, a few miles from Manassas. For hours, men on each side hammered one another with a courage that they could not have acquired from hard training or battlefield experience, for they had neither. Confusion in identifying uniforms aided the secessionists. In one sector, Union artillery pounding the rebels held its fire while soldiers in blue entered the field. But these were rebels, and once they were in place they pummeled their opponents. Also contributing to the Confederate victory that day was a brigade of Virginia troops under the brilliant, cranky religious zealot, General Thomas J. Jackson, a former professor at the Virginia Military Institute. At one point, his steadfastness prompted a fellow general to exclaim something like "There is Jackson standing like a stone wall" and urge his own rattled men to rally to Jackson's Virginians. Jackson's troops remained steady in breaking a federal assault, and thereafter he became known as "Stonewall" Jackson. In the course of the day, some slight shift in fortunes could have cracked the green yet plucky soldiers of either side, but by the end of the battle, the exhausted Union forces broke. The rout not only sent them in flight but scattered the sightseers from nearby Washington who had come to picnic and watch a Union victory. The Battle of Bull Run or Manassas, as the rebels called it, humiliated the North and deepened the conviction among secessionists that southerners could thrash any number of northern soldiers.

SETTLING IN FOR A LONG WAR

Lincoln now knew for certain that reunion would require not a few skirmishes and some negotiation but a hard-fought road to victory. Just after Bull Run, he signed two bills that together authorized him to enlist a million volunteers for a three-year term of service. For fighting a long war, the Union had a population of twenty-two million, the Confederacy nine million, over a third of them slaves. The slaves counted; their labor freed white men for military service. The Union states together had a diverse economy, and the Northeast was highly advanced industrially. The Confederacy had a few large ironworks quickly converted to arms manufacture. Much of its agriculture was in subsistence farming, in which families grow food mostly for their own consumption. It also had a range of agricultural products for trade abroad. For a time southern leaders mistakenly hoped that the British and continental European powers, craving cotton for their textile industries, would seek an alliance with Richmond and move to break the federal blockade.

The war, as Lincoln defined it, aimed to defend freedom. In retrospect, it is easy to assume that he meant from the beginning freeing the slaves, but in 1861 he meant no such thing. The freedom he had in mind was that of republican institutions offering civil liberties and government officials elected by popular vote. At that time much of the world still viewed republics, beyond the city-state boundaries of ancient and later times, as dangerous experiments. Between 1789 and the 1860s France, for example, had lived successively under a republic, an imperial regime under Napoleon, a restored monarchy, a second republic, and another emperor, Napoleon III. And the republics on the American continent south of the United States looked unstable. Were republics inherently weak, it was wondered, unable to survive under the corroding influences of political freedom and popular elections? If the Confederate rebellion succeeded, skeptics would have additional evidence that a republican government on the French or the American model could not endure. So Lincoln determined to show that government could be at once free and democratic (even if only for whites) and strong enough to put down a major insurrection. Not until circumstances changed would the president be able to extend his vision beyond preserving the freedoms of the old Union and look to making black Americans free as well.

Because the federal government operated on the assumption that secession was illegal, it might have treated every Confederate prisoner as a criminal suspect, entitled to trial by jury and subject to punishment that could include execution. But Lincoln, always prepared to go for substance over technical detail, chose to ignore such matters. Despite the illegality of secession, the Confederate army clearly met the norms for soldiers: uniforms, chains of command, and all the rest. The Union leaders decided, wisely, to live with a contradiction: to treat captives as prisoners of war, as though they had fought as troops of a legitimate government.

The Union Command

Winfield Scott, a leading general in the Mexican War, at the war's beginning held overall command of the Union army, second only to Lincoln as commander-in-chief. Scott was a Virginian, and another southerner who stood by the United States against the secessionists. Though infirm, he was able to plan the Union's overarching military strategy, which critics derisively named the Anaconda plan after a snake that coils around its prey. It called for blockading the southern coast, seizing the Mississippi, and thereby pinching off the eastern Confederacy from the outside world. Given the superiority of the North in men and production, it was a sensible strategy. To it Washington would add several invasions of the South. Lincoln replaced McDowell, who had conducted the troops at Bull Run, with George McClellan, whose task required drilling recruits and turning them into a seasoned military force. Upon Scott's retirement near the end of 1861, McClellan took his place. By 1862 Union officers in the West included Ulysses S. Grant and George H.

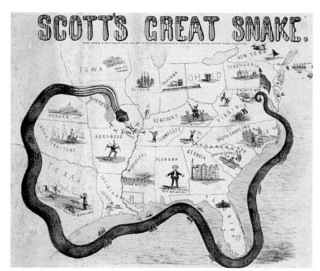

The elderly General Winfield Scott's "Anaconda Plan" was well thought out, shutting down the Confederate economy; his strategy would ultimately prevail. (Courtesy, Library of Congress)

Thomas of Virginia, another southerner who stayed with the old republic.

The War in the West

The West, laced with river systems that offer control of large reaches of land, continued to be the more promising theater of war for the Union. The largest, of course, was the Mississippi. But the Tennessee, cutting though that state on its way northward to the Ohio, provided a route for federal forces into the Deep South; and the nearby Cumberland, another tributary of the Ohio, offered a water pathway to Nashville, the capital of Tennessee. Two Confederate posts just within the northern border of Tennessee were essential to southern control of the river system: Fort Henry on the Tennessee River, and Fort Donelson on the Cumberland. In February Union troops took both. Later that month, Nashville fell.

These successes, important in themselves, also brought attention to an officer who later proved indispensable to Union victory. Ulysses S. Grant, a veteran of the Mexican War, had afterward resigned his commission and pursued business enterprises in his native state of Ohio. But the disease of alcoholism that had damaged his military career continued to assail him, and in commerce he went nowhere. Then the Civil War drew him back into military service and largely stopped his heavy drinking. His determination and coolness during the Tennessee campaign, during which the Union captured much of the state, was one sign of his readiness to take on the larger responsibilities he would eventually assume.

The climax of that campaign came in April 1862, at Shiloh church near the Tennessee River not far from the state's southern border. The total number of Union and Confederate troops in or near the battle came to nearly a hundred thousand. The secessionists were under the command of Albert Sidney Johnston and, after he was fatally wounded, General Beauregard. During the engagement, Union and rebel officers alike had the task of holding together troops disorganized in the fighting, and desertions shrank the numbers on both sides.

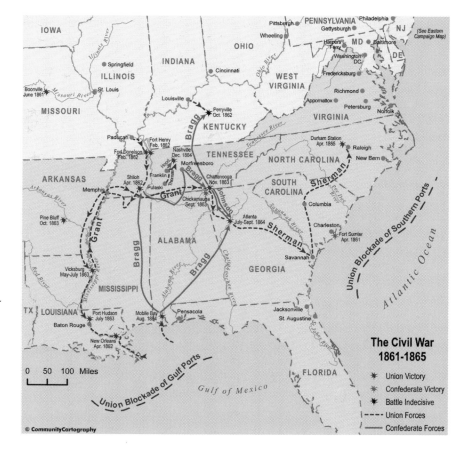

Union strategy involved blockading southern ports, splitting the Confederacy by gaining control of the Mississippi River Valley, and capturing Richmond. Confederate strategy included defending the South from attack, breaking the Union blockade, and splitting the Union by gaining control of Washington, D.C., Maryland, and central Pennsylvania.

William Tecumseh Sherman distinguished himself by his energy in rallying one unit after another of his unseasoned Union troops in the face of ferocious Confederate attacks. The Tennessee campaign thereby brought recognition to another major leader in the war's later stages. Grant's aggressiveness showed itself toward the end of the fight, when his forces had taken a bad pounding and some of his officers advised retreat before a rebel attack expected the following morning. Instead, the next day he and his troops assaulted the Confederate forces, startled to discover that their supposedly beaten foe had gone on the offensive. The Confederates had to withdraw, and Grant ultimately received credit for a substantial success. Lincoln, dismayed by the caution of other officers, saw in Grant what he was looking for. The Union had now become the dominant power in the strategically vital Mississippi Valley.

The Peninsular Campaign

Lincoln had reason to be frustrated at caution, chiefly that of George McClellan, whom the president had appointed as the overall commander of the Union armies. McClellan, born to a prosperous Philadelphia family and educated in private schools and at West Point, had about him an air of success. A Mexican War veteran and in private life a railroad executive, in 1861 he received the commission of major general in the Union armies. He believed himself altogether superior to Lincoln, whom he described as "no more than a well meaning baboon," and at least once this attitude found expression in an act of outright insolence. One evening Lincoln came to McClellan's home to speak to him, but the general declined to meet with his president and commander-in-chief, and simply went to bed. A Democrat who had no love of slavery but did not care to overturn southern institutions, he wanted, like Lincoln, a war that would bring the seceded states back into the Union on moderate terms. He also preferred drill and careful maneuvering to battle. His hesitancy in moving against the rebels impelled Lincoln to demote him, giving him command only over the Army of the Potomac and ordering him to advance upon Richmond.

In carrying out Lincoln's orders, McClellan chose not to move more directly southward but to go by way of the peninsula between the York and the James River in eastern Virginia. The Confederate defenders were led first by Joseph E. Johnston and then by Robert E. Lee, who had waged an unsuccessful campaign against Union forces in western

Lincoln's cabinet. The three most important are seated from the left: Secretary of State William H. Seward, Secretary of the Treasury Salmon P. Chase, and Secretary of War Edwin M. Stanton. (Courtesy, Corbis)

Virginia. But McClellan did not pursue his objective with any energy. Overestimating the numbers of enemy troops arrayed against him, he demanded that Washington send him reinforcements. That the president could not do, for he believed he needed them to protect the capital. Nor did McClellan require any more troops than he had. Outraged at the failure of the administration to give him what he wanted, the general allowed himself to go on the defensive, and after an engagement of seven days from late June into early July, the whole peninsula venture ended. Among officers prominent in the fighting on the Confederate side was the cavalryman J. E. B. (Jeb) Stuart.

That spring the Union encountered a danger from another quarter, Stonewall Jackson's successful campaign in the Shenandoah Valley of Virginia. Jackson's ingenious victories at a time when Lincoln and his secretary of war were making policy decisions created a menace even to the nation's capital, and required the diversion of Union troops. Toward the end of August Lincoln had to absorb more bad news, this time from the scene of the first major Union defeat more than a year earlier. General John Pope, who expected to be joined by McClellan on an inland route to Richmond, attacked Stonewall Jackson's troops near Bull Run, unaware that the Confederate general James Longstreet with his soldiers was stationed close by. The result was the Second Battle of Bull Run, in which the rebels drove the federal army from the field.

FIGHTING THE NAVAL AND DIPLOMATIC WAR

Over the battlefields of the American war hovered the shadow of Europe. The Confederacy hoped avidly that Britain, France, or some other European power would grant it diplomatic recognition as an independent nation; the Union dreaded that same prospect. Such recognition by one or more foreign countries would have mocked the claim of the federal government that the supposedly seceded states were still inseparably part of the United States, and would have defined the federal military campaign as an unjust war of conquest against a sovereign neighbor. Another and more immediately practical matter appeared to threaten the Union while enticing the Confederacy. The blockade of the South's coast, a component of the Anaconda strategy designed by Winfield Scott, aimed at strangling the Confederate economy. But if Britain in its hunger for southern cotton decided to break the blockade by force, the South would have acquired at once a military alliance with a foreign power and a widened access to needed commodities.

Cotton was the practical lure that might have drawn Britain to the Confederacy, that and the consideration that the splitting of the Union would weaken a young and growing power possibly competitive in time to the United Kingdom. France had its own reasons to wish for a disintegration of the United States. Emperor Napoleon III sought to establish in Mexico a regime that would turn the country effectively into a possession of the French empire. The United States could certainly be expected to oppose such a scheme. The sundering of a strong republic into two weaker nations would be to the advantage of the French. During the war the Confederacy and the emperor flirted with the idea of French recognition of the Confederacy and perhaps aid in breaking the Union blockade in return for southern cotton and support of France's designs on Mexico.

Especially in the case of Britain, ideology was also in play. The British were quick to sympathize with any movement for independence, such as southern secession, not directed against their own empire. Balanced against that consideration was the matter of slavery. Not even social conservatives in Britain and continental Europe wished to give comfort to that system. In spending the first year of the war ducking the issue of slavery, for he wished to maintain the loyalty of the border slave states, Lincoln made it easier for supporters of southern independence to ignore the question. By 1863 and Lincoln's Emancipation Proclamation, it was becoming clearer that a Union victory would bring abolition, and a Confederate triumph the continuance of slavery. That did not kill off British sympathy for the rebels, but made it more awkward. Historians continue to speculate over whether the majority of working-class British wanted the South to succeed—the economic interests of the Lancashire textile workers lay with cotton—or responded to the moral claims of abolition, defining slaveowners as enemies of labor. In public demonstrations, some portions of the British labor force did explicitly side with the Union, and others with the Confederacy. Ideology added, though only in a minor way, to the mixture of motives that might sway London to help the Confederacy or to shun it.

Neither Britain nor France, in any event, ventured to recognize the Confederacy and risk war with the United States unless a rebel victory looked to be an unclouded certainty. More than once that victory seemed near and the British government stood poised to exchange diplomats with Richmond. But the moment never came.

The Trent Affair

In November 1861 the British ship *Trent* was headed home carrying two rebel commissioners: James M. Mason, appointed to represent the Confederacy in London, and John Slidell, the designated representative in France. A Union warship commanded by Captain Charles Wilkes stopped the vessel and seized the two, claiming them as contraband—in effect, enemy property that a nation at war can take. The seizure was interpreted as an insult to Great Britain, and for a moment the British press talked of war. But the Lincoln administration could not afford to fight on a second front; for gunpowder, moreover, it desperately needed saltpeter from British India. In failing to take the *Trent* to a port to seek a ruling on the legality of his actions, Wilkes had acted contrary to international law. That gave Secretary of State Seward an excuse to release the two commissioners without seeming to back down before the British. The crisis ended.

Blockade

The Union, meanwhile, was maintaining a strong naval blockade around the South, and federal troops had taken several ports along the southern coastline. In early February 1862, Major General Ambrose E. Burnside, the possessor of distinctive whiskers that have since become known as "sideburns," won an important victory at Roanoke Island off North Carolina, which sat astride waterways that afforded to the rebel capital of Richmond in Virginia an access to the outside world. Union gunboats hammered down the shore defenses, and troops slogged through deep swamps to capture the Confederate post on the island. For the rebels, it amounted to a defeat serious enough to call for an investigation by a committee of the Confederate Congress.

In April, a naval force under Captain, and later Admiral, David Farragut pushed through to New Orleans at the mouth of the Mississippi, and General Benjamin F. Butler occupied that French- as well as English-speaking city. Remembered particularly for smashing the defenses and risking the floating mines at Mobile Bay, Alabama, in August 1864, a feat that sealed off one of the Confederacy's few remaining outlets to the ocean, the Tennessean Farragut figures as yet another southerner who contributed significantly to preservation of the Union cause.

On March 8, 1862, a lumbering, bulky craft that the North had begun to dread steamed to the mouth of the James River, a water route to Richmond. The hull of the United States ship *Merrimack*, earlier scuttled by the federal navy to keep it from falling into Confederate hands, had now become the rebel vessel *Virginia*. Plated with iron, and relatively invulnerable to cannon shot, it destroyed that day two federal vessels while a third ran aground. This first ironclad ship to enter combat seemed capable of destroying any vessel that did not sit in waters too shallow to accommodate the *Virginia*. But the next day appeared the second of all fighting ironclads, the Union ship *Monitor*. For hours the two floating piles of iron pounded away at each other. Neither could be sunk, but the crew of the damaged *Virginia* lost all hope of dominating the battle. The Union once again controlled the entrance to the James. Both sides went on to float other ironclads, a notable contribution of the Civil War to advances in naval combat.

King Cotton's Crown?

Ever since the early days of the war, as the Union blockade began to tighten around the South, the Confederacy had proceeded on a theory known then and after by the term "King Cotton." The bedrock of the British economy, or so the rebels assumed, was the textile industry, which in turn depended on southern cotton. In a short time, Britain would feel compelled to break the blockade by force. Richmond also drew on a proposition in international law ordaining that a blockade has to be effective; otherwise it amounts to no more than random harassment of neutral commerce. Since the blockade was not yet completely effective, so Confederate representatives pointed out to London, it was illegal and should be broken. But this argument contradicted the other simultaneous southern claim: that the blockade was effective enough to stifle the British textile industry. In pursuit of the belief that Great Britain had to have southern cotton and would intervene to get it, the Confederacy also instituted an unstated policy of withholding the commodity from export. But that attempt at arm-twisting awakened resentment. At the beginning of the war, England's storehouses were bursting with the fiber, and soon an increase in production in Egypt and India, both of them part of the British Empire, answered to the needs of textile manufacture. Cotton never wore a king's crown.

Britain and the Commerce Raiders

Once the *Monitor* confined the *Virginia* to a single day of glory, the South had no hope of taking on the federal navy in regular battle. One thing, though, the Confederacy could do: launch ships that raided Union commerce. For raiders, the South turned to Britain, or rather to the pro-Confederate city of Liverpool, which had once engaged in the slave trade. For London openly to permit the building in Liverpool of raiders commissioned by Richmond would have been an act bearing grave diplomatic consequences, as Charles Francis Adams, United States minister to the kingdom and son of John Quincy Adams, did not hesitate to point out to the British. But London did not act with sufficient alertness or resolve to stop the construction and launching of the *Florida*. Then in the summer of 1862 the *Alabama* slipped out of sympathetic Liverpool. Eventually the Union captured the *Florida* and sank the *Alabama*. But both ships, along with other Confederate raiders, so damaged the United States merchant marine that it would take decades to recover. After the war Washington lodged against London a demand, collectively known as the *Alabama* claims, for the harm done to Union commerce by Confederate raiders built in Britain, and in 1872 Great Britain agreed to pay the United States a sum settled upon by an international commission of arbitration.

A WAR OF EMANCIPATION

That the question of emancipation would elude President Lincoln's efforts to silence it is illustrated by an event in the late summer of 1861, when fed-eral forces in Missouri were taking a beating. Their commander, the dashing and impetuous abolitionist John C. Frémont, issued an order threatening execution for Confederate guerrillas operating within Union lines. Frémont commanded that the property of the state's rebels—which of course included their slaves—be confiscated and the slaves freed. In a private letter to Frémont, Lincoln instructed him to refrain from executing guerrillas without the president's approval, and requested that he adhere to the provisions of a congressional act mandating the confiscation only of rebel property employed in the war. Such property would include slaves, but the measure stopped far short of the emancipationist objective Frémont pursued. Responding to reports that Frémont's plan was rattling border-state Unionist sentiment, Lincoln later turned the request into an explicit order to desist.

Escaped slaves themselves pushed the issue further. Earlier that year Benjamin Butler, then commanding a Union force in Virginia, had begun taking in fugitive slaves and setting them to work at his encampment. As legal justification he claimed them as "contraband of war,"—enemy property subject to seizure. But Butler further insisted that if they were property, then they belonged to their military rescuers who, he made it clear, refused to hold human beings as property. Should the fugitives, he asked, not therefore be considered free?

Argument was by then becoming irrelevant. Slaves in increasing numbers were fleeing to Union lines. Late in 1861 Simon Cameron, Lincoln's secretary of war before being replaced by Edwin M. Stanton, raised the contraband issue in a way bound to please abolitionists. As "property" taken from the enemy, the refugees could be used for military purposes as might any other contraband property, and in the case of the fugitive slaves that might mean arming them for combat. Lincoln, however, was completely unready for a policy of turning ex-slaves into soldiers, and he attempted unsuccessfully to stop the publication of Cameron's report.

The flood of human contraband continued, and even when the fugitives did find shelter some Union soldiers treated them viciously. Yet the practice of taking them in became widespread. And while major elements of the Democratic Party were making opposition to emancipation a major component of their creed, abolitionists were pressing to transform the war from a mere effort against secession to a larger struggle for the destruction of slavery. Lincoln could in no way seal off the issue from public view. And he could not seal it off from his own conscience.

Emancipation Gathers Force

In March 1862 Congress cut through the confusion surrounding the treatment of slaves as contraband. A measure passed that a year earlier would have been politically unthinkable; it prohibited the military from returning fugitive slaves to their owners, even owners claiming to be Unionist. Soon after, Congress adopted a resolution Lincoln had proposed offering financial support to any state adopting a gradual end to slavery. The vote went almost exactly along party lines; all Republicans backed it, while the great majority of Democratic and border-state legislators in Congress were opposed. In July, Congress moved further toward emancipation. A militia act included a provision authorizing the president to enlist into the military men of African ancestry. Abolitionists had added to their argument for emancipation the practical military advantages of drawing slaves from their owners and thereby effecting the collapse of the Confederate economy and society. And Congress did then pass a measure that declared the confiscation of all property of rebels, their confiscated slaves to become thereupon free. Throughout the various theaters of war, Union officers now began, if they had not done so before, taking or destroying any rebel property they could get hold of with the aim of depleting Confederate resources. For the human property involved, that meant freedom. Slaves who fled to the Union forces deprived the Confederacy of labor much needed at a time when white men were away in military service.

A National Economy

As the Republican Congress and president moved toward effecting a social revolution, the two were at the same time envisioning a national economy significantly coordinated by the government. Federalists of the time of John Adams and Alexander Hamilton, National Republicans speaking through John Quincy Adams, and Whigs led by Henry Clay had nurtured earlier forms of the concept. Now, as the federal government fought a major war to assert its supremacy over the states, a body of legislation enacted in 1862 defined an economy founded on free labor in western farms and in eastern factories.

In May of that year, Congress passed the Homestead Act, as the Republican Party platform of 1860 had promised. It offered a 160-acre plot of federal land to any man or woman who lived on it for five years and made improvements encompassing anything in the way of cultivation or building. The idea of opening public land to small farming had been part of the antislavery program of the 1850s, for it looked to filling the new federal territories with free-labor agriculture as opposed to plantation slavery. A measure introduced by Representative Justin Morrill of Vermont in July provided for granting to every state a portion of federal land to be used for the creation of institutions of higher learning. The lands awarded to a state did not have to be within its borders; their usefulness consisted in their being sold by the state and the revenues employed for financing colleges. The statute defined the schools to be founded as stressing agriculture and technology, but land-grant colleges such as Berkeley have also become centers of learning in the liberal arts and the humanities. At the same time, Congress granted public lands for the building of a transcontinental railroad, soon to become one of the major industrial projects of the century.

Some of the innovative measures adopted by the national legislature resulted not from political or ideological motivation but simply from the necessity of paying for the war. These too, however, represented a more energetic centralized government and deepened its involvement in the economy. As secretary of the treasury, Salmon P. Chase had the task of overseeing much of the financing. He instituted the selling of war bonds, stimulated by an advertising campaign appealing to the patriotism of the people and foreshadowing the bond drives of the two twentieth-century world wars. Various tariffs also provided revenue for the wartime government. In 1861, Congress had enacted the first income tax in the nation's history. This and subsequent measures taxing incomes in proportion to their size were, however, technically unconstitutional. Not until ratification of the Sixteenth Amendment in 1913 would the federal government have the authority to impose a tax scaled to the income of the payer. But for a nation at war, legal niceties seemed irrelevant. The Legal Tender Act, adopted in February 1862 over the opposition of Democratic legislators, allowed the government wide latitude in issuing paper money, commonly known as greenbacks. A National Banking Act of 1863, passed with overwhelming Republican congressional support and resisted by all but a fraction of the Democrats, established a framework for the centralization of banking, weakening the ability of state banks to engage in reckless issues of paper currency.

The Sanitary Commission and the Ambulance Corps

While both Republican ideology and the demands of war were forming a stronger national government, private agencies pressed for a centralized and efficient medical system. The Sanitary Commission, which became an arm of the government, added its own contribution to the making of a more unified republic.

Beyond the carnage of the battlefields themselves hovered the most lethal force in the Civil War: disease. The medical profession of that day was almost totally ignorant of the true nature of infection and of the corresponding importance of sanitation and cleanliness, and in military camps where soldiers packed together water swarmed with germs. As for treatment of the wounded, to stop the spread of gangrene physicians had no recourse but amputation, with chloroform or ether if the patient was lucky, otherwise with enough alcohol to dull the senses slightly.

Much of the health care on both sides was at the hands of thousands of women who defied the conventional belief that ladies were too delicate to bear the sight and stench of raw suffering. As volunteer nurses serving in the medical arm of both the Union and the Confederate military, they brought food and water to soldier patients, dressed wounds, and otherwise made life a bit more endurable. Elizabeth Blackwell, who had earned a medical degree when such a thing was almost unimaginable for a woman, organized a training program for nurses serving the Union. From such beginnings came the United States Sanitary Commission. Headed by the Unitarian cleric Henry Bellows and Frederick Law Olmsted, one of the nation's most important architects, the Commission recruited nurses and solicited public donations of medicine, bandages, and other supplies. Inspectors sent out by the Commission worked to teach soldiers, for example, better standards of cleanliness in drainage, the placement of latrines, and the general hygienic arrangements of camps. Soon a trained ambulance corps emerged within the army. It became a model for ambulance services in European armies.

Antietam and the Emancipation Proclamation

In early September 1862, the fortunes of the Union war effort lay about as low as they would ever be. The Second Battle of Bull Run had brought a major defeat. Rebel forces were menacing Union positions in Kentucky and Tennessee. General Robert E. Lee and his troops were confident, the Army of the Potomac discouraged. Now Lee embarked on a daring scheme. Although he could not take Washington in a direct assault, he would invade Maryland, rally that state's large population of Confederate sympathizers, and generally throw into turmoil the region to the north of the Union capital. So on September 4 his Army of Northern Virginia, ragged and weary but in high spirits, crossed into Maryland.

General George McClellan was then in command of the Union's Army of the Potomac. On September 16, the two forcers met near Antietam Creek near Sharpsburg, Maryland. McClellan had at his disposal seventy thousand or so soldiers in place or within a short distance. Lee had half that number. But in his habitual way McClellan overestimated the strength of his enemy. In a day of fighting during which Union troops, stung by the humiliation of their previous failures, fought ferociously against ferocious rebels, the federal commander held back reserves who might have finished the fight. At the end of one of the most terrible clashes of the war, Lee's troops limped back to Virginia. Insofar as the battle stopped Lee's invasion of Maryland, it amounted to a technical victory for the Union. But McClellan's failure to go for the destruction of Lee's army sustained Lincoln's frustration at his general.

Yet this qualified federal success had important consequences. The British government, which had been seriously considering whether to extend diplomatic recognition to the Confederacy as a securely established, independent nation, now drew back. And Antietam gave Lincoln the opportunity to set a course he had determined on against the unanimous advice of his cabinet months earlier. This was

THE WOUND DRESSER

Bearing the bandages, water and sponge,
Straight and swift to my wounded I go,
Where they lie on the ground after the battle
brought in,
Where their priceless blood reddens the grass
the ground,
Or to the rows of the hospital tent, or under the
roof'd hospital,
To the long rows of cots up and down each side
I return,
To each and all one after another I draw near,
not one do I miss,
An attendant follows holding a tray, he carries a
refuse pail,
Soon to be fill'd with clotted rags and blood,
emptied, and fill'd again.

I onward go, I stop,
With hinged knees and steady hand to dress
wounds,
I am firm with each, the pangs are sharp yet
unavoidable,
One turns to me his appealing eyes—poor boy!
I never knew you,
Yet I think I could not refuse this moment to
die for you, if that would save you.

On, on I go, (open doors of time! open hospital
doors!)
The crush'd head I dress, (poor crazed hand tear
not the bandage away,)

The neck of the cavalry-man with the bullet
through and through I examine,
Hard the breathing rattles, quite glazed already
the eye, yet life struggles hard,
(Come, sweet death! be persuaded O beautiful
death! In mercy come quickly.)

Walt Whitman's Drum Taps *leaves haunting images
of wartime death, particularly this fragment of his
poem entitled "The Wound Dresser." (Courtesy,
National Portrait Gallery, Smithsonian Institution)*

a presidential proclamation decreeing, as in another form Congress had already decreed, that the slaves of rebels would be confiscated and set free. At a time when the Union seemed on the defensive, Lincoln had refrained from taking this action, concerned that such an order would appear to be an ineffective act of desperation. But Antietam eliminated that consideration.

The Emancipation Proclamation announced that wherever on or after January 1, 1863, rebellion still prevailed, the slaves there would be free. Critics were quick to observe that the edict applied only in places where it could not then be enforced: lands still under Confederate control. But criticism missed the point. The proclamation was essentially a military directive, ordering confiscation of rebel property as any Union officer might authorize the seizure of property in a hostile area. As president, Lincoln could not declare freedom for slaves throughout the nation; the Constitution does not endow the presidency with such sweeping powers. But as commander-in-chief of all the military, Lincoln had at least as much authority as any lieutenant or captain to order the seizure of property in areas where the rules of war governed.

The proclamation, then, did not encompass the

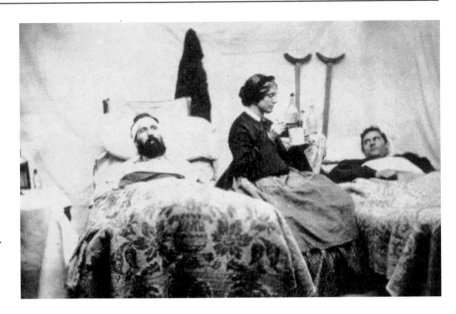

Women, southern and northern, saved lives and relieved suffering among war casualties. (Courtesy, Williamson Art Gallery and Museum, Birkenhead, England)

grand design of freeing all the slaves at a single stroke. Lincoln, in fact, might not have been unhappy if the threat of emancipation brought one or more of the seceded states back into the Union before January 1, with their slaves still in bondage. And yet he was also clearly aware of the moral component of his proclamation, and spoke of it as being in response to a covenant he had made with God. The significance of the order, as he knew, went far beyond its stated limits. In areas still in insurrection as of January 1, slaves were to become free as soon as Union troops could fight their way to these areas. And that would leave slavery everywhere else in severed remnants of a defeated system.

An Uncertain End to 1862

In the midterm elections of 1862, the Republicans held on to both Houses, even increasing their majority in the Senate, and prevailed as well in most state gubernatorial campaigns. But some sufficient Democratic gains made the results look like a rejection of administration policy.

In November the president, having failed to get McClellan to wage an active campaign in Virginia, replaced him with General Ambrose Burnside. The new commander showed the aggressiveness Lincoln was looking for, but with disastrous results. At Fredericksburg, Virginia, on December 13 as Burnside moved south toward Richmond, his troops clashed with the armies of Lee and Jackson. A failure to coordinate the Union forces sent one assault after another across terrain broken by ravines and a marsh and leading to a stone fence at the base of a hill, and from behind that wall Confederate soldiers systematically cut down the attackers. When it was over, the Union had suffered a defeat that added to the late autumn gloom.

A few days later, Lincoln faced another danger. Even as enemies of emancipation were attacking the administration from the right, it was under siege from the radical wing of the Republican Party, which thought that it moved too slowly. Believing

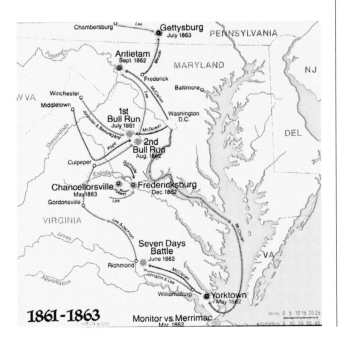

Secretary of State Seward to be responsible in particular for the government's caution, radicals in the Senate now tried to force the president to replace Seward with Salmon Chase, at the time the secretary of the treasury. Lincoln handled the matter deftly, inviting the senators to a meeting at which they found the full cabinet with the exception of Seward. The cabinet members, including Chase, supported Lincoln and the absent secretary of state, and the crisis ended.

On January 1, 1863, the president carried out his promise. Referring to his preliminary proclamation of September 22 declaring freedom for slaves in regions that had not returned to the Union by January 1, he identified those areas and announced: "I do order and declare that all persons held as slaves within said designated States and parts of States are, and henceforward shall be, free. . . ." He urged that liberated slaves commit no unnecessary violence and that whenever possible, "they labor faithfully for reasonable wages." Whether or not he expected these words to be taken as sincere, they amounted to a denial that he was encouraging the bloody slave uprisings foes of emancipation had predicted. Lincoln also declared that freed slaves "of suitable condition" would be accepted into military service.

WAR AND POLITICS UNDER THE POLICY OF EMANCIPATION

A war now plainly being fought for emancipation drew passionate responses. For abolitionists, black and white, the conflict now had a real moral purpose. Much of the Democratic Party, however, deplored this transformation of war aims. Peace Democrats were labeled "copperheads," apparently at first by Republicans referring to the copperhead snake, though later some antiwar Democrats took to wearing badges carrying the image of the goddess of liberty on the copper penny. Claiming that a war of emancipation was an assault on the freedoms of white Americans, they proposed withdrawing troops from the South and opening discussions for reunion.

In the Midwest, where in its lower territory much of the population had emigrated from the South, hostility to the new federal policy abounded. The National Banking Act of February 1863 further antagonized midwestern Democrats who believed that it would concentrate banking in the hands of eastern interests.

The Draft in the North and the South

A Conscription Act that Congress passed the next month by a predictable party-line vote fueled still greater anger in the Midwest. Among military units from the region, copperheads now circulated an appeal to desert. Protests against an earlier form of conscription had already brought arrests by federal authorities. Lincoln's general wartime limitations on access to the writ of *habeas corpus,* by which arrested suspects are enabled to appear before a court that will consider the charges against them, increased the legal difficulties of the detainees. Opponents of the war denounced what they defined as a violation of civil liberties.

General Burnside, having been transferred from the Army of the Potomac to the Army of the Ohio, issued an order in April 1863 stating that anyone engaging in explicitly or implicitly treasonable activities faced arrest and trial by military courts. Soon afterward Clement L. Vallandigham, an Ohio politician and antiwar Democrat, deliberately challenged Burnside's order by making a speech against the war. The general met the challenge: Vallandigham was seized, convicted by a military court, and sentenced to prison. Lincoln, however, sensing that the congressman might take on the status of martyr, banished him instead to the Confederacy. From there Vallandigham slipped off to Canada, where he conducted an unsuccessful campaign for governor of Ohio.

The Confederacy had its own dissidents. In 1862, in opposition to a general conscription of men between eighteen and thirty-four, some neighborhoods essentially ruled themselves outside Confederate law. The conscription statute allowed a potential draftee to hire a substitute, as northern policy would do. It also exempted a number of occupations, among them druggist, miner, teacher, large planter, and Confederate government employee. The provision applying only to holders of the largest numbers of slaves responded to the fear that in the absence of male owners, slaves might take to disruption and rebellion. These exemptions convinced many common soldiers that the Confederacy was being run for the benefit of the rich. Resentment rose against the draft coupled with hostility to a requirement that farmers turn over a portion of their crops, meat, and dairy products to the government. Food for the Confederate military was scarce, and provisions ran low for many civilians as well. As the war went on, bread riots broke out in southern cities. Women invaded shops and took what they needed. The best known of these disturbances occurred in Richmond in 1863, when the Confederate president Jefferson Davis in person had to confront the looters and order them to disperse.

In the Union draft calls, only about seven percent of the men whose names came up actually served. The rest hired substitutes, paid a commutation fee, or were turned down for health problems or other considerations. Draftees made up only a small percentage of Union soldiers; the rest had voluntarily enlisted or reenlisted. The real purpose of the draft was to encourage the alternative of voluntary service, whether by reason of patriotism, or to collect the fee for being a substitute, or to take the bounty that the military offered. During the war some men made a practice of enlisting, collecting the bounty, then disappearing and showing up to collect another fee.

Popular belief in the Union as well as the Confederacy held that the rich, making use of the various draft dodges, were sitting at home making money while the poor fought. But for neither side do the figures justify the folklore. One set of calculations for the Union military shows that a slightly higher proportion of farmers and farm laborers than of the affluent and the professional classes got out by commutation or substitution. Among all major occupational groups as the study ranks them, no fewer than about twenty-two percent and no more than thirty-one percent or so of men called were released by paying the commutation fee or finding a substitute. The poor did not have to pay out of their own money. Some communities collected funds by one means or another: property taxes or, in the case of New York City's Tammany Hall machine, soliciting contributions. Employers who wanted to keep their workforce paid the necessary fees.

Anger at conscription, however, ran wide, and was increased by anger at emancipation. Enrollment officers sometimes faced copperhead mobs. In New York City on July 13, 1863, a draft riot broke out among impoverished Irish Catholics steaming with race hatred and hostility toward what they thought to be the nation's Protestant establishment. The riot lasted for several days and led to over a hundred deaths. The rioters turned their fury both on black New Yorkers and on whites who looked affluent enough to pay the commutation fee on their own. They also attacked the property of bosses reputedly opposed to unions, and burned Protestant churches and missions. Surely the ugliest moment came with the torching of an asylum for black orphans. Troops from the Pennsylvania campaign had to be brought in to put down the insurgency.

Lee's Fortunes Crest

Antietam had brought respite to the Union and disappointment to Lee, but it merely put a halt to a venture in no way necessary for the triumph of the Confederacy. The victory of Lee and the success of the Army of Northern Virginia at Fredericksburg reestablished the supremacy of rebel forces in the region. The first days of May 1863 gave Lee increasing reason to believe that his troops could win the war.

To command the Army of the Potomac, Lincoln after Fredericksburg had chosen Joseph Hooker (like Burnside, the general contributed a word to the English language: the ladies for hire who plied

HANGING A NEGRO IN CLARKSON STREET.

As many as one hundred people died in rioting that began on July 13, 1863, with a march of thousands of poor mostly Irish laborers protesting exemptions from the draft. Black workers in competition for jobs were in some cases lynched. (Courtesy, The Granger Collection)

their trade among his troops called themselves Hooker's Division). Hooker seemed to promise an aggressive campaign. At Chancellorsville on May 1, in the course of yet another of the Union army's marches south through Virginia, his seventy thousand troops encountered Lee's forces numbering a bit more than half that number. In the battle that followed, Lee executed one of his riskiest and most daring maneuvers. Leaving only fifteen thousand men to face Hooker, he sent Stonewall Jackson westward to hit the vulnerable right flank of the Union army. His gamble succeeded: when the northern general detected this movement, he assumed that it signaled Lee's retreat and so concluded he had already won the encounter and took no further action. Launching its attack on the late afternoon of May 2, Stonewall Jackson's force smashed the unsuspecting Union's right section. Fighting continued for the next two days. By the evening of May 4, the Army of Northern Virginia had achieved one of its greatest victories, yet also sustained one of its greatest losses. In the course of the battle Jackson, mistaken for a Union soldier, was hit by Confederate fire. A few days later, he died.

Nothing, it now seemed, could prevail against Robert E. Lee. He was then inspired to undertake the boldest southern venture of the war. He would invade southern Pennsylvania, provisioning his ill-fed troops from the land, discouraging northerners who wished to continue the war, and correspondingly strengthening the hand of the peace Democrats. The copperheads, to be sure, wanted negotiations aimed at reunifying the country around the Constitution and its protections of slavery, while the rebels were determined to have nothing less than full separation from the North. But once Lee's plan succeeded and talks supported by Democrats began, the momentum toward Confederate independence would be unstoppable. Success in the Pennsylvania campaign could also help persuade European nations to recognize the Confederacy.

By early June of 1863, Lee was moving northward. At the end of the month, Lee's troops were living off provisions and supplies gathered in Pennsylvania. On June 28 Hooker resigned his command of the Army of the Potomac, and Lincoln appointed George Meade in his place.

Three days later, near the Pennsylvania town of Gettysburg, the two armies made contact. In the battle that followed, the North had fifteen thousand

General Robert E. Lee could not break with his region. (Courtesy, Bettmann Archives)

troops more than Lee. But the Confederates attacked and the Union soldiers went on the defensive. What Meade's forces defended most vigorously was the high ground of Cemetery Ridge. On July 2, a point on the ridge known as Little Round Top was held by Maine troops under the command of Colonel Joshua Chamberlain, a college professor whose prewar photograph reveals a bookish scholar. When under continuous assault his soldiers ran out of ammunition, Chamberlain ordered them to fix bayonets and charge down the slope. To the southern contingent assaulting the Little Round Top, the charge made no sense. They therefore broke, and that part of the field now lay in Union hands. That same day, 262 soldiers of a Minnesota unit defending another sector of Cemetery Ridge received orders to attack a Confederate force numbering 1,600. The Minnesotans did so, losing more than four-fifths of their men. But at the end of the day, the federal army remained in possession of the ridge.

James Longstreet, one of Lee's generals, throughout the battle argued for a more cautious strategy. But the next day, July 3, under orders from his commander and against his own judgment, Longstreet sent an attack on the center of Cemetery Ridge. For George Pickett, who led the major part of the Confederate assault, the venture is remembered as Pickett's Charge. In mid-afternoon fourteen thousand rebel troops advanced uphill on exposed ground in a grand sweep that would be one of the memorable moments of the Civil War. Union artillery, heretofore concealed, now opened up in concert with the massed fire of Union infantry. The charge reached the Union lines but then withered under the intense fire. The Battle of Gettysburg was over and with it Lee's northern campaign. Only about half the Confederate force survived intact.

Before Gettysburg Jefferson Davis was confident in the expectation that the Army of Northern Virginia would triumph in its northern foray and that Washington would then be ready to negotiate. Gettysburg now squelched the possibility of the Confederacy's winning diplomatic recognition abroad.

Lee knew that for once he had been soundly beaten. He withdrew from Pennsylvania, while Lincoln fretted that General Meade, like General McClellan before him, had failed to pursue him to deliver what might have been a final, crushing blow. But Lee would never again possess the field of battle he had held at Fredericksburg and Chancellorsville.

The Winning of the Mississippi

In the western theater, the Army of the Tennessee under General Ulysses S. Grant had the task of wrenching from the Confederacy the portion of the Mississippi River the enemy still held. Doing so would slice the Confederacy in two, sealing off Texas. It would also enable river commerce to move unimpeded between the North and the mouth of the Mississippi. The inability of the Midwest to send its goods down the Mississippi contributed significantly to copperhead sentiment in the region in favor of an accommodation with the rebels. The stronghold of Vicksburg, the chief obstacle, lay on the east bank of the river in southern Mississippi. General John C. Pemberton, a Pennsylvanian who had married into a southern family, headed the rebel defense. North of Vicksburg, Union gunboats roamed free. But batteries stationed in the city prevented their passage to the towns further downriver in federal hands: Natchez in Mississippi, Baton Rouge and New Orleans in Louisiana, all three of them having fallen to David Farragut, the naval commander who had helped implement the Union blockade.

Grant's supply line stretched to the western Tennessee city of Memphis. But he determined that his best approach to that city would be from the south. His solution ranks among the most innovative campaigns of the war. In April 1863, he moved his troops across the Mississippi from north of Vicksburg and then marched them south down the river's western bank. He ordered the Union gunboats to dash southward past Vicksburg's artillery defenses, a dangerous maneuver that most of them survived.

To divert Pemberton's attention, Grant meanwhile sent Union cavalry on a raid through the state of Mississippi. Early in the war, Confederate cavalry had been ascendant, and sweeps under the direction of Jeb Stuart in the East, Nathan Bedford Forrest and John Hunt Morgan in Tennessee, and Morgan in Kentucky brought fame to rebel horse soldiers.

Union General Ulysses S. Grant exhibited a relentless will that matched that of Robert E. Lee. (Courtesy, Library of Congress)

But by 1863 Union cavalry was making its own reputation. The raid through Mississippi stripped plantations bare of provisions, tore up railroad tracks and equipment carrying supplies to Pemberton's men, and in sixteen days reached the federal lines in Baton Rouge. Pemberton's troops could not find the invaders, for smaller units went scattering in different directions to confuse their pursuers.

Grant then advanced north. Having cut themselves off from their source of supplies in Memphis, his forces provisioned themselves from the land. By late May he held Vicksburg under siege. Grant's assault was aided by black troops who successfully defended a garrison at Milliken's Bend on the Mississippi above Vicksburg, an achievement that kept open another flow of supplies to Grant. The feat won the admiration of Union officers who had previously doubted the ability of freedmen to fight. But it was reported that outraged rebel troops at Milliken's Bend had killed some black prisoners and sold others into slavery.

Union artillery and gunboats now pounded Vicksburg, while engineers tunneled under Confederate lines. The assault choked off the city, and hunger added to the shelling drove Pemberton to surrender on July 4, 1863, the day after Lee's defeat at Gettysburg. Within a few days, the Union and the Confederacy both knew that that year's Fourth of July had been the most momentous since 1776.

On July 18, black troops of the Fifty-fourth Massachusetts Infantry led by the New England aristocrat Colonel Robert Gould Shaw—the federal army put black troops under white officers—carried out an attack against Fort Wagner on the South Carolina coast. The unit lost nearly half its numbers, including Shaw. In the course of the fighting, in which they had to cross open ground before the fortress, the black troops had gained part of its outer rim and held it for an hour. The widely publicized episode was a further answer to doubts in the North about the ability of black soldiers to do frontline duty. In an open letter in late August, Lincoln addressed the foes of emancipation. "You say you will not fight to free negroes. Some of them seem willing to fight for you . . . . So fight only to preserve the Union if you wish." But the Proclamation was to save the Union. And after the war some black men will remember that, "with silent tongue, and clenched teeth, and steady eye, and well-poised bayonet," they aided in the nation's victory, while some whites will remember that with malice and deceit, "they have strove to hinder it."

Gettysburg and Vicksburg had made a mockery of the defeatist vocabulary of the peace Democrats who wanted negotiations with the South. Fort Wagner was an answer to copperhead assaults on emancipation, and horror at the naked face of racism as it had revealed itself in the New York draft riots may have contributed to a shift in northern sentiment toward emancipation. Whatever the reasons, observers were noting that autumn a decline in anti-emancipation feeling in the North

This lithograph commemorates the 54th Massachusetts Colored Regiment charging Fort Wagner, South Carolina, in 1863. (Courtesy, Library of Congress)

and an embrace of abolition as an objective of the war. Gubernatorial elections in Pennsylvania and Ohio, two states containing a strong copperhead element, were tests of where public opinion was going. Republicans won both. The defeat of Vallandigham, conducting from Canadian exile his campaign for governor of Ohio, brought down the most notorious opponent of the war. Doubtless it was the Union battlefield successes of the preceding summer that had done most to weaken the copperheads in these and other elections. But their failure meant also the failure of the attempt to stem the progress of emancipation.

THE WAR AFTER GETTYSBURG AND VICKSBURG

Following the two great Union triumphs of July 1863, the war continued for nearly two years. The Confederacy continued to have moments of hope. In the summer of 1864, discouragement in the North threatened Republican prospects for that autumn's presidential election. A Democratic victory would turn the federal government over to a party that might negotiate with the Confederacy until the rebels acquired independence by default. But in general, the victory at Gettysburg and more especially Grant's triumph on the Mississippi had the Confederacy permanently on the defensive, subject to invasion and a steady erosion of its territory.

The Battle for East Tennessee

In the hill country of east Tennessee, a Unionist majority lived under Confederate occupation. The Union Army of the Cumberland under William S. Rosecrans made the liberation of the region a major objective. That summer of 1863 Rosecrans had pushed through middle Tennessee, and Confederate troops under Braxton Bragg in September abandoned Chattanooga, in southern Tennessee just north of the border with Georgia. Another Union army under Burnside had entered Knoxville, the biggest city in east Tennessee. In late September a force combining Bragg's army with twelve thousand troops from the Army of Northern Virginia led by Longstreet drove Rosecrans's army from Chickamauga Creek near Chattanooga. For checking a

Confederate advance, the Union loyalist Virginian general George H. Thomas became known as the Rock of Chickamauga. Bragg might have gone on to attack the Union forces now in possession of Chattanooga. But his own losses—twenty thousand killed, wounded, or missing—kept him from following up. Instead, he tightened the siege of the federal troops in the city, putting artillery on Lookout Mountain, foot soldiers on Missionary Ridge outside Chattanooga, and other men on the roads leading to the town. By mid-October, starvation threatened Rosecrans's army.

Rosecrans's campaign that summer had been a notable triumph of maneuver, but the inconclusive results prompted Lincoln to find a more aggressive leader. The president created a huge Division of the Mississippi, stretching all the way from that river to the Appalachians, the mountain spine running through Virginia to the south. He named Grant its commander, and Grant in turn replaced Rosecrans with George Thomas. The conqueror of Vicksburg himself went to Chattanooga taking over an operation that Rosecrans's staff had planned. Grant drove the rebels from the roads to the west of the city. Supplemented by a force led by Hooker from the Army of the Potomac and another under Sherman taken from the Army of the Mississippi, the federal force occupying Chattanooga numbered by the middle of November seventy-two thousand.

In a battle in late November, the Union troops broke what remained of the Confederate siege. Hooker's men took Lookout Mountain, but had trouble extending their advance on Missionary Ridge, and Sherman's assault on what turned out to be a detached ridge to the north was stalled by counterattacks. Then came one of the most surprising turns of the war.

Grant, assuming that the Army of the Cumberland had been too badly demoralized by Chickamauga to contribute to the main battle, ordered it on the afternoon of November 25 to create a diversionary attack against rebel trenches at the foot of Missionary Ridge. The Cumberland troops carried out this supposedly minor task, driving the Confederate defenders from the trenches. But they did not stop there. Spurred by a madness that appears to have stemmed from the sting of the humiliation they had suffered at Chickamauga and the disrespect with which they thought the rest of the federal army was treating them, they started up its steep and apparently unconquerable slope, taking advantage of the hill's broken surface, which provided gashes and mounds that they could move among for protection as they climbed. The assault was lunacy, and from lunatics the rebels fled. The Union had gained undisputed control of Chattanooga.

Grant's Campaign of No Retreat

After Vicksburg and Chattanooga, the Union forces launched a continuing assault on the Confederacy. In the spring of 1864 that effort intensified. Lincoln now promoted Grant to the newly-created rank of general-in-chief of all the Union armies. Putting Sherman in charge of troops in the western theater, Grant went east to be with the Army of the Potomac, of which Meade remained the commander though Grant had final control over its operations.

Grant sent Benjamin Butler to fight his way up the James River and Franz Siegel on a campaign in the Shenandoah Valley. But his main force, the Army of the Potomac numbering over a hundred thousand troops, he reserved for a direct confrontation with Lee.

What that meant became clear by early May. Grant's army engaged Lee's in the Wilderness, a spot of Virginia so dense with scrub growth that Grant's superiority in numbers did not give him the advantage it might have offered in an open field. Profiting from their knowledge of the terrain, the Confederate troops in about two days of fighting inflicted over seventeen thousand casualties on Union soldiers killed or otherwise put out of combat. Grant, however, chose not to consider this engagement as a lost battle calling for retreat. He continued the fight, on bad and good days alike. The mood of his troops turned from dispirited to exuberant as they discovered that they were advancing south, not withdrawing after another Confederate victory.

At Spotsylvania Courthouse shortly afterwards, Grant once again sustained heavy losses. Lee's army had built there a powerful defense line complete with trenches and breastworks. Union troops hurled themselves against it and met with temporary success. A rebel counterattack brought the two armies surging together in the trenches, fighting with bullets and bayonets until these gashes in the earth lay piled high with dead and wounded. At the end, Lee

withdrew. Both sides lost many men. In the first days of June, Grant struck once more, this time at a place bearing the eerie name Cold Harbor. This time the Confederate defenses were so visibly strong that many Union troops, anticipating the outcome, pinned slips of paper with their names on their uniforms so their bodies could be identified afterward. The assault failed and cost another several thousand Union casualties. Grant then shifted his army to the south of Richmond, attacking the town of Petersburg, only twenty miles from the rebel capital. In four days of inconclusive fighting in mid-June, Grant's army diminished by an additional eight thousand. He then laid siege to the town, locking the two armies in what turned out to be a nine-month contest.

In the course of it, some Pennsylvania miners in the federal army embarked under the leadership of a former mining engineer on a particularly ambitious venture. They tunneled under a stretch of Confederate lines, and placed there a huge cache of gunpowder. On July 30 they detonated the explosives, destroying a rebel regiment. Union troops then began an offensive against the confused and demoralized Confederate force on the sides of the crater the explosion had created. But in their zeal the federal soldiers rushed into the crater rather than around it, trapping themselves while the rebels fired artillery and mortars into the hole. As

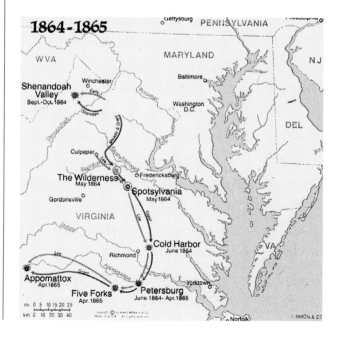

other Union troops retreated, a black unit moved through them to the front, only to be cut down by a Confederate counterattack. During the fight, rebels killed some of the black soldiers who tried to surrender. Union losses in the episode numbered eight thousand.

From Chattanooga to Atlanta

Back in May 1864, Sherman began an invasion of Georgia, aiming for Atlanta. Several armies, including Thomas's Army of the Cumberland, made up his force. Joseph E. Johnston, who had replaced Bragg, commanded the Confederate troops defending the state.

Johnston preferred skillful maneuver to direct assault. So did Sherman, in defiance of the reputation he has gained for being a hack-and-slash leader. And for much of the summer of 1864, the two generals practiced tactical dexterity, Sherman constantly trying to slip around Johnston or to hit him at weak points, his antagonist retreating when necessary. At Kennesaw Mountain on June 27, Sherman chose to attack his entrenched foe but failed and suffered a loss of three thousand men. Thereafter he reverted to the more successful tactic of getting around Johnston, steadily forcing the rebels to retreat to a new line of defense, closer and closer to Sherman's goal: Atlanta. By July he had almost reached the city. Jefferson Davis, frustrated at Johnston's apparent passivity, replaced him with John Bell Hood. The new commander demonstrated the aggressiveness Davis desired. In eight days of fighting beginning on July 20, Hood suffered fifteen thousand casualties and Sherman six thousand. The siege of Atlanta continued through August.

A Gloomy Northern Summer

In the summer of 1864, Lee's army shrank in numbers against Grant's assaults. But along with Sherman's apparently stalled effort to take Atlanta, the number of dead and wounded in Virginia spread disillusionment in the North. Farragut's capture of Mobile Bay that August, an important episode in strengthening the blockade of the Confederacy, went almost unnoted. The rebels looked close to winning the war—not on the field but in northern voting booths.

On July 29, the Democrats, meeting in Chicago, nominated General George McClellan for president.

The party platform advocated negotiations with the Confederacy with a view to ending the war peacefully, and by strong implication on terms acceptable to the South. Although McClellan refused to endorse the platform, it became evident that a triumph for the party that autumn would in fact lead to such negotiations. And these, clearly, would make an independent Confederacy a practical reality.

Amid all the war weariness so encouraged by the Democrats, Lincoln also had to face the anger of abolitionist radicals in his own party. In December 1863 he had proposed conditions for the readmission of seceded states: whenever in a rebel state eligible white voters amounting to as much as ten percent of the state's electorate in 1860 took an oath of future loyalty to the United States and to its laws and edicts against slavery, they could form a new government. Lincoln excluded from the process only high-ranking Confederate civil officials and military officers. The president, to be sure, could not force Congress to seat senators and representatives chosen under such a ten-percent rule; by long-

General William T. Sherman left terrorized civilians, wrecked railroad tracks, and destroyed city buildings in his march to make "Georgia howl." (Courtesy, Library of Congress)

standing British and American tradition, a legislature is the sole judge of the qualifications of its members. But Lincoln's plan, if Congress went along with it, would have put the seceded states on an easy path to full readmission, maintaining in place far more of the South's prewar political and social structure than radicals desired. Congress instead adopted a bill sponsored by Senator Benjamin Wade and Representative Henry Winter Davis setting stricter terms for reentry. Among other conditions, it included a requirement that only citizens who could swear to never having supported the rebellion could vote for delegates to a state convention. Lincoln accordingly pocket-vetoed the bill (killed it by refraining from acting on it before the end of the session, a device that a president can employ when only a few days of a session are left). Disturbed as they were by Lincoln's evident position to be lenient toward former rebels, some radicals thought of trying to find an alternative Republican nominee for that year's presidential contest.

An End to Defeatism

In late August of 1864 Sherman by stealth sent much of his army around to the south of Atlanta, where the Union soldiers tore up the last railroad tracks to the city. To save his army now completely isolated from the rest of the Confederacy, Hood abandoned Atlanta on September 1. The next day, just after after the Democrats nominated McClellan

and called for reunion with the South through a peaceful settlement, Sherman entered the city. Northerners cheered. Republicans, having temporarily merged at the presidential level with war Democrats into an organization called the Union Party, could now be more confident that their presidential ticket of Lincoln and the Tennessee Unionist Democrat Andrew Johnson would carry the election.

Upon leaving Atlanta, Hood attempted to undercut Sherman by going to his north and cutting his lines of supply to Tennessee. Sherman first spent some time chasing Hood. But he then came up with a better idea: abandon his supply line and march out of Atlanta, slashing eastward through the Deep South. His troops would live off provisions they gathered on their way through enemy territory. This would not only solve the problem of supply but wreak social and economic devastation on the Confederacy. So began a venture that would take Sherman to Savannah, Georgia, and then north through both Carolinas, while his men pillaged for their own sustenance and destroyed crops, train rails, and whatever else might keep the rebellion alive.

In the Shenandoah Valley of Virginia, the Union also made progress. First came a setback. By May the Confederate general Jubal A. Early had driven federal troops out of the area, and in early July he mounted a raid that reached almost to the city of Washington before being turned back. He then

Richmond, the Confederate capital, April 4, 1865. (Courtesy, Library of Congress)

retreated to the Shenandoah. But in September Philip Sheridan, a cavalry commander who had distinguished himself in the West and now had charge of the federal army in the Valley, defeated Early in two engagements. At Cedar Creek on October 19, Early scattered a force of federal troops. Thereupon Sheridan, dashing on horseback to the front, steadied his retreating men and led them forward in an attack that demolished the rebels just as they were celebrating their apparent victory. Sheridan's ride became instant legend. In the course of his Valley campaign he employed, like Sherman, the tactics that were hastening Confederate defeat in the Deep South: he stripped the countryside.

THE END OF THE REBELLION

As late as the summer of 1864, Lincoln continued to insist that he fought for one purpose: to save the Union. His Gettysburg Address, delivered on the previous November 19 during the dedication of a cemetery for troops fallen in battle there, speaks of preserving the government and the liberties it already embodied, not of extending liberty to the enslaved. (Only the reference to "a new birth of freedom" might have led listeners to imagine that the president had anything in mind beyond safeguarding the rights and liberties of Americans who already enjoyed them.) Emancipation and the enlistment of black Americans in the army and navy, perhaps 130,000 in August 1864, were in Lincoln's reasoning vital to the success of the Union. It also meant, however, an obligation to these enlistees, an obligation that the president and Grant both accepted. But a serious problem arose regarding the rebel treatment of black troops in federal uniform.

African Americans in the Union army could expect from their Confederate foes none of the respect that nineteenth-century convention required between wartime enemies. An especially notorious example occurred on April 12, 1864, at Fort Pillow on Tennessee's western border with the Mississippi River. There rebels led by Nathan Bedford Forrest overran a force of fewer than three hundred black soldiers, along with a roughly similar number of white troops in a Tennessee command loyal to the Union. Accounts at the time reported that some of the victors had gone on to slaughter black defenders of the post.

When in 1863 African Americans began to appear in significant numbers in the Union army, the Confederacy refused to treat its black captives as prisoners of war, exchangeable on the same terms as white troops. And the federal government itself did not give its black soldiers equal treatment. They were placed under white officers and until fairly late in the war did not receive equal pay with their white comrades. By the end of 1863, the Confederacy had become willing in theory to consider as legitimate prisoners of war black soldiers legally freed under previous laws. It claimed the right, however, to return to slavery fugitives who had joined the Union military. Under those conditions, Washington ceased exchanging prisoners altogether. Black troops would be treated as genuine soldiers or there would be no exchanges at all.

In the resulting impasse, Union prisoners languished in southern camps and rebel prisoners in federal compounds. The worst instance of misery was at Andersonville, a Confederate camp in Georgia. In a stockade built to contain ten thousand, over three times that number of Union captives lived in conditions of filth and deprivation. During that summer, sometimes over a hundred prisoners died daily. Though after the war the victorious Union tried and executed the camp commandant Henry Wirz, he was not fundamentally responsible for the horrors of Andersonville. They resulted from the Confederacy's lack of resources. During the later days of the war even rebel soldiers were on the shortest of rations.

In January 1865, Richmond acceded to the demand that captured black troops of whatever prior status of freedom or slavery be treated as military prisoners. By then, it was beginning to be clear even to southerners that however the war ended, slavery in its old forms could not endure. In the very last days of the conflict, the Confederate leadership was prepared to arm and promise freedom to black slaves who enlisted in the rebel military. This desperate proposal amounted to an admission that the social system that had led to the secession was dead.

The Momentum of Success

In early November 1864, meanwhile, the Confederacy suffered a defeat at the polls perhaps greater than any single defeat in battle. Farragut, Sherman, Grant, and Sheridan had together put to rout the

Democratic claim that the war was unwinnable. Democrats waged an overtly racist campaign, attacking emancipation and denouncing Lincoln for wasting white lives in pursuit of black freedom. But by now most northerners were associating the cause of abolition with that of Union and patriotism. Lincoln and Johnson carried every state except Delaware, New Jersey, and Kentucky. Even the border states of Maryland and Missouri went Republican. Republicans swept the congressional races as well.

At the time Sherman set out on his invasion of the Deep South from Atlanta to the sea, he put General Thomas in charge of troops confronting Hood in Tennessee. South of Nashville, Hood assaulted a well-entrenched federal army in a costly but inconclusive battle. By late December, Thomas had the rebels on the run. On December 22, while Hood's army was disintegrating in the West, Sherman took Georgia's coastal city Savannah. In mid-January Fort Fisher on the North Carolina coast fell to the Union. The post had until then served to protect blockade runners carrying supplies to Lee's force besieged at Petersburg.

On February 1 Sherman set out on the next phase of his campaign, a march northward through South Carolina. His troops relished the opportunity to trash the birthplace of secession, and in their movement through the state they left more desolation than they had inflicted on Georgia. Joseph E. Johnston received on February 22, 1865, the unenviable command of a ragtag army that was supposed to halt Sherman's progress through the Carolinas. But Sherman did not consider the destruction of Johnston an important task. His objective was to get to Virginia and join with Grant in the defeat of Lee.

He did not get there in time, and as things turned out he was not needed. Sheridan, having arrived from the Shenandoah Valley, participated in the crushing of what remained of Lee's army at Petersburg, already shrinking from desertions. On April 2, Lee decided he had to abandon Petersburg, and with it any hope of defending Richmond. He sent Jefferson Davis a telegram that reached the president of the Confederacy while he was attending an Easter Sunday service in the capital. The rebel government fled from the city, and Union forces captured it, encountering only scant resistance. Lincoln, who had been visiting Grant at Petersburg, immediately went to Richmond, where he received an emotional greeting from the black residents.

The Confederacy effectively came to an end on

Andersonville Prison provided no shelter for many of its inmates. The facility's death rate doubled that of other southern prisons. (Courtesy, Library of Congress)

April 9, when at Appomattox Courthouse Lee surrendered his exhausted army to Grant. Various remnants of rebel armies remained in the field. On April 18 Johnston capitulated to Sherman in North Carolina. The trans-Mississippi Confederate West, which had long been severed from the eastern half of the rebellion, yielded on May 26 when Kirby Smith, commander of the rebel forces there, surrendered at New Orleans. By then Jefferson Davis was already a Union prisoner.

From wounds or sickness, the war had killed about 258,000 Confederate troops: a fourth of the white male population eligible by age for military service in the states of the rebellion. Union deaths were just under 360,000. The end of the war left the economy of the South in ruins, while northern industry was thriving from the demands the conflict had put on it. The only Union enterprise to be set back by the war was the merchant marine, a victim of Confederate raiders. Throughout the late nineteenth century and well into the twentieth, the South would be a poor cousin of the North and its economy.

The Second Inaugural

After Appomattox Courthouse, Lincoln had only a few days of life remaining. Shaping a policy toward the defeated secessionist states would be left to others. But Lincoln had already given to the conflict the definition he himself so long evaded: a war not only for Union but for emancipation. On March 4, as the war's end clearly approached, he took the oath of office for a second time, delivering one of his most distinguished addresses. The Second Inaugural is best known for its call for reconciliation between the wartime enemies: "With malice toward none, with charity for all. . . . " But there was also a moment of speculation. Could it be that the war was retribution for the sin of slavery, that it would continue "until every drop of blood drawn with the lash shall be paid by another drawn by the sword?"

Suggested Readings

A fine overview of the Civil War is James M. McPherson, *Battle Cry of Freedom: The Civil War Era* (1988). Other excellent syntheses include Russell F. Weigley, *A Great Civil War: A Military and Political History, 1861–1865* (2000); Herman Hattaway, *Shades of Blue and Gray* (1997), and Charles P. Roland, *An American Iliad: The Story of the Civil War* (2nd. ed., 2002). For treatments of the war's immense historiography, see James M. McPherson and William J. Cooper Jr., eds., *Writing the Civil War: The Quest to Understand* (1998) and Steven E. Woodworth, ed., *The American Civil War: A Handbook of Literature and Research* (1996). The 131-page bibliography in J. G. Randall and David Donald, *The Civil War and Reconstruction* (2nd. ed., 1969) remains valuable despite its publication date.

All important Civil War generals and many secondary ones have found one or more biographers. Among the best of these studies are William S. McFeely, *Grant: A Biography* (1981); Emory M. Thomas, *Robert E. Lee: A Biography* (1995); John F. Marszalek, *Sherman: A Soldier's Passion for Order* (1993); Michael Fellman, *Citizen Sherman: A Life of William Tecumseh Sherman* (1995); Stephen W. Sears, *George B. McClellan: The Young Napoleon* (1988); and Craig L. Symonds, *Joseph E. Johnston* (1992). Provocative introductions to Civil War grand strategy include Richard E. Beringer, Herman Hattaway, Archer Jones, and William N. Still Jr., *Why the South Lost the Civil War* (1986) and Herman Hattaway and Archer Jones, *How the North Won: A Military History of the Civil War* (1983). Steven E. Woodworth, *Jefferson Davis and His Generals: The Failure of Con-federate Command in the West* (1990) and T. Harry Williams, *Lincoln and His Generals* (1952), explain how Richmond and Washington, worked out problems of high command. Virtually all major Civil War campaigns and battles, and even specific armies, are the subject of multiple books. For some of the best works in this genre, see Stephen W. Sears, *Landscape Turned Red: The Battle of Antietam* (1983); James Lee McDonough, *Shiloh—in Hell before Night* (1977); Peter Cozzens, *No Better Place to Die: The Battle of Stones River* (1990); Richard J. Sommers, *Richmond Redeemed: The Siege at Petersburg* (1981); Gabor S. Boritt, ed., *The Gettysburg Nobody Knows* (1997); Richard M. McMurry, *Atlanta 1864: Last Chance for the Confederacy* (2000); Thomas L. Connelly's *Army of the Heartland: The Army of Tennessee, 1861–1862* (1967) and *Autumn of Glory: The Army of Tennessee, 1862–1865* (1971). Two especially imaginative approaches to Civil War battles are Stephen Cushman, *Bloody Promenade* (1999) and Peter Svenson, *Battlefield: Forming a Civil War Battlefield* (1992). Of the many works about technology's impact on the Civil War, Milton F. Perry's, *Infernal Machines: The Story of Confederate Submarine and Mine Warfare* (1965) stands out for its relevance to modern military ethics. Civil War prisons receive comprehensive coverage in Lonnie R. Speer, *Portals to Hell: Military Prisons of the Civil War* (1997).

A vast literature covers the war's naval side. See, for a sampling, William C. Davis, *Duel Between the First Ironclads* (1975); Stephen R. Wise, *Lifeline of the Confederacy: Blockade Running During the Civil War* (1988); and William N. Still,

Jr., *Iron Afloat: The Story of the Confederate Armorclads* (1971). Two of the most compelling works about the Civil War's horrific guerrilla conflicts are Michael Fellman, *Inside War: The Guerrilla Conflict in Missouri During the Civil War* (1989) and Phillip Shaw Paludan, *Victims: A True Story of the Civil War* (1981). The often ignored fighting in Arizona and New Mexico receives a compelling treatment in Donald S. Frazier, *Blood and Treasure: Confederate Empire in the Southwest* (1995). David A. Nichols, *Lincoln and the Indians: Civil War Policy and Politics* (1978) and Laurence M. Hauptman, *Between Two Fires: American Indians in the Civil War* (1995) are two of the more significant works on Native American issues and participation in the Civil War. Elizabeth D. Leonard tells the long overlooked story of females who served the Union and Confederate armies in different capacities (sometimes disguising their gender and fighting in battle) in *All the Daring of the Soldier: Women of the Civil War Armies* (1999). Among many provocative recent works about the ideologies and experiences of Civil War common soldiers, Reid Mitchell's *The Vacant Chair: The Northern Soldier Leaves Home* (1993); James M. McPherson, *For Cause and Comrades: Why Men Fought in the Civil War* (1997); and Gerald F. Linderman, *Embattled Courage: The Experience of Combat in the American Civil War* (1987) are standouts.

D. P. Crook's *Diplomacy During the Civil War* (1975) provides a reliable overview of Union and Confederate relations with foreign powers, but supplement it with Howard Jones, *Abraham Lincoln and a New Birth of Freedom: The Union and Slavery in the Diplomacy of the Civil War* (1999); Richard J. M. Blackett, *Divided Hearts: Britain and the American Civil War* (2001); and Robert E. May, ed., *The Union, the Confederacy, and the Atlantic Rim* (1995). For Union politics and the northern home front during the conflict, see Phillip Shaw Paludan, *"A People's Contest": The Union and Civil War, 1861–1865* (1988) and *The Presidency of Abraham Lincoln* (1994); Mark E. Neely, Jr., *The Fate of Liberty: Abraham Lincoln and Civil Liberties* (1991); and Iver Bernstein, *The New York City Draft Riots: Their Significance for American Society and Politics in the Age of the Civil War* (1990). *Lincoln at Gettysburg: The Words That Remade America* (1992) by Garry Wills is a fascinating analysis of Lincoln's most memorable speech. But also consult the excellent biographies of Lincoln that are available, including David Herbert Donald, *Lincoln* (2000) and Mark E. Neely, Jr., *The Last Best Hope of Earth: Abraham Lincoln and the Promise of America* (1993). The rich literature on the Union's emancipation policy and the enlistment of African Americans in the Union military includes such works as John Hope Franklin, *The Emancipation Proclamation* (1963); Herman Belz, *A New Birth of Freedom: The Republican Party and Freedman's Rights, 1861–1866* (1976); Ira Berlin, Joseph P.

Reidy, and Leslie S. Rowland, eds., *Freedom's Soldiers: The Black Military Experience in the Civil War* (1998); Dudley Taylor Cornish, *The Sable Arm: Negro Troops in the Union Army, 1861–1865* (1956); and James M. McPherson, *The Struggle for Equality: Abolitionists and the Negro in the Civil War and Reconstruction* (1964). Union confiscatory policies in occupied Confederate territory receive dissection in Mark Grimsley, *The Hard Hand of War: Union Military Policy Toward Southern Civilians, 1861–1865* (1995). But see also Charles Royster, *The Destructive War: William Tecumseh Sherman, Stonewall Jackson, and the Americans* (1860) for how the Civil War became total war. Union wartime reconstruction policies and their implementation receive attention in William C. Harris, *With Charity for All: Lincoln and the Restoration of the Union* (1997); Willie Lee Rose, *Rehearsal for Reconstruction: The Port Royal Experiment* (1964); and Louis Gerteis, *From Contraband to Freedman: Federal Policy toward Southern Blacks, 1861–1865* (1973). For Confederate politics and the southern home front, see William C. Davis, *"A Government of Our Own": The Making of the Confederacy* (1994); Emory M. Thomas, *The Confederate Nation: 1861-1865* (1979); Gary W. Gallagher, *The Confederate War: How Popular Will, Nationalism, and Military Strategy Could Not Stave Off Defeat* (1997); George C. Rable, *The Confederate Republic: A Revolution Against Politics* (1994); Drew Gilpin Faust's *The Creation of Confederate Nationalism: Ideology and Identity in the Civil War South* (1988) and *Mothers of Invention: Women of the Slaveholding South in the Civil War* (1996); Steven V. Ash, *When the Yankees Came: Conflict and Chaos in the Occupied South, 1861–1865* (1995); and William J. Cooper, Jr., *Jefferson Davis, American* (2000). Confederate initiatives to emancipate and arm slaves to salvage a losing cause are covered in Robert F. Durden, *The Gray and the Black: The Confederate Debate on Emancipation* (1972). For the slaves' reaction to the war and emancipation, consult Leon F. Litwack's moving *'Been in the Storm So Long': The Aftermath of Slavery* (1979).

An imaginative analysis of the war's popular literature is Alice Fahs, *The Imagined Civil War: Popular Literature of the North and South, 1861–1865*. Also see Daniel Aaron, *The Unwritten War: American Writers and the Civil War* (1973) and Louis P. Masur, ed., *The Real War Will Never Get in the Books: Selections from Writers During the Civil War* (1993) for an understanding of writers and the war.

Eric T. Dean, *Shook Over Hell: Post-Traumatic Stress, Vietnam, and the Civil War* (1997) explores the long-term psychological damage of Civil War fighting on its soldiers. David W. Blight's moving *Race and Reunion: The Civil War in American Memory* (2001), which won multiple book prizes, explains the contest of Civil War memories in United States culture.

This somber scene of birds returning to roost at twilight can be interpreted as a visual meditation of the nation's weary mood at the end of the Civil War. Painted in 1866 by Jervis McEntee, the forlorn landscape, devoid of human faces, reflects the melancholy sentiments of national dreams deferred. Birds were seen as religious symbols—souls of the dead returning to their resting places. Yet the upright form of a man-made fence crossed by a young sapling as a crucifix promises hope nonetheless. *(Courtesy, Library of Congress)*

Reconstructing the South

★

LANDSCAPE OF CONFEDERATE DEFEAT

In their continuing invasion of the Deep South in the final months of the Civil War, General William Tecumseh Sherman's northern troops made the destruction of railroads into an art. His men would spread out for a mile on one side of the track. Grasping whatever rails were before them, they all lifted at a command, toppling the strip. One group of soldiers tore up the track. Another stacked the wooden ties and piled the steel rails on top. A third set the ties afire so the heat softened the rails until they could be bent and twisted into uselessness or wrapped around tree trunks.

The thoroughness and discipline of Sherman's operations bespoke the relentless progress of his war machine as it ground through the South. The burning of the business district of Atlanta, Georgia, during September 1864 is part of the folklore of the war. Retreating Confederates blew up locomotives and train cars filled with ammunition. Then the northern army of sixty thousand marched from that city to the sea, living off the land and leaving a swath of destruction sixty miles wide.

The invaders needed no instructions in methods of devastation. Every one of Sherman's "bummers," as they were called—tanned, dirty, bearded, and tough—was a gnawing, hacking demolition engine. Men repeatedly ventured out from the line of march to carry out their work. Farms were sacked and their animals taken, and clothing and other personal items were not spared; the possessions of blacks were sometimes stolen along with the goods of the planters. "[We] destroyed all we could not eat," a Union veteran would recall of the drive through Georgia, "stole their niggers, burned their cotton and gins, spilled their sorghum, burned and twisted their R. Rails, and raised Hell."

By the end of January 1865, Sherman's troops were marching on South Carolina's capital of Columbia, eager for revenge on the state where the war had started. "South Carolina cried out the first for war," wrote an Iowa volunteer. "And she shall have it to her heart's content." Sherman reduced Columbia to a shell. He blamed retreating rebels for setting Columbia ablaze, but given the orgy of drunkenness among his men, any number of them might have fired the city, purposely or not.

Sherman's troops had to subsist on what they could find, and they like their foes knew aching hunger. They were fighting a modern war, a war of whole peoples, in which winning required the exhaustion and demoralization of the civilian population. Even had the march been conducted with greater restraint, the conflict would have left the region desolate. Not only did federal troops take food from the people of the South; so did the Confederate military, leaving women and children to wring whatever thin provision they could from the soil. Blacks fled from plantations, not just toward freedom but away from the path of the war. Within Sherman's army, much of which was from states west of the Atlantic seaboard, were men as viciously racist as any southerner, and coarsened by the gleefully triumphal procession through the South. Yet as the Union soldiers marched into the city of Columbia, they sang the song of freedom, "John Brown's Body," to the cheers of the city's black population. After South Carolina the army moved through North Carolina with no significant opposition.

"All is gloom, despondency, and inactivity," wrote a South Carolinian early in 1865. "Our army is demoralized and the people panic stricken." When General Sherman said "War is all hell," he meant that it should be made as costly and terrible as possible for the opponent. Southerners would be quick to say that he had done so.

In the period of Reconstruction following the war, would the North have the will to reorder the rebel states with the same determination that the Union troops had brought to conquering them?

Not all of the destruction in Atlanta came at the hands of Sherman's forces; as the Confederate army retreated from Atlanta, it exploded munitions to keep them out of Union hands. The wreckage seen in this photograph is of a factory that retreating troops blew up. Union troops wrecked the remaining industries, including a nearby roundhouse and car repair shed. The devastation of Atlanta and southern Georgia during Sherman's march to the sea destroyed Confederate morale. (Courtesy, National Archives)

HISTORICAL EVENTS

1863
Lincoln presents "ten-percent plan" for reconstructing the South

1864
Lincoln "pocket vetoes" congressional plan of reconstruction, the Wade-Davis Bill • General Sherman burns Atlanta and makes his destructive march to the sea

1865
Civil War ends (April) • Thirteenth Amendment ends slavery • Freedmen's Bureau established • Lincoln assassinated April 14 • Andrew Johnson becomes president • black codes passed by white southern legislatures

1866
Civil Rights Act passed over President Johnson's veto • first Ku Klux Klan is organized • riots in Memphis and New Orleans • Radical Republicans capture both houses of Congress after President Johnson's "Swing Around the Circle" fails

1867
Tenure of Office Act • Johnson suspends Secretary of War Edwin Stanton

1868
Fourteenth Amendment • President Johnson is impeached by the House but acquitted by the Senate • Ulysses S. Grant is elected president

1869
Woman suffrage organizations disagree over Fifteenth Amendment

1870–
Enforcement Acts • Fifteenth Amendment is ratified

1872
Grant reelected president

1876
Rutherford B. Hayes elected president in disputed election

1877
Federal troops withdraw from the South

FREEDOM

On April 9, 1865, the main body of Confederate troops under Robert E. Lee surrendered to Ulysses S. Grant at Appomattox Courthouse in Virginia. Though rebel armies were still operating in the field, April 9 is the day customarily assigned to the defeat of the Confederacy. It is not, however, the day the slaves were freed.

The Moment of Liberation

President Lincoln's Emancipation Proclamation, taking effect on January 1, 1863, grew out of his primary war aim, to save the Union. He had, in fact,

a few months earlier told the New York publisher Horace Greeley: "If I could save the Union without freeing *any* slave I would do it, and if I could save it by freeing *all* the slaves I would do it. . . ." The Proclamation applied only to states still in rebellion, so it had no immediate practical effect. But it made the northern soldiers an army of liberation; the North now fought for freedom as well as for the Union, and slaves became free as enemy territory was conquered. By the time of General Lee's surrender, freedom had already come to much of the black population. It happened during 1863 in Maryland, a slave state that had never left the Union. Maryland abolished slavery on its own. At the end of 1863 emancipation came, technically, to the state of Tennessee, Confederate but divided in sentiment.

There the Unionist Andrew Johnson, appointed governor by Lincoln, declared the abolition of slavery. In sections of the state under Union control, abolition of slavery prevailed. Emancipation also arrived, at least momentarily, whenever Union troops on their way through the deeper South came to a plantation, looted it, and announced to the slaves that they were free. That might not mean much: the soldiers could be gone within hours, leaving blacks and whites alike confused as to what law would prevail the day after.

The arrival of Union troops could be a nightmare for slaves. The federal army was of no one mind on racial questions. Along with the growing number of blacks within its ranks were committed abolitionists, white racists, and some white troops who converted to abolitionism when they saw the scars that laced the backs of slaves. Whether at a given plantation the liberators were kindly or cruel was pretty much a matter of chance.

Even for slaves who were fortunate enough not to encounter the worst kind of Union soldiers, the last months of the war could be a particular horror. Hunger and misery were the lot of both races. And masters or mistresses sometimes became overwrought at the thought that their slaves were soon to be taken from them. An owner might go into a frenzy of whippings or killings, taking out his frustration and bitter disappointment on his slaves. Some owners reacted to emancipation by sinking into despair. A whole culture of dominance and deference, the very essence of life as they had known it, seemed to have vanished.

Even after the military conquest of the whole of the rebel South, moreover, freedom applied only to areas within the former Confederacy in which the Emancipation Proclamation prevailed or some Unionist regime decreed it. The Proclamation, though it rested on a deeper commitment to freedom, was technically a military order treating slaves as property to be taken by troops like any other goods in a combat zone. Lincoln as Commander-in-Chief could authorize seizures of slaves; he had no other constitutional power by which to declare their freedom. Freedom would not be the universal rule until the end of 1865, when a sufficient number of states had ratified the Thirteenth Amendment to the Constitution abolishing slavery and it took effect.

For many slaves, the instant of emancipation whenever it came was bewildering. A system of life and work had disappeared. Stories tell of mingled exaltation and sadness, feelings of affection and loyalty to masters and mistresses or, on the contrary, an urge to lash out at owners who sometimes had been at once friends, guardians, and oppressors, but often merely oppressors. The system now cast aside had trained neither race in how to live as free men and women. Liberation from slavery brought black southerners joy. But the collapse of slavery and the

Winslow Homer, A Visit from the Old Mistress, *1876.* (Courtesy, National Museum of American Art, Smithsonian Institution, Gift of William T. Evans)

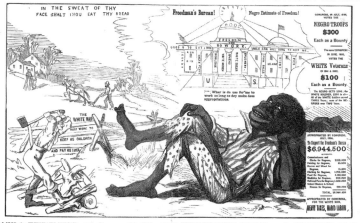

In 1866, and even before, attacks on the Freedmen's Bureau became openly racist. (Courtesy, Library of Congress)

ravages of the war forced them to rethink their lives.

The World Beyond the Plantations

One of the first choices the freedmen—the collective name for ex-slaves—had to face was whether to leave their plantation and encounter the insecurity of uncertain employment in the world beyond. Among planters the belief had been common that their slaves were happy and faithful. That was one of the foundation myths of their defense of slavery. Now they felt shock, hurt, and outrage at finding their trusted people to be so ungrateful as to desert them. For the slaves, leaving could be dangerous. In the early postwar period some planters refused to accept the reality that their former servants no longer belonged to them; local patrols would return, whip, or shoot freedmen whom the ex-rebels considered to be runaways. In an effort to keep freedmen from abandoning the countryside, Union military officers sometimes cooperated with planters. So, in many cases, did agents of the Freedmen's Bureau that the federal government had set up as a general welfare agency for the devastated South. At the end of the war a widespread view among the federal officials was that it would be to the advantage of former slaves to accept any kind of available employment. That conviction translated into a determination to keep the freed blacks on the plantations where work, however unsatisfactory, was available.

While many ex-slaves remained with their former masters, others took to the roads in sizable numbers, though often they migrated only a few miles. They left because they were curious about the opportunities beyond the borders of their captivity, or simply because leaving gave meaning to freedom. Or they left former masters and mistresses who were impossible to tolerate any longer. Some freedmen set out in a desperate effort to find children, spouses, or parents from whom they had been separated by sale. That search could bring joy at finding relatives or distress at discovering husbands and wives deceased or remarried.

Emergency projects arose to supply some freedmen with food, shelter, and employment. Much of the southern white population was scarcely better off. Widows had to provide for children in a land burned and despoiled. Veterans missing an arm or a leg needed to work as though they were whole. Planters comfortably off before the war put up makeshift shelters in place of the stately homes in which they had lived, or sought to regain their fortunes from fields no longer tended by slaves. In a few cases, their ex-slaves helped them out, for freedmen knew how helpless much of the planter class was at the prospect of survival by working.

The Freedmen's Bureau, the nation's first widespread and systematic welfare and antipoverty program, began under the direction of Major General Oliver Howard, one of Sherman's commanders and an evangelical Christian. In its earliest days, the Bureau did not even have a budget, only the occupying army and charitable organizations prepared to supply money and volunteers. With these—even supplemented by aid eventually provided by Congress—the Bureau had to scramble to care for needy southern blacks and whites, set up an educational system, and supervise labor contracts that replaced the system of slavery.

Lincoln's Assassination

President Lincoln was not given time to administer conditions within the ravaged South. But he put his moral force behind the Thirteenth Amendment abolishing slavery. The amendment from the moment of its drafting confirmed that slavery would not survive the defeat of the Confederacy, as the Emancipation Proclamation had promised.

On the day of Lee's surrender at Appomattox, Lincoln made a triumphal visit to Richmond, Virginia, the capital of the Confederacy, where he met a joyous reception by black civilians and soldiers. Shortly after his return to Washington, the president along with Mrs. Lincoln and friends went to Ford's Theater on April 14 to watch a performance of the comedy *Our American Cousin*. John Wilkes Booth, a Maryland actor with free access to the building, leapt into the president's theater box, shot the president, then fled crying "Sic semper tyrannis!"—"thus always to tyrants." A bullet lodged in Lincoln's head took his life within a few hours. Booth, who had been brooding over the defeat of the Confederacy, was soon hunted down and shot to death while resisting arrest, and some co-conspirators were hanged.

The death of Lincoln, at the instant of national victory and the formal liberation of a whole enslaved people, framed his life in glory. The task of designing in collaboration with Congress a policy for the defeated states now fell to Lincoln's vice president, Andrew Johnson. A Tennessee politician and a Democrat opposed to the rebellion, Johnson had run with Lincoln on the 1864 presidential ticket of the Union Party, a temporary combination

Drawing by J. A. Arthur of Washington welcoming Lincoln to Heaven with a crown of laurels, 1865. (Courtesy, Library of Congress)

of Republican and Democratic supporters of the war. While military governor of Tennessee, Johnson had endorsed emancipation. Yet in his prewar career, hostile to the slaveowning plantation class for its dominance of politics but not hostile to slavery itself, he had nothing in common with the abolitionist wing of the Republican Party.

THE SHAPE OF FREEDOM

For much of the white South, particularly the planter class, psychological disorientation accompanied physical ruin. Former rebels had to live with defeat in all its manifestations. And African Americans, once obliged to perform a thousand gestures acknowledging whites as their superiors, could no longer be counted on to humble themselves. A North Carolina planter was upset that a black Union soldier had bowed and greeted him:

President Andrew Johnson had been both a governor and a senator from Tennessee before becoming vice president and, after Lincoln's assassination, president. (Courtesy, Library of Congress)

the local custom was for blacks never to speak to whites before being spoken to first. One of innumerable reports of white indignation after the end of slavery was of a woman whipped for refusing to call her employer "master." Whites accustomed to locating their self-worth in their skin now had to base their identity elsewhere. For the shattered nerves of some of the vanquished, it was all too much.

Freedmen also suffered greatly from the destruction the war had brought to the southern economy and society. More than the whites, they were adrift. But they had the task of defining themselves in previously forbidden ways: as citizens, independent workers, people of education and acquired ability.

Freedmen
in Command of Their Lives

For a start, former slaves sought to establish families or to reunite in marriages and blood relationships that slavery had ruptured by sale. Marital arrangements took the conventional nineteenth-century form, the man heading the household. Despite all the disruptions that slavery had brought to family life, most black southerners in 1870 would be living in a two-parent home.

Freed slaves knew the significance of schooling. The antebellum rules prohibiting the teaching of the slave population alone suggested to them how important literacy was. Now poor black communities taxed themselves or took up collections to establish a school and hire a teacher. Churches, private homes, whatever space could serve as a classroom was put to use. Any break in the workday might be time for taking out a spelling book; children walked their parents through the alphabet. Northern men and women driven by a Puritan or evangelical Christian conscience, along with blacks from the North who had never known slavery, went south to become teachers.

Much of the life of the freedmen was centered in their churches. In Bible stories black Christians, like whites, found models for the tribulations of their own times. For slaves and ex-slaves, the years of captivity in Egypt endured by the Children of Israel carried particular meaning. Drawing on the richness of the Bible, the impassioned preaching

The Freedmen's Bureau employed teachers from northern missionary and abolitionist societies to staff thousands of schools for freed slaves and poor whites. (Courtesy, Valentine Museum, Richmond, VA)

common to black as well as white evangelical ministers made church services a powerful instrument of collective action. No matter what the specific subject of the sermon, it was always at least implicitly political. The church by its very existence affirmed that the freedmen had formed a community.

Outside the churches, the freed slaves engaged incessantly in fundamental acts of politics: meeting, speaking, arguing. Black rallies and petitions sought to win the vote and other rights. Organization and leadership varied in response to local conditions. In New Orleans, for example, an African American elite of some property and status that had been free before the Civil War figured prominently in the effort to bring equality to the newly emancipated.

Freedom Without Land?

The Constitution now affirmed the freedom of the black race. But what did that mean in a practical way? It was important that the emancipated slaves were free to meet and discuss, to read, to throw off their old customs of servility toward whites. But freedom, to be meaningful, required property or some means of productive activity. For skilled workers, especially in urban centers, such a life was often available. But the mass of the emancipated thought only of a future of agricultural labor. And for that, freedmen needed either land of their own or a way of gaining a decent wage and working conditions from whites who possessed the land.

On the Sea Islands off the coast of South Carolina that Union troops occupied during the war, the departure of the owners had left land that blacks treated as their own. Many of the blacks were Gullahs, who spoke a distinctive dialect. Some groups of ex-slaves collected enough money to buy patches of land. But northern investors or enterprising army officers, believing the wage system to be beneficial to the emancipated, attempted instead to establish plantation production of cotton, though by use of paid labor. Now black refugees from the fighting in South Carolina crowded into the area, so there were desperate newcomers to be fed as well.

Elsewhere in the South, no serious attempt was made to seize the lands of rebels and distribute them to the freedmen. Promises of "forty acres and a mule," a promise made by a Union officer just after the triumph of the Union, never materialized.

Instead they have remained as a ghostly whisper of a free South that might have been.

Why Land Was Not Provided

Why did the federal government not set out to remake the land and property distribution of the region, and so give freedom a solid foundation? The simplest answer is that the will to do so was not present. Andrew Johnson had some concern for the freedmen. But he was possessed by the racism of his region, and what was in truth the racism of the nation as a whole. He wished for blacks little more than formal freedom, and he had no intention of using the federal army to turn white property over to the emancipated. A peppery backcountry southerner accustomed to the attack mode of his region's rural politics, Johnson was to become increasingly combative in opposition to black rights. Nor was Congress of any one opinion as to how far black freedom should extend. One faction there, the Republican Radicals, did want the federal government to insure full equality for the freedmen. But within Radicalism itself, no clear vision existed of a Reconstruction to be achieved through distributing among southern blacks the land of former slaveholders. The Congress had no commitment to an economic remaking of the South to match their coming political reform of the region.

Lack of will, however, furnishes only part of the

To All Whom It May Concern

Edisto Island, August 15th, 1865 George Owens, having selected for settlement forty acres of Land, on Theodore Belad's Place, pursuant to Special Field Orders, No. 15, Headquarters Military Division of the Mississippi, Savannah, Ga., Jan. 16, 1865; he has permission to hold and occupy the said Tract, subject to such regulations as may be established by proper authority; and all persons are prohibited from interfering with him in his possession of the same.

By command of
 R. SAXTON
  Brev'tMaj. Gen.,
  Ass't. Comm.
  S.C., Ga., and Fla.

The Sea Islands off the Carolina coast honored black landowners.

explanation. The larger problem lay in a hitch in the thinking even of many of the Radical Republicans—those federal legislators who were prepared to press the question of equality further than was the North as a whole.

The Market Ideology

Most abolitionists and Radicals, along with Americans generally, closely identified political freedom with market capitalism. Freedom meant entering the marketplace to earn a wage or to start a business. Many Radicals assumed an almost magical ability on the part of the market to provide wages for workers and capital for business. Freedom, in this way of thinking, does not have to be built up and sustained; freedom simply happens when nothing gets in its way. The market ideology insisted also on the sanctity of private property. While the Radicals and abolitionists, at least, could perceive property in human beings as unnatural, and so applaud the elimination of slavery, landed property was a different matter. The bulk of the Radicals—though there were exceptions, most insistently Representative Thaddeus Stevens of Pennsylvania—ideologically opposed taking land from its owner.

Defenders of capitalism in its nineteenth-century form viewed human beings as meant to be hungry for possessions and for the satisfaction of material desires. Owning a piece of land and using it mainly for family subsistence betrayed a failure of ambition. It was better, economists thought, to be a wage earner. That way you could hunger for an ever-higher wage and an ever-better job. One argument for educating the freedmen was that schooling would bring an increase in wants that would drive the educated individual to greater effort. In this view, plantation gang labor for a wage was not merely a necessity but a positive good.

As Americans, black leaders had absorbed the pieties of capitalist economics and promoted them among their followers. In political meetings they spoke of the harmony of capital and labor, a notion consistent with the nineteenth-century concept of political liberty and the formal freedom to seek work. But freed slaves also understood, with an intimacy unavailable to their northern white sympathizers, the cruelty of gang labor—masses of workers watched and driven by an overseer. Gang labor in cotton production also fitted the prevailing form of American capitalism. Northern clothing mill owners had an insatiable appetite for southern cotton. It was not to their liking to have southern blacks own land and grow food on it. They preferred that the land and its labor force be put to producing cotton in bulk for a northern market. The northern capitalist economy, moreover, was increasingly hiring masses of factory hands who were placed under the direction of floor superintendents. Capitalists and their political allies naturally identified freedom not with independent labor but with wage-seeking among workers massed in controlled and supervised gangs.

Sharecropping, Cotton, and the Crop Lien System

Northerners would never adequately address the question of what economy the freedmen could best live under. The freedmen, to the contrary, did speak to it. Whenever they could, they pressed for labor contracts. These contracts the harried, understaffed, underfunded Freedmen's Bureau made some effort to enforce in the courts. Another solution that black field workers often worked out with white planters was sharecropping. Families would be given yearly a plot of land on which independently to grow a cotton crop, to be divided between sharecropper and landowner. The term "sharecropping" has long since come to be synonymous with the exploitation of black and poor white southerners. But at least initially blacks liked it better than planters did, for it allowed them to live as independent workers, free from the supervision of the plantation master. After the war, the system spread partly in response to the continuing weakness and marginality of the southern economy as a whole, which deprived landowners of the cash with which to pay gang workers. Sharecropping also spread among poor white farmers; by 1880 one in three of them in the cotton-producing states was a renter or sharecropper.

As much by habit and inertia as anything else, the South largely remained committed to growing cotton. And that commitment resulted in a self-perpetuating debt system. A sharecropper, or even a small landowner, needed supplies. Since cash was not available to buy them, the local storekeeper would provision the customer on condition of a lien, or mortgage, on a part of the crop. The crop would go to the store at the end of the season if the debtor could not sell his cotton independently.

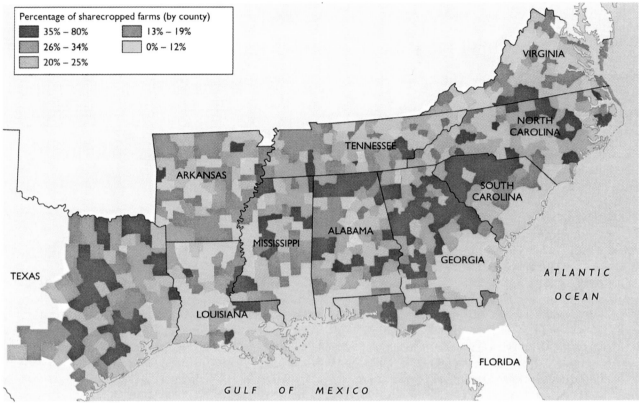

Percentage of sharecropped farms (by county)

- 35% – 80%
- 26% – 34%
- 20% – 25%
- 13% – 19%
- 0% – 12%

This map shows where sharecropping was most common in 1880.

COTTON PRICES IN NEW YORK (CENTS PER POUND)	
Year	**Real Prices (1880)**
1864	52.59
1865	45.07
1866	24.83
1867	19.50
1868	15.73
1869	19.21
1870	17.76
1871	13.04
1872	15.06
1873	13.49
1874	13.49
1875	12.71
1876	11.82
1877	11.07

Although the price of cotton fell sharply from 1864 to 1877, demand rose among northern manufacturers.
Source: M. B. Hammond, The Cotton Industry (Macmillan, 1897), reproduced in Gavin Wright, "Cotton Competition and the Post Bellum Recovery of the American South," Journal of Economic History, 34 (Sept., 1974), p. 611.

This made the land captive to cotton, the one crop a storekeeper could feel secure with. But prices were too low for sharecroppers, tenants, and small landowners of both races struggling to get themselves out of debt. So the crop lien system continued, year after year, to draw cotton from the grower, which in turn extracted from the soil the nutrients that the cotton needed, leaving fields exhausted. The storekeeper, whether greedy or fair-minded, was caught in the same dilemma, required to demand cotton as a safe crop to be turned into the means of purchasing tools and other supplies. So ruinous was the whole process that when in the next century the boll weevil ravaged the region's cotton, one town, so it is said, put up a statue to the insect for liberating the South from its one-crop bondage.

WHITE SOUTHERN DEFIANCE

Much of the white South sought to regain the social dominance that whites, whether slaveowners

In the aftermath of the Civil War, the end of slavery and the poverty of the South badly disrupted southern agriculture. Even by 1870 cotton production remained half of what it had been in the 1850s. Large plantations, tended now neither by slave gangs nor by hired freedmen, broke up into smaller holdings. But the capital needed for an attempt at making agriculture profitable again meant that control of the land remained in the hands of elite merchants and landholders.

New ways of financing southern agriculture included tenants working on leased land, and landowners giving liens on their crops to get financing for seed and fertilizer. The most common mechanism of all was sharecropping. Agreements like the Grimes family's sharecrop contract, printed below, shaped the lives of thousands of poor rural families in the new South. Both African American and white families, lacking their own money for agriculture, received seed, implements, and credit for food and other necessities to keep them until the crops were harvested and sold. Accounts were then settled. In this situation, only a small number of landowners made enough money eventually to acquire land themselves. Most sharecroppers found themselves deeper in debt at the end of each successive year.

GRIMES FAMILY PAPERS

To every one applying to rent land upon shares, the following conditions must be read, and *agreed to*.

To every 30 or 35 acres, I agree to furnish the team, plow, and farming implements, except cotton planters, and I *do not* agree to furnish a cart to every cropper. The croppers are to have half of the cotton, corn and fodder (and peas and pumpkins and potatoes if any are planted) if the following conditions are compiled with, but—if not—they are to have only two fifths (2/5). Croppers are to have no part or interest in the cotton seed raised from the crop planted and worked by them. No vine crops of any description, that is, no watermelons, muskmelons, . . . squashes or anything of that kind, except peas and pumpkins, and potatoes, are to be planted in the cotton or corn. All must work under my direction. All plantation work to be done by the croppers. My part of the crop to be *housed* by them, and the fodder and oats to be hauled and put in the house.

All the cotton must be topped about 1st August. If any cropper fails from any cause to save all the fodder from his crop, I am to have enough fodder to make it equal to one half of the whole if the whole amount of fodder had been saved.

For every mule or horse furnished by me there must be 1000 good sized rails . . . hauled, and the fence repaired as far as they will go, the fence to be torn down and put up from the bottom if I so direct. All croppers to haul rails and work on fence whenever I may order. Rails to be split when I may say. Each cropper to clean out every ditch in his crop, and where a ditch runs between two croppers, the cleaning out of that ditch is to be divided equally between them. Every ditch bank in the crop must be shrubbed down and cleaned off before the crop is planted and must be cut down every time the land is worked with his hoe and when the crop is "laid by," the ditch banks must be left clean of bushes, weeds, and seeds. The cleaning out of all ditches must be done by the first of October. The rails must be split and the fence repaired before corn is planted.

Each cropper must keep in good repair all bridges in his crop or over ditches that he has to clean out and when a bridge needs repairing that is outside of all their crops, then anyone that I call on must repair it. Fence jams to be done as ditch banks. If any cotton is planted on the land outside of the plantation fence, I am to have *three fourths* of all the cotton made in those patches, that is to say, no cotton must be planted by croppers in their home patches.

All croppers must clean out stables and fill them with straw, and haul straw in front of stables whenever I direct. All the cotton must be manured, and enough fertilizer must be brought to manure each crop highly, the croppers to pay for one half of all manure bought, the quantity to be purchased for each crop must be left to me.

No cropper to work off the plantation when there is any work to be done on the land he has rented, or when his work is needed by me or other croppers. Trees to be cut down on Orchard, House field & Evanson fences, leaving such as I may designate.

or not, had once enjoyed. Much of Reconstruction is the story not of measures imposed by the Union but of efforts on the part of the defeated Confederates to return to their past. It could do so, however, only in the absence of any major interference from its conquerors.

The Ten-Percent and Wade-Davis Plans

The earliest wartime program of Reconstruction, drafted by Lincoln in December 1863, had promised ex-rebels an astonishingly easy reentrance into full citizenship. Once a Confederate state had been militarily subdued, the program required that white male residents constituting as little as ten percent of the total number of voters registered in 1860 take an oath of future loyalty to the United States. They would thereupon be required to adopt a state constitution abolishing slavery. No substantial further accommodation to the rights or freedoms of the black population was necessary. Among the few groups excluded from participation in this "ten-percent plan" were high civil and military officers of the Confederacy. The scheme was essentially a war measure. It looked less to a settled future than to enticing as many southerners as possible to accept emancipation, at the time a daring and untested objective.

Still, as the war progressed the determination grew to demand of the rebel states, once they had been subdued, something more substantial. Congress formulated in the Wade-Davis Bill what it considered the proper conditions for reinstatement. The bill that Congress passed as an alternative to Lincoln's ten-percent plan provided that in any former Confederate state seeking to regain its full status within the Union fifty percent of its white male population first pledge loyalty to the Union. After that, citizens who could take the Ironclad Oath that they had never supported secession were to elect delegates to a convention for drawing up a state constitution. Going beyond mere emancipation, the Wade-Davis Bill stipulated that the state must give blacks equality before the law, though it did not insist upon their being granted the vote. Lincoln, thinking the plan too severe, refused to sign the measure and in 1864 pocket-vetoed it, which occurs when Congress is about to go out of session and the president holds a bill without signing it until the legislature adjourns. And there, at the end of the war, was where matters stood.

President Andrew Johnson's Reconstruction Plan

Johnson came to the presidency in 1865 with a political outlook shaped in large part by his identification with the poorer whites of the South for whom the plantation aristocracy had been the enemy. Having recognized like Lincoln the governments of Tennessee, Arkansas, Louisiana, and Virginia, he outlined his own plan for restoring the Confederate states to the Union. For the mass of rebels he issued a blanket pardon that applied to any person who pledged loyalty to the United States and support of black emancipation. Important officials in the Confederacy and owners of substantial taxable property, however, were excluded; they had to apply individually for a pardon from the president. Except for ex-rebels specifically excluded, whoever in a former Confederate state was able to meet the state's eligibility requirements for the vote could select delegates to a state constitutional convention. Johnson demanded only that the new state governments ratify the Thirteenth Amendment and repudiate state debts incurred under the Confederacy.

For southerners looking essentially to restore their old prewar society, Johnson's plan could hardly have been better. The former rebels proceeded to establish state governments that went as far as they could to negate the victory of the Union armies. Sending to Congress officials of the defeated Confederacy, including its vice president, Alexander Stephens of Georgia, came close to mocking the whole process. The most extensive act of defiance, however, was the adoption of rules governing African American residents. These regulations are remembered as the Black Codes.

The Black Codes

The rules varied from one state to another. They were not entirely vicious: a typical state code might grant blacks the right to marry, hold property, and gain at least partial access to the courts. But their main thrust was to keep the black race in place as a docile labor force. Mississippi's black code, for example, required African Americans to provide evidence every January that they had employment for the new year. Any black who during that year left the job contracted for was subject to arrest.

Another Mississippi law prohibited blacks from renting town land, which further restricted their economic options. South Carolina statutes forbade workers to leave their plantation without permission from their employer. Various states made it illegal for an employer to entice away a worker already under contract to another. Orphans and children whose parents were judged incapable of supporting them could be assigned to whites as apprentices. Rules against vagrancy were another way of insuring that black southerners would remain working for whites. Militia units, some of them including war veterans still wearing their Confederate uniforms, policed the countryside enforcing regulations against blacks.

During their ascendancy for a year or so after the war's end, the Black Codes did not completely dominate southern society. After the initial legislation, white southerners began wording laws so as to avoid the specific references to race that invited retaliation from the federal government. No one was in any doubt, of course, what part of the population all of them aimed at. The Codes collectively made clear to black southerners, along with white northerners concerned with justice in the defeated Confederacy, exactly how little justice the emancipated slaves were likely to get.

The Black Codes were not only a moral abomination but a major political mistake. Added to the South's election of prominent ex-rebels to Congress, they revealed even to northerners only mildly interested in racial justice that the region needed more reconstructing than the Johnson administration was prepared to impose. The consequence was that a frustrated national legislature turned toward more severe measures against a rebel South that had not sufficiently accepted the fact of its defeat.

CONGRESS CHARTS A POLICY

When a new Congress assembled early in 1866, opinion on the course of Reconstruction had not yet settled into clearly opposing camps. But the large Republican majority in each of the two Houses of Congress was opposed to the newly established southern state governments that President Johnson had endorsed. In accordance with their constitutional privilege, the Radical Republicans denied

Mathew Brady took this photograph of the Radical Republican Thaddeus Stevens of the House of Representatives. (Courtesy, Library of Congress)

membership in Congress to the senators and representatives elected under those regimes. The South would have to be reconstructed under principles differing from Johnson's. As an agency for investigating conditions in the states of the defeated Confederacy and deciding on proper policy, Congress set up a Joint Committee on Reconstruction.

The Legal Standing of the Former Confederate States

The decision by Congress to pursue an extensive program of Reconstruction raised a potential constitutional problem. The Union had fought the Civil War on the principle that secession was meaningless, a constitutional impossibility. This meant in theory that the Confederacy as a legal entity had never existed. Its officers and armies composed merely a criminal uprising within eleven states that had remained throughout, and were now, as much a part of the Union as ever. Its gray and butternut uniforms were no more than the costumes of a private gun club; its flags, the sheets and trappings of a stage play. But if that were the case, defenders of southern states' rights argued, then as of the end of the war the eleven states in question were in possession of exactly the same rights under the Constitution as any other state. Clearly, Congress and the national government in general had no authority completely to control the internal affairs of a state. Then how could Congress presume to establish a plan of Reconstruction over those states merely because their inhabitants had for four years behaved, falsely, as though they had seceded from the Union?

Lincoln had simply dismissed such constitutional tangles. From a practical standpoint, he reasoned, the seceded states were out of the Union; the thing was to bring them back into the nation by some workable plan. That was the purpose of his ten-percent scheme, annulled by Congress. But when it became clear that Johnson's course too had failed to produce a meaningfully reformed South, some legislators questioned how the national government could legally justify the authority Congress was now prepared to exercise over the ex-rebels.

One answer was that the eleven states were "conquered provinces," as advocates phrased it. If they were, then Congress could wield over them the power that conquerors are expected to deploy. Victors do not customarily rush to consult pieces of constitutional parchment to see whether they can permit themselves to act like victors. The South was conquered territory; the rebel organizers of the first postwar governments simply had not gotten that clear. For some in Congress, however, defining the South that way simply did not suit. Congressmen wished to be legislators, not field marshals.

More interesting from a legal point of view was the use that might be made of a passage in Article IV of the Constitution: "The United States shall guarantee to every State in this Union a Republican Form of Government. . . ." In particular Senator Charles Sumner of Massachusetts, one of the early antislavery leaders of the Republican Party, insisted on the applicability of this generally neglected passage. Rightly interpreted, he believed, it might empower the federal government to impose on the southern states conditions of justice toward the black populace that would make them genuinely republican.

The argument stumbles on the obscurity of the passage. What exactly is a republican government? History has given the label "republic" to many aristocratic states: the Greek cities, Rome, Venice, some of them governed, to one degree or another, by an upper class of slaveholders. And there was the United States itself at the time of the adoption of Article IV: proudly proclaiming itself a republic and yet carefully protecting the institution of slavery. How could any meaning be gleaned from Article IV that would give the federal government the authority to equate republicanism with racial justice and remake the South accordingly?

Like the concept of conquered provinces, the idea that the Constitution committed the nation to a republican destiny failed to provide a fully satisfactory rationale for the exercise of national authority over the vanquished southern states. In the end, Congress legislated for the South because it needed to do so.

The effort within Congress to establish a plan of Reconstruction began with a Civil Rights Act of 1866 that aimed at a thorough remaking of racial relations in the South. The bill specifically granted black southerners the right to make contracts, bring lawsuits, and have equal benefit of laws bearing on "security of person and property." Another bill would strengthen the Freedmen's Bureau, and still another gave it a budget. Against violations, Bureau and other government officials could begin legal proceedings in federal court, and punishment was specified for guilty parties.

President Johnson's friendliness toward the state governments devised by former secessionists was well known. Now Johnson quickly dispelled whatever illusions may have remained among Republicans as to the possibility that he would support significant resistance to southern racism. Vetoing both bills, he began a course of confrontation with Radicals and moderate Republicans alike. By the two-thirds vote necessary to override a presidential veto, both Houses of Congress enacted the Civil Rights Bill into law.

To deepen the legal force of civil rights, the Republicans also turned to the device of a constitutional amendment, which did not involve a presidential signature. Debate and compromise produced one of the most remarkable measures in American constitutional and legal history, the Fourteenth Amendment. It was ratified in 1868 by the necessary three-fourths of the states, among them a

AMENDMENT XIV [1868]

Section 1— All persons born or naturalized in the United States, and subject to the jurisdiction thereof, are citizens of the United States and of the State wherein they reside. No State shall make or enforce any law which shall abridge the privileges or immunities of citizens of the United States; nor shall any State deprive any person of life, liberty, or property, without due process of law; nor deny to any person within its jurisdiction the equal protection of the laws.

Section 2— Representatives shall be apportioned among the several States according to their respective numbers, counting the whole number of persons in each State, excluding Indians not taxed. But when the right to vote at any election for the choice of electors for President and Vice-President of the United States, Representatives in Congress, the Executive and Judicial officers of a State, or the members of the Legislature thereof, is denied to any of the male inhabitants of such State, being twenty-one years of age, and citizens of the United States, or in any way abridged, except for participation in rebellion, or other crime, the basis of representation therein shall be reduced in the proportion which the number of such male citizens shall bear to the whole number of male citizens twenty-one years of age in such State.

Section 3— No person shall be a Senator or Representative in Congress, or elector of President and Vice-President, or hold any office, civil or military, under the United States, or under any State, who, having previously taken an oath, as a member of Congress, or as an officer of the United States, or as a member of any State legislature, or as an executive or judicial officer of any State, to support the Constitution of the United States, shall have engaged in insurrection or rebellion against the same, and given aid or comfort to the enemies thereof. But Congress may by a vote of two-thirds of each House, remove such disability.

Section 4— The validity of the public debt of the United States, authorized by law, including debts incurred for payment of pensions and bounties for services in suppressing insurrection or rebellion, shall not be questioned. But neither the United States nor any State shall assume or pay any debt or obligation incurred in aid of insurrection or rebellion against the United States, or any claim for the loss or emancipation of any slave; but all such debts, obligations, and claims shall be held illegal and void.

Section 5— The Congress shall have power to enforce, by appropriate legislation, the provisions of this article.

few southern states required to accept the Amendment as a condition for reentry into Congress.

Equality and the Fourteenth Amendment

The Fourteenth Amendment begins by declaring, "All persons born or naturalized in the United States . . . are citizens of the United States and of the State wherein they reside." Intended to insure that blacks would thereafter be recognized as citizens, it is notable for being the first constitutional definition of American citizenship. Next comes the declaration: "No State shall make or enforce any law which shall abridge the privileges or immunities of citizens of the United States. . . ." Initially this provision looked to be central to the whole Amendment, but it soon became subject to conflicting

interpretations. Did it merely forbid the states from interfering with relations the citizen enjoys with the federal government? Or did it go further, requiring each state to behave toward its citizens the way Congress and the president must behave? A clearer wording might have changed the whole subsequent course of American law.

Then appears the injunction: " . . . nor shall any State deprive any person of life, liberty, or property, without due process of law; nor deny to any person within its jurisdiction the equal protection of the laws." Here is the enduring core of Section 1 of the Amendment. It contains the two essential components of the concept of civil rights as they were then understood: equality before the law, and access to the courts with their honored and seasoned guarantees of justice to the individual. The phrase "due process of law" was to invite in later years definitions that have generated a mass of important Supreme Court decisions. At the time, it served as a statement to the South that from then onward rights would be as fully the possession of black Americans as they were of whites.

The Fourteenth Amendment and the Vote

Section 2 of the Fourteenth Amendment implicitly encourages, but in an indirect way, that states grant the vote to the black race. Today, when suffrage is widely considered a right of every adult citizen who has not legally forfeited it, Section 2 may seem to contradict Section 1. It clearly contemplates and accepts the possibility that states will deny black citizens the vote. That appears to clash with the requirement in Section 1 that states must provide their citizens with legal equality. But at the time, Americans were not fully prepared to put the vote on the same plane as equal treatment in legislation and the courts. Section 2 considers the case of any state that denies to a portion of its male inhabitants the right to vote in federal or state elections. In such instances, the state's seats in the House of Representatives would shrink in the proportion that the number of adult males in the excluded group bore to those in the state as a whole.

This formula speaks among other things to what at the time was a constitutional dilemma. States hold seats in the House of Representatives in proportion to the size of their population. The Constitution had provided that in counting a state's population, three-fifths of all slaves—a word the drafters had prudishly avoided, but the references are clear enough—would be included. But slavery no longer existed: the Thirteenth Amendment had outlawed it. Every black southerner, then, was now recognized as a full human being. As a consequence, though, the secessionist states were now in a position actually to increase their representation in the lower House, and with a minimal concession to emancipation. Has defeat ever been sweeter to the vanquished? So the Fourteenth Amendment said in effect to the white South: give the vote to your adult male blacks, and your seating in the lower House will grow; deny it, and your representation will diminish.

The section stopped far short of Radicalism. Sponsors of the Amendment might hope that its eventual effect would be favorable to black suffrage, that the lure of gaining seats in the lower House could in time lead former Confederate states to enfranchise their black inhabitants. Yet it allowed white southerners to deny suffrage to their black neighbors. For that denial, Section 2 makes clear, southern states would pay a price, but there were indications that white racists were ready to pay it.

The Amendment and the Confederacy

Two other sections of the Amendment were directed essentially at the Confederacy itself. Section 3 decrees that no one who as a state or federal official had taken an oath to support the Constitution and then engaged in insurrection thereafter is to hold federal or state office. A considerable portion of the South's wartime leadership had previously held official positions in the old Union. That included even John Tyler of Virginia, a former president of the United States who died early in the war. The Amendment adds, however, that by a vote of two-thirds of each of its branches Congress can lift the prohibition. Section 4 forbids federal or state payment of debts incurred in support of rebellion or in compensation for the loss of slaves.

If there had been any possibility of cooperation between President Johnson and Congress, the president now stifled it. He advised the former rebel states to reject the Amendment, and in its initial circulation through the country for ratification all of them did so except his own Tennessee. Johnson combined racism (somewhat tempered by a vague wish to help the freedmen), belief in states' rights, and quickness to think that people meant to do him harm. For the next two years, Republicans not necessarily in the Radical camp would have to accept the reality that they were at political war with the president. And that deepened their recognition that they were also in opposition to much of the white South.

Riot in Memphis

Local politics in Memphis, Tennessee, in 1866 did not conform to stereotypes for southern river and plantation culture. Memphis had a considerable immigrant Irish population that had achieved effective political control of the city. A minor incident there in late spring led to an essentially white riot. Police and firemen, many of them Irish, attacked

Armed whites are shown here shooting blacks during the three-day race riot of May 1866 in Memphis, TN. (Courtesy, The Granger Collection)

black bystanders and rampaged through a dilapidated neighborhood inhabited by families of black soldiers at a nearby military base. The mob killed at least forty-eight people, only two of them white. Black homes, churches, and schools were pillaged or torched. The Freedmen's Bureau was helpless.

The army was the only institution at the time with any serious power to protect black people in the South, and that power was limited by the scarcity of federal troops throughout the region. But in the Memphis riot the army did not intervene even to protect the families of its own soldiers. And

some blacks who were free before federal emancipation had distanced themselves from the rural former slaves and proposed their removal, calling them a cause of tension.

The mere banning of ex-rebels from Tennessee's government did not suffice to bring racial justice to the state. A few weeks after Memphis came a riot in New Orleans that pushed northern opinion beyond the limit of tolerance toward the unreconstructed South.

New Orleans Erupts

Louisiana's great port city, New Orleans, under Union occupation during much of the conflict, possessed a rich mingling of cultures. Before the war the city had within its black population a considerable free-born element, typically light-skinned and at its highest levels scarcely distinguishable from the white aristocracy in property, manners, and standing. Some of its members were slaveowners themselves. Among both free and newly emancipated blacks as among whites, French was in frequent use. African rituals survived in the city more than elsewhere in American slave society. And yet this city, so cosmopolitan, so much more open and tolerant than other southern urban centers, was to become a battleground, at times literally so, pitting Unionists black and white against unreconstructed southern white rebels.

New Orleans by 1866 had well-defined political

Whites are shown firing on blacks during the July 1866 New Orleans race riot. (Courtesy, National Archives)

factions. An active black politics took its leadership from members of the free-born middle and upper classes. Most whites mourned the defeat of the Confederacy and resented military and civilian control by the federal authorities. Other whites had been loyal to the Union during the war and, like the black populace, looked to the federal government for support. This was the context for the New Orleans race riot of 1866.

On July 30 a convention of blacks and Unionist whites met to support a strong policy of Reconstruction. At noon blacks, braving gunfire and scuffles, marched in a parade to the convention hall. As a white mob surrounding the convention fired into their midst, some marchers scattered while others entered the building. There they came under siege along with the small interracial gathering already present. Through the windows, city police opened fire on the assembly. Assaults on blacks meanwhile continued outside on the streets. In mid-afternoon, federal troops arrived to subdue the violence. One estimate put the number of blacks dead at thirty-four. The deaths of three white Unionists were also reported.

Johnson's "Swing Around the Circle"

The ultimate betrayal of the black population of Louisiana and of the South in general was still several years in the future. For the moment, Memphis and New Orleans alienated northern whites who might otherwise have been sympathetic to a program going easy on the rebel South. And President Johnson, now sharply profiled as an ally of the most racist southern whites, actually proceeded to bait northerners yet again. During the 1866 congressional campaign Johnson, seeking to shape a politics opposite to that of the Radicals, took what he called a "swing around the circle," a tour of the North attacking his opponents. When he got to the Midwest, his belligerence took control of him. When a heckler suggested hanging Jefferson Davis, president of the Confederacy, he shot back, "Why not hang Thad Stevens and Wendell Phillips?" naming two of the country's most prominent Radicals. And he insisted on framing the controversy as a vicious personal attack on him.

The nineteenth-century public was prepared for political rhetoric flamboyant by today's standards, ranging from soaring eloquence to slashing denun-

ciation. It was not prepared for Johnson. As he destroyed himself, he also wrecked the policy he promoted. The autumn elections piled up in both Houses of Congress Radical majorities that ran above the two-thirds necessary to override a presidential veto of their Reconstruction bills.

A Political Base of Radical Reconstruction

A more systematic reconstruction of the South than the federal government had yet attempted required the establishment of major power bases in the region. In the absence of any effective restraint on the white planters, the Old South would be revived. Where else could northern legislators look?

One source was the black population. By the war's end, leaders in the Radical wing of the Republican Party were determined to give black southerners the vote. But outside of Radical circles, the idea did not yet have major support. Racism ran too deep in American society. Northern reformers, moreover, were unsure of how the freedmen would conduct themselves politically. And of course, Republican legislators knew the depth of opposition within the South's white populace to black political activity. Nonetheless, events were compelling rapid change in northern attitudes about rights for black southerners.

Within the white population of the South as well there existed pools of potential supporters of Republican, congressional Reconstruction. The southern hills and mountains nurtured a deep antagonism to the wealthy planter class of the low country. Enraged by state laws that gave disproportionate representation to the planter lowlands, white hill people before the war had perceived the large slaveowners as haughty and insolent. Hostility to slavery on moral and humane grounds did not figure heavily in the hill country. Prejudice against blacks was common, and opposition to the slaveowners went easily with resentment toward slaves as instruments, however unwilling, of planter domination. Yet hill and mountain people recognized that the power of the lash that slavery wielded over its human captives fed the arrogance of the planters.

During the Civil War, Unionist sentiment was so strong in the western part of Virginia that the region broke away from the secessionist state and joined the Union as the new state of West Virginia. Mountainous western North Carolina and eastern

Tennessee seethed with resistance to the Confederacy. Draft agents seeking to force enlistment into the rebel army were perceived as foreign invaders and hardened local bitterness toward the secessionists. An underground movement smuggled Union loyalists out of the hands of the authorities. Hill folk volunteered in great numbers for the federal army. Especially in eastern Tennessee, loyalty to the Union translated into a long-standing adherence to the Republican Party. A southern mountaineer decades after the fighting expressed a sentiment common among the hill people when he declared that Democrats were "nothing but yellow-livered rebels."

Elsewhere in the South, wartime conditions and decisions had alienated many people at first eager to support secession. Fearing that unattended slaves would become insubordinate, the Confederacy exempted the largest slaveholders from conscription. The draft fell heaviest on small farmers, whose removal into the military left their families to scratch out a living within a South generally impoverished by the conflict. And amidst the wreckage of the region after the Confederate defeat, anger smoldered against the architects of secession. So it was that among low-country whites as within the hill neighborhoods, Republicans might hope to find allies in Reconstruction.

Such feelings fed into the one scheme of the era that involved a revolutionary rethinking of the southern economy, society, and culture. In the House of Representatives, the Radical Thaddeus Stevens of Pennsylvania envisaged a division of the larger plantations into small plots of forty acres each that would go to freedmen. Any land remaining would then be put up for public sale, the proceeds to be awarded to southern white Unionists as compensation for their losses in the war. Stevens conceived a future for the South of small property holders, black and white, who would wield the political power once possessed by the planter slave regime.

RECONSTRUCTION TAKES HOLD

The former Confederacy, in sum, was not what its early postwar governments made it seem, a solid block of determination to reestablish as much of the Old South as possible. Black southerners; Union loyalists opposed to the South's return to its prewar planter leadership; reluctant secessionists who might be drawn into a Republican future: some combination of these elements could shape an enduring Reconstruction.

Radical Reconstruction

A Republican victory in the midterm elections of 1866, together with the increasing force of Radicalism in public opinion, made it clear that the immediate future belonged not to the president but to Congress. An active pursuit of deep change in southern politics and society now seemed possible. Central to this prospect was black suffrage, which would be a critical means of breaking the power of the defiant ex-rebels, and so achieving the final victory over slavery that a half-decade before had been a mere dream.

Early in 1867, Congress thrashed out a plan to place under federal control all of the old Confederacy except Tennessee, which had gained full readmission into the Union. Under the Military Reconstruction Act of 1867, which became law over Johnson's predictable veto, the region from Virginia through Texas was divided into five military districts. Within them elections were to be held for state constitutional conventions. Among the voters for delegates, male blacks were included. But ex-rebels excluded from office under the Fourteenth Amendment could neither be delegates nor vote for them. The resulting constitutions must formally enfranchise male blacks. After voters approved such a constitution and the state ratified the Fourteenth Amendment, it could apply for resumption of its place in Congress. A supplementary law provided that military commanders set up the election process. The Military Reconstruction Act in effect swept away the governments already in place.

The Habeas Corpus Act, also passed in 1867, strengthened the ability of citizens to have their cases removed to the federal courts. This would make possible a greater degree of justice in civil rights matters than was likely to be forthcoming from state courts. The Habeas Corpus Act also outlawed peonage, the practice of forcing a person to continue in service to an employer until payment of a debt. Peonage was among the devices by which the former Confederate states had tried to reinstitute slavery under another form.

Impeachment

Between Congress and President Johnson, disagreement darkened into hostility. The president set about firing federal officeholders who aligned themselves with congressional policy. In response Congress in 1867 passed the Tenure of Office Act. This measure, which violated the normal constitutional separation between legislative and executive powers, declared that the president could not dismiss federal officers without the consent of the Senate. Another point of contention between Johnson and Congress was that the president, acting as Commander-in-Chief, had issued orders restraining military officials from carrying out Reconstruction measures. The congressional reply to that was the Command of the Army Act of 1867. It provided that the president could issue orders only through the commander of the army, at the time General Ulysses S. Grant.

Still holding the post of secretary of war was Lincoln's appointee Edwin M. Stanton, a friend to the Radicals. In August 1867 Johnson, true to his habit of transforming stubbornness into full combat, dismissed Stanton in an open challenge to the Tenure of Office Act. Stanton thereupon holed up in his office for two months, while the successor designated by Johnson periodically pounded on the door urging him to leave.

Johnson had now violated the law—if, of course, the constitutionally questionable Tenure of Office Act could be considered a real law. In February 1868, the House of Representatives impeached him, that is, called him to stand trial before the

Andrew Johnson was the first president to be impeached and then tried before the United States Senate. He successfully argued that he had legitimately used the power of the executive branch of government. (Courtesy, Library of Congress)

Senate. By a vote of two-thirds, the Senate could remove the president. But the only grounds for impeachment and removal specified by the Constitution are "Treason, Bribery, or other high Crimes and Misdemeanors." Had Johnson done anything that could fall into any of these categories?

The Senate trial took three months. Everyone knew that the core of the matter was the dispute between Congress and the president. But a quarrel with Congress is not a high crime and misdemeanor. In the end, seven Republican senators voted against conviction, which kept the count just below the two-thirds required for removal.

A New Alliance

News of the passage of Radical Reconstruction gave black southerners a second chance: the first, emancipation itself, had nearly been lost when, in the Black Codes, some southern states came close to reestablishing slavery in other guises. Now interest in politics quickened among the freedmen. Literate blacks passed on information to their unschooled brethren. Rallies were common; some ministers of black congregations became political organizers. Prominent in this time of renewed hope was the growth of the patriotic Union League, an organization founded in the North that now expanded enormously in the South, attracting both blacks and white southern Unionists. Its local branches met in churches, in homes, or in the open, administering

A ticket to the United States Senate trial of President Andrew Johnson. (Courtesy, Collection of David J. and Janice L. Frent)

oaths to new members and confirming allegiance to the principles of the Declaration of Independence and the Republican Party. Black units of the League worked for improved schools and churches and protested such local injustices as the exclusion of blacks from juries.

At first, much of the leadership consisted of blacks free since birth, accustomed to some degree of independence. Among new African Americans in Charleston and New Orleans, freedom had included a measure of social status, though of course separate from that of whites. From Charleston members of that class went into the South Carolina countryside following the war, organizing the freed slaves. After 1867, when the congressional Reconstruction Act seemed to promise the black southern populace a serious political future, black northerners were prominent in attempting to guide it. Many had gone south as members of the military, others as workers for the Freedmen's Bureau, ministers in black churches, or teachers sent by missionary groups. A few were the children of free blacks whose parents had sent them north before the war for their education.

Carpetbaggers and Scalawags

The teachers who went south were among northern migrants known among former rebels as carpetbaggers: they were reputed to arrive carrying their possessions in a kind of suitcase called a carpetbag. Ambition to make money out of a region in the midst of rebuilding its economy drew many carpetbaggers. So did the possibility of entering southern politics, which Congress had now laid open to all kinds of adventurers, idealistic or self-serving.

Southern whites who sided with Radical Reconstruction the rebels called scalawags, a term meaning something close to "rascal." Continuing their hostility to the old planter class, they hoped to rebuild the South on a foundation of small farms. And even in the midst of racial hatred, the idea of a political alliance between the races, or recognition of its necessity, became not uncommon. A Unionist group in Georgia that proposed the confiscation of the land of wealthy planters and its distribution to both races illustrates how far the vision of a transformed society might go. Other scalawags were previous supporters of the rebellion who now simply decided that cooperation with Congress would

A carpetbag, the namesake of northerners who went south to take part in Reconstruction. (Courtesy, Collection of Antique Textile Resources, Nancy Gerwin)

benefit the South. Among this last group were even a few Confederate veterans, the best-known being James Longstreet, Robert E. Lee's general at Gettysburg who had reluctantly ordered George Pickett's disastrous charge.

The State Constitutions

In elections for delegates to the state constitutional conventions, many ex-rebels refused to participate because Confederate officials were excluded. The process was therefore left mostly, though not entirely, to Republicans of one kind or another. A profile of the conventions represents the varieties of southern Unionists and Republicanism in the region.

Overall, one-sixth of the delegates to these conventions were carpetbaggers, most of them representing voters in the black belt with its large concentration of freedmen, and many of them Union military veterans. Carpetbaggers were among the best educated of the delegates, and of any group they had the most professionals. Many became leaders of their delegations and took a major role in drafting parts of the state constitutions. Southern white delegates brought with them some if not all the race prejudice of their region. This came out with particular clarity in the widespread opposition among scalawag delegates to integrated schooling, though public schooling for blacks had their general assent or acquiescence. Yet some white Unionists recognized the justice of racial equality, along with the wisdom of banding with blacks against the powerful forces of unreconstructed rebels. Then there were the black delegates, both free-born and freed. Only in South Carolina were blacks in the majority. There and in the Louisiana convention, a black free-born elite took positions of leadership. Elsewhere, most black delegates who spoke up were artisans, farmers, teachers, or ministers.

Delegates reflected their class and social interests. Among the hill country white Unionists of the wartime era, the idea of restricting the power of ex-rebel planters was popular. Accustomed at least to some degree of public respect and therefore quick to resent the exclusion of blacks from public facilities, southern black free-born delegates and black northerners were the most energetic in supporting provisions guaranteeing equal access to public transportation and accommodations. Freedmen agreed. But divisions among scalawags and white carpetbaggers on the issue deflected it; only Louisiana's constitution mandated equal treatment in transportation and businesses licensed by the state. Proposals addressing the economy—for debt relief, fair taxation, and land distribution—appealed to many sectors of the delegations, white and black alike. Several new state constitutions adopted a general property tax that increased the levy on landowners, large and small, and was to the advantage of artisans, professionals, merchants, and freedmen with no property.

Most important is that these constitutions, for all their limitations, did generally decree basic civil rights for all citizens, including the right to vote. The new order was now to include also the institution of free publicly funded schooling, unknown to the Old South. Texas and South Carolina made school attendance compulsory. Fearful of losing their fragile grip on white Republican constituencies, Reconstruction governments avoided integrating their educational systems. But public schooling itself was an astonishingly ambitious new institution in the region. By 1875 half the children of both races in South Carolina, Florida, and Mississippi were attending school. Provisions for the establishment of orphanages, insane asylums, and other public services took the South farther along the course of active modern government.

The New Governments

After the conventions ratified the new constitutions, elections chose state officials. North and South Carolina, Florida, Georgia, Alabama, Louisiana, and Arkansas, having adopted constitutions acceptable under the terms of congressional Reconstruction, all regained in 1868 their status as states within the Union. Only three states remained outside: Virginia, Mississippi, and Texas. The seven restored states reentered the Union in time to participate in the national elections of that year, a presidential election year. Wherever in those states it was physically safe to vote, black southerners usually did so.

Still, the new constitutions did not mean the clear triumph of Radical Reconstruction. White Republican officials in the South were timid or hesitant about granting full equality to blacks. Preju-

Successful blacks during Reconstruction. The man at the top in the center is Frederick Douglass, long an abolitionist leader. (Courtesy, Library of Congress)

dice on their own part coupled with a desire to win over unreconciled white southerners contributed to their hesitancy. How far the South was from a strongly founded equality is illustrated by an episode in Georgia. In September 1868 Democrats in the legislature acted to remove its black members, arguing that the state's new constitution did not specifically guarantee the rights of blacks to hold public office. The Democrats achieved their expulsion. The action, though temporary, added to the complexity of race relations during Reconstruction.

The National Elections of 1868

The elections of 1868 centered on the issue of Reconstruction. For the North, that meant whether to endorse the Radical program. Southern voters, black and white, Unionist and ex-secessionist, had to consider how to align their states to conform to that program.

The Republican presidential nominee was the North's wartime hero, General Ulysses S. Grant. Though not a supporter of the Radicals, he could be relied on to carry out the provisions of the Military Reconstruction Act. A major aim of the Democratic presidential ticket was to attract rebel white southerners. New York's former governor Horatio Seymour, its nominee for president, was a lackluster figure. His running mate Francis P. Blair, Jr., of Missouri was worse as the vice-presidential choice. During the campaign he went, against Seymour's wishes, on a speaking tour during which he expressed blatantly racist sentiments, warning against the "semi-barbarous" people to whom the Republicans would consign the fortunes of the South and innocent white women.

In the South the Democratic Party, often taking the name Conservative, explicitly defined the election as determining whether the white race would be toppled from its rightful throne. To ensure that this would not happen, white mobs and the Ku Klux Klan, then two years old, spread violence through the region. A congressman from Arkansas, three members of South Carolina's legislature, and several delegates to state constitutional conventions were killed. In northern Alabama poor whites were reported to be as terrified as blacks. A crowd in the Louisiana parish of St. Landry killed upward of two hundred blacks. The violence allowed Seymour to win Georgia and Louisiana. Still, enough blacks and

scalawags voted throughout the South to make for a substantial Republican presence. In the Unionist mountain regions, Grant drew more than six votes out of every ten.

Grant won the election, and the statewide southern Republican parties remained strong enough to control much of the region. But Reconstruction emerged with at best a shaky hold on the South.

The Fifteenth Amendment

Strengthening the grip of Reconstruction was an objective of the Fifteenth Amendment, which Congress in 1869 adopted and sent to the states for ratification. The Amendment prohibits federal and state authorities from using "race, color, or previous condition of servitude" as a basis for denying the right to vote. Congress was thereby risking a backlash from the northern public; few northern states allowed blacks to vote. Nonetheless, the Amend-

Susan B. Anthony (left) joined Elizabeth Cady Stanton in forming the National Woman Suffrage Association. (Courtesy, Library of Congress)

ment won approval by the requisite number of states and became part of the Constitution.

Notably absent from the Fifteenth Amendment is any guarantee of a right to vote regardless of sex. The unwillingness of Republicans to extend voting rights to women drew the anger of feminists who had worked for an end to slavery. A woman's convention in 1869 split apart over the issue. Lucy Stone was prominent in a faction that supported the Amendment and formed the American Woman Suffrage Association. The other camp, the National Woman Suffrage Association, turned away from the issue of racial justice. Susan B. Anthony was a leader in the National Association, along with Elizabeth Cady Stanton, whose anger at the denial of woman suffrage was such that it found expression in racial and ethnic prejudice. She recoiled at the thought that "Patrick and Sambo and Hans and Ung Tung"—Irish, black, German, and Chinese men—would make laws for white ladies of standing.

As a supplement to passage of the Fifteenth Amendment, Congress required the three unrestored rebel states to ratify it as a condition of readmission. On meeting this provision, Virginia, Texas, and Mississippi were granted their full rights. For some time, Reconstruction would continue in much of the South. Republicans would hold there some of the political base they had built when the region was under federal occupation. And a series of laws passed after 1870 gave the national government authority to intervene with troops and courts in instances of violation of civil rights.

Reconstruction in the States

Under congressional Reconstruction, timidity on race questions soon gave way to a bolder policy invigorated by the increased assertiveness of black southerners. Emancipated slaves came to take an increasingly large role alongside their free-born brethren. But they were almost always dependent on a white Republican leadership enjoying the advantages of background and connection to sources of power.

During Reconstruction, twenty-one high-level positions in the ex-rebel states went at some point to blacks: six lieutenant governors—one of whom briefly served as governor of Louisiana, two state treasurers, four superintendents of education, and eight secretaries of state. Nearly all of these officials

had been born free. Fourteen blacks served in the federal Congress, and over six hundred sat in state legislatures, a large proportion of them freed slaves rather than free by birth. South Carolina, distinctive like Louisiana in the extent of leadership provided by the free-born, was unique in the strength of the black contingent of its legislature. Throughout Reconstruction, blacks predominated in that state's House of Representatives and controlled its important committees.

Blacks won some control in local government as well. In Louisiana and Mississippi together, thirty-four counties had a black sheriff at one time or another. County supervisor, school board member, court judge, justice of the peace, and in a few cases mayor were among offices that gave blacks a presence. For a time, blacks made up a third of Nashville's city council; so did a majority in Little Rock's. Tallahassee and Little Rock had black police chiefs, New Orleans and Vicksburg black captains, and Montgomery along with Vicksburg a police force half black. In New Orleans, Mobile, Alabama, and Petersburg, Virginia, a substantial portion of the police was black. Such gains, along with placing of black southerners on juries, were revolutionary for the time, though far from giving blacks power in relation to their numbers.

One of the many injustices of the early postwar governments had been laws holding that a crop lien to merchants who had advanced supplies to planters or farmers took precedence over other debts the borrowers had incurred. After the lien holder took his share, there might be nothing left over for the laborer. New laws gave the initial lien to workers instead. South Carolina instituted a serious program of land redistribution, purchasing real estate and reselling it on easy credit. By 1876 about one-seventh of the state's black populace and a few whites had been settled on homesteads. Several states employed property taxes to free up unproductive land that could not meet the tax burden. But while this land was intended to go in small lots to the poor, speculators gobbled up much of it instead.

Mindful of their hill country white populations, Republican governments initiated some schemes of debtor relief. At what must have been great political risk, several state governments even attempted to go beyond their new constitutions and outlaw discrimination in businesses serving the public. Such laws had little effect. But they, along with

The unknown artist of this glorification of Reconstruction in 1867 centers on raising the missing pillars, which represent the returning southern states, to form a rotunda of the reunited Republic. Clasped hands over the eagle bear the words "Union and Liberty, Forever." From heaven, the country's great past leaders look down approvingly. (Courtesy, Library of Congress)

major efforts to address land and labor issues and an enormous expansion in public services, gave to much of Reconstruction the right to claim the title of radical.

The Precariousness of Reconstruction

Reconstruction rested on frail foundations. There was the seething anger of ex-rebels who had returned grudgingly to the Union. They were infuriated at every faltering attempt to raise the status of the black race, smarting at every demand by blacks for respect that in their eyes was often construed as insolence. Then there were the Republi-

cans among the small farmers. How far could the Republican regimes go before an ingrained racism asserted itself and white voters turned Democratic? Added to prejudice was the costliness of the Reconstruction governments. The size of their undertakings for education and welfare, particularly in face of the devastation the war had wrought on the region, made it inevitable that their expenditures would soar above the budgets of the prewar South. Ventures in inviting railroad enterprises into the region ran costs higher. And in the wide-open conditions of Reconstruction, corruption was inevitable. Corruption flourished in the North as well, but northern states could far better afford it.

Thomas Nast of Harper's Weekly, *though in favor of rights for African Americans, in 1874 drew this caricature of African Americans running a southern legislature. The image dominated popular thinking and historical accounts for some eighty years.*

Quick to assume that black rule prevailed and that blacks were showing themselves to be as unfit to govern as white Americans had always thought, the national press subjected the South to microscopic scrutiny. But in fact, even to conceive of a South ruled by Republican regimes is misleading. Much of the region's local rule was in the hands of Conservatives, so state governments presided shakily over stretches of population and territory controlled by their enemies. And in those vast reaches, Republican Reconstruction was met by incessant terrorist warfare, commonly known by its most famous agent, the Ku Klux Klan.

The Ku Klux Klan

Along with its western part, the central portion of Tennessee had been secessionist during the Civil War. There, in 1866 in the town of Pulaski, a small band of Confederate veterans formed a secret society

akin to a college fraternity. "Ku Klux," the first two words in the name it adopted, seem to have been taken from the Greek *kuklos* meaning band or association; a well-known southern fraternity had used *Kuklos* in its name. The word "Klan" was technically unnecessary, but the string of "k" sounds was striking. The Ku Klux Klan adopted rituals together with impressive titles for its officers such as Grand Wizard and Grand Cyclops; and it encouraged outlandish costumes.

The masquerade society transformed itself quickly into a terrorist organization. Disruptions brought on by a war fought over much of southern territory heated the emotions of a region that was volatile to begin with. The mood of the South was exactly suited for quick tempers and quarrels that turned into shooting and lynching sprees. A code of honor prevailed that had nothing much to do with fighting fair and everything to do with beating or killing anyone who had injured the touchy self-esteem of the attacker. Country boys during their times of leisure had opportunities for boasting, drinking, and plotting mischief on steamy summer afternoons that invited a sense of limitless freedom. Before the war, playing cruel pranks on slaves who could not retaliate had sharpened the habit of bullying. And however deferentially much of the black population continued to find it convenient to behave, whites recognized, to their enraged confusion, that pride and self-assertion were growing among the freedmen. Add to all this that Tennessee was home to veterans of two armies, some of them restless like returned soldiers of all wars. The violent course the Ku Klux Klan took as it spread throughout the South fed on these conditions.

At its turn to terrorism, the Klan made much of its taste for costumes and ritual. None of this included burning crosses, a practice first adopted by the revived Klan of the twentieth century. Nor were white sheets the required garb. A robe of any available color would be topped by a headpiece containing horns or other supposedly frightening objects, such as a long red cloth tongue. The hoods and masks were in part for disguise. But Klansmen believed that blacks were superstitious and would be frightened by the ghostly riders, some of them claiming to be risen Confederate war dead. One trick was to fasten underneath their costumes a large container. The "ghost" would make a great show of drinking bucket after bucket of water (the stunt was to let the water pour into the hidden ves-

This group of Klansmen, some with horns sticking out of their hats, contemplates the murder of a white Republican. (Courtesy, Library of Congress)

sel), explaining to his victim that he had not had a drink of water since his death. The costumes and the play at being the risen dead did frighten freedmen, not out of any belief in ghosts but because they knew the real and earthly enemy lurking behind the masks. But members enjoyed the rituals for their own sake, and they cemented group loyalty. Notices aimed at the public in general perpetuated the show of shadowy horror and mystery:

> The Great High Giant commands you. The dark and dismal hour will soon be. . . . In the dark caves, in the mountain recesses, everywhere our brotherhood appears. Traitors, beware!

So proclaimed a Great Grand Cyclops on posters displayed in Montgomery, Alabama.

The Klan was a somewhat loose term. The KKK overlapped other organizations, such as the Masons: at least one victim saved himself by making a Masonic sign recognizable to a member of the raiding party. The groups that sprang up in one locality after another were often no more than mobs of thugs with only the barest pretense of organization. But they all had a similarity of purpose and method, and it became common to refer to all of them under the heading of the Klan.

Chief among the reasons for the attacks on the homes of blacks and white southern Unionists was to scare people away from supporting the Republicans. Whippings, shootings, hangings served not only to eliminate some particular victim but to warn other Republicans against political activity. In this the bands of terrorists had a remarkable success. At a time when ballots were open rather than cast in secrecy, a county that had gone heavily Republican before the coming of the Klan might in the next election cast only a handful of Republican votes. Or the objective might be to stop some activity offensive to white supremacists. In parts of Mississippi, blacks who owned or rented land were targets; the black race was not supposed to have the independence that comes from working a separate plot of land. In North Carolina an elderly man who had distributed land to his former slaves was whipped. Klan-like groups would attack blacks who went to school—cultivating intelligence was also defined as an act of impudence—or drive off their teachers of either race. Some school buildings were burned to the ground.

Reconstruction Regimes Fight Back

But the Klans, or whatever they might choose to call themselves, were operating on a wide-open frontier where armed bands could also gather against them. The most promising of these, though they varied in effectiveness, were the militias organized by Republican state governments. In the Upper South, recruits came from the white Unionist hills and mountains. Elsewhere they were more likely to be blacks. Governor Powell Clayton of Arkansas got the Klan on the run when, late in 1868, he organized a militia of white Unionists and blacks that seized suspects and tried them by military commission. Early in 1869, Governor William G. "Parson" Brownlow declared martial law in parts of Tennessee, and Klan terrorism thereupon declined. The Reconstruction government of North Carolina similarly made an effort to crush the Klan by a militia campaign.

Among ex-rebels, attitudes toward the Klan and its counterparts were not all of a piece. Much of the Democratic, or Conservative, population sympathized with the objectives of the Klan. In time, it became the tendency among Conservatives to deplore violence and wish privately that the Klan would temper its conduct. The Conservatives especially feared state militia intervention, or action by the federal government. This reinforced a growing distaste for the Klan's brutality. A few Democratic papers spoke out against the terrorists. Even

Nathan Bedford Forrest, a hero of the Confederacy and for a time the Grand Wizard of the early Klan, came out publicly against the course that the organization had taken. At the same time, the fear of intensifying white hostility often left Republican state governments perplexed as to how they should proceed. In areas where the law officers and juries who would have to carry out an anti-Klan policy had no interest in doing so, vigorous prosecution of the organization was pointless.

The Federal Government Acts

As terrorist attacks against blacks and Republicans spread, Congress passed Enforcement Acts authorizing the federal government to intervene, essentially militarily, where citizens were being systematically denied constitutional rights. Also adopted was the Ku Klux Klan Act of 1871, which outlawed any conspiracy to deprive citizens of such rights as the vote, officeholding, and jury service. For extreme cases the law now authorized federal military force and the suspension of the writ of habeas corpus, the procedure by which a jailed suspect could get quick access to a court hearing.

The Klan law was unprecedented in allowing the national government to act against not only state officials but private citizens engaging in the use of force or intimidation. Like white supremacists nearly a century later, opponents of federal intervention appealed to the doctrine of states' rights. Republicans knew, to the contrary, that the Union victory on the battlefield and the constitutional amendments of the period had changed the relations of the federal government to the states.

At a time when the people of the North were largely losing interest in racial justice and Democrats in the South were assaulting the rights of their black citizens, the new measures were surprisingly effective. In a campaign that included President Grant's suspension in 1871 of the writ of habeas corpus in nine South Carolina counties and brought military occupation of the region, the Klan was broken.

THE WANING OF RECONSTRUCTION

The suggestion that there might be any greater danger to Reconstruction than the Klan strains the imagination. But there was. The ultimate threat was the growing indifference in the North to conditions in the South. It was grounded in part on the conviction that the Constitution now provided black southerners with all the rights and protections they needed.

The Liberal Republicans

This attitude in the North was most clearly embodied by a faction within the Republican Party that came to be termed the Liberal Republicans. The hostility among Liberals to the continuance of Reconstruction was embedded within a whole range of concerns. They were reacting against political corruption in the North and what they thought to be bungled administration in the South. Most favored government by an elite defined by ability, education, and high moral standards. Clean government was their passion. They advocated civil service reform that would replace patronage with ability proved in examinations. They embraced the economics then conventional in universities, which trusted to the free operation of market forces and opposed tariffs, high taxes, and government interference. Integral to their outlook was a fear of class warfare. Demands for inflated currency that would cheapen the dollars debtors paid to lenders, legislation favoring labor in its struggles with capitalists, the exclusion from office of numbers of the old southern ruling class: such politics the reformers defined as an attack on the "better sort of people."

The Grant administration was accumulating, justifiably, a reputation for corruption. Himself a plain-thinking old soldier with little feel for politics—a contempt, in fact, for the whole grubby thing—Grant had nothing to gain from larceny. He simply ignored the increasing evidence of shady dealings some of his associates practiced.

Officers of the Crédit Mobilier, a construction company under French ownership that had contributed to building the Union Pacific Railroad, defrauded the government and the railroad and tried to protect themselves by providing stock to members of Congress. Later it was revealed that officials in the administration had belonged to a Whiskey Ring that cheated the government of liquor taxes. Scandal also touched a trading post in Indian country. One of the schemes that did interest President Grant he appears to have embraced out of naive idealism. For a time, he tried to get through the Senate a treaty that would annex the Caribbean republic of Santo Domingo, formerly a Spanish possession and inhabited by the descendants of pre-Columbian natives, African slaves, and Spanish colonists. As best his thinking on the matter can be understood, he thought of such an annexation as an extension to the outside world of American institutions of liberty and justice. The treaty was defeated. High among the reasons was a widespread racist disdain for the people of Santo Domingo, an attitude shared by many elitist Republicans who joined in the plan's rejection.

The Election of 1872

In 1872 the Liberal Republicans formed a separate party on the national level, and nominated as their presidential candidate the powerful journalist Horace Greeley. The Democratic Party thereupon endorsed him as its candidate as well. The regular Republicans renominated Grant, who was still popular. The national election again turned essentially on whether federal intervention in defense of racial justice should be continued or ended. Northern Democrats, modifying the racist vocabulary they had previously adopted, joined with the Liberal Republicans in arguing that Reconstruction had run its course and should now be scrapped. Yet Grant won in the North and in most of the ex-rebel states.

Still, the challenge posed by the Liberals indicated that much of the Republican Party had moved beyond the issues of race and secession. Reconstruction was being abandoned long before the time when anything like racial equality had been firmly implanted in the southern mentality.

The End of Reconstruction

During Grant's second administration, the federal government continued to impose Reconstruction policies. In 1873, freedmen in Grant Parish, Louisiana, fearing that Democrats were planning a coup, seized the town of Colfax and under the command of black Civil War veterans and militia officers fortified it for an assault. After three weeks a white force broke through the defenses; the carnage included the slaughter of about fifty blacks after their surrender. In the late summer of 1874 the anti-Reconstruction White League defeated in armed conflict the New Orleans police force commanded by James Longstreet, the former Confederate general who was now a supporter of Recon-

In the election of 1872 some northerners tried to conciliate the South. Here the cartoonist Thomas Nast of Harper's Weekly *shows the liberal Republican Horace Greeley of New York pushing a black man to shake hands with a Klansman.*

struction. But President Grant, determined to enforce orderly government in the South, used troops to reestablish the city's rightful officials.

Even after the congressional elections of 1874, which gave the Democrats control of the House of Representatives while the Republicans retained the Senate, the Republicans continued to legislate for racial justice. The lame-duck Republican House, in its final days before the new Democratic representatives were seated, debated a civil rights bill that the Senate had already passed. Initiated by the Massachusetts Radical Senator Charles Sumner, who had died in 1874, it contemplated a daring employment of federal power: private businesses serving the public would be prohibited from rejecting patrons on the basis of race. Representative Benjamin Butler of Massachusetts, a Union general faithful to the principles of Radicalism, pressed for passage of the measure in the House. After Butler decided to drop its most politically sensitive provision, the outlawing of discrimination in public schools, the bill passed and Grant signed it. But its enforcement

mechanisms were weak, and in any event the Supreme Court in 1883 ruled it an unconstitutional extension of federal authority.

This Civil Rights Act of 1874 stood almost alone as a latter-day effort to strengthen the meaning of equality. The northern public was losing whatever interest in the plight of black southerners it had ever possessed. Northern Republican politicians were interesting themselves in other questions: the tariff, currency, and the general promotion of business interests.

In the South, matters were worse. Whites once attracted to the Republican Party were responding to racist appeals by Democrats. Violence and murder were again discouraging Republicans from voting. In Mississippi during 1874, the same year that Grant acted to put down white insurrection in New Orleans, he chose not to intervene in any major way in the face of a successful campaign of terror against Republican voters. In January 1875 he did send troops to Mississippi to restore to office a city government in Vicksburg that white supremacists had driven out by an armed invasion and occupation. Southern Republicans meanwhile divided over Reconstruction policy, their white leadership increasingly wary of racial questions. By the late 1870s, the last of the southern states had been "redeemed," a southern Democratic term for the capture of state governments by white supremacists.

The Republican Party essentially abandoned Reconstruction in the presidential election of 1876. That election and its aftermath mark a turning of the party to another phase of its career.

Suggested Readings

A recent collection of valuable essays is Eric Anderson and Alfred A. Moss Jr., eds., *The Facts of Reconstruction: Essays in Honor of John Hope Franklin* (1991). Richard Franklin Bensel, *Yankee Leviathan: The Origins of Central State Authority in America, 1859–1877* (1990) is a political analysis of the partial transformation of American government during and after the Civil War. David W. Blight, *Race and Reunion: The Civil War in American Memory* (2001) explores ways in which black memories and white memories of the war diverged, as whites in the North and in the South found a means to find unity with each other through their selective understanding of the war.

Paul A. Cimbala and Randall M. Miller, eds., *Reconstruction: Reconsiderations* (1999) is a collection of essays by the latest generation of historians about the Freedmen's Bureau. William Cohen, *At Freedom's Edge: Black Mobility and the Southern White Quest for Racial Control, 1861–1915* (1991) is an important exploration of the black southern quest for mobility after slavery was abolished, together with continuing efforts by white southerns to bring blacks under white control. Richard Nelson Current, *Those Terrible Carpetbaggers: A Reinterpretation* (1988), adopting an ironic title, reexamines some of the leading white men who went South after the Civil War, and rehabilitates them. Michael Kent Curtis, *No State Shall Abridge: The Fourteenth Amendment and the Bill of Rights* (1986) examines the origins of the Fourteenth Amendment and concludes that the framers did intend to incorporate the Bill of Rights in Section One. Jane Dailey, *Before Jim Crow: The Politics of Race in Postemancipation Virginia* (2000) is a provocative reexamination of the politics of Reconstruction and the rise to power, after 1877 of a biracial coalition in one former Confederate state. Laura F. Edwards, *Gendered Strife and Confusion: The Political Culture of Reconstruction* (1997) is a striking reconsideration of Reconstruction in the South—what it was about, how long it lasted, and what it meant to blacks and whites, men and women, rich and poor, Democrats and Republicans.

Eric Foner, *Reconstruction: America's Unfinished Revolution, 1863–1877* (1988) is a masterful modern synthesis. Gaines M. Foster, *Moral Reconstruction: Christian Lobbyists and the Federal Legislation of Morality, 1865–1920* (2002) enlarges the study of Reconstruction beyond race and politics in the dozen years after the Civil War. Richard Paul Fuke, *Imperfect Equality: African Americans and the Confines of White Ideology in Post-Emancipation Maryland* (1999) closely examines the aftermath of slavery in a state that did not secede. Leon

F. Litwack, *'Been in the Storm So Long'* : *The Aftermath of Slavery* (1979) is a richly detailed exploration of black southern life as emancipation opened all kinds of new possibilities for former slaves.

Frank McGlynn and Seymour Drescher, eds., *The Meaning of Freedom*: *Economics, Politics, and Culture after Slavery* (1992), is a collection of essays, some of them on the American South, others developing the story in other New World societies after emancipation, and others expressly evaluating the experience of the United States in a comparative context. William E. Nelson, *The Fourteenth Amendment: From Political Principle to Judicial Doctrine* (1988) is about the emergence of the legal core of the Republican program for the postwar nation. Michael Perman, *The Road to Redemption: Southern Politics, 1869–1979* (1984) boldly interprets southern politics during Reconstruction and the rise to power of the Bourbons. Howard N. Rabinowitz, ed., *Southern Black Leaders of the Reconstruction Era* (1982) is a fine collection of essays about many of the black leaders of the Reconstruction South. George C. Rable, *But There Was No Peace: The Role of Violence in the Politics of Reconstruction* (1984) reveals that after the Civil War's technical ending the war continued in the South, and normal politics could not unfold the way individual voters might have determined, nor could Reconstruction thrive.

Heather Cox Richardson, *The Death of Reconstruction: Race, Labor, and Politics in the Post-Civil War North, 1865–1901* (2001) is another among the recent explorations of Reconstruction that broadens it out in time and topic. This work concentrating on the North addresses questions of class as well as race.

James L. Roark, *Masters without Slaves: Southern Planters in the Civil War and Reconstruction* (1977) is a marvelous social history of the southern planter elite as slavery was being abolished. Mark W. Summers, *Railroads, Reconstruction, and the Gospel of Prosperity*: *Aid under the Radical Republicans, 1865-1877* (1984) analyzes a question of economic policy in the states of the Reconstruction South. Peter Wallenstein, *Tell the Court I Love My Wife: Race, Marriage, and Law—An American History* (2002) considers post-Civil War American race relations and political power from the perspective of rapid shifts in law and policy as they related to interracial marriage. Xi Wang, *The Trial of Democracy: Black Suffrage and Northern Republicans, 1860–1910* (1997) is an essential study of black political rights.

Sherlock Holmes wearing his detective garb. *(Courtesy, Movie Stills, Inc.)*

Raiding the Continent

CHAPTER 16

★

A BRITISH LOOK AT AMERICAN CULTURE

Beginning in 1887, Sir Arthur Conan Doyle wrote thousands of pages of short stories featuring his masterful sleuth Sherlock Holmes and his assistant Dr. Watson. In most of them, the crimes occur in London or the English countryside. But the reunited American nation that emerged in the years following the Civil War also held a powerful grip on Conan Doyle's imagination. For him and many other Europeans the United States was flat-out bizarre, the only place in the world where an eccentric millionaire

> "The ship reached Cape Town last night. I received this cable from Mrs. Douglas this morning:
>
> Jack has been lost overboard in gale off St. Helena. No one knows how accident occurred.
>
> Ivy Douglas"
>
> "Ha! It came like that, did it?" said Sherlock Holmes thoughtfully. "Well, I've no doubt it was well stage-managed."
>
> "You mean that you think there was no accident?"
>
> "None in the world."
>
> "He was murdered?"
>
> "Surely!"
>
> "So I think also. These infernal Scowrers, this cursed vindictive nest of criminals—"
>
> "No, no, my good sir," said Holmes. "There is a master hand here. It is no case of sawed-off shotguns and clumsy six-shooters. You can tell an old master by the sweep of his brush. . . . This crime came from London, not from America."

might leave a bequest that offered redheaded men easy money for copying the dictionary ("The Red Headed League"). It was the exotic, sensual home of Mormon polygamy, where hard men struggled with the western deserts and kept harems in mountain strongholds (one of the author's four novels, *A Study in Scarlet*). It spawned the mysterious Ku Klux Klan, whose long arm reached across the Atlantic to leave orange seeds warning of murder ("The Five Orange Pips"). Its cities housed organized criminal gangs run by ruthless men with the harsh accents of ethnic immigrants ("The Dancing Men"). On its western goldfields, men became rich and women were raised to be simple and natural, lacking the niceties but also the repressions of Victorian culture ("The Adventure of the Noble Bachelor"). Its workers gathered in violence-prone fraternities like the Scowrers whom Doyle placed in the Pennsylvania coalfields. Breaking them might call for the courage of undercover Pinkerton detectives like the unfortunate Jack Douglas, gone into hiding after having broken the Scowrers (*The Valley of Fear*).

At the same time, Sherlock Holmes and Dr. Watson understood the strange republic across the seas as part of a tightly interconnected Atlantic world sewn together by the transnational tours of upper-class tourists, the cargoes of merchant ships, the dank holds of transports carrying immigrants and imports from Europe, and the exchange of printed and wireless news across the vast ocean. The United States, however defiantly independent, remained part of the world system defined in considerable part by the British empire, and its macabre American criminals might be lumped together with the curiosities of India or Australia.

For all his fascination with America as a singular place, then, Arthur Conan Doyle also felt a connection to it. His notions differed little from attitudes widely held among Americans about their own country. He viewed Mormons, radical workers, and immigrants, for example, as criminals; cast the West as a land of refuge, economic opportunity, and fresh starts; ignored Indians, Latinos, African Americans, and Asians; and casually aligned himself with the interests of economic elites. Looking across the Atlantic, Doyle offers an oblique look at the nation in the years following the Civil War and Reconstruction, his vision capturing the oddities, the complexities, and the transformations of this land during a period as complicated as any in American history.

HISTORICAL EVENTS

1869
Transcontinental railroad completed

1872
Yellowstone National Park established

1876
Centennial Exhibition, Philadelphia • Colonel George Custer's Seventh Cavalry slaughtered by Sioux at the Little Big Horn River in Montana territory • Rutherford Hayes elected president in a disputed election similar to that of 2000 and resolved in 1877 • National [Baseball] League established

1877
End of Reconstruction era • major strikes in Pittsburgh and elsewhere

1879
Terence Powderly becomes Grand Master of Knights of Labor

1880
James B. Garfield elected president

1881
Helen Hunt Jackson, *A Century of Dishonor* • Chester Alan Arthur becomes president after Garfield is assassinated

1882
Chinese Exclusion Act

1883
Pendleton Civil Service Act

1884
Grover Cleveland elected president

1886
Bomb explodes killing seven in Haymarket Square, Chicago

1887
Dawes Severalty Act attempts to break up Indian reservations • Interstate Commerce Commission created

1888
Benjamin Harrison elected president

1890
Sherman Silver Purchase Act • Sioux massacred at Battle of Wounded Knee

1892
Grover Cleveland elected president again, the only Chief Executive to serve two nonconsecutive terms

THE CENTENNIAL EXPOSITION OF 1876

While North and South struggled over the fading policies of Reconstruction, Americans flocked to Philadelphia to see the 1876 Centennial Exposition, a grand fair meant to celebrate the hundredth anniversary of the nation's independence. With sections devoted to horticulture, agriculture, art, and machines, the main structure stretched almost two thousand feet in length—the largest edifice in the entire world. The huge Mechanical Building, powered by the enormous Corliss Engine, instructed the visitors on the nation's industrial might, while astonishing innovativeness demonstrated its triumphs in the telegraph, the Westinghouse air brake, refrigeration, and other marvels. The 1876 fair heralded an enormous boom in expositions over the next century that would teach Americans not only to produce but to gobble up the vast products of their industry. Commercial displays in the Centennial's Singer Sewing Machine building and the shoe-and-leather building, among many others, foreshadowed the consumer culture of the twentieth century, and the twenty-first.

At *the opening of the Centennial Exposition of 1876 in Philadelphia, President Grant is starting the great Corliss steam engine.* (Courtesy, Library of Congress)

The white South, with little to celebrate of the nation's triumphs, made a meager effort to have a presence at the fair. If black Americans had hoped to appear there as full participants, offering a visible image of the equality and inclusiveness promised under Reconstruction, they were disappointed. The Exposition offered spots only to a token African American artist or two; most of the blacks involved served as waiters or backstage workers. White women, too, hoped to make the case for their full participation in the national pageant, and they fought hard to be included. Black women had no place among the group of middle- and upper-class white ladies agitating for a woman's rights pavilion, which they obtained.

While the Exposition pushed black Americans to its margins, organizers made a point of bringing American Indians to the fair. This difference mirrored a persistent distinction between relations whites had with blacks and their relations with Indians that would structure racial conditions for the next century. African Americans sought integration only to be rejected, particularly by "Jim Crow" segregation laws soon to be passed in southern states. But white Americans, aside from frontier settlers many of whom hated Indians, either romanticized them as brave and honorable children of the forest or attempted to assimilate Indian people, most of whom spurned the offer.

At the height of the celebration, which was portraying Indians as quaint but admirable features of the American landscape, the news came that Indians had wiped out Colonel George Custer and his Seventh Cavalry at the Little Big Horn River in Montana territory. The battle was part of a conflict that sprawled across the northern Plains over the ownership of the gold-rich South Dakota Black Hills, guaranteed to the Sioux nation by treaty in 1868. At the Little Big Horn, the wave of Indian resistance led by Sitting Bull—represented by the Lakota, Cheyenne, and Arapahoe warriors who overran Custer's regiment—reached its zenith. Shortly afterward, during the winter of 1877, the United States army launched a devastating campaign that forced Indians on the northern Plains into confinement on reservations. Now, federal negotiators forced a small number of Lakotas to sign the Agreement of 1877, a blatantly illegal compact that ceded the Black Hills to the United States. It would be repudiated by the Supreme Court in 1980—a century too late for the Sioux. The winter campaign, paired with earlier defeats of the Comanches, Kiowas, and Cheyennes on the southern Plains, and subsequent forays against the Apaches, helped clear the West.

In 1888 a new religion arose among the Paiute Indians. Its central rite, a ghost dance, promised a return to the order existing before the white man had destroyed the Indians' homelands. Quickly spreading across the desert and Great Plains, the new rites came to Sitting Bull, still defiant although long confined to Sioux reservations in the Dakotas. Under his leadership, the Ghost Dance movement became more belligerent. Indian agents and the army tried to forbid the dancing that went with it and to disarm Sioux warriors who began to believe that wearing garments painted with sacred symbols would protect them against the white man's bullets. Then troops of the Seventh Cavalry—Custer's old regiment—initiated a search for arms in an Indian village at Wounded Knee Creek. In an earlier incident Sitting Bull had died. Soon after

In 1890 United States soldiers massacred 146 Sioux Indians, including women and children, in the Battle of Wounded Knee in South Dakota. It was the last large encounter on the northern Plains between the army and Native Americans. (Courtesy, National Anthropological Archives, The Smithsonian Institution, Washington, DC)

entering Wounded Knee the soldiers slaughtered every Indian in sight. Bodies of women and children were later found as far as three miles away from the village. Through the ghost dance excitement, and even after Wounded Knee, there had not been a single raid on a white settlement. Thenceforth there would be more agricultural settlement along with widespread resource extraction from the land, water diversion, and reclamation, and the setting aside of parklands, emptied now of people and renamed "wilderness."

1877

The almost unprecedented outcome of the 2000 election led Americans to pay renewed attention to a contest that had long since fallen into obscurity. In a manner similar to the campaign pitting George W. Bush against Al Gore, that of 1876 between the Republican Rutherford B. Hayes and the Democrat Samuel Tilden stalled at a small margin of difference in the Electoral College and disputed popular votes in Florida. In the nineteenth-century election the votes cast in Louisiana, South Carolina, and Oregon were also in question. In 1876 as in 2000, the power to decide the outcome rested with a small bipartisan, supposedly neutral group (in that earlier dispute, a specially appointed commission) that split its votes along party lines and favored the Republican. The commission appointed in 1876 by a Republican Congress gave its party one more commissioner than the Democrats. Hayes's marginal victory—like George W. Bush, he lost the popular vote—was negotiated in part by southern Democrats willing to accept a Republican who would end Reconstruction. The moment was ripe. By this time a series of Supreme Court decisions had weakened the Fourteenth and Fifteenth Amendments recently added to the Constitution, suggesting that the states rather than the federal government should enforce their protections of equal rights. Hayes's "Let 'Em Alone" policy toward the South embodied precisely that line, and in the years that followed black Americans would encounter increasing difficulty in exercising their rights.

A New Labor Militancy

Americans got another shock in 1877 when unionized railroad workers across the country struck to protest cuts in wages. Burning buildings and derailing trains, the strikers won support among other laborers. But the railroads hired strikebreakers and gained the backing of state authorities who called out local militias. In Pittsburgh, in July 1877, a pitched battle left thirty strikers dead and over a hundred engines along with more than a thousand railroad cars destroyed. After a month of widespread violence came close to shutting down the whole nation, President Hayes called out federal troops to put an end to the rail strike. The national scope of the strike and the violence that accompanied it opened a turbulent period in the struggle between American workers and capital. And the government, which had abandoned the use of its military to protect black citizens, now used the army not only on western Indians but on the working classes.

In the tumult surrounding that national exposition, the disputed election, labor riots, warfare against the Plains Indians, and the ending of Reconstruction, forces emerged that were to shape the rest of the century. The rise of an industrial economy characterized by technological innovation and resource extraction led to class struggles, in both the cities and the countryside. In the South and West in particular, racial lines between whites and blacks, Indians, Asians, and Latinos perceptibly hardened. Perhaps Conan Doyle would not have recognized these as important elements in the republic following Reconstruction. They nevertheless permeate his Sherlock Holmes stories.

THE NEW INDUSTRIAL ECONOMY

Like other wars, that between North and South spurred new inventions and manufacturing processes. It is commonly argued that the North's vastly superior industrial capacity ensured its victory. From uniforms to ordnance, Union factories found ways to speed up manufacturing, and industrialists refined those lessons in the years following the war. Much of this came from new machines that allowed manufacturing to occur at a pace and on a scale unimaginable only a few years earlier. Perhaps most significant was a shift in the sources of power. To drive shafts and belts, American industry had relied first upon the power of falling water, and then turned to steam. By the 1880s, manufacturers began to look at electricity. Thomas Edison had established a laboratory for inventors in Menlo Park, New Jersey, and with a small power plant up and running in 1882 succeeded in lighting the Wall Street financial district. Factory buildings had once risen multiple stories astride rivers and canals in order to take advantage of waterwheels underneath; with the advent of steam power successors spread along the ground. Soon electricity would allow factories to expand to accommodate rows of machines and before long, the assembly line.

This "Pyramid of [the] Capitalist System" shows workers at the base who by muscle and sweat support the wealthy at the top who worship money. Soldiers, ministers, and politicians protect the capitalists. (Courtesy, The Granger Collection)

The Free Market in Labor

The men and women who took charge of these machines were a workforce newly positioned in the productive process. Earlier generations had considered themselves producers or craftsmen, making complete items—a pair of shoes, for example—directly for the consumers who used them. Only a few, for instance in the New England textile mills, toiled instead in factories driven by power of one sort or another apart from the muscle of the workers. Now, increasing numbers of workers were defined as employees, performing a specific, in most cases repetitive task assigned by an employer, perhaps operating a machine that fixed soles to shoes. Shoes themselves instead of receiving the shape wrought by an individual worker were now the impersonal and uniform product of an anonymous company. The act of labor itself had become a commodity, to be measured in time and productivity, and to be bought and sold on the open market. Cobblers a century earlier had sold shoes; workers at a mechanized shoe factory now sold their labor time in exchange for a wage, and the employer sold the shoes.

The term "free market" in labor took much of its meaning from the thriving capitalist economy in contrast to the recently abolished system of slavery. Under the regime of American liberty, employers argued, workers could sell their labor to any boss they chose. Yet this freedom, as southern critics at the emergence of the American factory system paced by water or steam power had pointed out, veiled what they called "wage slavery"—a system they claimed to be as exploitative as slavery itself. Employers uniformly held wages down and kept hours long; they took no responsibility for their workers' health or safety; and they viciously fought any efforts on the part of employees to act together in pressing for reforms. The market in commodities was "free," and labor became simply one more commodity. That left sections of the working class to be treated like other commodities on the market: priced and otherwise disposed of according to its whims.

Industrialists

Industrialists increasingly sought to develop concentrations of power and resources in their businesses. They used either of two ways, one going by the name "horizontal" and the other termed "vertical." The owner of a steel mill, for example, might acquire as many other steel mills as possible, stretching his grasp horizontally across the landscape of the industry. Another capitalist or even the same owner would attempt to control the processes that brought raw material to his mill, the digging of raw iron and its transportation that together are best imagined as taking an upward course to the factory. That kind of extended ownership received the label "vertical integration." Few people succeeded in mustering such total control over their businesses, but in addition to allowing a number of monopolies, the system produced an elite cluster of owners with intricately interlocking interests and rivalries. They began creating the culture of money that would give the era the name "Gilded Age" after the 1873 novel of that title by Mark Twain and Charles Dudley Warner, and produced a range of cultural expressions of wealth. In Newport, Rhode

The William Vanderbilt Mansion, Newport, Rhode Island. (Courtesy, private collector)

Island, industrialists constructed summer mansions out of Italian marble, with gold fittings, mammoth dining rooms, and long, sloping lawns. They were the newly rich clientele that supported ornate hotels and yacht races and toured Europe, mingling with Old World aristocracy hoping some aura of ancient pedigree might rub off on them. Some of the Old World aristocrats were looking for American money to rub off on them. So the arrangement worked well for both parties.

The excesses of industrialists made the situation of workers that much more severe. The courts consistently ruled that wages were the result of an individual contract between employer and employee, and they rejected efforts among workers to organize and to bargain as a group. Many industries moved through cycles of excessive production and under-production that slashed jobs. And as immigration increased through the 1870s and 1880s, the low-end labor pool was endlessly refreshed by new blood.

Factory Workers

Traditionally in the United States, land had been inexpensive. The consequence was that labor, with a whole continent open to it, was expensive. In the years after the Civil War, this equation was tempered. The federal government continued to offer inexpensive land in the West; Americans continued to take up homesteads there until well into the twentieth century. But in urban areas along the coasts, in the booming industrial heartlands, and in the mining outposts of the West, immigration often helped maintain the floating population of unemployed workers necessary to hold wages to a minimum. And employers could, if necessary, count on other populations to serve as low-end workers and strikebreakers. Women and children might be brought into the workforce to join black or, in the West, Mexican or Chinese immigrant workers.

Chinese, for example, had helped construct the first transcontinental railroad, and, along with Mexican railroad labor, dispersed throughout the West, working in mining, agriculture, and other industries. When white workers organized, they attacked the upper reaches of the industrial system—monopolists and managers who accumulated wealth at their expense—but they also turned on members of the low-end labor pool who worked for cheap wages. It was a splendid instance of the tradition within the American working class of turning upon the weaker part of itself. So in California, Wyoming, Colorado, Washington, and other states, white labor led anti-Chinese riots. This antagonism, along with a particularly racialized politics, produced in 1882 the Chinese Exclusion Act, which banned further immigration from China and prevented Chinese immigrants from becoming American citizens. In 1881 about forty thousand Chinese immigrants had entered the country; the next year the total shrank to a handful.

The Knights of Labor

Yet the first significant national labor organization—the Knights of Labor—at least on occasion reached out to workers outside the relatively favored white labor force. Founded in Philadelphia in 1869, the Knights added chapters in other cities throughout the 1870s. When Terence Powderly became Grand Master in 1879, the organization was primed for growth, and it drew in African Americans, women, immigrants, and workers without the traditional skills, such as shoemaking or carpentry, that had sustained previous craft unions. The organization was a leader in the movement for an eight-hour day. By the mid-1880s, membership had risen to 730,000, in no small part because the stress among the Knights on the rights and nobility of work, along with their inclusive attention to the lower ranks of the labor pool, mixed with a kind of fraternalism that drew from their era's culture.

Throughout the country in the years following the Civil War, fraternal organizations sprouted or spread. A Knight of Labor might also be a Knight of Pythias, an Oddfellow, or a member of the Improved Order of Redmen. It is said that by making the secret Masonic sign, a white victim of the Ku Klux Klan gained the protection of one of his confronters. Weekly gatherings, with quasi-secret rituals, open fellowship, and elections to a chain of offices helped American men and, in auxiliaries, American women move toward a renewed sense of community in the wake of a conflict that in some

Chinese miners in Idaho operate water cannons employed in hydraulic mining, a practice destructive of the environment. Technological innovations made most miners wage earners for companies. (Courtesy, Idaho State Historical Society)

A black delegate introduces Terence V. Powderly at a Knights of Labor convention. The union had as many as 60,000 black members. (Courtesy, Library of Congress)

regions had pitted neighbor against neighbor. The fraternal form appealed to the Knights, who used it to articulate a new vision for American society. Powderly and others thought to make every worker the owner of his work. If labor owned and operated cooperative railroads, mines, and factories, then each person would, at least in part, be an employer. Such a society would leave little room for capitalists who built industries through contractual relations with workers.

Offering an image of social transformation, the Knights possessed little power to bring it about. Powderly and the national leadership opposed strikes as futile short-term endeavors that distracted members from long-range goals. Some members disagreed, however, and in 1886 they launched a disastrous strike for wages against the railroad magnate Jay Gould. When Powderly called off the strike and Gould refused to respond with concessions, more militant groups began to peel off from the organization, which thereafter declined rapidly.

Yet while the Knights at their height never attained real economic or political power, their widespread articulation of a utopian alternative to capitalism did indeed pose, so their critics thought, a threat. *The Valley of Fear*, one of Arthur Conan

Doyle's novels, pitted his Pinkerton hero against a group very much like the Knights of Labor. The novel's Eminent Order of Freemen exists as a national fraternal organization, comprised largely of immigrant workers, and led by a "bodymaster." In the mining districts of Pennsylvania, imagined Doyle, the organization's rhetoric about workers' rights has turned to militant criminal terrorism. "What is it," declares the local boss of the Freemen, "but a war between two classes and we hit back where best we can?" Conan Doyle, like many of his elite status, identified labor militancy with violence. One of the murdered victims in Doyle's tale, for example, is "a model employer" whose only crime was insisting upon "efficiency in the work."

The readiness of employers in the new industrial age to equate efficiency with low wages and long hours guaranteed increasing dissatisfaction among workers. As the Knights of Labor attempted unsuccessfully to raise the wages of railroad employees, for example, laborers in Chicago campaigned for an eight-hour workday. After a few days of skirmishes between demonstrators and police, a crowd gathered on May 4, 1886, at Haymarket Square to protest the behavior of the police. A bomb exploded, killing seven people and wounding ten times that number. Among the Chicago militants were radical anarchists who believed in using violence to effect social change. In the ensuing crackdown, several of them were arrested, tried, and convicted; eventually four were executed.

Authorities and employers now ranged more widely, pursuing not only immigrant anarchists but protestors more generally. Across the country, employers began assembling private police and blacklisting worker activists. State and local governments also beefed up their forces, evidently prepared to bring the full power of the law on whoever challenged the dominance of capitalism itself. Combined with the failure of the Knights, the Haymarket explosion and the ensuing wave of repression made new labor strategies almost inevitable.

In the aftermath of 1886, skilled workers such as printers, bakers, and carpenters preferred to gather in craft unions built on the distinctiveness of their trade. Turning away from unskilled and marginal laborers, they formed an alliance of craft unions, the American Federation of Labor. Workers possessing a skill they could withhold from employers feared that their power would be weakened if they joined with the more vulnerable unskilled. The AFL understood the meaning of the events of 1886: the industrial system was here to stay, the place of workers in that system was also permanent, and they must content themselves with working for reforms within it. AFL strategists rejected the utopian goals of the Knights of Labor in favor of three concrete aims: better wages, shorter hours, and the right to bargain collectively in order to attain the other two goals. Throughout the late nineteenth century and the early twentieth, the AFL became the dominant labor organization in the country.

Feeding the Industrial Machine

Urban workers and their machines produced commodities out of raw materials. Laborers in the great stretches of the nation's interior produced those raw materials. Shoemaking required leather, which needed cattle or occasionally other livestock. Furniture production required lumber, which needed logging. Amid all the other resources being produced for urban processing and consumption, workers themselves needed bread and meat, which demanded market farming and the large-scale production of beef and pork. Among all regions of the country, that most primed to produce these resources was the West. And perhaps no other city existed so well positioned to structure the flow of resources as Chicago.

Trees in Michigan and Wisconsin, cut down and called lumber, could be floated down river to Chicago's factories, there to be reworked and redefined as tool handles or prefabricated houses, shingles or fence posts, all of which could be shipped by railroad to remote farms in the West. Desks, chairs, pianos, railroad ties: Chicago's workers remade nature into products. The cattle of the Dakotas and the Great Plains, the pigs and corn of Iowa, the wheat of Kansas and Montana, the fish of the Great Lakes, all these things came to the city to be processed and shipped to consumers across the nation. But in building a future, industry was plundering a land.

Just as the timber industry had earlier stripped the Northeast of much of the forest there, it now systematically clear-cut swaths of Michigan, Wisconsin, and Minnesota, taking first the hardwoods and pines for lumber and turning later to birches and other trees to make paper products. This ravaging of the forests was simple and direct. More

complex and less easy to predict was the damage to grasslands, rivers, and wildlife.

An early victim of industrial progress was the bison population of the Plains, commonly termed "buffalo." Imperiled for years by overhunting, railroad development, European diseases, drought, and competition from horses and cattle, the bison were nearly swept away in a final round of hunting that accompanied the Plains Indian wars of the 1870s. For a time, trains passing through the Plains would stop to allow passengers to get off and shoot at the animals for sport. The discovery at about the same time that buffalo skins were desirable for leather sent hunters scouring the region, killing the beasts, skinning them, and leaving their carcasses. Soon the number of bison left in the West could be counted with an exactitude that had been unimaginable only a few years earlier, when they darkened the surface of the ground. By the late 1880s, they numbered only in the hundreds. Bone hunters, feeding the market for fertilizer, searched the Plains for the remnants of slaughtered bison. Ranchers filled the empty grasslands with cattle to feed the meat and hide markets of Chicago. In 1903 only thirty-four buffalo were known to exist. From this tiny remnant, conservationists were later to breed and protect enough to bring the animal back from total disappearance.

A relatively recent phenomenon, the Plains Indians culture had depended greatly on one European importation, the horse, and secondarily on European weaponry, though with bow and arrow the Plains people were magnificent hunters and warriors on horseback. The way of life of the Plains also relied on bison. The vast herds supplied meat: fresh and, for journeys, dried. Buffalo skins clothed the Plains Indians and made up their tents; sinews extracted from the animals were usable for cord and bowstrings. In a region offering little wood, large chips of dried bison droppings provided fuel for fires as they did for early European Americans in the region. The thinning of the buffalo herds almost to extinction together with the filling of the range with farms, sheepherding, and the cattle industry, all of it crowding out bison and Indians alike, brought an end to Plains culture.

In the years following the Civil War, Texas ranchers relied upon the unfenced open range, cowboys driving their cattle north to railheads in Kansas. During the first years after the confinement of Indian people to reservations, the open-range system worked well enough for the cattle ranchers spread across the West. Proceeding in warm weather when the green grass could feed the traveling herds, they were the most dramatic events in the lives of the ranch workers. Their typical labor was on the ranch rather than the trail. But in a bone-cold winter they chopped through the ice to liberate water for cattle, among the most helplessly passive of animals. Branding cattle was another task, the means by which the owner marked off a herd from the others on the open range. Though cattle were not so gentle on the Plains grasses as the bison had been, at first they moved around enough to keep the range relatively undamaged.

Exploiting Western Lands

By the 1880s, however, most of the Texas cattle drives came to an end, victims in part to state restrictions on the use of land, the loss of cattle weight associated with driving them, and the spread of the railway network, which allowed close access to shipping points. But most directly ranch-

ers faced competition from sheepherders and homesteaders. Homesteading farmers, or rival cattle ranchers, caused problems for free-ranging cattle. And cattle caused problems for homesteading farmers. "Good fences make good neighbors," the poet Robert Frost has written in ironic intent; and western ranchers whose fencing of the range forced the end of the open-range system reinforce the mockery in Frost's words. Increasingly confined on smaller pastures, cattle by overgrazing destroyed the rich native grasses. And when a series of devastating blizzards arrived in the winter of 1887 and 1888, the winds pushed the animals to the corners of their pastures, where fences trapped them. When the spring thaw finally arrived, many ranchers found themselves out of business, their pastures' corners packed with dead, bloated cattle. Like other industries, cattle ranching proved ripe for consolidation, and entrepreneurs with capital, much of it European, acquired the holdings of venturers who had gone under.

As railroads expanded and sprouted branch lines throughout the 1870s and 1880s, farmers flooded

Passengers shot buffalo by the thousands from trains en route west, contributing to depleting the herds that became almost extinct by late in the nineteenth century. (Courtesy, The Granger Collection)

western landscapes. In many cases, they came not as homesteaders—people who received a standard allocation of land under the Homestead Act of 1862—but as purchasers of the land grants the federal government had offered railroad companies to subsidize construction. Many came from Europe, large numbers of them participants in chain migrations that brought one family, then assorted relatives, then other residents from the Old World town of origin. Across the Plains, communities of Swedes, Poles, Germans, and others remain even today.

With them they brought European seeds particularly well adapted to the arid West, such as the Turkey Red variety of wheat, a hardy winter wheat introduced by Russian Mennonite immigrants in 1874. The winter wheat gave farmers an extra crop, for a field could now be planted in both the fall and the spring. Steel plows cut through the matted Plains and prairie grasses, exposing fragile topsoil, creating a type of agriculture that did not confine itself to feeding the farm family. Crops produced for a nationwide market needed to draw on sources of energy outside the local ecological system. To make the wheat that made the bread that fed the Chicago laborer, for example, the Colorado farmer had to purchase not only seeds but also fertilizer to boost the productivity of his overworked fields. And the farm needed water to supplement the natural but unreliable allotment from the sky. Arguments arising over the use of water were usually worked out locally through mutual irrigation companies and claims settled by the state or territory. The authorities had the hard task of deciding who had first gotten to a source of water and therefore had first use of it. Fertilizer, moreover, came from a factory, perhaps a plant in Chicago that processed bison bones from the Plains. In that instance, a western product went eastward, then back to the West. Industry and agriculture, in sum, were cooperative and antagonistic in ways beyond any simple description. The new industrial economy only looked urban. In reality, it rested firmly on the resources of its lands in the West and South.

Mining the Land

Perhaps the most visible resource extraction from the land was western mining. Although the California gold rush was long since over, rushes continued for gold and for other minerals just starting to come into their own. Spreading throughout Colorado, Oregon, Idaho, Montana, and British Columbia, miners as late as the turn of the century hustled north to Alaska. Like the mines in California, these became industrial endeavors, requiring railroad access, powerful digging, blasting, and processing equipment, and a low-wage labor force. Entrepreneurs stripped hillsides and hollowed out mountains, leaving acid-leaching piles of waste rock behind, all part of the rapid industrialization of the western landscape.

Creole, Colorado, a mining town. Another Colorado mining town, Leadville, had two hundred fifty saloons, one hundred and twenty gambling dens, one hundred houses of prostitution, and four churches. (Courtesy, Henry Ford Museum and Greenfield Village)

For Americans watching quick fortunes being made in industry, railroading, and land speculation, mineral prospecting had deep cultural meanings. Ordinary workers had only a slight chance of pulling together the necessary capital to build an industrial fortune. Prospecting seemed one mode of capital accumulation that catered to a poor man's luck. And the romance of mining fortunes outstripped reality. *The Valley of Fear* and other stories by Conan Doyle capture the myth of quick mining wealth that had prevailed since the early days of the California gold rush. The character Jack Douglas flees the vengeance of his criminal adversaries by striking it rich and retiring to England.

Douglas's dream of economic independence was that of many who fanned out across the West. In Colorado, the quest was for silver. Montana and Arizona began supplying copper to meet the new demands placed by a nation generating electricity. In the last years of the nineteenth century and the first years of the twentieth, mining western minerals would become a boom-and-bust endeavor as the markets in these materials fluctuated. Prospectors turned to oil, tungsten, and coal, and later bauxite (aluminum ore), molybdenum (used to strengthen and harden steel), and other minerals, each valuable to the new industrial economy.

Mining the Soil

American agriculture, both in fact and in the imagination, had once been assigned to provide the farm family with its own food and much of the rest of its needs or sustenance. This self-reliance lay at the core of Thomas Jefferson's vision of a nation of republican yeoman farmers. Farming, in many ways, was a critical part of the American identity. In both the South and the West, however, the nature of agriculture changed during the years following the Civil War. Increasingly, farm families came to rely upon commodities, including food, that they bought with cash from selling their excess yields on the market. On the Great Plains, for example, planting vast fields of wheat seemed a more profitable bet than sowing a few acres each of corn, wheat, potatoes or some other marketable vegetable; tending a garden; and raising a few cattle. Farmers increased their acreage, bought fertilizer, and purchased or rented machines to aid in planting and harvesting. In order to afford these aids to productivity, they needed more cash and so produced

even more. But when a whole region of farmers produced the same single crop in huge volume, the result was an oversupply that brought down the price of that crop, which forced them to plant even more and thus set up a descending spiral of overproduction and falling prices. Not until the twentieth century, when the severely punished land had turned to dust whipped by the wind, would market farming be revealed for what it had always been: a mining industry. From the land it drew not coal or iron or silver but the nutrients that went into crops.

Railroad rates responded to the problems inherent in carrying goods between urban and rural areas. A railroad might need to send out a huge number of boxcars to gather in wheat or other agricultural products. As inbound cargo, the wheat could pay for itself. But for the outbound trip to the grainfields, the railroad would often have to send near-empty trains that burned fuel without profit. To make up for the loss, railroads would charge higher rates than for traffic within heavily developed regions, where they could expect always to have their cars packed with goods going from one point to another.

Southern farmers, both black and white, faced problems similar to the troubles of westerners, though in the South these took shape within the context of the sharecropping system that began in the era of Reconstruction. Like the Great Plains, the South became victim to production of a single primary commercial crop—in this case, cotton. Southerners, prosperous white planters and sharecroppers alike, were trapped in an endless cycle. They had to produce cotton in order to get needed commodities, and the resulting debts had to be met by further production. The system bore steadily down on its most impoverished producers.

In the late nineteenth century, distressed farmers formed local groups called Granges. Initially social gatherings, they eventually turned political, seeking laws regulating railroad and grain elevator rates. On occasion, they attempted to band together in cooperative efforts. They also lobbied for agricultural colleges and education. In general, however, the Grangers lacked the economic power either to build cooperatives or to influence the political process in significant ways, and by the late 1870s they had started to decline. They were, however, like the Knights of Labor in being an early instance of what was to become widespread rebellion. A decade later, farm radicalism would reappear in the

This lithograph of 1873, "The Purposes of the Grange," idealizes the common farmer and expresses his centrality in the economic order. (Courtesy, *American Heritage*)

form of the Farmers' Alliances, networks based initially in Texas and the South and later, the Great Plains, Midwest, and West. In 1889, the Southern Alliance had two million members, and its northern partner a like number, while a separate Colored Farmers' National Alliance boasted yet another million. The next year, the Alliances controlled four governorships, eight state legislatures, and forty-seven congressional seats. Out of their success came the Populist Party, which in 1892 and 1896 would launch one of the most important third-party challenges to the status quo in American history.

NEW SOCIAL RELATIONS

In the 1870s and 1880s, the word "race" did not mean what it does today. It referred rather to any number of people identifiable by a mixture of ethnicity and nationality. While Americans did speak of the Indian or Negro race, they might just as easily have used the word for people from Ireland, or from eastern or southern Europe. In this way, the word sifted out small, semi-national groups, most of them Europeans, while lumping together hundreds of other distinct peoples under labels such as Indian or Asian or Negro. It also meant that skin color, while important, was by no means the only way of defining race. There might be different racial ways, for example, of being white. And among these, the most favored was to be Anglo-Saxon, a term that assumes that the person so defined was of British and ultimately Germanic ancestry.

A New Mingling

By the turn of the twentieth century, immigration to the United States by groups from Britain and elsewhere in northwestern Europe was becoming overwhelmed in numbers by peoples of lower social repute among old-stock Americans. Particularly to the eastern half of the United States came immigrants from southern and eastern Europe of slightly darker skin shadings. In the West, Japanese supplemented continuing immigration of Mexicans. Unskilled, poor, and destined for more poverty, knowing only scraps of English if that much, the newcomers were widely thought to be ill-fitted to adapt to their new surroundings. That

they were likely to be Roman Catholic or Jewish rather than Protestant, and so outside what Americans took to be their country's religious consensus, supported the opinion many Americans had of them. Japanese and Chinese seemed more outlandish still. In both cities and the countryside, great numbers of the newly arrived ended up in ethnic or racial ghettoes. Yet immigrants and natives mingled in many ways, setting off complicated patterns of social relations. Immigrants themselves sought to preserve their Old World cultures within the bounds of the United States; their offspring over time learned the ways of the new nation and moved freely outside the neighborhood. Some Americans wanted to confine immigrants to specific areas; others wished to see them assimilate. Immigrants themselves differed over the matter of absorption into American culture. Inevitably, most customs and languages of the old country gave way to American slang and the ways of the city streets.

People also constantly moved about within the nation. Though not in the epic numbers of the Great Migration of the era of World War I, black Americans moved north, south, and west into urban and rural areas. In the wake of the repudiation of Reconstruction, for example, black "Exodusters" fled from parts of the South to Kansas in the late 1870s to establish farm communities; others headed to midwestern cities, or turned farther west to Texas and the Southwest. A good proportion of western cowboys, especially in Texas, was black. In the East, cities grew diverse; in the West, both rural and urban landscapes mixed Mexicans, Indians, Asians, African Americans, and all manner of white ethnicities. Amid this extensive mingling and blending of peoples and cultures, the idea of a white race sprawled over groups so diverse, or excluded so many among the newly arrived, as to cease to have any definite meaning.

Race is a category, a dividing line that human beings imagine into being and act upon in real and physical ways. Any effort to mark off racial differences is threatened when actual people cross the dividing lines of race and culture. And real people, when placed in multiracial situations—cattle ranch, mine, or urban street—cross those lines by interbreeding or by cultural melding. One central paradox of race in the United States—that we constantly both destroy and remake race boundaries—began to take on its modern shape in the years following Reconstruction.

These southern black "Exodusters" camp out on the Mississippi River on their way to Kansas after being driven by terror from the South. (Courtesy, Library of Congress)

Conan Doyle's relish for the far corners and margins of American society produced in "The Five Orange Pips" a story of the Ku Klux Klan, the obligatory murder victim having spirited off to England the organization's secret records. Doyle painted the turncoat as an unpleasant man, more Klan-like than the Klan, whose leaving the United States reflected his "aversion to the negros and his dislike of the Republican policy in extending the franchise to them."

While Conan Doyle expresses no open racism, African Americans scarcely appear in the tale. The Klan as Doyle portrays it shows less concern with terrorizing former slaves than with policing its own secrecy and so its victims are white rather than black. Doyle the Anglo-Irishman was thinking like

a white American northerner of the time after the collapse of Reconstruction. It was a time when people outside the South were not so much hostile to black Americans as indifferent to their existence. That attitude permitted reconciliation between North and South on the basis of a shared whiteness.

The South after Reconstruction

Reconstruction's promise of political equality carried within it the means of breaking down the deeply etched social and cultural lines that defined black Americans in racial terms. And that frightened whites. Nothing more seriously blurred the line than sexual contact across the boundaries. From the time of the first Ku Klux Klan through the

Studies of cowboys estimate that as many as one third were black or Mexican. This photograph was taken in Texas. (Courtesy, Library of Congress)

lynchings that threatened black southerners well into the 1920s, interracial sex was always and everywhere the supreme threat used to justify white violence. Instead of breaking down racial boundaries, then, Reconstruction pushed white southerners to reinforce them. And upon the withdrawal of federal troops and support after Rutherford B. Hayes became president, those lines hardened even more.

Even after the official dissolution of the Klan in the early 1870s, blacks continued to suffer from nightriding raids and other forms of terrorism. Lynching, murder, beating, and harassment all kept freed men and women in what the white South defined as their place. And that place was essentially the same as in the days of slavery—agricultural labor and domestic service. In 1880, the great majority of southern blacks remained either in the field tilling land owned by whites, or in the new equivalents of the plantation Big House. Millions of whites too scratched a living from land that they worked only as tenants or sharecroppers. Initially, even the end of Reconstruction did not prevent African Americans from voting, and in some states, black legislators continued to be elected into the 1890s. But in many places, the tenuous power of the Republican Party relied upon fragile coalitions of black and poor white voters able to perceive and willing to act on their shared class interests, which took shape in opposition to white economic elites.

In no small part, the political power of these elites depended upon the reaffirmation of white supremacy, which convinced poor whites that their interests were racial and deflected them from questions of class and economic condition. And that social and cultural reaffirmation went hand in hand with a series of legal and political maneuvers designed to curtail black voting and eventually, to install full-fledged racial segregation. Following the lead of Florida in 1889, for example, southern states instituted poll taxes, usually a dollar, on all voters. Innumerable African Americans, caught in the debt cycle imposed by sharecropping, could not spare the money to vote. Other laws, passed at about the turn of the twentieth century, included property ownership requirements and literacy tests designed to stump potential black voters. Electoral participation by black southerners plummeted. But the same laws theoretically put up obstacles to voting by poor whites as well, which went against the intention of southern legislators to disfranchise only blacks. A solution was the grandfather clause.

THE GRANDFATHER CLAUSE

Some states included a grandfather clause to the effect that anyone whose father or grandfather could have voted before passage of the Fifteenth Amendment was exempt from having to meet the literacy qualifications. Since that provision did not specifically refer to race, the state might claim that whites were not being given special privileges forbidden by the Constitution. Yet the purpose of the grandfather laws was so blatant that in 1915 the Supreme Court struck them down.

The solidifying of racial difference and inequality also required physical markers, and these took the form of increasingly segregated spaces. In a series of cases, courts ruled that the federal government lacked authority over the discriminatory actions of individuals or private organizations. The Fourteenth Amendment, moreover, protected freedmen's rights only against discrimination by a state government. Freedmen wishing to contest private discrimination must turn not to the federal government, but to the states, within which they were most unlikely to win sympathy. In 1883, the Supreme Court overturned the 1875 Civil Rights Act, which prohibited discrimination in public facilities. Other courts began toying with the idea that states imposing segregation did not violate the Fourteenth Amendment so long as the facilities provided the separate races were equal in quality. In *Plessy* v. *Ferguson*, decided in 1896, that principle got the full endorsement of the Supreme Court.

The Fate of American Indians

In the late 1870s and 1880s came the final phase of the struggle by Indians in the West against white domination and occupation. It ended with their being forced onto reservations, usually desolate wastelands shunned by white settlers. After Custer's defeat at the Little Big Horn, General Nelson Miles by use of railroads and modern technology devastated the Lakota and Cheyenne people during the winter of 1876 and 1877. Sitting Bull and his people were compelled to flee to Canada and Crazy

Ensconced in the narrow valleys between the Cascade and Bitterroot mountains (lands now parts of Idaho, Washington, and Oregon), the Nez Percé apparently never attacked settlers before their great war with the whites in 1877. They had aided Lewis and Clark in 1805. The Nez Percé welcomed outsiders and were quick to learn from and trade with them. They even survived a gold rush into their lands in the 1860s, remaining at peace despite numerous outrages by the miners. Nonetheless, friction sharpened in the 1860s as cattle ranchers eyed lands on which Indian horses grazed. In 1863 the federal government negotiated a treaty to delimit Indian land titles, but a group of braves, loosely led by Old Joseph, the father of a more famous Joseph, rejected it. Turning away from the Christianity they had learned from missionaries, they began a peaceful but determined resistance to the white man's designs on their ancestral lands. "My son," Old Joseph whispered, as he lay dying, "you are the chief. . . . You must stop your ears whenever you are asked to sign a treaty selling your home. . . . This country holds your father's body. Never sell the bones of your father and your mother"

Chief Joseph was ever true to this stern injunction. Although he struggled to avoid conflict, his people's fate was typical: rapacious settlers pressing for land, unfeeling Indian agents, bungling in governmental departments, an unsympathetic general, a forced and hurried evacuation of their lands, and finally young braves driven to fury and terrible violence. Once at war, Joseph and his tribe enacted one of the great feats of military prowess and human endurance (for this army traveled with its women and children, its sick and aged). A United States Army ROTC instruction manual describes Joseph's achievement: "In 11 weeks, he had moved his tribe 1600 miles, engaged 10 separate U.S. commands in 13 battles and skirmishes, and in nearly every instance had either defeated them or fought them to a stand-still." Joseph and fewer than two hundred braves withstood an army. The effort, of course, was doomed to failure, and with its failure, the Nez Percé would no longer exist as an independent people. Chief Joseph surrendered on Octo-

Chief Joseph of the Nez Percé. (Courtesy, Library of Congress)

ber 5, 1877. His memorable speech gave all the reasons:

I am tired of fighting. Our chiefs are killed. . . . The old men are all killed; It is the young men who say yes or no. He who led the young men is dead. It is cold and we have no blankets. The little children are freezing to death. My people, some of them, have run away to the hills and have no blankets, no food; no one knows where they are, perhaps freezing to death. I want time to look for my children and see how many of them I can find. Maybe I shall find them among the dead. Hear me, my chiefs, I am tired; my heart is sick and sad. From where the sun now stands, I will fight no more forever.

The Nez Percé's fighting days were over.

In his new home in western Washington, Joseph became an Indian elder stateman, a national symbol of courage and freedom. He returned to the Wallowa Valley but once, in 1900, an old man. There he found only the consolation that a settler—a man with, as he said, "a spirit too rare among his kind"—had enclosed and cared for his father's grave.

by Robert D. Marcus

Horse to lead his followers to the Indian agency at Fort Robinson, Nebraska, where he was killed. After successfully evading the United States Army on a 1400-mile trek whose course ran through the new Yellowstone National Park, Chief Joseph and his Nez Percé people surrendered in 1877, just miles from the Canadian border. And following a long series of futile campaigns, the Apache leader Goyathlay (Geronimo) surrendered with his followers in 1886, a handful defending their homeland, many of whom would remain for life on an Oklahoma reservation. In California and the Pacific Northwest, too, Indian people were confined to small areas, with the great bulk of their lands opened up to settlement.

Some Americans, among them the writer Helen Hunt Jackson, looked back with dismay over the history of the long war that whites had waged against Indians. Her book *A Century of Dishonor*, published in 1881, reminded the nation of its dismal record of lying, cheating, and mismanaging Indian affairs. Others, such as Buffalo Bill Cody, barnstorming the nation and Europe with his Wild West extravaganza, celebrated the conflicts that had shaped American character by pitting settlers against a worthy foe. Still others, moving from the cause of abolition to that of Indian reform, argued that the conquest now complete, the United States had an obligation to assimilate Indian people into the nation. Eastern reformers, in particular, tended to see Indians not so much as an absolutely distinct race—that would come later—but as a people frozen in time. Look at an Indian, they supposed, and you will see your own society at an earlier stage of development. On that assumption, the need was merely to transform native cultures, to bring Indians rapidly up to the present.

For reformers, such speeded development ought to take place in the spheres of work, land, education, and religion. Accordingly, they sent missionaries to reservations, brought children to boarding schools to be given a basic education and trained for work, and, with devastating results, changed the nature of reservation land ownership. Traditionally, in almost all Indian societies, land was not divided among individuals but held in common, and initially reservation lands also belonged to the whole tribe. But the Dawes or General Allotment Act, passed in 1887, ordained the breakup of these lands into individual parcels, commonly 160 acres each,

and specified that whatever land remained was to be sold off to homesteaders. Given some assistance, so the legislators believed, Indian people would farm their parcels, taking their cue from white agrarian neighbors. Hard work and productive crop yields would integrate them into the urban industrial marketplace, and they would turn their backs on the old ways and in no time at all become regular Americans.

But while the reformers generally had good intentions, they ignored facts. Many of the allotted tribes had not traditionally practiced agriculture, or had done so to a very limited extent; most considered planting and harvesting to be the work of women, and the men resisted being forced into it. Much of the reservation land, moreover, had soil inadequate for farming. In general, the West was too dry to be farmed reliably in small lots: the minimum area desirable might be 640 acres with a water source rather than 160 acres without. And what happened when allotment holders died? Frequently the parcels, divided among the survivors, so fragmented the land that within a generation or two land ownership became utterly impossible to manage. The Dawes Act stipulated that the government would hold title to the land for twenty-five years, but later provisions gave deeds to individuals, many of whom sold the land. And an Indian farmer who managed to overcome all of these problems still confronted the disastrous agricultural market then driving farmers both black and white into the militant Farmers' Alliances.

The great irony of Indian allotment and assimilation policies can be seen in their relation to the rest of post-Reconstruction racial consciousness. White southerners vehemently rejected the idea that black and white could live side by side. Americans of older stock expressed increasing concern about the people emigrating from what they took to be the wrong parts of Europe. In California and other western states, whites rigorously excluded Chinese immigrants and workers and forced Mexicans into segregated barrios. And yet a consensus—among legislators, administrators, and reformer missionaries, if not across the entire society—had formed around the idea that Indians must be brought within the boundaries of white nationhood. Against the deeper reserves of white racism, that belief had little chance of sustaining itself. Within a few decades, Indians would remain with black Americans and other peoples of color at the bottom of the racial hierarchy.

Polygamy and the Mormons

Nor were the dynamics of exclusion and forced assimilation applied solely to people of color. The practice of plural marriage among male adherents to Mormonism, the Church of Jesus Christ of Latter Day Saints, marked the church as unacceptably and outrageously threatening. More ominous, perhaps, was its political and economic control over Utah Territory. Mormons voted in a bloc, pooled their resources, and believed firmly in their own uniqueness. They had faced persecution since the 1820s, forced from New York to Ohio to Illinois and finally, in 1846, to the isolation of the mountain West. And when in 1852 they publicly revealed their doctrines of plural marriage, politicians, Protestant ministers, and female reformers rallied against the church.

Five years later, the United States army entered Utah determined to topple Brigham Young, who both led the church and served as territorial governor, and to install a government not beholden to Mormon authority. But although Young agreed to step down, changes in Utah were superficial. In 1862, Congress passed an antibigamy act aimed at the Mormons, but local judges and juries refused to convict the few people actually brought to trial. Two decades later, however, a new act declared polygamy a felony and empowered federal officials to pursue Mormon leaders, who immediately went underground, moving from safe house to safe house, one step ahead of the marshals. Even this harassment did not deter the Mormons, and so in 1887 Congress passed the Edmunds-Tucker Act, which prescribed the legal dissolution of the church itself and the seizure and redistribution of its substantial holdings.

In characterizing the Mormon Church as "Asiatic," critics sought to make its members analogous to an alien race, but they did so with an assimilationist bent. "Throw off the yoke of the Priesthood," one opponent implored. "Do as we do and be Americans in deed as well as name." During the summer of 1890, as Congress prepared to disfranchise all Mormons, the church's president and his council issued a manifesto outlawing polygamy and declaring their intention to submit to the laws of the United States. Within the next six years, the

Polygamy, it was argued as a defense, helped absorb widowed and single women into Mormon communities. (Courtesy, Library of Congress)

church's property would be returned, and the Mormons agreed not to attempt to reclaim their ironclad control over the territory's politics and economy. In exchange, Utah entered the Union as a state in 1896.

The Mormons were a phenomenon striking enough to catch the attention of Arthur Conan Doyle. In *A Study in Scarlet*, set in 1878, Sherlock Holmes solves the mysterious murders of two men who turn out to be Mormon polygamists visiting London. The motive? Revenge—a killing by a man who had seen his lover forced into a polygamous marriage, the horror of which had driven her to an early death. Like American opponents of the Mormons, Doyle connected polygamy and slavery, repeating Harriet Beecher Stowe's appeal to the women of her country: "Let every happy wife and mother who reads these lines give her sympathy, prayers and efforts to free her sisters from this degrading bondage." Polygamy displayed a form of bondage explicitly sexual, directly the enemy of the "happy wife and mother" who was imagined to be the pinnacle of white womanhood.

Woman Suffrage

The attack on the Mormons demonstrated the impulse to reform similar to that which had driven the antislavery campaigns before the war and propelled the movement for Indian reform. And it was fitting that both abolitionism and opposition to the Mormons spoke in defense of the virtues of women.

Reform was increasingly defined as an effort to bring to public life the order and virtue that ideally prevailed in the private home and family, a realm that was supposed to be in the keeping of women. The public as a national household, so such reasoning went, could be moral only insofar as the women who inhabited it were protected in their virtue and granted their due honor. But if women assumed the role of particular guardians of virtue, reason argued for bringing them directly into the public sphere, specifically by giving them the vote. Would male reformers be true to this implication of the idea of reform as setting the national household in order? When, in 1869, the Fifteenth Amendment granted the vote to all men regardless of "race, color, or previous condition of servitude" but not to women, women's rights activists, disappointed and energized, set to work on woman suffrage almost immediately.

The American Woman Suffrage Association came out of the tradition of abolitionist reform. Led by Lucy Stone and Thomas Wentworth Higginson, it sought women's voting rights at the state level, working to amend state constitutions. In 1870 Utah, presumed to be the solid lair of male supremacy in the form of polygamy, became the second territory to grant women the vote a year, after Wyoming. The more militant National Woman Suffrage Association, led by Elizabeth Cady Stanton and Susan B. Anthony, articulated a larger vision of women's rights, looking beyond the abolitionist model and seeking to win for women something like the civil rights that Reconstruction was seeking for blacks. Equality, the two women and their followers believed, needed to happen not only at election time but every day, in the courts, the legislatures, and the workplace.

In 1878, Susan B. Anthony succeeded in finding a sympathetic senator to introduce a constitutional amendment stating that the rights of American citizens to vote "shall not be denied or abridged by the United States or by any state on account of sex." The amendment died in a Senate committee, to be reintroduced regularly over the next eighteen years. When the amendment came up for a vote, it was easily defeated with the argument that voting was inconsistent with women's family obligations. The concept of reform as extending to politics the virtues of the household bumped up against itself. As the keepers of domestic virtue, women should be among the most valuable of voters. But granting the vote, so opponents were convinced, would undermine the place of women in the private household, where their virtue had its foundation and was most deeply sustained.

KNITTING THE COUNTRY TOGETHER

The concept of their nation as a white man's country was but one way Americans found of conceiving themselves as a united people with a coherent society. Even as its population sprawled ever westward and the ethnic diversities among its immigrants multiplied, the United States was tightening politically, technologically, and in some ways culturally.

Reconciliation

Prominent among postwar fraternal orders was the Grand Army of the Republic, a society of former Union soldiers. As the debates over Reconstruction faded, Union and Confederate soldiers began meeting together, tentatively at first, discussing what were rapidly becoming the old days. For many veterans of both armies, of course, the war would always remain a bitter memory. When the Democratic president Grover Cleveland in 1887 ordered the return to the South of Confederate battle flags captured in the war, northern veterans protested and Cleveland withdrew the directive. Still, during the 1870s and 1880s cities and towns found ways to commemorate the conflict, to turn the present away from overt hostility and toward a glorious history. Statuary and cannon on courthouse lawns expressed specifically Union or rebel sympathies. But together they developed a sense of the war's having been not so much about abolitionism or states' rights as a cultural event in the lives of boys from this or that neighborhood, their quarrel ultimately submerged in their common experience of combat.

Wilderness: A National Possession

The nation came together also in its startling discovery of its magnificent natural heritage, which earlier generations of settlers had exploited with

Yellowstone Falls, 1881, painted by Albert Bierstadt. (Courtesy, Buffalo Bill Historical Center, Cody, WY)

hardly a thought, so it seemed, to its wonders. As early as the 1830s the artist George Catlin had suggested the establishment of a national park, and in 1864 the federal government deeded Yosemite to California to be established as a state park. In 1872, Yellowstone, in Wyoming, became the country's first formal national park. While the boom years of park formation lay ahead in the first decades of the twentieth century, the urban middle class was already seeking experiences in the rugged outdoors. Along the East Coast, railroads allowed quick access to hunting camps, where urban men might reaffirm their own experience of a wild and hardy frontier that Americans feared to be vanishing. And in the West, visitors were drawn to the grand railroad hotels, such as the Old Faithful Inn at Yellowstone, or El Tovar at the Grand Canyon. In 1890, Yosemite reverted to the federal government, now as a national park. Two years later, John Muir founded the Sierra Club, which in the twentieth century would turn into one of the nation's more effective political organizations lobbying for the environment.

The Bonds of Technology

A lacing of steel rails drew together the vast stretches of the republic. The first great transcontinental railroad was completed in 1869 when the meeting of the Union Pacific and the Central Pacific at Promontory Point, Utah, was commemorated with the driving of a golden spike, the last nail binding the track that was now as long as a continent. Five other lines eventually crossed the country. By 1881, the Southern Pacific made the connection in the South. Two years later the Northern Pacific crossed the northern tier. The Great Northern, completed in 1893, the last of the great transcontinentals, was built without any of the government subsidies required by the other lines. In the 1860s, it had taken several months to move

from the East to the West Coast; now a passenger could leave New York on a Monday and stand amid the geyser basins of Wyoming the following Thursday. Such easy access to great distances required Americans to revisualize their nation.

No less important was the telegraph, first employed in a major way in the 1850s, and grown to common use during the Civil War. As the golden spike was hammered into the track in celebration of the meeting of the Union Pacific with the Central Pacific, a telegraph carried the sound east across the continent. Newspapers, which had been aiming at mass audiences since the penny press papers, could now use the telegraph to gather information from a range of national sources, and they came fully into their own as a form of mass popular culture. Critical to the newspaper revolution was Joseph Pulitzer, who bought the *New York World* in 1883 and successfully centered its attention on the sensational and the scandalous. The *World* transformed newspapers, adding large headlines, sections devoted to sports, the household and fashion, and comics, printed with yellow ink. The term "yellow journalism" quickly arose to define the journalistic style pioneered by the *World*, combining sentimental stories with sensational reports of crimes and disasters. Others soon imitated Pulitzer's success. Informing Americans of events across the country, newspaper chains created a consciousness that every American was a daily participant in a collective nationwide experience.

Literacy and Entertainment

The spread of literacy benefited other forms of publishing as well. Supplementing the elite literary journals of previous years, publishers began reaching out to larger audiences through such magazines as the *Saturday Evening Post,* the *Ladies' Home Journal, Collier's, McClure's,* and *Harper's.* To the homes of an increasingly educated middle class they car-

The Golden Spike. (Courtesy, Union Pacific Corporation)

ried news, fiction, human-interest stories, photographs, artwork, advertising, and advice. "Dime novels" had proliferated in the years before and during the Civil War; by the 1870s they were giving way to the "cheap library," publications of from sixteen to thirty-two pages of three-column print that combined the form of a book with the appearance of a newspaper. Aimed at a less educated clientele than did the likes of *McClure's* or the *Ladies' Home Journal*, they included frontier adventure and urban crime stories.

In sum, print culture now stood in the vanguard of a new form of mass leisure, which came into being as the result of the urban industrial economy of the postwar period. The technological progress that allowed publishers to reach in new ways a mass public also extended the range of access to popular entertainment.

A new form of popular culture performance was the circus. Although traveling entertainment was nothing new in the United States, the circus fused with the new transportation technologies of the railroad the performance tradition of acrobats and animals popularized in the early shows of P. T. Barnum's museum. As a museum entrepreneur, Barnum had continually sought out novelty; getting the same customers to return depended on presenting them with something they had not seen on their last visit. As a circus manager, he did the exact opposite, crafting a scripted show and taking it on the road. Railroad systems allowed circuses access to a never-ending supply of new locations.

Beginning in 1883, Buffalo Bill Cody used the railroads to create another hybrid form of performance; his highly successful Wild West show mingled circus excitement, dime-novel western adventure, and stage melodrama. Like black entertainers in the minstrel show, Indian and later Mexican riders presented images of themselves to white audiences, in the process traversing the nation and the world. The content of the shows, which reinforced myths about the struggle for the frontier, and their enactment before differing audiences throughout the country deepened the sense among Americans of being participants in a single nationwide experience.

Leisure Diversions

The national tour of the Cincinnati Red Stockings baseball club in 1869 and the founding of the

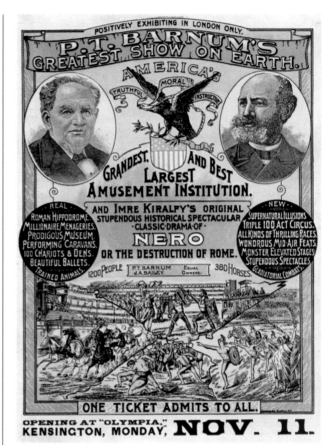

P. T. Barnum's "Greatest Show on Earth" traveled worldwide as well as throughout the United States. (Courtesy, American Heritage)

National League in 1876 strengthened the status of baseball as yet another enterprise that Americans across the country could share and know themselves to be sharing. Fans quickly developed loyalties to home teams; league play required certain knowledge of other places and a vision of the nation of linked communities, all speaking the same language of strikes and runs and outs.

Baseball, a participatory as well as a spectator sport, invited Americans across the country to turn empty lots into ball diamonds. Joining baseball as a widespread activity was cycling. After the development in 1885 of the safety bicycle, which had inflated tires and same-size wheels, cycling swept the country. Cycling tracks, cycling clubs, professional and local races, lobbying groups for better roads: all these became part of the culture of cycling, which, not incidentally, required some freeing up in the dress and comportment of the hitherto constrained Victorian woman of late nineteenth-century America.

Other kinds of popular culture changed more slowly. Stage performances continued to rely upon familiar forms—the sentimental melodrama, the minstrel show, the musical comedy. Burlesque, later associated with striptease, had its origins in postwar days as an all-woman musical theater performance. Vaudeville would in time grow out of the minstrel show, but until the 1890s minstrelsy continued to present the racial stereotyping that had characterized it since its origins in the 1830s. Postwar minstrelsy did, however, open up new—though, in their implications, conflicted—opportunities for African Americans, many of whom formed successful minstrel troupes of their own. But they felt obliged to present the comic caricatures of blacks that their white audiences expected.

Bicycling became a healthy form of exercise for both men and women in the late 1880s and 1890s. It also brought them together socially on outings. (Courtesy, The New-York Historical Society)

Altogether, these activities and pursuits reflected the appearance of organized leisure, passive or strenuous, a new component in the American economy and society. Despite the continuing reality of exhausting work and long hours, many Americans were finding that mechanization had in fact created shorter workweeks and more free time for their own. The widespread demand within the labor movement for an eight-hour day made sense only insofar as mechanical production dictated work for a specific number of hours clearly marked off from the remainder. And as the Philadelphia Exposition of 1876 had hinted, the American economy could not survive merely through efficient production. Its workers needed to be able, and willing, to buy their own products, or industry would not make the profits it needed to continue producing. The purveyors of leisure entertainment and activities led the way in training Americans to be consumers, an activity that was gaining an increasing social status of its own.

POLITICS AFTER RECONSTRUCTION

Politics is more than presidents, but the period between 1877 and 1890 perhaps can best be described by reference to its chief executives. President Rutherford B. Hayes's successor, James Garfield, governed briefly in 1881 before being cut down by an assassin, whereupon his vice president, Chester Alan Arthur, completed his term. From 1885 to 1889 the chief executive, Grover Cleveland, served as the lone Democratic president of the time. From the presidency of Hayes through Cleveland's first administration (after losing the next election he would win a second term), American politics had a distinctive moment. It was marked by balances of power among the three sections, East, South, and West, between factions within parties and within Congress, and among the three branches of the federal government: Congress, the courts, and the executive. At no time during that period, for example, did the same party control both the presidency and both houses of Congress. That would await the inauguration of Benjamin Harrison in 1889. In most cases, beginning of course with Hayes's contest, the elections were extremely close. As a result these presidents, who were by and large

This Republican campaign poster from the 1888 presidential election is aimed at the Democratic candidate, Grover Cleveland, who admitted to having fathered a child out of wedlock. (Courtesy, Corbis-Bettmann)

competent and honest men, served unremarkable terms characterized by legislation that sought to manage the industrial economy and the society that followed Reconstruction. That management was, inevitably, the product of the rivalries and near-equal balances of political power.

From the end of Reconstruction, American political argument turned upon questions new to the country, for they engaged the extraordinary advance in the nation's technological and productive capacities. Even monetary policy, an American preoccupation as far back as the colonial days, now took its urgency from economic disruptions stemming from industrialism. Large segments of American society

PRESIDENTS, 1877–1901

Rutherford B. Hayes. . . .	1877–1881
James Garfield	1881
Chester A. Arthur.	1881–1885
Grover Cleveland	1885–89; 1893–97
Benjamin Harrison	1889–1893
William McKinley	1897–1901

were either excluded from participation in the political debates of the time or pressed as far to the edges as the more powerful economic and governmental interests could manage. African Americans were denied civil and voting rights without significant protest from Congress or the presidency. Courts consistently ruled against workers, and supported businesses when they protested state regulation of pricing or labor conditions. Bringing several new states into the Union—in 1889, both Dakotas, Montana, and Washington, the following year Idaho and Wyoming, Utah in 1896 and in 1907 Oklahoma—the American political system attacked Mormons, excluded Chinese immigrants, and effected disastrous reforms in Indian policy. It brought little peace to a time when lynching and terror became a way of life in the South, when the Sioux, seeking to escape starvation, were massacred. Yet in the midst of much selfishness, much bigotry, and most of all much ignorance, American politicians and popular leaders stumbled toward an understanding of the industrial future and a redefinition of the role of government.

An Assassination and Its Reform Aftermath

Abraham Lincoln's assassination in 1865 burns in our collective consciousness. We have, as a culture, decided to remember the details—the shot from behind, John Wilkes Booth's dramatic jump to the stage of Ford's Theater, his shouted Latin admonition—in English, "Thus always to Tyrants!"— and we have assigned meaning to the passing of Lincoln. It enacted the last scene of the Civil War, the disaster that put Andrew Johnson in the Executive Mansion. In contrast to Abraham Lincoln, James Garfield at his death had not just finished winning our nation's greatest military conflict, and his assassination, in the first year of his presidency, has faded from our historical memory. His killing did not come of some large political principle as had struck down Lincoln; it was by a frustrated seeker for a government job. The system of awarding federal positions had invited, from before the Civil War, an open scramble uncontrolled by questions of competence. Federal jobs went to people loyal to the politician who had arranged the appointment. As a result, many Indian agents knew nothing of Indians, postal inspectors little of the mail system, and diplomats a few scraps of information about the countries to which they were posted. Appointees used their influence to support their patrons; sometimes they kicked back part of their salaries. This system permeated all levels of government, but the plum appointments lay in the hands of presidents and other high-ranking officials, who were besieged by office seekers. So it was really that system that bears responsibility for Garfield's death. In the wake of the murder there began, in a modest way, the transformation of government that would crest during the early twentieth-century Progressive Era and peak during the New Deal of the 1930s.

Protests against the spoils system had been ongoing—the Grant scandals directly involved corrupt

"Let Us Prey" The Tweed Ring. Corruption in New York City was attacked by Thomas Nast, a political cartoonist. Boss William M. Tweed of Tammany Hall stole $100 million from the city. (Courtesy, The New York Public Library)

patronage appointments. Now Garfield's assassination helped crystallize a broad movement to replace spoils and patronage with merit as the standard for awarding federal positions. In 1883, the year after the assassination, Congress passed the Pendleton Civil Service Act, which established a Civil Service Commission charged with administering competitive examinations for appointment. Chester Arthur, Garfield's vice president and successor, had been known as a spoilsman, but as president he supported the reform. The Pendleton Act was only a small beginning—it covered only ten percent of federal jobs and nothing at state or local levels—but it set the tone for government, putting proven expertise above bribes or influence-peddling. When wedded to the technical skills in social science advocated by subsequent reformers, the new civil service would become the activist institution of the early twentieth century.

The Politics of Industrialism

More immediately pressing for politicians after the end of Reconstruction were issues about the new industrial economy and how it might be regulated, if at all. Organized labor had demands to make. But farmers pushed hardest.

Farmers were distressed by railroad rates that fluctuated as rail operators waged price wars with one another, shifting high prices to less frequently used routes in order to keep competitive routes low. In an 1877 decision, the Supreme Court agreed that states might regulate railroad rates within their borders. Fourteen states were already doing so. Congress, however, had the major authority to regulate commerce that flows over state boundaries. Pushed by reformers, the national legislature did just that. The Interstate Commerce Act of 1887 created an oversight bureau, the Interstate Commerce Commission, and prohibited a number of railroad rate-setting policies. The ICC had only little power of enforcement, but the act marked a shift to a more extensive brand of government regulation of the economy.

So, too, did the debates that took place over gold and silver coinage. Militant farmers again led the way. Faced by falling prices as a result of overproduction, they argued that the government should increase the supply of money in the system by expanding the coinage of silver, driving down the value of a dollar and thereby allowing them to repay their debts with relatively cheap currency. Creditors, on the other hand, argued that the economy needed a stable supply of money backed only by gold. After the United States in 1873 stopped buying silver, the nation along with many of its trading partners unofficially adopted gold as the exclusive monetary standard. By the mid-1870s, however, silver production in the West had increased. Joined by farmers seeking as always to cheapen the value of the dollar, silver miners began lobbying for a return to their favorite metal. In 1878, Congress authorized the Treasury to buy between $2 million and $4 million of silver each month. This was enough to keep the western mines profitable, although it never expanded the money supply in ways that satisfied debtors. The Sherman Silver Purchase Act of 1890 was a substantial victory for the farmer and silver interests.

Gold and silver stood for more than technical questions of finance. Many farmers and miners saw in silver a lifeline that would lift them from trouble and take them to prosperity. From the East, the seat of creditor forces, streamed arguments for a stable, limited gold standard. In the West and South lived farmers, so often in debt, and in the West silver miners. Among both groups, gold was the enemy, the metal of the rich, while silver belonged to the people. The class lines here divided not so much laborers from industrialists as debtors and producers from creditor financiers. The emotional energy generated by the debates over gold and silver empowered Farmers' Alliances and propelled the challenges of the new Populist Party in the 1890s. When the nation, following a financial panic in 1893, abandoned the Sherman Silver Purchase Act, western mining towns collapsed one after another.

The Sherman Silver Purchase Act came in the year of the Sherman Antitrust Act, Sherman being in both cases the Republican senator John Sherman of Ohio. The law responded to a problem far overshadowing the quarrel over money and currency: the growth of business corporations that alone or in concert could dominate vast swashes of the country's economic life. The legislation was quite mild. In effect, it outlawed combinations that could crush competitors engaged in interstate commerce, a realm that the Constitution gave Congress the power to regulate. For a time, it had little effect, and the Supreme Court narrowed its scope. But it was a beginning to considering the massive industrial and financial forces that industrial technology had made possible.

THE SHAPE OF AN ERA

To define a period of history by an opening and a closing year is necessarily arbitrary, but we do so because splitting up into periods can clarify the meaning of events. The year 1877 is a touchstone in American history, for it marks the end of Reconstruction. The coming of the year 1890 offers another useful marker, for in 1890 the federal Bureau of the Census announced, on arbitrary statistical grounds but with enormous symbolic significance, the disappearance of the frontier. In between these dates an interconnected set of transformations unfolded.

One of these transformations amounted to new and intensive kinds of exploitation of the land. The industrial system normally associated with urban places also applied to logging, farming, mining, ranching, reclamation, and other kinds of extraction from the land. If the frontier that allegedly promoted democracy and individualism could be said to have ended in 1890, it was perhaps only secondarily because of the growing density of people on the land, the measure the census applied. More deeply, the closing of the frontier signified a qualitative change. As between subsistence farming by a family living off of its own produce and market farming for distant consumers, for example, the scale now tilted more heavily toward the market. Market farming does not cultivate small and varied plots supplying the family with corn and greens but draws from the soil a continuing produce for customers far away. And by the end of the nineteenth century, farms were becoming industrialized, making increasing use of machinery. The consequences of this exploitation of nature's bounty would only slowly become apparent to Americans, but the first signs appeared in the near-extinction of the bison, the worsening plight of open-range ranching and dryland farming, and the waste rockpiles and warm, silty rivers left behind by miners.

The exploitation of the land depended upon three social conditions. It required the clearance of the previous occupants. Across the West, Indians (and to some extent, Latinos) were forcibly consolidated on bounded parcels of land, the last great roundup in a long history of conquests and dislocations. Exploiting the land also required the presence of local workers. Whether cowboys, miners, loggers, or farm labor, whether Chinese or Mexican, Greek or Italian, black or Indian, mobile wage workers extracted the resources that traveled to the cities. And it needed other laborers, clustered in cities under their own particular forms of exploitation. The hallmark of the West, "free land," was as much a mockery as the hallmark of the industrial East, "free labor," and the bitter joke on blacks in the South, "freed people."

These differing kinds of activity existed in relation to a rising industrial market economy that strove to consolidate capital, control costs, and produce on a mass scale. The market system placed power in the hands of an elite few, but it also created limited though genuine opportunities for workers to resist or transform the system. The Grange, the Farmers' Alliances, the Knights of Labor, the American Federation of Labor, the American Woman Suffrage Association all sought to use for purposes of change the economic, social, and political systems then in place. The period is also notable in the ways that the political systems and mechanisms of governance, judicial, legislative, and executive, worked both to preserve and to reshape the developing economy. Some courts might allow states to regulate railroad rates, for instance, while others consistently upheld the interests of business elites or in the South, a planter class that along with poor whites insisted upon white supremacy. Congress established the Civil Service Commission, which made merit and appropriate qualifications the standard for government service. The Interstate Commerce Commission created by Congress in 1887 set standards and regulated commerce in the public interest. The national legislators passed an antitrust act that tried to impose on giant business a publicly responsible structure. Yet congressmen often cut backroom deals to support industry. The

political system of the time permitted the new industrial economy to consolidate and thrive, yet it allowed enough reform to ward off more serious challenges to the system.

The social, economic, technological, and political systems of the time bore also on the making of culture: books, leisure pursuits, sports, and entertainment. Leisure, for example, was more than just a diversion from the strains and pressures of work. On the whole, brought consumers enough pleasure and contentment to elicit a sense of satisfaction with politics, economics, and society as these existed. But just as the political system was open to slow change though closed to significant transformation, so too did opportunities for leisure permit a degree of questioning while chiefly reinforcing social and cultural like-mindedness. Dime novels, Wild West shows, and expositions offered certain messages about American culture; just as surely, however, individuals used mass media in their own ways to challenge the status quo.

This chapter began with a discussion of Arthur Conan Doyle's use of his Sherlock Holmes character to illumine American social and cultural realities. Conan Doyle drew significantly from an American predecessor. Edgar Allan Poe, with his hero Auguste Dupin, was the effective founder of the detective genre. In the methodical ways of the French police and the dry urbanity of Dupin, Poe gave a characterization of France; Doyle caught many images of the United States. Each of the two illustrates how a nation may reveal itself through the eyes of an outsider. Doyle's vision took account of American realities: western opportunity, urban danger, industrial management and class warfare, racial antipathy, and general eccentricity. He turned those realities into fiction that borders on the grotesque. Yet even there he caught accurate glimpses of the disruptions and violence that this land was undergoing as it transported itself from an earlier world into the era that we recognize as modern.

Suggested Readings

John Dickson Carr's *The Life of Sir Arthur Conan Doyle* (1949) is still the most reliable biography of the author whose work so richly chronicled American cultural stereotypes. For a penetrating analysis of national expositions, see Robert W. Rydell, *All the World's a Fair: Visions of Empire at American International Expositions, 1876–1916* (1984).

For a general overview of the industrial period, Alan Dawley, *Struggles for Justice: Social Responsibility and the Liberal State* (1991) and Nell Irvin Painter, *Standing at Armageddon: The United States 1877–1919* (1987) are especially strong on social history. The classic work on the rise of the industrial corporation is Alfred D. Chandler, Jr., *The Visible Hand: The Managerial Revolution in American Business* (1977). Also useful is Richard Tedlow, *The Rise of the American Business Corporation* (1991) and Naomi Lamoreaux, *The Great Merger Movement in American Business, 1895–1904* (1985).

The legal and political changes underlying the triumph of the corporation are the subject of Martin J. Sklar, *The Corporate Reconstruction of American Capitalism, 1890–1916: The Market, The Law and Politics* (1988). Alan Trachtenberg's brilliant *The Incorporation of America: Culture and Society in the Gilded Age* (1982) shows how anxieties over the clash of labor and capital pervaded literature, philosophy, and popular culture.

David Nye's *Electrifying America: Social Meanings of a New Technology, 1890–1940* (1990) explores the social consequences of the new energy technology while David F. Noble, *America by Design: Science, Technology and the Rise of Corporate Capitalism* (1977) looks more closely at the alliance between corporations and science.

The railroad's transformation of economy and culture is the subject of Alfred D. Chandler, Jr., *The Railroads: The Nation's First Big Business* (1965) and Albro Martin, *Railroads Triumphant: The Growth, Rejection, and Rebirth of a Vital American Force* (1992). Gabriel Kolko's *Railroads and Regulation, 1877–1915* (1965) and Ari and Olive Hoogenboom, *A History of the ICC* (1976) investigate the response to industrialism and the rise of a regulatory antitrust movement.

Critical biographies of the industrial and financial tycoons who shaped industrial America include Harold Livesay, *Andrew Carnegie and the Rise of Big Business* (1975); Ron Chernow, *The House of Morgan* (1990); and Chernow, *Titan: The Life of John D. Rockefeller, Sr.* (1998).

A strong overview of the industrial workers' struggle for control of their labor is David Montgomery's classic *The Fall of the House of Labor* (1987). Also useful is David Brody, *Steelworkers in America: The Nonunion Era* (1960) and *Workers in Industrial America: Essays on the Twentieth Century Struggle* (1980); Herbert G. Gutman, *Work, Culture, and Society in Industrializing America* (1976); and Melvyn Dubofsky, *Industrialism and the American Worker, 1865–1920*, 2nd ed. (1985).

The classic work on the immigrant experience is Oscar Handlin, *The Uprooted: The Epic Story of the Great Migrations That Made the American People* (1951). John Bodnar's *The Transplanted: A History of Immigrants in Urban America* (1985) corrects Handlin's preoccupation with alienation and shifts the focus to family ties and ethnic autonomy. Ronald Takaki, *A Different Mirror: A History of Multicultural America* (1993) weaves the stories of African, Asian, and Latin American immigrants into the story. Olivier Zunz, *The Changing Face of Inequality: Urbanization, Industrial Development and Immigrants in Detroit, 1880–1920* (1982) compares several European American groups in one city. A more recent body of scholarship, notably David R. Roediger, *The Wages of Whiteness: Race and the Making of the American Working Class* (1991) and Matthew Frye Jacobson, *Whiteness of a Different Color: European Americans and the Alchemy of Race* (1998), explores the interplay between "white" racial identity and class affiliation.

The industrial system's making nature into commodities, and the resulting impact on the environment, is the subject of a growing body of work led by William Cronon, *Nature's Metropolis: Chicago and the Great West* (1991). The bison and other threatened flora and fauna in the Great Plains are addressed in Andrew Isenberg, *The Destruction of the Bison: An Environmental History, 1750–1920* (2000) and Dan L. Flores, *The Natural West: Environmental History in the Great Plains and Rocky Mountains* (2001).

Historical interpretations of the West are also changing quickly. Working beyond more traditional works like Howard Lamar's *The Far Southwest, 1846–1912* (1970) are Patricia N. Limerick, *The Legacy of Conquest: The Unbroken Past of the American West* (1987); William Cronon, George Miles, and Jay Gitlin, eds., *Under an Open Sky: Rethinking America's Western Past* (1992); and Richard White's sweeping narrative text *"It's Your Misfortune and None of My Own": A History of the American West* (1991). Critical takes on the saga of the ranching frontier and the cowboy can be found in Edward E. Dale, *The Range Cattle Industry*, rev. ed., (1969); Robert Dykstra, *The Cattle Towns* (1968); and William L. Katz, *The Black West* (1971). The mining frontier is most thoroughly chronicled in Elliott West, *The Contested Plains: Indians, Goldseekers, and the Rush to Colorado* (1998). A fresh new look at how European immigrants coped with the clash between autonomy and assimilation can be found in Jon Gjerde, *The Minds of the West: Ethnocultural Evolution in the Rural Middle West, 1830–1917* (1997), an update of the still-useful Fred Shannon, *The Farmers' Last Frontier, 1860–1897* (1945). On the Mormons' history, see Jan Shipps, *Mormonism: The Story of a New Religious Tradition* (1985).

The New South, warts and all, is the subject of the *Origins of the New South, 1877–1913* (1951) by C. Vann Woodward, which has been supplemented by Edward L. Ayers, *The Promise of the New South: Life after Reconstruction* (1992). For the post-war southern economy, see Gavin Wright, *Old South, New South: Revolutions in the Southern Economy Since the Civil War* (1986). The rising tide of racism is described in Joel Williamson, *The Crucible of Race: Black-White Relations in the American South since Emancipation* (1984); Howard B. Rabinowitz, *Race Relations in the Urban South 1865–1890* (1978); and Leon F. Litwack, *Trouble in Mind: Black Southerners in the Age of Jim Crow* (1998).

For brief surveys of Native Americans and their relations with whites, see Robert M. Utley, *The Indian Frontier of the American West, 1846–1890* (1984), and Dee Alexander Brown, *Bury My Heart at Wounded Knee: An Indian History of the American West* (1971). Custer's story and mythology are the subject of Robert M. Utley, *Cavalier in Buckskin: George Armstrong Custer and the Western Military Frontier* (1988). See also Vine Deloria, *Custer Died for Our Sins* (1969).

Sophisticated interpretations of women's activism in the years before they gained the vote can be found in Paula Baker, "The Domestication of Politics: Women and American Political Society, 1780–1920," *American Historical Review* 89 (June 1984): 620-47, and Robyn Muncy, *Creating a Female Dominion in American Reform, 1890–1935* (1991).

The political stalemate that paralyzed national politics during the Gilded Age is explained in John A. Garraty, *The New Commonwealth, 1877–1890* (1968) and Paul Kleppner, *The Third Electoral System, 1835–1892* (1979). Stuart McConnell's *Glorious Contentment: The Grand Army of the Republic, 1865-1990* (1992) considers the continuing resonance of the Civil War in political culture. David M. Tucker's *Mugwumps: Public Moralists of the Gilded Age* (1998) addresses elite reformers.

The White City at the Columbian Exposition, Chicago 1893. *(Courtesy, Chicago Historical Society)*

The Search for New Frontiers

★

CHICAGO 1893:
THE COLUMBIAN EXPOSITION AND THE FRONTIER

In 1890 Congress appointed Chicago as the site of the World's Fair of 1893 observing the three-hundredth anniversary of Columbus's first voyage to the Americas. The city went to work immediately in preparation. It was a Chicago project, heavily financed by entrepreneurs in alliance with architects. In this most energetic of cities, the planners conceived of the Exposition as demonstrating the new forces of industry and science. They took pains to construct a little city within Chicago, clean and carefully arranged. Beginning in 1891, forty thousand employees (including Walt Disney's father, who throughout his son's childhood would recount stories of the wondrous other-world experience the fair offered) worked across the Exposition grounds, estimated at 685 acres. They constructed more than sixty million square feet of buildings. Every week for two years before the official opening, the setting up of the fair attracted thousands of spectators, each paying twenty-five cents for a tour. By the time it opened in May, the total cost had reached $28 million.

Over the next five months, the event played heavily on the American imagination. By one account twenty-seven million visited the Exposition, about a fourth of the country's entire population. Much of the remainder enjoyed it through media reports, guidebooks, and personal accounts by family and friends. The layout of the Exposition itself fascinated the public. The designers had achieved what they wanted: a spacious and ordered city of the future, in gleaming white that earned it the title the White City.

While the fair was in progress, a history professor at the University of Wisconsin took the speaker's podium at a gathering of historians inside the Exposition grounds. In a paper entitled "The Significance of the Frontier in American History," Frederick Jackson Turner declared that the nation had turned an important corner in its history. He pointed to the finding of the 1890 census that the frontier, defined as a geographic area populated by fewer than two people per square mile, no longer existed. Turner was looking beyond the statistics to the reality that the West was no longer a wild unsettled territory: that something was happening qualitatively to the lands once thought to reach endlessly beyond the developed portions of the United States. Turner was speaking and writing about shifts in habits and methods. By the time of Turner's essay, the buffalo had been mostly annihilated, the Indians put on reservations, and much of the Great Plains settled along a crisscrossed web of railroad lines and telegraph poles. If the unique American character resulted from a constantly moving frontier, as Turner believed, then the disappearance of the frontier foretold a different future. Ever since, Americans besides Turner have wondered about what that disappearance meant. Without the challenges of the frontier—wild animals, terrain inhospitable to easy travel, the disorder of young settlements—how would later generations form American identities? And without a safety valve of unsettled land, what would become of the landless immigrants or native sons, without inherited farms, who in an earlier time in the nation's history could have picked up and gone farther west? Were the nation and the national character doomed?

Few recent historians have found Turner's ideas persuasive. The statistical criterion the census employed for defining a frontier was arbitrary. Even the West as it is today has been described as a region of urban and suburban cores surrounded by long tracts of unsettled land. Vast stretches of frontier endure into the twenty-first century. Only one major element of the frontier could be said to have disappeared near the year 1890. In 1887 the cattle kingdom collapsed, to be replaced by the confined raising of beef such as continues to this day.

Turner helped begin one of the most important discussions among Americans wishing to understand their culture. His inquiry, though, was bounded by his preoccupation with white settlers: he largely ignored Indians, African Americans, and Mexicans. Historians today are less likely to view the frontier as a symbol of adventure and opportunity but see the West as a breeder of a mythology: in particular, the folklore that justified the white invasion, conquest, and settlement of western lands. Turner was as much a participant in the formation of the myth of the West as he was an unbiased chronicler of the past.

Turner's paper was mostly ignored in the immediate weeks following his presentation, but the country's fascination with the mythic frontier was demonstrated daily just outside the grounds of the Exposition. Fairgoers might grow tired of looking at California's statue of a medieval knight made entirely of prunes,

Thomas Edison's eighty-two-foot Tower of Light with its eighteen thousand lightbulbs, the Exposition's elevated train, the restaurant that seated seven thousand, or Little Cairo's scantily-clad Egyptian bellydancers. In that case they could leave the fairgrounds, cross one crowded street, and enter a recent, receding past at Buffalo Bill Cody's Wild West Show. Together the World's Fair and Cody's portrayal of the West catch an American desire to see their national experience as a continuing romance: the drama of the frontier, the magic of a future made bright with electrical lighting.

HISTORICAL EVENTS

1872
Aaron Montgomery Ward establishes first large mail-order business

1875
Andrew Carnegie opens world's largest steel plant

1877
Munn v. *Illinois*

1878
Bland-Allison Act

1879
Henry George publishes *Progress and Poverty*

1883
Anaconda copper mine begins operations in Montana under Marcus Daly

1885
First skyscraper built in Chicago

1886
Wabash, St. Louis and Pacific R.R. v. *Illinois*

1887
Dawes Severalty Act

1888
Edward Bellamy publishes *Looking Backward* • Benjamin Harrison elected president

1890
Jane Addams opens Hull House in Chicago to do settlement work

1892
Homestead steel strike, Homestead, Pennsylvania • Grover Cleveland elected president for a second nonconsecutive term

1893
Columbian Exposition in Chicago • Frederick Jackson Turner presents his frontier thesis

1894
Strike in Pullman, Illinois

1896
William McKinley elected president, defeating William Jennings Bryan

INDUSTRIALISTS AND WORKERS

In the remainder of the 1890s as western cities grew, among them San Francisco and Denver, the West continued for much of the country to be a landscape of dreams. Yet what many thousands of settlers in the West during the last decade of the century were really looking for in the way of possibilities came closer to what the industrial East provided than to the thinner benefits of some barely cultivated, sparsely inhabited backland beyond civilization. People who moved to Butte, Montana, in the 1880s and 1890s, for instance, had the West of one Marcus Daly to envy, imitate, make use of, or resist, not cowboys and Indians.

In 1856, at age fifteen, Daly had emigrated from Ireland to the United States. For more than two decades he worked in mines across the West. In 1883, when he discovered a large copper vein three hundred feet underground in a Butte silver mine known as the Anaconda, Daly was well on his way toward vast wealth. Copper was necessary for building a fully wired and electrified nation. That year Daly gathered investors and gambled his future on the reddish metal. He secretly bought claims surrounding the mine, then built the world's largest copper smelter southwest of Butte in a cow field that became the company town of Anaconda. Then Daly constructed a railroad that ran between the new town and his mines. In order to supply timbers for underground mine shafts, he got control of thousands of acres of forest in the mountains of western Montana and Idaho. Not content with mining alone, he raised cattle on his ten-thousand acre Bitterroot Valley ranch, known as the Bitterroot Stock Farm, and shipped beef and milk to the Montana towns of Missoula and Butte as well as Anaconda. Bribes and threats of violence landed a number of Montana's politicians in his pocket. Daly's Anaconda Company earned from Montanans the nickname "the snake," appropriately enough for a business that adopted the name of the serpent that squeezes its prey to death.

"Butte grew," it is said, "from a heart of copper," but growth could never have happened without Daly's organizational skills and without the backbreaking, dangerous work of thousands of European immigrants. By 1916, Butte's population had increased sixty-fold from three thousand in 1880.

During roughly the same period, the percentage of European-born men and women in the Rocky Mountain states rose to be higher than in any other region of the country. In Cripple Creek, Aspen, Leadville, and Telluride in Colorado, in Coeur d'Alene, Idaho, and in Park City, Utah, neighborhoods formed by ethnic origins: Swedes, Finns, Germans, Welsh, Chinese, Greeks, and Italians among other immigrants who settled there. By the end of the century, Butte's Irish constituted the largest percentage of men and women Irish by birth in any American city.

The pace of invention and scientific discovery in the late nineteenth century made it possible for such businessmen as Daly to tap into sources of power and wealth unimaginable to earlier generations, and for other Americans to negotiate their surroundings in widely new ways. In 1873, for example, typewriters were being made in quantity. Alexander Graham Bell got his patent for the telephone in 1876, and by 1900 there would be nearly a million and a half phones in the nation. Thomas A. Edison invented the phonograph in 1877, and two years later an incandescent electric lightbulb. This most productive of technicians also did much to advance motion pictures during their turn-of-the-century infancy. By 1880 refrigeration allowed year-round shipping of meat, and before the end of the century Chicago had become the center of the slaughtering and meatpacking industries. There Gustavus Swift, who like Daly numbered among the minority of great industrialists to have risen from poverty, built an empire through what is called vertical integration. He bought cattle in the West, slaughtered them in Chicago, and shipped the meat by his own refrigerated cars to eastern markets. George Westinghouse's invention of air brakes increased the safety of railroads, as did steel rails. Steel itself, formerly of little use, became a major commodity. Two new processes made possible its mass production. Just after midcentury the British inventor Henry Bessemer introduced a method for forcing air into iron and thereby burning off excess carbon. The other innovation, the open hearth, subjected iron to enormous heat that dissolved impurities. The great strength of steel enabled architects to design buildings with a cleaner, less bulky look than the constructions that had required thick walls for support. Steel also made possible the skyscrapers that began to appear by the end of the century: iron girders would not have been sufficiently strong.

The uses Daly and his fellow mining barons made of advanced technology illustrate what was happening to industry as a whole. Montanans mined and smelted copper, then sent their products to factories in Illinois, Pennsylvania, New Jersey, and elsewhere so that it could be turned into wires and other parts used in lighting fixtures and telephones. In Telluride, mining and electricity came together in yet another way that had new and profound repercussions for the use of electric energy. There in 1890, the Gold King Mining Company and Westinghouse Electric and Manufacturing used alternating current—Edison and others used direct current—to power mine machinery. Gold King and Westinghouse proved for the first time that electrical energy might be transported long distances through the use of transformers that allowed current to be moved and stored at varying voltage levels.

A Tycoon on the Southern Frontier

For several decades after winning statehood in 1845, Florida slept in the sun, aroused only momentarily to join the Confederacy during the Civil War. Then Henry Flagler, a visitor from the North, discovered it, and Florida awakened to commercial success.

Even without Florida, Flagler's career is a study in nineteenth-century enterprise. Failing in the salt industry in Michigan during the Civil War, Flagler returned to Ohio and got started again in the grain business, work he had begun as a fourteen-year-old after dropping out of school. The embarrassing return to Ohio and grain dealing turned out well. Flagler's experience there demonstrates a truth about millionaires: that more often than not, they are simply in the right place at the right time. In Ohio Flagler made the acquaintance of John D. Rockefeller, another grain merchant, who encouraged his young friend to invest borrowed money in a new oil company. By 1877, when Standard Oil under Rockefeller and Flagler controlled most of the oil refining industry, making both of them rich beyond their greatest imaginations, Flagler could sit like a king on his throne in a mansion on New York City's fashionable Fifth Avenue. His career illustrates another fact about millionaires: earning

their first million is the hardest, and then they have the money for making more money.

When Flagler's wife became sick, the two traveled to Jacksonville, Florida, where he saw opportunity wave at him like a palm tree bending in the breeze. He recognized that Florida, glorious with its sun and warmth in winter, might attract northerners by the thousands if only trains and proper accommodations could be built to serve them. By 1885, Flagler had begun building St. Augustine's Hotel Ponce de Leon. With a vision of hotels lining Florida's Atlantic coast, Flagler eventually also created the Florida East Coast Railway to deliver the well-to-do from Boston or Cleveland to Palm Beach and Miami.

When in 1897 Flagler opened the Royal Palm

John D. Rockefeller moved his Standard Oil office from Cleveland to New York City in 1884. He and Henry Flagler had created a monopoly in oil. (Courtesy, Rockefeller Archive Center)

Hotel in the little village of barely a thousand people by Biscayne Bay, Florida was known up and down the East Coast as a burgeoning tourist destination. Four years earlier, in preparation for the Chicago World's Fair, the American Press Association had asked prominent Americans to think about what the country might be like a hundred years later in the 1990s. The opinions ran in newspapers nationwide for several months prior to the Exposition's opening. In a piece entitled "The Wonderful Development of Florida," a commentator wrote that the state would come to rival Mediterranean resorts. "I think I am not making a wild prediction," declared the author, "when I say that, in the next century, the value of Florida to the United States will be of more commercial importance than are some of the states in which even bonanza mines have been discovered." As the United States inched toward a gold standard that eventually shut down many western mining towns, Florida's role of destination resort for the newer wealthy classes became clearer with each passing year.

In 1898, a year that brought war with Spain, Flagler persuaded politicians to make Miami an army camp, knowing that his hotel (emptied by Miami's summer heat, but ideal as an officers' quarters) and his railroad would benefit most. There is no "pleasanter location on the Atlantic Coast, south of Bar Harbor [Maine]," Flagler wrote one influential senator, "to spend the summer in than Miami." Once the army sent seven thousand men to Miami, it became apparent that Camp Miami was, in fact, quite unhealthy. The filthy drinking water and sanitation facilities made hundreds of troops sick from diarrhea and dysentery. One man contrasted Flagler's paradise to the camp for enlisted soldiers: "There was a most magnificent and gorgeously appointed hotel right in the midst of a perfect paradise of tropical trees and bushes. But one had to walk scarce a quarter of a mile until one came to such a waste wilderness [the campsite] as can be conceived of only in rare nightmares."

Dismal heat and camp conditions encouraged the dismal attitudes of white soldiers toward African Americans. In addition to swimming nude in Biscayne Bay and shooting coconuts for target practice, white soldiers in 1898 fired guns at black Floridians and harassed others for refusing to step off sidewalks. "The constant friction between the troops and the colored people," one early Miami resident noted, "was a continual source of anxiety." But for Americans more fortunate than the enlisted men or the state's African Americans of 1898, the Florida climate offered a glorious future.

The Rich and Their Ways

New technologies only partially explain how capitalists of the late years of the nineteenth century were able to thrive. The styles of men like Daly, Andrew Carnegie, William Vanderbilt, Flagler, and Rockefeller depended in some cases on inheritance, and almost always on luck and considerable business skill in putting to profitable use the latest technologies. But their extravagances, besides drawing on the hard work of millions of employees whose unions they were prepared to break, profited from a politics and an economy rife with corruption and open to exploitation. For crippling unions, they had the aid not only of federal and state troops but also of the Pinkertons, the detective agency that in the nineteenth century even Washington made use of in the absence of an FBI.

In 1873, when labor troubles in the Pennsylvania coal fields were attributed to a shadow organization, real or fictional, labeled the Molly Maguires, a railroad executive who was also a mine owner hired James McParlan, a Pinkerton. McParlan circulated among the workers, buying them drinks and silently gathering information. At the end of months of strife in which strikebreakers and company police clashed with militant workers, McParlan was chief prosecution witness in a trial that sent ten miners to hang and fourteen others to prison.

Henry Clay Frick, general manager at Carnegie's Homestead Steel plant in Pennsylvania, made a different use of Pinkertons in 1892. Workers there belonged to the Amalgamated Association of Iron and Steel Workers. With a membership of twenty-five thousand workers, it was possibly the strongest union in the country, just as Carnegie's steel corporation, forerunner of United States Steel, ranked among the most powerful corporations. Owing, he said, to hard times, Carnegie refused to renew a collective bargaining agreement that he had accepted three years earlier. Instead, he announced that he would renew contracts individually without union participation. Just before the workers' contracts were to expire, Frick proceeded toward instituting a lockout. Planning to hire scabs—the name given workers willing to take the place of strikers or union labor—he fortified the plant grounds with searchlights and board fences with gun holes and barbed wire. Frick also hired three hundred Pinkerton agents. When the armed Pinkertons arrived by barge, a pitched battle broke out that left three of them and nine strikers dead. The remaining Pinkertons were taken prisoner and confined in a skating rink. Pennsylvania's governor called in the state militia to control the situation. Although workers believed that the militia had come to protect them from Frick's hired guns, it quickly became apparent that the governor had more concern for protecting Carnegie's property than for shielding his workers. During the troubles an anarchist stormed Frick's office, shooting and stabbing him. Frick survived. A member of the Pennsylvania militia who suggested to his fellow soldiers that they give "three cheers for the man who shot Frick" was court-martialed and strung up by his thumbs. The assault on Frick contributed to public hostility toward labor agitation.

One route by which the rich gained power was by pure manipulation and speculator investment. Jay Gould made his reputation that way. His best known moment was in 1869, when he spread rumors that the government was going to buy gold. The story created a run on the precious metal. In the end, the gold market crashed and brought panic to New York City's Wall Street, which had already become the center of much of the nation's high finance. For consolidation and monopoly, industrialists had stodgier but equally effective methods. In a trust, stockholders in various companies in a single industry surrendered their company votes to a board of trustees, who then could regulate the enterprises in such a way that they would not compete with one another and instead could monopolize the trade. Rockefeller pioneered in the device. The trusts eventually came under federal and state legal assault. The alternative was the holding company, which acquired stock in several enterprises, controlling them in much the same manner as a trust. And at the same time that powerful companies were turning to monopoly, they were coming under the influence of another group of capitalists, the investment bankers. These neither invented a steel-making process or a conductor of electricity or an internal-combustion engine nor directly managed, as Carnegie did, the daily workings of some industry making use of inventors. Centered particularly on Wall Street, where the formidable J. P. Morgan reigned, investment banking lent the

money for productive enterprises, and in the process gained a large measure of control over much of American industry.

Some, like Daly, had tactics that are hard to pin down; he avoided long and possibly incriminating paper trails by writing numbers in pencil on his washable shirtsleeves. When he died, his few existing papers were immediately burned in the furnace at his ranch. Yet big industrialists did not always have their way. Standard Oil became so notoriously cutthroat in controlling the petroleum refining industry that in 1911 the Supreme Court forced the parent company to dissolve.

Beneficiaries of capitalist industrialism built themselves gaudy mansions on what became known as "millionaires' row," New York City's Fifth Ave-

This 1899 cartoon from the magazine The Verdict *portrays a greedy vulture with the name of the Republican Party boss Mark Hanna pinning down "labor" with his claws.* (Courtesy, *The Verdict*, November 13, 1899)

nue. They primed their daughters and sons for education and marriages befitting a class that aspired to move as fast as possible from the status of new wealth to that of Old Money. But while some new capitalists used their treasure chests to buy the manners of the upper class, Daly clung to cruder ways. To be sure, he built mansions in Butte, on his Bitterroot ranch, and on Fifth Avenue. He owned private train cars, swimming pools, hotels, and dozens of thoroughbred horses. These included a champion racehorse he named Tammany in honor of New York's political machine. The new rich with loftier aspirations to Old World elegance would not have risked honoring an organization that represented the saloon politics of immigrant Irish. At any given time, Daly gambled thousands of dollars on a hand of cards, a horse race, or a boxing match. He loved to tell the story of the salesman who had unwittingly seated himself at the backroom poker table in Daly's own plush Montana Hotel in Anaconda. When the man saw the piles of chips spread around the table, he asked the dealer for a hundred dollars worth. An amused Daly relished in telling the dealer, quite loudly, that he had heard the gentleman correctly, and that the salesman should receive his one solitary chip.

Some millionaires donated huge sums to charity. Carnegie built at least two thousand libraries in small towns across the country. He founded the Carnegie Institute of Technology, and the Peace Palace for the International Court at the Hague in the Netherlands, and his commitment to peace made him an opponent of the American occupation of the Philippines early in the twentieth century. "Like the man himself," one writer notes, "Carnegie's libraries were a mixture of sincere generosity and naked self-interest." Carnegie seems genuinely to have believed in the socially responsible use of wealth. Yet in the gaining of wealth he put his conscience on hold. And refusing to pamper himself at work, the rugged Scotsman apparently had no respect for the rich who used their money to coddle their slightest needs. Though he knew nothing, or next to nothing, of steel making—he was not an inventor like Edison—he brought to his industry an appetite for hard work and skill in efficient management. He ranked with Swift and Daly in having experienced poverty, unlike most immensely wealthy barons of industry. A well-known cartoon in his day showed Carnegie as his own conjoined twin. One Carnegie presents a library to a factory

One of the few "industrial statesmen" or "robber barons"—take your pick—Andrew Carnegie summed up the cost savings of vertical integration this way: ". . . two pounds of iron-stone purchased on the shores of Lake Superior and transported to Pittsburgh; two pounds of coal mined in Connellsville and manufactured into coke and brought to Pittsburgh; one half pound of limestone mixed east of the Alleghenies and brought to Pittsburgh; a little manganese ore, mined in Virginia and brought to Pittsburgh. . . . That's all that needs to be said about the steel business." (Courtesy, The Granger Collection)

town; the other demands a wage cut from the factory's employees.

Horatio Alger

During the late nineteenth century, an author of popular stories directed to children and adolescents, especially boys, gave a different account of business success. Horatio Alger wrote more than one hundred novels carrying such explanatory titles as *Work and Win* and *Strive and Succeed*. Typically a lad (in one case, *Tattered Tom*, a young girl disguised as a boy) succeeds, but not by competition. He combines with earnest industriousness the virtue of honesty, not the most conspicuous character trait of actual entrepreneurs on the make. His success comes also by luck, such as rescuing from drowning the daughter of a rich man who thereafter looks after him. The Alger hero represents what Americans wanted to see in business: essentially a remaking, sometimes in an urban setting, of the nobility of Jefferson's honorable and hardworking farmer. Insofar as the Horatio Alger stories might be taken to imply that virtue and hard work lead to riches, the facts of wealth-making in the nineteenth century prove that wrong. As a description of how entrepreneurs wished to think of themselves, he is not to be quickly dismissed. Most businessmen were small merchants and manufacturers, neither the vulgar rich nor hirers of company police or thugs to break strikes. Commercial farmers themselves operated as small-scale business adventurers.

Readers of Horatio Alger books numbered in the millions. In this story set in a rural landscape, Harry Vane, a poor but earnest lad, succeeded in the world despite countless obstacles he faced. (Courtesy, Frank and Marie-Therese Wood Print Collections, Alexandria, Virginia)

Doubtless millions of such people survived by work and upheld by honest dealings the worth of their shops, their crafts, their farms. However typical or imagined, the Alger heroes defined one way of looking at the thumpingly energetic economy and society of his times, as the Fifth Avenue wealthy defined another.

Alger is an excellent representative of popular culture, the writer of undistinguished but influential and widely read works. His novels were popular without being great. The author had a keen ear for what his readers wanted to hear and believe. One of his characters, Ragged Dick, achieved not wealth but respectability. This is a story of moral uplift and transformation, reassuring to his readers that the old-fashioned virtues were still alive in a swiftly changing world. Though naughty at times and reckless at others, Dick is essentially a good and decent boy. Alger was read even more widely after his death in 1899, particularly in the 1920s. Tattered Tom, a girl but one who takes on the mannerisms of a boy and a tough one at that, is ultimately adopted and slowly made into a young Victorian woman displaying feminine grace and style. Many of Alger's stories demonstrate some degree of eroticism toward adolescents; after attending Harvard Divinity School he was dismissed from the pulpit for molesting young boys—and Tattered Tom adds crossdressing to the mix. This leaves the careful reader to wonder whether Alger was as much an apostle of free enterprise as the teller of stories of a boys' world that had its special attractions to him.

Consumer Spending

From the new technology the wealthy drew their riches, and their high living. At the same time, industrial progress was providing a more modest form of consumption to Americans with a little extra money to spend on it. And to spread the products of industry, business was developing retail outlets that had something of the efficiency and standardization that advanced the productivity of machines.

In 1846 A. T. Stewart set up in New York City a dry-goods retail house that is considered the first department store. Soon afterwards John Wanamaker established a similar store in Philadelphia. Macy's in New York City, in Chicago Marshall Field's: these figure among many stores that in the late nineteenth century sold a variety of goods to a range of customers. They along with other enterprises replaced the ancient practice of haggling with a system of one uniform price for an item, and thereby contributed to the conformity of processes that also characterized industrial technology. And prices for goods were relatively cheap, since department stores commanded such a volume that they could go directly to manufacturers and cut out middlemen, besides persuading the manufacturers that it was good business to sell to them at low rates. Mass retailing gained as well from chain stores. The Great Atlantic and Pacific Tea Company or A & P, which had begun under another name as a seller of teas and spices, operated in 1876 a hundred stores. About three years later the first five-and-dime, as such enterprises are now known, opened in Lancaster, Pennsylvania, under the ownership of the F. W. Woolworth Company.

These businesses catered to urban centers. But in 1872 Aaron Montgomery Ward established in Chicago a mail-order business that tapped the countryside. Sears, Roebuck soon competed with Montgomery Ward in reaching out to farmers. Farm families could not only enjoy buying affordable goods but also delight in browsing through the mail-order catalogs, savoring the rich variety of products attractively presented. Probably more so than the department and chain stores, the mail-order business bound the country together, offering the common pleasure of wondering what to buy, in the knowledge that across the country other customers were thumbing through the same catalogues, wondering the same thing.

Americans at Work

The industrialists had an energetic workforce to draw on: they themselves, in one way or another, were a part of it. And among immigrants they could draw upon fresh sources of labor eager to toil for wages that, however small they may seem today, were sufficient to draw millions from the rest of the world. In 1890 factory hands worked on average sixty hours a week. But Americans were also inwardly driven. An immigrant described them as "savagely wild in devouring their work."

In 1900 about two-thirds of the labor force consisted of the hired employee, not the self-employed. Much of the wage-earning population lived well enough but insecurely. Only personal savings painstakingly gathered cushioned the loss of a job. In

This photograph of a Sears, Roebuck catalog argues that consumers can buy items more inexpensively from the mail order company than from local shopkeepers. (Courtesy, Chicago Historical Society)

the later years of the nineteenth century an average of thirty-five thousand Americans died every year in industrial accidents, six thousand of these in railroad work. Fires, boiler explosions, mine disasters numbered among the hazards. Gas ignited in a mine set the air afire through the many adjoining passages, scorching the lungs of a worker who did not have time to fall to the floor where the air escaped the streaking flame. A mine explosion might hurl the heavy door at the entrance as far away as a mile. Among industries illness threatened, especially tuberculosis from crowding and the weakness attending overwork and malnutrition. A maimed or sickened laborer ceased to be a breadwinner for a family already scratching out a living.

Woman and Child Labor

Most women worked at home, often as seamstresses for outside employers. These were not counted in the census for working women. Nor were women who did housework or farm labor for their families. Most women who worked outside the home did so for only part of their lives. Except in the South, domestic service drew immigrant rather than native-born women. By 1880 women accounted for 2.6 million, or about one-seventh, of the paid labor force. In the same year females made up sixty percent of public-school teachers. Other opportunities lay in nursing and social work. Clerical jobs were opening to women, along with sales positions in stores. By 1900 a few hundred women had earned medical degrees, but there were no women in the legal profession. Nonetheless, the founding of coeducational land-grant colleges considerably improved women's opportunities for education, though "feminine" courses such as home economics were emphasized. In the 1890s the new University of Chicago became the first graduate school to train significant numbers of women, especially in sociology and the other social sciences.

Children between ten and fifteen years of age held about seven hundred thousand jobs outside the farm at the turn of the century. Some worked as shoeshine or errand boys. In coalfields, youngsters working for as long as ten hours a day picked slate and stones out of coal conveyed past them by belts.

"Breaker Boys" take a rest from their twelve-hour day in an Appalachian coal mine. (Courtesy, Brown Brothers)

Children below the age of ten, especially girls, not infrequently worked in southern textile mills from sunup to sundown. In the 1890s the New York and Chicago woman members of the National Consumers' League demanded the abolition of child labor. Educators attacked it for interfering with schooling. But it had its defenders as well: employers anxious to keep down labor costs and many working-class parents who saw nothing wrong with supplementing family income out of children working—or found they had no choice.

Laboring Families and Strikes

In their ethnic neighborhoods and their industry-driven economies, small manufacturing towns like Homestead, Pennsylvania, resembled the mining communities of the West and the working-class neighborhoods of bigger cities. Laborers spent much of their free time fraternizing with members of their own clannish groups in national churches, mutual benefit societies, and saloons. Their world combined heavy work, much of it dangerous, with little reward, and they understood their situation quite well. In his novel *Out of This Furnace* about three generations of a Polish family in the western Pennsylvania steel country around Homestead, Thomas Bell's character Dubik shows that he grasps how the big industrialists operate. "I suppose," he remarks, that if Frick triumphs over the workers, "he will give them a library."

Homestead, along with the great railway strike of 1877, expressed a militancy within the portion of the labor force responding to a relatively new condition: the massing of workers within large capitalist enterprises driven by modern technologies. Strikes reflected the angry side of the workforce, as the Knights of Labor and the AFL represented the effort of workers to find continuing means of defining themselves and their needs. The National Labor Union that preceded the Knights and the AFL, the spreading strikes, the demand for the eight-hour day announced that labor, as a separate category within the industrial system, was seeking, and gaining, its own identity.

Conditions in the West awakened labor to the same issues as affected its brothers and sisters to the east. In the spring of 1892, silver miners and owners clashed in Coeur d'Alene, Idaho. The owners argued that in light of the uncertain state of the silver-mining economy, the daily wage of $3.50

should be reduced to $3.00. In response, mine workers decided to strike. After miners dynamited a guard's barracks, the state and federal troops brought in to insure peace placed the strikers in a fenced pen. Partially as a result of the unrest at Coeur d'Alene, several local mining unions from around the Rocky Mountain states met together in Butte in 1893 and formed the Western Federation of Miners. Over the next eight years, the union led strikes in Cripple Creek, Leadville, Telluride, and time and again, in Coeur d'Alene.

Labor Divided Against Itself

Mine owners and other industrialists are said to have made it a practice to use race and ethnicity to set workers against one another. If so, they did not need much skill at it: workers were entirely willing to act on their own prejudices. When the owners at Coeur d'Alene brought in scabs from other states, the miners spoke of them as foreigners, "scum . . . more fitted for their condition of slavery than ever were the blacks of Africa." Another illustration of the antagonism that divided worker from worker occurred in a labor conflict farther to the east.

The workers outside Chicago who constructed railroad sleeping cars for the Pullman Palace Company were white. Once the cars left the factory and went to a railroad, black porters and waiters tended them, serving passengers food and drinks and furnishing their bunks with fresh linens as the train rolled along. The white workers belonged to the American Railway Union; in conformity with racial customs at the time, the black porters and waiters did not. It took a strike to reveal the full implications of that policy.

At Chicago's outskirts, the industrialist George Pullman had built for his employees a town with trees and shrubs, boasting also a theater, a school, and a church. There is no reason to doubt that Pullman combined genuinely humane motives with the objective of creating a contented and productive workforce. His effort failed. "We are born in a Pullman house, fed from the Pullman shop, taught in the Pullman school, catechized in the Pullman church, and when we die we shall be buried in the Pullman cemetery and go to the Pullman hell," explained one employee. In 1894 the workers struck when Pullman tried to cut labor costs in response to the slowdown in his business resulting from the

depression of the early 1890s. In support, fellow members of the American Railway Union declined to handle Pullman cars. President Grover Cleveland's attorney general Richard Olney, a former lawyer for the railroad owners, sent troops to Chicago and a federal court issued an injunction against the strike. Governor John Peter Altgeld of Illinois, who on the grounds of the injustice of their trial had released three defendants in the Haymarket bombing of 1886, protested the dispatch of federal troops. That the courts and the government would act against the strikers could be predicted. More notable is the attitude of the strikers, like that of

A black waiter attending to white passengers appeared in the late nineteenth century to be part of the natural order. (Courtesy, New-York Historical Society)

the miners at Coeur d'Alene, toward their fellow workers. By any reasonable interpretation of what it is to work for a railroad, the black waiters and porters should have belonged to the American Railway Union. And by any reasonable calculation of what the Pullman strikers needed, it would have been wise to enlist the aid of the black workers. Americans used to having their beds made and their drinks brought by black servants as they traveled by rail would have been unhappy to have such services withheld. The union's leader, Eugene Debs, argued to his members that admitting black railroad workers would help their cause. Yet white unionists refused him. "If they had only admitted these porters and waiters," Debs wrote later, "there would have been a different story of that strike." But at Pullman, race counted for more than labor solidarity.

The reaction of white American labor to stran-

Here white citizens of Denver are shown attacking the Chinese community of the city in 1880, beating many of the residents senseless and vandalizing their homes and businesses. (Courtesy, Bettmann)

gers of any sort had already contributed to federal legislation. By 1870, the Chinese in San Francisco made up forty-six percent of all employees in the city's four main industries. And nearly all of San Francisco's Chinese eventually lived in what became known as Chinatown, an area of roughly twenty-four blocks that line Grant Avenue on the city's east side. In western towns violence occasionally flared against the Chinese, several of whom were murdered. Just after passage of the law that at the demand of American labor excluded Chinese immigration, only a handful were able to enter. The periodically renewed legislation was not airtight: it allowed for some exceptions. But at a time close to the end of the century when newcomers came flooding in from Europe, fewer than thirty thousand Chinese gained admittance. With financial help from organizations such as the Chinese Six Companies, immigrants from China hired lawyers and fought restrictions in federal courts, in the process influencing American immigration laws for other ethnic groups. To prevent such use of the courts, Congress passed a law that put immigration under the complete control of the Bureau of Immigration, giving that agency more power to combat resisters. "Thus the West and its immigrants," one scholar has written, "often treated by historians as peripheral to . . . the immigration on the East Coast, had a powerful effect on the shape and enforcement of immigration laws throughout the nation."

INJUSTICES AND REFORMERS

In every era since the American Revolution, reform movements have taken on a character shaped by the particular moral tone of their time and by the specific phenomena they aimed to correct. The later years of the nineteenth century presented conditions only glimpsed before the Civil War. Capital had gathered into massive concentrations owned either by corporations or individuals. Factories driven by new sources of power submitted to their discipline a labor force that earlier would have worked out of small shops. Great cities packed immigrants into wretchedly poor and crowded neighborhoods. Natural resources once seen as endless were shrinking before the advance of farming and logging. Among a range of responses, numbers of them applied specific programs designed to relieve particular ills while others projected a re-making of the economy and society. For the most part, reformers embraced some elements of the age, especially its science and technology, incorporating these within their proposals.

Hull House

In 1888, Jane Addams traveled from the United States to London and visited Toynbee Hall in the city's poor East End. There she witnessed Oxford University students living among the working-class poor and teaching them. Taking privileged university students from the future ruling English elite and putting them to work with London's poor, Toynbee Hall created a foundation for long-term social reform in Great Britain. Jane Addams upon returning to the United States went to Chicago and rented the former home of Charles Hull, a wealthy

Alice Kellog Tyler, Jane Addams. *Alice Tyler was an artist who lived at Hull House.* (Courtesy, Chicago Historical Society)

businessman. Hull House, as her own version of Toynbee Hall became known, stood at the heart of the city's Near West Side in the nineteenth ward. It began operation as a "settlement" house in 1890.

As Chicago's population and industry grew, land-lords divided the houses of the Near West Side—once a suburb of large, singlefamily homes—into four or five smaller apartments for families of immigrant laborers. Germans, Greeks, Italians, Irish, and Jews from Russia and Poland moved into the ward and worked in the garment industry and other trades. Sewing and stitching workers, known collectively as "sweaters," labored at home in their apartments, where they converted living rooms and kitchens into small-scale operations for cutting cloth and sewing clothes for large distributors. Children helped their parents in the garment trades, while others worked in candy factories or on the streets shining shoes or collecting garbage. A social worker at Hull House described the home factories as breeding grounds for smallpox, typhoid, scarlet fever, and other diseases. The families lucky enough to escape illness risked other hazards related to the exhausting jobs they performed. Foot-powered sewing machines drained the sweaters, and many of them contracted severe respiratory congestion from the buckets of noxious dyes stored in their kitchens. A millionaire philanthropist, a report on such conditions noted, was once asked why as the head of one of the largest clothing houses in the world he did not employ directly the people who made his goods, and furnish them with steam-power, thereby preventing a heavy burden upon their health. "So far," he replied, "we have found leg-power and the sweater cheaper."

In its original conception, Hull House set out to respond to individual and family distress. But Jane Addams soon decided this was not sufficient. Securing a job for a laborer seeking employment, for example, would help his family but do nothing to ease the obstacles built into the whole social and economic system. To "treat an isolated episode is almost sure to invite blundering," the ambitious reformer wrote. For the living and working conditions of the poor, she blamed the tenement realtors, who in response to the influx of residents permitted conditions "which would be regarded with horror if they were considered permanent. Meanwhile, the wretched conditions persist until at least two generations of children have been born and reared in them." The staff at Hull House proceeded to weave the settlement house into the fabric of the community, where it could bring hope and ideas to the neighborhood while serving as its political advocate.

Jane Addams, who would win a Nobel Peace Prize in 1935 for her work with the Women's International League for Peace and Freedom, organized kindergarten and daycare facilities for children of the ward's working mothers. Hull House also served as an employment bureau and art gallery, and provided a library and classrooms for music and art programs that served both children and adults. By 1900, the operation expanded to include a cooperative residence for working women. At the same time, Hull House ran a Labor Museum and offered regular entertainment through its community theater productions. Sharing the confidence that intellectuals placed in the scientific methods of inquiry, Hull House soon welcomed visiting investigators seeking to study conditions of poverty and immigration. Its main purpose, of course, aimed to assimilate foreigners into American life. Some of the volunteers, notably Florence Kelley, went on to serve in governmental reform agencies during the Progressive Era in the early twentieth century.

Ida B. Wells-Barnett and the Fight against Lynching

The problems that Hull House confronted were bad enough. But during this period, the South was busy dismantling much of the remaining racial accomplishments of Reconstruction. The black population, some of its members having enjoyed the vote for years, faced disfranchisement. Segregation, only spottily practiced before, increasingly became public policy. Segregation rules went by the name Jim Crow, after a stage figure played insultingly by white actors in blackface.

In Memphis, Tennessee, lived a young black journalist, Ida B. Wells. In 1884, she had refused to relinquish her seat reserved for whites in a railroad passenger car, and two porters dragged her to a smoking car. She sued the railroad for discrimination and won a lower-court ruling that the Tennessee Supreme Court overturned. In 1892 a white mob attacked a black grocery that competed with white stores. Three co-owners fought back, wounding three whites. Later the three black grocers were lynched. Ida Wells wrote editorials in African American newspapers denouncing the event. In

Ida Wells-Bennett, an angry opponent of lynchings, moved to New York City after a lynching in her home city of Memphis, Tennessee. She became a national civil rights leader. (Courtesy, The Granger Collection)

deeper defiance of white sentiment, she also insisted that in some instances in which black men stood accused of raping white women, the women involved had probably sought the sexual encounter. After a journey to New York City, she received information that her return to Memphis would be inadvisable. For the moment she settled in New York, conducting a campaign to arouse public opinion against lynching. She became sought after as a lecturer, and made two journeys to Great Britain to speak on lynching. In 1895 she married, thereupon giving her family name as "Wells-Barnett" and moving to her husband's home in Chicago. To her attack on lynching, she added the cause of woman suffrage.

What this determined publicist had to overcome in her campaign against lynching was not anything like approval of the mob murders. Even white racists felt uncomfortable about the custom; the remnant who did not oppose it were beyond converting. The real enemy, rather, was indifference. In one of the darkest decades between the end of Reconstruction and the successes of the civil-rights movement of the 1950s and sixties, Ida Wells struggled to overcome the indifference.

Schooling Indians?

Much of the effort of reformers to right injustices went not to African Americans but to Indians. The Dawes Severalty Act of 1887 had the best of purposes, but in breaking up common reservation land and parceling it to individual Indians the law disrupted established relationships, rendering many of the intended recipients impoverished. "Although it seems paternalistic and misguided to us today," one historian observes, "in its conception [it] embraced the most sincerely humanitarian thinking of the time."

Enlightened reformers brought the same good intentions to the effort to provide schooling for Indian children. In the 1890s, almost a thousand Indian students, representing thirty-nine tribes, attended the Carlisle school in Pennsylvania. There they received training in skilled trades together with basic math and grammar. But first the schoolmaster Richard Henry Pratt saw to it that they dressed in Euro-American clothing—following trips to the barber. Pratt required students to speak English instead of their native languages. He desired, in his words, to "kill the Indian, save the man." Some Indians became physicians, teachers, or clergy. But much to Pratt's dismay, many Carlisle alumni at the end of their schooling grew their hair long again and relished their return to Indian identities. Other graduates frustrated Pratt when they left school and gained work as actors in Buffalo Bill's Wild West Show, or inside the grounds of the Columbian Exposition at the Indian Village. There they acted out stereotypical conceptions of Indian ways in what one guidebook described as "the aborigines of this country . . . an almost extinct civilization, if civilization it is to be called." The same book urged visitors to Chicago to see the Indians, since the Exposition likely offered "the last opportunity for an acquaintance with the 'noble red-man' before he achieves annihilation, or at least loss of identity." At the moment that Frederick Jackson Turner announced the implications of the frontier's closing,

visitors to the Exposition understood that the real frontier and the real Indian no longer existed.

Hispanics

In the Southwest lived descendants of the Mexicans who had been absorbed into the United States with the country's acquisitions, and their numbers were supplemented with immigration from Mexico. They had the coherence of long-established communities; some of them held large tracts of land, and there existed a substantial middle class. They did not have the burdens, psychological and social, of blacks recently freed from slavery, and prejudice did not run so deep as to prohibit intermarriage with Anglo-Americans. Yet prejudice there was considerable sharpened by the land hunger among Anglos that spelled trouble for Indians as well. In the treaty that ended the Mexican War, the United States had guaranteed *mexicanos* citizenship and freedom of religion (they practiced Catholicism in a largely Protestant country still harboring much hostility to that religion). The treaty also promised security in their landholdings. That assurance, however, stood in face of the conviction among settlers from other parts of the United States that the land belonged to Anglos. In matters of competing claims, a Board of Land Commissioners in California proceeded to rule in favor of settlers who simply squatted on the land of the Mexicans, known as *californios* in that state. In cases when the Board ruled for the Hispanics the squatters managed to remain for years while the question crept through federal courts. In Texas, tax policy had the effect of forcing Mexicans, known as *tejanos*, off the land, and later in the century Texas Rangers sided with Anglo landowners, sometimes gunning down the Mexicans. Law in the territory of New Mexico similarly supported Anglo appetite for land.

The plight of southwesterners of Mexican origin did not receive the national notice that injustice to Indians and African Americans drew. They had to make do with their own forms of resistance. In New Mexico in the 1880s, *Garras Blancas* ("White Caps") cut the barbed wire protecting land Anglos had appropriated. La Alianza Hispano-Americana tried to take a political route. But even early in the twenty-first century *mexicanos*, by now widely known as *chicanos*, still continued to face problems that by then had centered not on land but on labor conditions among immigrant farm workers.

THE INTELLECTUAL RESPONSE TO INDUSTRIALISM

Middle-class Americans showed reluctance to debate the race question, and their best efforts did not provide a satisfactory solution to the needs of American Indians. Yet they had a considerable taste for utopian alternatives to a free-market industrial society.

Edward Bellamy and a Utopian Future

In his 1888 novel *Looking Backward*, Edward Bellamy imagined an American society in the year 2000, where everyone shares equally in the country's wealth. Healthy men and women populate

Edward Bellamy preached a gentle utopian socialism that won millions to the cause. (Courtesy, Library of Congress)

Bellamy's futuristic world. They work only four hours a day, then dedicate the rest of their time to the pursuit of education and leisure. There are no Carnegies in Bellamy's story, and therefore no need for philanthropic libraries. Bellamy's Americans are their own bosses, their own teachers, capable of building great institutions independently and collectively. Though he went far beyond other reformers in imagining an alternative to the conditions of his own day, Bellamy did not follow the path of some radicals in hoping for a dismantlement of industrial technology. His future is lightened by all sorts of gadgets, such as music piped from a central source, a crude anticipation of the radio.

Bellamy's egalitarian ideas influenced a movement of seekers after a better life who called themselves Nationalists and settled in organized communities. The Theosophical Temple and Homestead at Point Loma, California, founded in 1897, became the best known of the communes inspired by Bellamy. Some five hundred residents there made their own clothes, grew their own food, and educated the settlement's children, who lived together in dormitories once they were old enough to attend the Homestead's school. The Homestead survived into the 1950s, but only through the financial support of a sympathetic millionaire—a support that contradicted Bellamy's vision.

Socialism

The word "socialism" today is ordinarily applied narrowly to societies under tight governmental planning. It has been slandered by its identification in the public mind with the totalitarianism of the Soviet Union and other Communist nations that applied the label to themselves. In the course of its history the term has referred to a full spectrum of movements. The goal that socialists have in common insures the worker, either individually or in self-governing communities and factories, full freedom and power over the processes of production and distribution. Socialism emerged in part out of a conviction that machinery robs those operating it of independence and capitalist owners complete their enslavement. But many socialists have put their hope in modern technical methods, believing that these refine the act of work and require new levels of intelligence on the part of the workforce. Socialists have differed over how to restore society to preindustrial agriculture and craftsmanship, or, to the contrary, how to put the machine fully in control of its operators. Some socialists have believed government as well as capitalists and the owners of private property to be the enemy. The future to which they look is anarchist: they want everyone freed from government and other repressive institutions, to cooperate out of choice and a commitment to the general good. By the end of the century a great number of socialists were accepting the necessity of government, at least as a temporary instrument on the way to a full reconstitution of society. But socialists true to the original ideal of freedom, though recognizing the place of government, continued to prefer that decision-making originate in individual workers and their communities.

By the last years of the century much, although by no means all, of socialism had adopted elements of the thought of the German radical theorist Karl Marx. Marxism describes a progression of historical stages driven by a process that is termed dialectical. An exploiter class of one kind or another comes to dominate a working force until the exploited overcomes the oppressor, and out of that victory

emerges a new ruling class. In more recent times, according to Marxists, the conflict occurs between capitalism and the workers in modern industry: between the most sophisticated oppressor force in history and the most intelligent labor force. The triumph, according to Marxist theory, of the new working class will end class divisions and bring about a future liberated from injustice, a future created from moment to moment by the workers.

Bits of Marxism quickly scattered themselves throughout much of socialist ideology. Radicals among German and other immigrants took to one form or another of Marxist socialism, planning to hasten the process to its fulfillment, the full liberation of the industrial working class. Some anticipated violent revolution; others hoped for peaceful political action. Still other socialists rejected Marxism, seeing in it a quest for dominance by a new ruling party, only claiming to speak for the workers. The sociologist Richard T. Ely espoused a non-Marxist version of the socialist idea to which he attached the term "Christian socialism," a phrase also applied to other radicals who combined socialism with religion. Socialism in the United States

Eugene Debs campaigned for president five times and twice polled almost a million votes. Here he is seen on the "Socialist Presidential Special," a campaign train that crossed the country. (Courtesy, Indiana State University)

reached its highest point during the election of 1912, when for president the Socialist Party nominated Eugene V. Debs, leader of the Pullman strike, and got nine hundred thousand votes. The party also had considerable success in some local elections.

While few Americans officially have identified themselves as socialists, the ideology once wielded an important influence. It kept alive a fundamental critique of capitalism that inspired less radical reformers to chip away at the rough edges of the capitalist economy and society.

Henry George and the Land Question

Another proposal for eliminating the concentration of power did not even oppose capitalism itself but would employ a simple tax policy to destroy its injustices. The chief promoter, Henry George, explained his plan in *Progress and Poverty*, published in 1879.

George, after a boyhood in Philadelphia and on the sea, spent several years in California, and was moved perhaps primarily by his western years to see the land—soil, ore deposits, water—as a divine gift to the human race as a whole. To appropriate it as private property is theft. The appropriation gives to the holders of land essentially a slavemaster's power over everyone else, for the landless cannot grow or make anything with which to keep themselves alive. Ownership of land became the basis of the particular forms that oppression had taken in George's time, so he thought. Land must be parceled out in some way to farmers, factory owners, and mine operators. If, then, land becomes rightly the possession of the human community, how can it be divided in some way, as it must if humanity is to make any good use of it?

George's answer depends on a distinction, already familiar to economists of the time, between the unimproved and the improved value of land. Land can be classified as unimproved before human hands have worked it in any way: enriched its soil with fertilizer, for instance, or built a factory on it. Its value lies in its natural resources, perhaps a vein of coal buried within it. The land's location also determines its value. The closer to a center of population, the more commercially desirable it will be. Whoever owns land naturally richer in soil, or thicker in coal and ores, or closer to a thriving urban center than are other tracts of land benefits

from sheer luck. George proposed a tax appropriating for the common good all the value that the land possesses apart from that added to it by human labor. Such a tax would force onto the market land that a speculator might have been holding until the pressure of a settled population around it pushes up its value to some desired sum. The tax, then, would free land for general use. No other taxes, Georgists believed, would be necessary: his plan is often referred to as the "single tax."

George's ideas affirmed technological progress. Just as land transformed by agriculture into corn and potatoes feeds the human race, land serves humanity when human effort and intelligence have turned timber into a bench, iron ore into steel, or sand into glass. The only problem was to make land fully available to human effort and human technology. That, George's adherents believed, the land tax would do.

The federal government considered a far different way to make nature fully the possession of the human race. As empty land dwindled under the press of population and industrial development, the idea of permanently protecting at least a portion of it gained force in the form of the conservation movement.

Conservation

As important as the Homestead Act of 1862 was in mapping out a plan for the settlement of the trans-Mississippi West, its provision for allotments of 160 acres per settler reflected an ignorance of the character of the vast country to be divided. Much of the region required dry farming—a process of irrigation, digging for wells, and in every possible way compensating for the scarceness of water; and survival demanded larger farmsteads than the law defined. Keeping the West fully habitable and productive, it appeared, made necessary a large effort to defend and reclaim its resources. George Perkins Marsh's *Man and Nature*, published in 1864, explained the desert climate in much of the Mediterranean as the result of earlier massive deforestation in the region's mountains. Scientists and conservationists became concerned that the country's mountain watersheds, stripped entirely of timber, might undergo the same fate. That would mean the arid sterilization of the entire inter-mountain West. As a beginning to an awareness of the needs of the West, the Timber Culture Act of 1873 offered additional land to settlers willing to plant trees. In 1877 Congress, now defining larger holdings than the original Homestead Act had established, passed the Desert Land Act, selling at a cheap price 640 acres to settlers who agreed to irrigate their allotments. Irrigation, however, cost more than most small farmers could afford. In any case, speculators and well-to-do seekers after kingly landed estates manipulated the federal policy for their own ends.

Marcus Daly's Bitterroot Valley, essentially his own private Montana fiefdom, offers a detailed example of the strategy of land grabbing and an illustration of why the nation's wildlands needed protection. In 1872, the future president James Garfield had traveled to the valley and sealed with the Salish Indian chief Charlot an agreement providing for the removal of the Indians from the valley. More than a decade later, the railroad reached the Bitterroot, and a local paper soon estimated that upwards of fifteen to thirty ranches appeared in parts of the valley every month. Many of these sprang up in thickly covered timberlands purchased for $1.25 an acre through the Preemption Act of 1841, or claimed by way of the 1862 Homestead Act. On some of the allotments, farmers cleared the trees and began raising livestock, but on a large number of the claims the tree-covered plots soon were sold to Daly's Anaconda or other large corporations eager to control large blocks of forested land. This type of land transfer occurred under the 1878 Timber and Stone Act. The law was intended to allow individual settlers to make use, for their own and their family's sustenance, of timber and stone resources from federally owned lands. Claims were to be made on 160 acres of non-cultivatable public domain land. In reality, the Timber and Stone Act ended up by being at times almost unenforceable, a joke and a scandal. Daly and others hired "dummy" entry men to apply for plots that they then passed on to the industrialists.

That this happened in the Bitterroot Valley was predictable, given the immense forest resources and the proximity of the timber-hungry mines in Butte. When William Clark, a mine owner, served as one of Montana's senators after statehood in 1889, he was charged with conspiracy to gain control of twenty-one thousand acres of timberlands in the western part of the state. Courts indicted his agents for obtaining the services of at least eighty entry men.

In 1891, in large part because of what had occurred with the illegal removal of public timber in the mountains around Daly's Bitterroot Valley, the rest of Montana, as well as elsewhere in the mountain regions of the West, Congress passed the General Land Law Revision Act. The act emerged mainly from the work of lobbyists for the American Forestry Association and the American Association for the Advancement of Science. They explained to Congress that forest health depends on regulated, scientific management of trees and the watersheds that trees protect. The General Revision Act repealed several of the earlier laws that had allowed for easy snatching of public timber, and gave the president the authority to create Forest Reserves, called since 1907 National Forests.

POLITICS AT THE WANING OF THE FRONTIER

Grover Cleveland defeated the incumbent Benjamin Harrison in 1892 for the presidency in a contest in which the two major parties had defined the tariff as the issue, the Republicans supporting a protective tariff while the Democrats called for a more open international market. Cleveland's victory was the only time in American history that a former president regained the office after a four-year forced absence: he had served from 1885 to 1889 before losing to Harrison in the election of 1888. By 1892 Cleveland, all 280 pounds of him, had several things working in his favor.

For one thing, the Democratic candidate could remind voters that he had received more of the popular vote in the previous election than Harrison, the Republican winning in the electoral college only because he took Cleveland's home state of New York. Cleveland refreshed the country's memory about the reason for Harrison's success in New York in 1888. Years earlier, as the state's governor, Cleveland had gained the disfavor of New York City's corrupt Tammany Hall after he cracked down on that political machine. Tammany thereupon backed Harrison and handed him thousands of votes in 1888. In 1892 Cleveland benefited as well from the Republican alienation of midwestern immigrant voters, among them Milwaukee's Germans, offended that nativist Republicans wanted to outlaw alcohol, beer particularly having a traditional association with Germans. Cleveland, as a Democrat, won the solid South, a region that Democrats would rely upon for votes until fairly late in the twentieth century.

The Populist Party and Its Forerunners

A third party known as the People's Party, or Populists, indirectly aided Cleveland by keeping Harrison from the successes he had enjoyed in the West four years earlier. The Populists sprang from agricultural cooperatives and other mutual-support farmers' organizations. Among these were the Patrons of Husbandry, or the Grange—the word has origins in a word for a farm building—and the Farmers' Alliances. Both organizations, like the Populists and the Knights of Labor, admitted women to their ranks. That the Alliances acknowledged the existence of a separate Colored Farmers' National Alliance might seem a small matter, besides being an instance of informal segregation. At the same time, however, it was noteworthy of a movement that had a strong base in the white South.

In the West and elsewhere, even small farmers were increasing their use of machinery. Some of them as well willingly sought to learn new methods of enriching the soil. In the dry regions of the West, they needed to learn how to farm by using machinery to drill wells, windmill pumps to draw up water. And in those harsh terrains, they faced droughts, blizzards, and infestations of grasshoppers. Farmers began integrating into the economy of industrialism and acquiring much of its spirit.

Yet so long as they remained individual, isolated producers, farmers lacked the power of the conglomerates formed in industry and finance with which they had to do business. The railroads and grain companies set rates and prices. Small farmers had very little control over profitability and the cost of living. They worked in blistering sun and driving rainstorms to get a return that barely, if at all, paid the bills. They also carried on their shoulders the debts that were the lot of nineteenth-century commercial agriculture. For that reason, countless farmers advocated cheap currency, in silver or in paper backed by silver. They defined gold as their enemy, for it made more valuable the dollars with which they had to repay their debts. Farm families were used to cooperation of a neighborly kind: lending tools, bartering eggs for milk, gathering to go from one homestead to another to aid in harvesting.

Now they tried banding together on a larger scale. Farm organizations attempted, falteringly, to set up cooperatives for buying farm supplies and selling their crops, owning grain silos for storage of produce, and otherwise dealing collectively over the forces with which the individual farmer had no negotiating power.

The most successful producers, a small minority, owned huge bonanza farms in California and elsewhere, growing grain or fruit. These were operated like industrial enterprises, standing out from the rest of the economy as did the great manufacturing plants of the East. And like eastern industries, bonanza farms made major use of machinery, such as giant reapers that crawled through the grain fields, cutting and bundling a crop as they went.

Farm activism made a mark on legislation. The Grangers in the farm states enacted a series of measures to regulate railroad and grain elevator rates. In 1877 the Supreme Court in *Munn* v. *Illinois* made a decision covering a number of cases involving what were called Granger laws. The Court held that an Illinois law establishing maximum rates for grain storage did not unconstitutionally interfere with the authority of Congress over interstate commerce. Insofar as *Munn* justified a wider role in the supposedly free market, it was a remarkable ruling, but premature. In 1886, the Supreme Court in *Wabash, St. Louis and Pacific R.R.* v. *Illinois* weakened the effect of *Munn*, invalidating a state law regulating transportation that crossed the state. The law, claimed the decision, trespassed on the authority of Congress over interstate commerce. For the moment, much of commerce remained free of regulation. The *Wabash* case hobbled the states, and Congress showed no inclination to intervene forcefully against the interests of big business.

In 1891 disgruntled farmers formed the People's Party. Among the leaders of the Populists were Georgia's Tom Watson, "Sockless Jerry" Simpson of Kansas—actually a fastidious and elegant dresser— and Ignatius Donnelly of Minnesota, an aggressive promoter of radical ideas and a writer of utopian fiction.

In the presidential campaign of 1892 the Populists presented a broad program. They demanded, of course, a cheap currency. That this included the extensive coinage of silver appealed not only to indebted farmers but to silver miners in the West. Populists, in reaction to private monopolies, wanted government ownership of railroads, tele-

Gun-carrying Populists at one point in 1893 nearly seized control of the Kansas state legislature. (Courtesy, Kansas State Historical Society)

graphs, and telephone systems. Such federal programs would give farmers the ability to communicate with one another and with buyers of their goods, bargain for the best price, and then transport their products on set, trustworthy terms. Populists, standing in a tradition of American radicalism wedded to cheap and inflationary money, wanted a national currency that included paper and silver. They called for a system of warehouses, where farmers could store crops and receive government credit based on the crop's value. The warehouses could hold the produce until its price rose. To these demands they added a graduated federal income tax and direct election of United States senators.

The Populists were a farm party. Yet they wished to be seen as a workers' movement in general, and they hoped to gain the support of labor. To their credit in a decade of growing hostility in the South to the remnants of rights that African Americans had won during Reconstruction, Populists also made some effort to include black southerners. Almost certainly, few white southern Populists would

have welcomed anything like racial equality. But in the South the polls had not been completely closed to all but whites, and the party did not disdain votes whatever their source.

The party chose as its presidential candidate in 1892 James Baird Weaver, a Union general in the Civil War. Weaver had been a leader in the Greenback Labor Party. That party, formed in 1878, endorsed a number of reforms including a graduated income tax but took its name from its demand for an extensive issue of paper money, such as the government had printed out of necessity during the Civil War. That same year the Bland-Allison Act responded in part to the wishes of farmers and silver miners by providing for a considerable though not unlimited coinage of silver. In 1884 the Greenback Party ran as its last separate presidential candidate another Union general, Benjamin Butler. Now in 1892 Weaver had in the Populist Party a new forum with which to carry on the fight for cheap currency, and so to capture both farmers and western silver-mining interests. He won Colorado,

This cartoon subjects the Populist, or People's, Party to charges of lunacy. ("A Party of Patches," *Judge*, June 6, 1891)

Nevada, and Kansas, three Harrison states in 1888. He also carried Idaho, which had been a territory in 1888 and therefore unable to vote for president. Weaver's candidacy, despite being weakened by the South's reluctance to support a former Union officer, made a remarkable showing for a third-party nominee.

The Populists had their own style. A commentator on one Populist convention noted the number of beards at a time when they were going out of style. The Populists also had Mary Elizabeth Lease, one of the earlier women to achieve admission to the law profession. Her temper is captured in her famous recommendation to Kansas to raise less corn and more hell. The movement had its tract, *Coin's Financial School* by William H. "Coin" Harvey. (Any explanation of the money question must have been welcome. A legend told of one man who, devoting his life to studying it, ended up insane.)

Populism also gave birth to one of the most loved books in the American library: L. Frank Baum's fantasy *The Wonderful Wizard of Oz*. Not published until 1900 when the Populist moment had passed, it is sometimes interpreted as an elaborate allegory describing the political forces in contest. Baum himself had been the editor of a Populist newspaper. The wicked witch of the East, on whom Dorothy's Kansas house lands, represents the gold standard, and the good witch of the West ("Glinda the Good") gives Dorothy her magical silver slippers. The poor bumbling wizard suggests the country's presidents who were incapable of solving the money problem. The tin man, whose joints need constant oiling, stands for the eastern workingmen, who had not banded together in effective unions. At the end of the story the wicked witch of the West is destroyed by water—the farmer's friend.

As an effort at wielding a nationwide third-party politics, agrarian radicalism soon failed. But in these times of farm agitation, growers had been discovering that in face of the vast market on which they depended, they could not act as isolated individuals. The attempt to establish cooperatives, and the extensive federal programs that the Populists advocated, signified that they were learning the advantages of social cooperation on a vast scale.

Popular Unrest Under President Cleveland

In 1893, when the newly reelected President Cleveland presided over repeal of the 1890 Sherman Silver Purchase Act, farmers and miners in the West united in opposition. The Sherman Act, enacted under Harrison, allowed paper money to be backed by silver. It also required the government to buy a set amount of silver each month for coinage. Miners liked a law that helped keep them working; debt-ridden farmers rejoiced in a measure expected to

The tin man, Dorothy Gale, and the straw man march on the yellow brick road, symbolizing the money power, to seek help from the wizard of Oz. (Courtesy, Historical Film Archives)

cheapen the dollar. But financiers felt more comfortable with heavy gold in hand or with paper backed by that most precious of metals. As a result, panicked investors cashed in their paper currency for gold and depleted the country's gold reserves. Democrats and Republicans who favored gold could therefore blame on the Silver Purchase Act the depression that followed the run on gold. Events, in any case, put politics into a peculiar spin. A silver act pressed, though unenthusiastically, by Senator John Sherman of Ohio and signed in 1890 by President Benjamin Harrison, both belonging to the Republican Party, was repealed at the insistence of the Democratic President Grover Cleveland.

Coxey's Army

The depression and unemployment that followed the panic brought from some sectors of the public a unique response. Jacob Coxey, a wealthy businessman and a Populist, was a visionary. He teamed up with another: Carl Browne, bearded, long-haired, wearing a cowboy hat and at times a buckskin jacket adorned with buttons made of silver half-dollars, the people's currency. Browne thrived on oratory, and he had a notion that a divine mission had settled upon him, Coxey, and their comrades throughout the population. Coxey had a plan that resembled the federal works projects of a later depression era. He wanted Congress to appropriate money to improve the nation's roads. This would put the unemployed to work. It would also send money flowing through the economy: cheap money such as radicals favored. Coxey knew that he could not expect Congress willingly to enact his scheme. So he arranged to lead a march on Washington carrying his demands. For the marchers Browne devised a roughly military organization and chain of command. The movement had more good sense than it was given credit for.

In advance publicity, Coxey had projected that as many as a hundred thousand would converge on the nation's capital. When he started out on Easter Sunday, 1894, from a little town in Ohio, the marchers numbered only a disappointing hundred or so, but the organizers hoped that his following would grow. They did, though to only a tiny fraction of what Coxey had wanted. In one sample among members of the Army of the Commonweal, as the marchers called themselves, perhaps half were immigrants and only two in three spoke English as

Jacob Coxey's army of the unemployed on the march.
(Courtesy, Library of Congress)

their primary language. Another fifty percent or so were skilled workers and so not at the low end of the labor scale; but a fourth reported having needed charity to survive the previous winter. On its way to Washington, the army found provisions. Towns opened their jail cells to overnight sleepers and took up collections for food. The reason for the hospitality seems to have varied: in some cases, a desire to hasten the marchers out of town; in others, genuine sympathy with the little band. Other separate marches meanwhile started out, one of them from San Francisco.

At one point, the command of Carl Browne faced a challenge from a marcher terming himself The Great Unknown and accompanied by a veiled woman. Coxey stilled the conflict. In Montana, the movement had a setback. Supporters from the West had been using boxcars as transportation to the rally. An attempt at Butte to occupy boxcars led to a fight with the city authorities, whereupon President Cleveland sent troops to put down the disorder.

On May 1, the Army of the Commonweal having arrived in Washington marched towards the Capitol building where Congress met. By that time the participants fizzled into something like five hundred; other groups had not made it to the city. Coxey, Browne, and one other soldier in the army were arrested. Coxey was charged with stepping on the grass. A movement compounded of clownishness, political daring, and a simple awkward dignity had been stilled.

The Army of the Commonweal was crushed, but the repeal of the Silver Purchase Act combined with the spread of economic distress had a separate effect. Populists during the midterm elections of 1894 won forty-two percent more votes than they had in 1892. But the Republicans gained the most power: 113 Democrats lost seats in Congress in one swoop. The silver debate split the Democratic Party in both the 1896 and the 1900 elections, allowing Republicans to control national politics for sixteen years, first under the presidency of William McKinley, and then under the quite different leadership of Theodore Roosevelt and William Howard Taft.

The Election of 1896

In the election of 1896, the Democrats chose William Jennings Bryan of Nebraska as their candidate for president. Bryan, a former member of the House of Representatives, at thirty-six was the youngest man up to that time to run for president on a major-party ticket. At the Democratic Convention in Chicago he had delivered one of the most stirring speeches in American political history. "You shall not press down upon the brow of labor this crown of thorns," he warned the defenders of the gold standard against silver. "You shall not crucify mankind upon a cross of gold." At that moment the young orator won the passion of the delegates and became their choice. Bryan electrified not only Democrats but also the Populists, so much so that they too nominated him at their own convention. But they balked at his vice-presidential nominee, a banker from Maine, selected to placate conservative members of the party. For vice president the Populists chose from among their own number, nominating Tom Watson. A small band of Republicans embracing silver endorsed the Democratic candidate, while some Democrats who wished to defend the gold standard entered their own contestant. A Socialist and a prohibitionist also joined the race.

The Populists' decision to back Bryan gave the upstart party its last significant run in a national election. By joining the Populists and the Democrats, he had created something of a symbolic battle between the rich and the poor. The tally was fairly close, Bryan winning about six-and-a-half million popular votes to McKinley's seven million. Bryan had traveled thousands of miles around the country, lectured from the backs of trains, and kissed babies in a forerunner of modern campaign tactics. McKinley stayed at home in his rocking chair in a strategy known as the Front-Porch Campaign. While McKinley rocked, the agrarian and miner revolt in the cause of silver died with Bryan's split-party backing and his defeat.

The Last Civil War President

Historians usually mark McKinley's presidency by two events: the rise of American imperialism upon the onset of the Spanish American War in 1898, and the coming of Theodore Roosevelt to the office upon McKinley's assassination in 1901. Yet McKinley deserves recognition in his own right for being a memorable and important figure in the nation's story.

In many ways, McKinley represents the typical postwar success story in politics, the embodiment of a new country rising from the ashes of the Civil War and Radical Reconstruction while trying to forget or ignore how hot those fires had really burned. Like many other Ohioans of his generation, and following in the path of every other Republican president from Ulysses S. Grant through Benjamin Harrison, McKinley had served in the Union army. As a private under Colonel Rutherford B. Hayes, McKinley had proved himself in the conflict and by the war's end was a major. He studied law. Afterwards his connections with Hayes, president from 1877 to 1881, and the Ohio political machine boss Mark Hanna advanced his political career. He served in Congress from 1877 to 1891, and then was elected Ohio's governor. While in Congress, McKinley concentrated his efforts on protecting American business from foreign trade, and in the process became one of the most important Republicans on Capitol Hill. His McKinley Tariff of 1890 won praise from industrialists and urban workers dependent on manufacturing jobs and ire from farmers needing cheap manufactured goods.

When McKinley came into office, customs duties brought more money—$160 million annu-

McKinley campaigned for president in 1896 from his front porch in Ohio. (Courtesy, American Heritage)

ally—into government coffers than any other program or policy. McKinley urged even higher tariffs. The passage in 1897 of the Dingley Tariff, which raised rates on average by forty-nine percent, fulfilled his wish, appeasing big business and portions of labor. As president, McKinley also must be recognized for exploring the possibilities of silver, a policy alien to most of the Republican leadership. In an appeal to western voters, he announced that he would support money backed by both gold and silver if Britain, France, and other European powers followed a similar course. When they refused, he endorsed the Gold Standard Act of 1900, which backed all currency with gold. At the same time, an increase in the worldwide supply of gold sufficiently cheapened the value of the metal as partially to weaken the argument for silver as the more inflationary debtors' ore. That and the Gold Standard Act consigned the silver movement to the past.

McKinley's presidency is important as well for what he failed to do. His administration ignored the 1896 Supreme Court case *Plessy* v. *Ferguson*, involving railroad facilities that Louisiana state law had segregated. The Court declared segregated facilities for blacks and whites legal as long as they were equivalent. In the wake of a more recent awareness that all racial segregation is discriminatory against African Americans, *Plessy* stands out as a starkly racist decision. Yet had its insistence been taken seriously that segregation required that provisions equal in quality be given to both races, they would have gotten a better deal than they were getting. In practice, the country embraced only the permission *Plessy* gave to segregation, not its demand for equality in segregated facilities. By the time of the decision, the federal government had made it a practice to ignore disfranchisement and violence against blacks in the former Confederate states. The government did so despite clear constitutional prohibitions against state measures enforcing racial inequality, prohibitions made possible by the Union victory in which McKinley had participated.

In much of McKinley's career, then, he was much a figure of his times. Returning from war service, he had joined up with a big state's well-greased political machine, at a time when the machine dominated politics. Like his party in general and a portion of the Democrats, he responded more to the interests of business, and to a lesser extent labor, than to the plight of agriculture. Even his slight deviation from that political course in a brief flirtation with silver put him alongside politicians and legislators trying to make their way through the elusive economics of money. McKinley drifted with the Republican Party as a whole in its abandonment of the black southerners who for a time had founded their hope in its friendship.

To years into his presidency McKinley presided over a war with Spain that he had not wanted but the public demanded. The war made a hero of Theodore Roosevelt, the colorful offspring of an old New York State family, who had gotten himself commissioned a colonel in order to take part in the fight. Roosevelt became McKinley's vice-presidential running mate in their successful campaign of 1900. When the president died of an assassin's bullet in 1901, Roosevelt inherited both the presidency and an empire wrested from Spain. The politics that had defined the time of McKinley did not disappear: protective tariffs, for example, remained an issue and remain so today. But the passing of the last presidential veteran of the Civil War introduced an era of federal activism in both domestic and foreign policy.

Suggested Readings

Henry Adams's intellectual autobiography is *The Education of Henry Adams* (1918). Although too much ink has been spilled in proving or disproving Frederick Jackson Turner's thesis regarding "The Significance of the Frontier in American History" (1893), historians generally agree that the mythology surrounding the frontier has been a powerful force in American culture and ideas. See Roderick Nash, *Wilderness and the American Mind* (1967); Henry Nash Smith, *Virgin Land: The American West as Symbol and Myth* (1950); G. Edward White, *The Eastern Establishment and the Western Experience* (1968); and Richard Slotkin, *The Fatal Environment: The Myth of the Frontier in the Age of Industrialization, 1800–1890* (1985). Dorothy Ross's *The Origins of American Social Science* (1991) links frontier mythology to the assumption of American exceptionalism underlying the early American social science community. On Henry Flagler and Florida's tourist frontier, see David Chandler, *Henry Flagler* (1986).

The scholarship on worker protest in the late nineteenth century is vast. P. K. Edwards, *Strikes in the United States* (1981); John Bodnar, *Workers' World: Kinship, Community, and Protest in an Industrial Society, 1900–1940* (1982); and Jacqueline Jones, *The Dispossessed: America's Underclass from the Civil War to the Present* (1992) provide sweeping overviews of the topic. The most useful studies of individual strikes or protest movements include Leon Wolf, *Lockout: The Story of the Homestead Strike of 1892* (1965); David A. Corbin, *Life, Work and Rebellion in the Fields: The Southern West Virginia Coal Miners, 1880–1922* (1981); James Barrett, *Work and Community in the Jungle: Chicago's Packinghouse Workers, 1894–1922* (1987); David Emmons, *The Butte Irish: Class and Ethnicity in an American Mining Town, 1875–1925* (1989); and Susan Glenn, *Daughters of the Shtetl: Life and Labor in the Immigrant Generation* (1990). The struggle to define working-class culture through leisure is the subject of Roy Rosenzweig's pioneering *Eight Hours for What We Will: Workers and Leisure in an Industrial City,* *1870–1920* (1983) and Kathy Peiss, *Cheap Amusements: Working Women and Leisure in New York City, 1880 to 1920* (1986).

Paul Boyer's sweeping survey in *Urban Masses and Moral Order, 1820–1920* (1978) and Robert Wiebe, *The Search for Order, 1877–1920* (1967) present the reform movements of the late nineteenth century as outgrowths of a new class consciousness among America's urban middling sorts. Oliver Zunz looks more closely at the culture of middle management in *Making America Corporate, 1870–1920* (1990). Jane Addams, *Twenty Years at Hull House* (1910) makes for good reading and provides revealing insights into the mindset of bourgeois reformers. For more on mugwumps, muckrakers, and settlement houses, see John G. Sproat, *The Best Men: Liberal Reformers in the Gilded Age* (1968); Walter M. Brasch, *Forerunners of Revolution: Muckrakers and the American Social Conscience* (1990); and Allen F. Davis, *Spearheads for Reform: The Social Settlements and the Progressive Movement, 1890–1914* (1967). For utopian and socialist alternatives to traditional reform, read Edward Bellamy's fascinating *Looking Backward* (1889). See also John H. M. Laslett, *Labor and the Left* (1970); Irving Howe, *Socialism in America* (1985); and Mary Jo Buhle, *Women and American Socialism, 1870–1930* (1981).

The conservation movement and the origins of environmentalism are topics explored in Stephen Fox, *The American Conservation Movement* (1981); Donald Worster, *Nature's Economy*, 2nd ed. (1994); and Willet Kempton, James S. Boster, and Jennifer A. Hartley, *Environmental Values in American Culture* (1995).

Among the many fine books on the Populist movement is Lawrence Goodwyn, *Democratic Promise: The Populist Moment in America* (1976), later abridged and published with the title *The Populist Moment* (1978). Also useful are Steven Hahn, *The Roots of Southern Populism* (1983); Robert C. McMath Jr., *American Populism: A Social History, 1877–1898* (1993); and Gretchen Ritter, *Goldbugs and Greenbacks: The*

Antimonopoly Tradition and the Politics of Finance in America, 1865–1896 (1997). For more on the social context in which rural radicalism flourished in the late nineteenth century, see Hal S. Barron, *Those Who Stayed Behind: Rural Society in Nineteenth-Century New England* (1984) and Glenda Riley, *The Female Frontier: A Comparative View of Women on the Prairie and the Plains* (1988). The turbulent politics that culminated with the election of 1896 are addressed in J. Rogers Hollingsworth, *The Whirligig of Politics: The Democracy of Cleveland and Bryan* (1963) and Paul W. Glad's beautifully crafted *McKinley, Bryan, and the People* (1964).

A rally on the West Coast of the labor organization, the Industrial Workers of the World (date unknown). *(Courtesy, Library of Congress)*

Taming the Forces of Social Change

18

★

THE IWW

"'Tis the final conflict.
Let each stand in his place.
The International
Shall be the human race."

—Socialist anthem

In 1905 a coalition of Socialists and labor union members formed the IWW, the Industrial Workers of the World. Soon referred to as the Wobblies, they intended to empower the most miserably exploited portions of the American labor force: migrants, blacks, women, immigrants, and the unskilled. Such people had little place in the American Federation of Labor, which represented the unions of skilled craft workers, the best paid, most easily organized elements of the workforce. The AFL feared that any alliance with the downtrodden would weaken its bargaining position.

When in Spokane, Washington, in 1909 organizers from the IWW tried to speak in public, they were arrested and confined, up to thirty in a small overheated cell, the walls bloodstained from beatings by the police. Next their jailers threw them without blankets into a room as cold as their initial confinement had been sweltering. Once a week they were stripped, given a cold shower, and herded back to their prison cells, this in the dead of winter. Then the city tried blocking all IWW meetings. Unbroken and willing to continue their nonviolent resistance, the Industrial Workers wore down the Spokane authorities, who ultimately allowed them their constitutional right to speak.

On a December night in 1910, authorities in Fresno, California, tried another method on the Wobblies, who even in jail had refused to silence their taunting of the police. Firemen turned on pressure hoses that flung the prisoners about until their clothes hung in tatters from their bruised bodies. They were then left to spend the rest of the winter night knee-deep in water. Yet in time Fresno too gave in. San Diego did not. There, in early 1912, vigilantes took about 140 IWW members from a freight train approaching the city. They forced their victims to kiss the flag and go through a gauntlet of beatings.

What beliefs sustained rebelliousness so stubborn; inflamed the frail, pregnant Elizabeth Gurley Flynn, the Rebel Girl of the movement; and sent Frank Little, part American Indian, from one jailing or beating to another until his lynching in Montana on August 1, 1917? And why did so many Americans feel threatened by a small movement among the most economically vulnerable of workers?

In its determination to fulfill the promise of the great socialist idea captured in the declaration of the anthem, that the international body of workers would be the human race, the IWW was more daring in vision than the most committed Marxist. Its revolution would not go through the socialist government that Marxists believed must precede humanity's full emancipation. Nor did IWW members wait patiently for the revolution to gather its legions, collect its rifles, and carry out a military assault on the state. Instead, each Wobbly was supposed to stand ready to live freedom and the revolution directly, to achieve emancipation at once by refusing to obey orders and by banding with fellow workers. An act of sabotage (from *sabot*, the wooden shoe of the French peasant, thought to be a clumsy obstacle to motion and good for throwing into machinery) became an act of freedom. Sabotage could be anything from a slowdown in work to the destruction of tools owned by the bosses. And together workers smashing property, crippling capitalism, and overthrowing government would be forming One Big Union, a community taking possession of the machines and railroads and telephones that labor had created.

In the most active years of the IWW early in the twentieth century, between two and three million workers joined the organization at one time or another, though in any given month the membership probably did not exceed sixty thousand. Lacking a close association with a particular job or skill, ordinary laborers could draw from the Industrial Workers a valuable identity of another sort. They belonged to the working class as a whole. And they could take satisfaction in the sheer orneriness that befitted the image of the Wobbly. To be a migrant logger "bindle-stiff," named after the bedding that timber workers had to take with them to the lumber camps, or to have a job that could terminate at any moment now meant not degradation but freedom. And there remained the core of organizers, such as the enormous, gentle William "Big Bill" Haywood, who kept the Wobbly faith in the worst of times. For such as Haywood the concept of One Big Union meant not only an ideology but a way of life and action.

Much of the IWW membership drifted across the western states, riding in boxcars to wheat fields and lumber camps. The union's greatest triumph, however, resulted from a strike of immigrant textile workers in Lawrence, Massachusetts, in 1912. A well-publicized rescue effort for the strikers' children, suffering from the long cutoff in pay, prompted families in New York City to take in some of them. The plight of the children increased public sympathy for the strikers, who eventually won a pay raise. The ability of the Wobblies to convert weakness into strength found another outlet on the racially and ethnically divided Philadelphia docks. Longshoremen had been helpless to change the system of daily arbitrary hiring by the shippers. Beginning its organizing there in 1913, the IWW insisted that black and white dockworkers collaborate. Not long after the end of the First World War the rival AFL affiliate, which was among the few unions to deviate from the AFL's widespread exclusion of blacks, actually fashioned itself into a race-conscious black union. Eventually the IWW union folded, but meanwhile it had converted the Philadelphia longshoremen from passive victims to active industrial unionists.

For opposing their country's participation in the First World War, the Wobblies endured mob violence. Though some members eventually became Communists, the IWW as a whole had nothing in common with the repressive Soviet Union that emerged from the war. A few members kept the organization alive, but its quest for the purest freedom combined with the purest community had no chance against the capitalist, fascist, and Communist regimes of the twentieth century. The Wobblies have nonetheless lived in cultural memory for carrying on their heroically fruitless battle against every obstacle to freedom and justice that they defined.

THE PREACHER AND THE SLAVE

Joe Hill, songwriter for the IWW, parodied the popular Salvation Army gospel hymn, "In the Sweet Bye and Bye."

Long-haired preachers come out every night,
Try to tell you what's wrong and what's right;
But when asked how 'bout something to eat
They will answer with voices so sweet:

CHORUS
You will eat, bye and bye,
In that glorious land above the sky;
Work and pray, live on hay,
You'll get pie in the sky when you die.

And the starvation army they play,
And they sing and they clap and they pray,
Till they get all your coin on the drum,
Then they'll tell you when you're on the bum:

Holy Rollers and jumpers come out,
And they holler, they jump and they shout.
"Give your money to Jesus," they say,
"He will cure all diseases today."

If you fight hard for children and wife—
Try to get something good in this life—
You're a sinner and bad man, they tell,
When you die you will sure go to hell.

Workingmen of all countries, unite,
Side by side we for freedom will fight:
When the world and its wealth we have gained
To the grafters we'll sing this refrain:

LAST CHORUS
You will eat, bye and bye,
When you've learned how to cook and to fry.
Chop some wood, 'twill do you good,
And you'll eat in the sweet bye and bye.

HISTORICAL EVENTS

1880–1921
23,500,000 immigrants, predominantly from Southern and Eastern Europe, come to the United States

1886
Founding of American Federation of Labor under leadership of Samuel Gompers

1895
Booker T. Washington, Atlanta Exposition speech • Stephen Crane, *The Red Badge of Courage*

1899
Thorstein Veblen, *The Theory of the Leisure Class*

1901
New York City passes law regulating tenements' sanitary facilities

1905
Lochner v. *New York* • W. E. B. Du Bois and other African American leaders start Niagara Movement • Industrial Workers of the World (IWW) formed

1908
Israel Zangwill, *The Melting Pot*

1909
Founding of National Association for the Advancement of Colored People (NAACP)

1911
Triangle Shirtwaist factory fire in New York City

1915
D. W. Griffith's racist film, *The Birth of a Nation*

CONDITIONS FOR REFORM

By the early twentieth century, the word "progressive" was commonly used to refer to a wide range of initiatives. In 1912 Republicans following Theodore Roosevelt put together a third political party that explicitly took the name Progressive. The phrase became so pervasive that historians have long spoken of the first part of the twentieth century as the Progressive Era. Yet the meanings attached to the word are conflicting. Some politicians to whom the term is applied favored a protective tariff; others supported free trade. Some held racist views toward recent immigrants as well as blacks; some helped organize the National Association for the Advancement of Colored People. Nor can the Progressive Era be sharply marked off from reform impulses of the preceding years. Henry George, Edward Bellamy, the Farmers' Alliances, the Populist Party, and Jane Addams's Hull House all foreshadowed the activism of the progressive period. A few big-city mayors, among them Samuel M. "Golden Rule" Jones of Toledo and Tom Johnson of Cleveland, instituted reforms that anticipated the more widespread progressive program. City-wide measures for unemployment relief, minimum wages, the length of the working day, and municipal ownership of utilities defined a more activist local government.

Progressivism as historians studying the early twentieth century use the word refers to an effort to put industry, labor, and the professions under enough direction, typically by government, to make them instruments of the common good. Progressivism so defined put confidence in trained experts to solve social problems. The movement reacted to the huge disruptions that the forces of machinery, electrical power, and giant corporations appeared to be effecting in American life. But like reformers and radicals just preceding them, they did not want to dismantle industrialism. They wished to the contrary to employ for progress the science and technology, the rationality and organization that formed the core of industrialism. And in what one historian of progressivism has called the search for order, progressives agreed with prominent figures outside of political reform circles. Thomas Edison, whose harnessing of electrical power late in the nineteenth century was itself a triumph of order, complained of the waste that he saw about him in a society that had not learned to organize itself for the common benefit.

AN UNRESTRAINED DEMON.

At first many people feared Thomas Alva Edison's new technology of electricity. This cartoon, printed in 1889, shows pedestrians being electrocuted, a horse and buggy collapsing, and a policeman running for help. The skull in the wires attached to the lightbulb warns of potential deadliness. (Courtesy, The Granger Collection)

Progressives did their work amid enormous energies generated outside government, in labor, immigration, industrialism, and the cities. These embodied both the disorder they wished to overcome and the forces they aimed to channel toward economic and social progress.

LABOR

In the late nineteenth century, American workers clocked on average over sixty hours weekly. By 1910 the average workweek in manufacturing had dropped to about fifty-two hours. Reduction in working hours would make more endurable the heightened speed imposed by the continuously moving assembly line, introduced during the second decade of the new century; and management was learning to improve the safety and convenience of the factory floor. Yet the laborer's conditions of employment remained risky, dirty, and often brutally supervised.

The American Federation of Labor

Of all labor movements, the IWW is historically the most radical and most colorful. Both characteristics, however, denied it wide success, which went instead to the American Federation of Labor, founded in 1886 and led for years by Samuel Gompers, a skilled cigar-maker. Though limited to craft workers and thereby excluding ordinary laborers, membership of the AFL by 1914 reached two million. Still, even at that date unions enlisted only about a tenth of the wage force. The Federation centered its efforts in getting better wages and working conditions, sometimes employing strikes for leverage in bargaining. Having abandoned socialism, Gompers also forsook idealism. He and his union fought day by day for quickly realizable ends. The elite AFL got somewhere largely because its trained workers could not easily be replaced. AFL officials did advocate government allotments for the aged, but the leadership was unenthusiastic about government laws concerning wages and hours. In general, the organization preferred the flexibility and power it might exercise in bargaining independently with employers.

Whatever labor radicalism existed within the AFL

lived in a few member unions. The International Ladies' Garment Workers Union, or ILGWU, organized European Jews and Italians in New York City. There, just at the end of the working day at 4:30 p.m., Saturday, March 25, 1911, a flash fire broke out at the Triangle Shirtwaist factory, which employed young Italian and Jewish immigrant woman workers. The factory building, constructed entirely of wood without a sprinkler system in accord with existing construction standards, constituted tinder for the fire, as were the dry goods, including thin cotton, on the shop floor. Lacking access to adequate fire exits, employees rather than burn to death in the building plunged to the street beneath, their bodies resembling bales of cloth that passersby thought the owners were trying to save. "Thud, dead. Thud, dead," began the eyewitness story by a United Press reporter. A year before some

of the girls had demonstrated for more safety precautions. The journalist wrote: "These dead bodies were the answer." Others died within the building. None of the owners went to jail. The disaster, which took 146 lives, led both to path-breaking state factory legislation and to accelerated growth in the ILGWU. It also furthered the political careers of New York State legislators Alfred E. Smith and Robert F. Wagner, Sr., both of them leading progressives who joined in the struggle for industrial safety by writing strict new laws governing factory working conditions.

Another major event in the labor history of the times occurred in the coalfields of Ludlow, Colorado, in 1914. Banding together in a tent community, strikers for the United Mine Workers demanded recognition of their union. There in the midst of a clash with the state militia, a fire and

When a fire broke out at the Triangle Shirtwaist factory in New York City during 1911, the women employees were trapped, for the management had kept the emergency exits locked to prevent workers from taking long breaks. The death toll was 146. Some died within the factory. Others leapt to their death; fire ladders could not reach to the eighth floor of the building. (Courtesy, Brown Brothers)

WORKING FOR THE TRIANGLE SHIRTWAIST COMPANY

Pauline Newman, an organizer and educational director for the International Ladies' Garment Workers Union who lived until 1986, had once been employed at the Triangle Shirtwaist factory.

A cousin of mine worked for the Triangle Shirtwaist Company and she got me on there in October of 1901. It was probably the largest shirtwaist factory in the city of New York then. They had more than two hundred operators, cutters, examiners, and finishers. . . .

We started work at seven-thirty in the morning and during the busy season we worked until nine in the evening. They didn't pay you any overtime and they didn't give you anything for supper money. Sometimes they'd give you a little apple pie if you had to work very late.

What I had to do was not really very difficult. It was just monotonous. When the Shirtwaists were finished at the machine there were some threads that were left and all the youngsters—we had a corner on the floor that resembled a kindergarten—we were given little scissors to cut the threads off. . . .

Well, of course, there were laws on the books [against child labor], but no one bothered to enforce them. The employers were always tipped off if there was going to be an inspection. "Quick," they'd say, "into the boxes!" And we children would climb in the big boxes the finished shirts were stored in. Then some shirts were piled on top of us, and when the inspector came—no children. The factory always got an okay from the inspector, and I suppose someone at City Hall got a little something too. . . . I stopped working at the Triangle Factory . . . in 1909. . . .

I wasn't at the Triangle Shirtwaist Factory when the fire broke out, but a lot of my friends were. . . . It's very difficult to describe the feeling because I knew the place and I knew so many of the girls. The thing that bothered me was the employers got a lawyer. How anyone could have *defended* them. . . . And when they testified that the door to the fire escape was open, it was a lie! It was never open. Locked all the time. One hundred and forty-six people were sacrificed and the judge fined Blank and Harris seventy-five dollars!

Now I am a little discouraged sometimes when I see the workers spending their free hours watching television—trash. We fought so hard for those hours and they waste them. We used to read Tolstoy, Dickens, Shelley, by candlelight, and they watch the "Hollywood Squares." Well, they're free to do what they want. That's what we fought for.

(Courtesy, Joan Morrison and Charlotte Fox Sabuskey, eds., *American Mosaic: The Immigrant Experience in the Words of Those Who Lived It,* [New York: E.P. Dutton, 1980], pp. 9–14.)

---

subsequent collapse of a shelter at the strikers' makeshift camp killed ten men, two women, and twelve children. The incident is remembered in labor history as the Ludlow Massacre. Within the AFL itself, however, such incidents rarely happened, for the national Federation favored businesslike arrangements that would make it a partner in the capitalist system.

Chicago: City of Labor

American labor, skilled and unskilled, native and immigrant, built mighty industrial cities. Of these, the most sprawling and astonishing was Chicago, the midwestern poet Carl Sandburg's City of the Big Shoulders. A horror to some visitors and captivating to others, Chicago symbolized the giant era of work and industry that lay ahead. In that city during 1886 had occurred the Haymarket affair, involving the bombing and killing of city police and up to that time the most widely publicized incident of labor radicalism. Chicago's architects experimented with buildings making use of the steel skeleton that would become typical of big-city construction. Structures by the architectural theorist Louis Sullivan had a clean-lined solidity. Sullivan was the forerunner of architects across the nation who emphasized more openly than he the lean po-

Louis Sullivan's Prudential Building, *Chicago.*
(Courtesy, American Heritage)

wer of slender supports. In the early twentieth century, Chicago and its surroundings grew to bursting with industries. Grain streamed through the city on its way from western farms to distant markets. Beef, lumber, steel, chemicals, agricultural machinery, printing and publishing, clothing manufacture, and for a time small automobile factories and a sprouting moving-picture industry broadened the shoulders of Sandburg's growing metropolis.

Residential areas for the poor, others for the middle classes, and even semi-rural communities added to Chicago's diversity. Waves of immigrants moved into neighborhoods and then, growing more prosperous, moved out again as a new group took their place. The immigrant neighborhoods were not in appearance slums of a kind that the word now suggests. After the city's great fire of 1871 only brick and stone structures could legally be built in the city's center. Chicagoans of every class passed with fluid ease through the crammed and thickly peopled metropolis. The city, for its time, was distinctive though not unique among urban centers for its elaborate electric-powered street railways, elevated streetcars, and commuter rail trains. "The sky is of iron," reported a French artist, "and perpetually growls a rolling thunder."

As more and more of the city became crowded with people and enterprises, industrialists looked farther out. On the sand dunes of nearby northern Indiana, United States Steel built a plant. In 1906 the company founded the city of Gary, ambitiously providing accommodations for as many as two hundred thousand residents. Pressed outward by congestion and spreading along the networks of its elaborate electric transportation, Chicago was emblematic of the industrialism of its time. It created a new urban landscape for its workers along with different and more constraining forms of work. Labor unions yet to come would crack through the bounds that industry attempted to set up against them.

IMMIGRATION

In the late nineteenth century and the early twentieth occurred possibly the greatest migration of peoples in the whole of human experience, continuing major population movements that for centuries had stirred within Europe and beyond. On

both the American and the European continent, people were adrift: wandering within or across national borders in Europe, and in the United States migrating westward. On both continents, migrants left the countryside for the growing industrial cities. And most visible was the passage from the Old World to new lands, the United States receiving the greatest number of newcomers. From them came much of the labor that sustained American industrial progress.

Misery goaded migration. Eastern European Jews, for example, fled Christian mob violence known as pogroms. But desperation does not adequately explain the restlessness that beset the world, especially in the later nineteenth century and into the next. Not suffering but opportunity constituted the larger reason for the extraordinary mobility. Industry drew European peasants to production centers in their own or neighboring countries or to the United States; it pulled French Canadians southward to New England, and jobs tempted Mexicans to cross the Rio Grande. A thriving economy lured Asians to the West Coast. The great advance in ease of transportation contributed to this mass exodus. Though much of the migration within Europe went by horse-drawn cart or on foot, railroads increasingly facilitated access to ocean steamers. Steamships, replacing the slower and more dangerous sailing vessels that had carried immigrants earlier in the nineteenth century, turned oceans into pathways to a new life. And within the United States railways quickened the journeys of native-born citizens and immigrants alike.

Between 1880 and 1921, when the first comprehensive law restricting immigration went into effect, more than 23,500,000 immigrants came to the United States. At one time most newcomers had come from Western Europe. But the bulk of the peoples arriving from the end of the century onward came either from the south of Europe—Italy, Greece, or the Balkans—or the north of Central and Eastern Europe: Russia, Poland, and neighboring states. They spoke languages that turned city streets into clashing choruses of words and tones and lilts. Irish and many Germans of earlier immigrant waves had been Catholics, and therefore disturbing to Protestant Americans. The new influx added Jews. Together the people from these regions more to the south and east of Europe became known as New Immigrants. At the same time, and contributing to the mixture of peoples other than

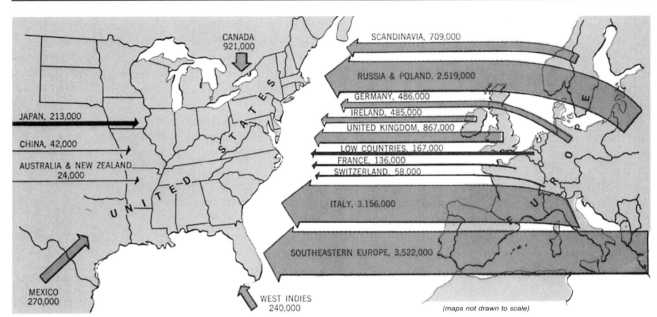

Immigration to the United States, 1900–1920. (Courtesy, Historical Statistics of the United States from Colonial Times to 1970, Kraus International, 1989)

The Crossing

The New Immigrants commonly held the conviction that officials in general were the enemy, collaborators with wealth and power. Even among the many concerned mainly with economic advantage rather than with flight from the repression or the hatreds of the Old World, that belief ran deep.

Often the first encounter with American authorities did nothing to lessen the distrust. Physicians employed by United States consulates in Europe or by the Hamburg-Amerika ship lines, a major carrier of immigrants, examined them for defects that might prevent their entry into the United States. Steamship companies had a financial reason for this. They had to absorb the expense of returning passengers rejected at an American port. At Hamburg, a main point of embarkation for the flow of travelers from Eastern Europe to the United States, the German government took precautions against the spread of scalp-borne disease. To the shaved heads of men and boys awaiting passage, officials applied a chemical cleanser to destroy lice and infections;

English-speaking Protestants, came Catholics from Mexico and French Canada, together with Japanese, and, after 1900, Filipinos.

they scraped with metal combs the hair of women and girls. However legitimate and pressing the problems that the authorities had to address, their solutions measured the distance between the mighty who enforced the standards and the lowly who were subjected to them.

For the great majority who could not afford better accommodations, the steamship journey from Europe to the United States made for further misery. Crammed into steerage, so named for the empty portions of the ship that had once held steering mechanisms, immigrants had little privacy and endured wretched sanitation facilities. Early in the twentieth century, some steamship companies that competed for immigrants installed better amenities for their customers.

Then came yet another stressful encounter. The immigrants who entered the United States at Ellis Island outside New York City, recently established as the largest processing center, faced a second medical examination even if they had already undergone a checkup before the ocean voyage. After 1917 they had also to demonstrate some literacy in at least their own language. An official unacquainted with the language of the applicant might hand a card commanding something—perhaps "Touch your nose"—in that native tongue; the proper response

Immigrants arriving in about 1900 at Ellis Island in New York harbor. (Courtesy, Scribner's Archives)

constituted proof of literacy. The immigration officers, particularly because some wore a uniform that looked military, instilled a largely unwarranted fear. Not on the whole unsympathetic, they allowed in far more newcomers than they turned back. But the impersonality of the process, together with the possibility of its ending in rejection, must have suggested to many immigrants that entry meant exchanging one set of arbitrary officials in the old country for another in the new.

Going to Work

A large portion of the New Immigrants, especially before 1900, had been men unaccompanied by a family. Some planned to win a little economic security before bringing over their wives and children; many had no intention of staying and expected instead to make money to take home. That

often changed as newcomers became settled. Still, in an average year early in the twentieth century, twenty or thirty percent of the New Immigrant population left the United States. The pattern varied from group to group. Russian Jews came as families and planned to stay. Nothing awaited them in their homeland but Christian hatred.

Most of the new arrivals settled in northern cities as far west as Chicago. There they could find people from their native localities and extended families; in much of the Old World, loyalties and connections were substantially more local than national, and often these passed more or less intact to the United States. In Italy, a village prayed to its particular saint, and a yearly feast honored its protector, whose statue would be carried in a procession. In an American city, the transported villagers might still march yearly through the streets, enacting rites and customs new to their largely Protestant adopted nation. The chief reason for settlement in cities, though, rested with the abundance of jobs, ill-paying as they were. Some Old World skills, such as tailoring among the Jews and for many nationalities the preparation of native food, could be carried out in the United States at home or in small shops. But many crafts of the Old World became obsolete in the new, and masses of immigrants had to begin again with raw muscle. Even so, New Immigrants were not simply victims of the economy, driven to the first job that would keep them alive. In the availability of work however badly paid, the new land was generous. And so immigrants chose jobs and regions according to cultural connections and individual objectives.

Poles and other Slavic peoples, for instance, generally planned to make money fast and return enriched to the homeland. The Slavs gravitated to mining, brutally hard work handled in massive doses for good pay. Yet about one in three Poles chose to farm the land, which made for a strong pull toward permanent residence. With very little capital the immigrants could rent or buy a plot for truck gardening in the East, providing tomatoes, onions, asparagus, and other vegetables for a local market. In the Midwest they grew corn and wheat. Italian men, also intending originally only to make money and leave, took to manual labor along with a specialty, expert stonecutting. At the end of the nineteenth century, Italians made up about three-fourths of the construction workers in New York

City, carving and shaping the great city they had made their home. Cultural preference may have dictated the Italian clustering to outdoor work: urban construction as well as California vineyards. Much of the Italian workforce was organized around the *padrone* system. The *padrone* (patron or boss), likely an immigrant himself, connected employers with laborers seeking work. The system was generally efficient, but an unscrupulous *padrone* could divert much of the worker's money to himself.

Many Jews came with usable skills in such trades as clothing manufacture. In New York City by 1897, Jews numbered about six in ten of the workers in the garment industry. Early in the twentieth century, garment sweatshops in the city might demand brutally long work hours. Yet among some of the garment shops, the Jewish owner would labor alongside his unmarried female Jewish employees, a father figure dispensing advice, lending money, and contributing to ship passage for relatives of his workers.

Tradition disposed Jews to prize education and scholarship. They also sought to establish themselves in a profession. For ambitious newcomers the two-wheeled pushcart, carrying dry goods and the ethnic foods for which the immigrants of a particular nationality hungered, boosted their fortunes. Jewish pushcart peddlers figured prominently in the trade. Fridays on New York's Lower East Side were good for business. Peddlers could hawk their wares for the Sabbath, the devout and celebrative weekly occasion that began on Friday evening. Forbidden by their religion to work during the hours from sunset on Friday to Saturday nightfall, peddlers and shopkeepers suffered from Sunday closing laws responsive to Protestant piety. To avoid losing one more day out of the week, they paid the police to look the other way.

Chinese immigrants had gone to cities on the West Coast. Their penchant for laundering was practical, for other groups avoided it. And with very small capital and a washboard they could go it on their own and not have to labor directly for Americans seething with prejudice against them. Mob violence, the anti-Chinese Workingmen's Party organized in California in 1877 by the Irish immigrant Dennis Kearney, and legal efforts to exclude them were the welcome the Chinese got. Japanese in Hawaii, that island still a sovereign nation until 1898, worked in the sugarcane fields, planning like many other immigrants to earn enough to improve their lot in their homeland. On the West Coast, some Japanese took to shopkeeping.

The Tenements

For the New Immigrants, the first years in their new country could be especially hard. Put up for them in densely populated parts of New York City, tenements of a construction called "dumb-bell" had sets of three- or four-room apartments balanced like dumbbell weights against central airshafts. These shafts along with a window in each apartment provided ventilation; toilet facilities were communal. Locked outhouses served tenements on the Lower East Side, each family having a key. A child playing in the streets would call up for the key to be dropped down. Children could make a penny by letting a stranger use the privy. In already crowded rooms, impoverished tenants supplemented their incomes by taking in boarders or lodgers. To relieve the pressure on living space, some tenants piled belongings onto the fire escapes, turning their apartments into deadly firetraps. For the tenements New York City required only rudimentary health regulations; a city law of 1901, inadequate by modern standards, provided for improvements in sanitary facilities in the old buildings and prescribed rules for new construction. But fear of being evicted from an overcrowded apartment kept residents from showing inspectors the filth and hazards amid which they had to endure their cramped lives.

Immigrant Cultures

Alienation from well-meaning authorities defines the fragile relationship that the New Immigrants sustained with their adopted land. An ingrained belief that government did not wish them well made them more comfortable with political bosses who supplied patronage with warmth that came of long association with immigrant groups. New York City's Irish had a way with the Jews. Irish police picked up some Yiddish, the language with old German roots common among Eastern European Jews, and wore Jewish good-luck tokens. The Tammany Hall ward boss John F. Ahern did so many favors, notably in aiding Jewish peddlers to get around the law, that he became a beloved figure on the Lower East Side. The college-educated reformers who ran the settlement houses

Hester Street, New York City, then one of the most densely populated spots on earth. (Courtesy, Library of Congress)

could not draw naturally on the spontaneous good fellowship that marked a city politician. They had to take care to reconcile their middle-class, Anglo-American world with the manners of the Jewish ghetto or the Italian peasant village. At times relations between organized labor and the New Immigrants were precarious. To protect the jobs of native-born workers, the AFL supported restrictions on immigration; on their side, newcomers who expected to return to their native countries saw little to connect them to the American labor movement, and some served as strikebreakers. Yet much of the IWW's membership came from immigrants.

Immigrants at first built much of their lives around their own cultures. In the Southwest, Mexicans who had recently crossed the border mixed with the descendants of Mexican residents from the time when the United States acquired their territory. Knowing the hostility and exploitation they could expect from many of their Anglo neighbors, the two groups were numerous enough that retaining their languages and culture, they could impart a substantial Hispanic flavor to the region. Various immigrant communities relied on mutual aid societies and other institutions that could lend a little

cash. Italians coming from a particular locality in their homeland would organize a society that collected dues to be dispensed to sick or destitute members. Japanese, also grouping according to place of origin in the old country, had elaborate organizations that in addition to providing social gatherings supplied relief, legal service, and assistance in seeking employment. Japanese communities maintained rotating credit programs to support new enterprises. The Chinese *tongs* of the West Coast, which in time turned to racketeering and gang warfare, began as fraternal organizations. Jews had the Yiddish theater, raucous and emotional, with Shakespeare in Yiddish especially popular. The portrayal of King Lear, the lonely father rejected by his children perhaps as elderly immigrants felt abandoned by their Anglicized offspring, drew such sympathy that sometimes a patron would rush on stage to comfort the poor old man.

Working Girls and Dance Halls

Among the challenges to traditional ways that the new land and especially its cities presented is that by 1910, nearly one in four American women

Thomas Allen, Market Plaza. *A traditional market bazaar run by Mexican Americans in late nineteenth-century San Antonio. Women sold handicrafts for cash or bartered them for food or clothing.* (Courtesy, Witte Museum, San Antonio, TX)

worked outside the home and perhaps sixty percent of women between sixteen and twenty were earning pay. This did not amount to the degree of independence that more recent generations of women have attained. It was common for these working girls to live at home and to turn over their wages to the family. And for higher education, the household fund would typically go to sons. But getting out of the house, mixing with other workers, perhaps in the capacity of saleslady dealing skillfully with a variety of customers, made for a new kind of woman: confident, quick-witted, direct in speech. In 1870 almost two out of three employed women had been servants. By 1910 nearly three quarters of working women had other kinds of occupations, such as clerk, secretary, typist, and factory laborer.

For the new woman, clothing design freed her of some of the bulk that had confined her mother. And if she had a little daring, she could mix at the dance halls with others of her age of both genders. A recent innovation in social life, these establishments featured such marks of the times as ragtime and faddish dance steps. The distinctive contribution of the dance halls to social manners is the ease and casualness of the encounters they encouraged. Young women went in groups and without male escorts. Young men also went there together. As the evening progressed, strangers would dance, trying out new steps. No doubt the intimacies of the evening occasionally went further. But that openness to whatever the encounter with a stranger might bring, which provided the young woman with the opportunity to say "no" as well as "yes," looked to a freer future. The girl whose parents remained distant from American culture and from the very thought of independent womanhood could define for herself a place in American society in concert with her fellow workers of longer American ancestry.

A Melting Pot?

Americans sympathetic to the presence of the New Immigrants divided loosely into two camps. One of them aimed at turning these foreign peoples into Anglo-Americans. Social workers argued, with some reason, that continued psychological dependency on the languages and customs the New Immigrants had brought with them might hinder their successful economic entry into American society.

Another ideal, known by the phrase "melting pot," expected that the different cultures of the immigrants together with that of Anglo-Americans would melt into a new American whole. Most vocal of the advocates of the melting pot, the author of a play of that name that opened in 1908, was Israel Zangwill, a Jewish writer from Britain commenting on the United States.

While assimilation and the idea of the melting pot offered their versions of an American future, immigrants worked out their own individual solutions to the competing demands of their heritage and their American environment.

Among Jews Abraham Cahan, himself a product of the Yiddish-speaking Jewry of Central and Eastern Europe, became a major figure. The journalist Cahan gave advice to Jews caught between two worlds. On one side, his correspondents knew the densely populated, clamoring Lower East Side, its pushcarts and bearded scholars, its little shops carrying the scents of kosher food and the colors of Old World village shawls and dresses. On the other loomed the cold mechanized culture of the Anglo-Americans. In a Yiddish newspaper of which the title translates as *The Forward*, Cahan ran a column titled *Bintel Brief*, or "bundle of letters," wherein he published correspondence from immigrants. To a woman whose husband objected to her ambition to go to school, Cahan defied Old World presuppositions about a woman's place and encouraged her to continue. One ashamed young man complained of his father's speaking Yiddish when the two entered a fancy store. Scolding the son for his insensitivity, Cahan nonetheless urged the father to recognize the importance of English.

Education, particularly learning English and using it in school, presented at once a point of conflict and a source of entry into the wider American society. Even the hot meals served at school could cause dispute. Italians, accustomed to a big noonday family meal, objected that their children were not allowed to go home for that purpose. The Talmudic learning and the Orthodox practices of the Jewish devout found a competitor in the public schools, where their youth mixed with peers who turned them into slangy, street-smart American kids. Jewish immigrants and their offspring hungry for education outside the confines of tradition could turn also to the Educational Alliances, formed by uptown German Jews. Sometimes accused of conde-

"BINTEL BRIEF"

in Yiddish means bundle of letters. Abraham Cahan answered these questions for his immigrant readers in the Jewish Daily Forward. The letters are from the early twentieth century.

Dear Editor,

Since I do not want my conscience to bother me, I ask you to decide whether a married woman has the right to go to school two evenings a week. My husband thinks I have no right to do this.

I admit that I cannot be satisfied to be just a wife and mother. I am still young and I want to learn and enjoy life. My children and my house are not neglected, but I go to evening high school twice a week. My husband is not pleased and when I come home at night and ring the bell, he lets me stand outside a long time intentionally, and doesn't hurry to open the door.

Now he has announced a new decision. Because I send out the laundry to be done, it seems to him that I have too much time for myself, even enough to go to school. So from now on he will count out every penny for anything I have to buy for the house, so I will not be able to send out the laundry any more. And when I have to do the work myself there won't be any time left for such "foolishness" as going to school. I told him that I'm willing to do my own washing but that I would still be able to find time for study.

When I am alone with my thoughts, I feel I may not be right. Perhaps I should not go to school. I want to say that my husband is an intelligent man and he wanted to marry a woman who was educated. The fact that he is intelligent makes me more annoyed with him. He is in favor of the emancipation of women, yet in real life he acts contrary to his beliefs.

Awaiting your opinion on this, I remain,
Your reader,
The Discontented Wife

Since this man is intelligent and an adherent of the women's emancipation movement, he is scolded severely in the answer for wanting to keep his wife so enslaved. Also the opinion is expressed that the wife absolutely has the right to go to school two evenings a week.

I am a girl sixteen years old. I live together with my parents and my two old sisters. Last year I met a young man. We love one another. He is a very respectable man, and makes a fine living. My sisters have no fiances. I know that should I marry they will never talk to me. My parents are also strongly against it since I am the youngest child. I do not want to lose my parents' love, and neither do I want to lose my lover because that would break my heart. Give me some advice, dear Editor!

I am in favor of giving women full rights, but most of my friends are against it. They argue that the woman would then no longer be the housewife, the mother to her children, the wife to her husband—in a word, everything would be destroyed. I do not agree because a woman is a human being just like a man, and if women are recognized as human beings, they must be granted all the rights of human beings.

I am a Russian revolutionist and a freethinker. Here in America I became acquainted with a girl who is also a freethinker. We decided to marry, but the problem is that she has Orthodox parents, and if we refuse a religious ceremony we will be cut off from them forever. I don't know what to do. Therefore, I ask you to advise me how to act. *Answer.* There are times when it is better to be kind in order not to grieve old parents.

To a man everything is permissible, to a woman nothing. A man is king over us and may do his will. When I argue that morality is more demanding on women, my husband gets angry and denies it with all his might. There is no such thing as a man with a bad name, but just let one spot fall upon a woman . . . . Why?!

I was born in a small town in Russia, and until I was sixteen I studied in Talmud Torahs and yeshivas, but when I came to America I developed spiritually and became a freethinker. Yet every year when the time of Rosh Hashana and Yom Kippur comes around I become very gloomy. . . . So strong are my feelings that I enter the synagogue, not in order to pray to God but to heal and refresh my aching soul by sitting among landsleit [countrymen] and listening to the cantor's sweet melodies. The members of my Progressive Society don't understand. They say I am a hypocrite. . . . What do you think?

scension towards Eastern European Jews, the institution provided a passage to American and Western European culture, and from it came some of the twentieth century's prominent artists and intellectuals. Parents wanted their children to speak the old language along with the new. But the young, such as many of Cahan's correspondents, wished to show how thoroughly Anglicized they had become, especially in speech. Or this relation of old to new generation could be exactly reversed. One family of more recent Lebanese immigrants who themselves spoke Arabic at home strictly forbade their sons to use it. They wanted their children to be American. Such have been the complexities of interaction between parents and offspring on matters of social adjustment.

Questions of how the communities that made up the American people would come to relate to one another meanwhile took another form. While the Yiddish theater sustained Jewish immigrants and Italians celebrated Old World village festivals, one policy that reformers attempted toward American Indians aimed at educating them away from speaking their own languages and practicing their religions. At the same time, however, intellectuals sometimes looked longingly in the direction of native peoples, seeing in them an embodiment of an American land and spirit. A group of Indian actors, writers, and political activists who made their own migration to the city sought to take advantage of this sentiment, using the idea of Indian contributions to the melting pot to argue against forced assimilation.

The Permanent Stamp

Beyond the bringing of new folkways, the New Immigrants changed the character of the country. They sped its urbanization, hastening the time when its cultural center of gravity would no longer be in its farms and villages. Urban crowding and poverty spurred the policies of the Progressive Era. Though at first distant from organized labor, the New Immigrants in time contributed to a robust trade union movement going beyond the craft unions of the AFL. And in both expanding the size of the American Catholic laity and making Judaism a visible presence in the big cities, they made it clear that Protestantism would no longer have indisputable dominance in American culture.

IN QUEST OF AN ETHICAL INDUSTRIALISM

Giant corporations presided over such industries as iron and steel, railroads, petroleum, electricity, and meatpacking. In 1909, just one percent of the nation's industrial companies produced nearly half of American manufactures. Investment firms such as J. P. Morgan and Kuhn, Loeb provided enough credit virtually to control huge companies. So some businesses that manufactured actual products had to submit to the dictates of enterprises that produced nothing in themselves but money. By the late nineteenth century, some state and federal legislation to restrain abuses of monopoly power had already appeared. But reformers in the Progressive Era believed in just what the label says: progress. Rational industrial consolidation could make for efficient ordering of resources and productive processes. Well-administered industries, regulated by government, made more sense to progressives than a full-scale attack on business.

Not until the height of progressivism in the early twentieth century would reformers make it a clear goal of national politics to achieve an ordered economy. And even then order meant different things to different people. But the idea of administration by experts was winning popularity among reformers. The conviction grew that trained administrators could solve social problems with the same kind of objectivity that measured to a microscopic tolerance the width of a steel bar.

The Social Gospel

American Protestant reformers, prominent among them Washington Gladden and Walter Rauschenbusch, began formulating a body of thought known as the social gospel. Rauschenbusch argued for turning Christianity from a pale abhorrence of this world in favor of the next and recasting it as a life-loving religion of earthly striving and social justice. Theologians of the social gospel commonly believed that the divine Kingdom to come invoked in the Lord's Prayer—"thy Kingdom come"—was a Kingdom to come on earth. It would be a time of moral regeneration founded in part on just social and economic relations. Legislation improving the treatment of factory workers or restricting the liquor trade would be an advance, however small, toward the Kingdom. The social gospel led to the founding of the Federal Council of Churches of Christ.

Some Roman Catholic theologians came to parallel conclusions. In the last years of the nineteenth century Pope Leo XIII in his best-known letter to the bishops, *Rerum novarum*, had moved his church toward reconciliation with the political and economic forces of the time. Recognizing that the democratic revolutions Rome had earlier detested were irreversible, and wishing to create an alternative to socialism, the Pope urged capitalists to make peace with labor and to establish decent working conditions. Catholics of Leo's persuasion favored a social order of cooperative institutions, modeled on the family, that could transcend both the selfish individualism of capitalist economics and the radicalism of the socialists.

The Social Housekeeping of Woman Reformers

Through much of the nineteenth century, middle-class men and women each had expected the other to inhabit a separate social sphere. Men, rational and competitive, lived in the public world of work and politics. Women, emotional and sensitive, were supposed to occupy the private world of home and children. This domesticity, of course, fitted primarily the experience of women from more affluent families, not that of farm wives, or servants, or female factory labor. In the early twentieth century, however, the participation or leadership of well-to-do women in reform efforts became commonplace. Part of the explanation lies in the suffrage movement, led in the new century by Carrie Chapman Catt's National American Women's Suffrage Association and by the more militant Alice Paul. The issue of winning the vote stirred women toward reform in general. And it reinforced the idea that their gender had something distinctive to bring to the cause of social betterment.

Already in the late nineteenth century, that conviction about the special insights that women could offer to reform had inspired the Women's Christian Temperance Union. As victims of drunken males and mothers of children beaten by liquor-maddened fathers, women had particular reason to speak out against alcohol abuse. That Frances Willard, a

Members of the National Woman's Party picket outside the White House. (Courtesy, Library of Congress)

founder of the organization, was also a labor radical reveals the breadth of the reform efforts among women. Their politics were moving from private concerns to public, from household issues such as temperance to the public questions surrounding labor and work.

Florence Kelley is illustrative. She was instrumental in the passage of Illinois legislation regulating the hours and working conditions of women and children. Thereupon, as the state's first chief factory inspector, she set about to enforce the new rules, finishing a law degree so that she could prosecute violators. In 1895 the supreme court of Illinois ruled against the part of the law limiting the working day, but she went on to become a major reformer on the national level. Testifying in 1914 before a congressional committee on child labor, she recalled:

The superintendent of a glass-bottle company told me himself that this occurred once when he was rushed with work: A widow had come in bringing two little boys, one still in kilts and one in knee breeches. She told him that their father had just been killed on the railroad, and that they were penniless; and she wanted the older little boy to go to work in the glass-works, where he would get 40 cents a day. The superintendent was pressed for boys, and said, 'I won't take the bigger fellow alone, but if you will take the baby back home and put him into knee pants, and then bring them both back in trousers, I will take them both.' Both went to work on the night shift.

Along with the suffrage movement came an increasing push to open the professions to women. By 1900 eighty thousand women went beyond high school each year, and the numbers were expanding rapidly. Women desiring fully to enter the social and political realm would have to come to terms with statistics, legal processes, and studies of the brutal conditions of poverty and vice. All this be-

A number of states and territories, beginning with Wyoming in 1869, permitted women to vote. But the first full nationwide participation, in the election of 1920, came after the Nineteenth Amendment forbidding sexual discrimination in voting. (Courtesy, Historical Statistics of the United States, Colonial Times to 1970, Kraus International, 1989)

Florence Kelley's National Consumers' league led the campaign for restricting the working hours of women and children. (Courtesy, Bettmann-Corbis)

longed to the domains of material hardship, sexual brutality, and intellectual combat that earlier generations of men and middle-class women had thought the female psyche too frail to encounter. Among woman reformers and radicals who chose medicine or other occupations related to preserving health was the revolutionary anarchist Emma Goldman, who for a time studied to be a midwife. The physician Alice Hamilton investigated industrial illnesses. Margaret Sanger, a social worker rather than a medical student, had seen the burden that unplanned births placed upon poor women. Herself one of seven children whose mother had died in childbirth, she fought against laws banning the spread of contraceptive information. Yet the birth-control movement, compassionate as it was toward impoverished women, illustrates as well a ruthlessly scientific side of progressivism. Some birth-control reformers hoped that contraception would be a means of holding down the numbers of what they considered the "unfit," a term that hinted of people of immigrant stock.

An inspiration to women reformers was the settlement-house idea. Florence Kelley started her reform career at Hull House. The women's clubs that sprouted or grew during this period gave female professionals a broader range of opportunities. Women banded together under the umbrella organization of the General Federation of Women's Clubs.

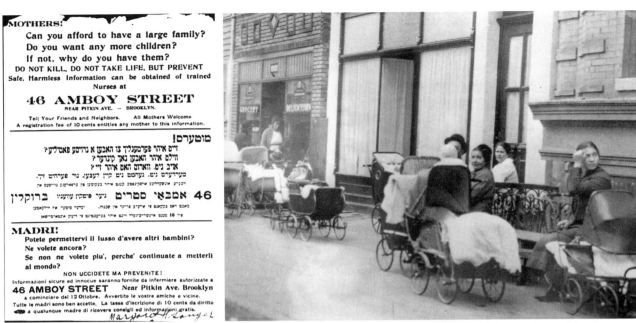

During the Progressive Era, Margaret Sanger opened the first birth control clinic in the United States. Located in the Brownsville section of Brooklyn, the clinic was shut down by police. In its first nine days of operation some four hundred Roman Catholic and Jewish immigrant women showed that they wanted to learn about birth control as much as Protestants. (Courtesy, Sophia Smith Collection, Smith College)

Prostitution

As modern capitalism along with consumerism grew in the last years of the nineteenth century, both had an impact on an ancient and desperate trade. Once practiced largely on a casual basis by women working independently, prostitution now became organized around brothels, concentrated in districts tolerated by many city governments. At luxurious establishments featuring the best food and wine, gentlemen of property and status gathered for business as well as pleasure and sociability, while madams who could be trusted not to talk about the customers saw after their every need. At the other extreme stood wretched hole-in-the-wall brothels where customers were not so much served as processed in quick succession by women driven to increase the take.

A widespread assumption among reformers held that immigrant women made up a disproportionate share of the flesh trade. Immigrants themselves, in fact, seem to have been less likely than native-born Americans to engage in it. But the offspring of immigrants, raised in communities in which the Old World family and its customs were coming apart, did contribute heavily to the business. Another popular idea at the time had it that many prostitutes were innocent country girls lured to the city and entrapped there. The evidence does not bear out this notion. Most prostitutes certainly came from relatively impoverished backgrounds. Yet the majority of poor women did not turn to the brothels, and so cultural and personal circumstances must also have factored in. Many prostitutes, for example, had been subjected to early sexual experiences, in some cases with family members.

Prostitution ranked high among the social conditions that progressivism addressed for a combination of moral, humane, and scientific reasons. Woman reformers expressed particular indignation at the claim that the commerce in sex protected virtuous women from male lust and seduction. In general, progressives must have been aware of the double standard that pardoned a degree of male sporting while females came to be labeled pure or lost and wanton. A few radicals demanded equal sexual freedom for both genders; most progressives probably preferred that both abstain from all sex outside of marriage. The common reform belief assuming that prostitution must have its roots in poverty went with the progressive determination to improve wages and working conditions.

The differing strands of progressivism came together in a wide though not a universal demand for closing brothels. Only a minority advocated instead the licensing and regulation of prostitution, which would require medical exams and thereby cut down on the spread of venereal disease. By the new century's second decade, cities were outlawing the zones and the trade. But destroying the brothel districts threw the women out of the only environment in which they had enjoyed a measure of shelter and stability. Henceforth they had to practice a fugitive profession, harried by police and dependent on the dubious protection of pimps.

Pawnshops, Loan Sharks, and Honest Credit

The attack on organized prostitution is but one of several instances in which progressives believed that redeeming society from abusive economic and political conditions would at the same time make for a reformation of personal character. The prohibitionist attack on the liquor industry is another clear case in point. Turning heavy drinkers into steady workers and husbands would improve the lot of the men, make life safer for wives and children, and cleanse politics of the evil of the bossism that operated out of saloons. Another problem that engaged reformers went deep into the very character of an industrial economy. The borrowing habits that the poor practiced in the face of the want that forever threatened them exacted heavy interest rates. Typical annual charges imposed by illegal small-loan agencies ranged from twenty to three hundred percent.

Well before the Progressive Era, American culture had made a rough distinction between sober and reckless borrowing. It was admirable to take out a big loan to start a productive enterprise: to buy farmland, for example, or a shoe shop. Borrowing from a pawnbroker for the purpose of answering an immediate need, to the contrary, could be justified only under desperate conditions, such as illness or near starvation in a borrower's family.

A common kind of small loan for immediate consumption came from pawnbrokers. Clothing, musical instruments, clocks, tools during slack work seasons, furniture, anything that could be appraised as having some substantial value could be used as security for small loans. Pawning articles could bring public shame. So a pawnshop might have an inconspicuous side entrance, or a row of booths strung along a counter, all opening to the broker but isolating the borrowers from one another. But pawning goods was also integrated into the culture of the poorer urban wage workers. Some families made pawning a regular, matter-of-fact component of their budget. A Sunday suit of clothes could be pawned on Monday, redeemed on Saturday, worn the next day, and brought back on Monday, in a rhythm providing a means of living while the customer waited for the weekly wage.

For the poor, buying on installments constituted another system of credit. Immigrants purchased clothing and furniture from so-called borax stores—"borax" here apparently comes from the Yiddish *borgs*, meaning "credit"—that after checking out a potential customer for employment and character accepted weekly payments. The sales techniques were aggressive, the goods flimsy, and the prices inflated. More reasonable were immigrant peddlers who, working with a store or warehouse, would sell on an installment plan a variety of goods in their own neighborhoods. Establishing personal contacts with customers, such peddlers could serve as advisers to newcomers unfamiliar with the ways and language of American retail buying.

Progressive reformers set out to liberate the poor and the lower middle classes from the clutches of oppressive lending agencies and from what they thought to be the undisciplined and uninformed habits of the borrowers. Remedial loan societies, the earliest of them having been formed before the progressive period, offered a combination of civic-minded objectives and efficient business methods. Drawing on funds from contributors willing to settle for a moderate return on their investment, these associations provided reasonable credit terms to struggling customers. They set out as well to instruct prospective lenders in careful planning for repayment, and to discourage frivolous borrowing. Reformers pressed for enforcement of laws already enacted banning excessive interest rates and for creating a model lending law. One provision would require that when borrowers put up wages as security to be seized by the loan company in the case of default, wives and employers must consent to the arrangement.

A number of illegal lenders, themselves wishing to win respectability, joined with the remedial loan societies in devising a model law. By 1932 twenty-five states had adopted it in some form. Sharks defied the state regulations and did big business, but the loan industry began to take on a new face. It now presented itself as serving responsible workers who sought to better their lives, and as discouraging loans for trivial habits of consumption. But poor people of all races, especially minorities, continued to be victims of loan sharks.

The Niagara Movement, the NAACP, and the Struggle for Equality

In 1900, the great majority of the ten million or so black Americans, only about fifteen percent of whom lived outside the South, suffered like their predecessors from pervasive, grinding poverty. In the South three out of four black farmers were tenants or sharecroppers, a status also common among whites. In 1910, less than one percent of that region's black adolescents went to high school. For a time after the Civil War, the South had seemed to be making some progress toward the softening of racial barriers. Now that had ended. Beginning in the 1880s, black southerners faced systematic exclusion from the ballot, and segregation before long

LYNCHINGS IN THE SOUTH 1891–1907	
Year	No.
1891	192
1892	235
1893	200
1894	190
1895	171
1896	131
1897	166
1898	127
1899	107
1900	116
1901	135
1902	96
1903	104
1904	87
1905	66
1906	73
1907	56

(Courtesy, *Historical Statistics of the United States, Colonial Times to 1970*, Kraus International, 1989)

This grim photograph shows the death of five African Americans lynched in the early twentieth-century South. Lynchings declined in the 1920s but continued into the 1950s. (Courtesy, The Granger Collection)

extended to the most trivial details of their lives. The threat of lynching hovered over them. A final insult awaited the presidency of Woodrow Wilson, beginning in 1913. In the administration of that Virginian and his Democratic Party, the party of southern white racism, the federal civil service became segregated. Yet in the early twentieth century, a handful of black leaders launched the ideologies and projects that decades later would break open the nation's white-supremacist institutions.

In 1903 W. E. B. [William Edward Burghardt] Du Bois, a young black intellectual with a doctorate from Harvard, publicly questioned the teachings of Tuskegee Institute's Booker T. Washington. Included in Du Bois's classic *The Souls of Black Folk* was a specific attack on what in Washington's speech at the Atlanta Exposition in 1895 he called the Atlanta Compromise. Du Bois was referring to Washington's implicit offer to the white race: give black Americans at least some tolerable place in the economy and they will put off the question of social equality. An essay in Du Bois's book, "The Talented Tenth," urges African Americans to provide for the higher education of their most promising members

(Left) W. E. B. Du Bois, a northerner, belittled Booker T. Washington and offered intellectual leadership. (Right) Washington, a southerner, was a complex leader of African Americans who would begin by winning improvements in black economic life before pressing for political goals. (Courtesy, Library of Congress)

and then follow their lead. Du Bois was proposing not outright confrontation of whites but a course of action settling for nothing short of absolute equality, especially in higher education.

At the time, nothing remotely like acceptance of Du Bois's proposals was conceivable among whites. He focused as much on what his program would do within the black community as on how it might force open an entrance into the privileges of the white. In this he differed not so far from Booker T. Washington as he perhaps thought. With more than a touch of condescension, Du Bois dismissed the training in agriculture and manual work to which Washington had devoted much of his life. But Washington believed, and argued eloquently, that careful work of any kind goes beyond merely practical objectives and makes for the building of character. Still, Du Bois's criticism of Washington's more modest immediate goals was on the side of the future.

In 1905 a group of prominent black citizens, Du Bois conspicuous among them, gathered at Buffalo, New York, to form the Niagara Movement. The conference made direct demands for racial equality. Four years later black and white reformers together founded the National Association for the Advancement of Colored People. *The Crisis*, a journal edited by Du Bois, gave the organization an outlet for a steady source of news. For decades, the NAACP remained the foremost organization pursuing equality between the races.

Another demand for racial equality found a voice in the wake of a 1911 meeting in Columbus, Ohio (and on Columbus Day no less), of the intellectuals Arthur C. Parker of the Seneca tribe, Henry Roe Cloud, the Winnebago spokesman, Sherman Coolidge of the Arapahoe, and others. Out of it came the Society of American Indians, a political and cultural lobbying organization that subsequent Indian political groups grew from. Although not active, Du Bois held an associate membership. A few years later appeared LULAC, the League of United Latin American Citizens. Over the course of time, these and other groups pressed, like the NAACP, for equality and reform.

Culture, Schooling, and Entertainment

At the turn of the twentieth century, the national literacy rate stood at about ninety percent. As many as three hundred thousand students attended colleges or universities, and women comprised almost a third of these. However modest these figures now seem, they demonstrate an enormous growth in the demand that an increasingly literate and urban society made for formal education. In small towns across the country, young people went not only to grade school but to high school. Immigrant children in major cities were learning the language and the skills they would need to negotiate the world to which they or their parents had come. Many older immigrants attended night schools, aiming to gain facility in English.

CIRCULATION OF DAILY NEWSPAPERS AND MAGAZINES, 1880–1919

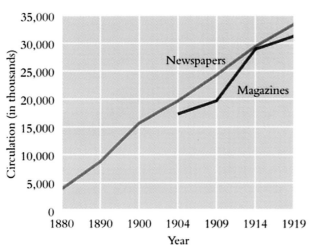

(Courtesy, *Historical Statistics of the United States, Colonial Times to 1970*, Kraus International, 1989)

Americans, like the peoples of other technically advanced nations, formed a reading public. Most read "yellow journal" newspapers, their headlines screaming the lurid stories that helped bring on war with Spain over the island of Cuba in 1898; or they turned to papers in their languages of origin. In both Europe and the United States, Yiddish, a tongue that educated Jews who spoke German or Russian had considered vulgar, became a living and vigorous literary vehicle. Newspapers and other periodicals in many languages supplied not merely entertainment or news but serious discussion of ideas. Socialists, anarchists, religious sectarians of varying kinds all had their own publications. And for at least a portion of the public, the printed word crammed with facts and figures gleaned by research aided in forming opinions about major issues. A handful of writers exposed corruption in politics and business. Theodore Roosevelt, who as president from 1901 to 1909 went on his own in pursuit of corporate misdoing, labeled them "muckrakers" after a passage in the old Protestant text *Pilgrim's Progress*. Ida Tarbell described the scheming that had created the Standard Oil Trust. Lincoln Steffens published a series of magazine articles on corrupt urban politics and in 1904 gathered some of them in book form under the title *The Shame of the Cities*. Other subjects the investigators combed through with their verbal rakes included child labor, insur-

ance practices, medical fraud, and unsanitary conditions in the Chicago meatpacking industry.

Entertainment came in new and creative forms. Beginning as simple, brief affairs telling some short event of adventure or humor, movies evolved in the first years of the century to longer, more sophisticated stories, using editing and camera movements we would recognize today. From the brief, crude kinescope features of the early 1900s, film would cap off the era with the visually stunning *Birth of a Nation*, released in 1915. The phonograph, invented before the end of the previous century, brought music into homes. Baseball, played or watched, had been followed for decades, and spectators now had the major leagues to provide them with the most elegant of popular sports. Amusement parks, featuring George Ferris's giant revolving wheel and other rides, became commonplace. Dancing was popular among young men and women. Vaudeville presented its varieties of humorous and musical acts. Along with vaudeville the immigrant stage, discovering and exploring the customs and twists of humor peculiar to ethnic city-dwellers, made the theater a dynamic force in urban life. Since the late nineteenth century, the rural inland had enjoyed programs known as Chautauqua after a lake and village in New York State where the system began. These were summer lectures in politics, science, and other subjects of general interest offered to a population hungry for education and lacking the instant connection with

Steeplechase Park, pictured here, opened during 1897 at Coney Island, an amusement park in Brooklyn, New York. Crowds vied to ride the mechanical horses; only one won each race. (Courtesy, Brown Brothers)

THE BIRTH OF A NATION

The Great Train Robbery, the cinema's first western, appeared in 1903. Its director, the superb storyteller Edwin S. Porter, employed a technique labeled crosscutting. He alternated shots among events supposed to be happening at the same time and drew them together to produce a dramatic result. But Porter's most significant achievement was to help a young actor, David Wark Griffith, get his start in film.

Griffith won fame as the director of *The Birth of a Nation,* released in 1915. It is an adaptation of Thomas Dixon's novel *The Clansman*, an openly racist story set in the era of Reconstruction following the defeat of the Confederacy. Through two families, the northern Stonemans and the southern Camerons, the film presents an idealized view of the South. It tells of the return home to South Carolina of a Confederate soldier after the Civil War and his efforts to organize the Ku Klux Klan. His enemies, northern politicians determined to impose their rule on the South with the aid of African Americans, are depicted as thieves and eager proponents of racial intermarriage. Senator Stoneman represents the Radical Republican Pennsylvania congressman, Thaddeus Stevens.

The country's most infamous and most technologically innovative silent film, *The Birth of a Nation* is also the first lengthy movie with a modern narrative structure. Before Griffith, movies had shown only body shots of actors from head to toe, much as they appeared on the theater stage. Better to catch a character's emotions, he changed the camera distance during a scene. Other techniques he pioneered include the close-up and the flashback. His use of a split screen goes beyond crosscutting: instead of moving back and forth among different events, the film shows them simultaneously. It occurs in Griffith's presentation of northern and southern soldiers marching toward each other during the Civil War, and as they approach the battlefield the drama intensifies. The film also makes free use of symbols: a dove that flies into the hand of a gentle colonel, the dried-up corn on the plate of a Confederate soldier, the cruelty that Silas Lynch, of mixed African and white blood, displays toward animals.

Movie poster for D. W. Griffith's The Birth of a Nation. *(Courtesy, Library of Congress)*

To the American people in 1915, the events portrayed in *The Birth of a Nation* did not depict distant history. Many eyewitnesses to the events of the Civil War survived, and countless Americans might hear family memories of the conflict that had almost torn the Union asunder. The plot moves quickly, and Griffith mesmerizes the viewer with epic battle scenes recalling their disorganization and brutality, along with grand recreations of the burning of Atlanta and Sherman's march through Georgia. Though Griffith's adoption of the racist commonplaces of his time compromise the objectivity of the film, authenticity preoccupied him. He rebuilt Ford's Theater, the scene of Lincoln's assassination, and accurately recreated the South Carolina legislature's chamber.

That careful depiction, however, becomes the setting for Griffith's racial fantasies. As a bill allowing racial intermarriage is passed, freedmen drink in the hallowed sanctum of the South Carolina legislature, while white women and children cower in the gallery. A similar theme is masterfully conveyed in chase scenes filmed on location near Big Bear Lake in California. Bent on raping Ben Cameron's sister Flora, black Gus with crazed eyes chases her through the woods. The scene is cut so that the audience views three lines of action: Flora running from Gus, Gus chasing Flora, and Cameron racing to save her. Rather than give in to her pursuer, the white-clad Flora hurls herself off a cliff to her death. The Klan tracks Gus down and lynches him. Building towards its climax, the film shows the Klansmen riding through the countryside gathering strength as they prepare to assault a black uprising. In shots of decreasing length, hooded Klansmen rush in a crosscut with black looters. The supreme white power obliterates the uprising and with it any possibility of racial reconciliation.

Reaction to the film ranged from outrage to adulation. Griffith naively insisted that the historical accuracy of the film made it uncontroversial. He was out of touch with the founding of the NAACP and the Urban League then challenging white supremacy and its black stereotypes. The protests prompted Dixon, whose novel had inspired the movie, to arrange a showing in the White House occupied by his Princeton classmate Woodrow Wilson, and the southern-born president pronounced the film "history written by lightning." That the president and a prominent member of the Supreme Court had seen and admired the film assured its wide distribution. Publicity events included horsemen dressed in full Klan regalia riding down the street where the movie played. An estimated one hundred fifty million people have seen the film.

Charges of racial prejudice haunted Griffith. The revival of the Ku Klux Klan in the years from 1915 to 1925 added to his soiled reputation. His ambitious *Intolerance*, a later film portraying historical instances of bigotry, has been interpreted as his attempt to erase his image of hate-monger. *The Birth of a Nation*, ranked by the American Film Institute as one of the country's best, continues to have power to transfix the viewer with spectacle while repulsing the audience through its message.

urban centers that radio and television have since provided.

For pure consumption of the items industrialism made widely available, whoever could afford to do so might patronize the department stores that had grown up in American cities in the late nineteenth century. New York City had Macy's along with Lord & Taylor, Philadelphia as well as New York shopped at Wanamaker, and Marshall Field supplied Chicago. Mail-order stores included Montgomery Ward and Sears Roebuck, while the nation had as chain stores the Great Atlantic & Pacific Tea Company, or A&P, and Woolworth's.

NEW IDEAS

For all the unequal power that owners of industries held over labor, they lacked one final control: they could not fully dictate the pace of work. A worker who was clearly a slacker could be fired. But if employees agreed among themselves that a day's production be of defined quantity, the owners might be stymied. The labor force did not have to unionize or become otherwise openly defiant; it needed only to slow down, or rather, simply not speed up. Among individual workers, fear that quickening their pace might be treason to their fellow employees could be greater than fear of reprisal from the owner if they did not work faster. And dismissal of some major portion of a plant's workers would itself disrupt production; nor could it guarantee that replacements would be more compliant.

Workers, at any rate, had their own ideas of how their labors were to be used. Social theorists meanwhile were considering large questions about the nature of work, technology, and science. The pace of industrialism demanded that they do so, as no previous generation of investigators had felt obliged to do.

Reform Experts: Frederick Winslow Taylor and Thorstein Veblen

Toward the end of the nineteenth century, a number of companies began experimenting with wage incentive plans, such as higher pay for greater productivity. Some, wishing to placate their employees, gave attention to physical comfort on the job and introduced such amenities as opportunities for schooling and recreation. This approach was most common in industries that hired considerable numbers of women. The efforts to order the labor force and to increase a plant's efficiency produced a series of initiatives known today by the term "scientific management." Of the many scientific managers who by this time were leaving their mark on industry, Frederick Winslow Taylor is the most widely recognized.

As an engineer, Taylor had undertaken a number of advanced technical tasks, among them finding the ways in which cutting tools could most effectively slice through metal. He is best known, however, for investigating how to train to greater efficiency the worker, the most complex piece of machinery in a factory. Early in the twentieth century union leaders feared Taylorism as an instrument of capitalist control over labor. Some scientific managers, however, urged humane practices such as lessening the hours of work. A workday of reasonable length with fresh and spirited employees, that argument went, would make for a larger total daily productivity than a longer day with tired and dispirited machine-tenders.

Taylor served capitalism. His contemporary Thorstein Veblen despised the capitalist system. In sociological studies, of which the best known appeared in 1899 as *The Theory of the Leisure Class*, Veblen presented the nation's privileged: the "conspicuous consumption" of the wealthy with their extravagant spending and their pompous mansions; the ignorance, among business leaders, of the productive forces they commanded. Yet in *The Instinct of Workmanship*, published in 1914, Veblen defined in technology itself principles of order close to what Taylor had discovered there. Studying or operating modern technical processes, Veblen concluded, awakens more fully than earlier forms of labor an urge for workmanlike efficiency. Unlike Taylor, however, Veblen would remove science and technology from the control of capitalism. Over the course of his life, he imagined a time when technicians, not business in pursuit of profits, would control production while labor, now freed of capitalist management, might seek highly polished workmanship.

Social Darwinism

The hypothesis developed by the nineteenth-century British scientist Charles Darwin as to the origins of the innumerable plant and animal species had an extraordinary influence not only on science but on the human imagination, including in the United States. Darwin, like other scientists, thought it likely that differing species that have survived came from some common life source. But investigators had not been able to answer the questions: how does change occur? How does one species gradually evolve into another? Darwin's answer was more satisfactory than any other. Within any species, Darwinists held, individuals differ slightly from one another in some trait that will contribute to survival: swiftness, intelligence, strength, ability to digest available food. Individuals lucky enough to be better off in one or more of these traits are the most likely to live to bear children. If their beneficial characteristic results from some quirk in their genetic makeup that will be transmitted to their offspring, then over many generations their descendants will constitute a new and dominant species. From this kind of explanation as Darwinists presented it came the popular notions that evolution is a reality and that it occurs within species by a struggle for survival.

The proposition that the human species is related biologically to other living forms and grew out of pre-human ancestors disturbed many Christians, but on the whole theologians found little to quarrel with. Christianity, they argued, is about the human species; how humankind came about is at the disposal of the divine will, and if evolution was the method, so be it. The idea that life is evolving into ever higher forms, a view often called Reform Darwinism, gave hope to some social critics and activists.

The explanation that evolution is the result of a process by which one individual survives and another dies off took its own course. Scientists were widely misunderstood to be claiming that individuals survive by killing or outdoing their rivals. But the survival of a sharp-clawed cat, for example, results not from some brutal triumph over another of its species, but simply by possessing a better means of staying alive. Yet concepts of a struggle for existence and survival of the fittest, terms that came soon into wide use, pleased theorists and ideologues of various sorts. Among political and economic conservatives, these ideas took a form known as Social Darwinism. It appealed to defenders of slash-and-burn capitalism, to nationalists seeing the country across the border as the enemy, and to imperialists seeking conquest of African or Asian peoples. A body of thought popular in American universities, at that time almost universally conservative institutions, held especially that economic progress comes of one industrialist's driving another to ruin.

Pragmatism

American scholars influenced by the sciences reexamined ways of defining truth. William James, a student of medicine who became a university professor, joined with other philosophers in developing a new way of understanding the truth of statements, whether scientific or everyday. A statement is true, James decided, insofar as an expectation it raises will prove out in concrete experience. Only if the predicted experience occurs can the statement be called true. This concept of truth, which came to be labeled "pragmatism," originated in the realm of philosophy. But the project of fitting language flex-

In his writings about how children should be educated, John Dewey influenced several generations of American teachers. (Courtesy, Library of Congress)

The Harvard philosopher and psychologist William James. (Courtesy, Library of Congress)

ibly to common life inspired reformers whose concern was with social problems. James lectured widely and reached popular as well as professional audiences. John Dewey, a younger philosopher essentially of the same school of thought, applied the pragmatic method to education. He argued for schooling that would teach pupils by giving them activities and investigations that make ideas spring to life.

The New England jurist Oliver Wendell Holmes, Jr., an aristocrat and combat veteran of the Civil War, applied to law a similar pragmatism. Holmes argued against reading law rigidly, as a reflection of a fixed natural law. The words of statutes, courts, and constitutions, Holmes contended, ultimately are no more than rough statements of public opinion attempting to find practical solutions to concrete problems. So understood, a constitutional passage should be interpreted not according to some abstract reading of its words but historically as an effort by its framers to solve some tangible difficulty. In 1905 the Supreme Court in *Lochner* v. *New York* threw out a New York State law limiting the hours of work of employees in the baking industry. The legislation, the majority held,

The photographer Jacob Riis posed this picture of homeless newsboys sleeping in an alley. The conditions he depicted were not inaccurate, but the photo is far from being a lucky snapshot. (Courtesy, The Jacob A. Riis Collection, #121. Museum of the City of New York)

violated the right of owners and workers to enter into a contract, a right that the justices believed to be implicitly protected by the Fourteenth Amendment. As an associate justice on the Court, Holmes dissented, finding that its arbitrarily narrow interpretation of the Constitution wrongly limited the power of the people to address a public issue though their state legislatures.

Art and Literature

Among artists who interpreted their industrial surroundings to the public were photographers. Far from presenting reality in an objective fashion, good photography involves personal, informed judgment. Alfred Stieglitz, Lewis Hine, and Jacob Riis, whose photographs of urban poverty may seem free of human bias, in reality pioneered in the use of staged images of social conditions. The newspaper boys photographed sleeping on a street no doubt represented children who had to spend their nights on the street, but photographic journalists did not hesitate to pose paperboys sleeping. Painting offered still greater freedom of investigation than photography. Early in the century the Ashcan School, centered in New York City's Greenwich Village, presented gritty scenes of city life that more traditional artists would have rejected. Experimental painters soon set about interpreting the world still more aggressively. The Brooklyn Bridge as John Marin captured it in dashes of color ceases to be a mere object for conveying traffic and becomes a thing of massed energies, perhaps as a physicist might view it.

Existence as rendered by leading writers, such as Theodore Dreiser in his portrayal in *The Titan* of the ruthless industrialist Frank Cowperwood, on the surface is reduced to crude formulations of Darwinism. Cowperwood takes what he wants from the world, and the impression in the novel is that he does so because the life force in him has a power of its own, and an insatiable hunger: the power and the hunger of some beast out of the evolutionary past who survives because he is the fittest.

A more subtle exploration of the forces that motivate conduct, however, is Stephen Crane's *The Red Badge of Courage,* published in 1895. Crane's young Union soldier Henry Fleming is initially depicted as subject to no more than biological drives. Animal fear sends him in flight from battle, ashamed but unable to go against his fear. Then, when guilt sends him back to the Union lines, a rush of primitive excitement impels him to grab a battle flag and lead his unit in a heroic assault against the rebel lines. So far, Fleming seems no more than a creature of biology that at first sends him into flight, then hurls him in aggression against the enemy. Yet the young soldier, facing his first hours of combat, has free will. He observes his own conduct and reflects upon it; painful self-recognition never completely disappears. Biology presses upon Fleming its conflicting impulses toward safety and toward aggression. But at the end of the battle, he has come to know himself and to be prepared, in the future, to act as reason and honor dictate. It is remarkable that Crane, whose composition of the novel drew wholly upon reminiscences of Union soldiers and other bits of secondary information, discovered soon afterwards as a war correspondent that he had gotten it right.

The Octopus, which Frank Norris published in 1901, achieves a different reconciliation of biology and human virtue. It presents a conflict between California wheat farmers and the railroad that makes them products of nature as much as the earth and grain themselves. Again, the first impression is of mindless biological energies. The wheat joins with hungry markets in calling into being the farms and the railroads. But by the end of the novel Norris has suggested that a positive force is in all of them, ultimately giving life to farmers and markets and golden wheat and bringing them to unity. In the seeming disorder of nature, Crane and Norris were finding meaning and deliverance.

Politicians and social critics meanwhile were seeking to tame the human world within the universe that Crane and Norris, James and the Darwinists sought to understand. Their efforts define much of the coming legislation of the new Progressive Era.

Suggested Readings

The Wobblies are chronicled in Patrick Renshaw, *The Wobblies: The Story of Syndicalism in the United States* (1967); Melvyn Dubofsky, *We Shall Be All: A History of the Industrial Workers of the World* (1969); and Joseph R. Conlin, *At the Point of Production: The Local History of the I.W.W.* (1981). Broader views of labor in the Progressive Era can be found in Bruno Ramirez, *When Workers Fight: The Politics of Industrial Relations in the Progressive Era, 1898–1916* (1978) and Gary M. Fink, *Labor's Search for Political Order: The Political Behavior of the Missouri Labor Movement, 1890–1940* (1973). For more on the Chicago that Upton Sinclair portrayed in his classic muckraking work *The Jungle* (1906), see James Barrett, *Work and Community in the Jungle: Chicago's Packinghouse Workers, 1894–1922* (1987).

A number of sophisticated monographs focusing on immigrants have appeared in recent years. Virginia Yans-McLaughlin, *Family and Community* (1977) and Robert Anthony Orsi, *The Madonna of 115th Street* (1985) focus on Italians in Buffalo and New York. Irving Howe, *World of Our Fathers* (1976) charts the journey of Eastern European Jews to America. Sucheng Chan, *This Bittersweet Soil* (1986) examines Chinese communities in California. Yuji Ichioka, *The Issei* (1988) looks at Japanese immigrants. On Poles, see Dominic Pacyga, *Polish Immigrants and Industrial Chicago* (1991). Mexican-American immigrants are the subject of a growing body of scholarship led by George L. Sanchez, *Becoming Mexican American: Ethnicity, Culture and Identity in Chicano Los Angeles, 1900–1945* (1993). Hasia R. Diner, *Erin's Daughters in America* (1983); Timothy J. Meagher, *Inventing Irish America* (2001) is an analytical narrative about the Irish of Worcester, Massachesetts, from 1880 through 1928; Susan A. Glenn, *Daughters of the Shtetl* (1990); and Doris Weatherford, *Foreign and Female* (1986) explore the struggle of immigrant women in America.

Ronald White extolled the social gospel movement's embrace of social democracy while criticizing its over-reliance on volunteerism and charity in *The Social Gospel: Religion and Reform in Changing America* (1976). The links between the social gospel and the subsequent movement for secular reform are explored in Robert M. Crunden, *Ministers of Reform: The Progressives' Achievement in American Civilization, 1889–1920* (1982) and Andrew C. Rieser, *The Chautauqua Movement: Protestants, Progressives, and the Origins of Modern Liberalism, 1874–1920* (2003). A more critical view comes from Susan Curtis, *A Consuming Faith: The Social Gospel and Modern American Culture* (1991).

The Progressive Era continues to spark contentious debate among historians. Progressives often cast themselves as a movement of "the people" against the "special interests." But historians today tend to view such phrases with skepticism. Ever since Richard Hofstadter's *The Age of Reform: From Bryan to FDR* (1955), which portrayed progressivism as an expression of middle-class "status anxiety" in a rapidly industrializing era, historians have tended to view the reformers as protectors of class authority. Gabriel Kolko, *The Triumph of Conservatism: A Reinterpretation of American History* (1963) and James Weinstein, *The Corporate Ideal in the Liberal State, 1900–1918* (1969) went a step farther and argued that so-called "progressive" reforms were really designed to stabilize a dangerously unstable economy and preserve corporate profits. Arthur Link and Richard L. McCormick counterbalance critical and sympathetic perspectives in *Progressivism* (1983).

Richard L. McCormick, *The Party Period and Public Policy* (1986) explores the roots of state reform, while David P. Thelen, *The New Citizenship: Origins of Progressivism in Wisconsin, 1885–1900* (1972) and *Robert M. La Follette and the Insurgent Spirit* (1976) are best on Wisconsin progressivism. The California scene is depicted in George E. Mowry, *The California Progressives* (1951) and Michael Kazin, *Barons of Labor: The San Francisco Building Trades and Union Power in the Progressive Era* (1987).

The new regulatory capitalism of the Progressive Era relied upon the authority of the expert, argues a number of historians who have explored the rise of professionalism in American. See Burton Bledstein, *The Culture of Professionalism: The Middle Class and the Development of Higher Education in America* (1976); Samuel Haber, *The Quest for Authority and Honor in the America Professions, 1750–1900* (1991). Academia's on-again, off-again relationship with political reform is the subject of Lawrence Veysey, *The Emergence of the American University* (1965); Mary O. Furner, *Advocacy and Objectivity: A Crisis in the Professionalization of American Social Science, 1865–1905* (1975); and Thomas L. Haskell, *The Emergence of Professional Social Science* (1977). James T. Kloppenberg, *Uncertain Victory: Social Democracy and Progressivism in European and American Thought, 1870–1920* (1986) and Daniel T. Rodgers, *Atlantic Crossings: Social Politics in a Progressive Age* (1998) argued that progressivism is best understood in the context of a broader shift towards pragmatism, social democracy, and state interventionism in North America and Europe. On the doctrine of scientific management, see Robert Kanigel, *The One Best Way: Frederick Winslow Taylor and the Enigma of Efficiency* (1997).

The Progressives' moral intolerance, reflected in anti-vice reform, is the subject of Mary Odem, *Delinquent Daughters: Protecting and Policing Adolescent Female Sexuality in the United States, 1885–1920* (1995). Women's refusal to remain trapped in traditional roles helped to shape public policy, argues Robyn Muncy, *Creating a Female Dominion in American Reform, 1890–1935* (1991); Theda Skocpol, *Protecting Soldiers and Mothers: The Political Origins of Social Policy in the United States* (1992); and Linda Gordon, *Pitied but Not Entitled: Single Mothers and the History of Welfare, 1890–1935* (1994). On the WCTU, see Ruth Bordin, *Women and Temperance* (1980). On woman suffrage, see Anne F. Scott and Andrew M. Scott, *One Half the People: The Fight for Woman Suffrage* (1975); Eleanor Flexner, *Century of Struggle: The Woman's Rights Movement in the United States*, rev. ed. (1975); and Aileen Kraditor, *The Ideas of the Woman Suffrage Movement, 1890–1920* (1965). Nancy F. Cott's *The Grounding of Modern Feminism* (1987) is an important study of the feminist movement's origins.

On the African-American struggle in the Progressive Era, consult John Hope Franklin and Alfred A. Moss Jr., *From Slavery to Freedom: A History of Negro Americans,* 7th ed. (1994). Excellent books on the formation of urban black communities in the North are Allan H. Spear, *Black Chicago: The Making of a Negro Ghetto, 1890–1920* (1967) and James R. Grossman, *Land of Hope: Chicago, Black Southerners, and the Great Migration* (1989). On the rise of a new black middle class, see Evelyn Brooks Higginbotham, *Righteous Discontent: The Women's Movement in the Black Baptist Church, 1880–1920* (1993). The campaign for anti-lynching laws and black civil rights in general is the subject of August Meier and Elliott Rudwick, *Along the Color Line: Explorations in the Black Experience* (1976); Louis R. Harlan, *Booker T. Washington: Wizard of Tuskegee, 1901–1915* (1983); David Levering Lewis, *W.E.B. DuBois: Biography of a Race, 1868–1919* (1993); and W. Fitzhugh Brundage, *Lynching in the New South: Georgia and Virginia, 1880–1930* (1993).

The scholarship on literary modernism and the rise of mass culture is especially deep and complex. Some of the more important titles include Larzer Ziff, *The American 1890s: Life and Times of a Lost Generation* (1966); Robert Sklar, *Movie-Made America: A Social History of the American Movies* (1975); T.J. Jackson Lears, *No Place of Grace: Antimodernism and the Transformation of American Culture, 1880–1920* (1981); Warren I. Susman, *Culture as History: The Transformation of American Society in the Twentieth Century* (1984); and William Leach, *Land of Desire: Merchants, Power, and the Rise of a New American Culture* (1993).

During 1903 a bearded John Muir, founder of the Sierra Club, and President Theodore Roosevelt camped out together for four days in Yosemite National Park. Muir persuaded Roosevelt to add considerable land to the forest system and national parks, but never managed to convince him to abandon his goal of preserving it for the economic use of later generations. Muir wanted perpetual preservation of American scenic wonders. *(Courtesy, Bettmann Archives)*

Progressive Empire and Progressive Reform

★

HETCH HETCHY

Flowing near San Francisco is the Tuolumne River. Spilling over a cliff, it once formed a waterfall that the wilderness champion John Muir praised for "the fineness and marvelous distinctness of the various sun-illumined fabrics into which the water is woven." Beneath lay the valley of Hetch Hetchy, its upper part nurturing pine and oak, its lower region a meadow rich in grass and flowers. In Hetch Hetchy the American land displayed itself in its splendor, sweeping and grand in the whole, precise and delicate in the fine sunlit threads of the waterfall and the sprinklings of flowers.

The praise of Hetch Hetchy came from another phenomenon of the young land. In the mid-nineteenth century John Muir as a Scottish boy had come to the United States. When old enough to take off on his own, he gravitated to great wild spaces, where God, he believed, is most fully known. While raising a family, Muir for part of the time lived off the unspoiled reaches of the Far West, studying their detail with a naturalist's eye and a lover's devotion. He had about him an air of grizzled eccentricity that went well with the country's vast disordered outdoors. Even as an old man he retained his Scottish accent together with a rough gray beard that drooped above his lank frame.

Sharing mutual admiration for the wilderness, Muir and the young patrician politician and adventurer Theodore Roosevelt became friends and went camping together in Yosemite National Park. Roosevelt as president of the United States after 1901 ranked among the leading political defenders of the nation's backlands, the cause to which Muir lent his ragged Scots voice. Yet Hetch Hetchy came to symbolize a fundamental difference between Muir's sensibility toward the land and that of Roosevelt and his government associates.

Certainly Roosevelt did much that must have given joy to his friend. As president, he protected huge tracts of land as forest preserves. At a time when the nation lacked anything close to a science of forestry, the aristocratic Gifford Pinchot had studied the field in Europe. Head of the Division of Forestry, renamed the Forest Service in 1905, Pinchot was Roosevelt's ally in conservation. Much of the purpose was to maintain for all time the wide outdoors that Roosevelt the champion of rugged living craved. Only William Clinton, the last president in the twentieth century,

The scenic wonder, Hetch Hetchy Valley, is shown here being flooded to provide water for the city of San Francisco. The illustration above is an anonymous painting of the valley before it was destroyed. (Courtesy, Wadsworth Atheneum, Hartford, CT)

would surpass TR's record in the acreage of wilderness lands preserved.

But however much the members of Roosevelt's administration wished to save wilderness lands for their sacred beauty and grandeur, they also favored putting the land to productive service. The Newlands Act of 1902, for example, established a Reclamation Service and set aside a portion of funds from the sale of public lands to apply to irrigation projects and dam construction. Roosevelt the conservationist was increasingly the advocate of major government intervention into the economy that would make all human, industrial, and natural resources instruments of human well being. That included a recognition of the enormous power for progress that inhered in the forests and the plains, the mines, the timber, the rushing water as these might join with industry, science, and labor to develop a human future. And finding a right balance between preserving nature in its pristine condition and conserving its resources to be carefully portioned out for industrial use embroiled Hetch Hetchy in a major dispute among defenders of the nation's wildlands.

The city of San Francisco needed water. Damming the river that flowed through Hetch Hetchy and flooding the valley would produce a reservoir to slake the city's thirst. Against the project, which Roosevelt's secretary of the interior James R. Garfield approved in 1908, Muir waged a campaign enlisting the methods now familiar to environmental and other advocates, including letters to federal officials. "Dam Hetch Hetchy!" he exclaimed. "As well dam for water-tanks the people's cathedrals and churches, for no holier temple has ever been consecrated by the heart of man." But Gifford Pinchot supported the dam. The "fundamental principle of the whole conservation policy is that of use," declared Pinchot, no longer chief forester, before a House committee in 1913 looking into the matter. It is "to take every part of the land and its resources and put it to that use in which it will best serve the most people." Muir would not have disagreed with that. Where he parted company with Pinchot, who declared that "Wilderness is waste," was over what constituted best service. For Muir, leaving the waterfall and the valley intact could best serve the public; it provided a magnificent soul-refreshing view. Though damming the river deprived the land of much of its treasure in beauty, Pinchot would have observed that the benefit to San Francisco was greater than that loss. Yet Muir turned out to be correct in claiming that the city could have gotten its water supply elsewhere; it does so today.

HISTORICAL EVENTS

1867
Purchase of Alaska

1871
Alabama claims settled

1890
Alfred Thayer Mahan, *The Influence of Sea Power on History*

1895
U.S. v. *E. C. Knight Company*

1898
Spanish-American War • annexation of Hawaii • United States purchases the Philippines from Spain

1899–1900
Open Door in China

1901
President William McKinley is assassinated • Theodore Roosevelt becomes president • Platt Amendment settles status of Cuba • J. P. Morgan creates U.S. Steel

1902
Newlands Act • Emilio Aguinaldo subdued in the Philippines

1903
Hay-Bunau-Varilla Treaty with Panama

1904
Northern Securities Company v. *United States*

1906
Hepburn Act • Pure Food and Drug Act

1908
Muller v. *Oregon* • William Howard Taft elected president

1910
Mann-Elkins Act

1912
Woodrow Wilson elected president

1913
Federal Reserve Act • Sixteenth Amendment (income tax) • Seventeenth Amendment (direct election of senators)

1914
Federal Trade Commission • Clayton Antitrust Act

1916
Wilson reelected president

EMPIRE

In the 1890s the United States began exchanging ambassadors with foreign nations. Up until then the highest diplomatic representatives the nation sent abroad had held only the humbler rank of minister. Ambassadors, Americans thought, represented a culture of titles and privilege, of pomp and show incompatible with republican simplicity. The decision to upgrade the diplomatic corps by the addition of an ambassadorial level seems no great matter. But it reflected a growing sense of the nation's presence in the world beyond its borders.

And the movement for the protection of wilderness played into that same mentality. A people great in their continental heritage, employing it to nurture their civilization and their industries, should be fit to seek commercial and political frontiers that stretched beyond the landed frontier of which the historian Frederick Jackson Turner announced the passing.

Acquisitions

In 1867 Secretary of State William Seward persuaded Russia to sell Alaska. This huge and valuable region evoked little enthusiasm at the time;

critics termed it "Seward's Icebox." Alaska was the last acquisition of the United States in its expansion across the continent. To aid American shipping in the Pacific, Seward had the United States take possession of the island of Midway the same year. The Senate rejected President Grant's treaty with Santo Domingo (today the Dominican Republic) that would have brought that republic into the United States. In 1898 the nation annexed Hawaii and another Pacific island, Guam. The next year Britain and Germany agreed to American possession of a portion of the Samoan Islands; the United States also picked up Wake Island. Along with Midway, Hawaii, Guam, Wake, and a scattering of other islands, these additions gave the country a grasp of much of the Pacific, tightened after the Spanish-American War of 1898 by American possession of the Philippines. In the Caribbean the United States also received Puerto Rico from Spain. Later Washington bought from Denmark the West Indian possessions now called the Virgin Islands. And in 1903 the new republic of Panama, just seceded from the South American country of Colombia in a coup supported by Washington, ceded a strip of territory that was to be used for building a canal across the thin neck separating the Atlantic from the Pacific.

Merely as increases in American territory, the new acquisitions did not differ from the nation's earlier expansion. But especially in the case of Panama and the Pacific islands, the intention differed a great deal. With the exception perhaps of the annexation of Hawaii, the purpose was no longer to pull outlying lands into a self-contained United States. Instead Washington was gathering outposts from which to launch commercial and, if necessary, military sorties into the wider world.

Americans Face Outward

That world had never been so remote from American notice as its history before the late nineteenth century might at first suggest. During the Civil War, Europe became a major concern for the United States. Charles Francis Adams, the American minister to Britain, had to do his best trying to keep the British government from allowing shipbuilders to construct raiders on orders from the Confederacy. At that he was unsuccessful, but at least Britain never went so far as to extend full diplomatic recognition to the Confederate states.

France too allowed the building of ships for the rebels. The extension of the French empire into Mexico brought complaints from Washington that France heeded only after the Civil War when under General Philip Sheridan an army now freed from civil conflict gathered at the Mexican border. For several years the Americans pressed claims against Great Britain for damage that Confederate raiders built there, notably the *Alabama*, had done to American sea commerce. In 1871 London agreed to international settlement, and the next year a commission awarded the Americans a sum lower than they had earlier demanded. Persuading the French to leave Mexico, and London to attend to the *Alabama* claims, amounted to cleaning up business left over from the Civil War. But the United States, enormously strengthened by the victory over secession and by a spectacular growth in industry, now had a stature that as a loosely joined republic tainted by the institution of slavery it had not previously enjoyed. Its larger purposes abroad now awaited defining and fulfillment.

The task had an early advocate in James G. Blaine, the late nineteenth-century secretary of state. Blaine's interest centered in Latin America, ever since the Monroe Doctrine a region of special concern to the United States and from late in the century onward the subject of increasing involvement by Washington.

Hundreds of years earlier, explorers had nurtured a dream of overcoming the obstacle that the American continent made to trade by sea between Europe and Asia. They looked for a Northwest Passage, a water route that they hoped lay to the north of the discovered parts of the continent. In the nineteenth century, the dream endured. But in place of discovering a Northwest Passage, visionaries now had a far more practical scheme. It was to build a canal across the Isthmus of Panama in Central America that interposed its slender width between the two great oceans. For a time a promising site seemed to be not Panama, then a part of the South American nation of Colombia, but Nicaragua, also in Central America. Under the Clayton-Bulwer Treaty of 1850 between Great Britain and Washington, each of the two nations pledged that it would not exclusively occupy an isthmian canal or ban nationals of the other country from use of it. Blaine was among Americans who did not like the treaty. The location of the proposed canal, wherever in Central America that might be, put it more in the sphere of interest

This interesting late nineteenth-century photograph shows a German American family proud of its ethnic past and its newer American identity. Patriotism, then and now, was a powerful sentiment. (Courtesy, American Heritage)

of the United States than in that of Britain. When as secretary of state under Garfield's presidency Blaine learned that Colombia, the owner of pencil-thin Panama, was testing the possibility of giving Europeans access to a canal route, Blaine unsuccessfully tried to get his country free of the Clayton-Bulwer Treaty.

Trouble anywhere on the American continent might tempt interference on the part of European countries, which since the time of the Monroe Doctrine in 1823 the United States had been determined to resist. And anything Washington might do in offering its good offices toward resolving quarrels among other American countries could extend its influence, to its own advantage as well as that of Latin America. Such considerations suggest a larger view of the relations between the United States and the outside world than had been typical of earlier administrations. Blaine, it seems, had that view.

In his first brief tenure in the office of secretary of state, appointed by the Republican president James A. Garfield in 1881, Blaine attempted fruitlessly to mediate a number of disputes between Latin American republics, among them a war that set Chile against Bolivia and Peru. He also invited American nations to a general conference to be held in 1882. His successor canceled the invitations. But at the time of the first administration of the Democrat Grover Cleveland, Congress authorized the president to call such a meeting. When the conference assembled in 1889, the administration was again in Republican hands and Blaine under President Benjamin Harrison had once more become secretary of state. The secretary failed to get the Latin American representatives to agree to establish a mechanism for the settling of disputes. But the meeting established a bureau that would later become the Pan-American Union, an agency for communication among American nations, including the United States.

President Cleveland in his second administration projected the concerns of the United States in Latin America. In a dispute over the boundary with British Guiana, Venezuela sought intervention on the part of the northern republic to bring about a settlement. Cleveland's administration attempted to arbitrate, but Britain shunned the effort. Thereupon Secretary of State Richard Olney sent to London a warning that British action against Venezuela would violate the Monroe Doctrine, which had declared the American continent off-limits to any extension of European power. Olney's note pointed quite arrogantly to the dominant position of the United States on the continent. When again the British rebuffed intervention by Washington, Cleveland announced that his country would have the duty of resisting, "by every means in its power," any British intrusion into territory that the United States had found to be Venezuelan. London, which had larger rivalries with Germany to attend to, submitted to a process of arbitration that found for the most part in favor of the British claims. In 1899 the whole matter was put to rest.

A War Wins an Empire

In 1890 the American admiral Alfred Thayer Mahan published *The Influence of Sea Power on History*. His subject was the British Empire, but the title suggests his argument: a strong naval force well deployed to protect colonies and the merchant marine is essential to national greatness. To the mind of imperialists the navy embodied empire, the physical presence of the United States on the high seas and in the ports of the wide world. That presence would protect American business. But industrial interests were not the only or even the chief promoters of economic and military expansion. Imperialists actually thought their role in global commerce would result in a benevolent empire along with power and dominance. In 1880 the United States navy ranked twelfth in the world; by 1900, the fleet ranked third. Seven years later the Great White Fleet, steel battleships painted white, would begin a voyage that President Theodore Roosevelt intended to impress the world, particularly Japan.

The most strident moment of American imperialism, in fact, had at its origins not lust for power but moral outrage over what Americans thought to be the cruelties of power abroad. In the 1890s Cuban revolutionaries engaged in a guerrilla war with Spain, which ruled over their island. Critics of the Spanish bestowed on General Valeriano Weyler of the occupying forces the nickname Butcher Weyler. Among the policies of the Spanish authorities was the gathering of islanders, bystanders as well as insurrectionists, into guarded camps where they could be neutralized: concentration camps, as such centers are now called. Hunger and sickness stalked the internees. Still, the tactic represented, for the future as well as its own times, the terrible character of wars in which an occupying force decides that it has to treat a whole population as the enemy. Only a few years afterward, the American military itself would employ the practice to put down an insurrection in the Philippines, acquired at the end of a war the United States had fought for the liberation of Cuba. But during the 1890s the practice of concentrating civilians under military supervision had the appearance of newly-invented brutality. Much of the public in the United States was in a fury over the conduct of the Spanish. War fervor ignited from paper kindling, reams of newspaper accounts particularly from the journals published by Joseph Pulitzer and William Randolph Hearst. These two were the most prominent contributors to the "yellow press," a sensationalist brand of popular journalism that Pulitzer would later abandon.

The rebels burned sugar fields and mills, calculating that the damage to economic interests in the United States would bring intervention. They also had good luck. The revolutionaries in Cuba got hold of a letter written by Dupuy de Lôme, the Spanish minister to the United States, and turned it over to Hearst's *New York Journal*, which published it with gusto. De Lôme described President McKinley as "weak and a bidder for the admiration of the crowd" and otherwise dismissed him as a shifty politician. McKinley, said the minister, was appeasing his party's jingoes. (The word, often used at the time to designate patriots seized with war lust, came from a popular British song: "We don't want to fight, but by jingo, if we do, we've got the ships, we've got the men, we've got the money too.") The letter unfairly characterized McKinley, who as a Civil War veteran had seen enough of the battlefield and had no taste for the war passions of the moment. Yet as a hesitant, retiring man, McKinley did not have the sway over public sentiment that would have equipped him to stand against the clamor for action against Spain. In the same month, February 1898, the rebels had even more good fortune. In Havana's harbor the United States ship *Maine* exploded and 260 died. To this day the cause of the disaster eludes historians; the consensus favors some accident. Jingoes at the time, though, had no doubt as to the responsible party. That Spain would have been unspeakably stupid to blow up the *Maine* and incite war with the powerful nation to the north did

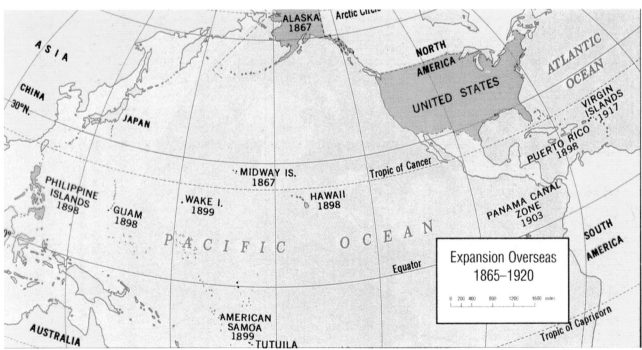

Expansionism swept from sea to sea, from the Philippine Islands in the far Pacific to Caribbean islands.

not bother the journalists who put out theory after conflicting theory about the disaster, all of them accusing the Spanish.

Spain did its best. Late in the preceding year, the government had recalled General Weyler and modified the detention camp program. After the release of his embarrassing letter, Dupuy de Lôme resigned. The McKinley administration, still hoping for peace, urged Spain to grant an armistice in Cuba, and the Spanish agreed. But in that impassioned year 1898, the public demanded war and got it. In April McKinley, before finding out about the Spanish concessions, gave in to popular pressure and called for intervention in Cuba. Congress passed a resolution recognizing the independence of the island, demanding Spanish withdrawal, and authorizing the use of the military by the president. It was

too much for Spain, which declared war on the United States.

At the time, Theodore Roosevelt was assistant secretary of the navy. But the young patrician for the moment deserted the navy for the army. In that day when gentlemen could get a military commission without undergoing any significant formal training, he was made a colonel. From among ranch hands, Indians, and the upper classes he recruited the Rough Riders. In Cuba Roosevelt led his storied charge over Kettle Hill and then on to San Juan Hill. In the Philippines, a Far Eastern cluster of islands, Admiral George Dewey on May 1 had steamed into Manila Bay and quickly defeated a Spanish fleet, turning that nation's ships into smoking hulls. In only a few months the war against Spain was over. Of over 5,400 American soldiers

William Randolph Hearst reports the calamity in his New York Journal, *February 17, 1898. (Courtesy, Columbia University Library)*

R. F. Zoogamy, Dewey at Manila. (Courtesy, Vermont State House, Montpelier, VT)

who died during the conflict or just after, fewer than four hundred perished in battle. Illness caused most of the remaining deaths in a war nearly as wretched in the military camp as in the field.

At a peace conference in Paris late in the year, Spain ceded Puerto Rico and Guam to the United States, and sold the Philippines to the Americans. Cuba won nominal freedom. The Teller Amendment to the war resolution had announced that the United States had no claim to control of the island, whose future would be up to its people. But at the end of the war the victorious troops administered Cuba for a period. And a military appropriations bill adopted by Congress in 1901 required the island to adopt as part of its constitution measures that compromised its sovereignty. One of them authorized the United States to intervene to protect Cuban independence and civil order; another had Cuba agree to sell or lease to the northern republic lands usable for naval or fueling stations. The provisions, known as the Platt Amendment, are contained in a treaty ratified by Cuba and the United States. Under a treaty signed in 1934, Washington renounced the insulting right to intervene in Cuba. But on into the twenty-first century the United States continued to maintain a base at Guantanamo Bay and would not consider relinquishing it to Cuba under Fidel Castro, at least not while relations between the two republics remained as bad as they were.

On the same August day in 1898 that Spain called for a cease-fire in Cuba, the republic of Hawaii abandoned its sovereignty and became a possession of the United States. That was exactly as the Americans on Hawaii wished who had overthrown the monarchy there and set up a republic. A decade later on Oahu in Hawaii, construction began on a naval base at Pearl Harbor, solidifying the claim of the United States to be a force to be reckoned with in the Pacific.

The question of whether to keep the Philippines raised a separate national debate. A number of prominent Americans opposed annexation of the islands. They included the philosopher William James and the industrialist Andrew Carnegie, whose denunciation of American brutality in the Philippines contrasts to the ruthlessness he had shown in his handling of relations with his workers. The local Filipino insurrectionists against Spain meanwhile found that they had to fight also against their American liberators. The conflict that followed, brutal by even the normal standards of warfare, ended in 1902 when the Filipinos, led by Emilio Aguinaldo, were subdued. Congress established a degree of local control, and under the governorship of William Howard Taft the islands were humanely administered. A 1935 law granted independence to come in about a decade.

The United States was now an imperial nation, not only possessing an empire of its own but projecting its force throughout the Pacific and the western Atlantic. The long military arm of American imperialism was the navy, exactly as Admiral Mahan had wished.

The Open Door

In 1899 John Hay, McKinley's secretary of state, spoke to other nations in a way that illustrates his country's expanded idea of its global place. He urged on them a policy toward China that is known as the Open Door, the principle that no nation would interfere in China with the trading rights there of any other country. Hay's purpose aimed at

In this political cartoon, competing imperial powers look on angrily as Uncle Sam hurtles into world affairs. (Courtesy, Prentice-Hall)

protecting what he hoped would be a profitable American commercial future in China. Though the Open Door implied a mild degree of respect for China's sovereignty and marginally assigned the United States a new role of guarding the rights of peoples outside the Western Hemisphere, its main assumption was that China would remain an area for Western exploitation. It projected not an equal relationship between a sovereign China and its trading partners but only a hope that the exploitation would be peaceable. Hay did not receive a clear assent among countries seeking advantages in Chinese trade. In 1900 American troops participated in an international intervention in China that put down an uprising by the Righteous Fists of Harmony, known in the West as the Boxers, whose aim was to drive foreign devils, so the Boxers called them, into the sea. The Open Door notes came at the same time that the United States was consolidating its grip on the Philippines. Nor did the China market work out. Businessmen were afraid to invest in an unstable country. Like many other dreams of American expansionists, this wish faded. It would take another century for commerce between China and the United States to become promising.

A year later, the American presidency went to a statesman fully prepared to live out the fullest possibilities of a nation that had become an imperial power.

THEODORE ROOSEVELT

When he goes to a wedding, his son said of Theodore Roosevelt, he wants to be the bride, and when he goes to a funeral he wants to be the corpse. The British ambassador once advised an acquaintance always to remember that the American president was about nine years old. He went in for strong opinions, at one time recommending shooting the Pullman strikers, and on a later occasion exclaiming, as president, "To hell with the Constitution when the people want coal." The conservative Republican House leader Joe Cannon sighed, "Roosevelt's got no more respect for the Constitution than a tomcat has for a marriage license."

Roosevelt demonstrated an extraordinarily boyish passion for life. As the offspring of an old land-

A FAIR FIELD AND NO FAVOR.
UNCLE SAM: "I'm out for commerce, not conquest."

The Open Door policy in China aimed to capture markets instead of colonies. (Courtesy, Special Collections, The University of Illinois at Chicago)

owning family going back to the time of Dutch possession of the colony that became New York State, he had an aristocrat's obligation to enter public service. In fragile health as a boy, he determined to master his own weaknesses. Committed as well to the intellectual life, he wrote, among other books, a study of the nation's westward expansion. For a time he ran a western ranch, and in that rugged country he had the pleasure of knocking down a bully at a saloon. In another career, he was police commissioner of New York City. And in yet another, he became assistant secretary of the navy. Then came his service in the war in Cuba. After winning election to the governorship of New York, the returning hero became vice president under William McKinley. For conservatives in the Republican Party that had been a way to get the unpredictable Roosevelt out of New York State.

Then in September 1901, McKinley was assassinated. McKinley's killer, his effort almost thwarted by the effort of an African American bystander to deflect the bullet, was revealed to be an anarchist. Thereupon a wave of popular rage erupted against revolutionary radicalism such as had followed the explosion in Chicago's Haymarket Square in 1886. The president's death ended a line of Union veterans of the Civil War who had become Chief Executive, their succession interrupted only twice, by Grover Cleveland. "Now look," complained the Republican boss Mark Hanna, "that damned cowboy is president of the United States."

The Rough Rider who ascended to the presidency brought to the office a boisterous, confidant energy such as it had likely never before contained. Just under forty-three years old when he took office so that he became the youngest president in American history, he crackled with restless energy. Apparently he did not choose to be addressed as "Teddy," but the public liked the term, naming teddy bears after him in honor of a bear cub he spared on a hunting trip. Roosevelt's ancestry, which made him as close to a titled aristocrat as the nation could produce, did not distance him from democratic politics. Combined with the physical and intellectual force that he cultivated, it made him fit for what he spontaneously sensed that the people wanted: leadership, full of drama and color. The White House, as the presidential mansion became known at the time, swelled with the enthusiasm its occupant gave to all his objectives. Guests

President Theodore Roosevelt's winning grin is caught in this photograph. (Courtesy, Library of Congress)

might include a Rough Rider, a poet, a wolf hunter, a Roman Catholic cardinal, or the cellist Pablo Casals, who played in the White House as he would for another president long after, John Fitzgerald Kennedy. And long after the country moved beyond his politics, Roosevelt would be known for his flashing teeth: gleaming in boisterous laughter or, as cartoonists would have it, clenched in angry determination.

It was appropriate for progressivism that Roosevelt was a Republican. While reform found adherents among Democrats, much of its energy came from within the Republican Party. Since the reform program involved setting limitations on the power of the wealthy and the corporations that Republican leaders in the House and Senate were quick to defend, the connections between progressivism and the GOP may seem puzzling. But the Republican Party from the time of its formation had supported far more than the Democrats the use of federal power for social and economic ends. In leading the cause of the Union against the Confederacy, the

THE WISCONSIN IDEA

During the tenure of Robert M. La Follette, who became Republican governor of Wisconsin in 1900, the state raised taxes on corporations, established a railroad-rate commission, enacted civil service reform, and restricted the workday for women and children. Wisconsin instituted direct primaries, in which voters rather than political leaders choose a party's candidates for the general election. Among the progressive reforms La Follette instituted was the initiative, under which voters by petition could offer a bill for legislative approval, and the use of the referendum, allowing a popular vote to decide the fate of a proposed measure, was extended. The electorate also gained the recall, the ability to remove officials before the end of their regular term. The governor urged the enactment of a state income tax to pay for progressive initiatives, and Wisconsin would become the first state to enact such a levy. In turning the University of Wisconsin into a research institution for the investigation of social and economic problems, La Follette's administration reflected a progressive's faith in the authority of experts.

All this suggests the range and diversity of projects that fall under the name of progressivism. The initiative, referendum, recall, and direct primaries widened opportunities for popular participation in government. So did the Seventeenth Amendment to the Constitution, ratified in 1913, which deprived state legislatures of the right to choose United States senators and substituted popular elections. Yet the research that La Follette's forces encouraged at the University of Wisconsin placed social policy in the hands of a few highly trained professionals, aloof from the brawl of democratic politics. The contradiction did not bother progressives. Both kinds of politics extended the possibilities for reform.

Though much of the Wisconsin brand of progressivism had precedents outside the state—Populists in South Dakota, for example, had already pressed for the initiative and referendum—La Follette and his state promoted reform so vigorously that their projects became known collectively as the Wisconsin Idea. In 1907 La Follette himself entered the United States Senate. By then his state had seeded innovations across the country. Progressivism, then, first initiated more reforms on the local and state level; but reformers increasingly contemplated the expansion of federal activity.

Governor Robert La Follette of Wisconsin (1901–1906). (Courtesy, State Historical Society of Wisconsin)

Plans circulating among reformers for pensions to the elderly ran up against the suspicion that they would turn into corrupt political patronage. Reformers also generally failed in their efforts to enact statewide minimum wage laws and limitations on the hours of work. Facing opposition from business and unable to gather massive labor support, they had little backing for their favorite proposals except that for employees injured at work. For social legislation, especially at the statewide level, success came in another guise. Reformers called on clubwomen to support legislation protecting their gender along with children at home and in the workplace. Many conservatives agreed with the conviction that women both needed protection as workers and deserved consideration as present or future mothers. In 1908, three years after the majority on the Supreme Court in the *Lochner* case ruled against New York State's legislation limiting hours of work for bakers, the justices in *Muller* v. *Oregon* upheld Oregon's law instituting a ten-hour daily ceiling on employment of women. The Court did not see itself as reversing *Lochner*; the justices were recognizing women as a distinctive category. The decision strengthened the case for special treatment of women and children. Statutes limiting the hours of particularly dangerous male employment also won the sympathy of the courts.

The states, then, were seedbeds of progressive reform. Notable reform governors included Albert Baird Cummins in Iowa, Joseph Folk in Missouri, Jeff Davis in Arkansas, Hiram Johnson in California, Hoke Smith in Georgia, Charles Evans Hughes in New York, and Woodrow Wil-

The lawyer Louis D. Brandeis, later appointed to the Supreme Court by President Woodrow Wilson, used statistical data about labor conditions to argue successfully in behalf of the state of Oregon in Muller v. Oregon, *1908. (Courtesy, The Granger Collection)*

son in New Jersey. In Denver, Colorado, Judge Ben Lindsay treated children not as criminals but as victims of their environment, pressing for vocational education, playgrounds, and social settlement houses. Most if not all of these reformers expressed gratitude to La Follette.

Republicans defined the national government as supreme over the states. The federal abolition of slavery overthrew a major social institution. The protective tariff, homestead acts providing for the settlement of the West, and land grants to railroads all identified the Republicans as the party of government and the aggressive promoter of the national economy. Much of progressivism, moreover, contemplated not breaking up the great corporations but controlling them for the common benefit. In these ways the Republican Party was a more log-

ical advocate of reform than the Democrats, the party of states' rights and limitation of governmental power.

Toward National Progressivism

In 1898 there existed only eighty-two relatively small trusts, financial organizations that through a series of mergers and acquisitions presided over great sections of the economy. John D. Rockefeller had pioneered the concept by establishing Standard

Oil in 1882. Andrew Carnegie, the railroad tycoon Jay Gould, and the investment banker J. P. Morgan used the trust to crush their competition. By 1904, 318 of these large combinations dominated the railroad, meatpacking, steel, tobacco, and petroleum industries. In 1901 Morgan created United States Steel, the nation's first billion dollar corporation. Soon just one percent of all the industrial firms in the country were producing almost half of the nation's manufactured goods. Thomas Nast, the late nineteenth-century political cartoonist, inflamed the public against large combinations with caricatures of powerful industrialists controlling everything from corn to Congress. In 1895 the Supreme Court, in the case of *U.S.* v. *E. C. Knight Company*, stripped the Sherman Antitrust Act of much of its power. The decision ruled that "the fact that an article is manufactured for export to another state does not of itself make it an article of interstate commerce" and so within the purview of the federal government.

J. P. Morgan, also in 1901, formed the four hundred million dollar Northern Securities Trust, a holding company—that is, a company that controlled large blocks of the stocks of several other firms—embracing much of the rail traffic in the Northwest. The new president soon took action on this "absolutely vital question." He decided to prosecute Northern Securities, which included such formidable industrialists as John D. Rockefeller and Edward Harriman, as a monopoly outlawed by the Sherman Act. A popular account has Morgan act toward the government as though he and it were on a par, proposing to Roosevelt that "my man"—Morgan's lawyer—get together with the president's "man"—Philander G. Knox, the nation's attorney general—and work something out. But Roosevelt, keenly aware of the dignity and power of the federal government, was not interested in Morgan's proposed negotiations. In 1904 the Supreme Court in *Northern Securities Company* v. *United States* upheld the government's action by a vote of five to four. The president, now known as a trustbuster, forced Congress to agree to establish a Bureau of Corporations empowered to investigate corporate activities, placing it in the new Department of Commerce and Labor. Under Roosevelt the executive department filed forty-three more antitrust suits. The year before the president had signed the Elkins Act, increasing the authority of the Interstate Commerce Commission and prohibiting railroads from giving

J. P. Morgan photographed by Edward Steichen. Morgan once announced: "I'm not in Wall Street for my health." (Courtesy, George Eastman House, Rochester, New York)

large shippers rebates on freight charges. The act had the support of railroads, whose primary customers had forced them to provide the rebates.

In May 1902 the United Mine Workers under John Mitchell began an anthracite coal strike in pursuit of higher wages. The owners, led by George F. Baer, refused to negotiate. The standoff threatened to subject the East to a winter of dwindling supplies for heating once the coal cars stopped rumbling over the Pennsylvania hills. New York schools closed for lack of heat. Angered by the stubborn arrogance of the owners, Roosevelt called both parties to the White House, where he threatened to throw the "insolent" Baer out of the window and, only a little less alarmingly, to use the military to seize the mines. Baer, who insisted that the miners "don't suffer; why, they can't even speak English," once remarked that "God in his infinite wisdom" had appointed the coal owners to their posts. The president subsequently appointed an arbitration commission to resolve the dispute, and eventually both sides submitted to the commission's judgment that the workers receive a wage hike and have limits set on their working hours. The operators, however, still refused to recognize the union. The commission also permitted them to raise the price of coal, passing on to consumers at least a portion of the wage increase. Yet the strike ended with a qualified victory for the mine workers and a heightened profile for Roosevelt and the federal government as a force that business must reckon with in its dealings with labor and the public interest.

The Square Deal

In 1904 Roosevelt, who so far had served as the successor to the assassinated President McKinley, became the Republican candidate seeking the office on his own merits. In the course of the campaign, he explained that in the coal strike he had sought a square deal for both sides. "Square Deal" caught on as a label for his program. So was born the first of the presidential Deals: "New Deal" would later encompass the policies of Theodore Roosevelt's Democratic distant cousin Franklin D. Roosevelt and "Fair Deal" the programs of FDR's successor Harry S Truman.

The expression in itself revealed little about the actual direction Roosevelt would take; it merely signified the president's wish to treat everyone fairly. That is not a fighting program. Over the next four years, Roosevelt defined more explicitly, though not in a fully coherent way, how government might achieve his developing concept of a just society.

After his election Roosevelt, pressing into the service of progressivism a Congress controlled by Republicans, responded to agricultural interests in the West and Middle West seeking relief from arbitrary railroad rates. Threatening the Senate with lowering the tariff on imported manufactured goods, the president won passage in 1906 of the Hepburn Act, which gave the Interstate Commerce Commission the power to set maximum railroad rates on the complaint of a shipper. Before setting the rates, the ICC could also examine a railroad's books and prescribe accounting standards in order to establish a railroad's value. For the first time, the government could open a company's books for the sake of setting rates.

The Pure Food and Drug Law, which passed the same year, was much indebted to the urgings of Dr. Harvey W. Wiley, the chief chemist of the Department of Agriculture. Wiley demanded federal reg-

ulation of the food processing and drug manufacturing industries. At a time when physicians and sellers of Coca Cola were widely promoting cocaine as a tonic and a curative, even for hay fever, policing the drug industry was very good medicine. A separate law compelling meat inspection owed much to Upton Sinclair's muckraking novel *The Jungle*. In the course of attacking the injustices the Chicago meatpacking industry inflicted on its workers, Sin-

Many tonics contained cocaine and other narcotics or large percentages of alcohol. One advertised that "it feels like a ball of fire going up and down your throat." (Courtesy, University of Virginia Library)

clair's book exposed the nauseating conditions on the packinghouse floor. He wrote:

> There was never the least attention paid to what was cut up for sausage; there would come all the way back from Europe old sausage that had been rejected, and that was moldy and white— it would be doused with borax and glycerin, dumped into the hoppers, and made over again for home consumption. There would be meat that had tumbled out on the floor, in the dirt and sawdust, where the workers had stamped and spit uncounted billions of consumption germs. There would be meat stored in great piles in rooms and the water from leaky roofs would drip over it, and thousands of rats would race about on it. It was too dark in these storage places to see well, but a man could run his hand over these piles of meat and sweep off handfuls of the dried dung of rats. These rats were nuisances, and the packers would put poisoned bread out for them; they would die, and then rats, bread, and meat would go into the hoppers together. . . . There was no place for the men to wash their hands before they ate their dinner, and so they made a practice of washing them in the water that was to be ladled into the sausage.

The resulting disgust inspired the novelist's comment that he had aimed at the public's heart and hit it in the stomach.

The president also urged but did not get restrictions on child labor as well as a system of federal incorporation of businesses engaged in interstate commerce, which would allow for more closely monitoring them. But incorporation remained under the

In this book published in 1906, Upton Sinclair exposed abuses in the Chicago meatpacking industry. (Courtesy, SUNY at New Paltz Library)

jurisdiction of individual states. Roosevelt wanted a constitutional amendment making possible a graduated tax on income. The Sixteenth Amendment would come in 1913, several years after he left office.

Yet Roosevelt was no archenemy of business. In an arrangement in 1907 that called on J. P. Morgan to calm a financial panic, the president allowed Morgan's United States Steel to take over the Tennessee Coal and Iron Company. This enormous extension of corporate power appeared to violate antitrust law. By the end of his second term, Roosevelt had not yet shaped an ideology reaching clearly beyond the broad general intention of playing square with everyone.

AN IMPERIAL PRESIDENT AND NATION

The restless Roosevelt could be no other than an imperialist. He savored power: power over whatever weakness he detected in himself, power of the federal government, the gathered power of the industry and labor and natural resources of the United States put to productive achievements. In Cuba during the encounter with a weakened Spain, he had gained enough experience in a relatively easy war to sharpen a taste for combat but not enough to recoil from its horrors. The language and the fantasies of warlike confrontation came easily to him. Yet despite his blusterings about military virtues, he had sufficient humanity and intelligence to recognize the superiority of negotiation to war. And negotiation, if shrewdly promoted by the United States, could enlarge the nation's global reach.

The Panama Canal

In the Hay-Pauncefote Treaty of 1901, Great Britain gave the United States the sole right to build and fortify a Central American canal, provided that other nations also have use of it. Washington then had to decide what would be the better route. Nicaragua had the advantage of offering passage across land at water level so that no locks would have to be built. Panama, then a part of the South American country of Colombia, consisted of a narrower strip of land. The solution was not so much technical as political. Nicaragua turned out to be too tough to bargain with. So did Colombia. But Panamanians wished to break away from Colombia in return for a canal deal with the United States. In 1903 a revolution in Panama succeeded with the aid of Colombian military officers willing to surrender for money. The presence of the United States navy further insured that Colombia would not intercede. It took Washington exactly one hour and sixteen minutes to recognize the new government. The new Panamanian republic signed the Hay-Bunau-Varilla Treaty granting the United States a strip of territory for the building of a canal in return for an initial payment and annual fees. Philippe Bunau-Varilla, Panama's new minister to Washington, had long been involved with transferring a canal venture to the United States.

A favorite saying of Roosevelt he took from an African admonition: talk softly and carry a big stick. A huge club ready to wield became a part of the cartoon portrayal of TR. The club had been in evidence throughout the Panama business, which the president claimed to have conducted "without the aid and advice of anyone," though his secretary of state, John Hay, had his name on the treaty with Panama. The president, demonstrating the racist streak that permeated the Progressive Era, had earlier fulminated about "those contemptible little creatures in Bogotá [Colombia's capital]." Negotiating with these "dagos," he said, was "like trying to nail currant jelly to the wall." After the understanding with the Panamanians, which included tens of thousands of dollars to high ranking military officials, Roosevelt declared that the process had been carried out "with the highest, finest, and nicest standards of public and governmental ethics." Payment of twenty-five million dollars to Colombia in 1921 said otherwise. Meanwhile, the Panama Canal, a magnificent feat of engineering opened to ship traffic in 1914, shortened the voyage between two oceans to a distance of little more than twenty miles.

The Roosevelt Corollary to the Monroe Doctrine

Since the announcement of the Monroe Doctrine in 1823, the United States had assumed the right to insure that European nations not attempt to carve out imperial domains in the Western Hemisphere beyond the few that already remained to them. Early in the twentieth century, several European countries threatened military force to collect debts owed them by various countries in the Americas. In a message to Congress, Roosevelt declared that the United States would act on its own to bring about the satisfaction of European claims: "The United States cannot see any European power occupy the territory of the Latin American republic, not even if this is the only way to collect its debts." Washington would act as an "international police power" in the event of "flagrant wrongdoing in the Western Hemisphere." The president had in mind especially a confrontation brewing over Santo Domingo. Some British and United States citizens had seized customhouses after the local government negotiated a repayment scheme not to their liking. Soon after, Roosevelt had marines occupy the country, and the Dominican regime agreed to allow customs receipts to be handled by a United States official who in turn would pay European claims. The American navy was also to enforce the arrangement and in the president's words "keep the island in the status quo." Americans would return from 1916 to 1924 to quell local opposition toward their intervention. In itself, the Roosevelt Corollary to the Monroe Doctrine seemed of limited scope, the assumption merely of a right to intervene in Latin America if international finances became an issue. Its larger implication, however, gave the United States the privilege of interfering, militarily if necessary, whenever conditions anywhere south of its borders were displeasing to Washington.

Roosevelt the Peacemaker

Entranced with navies, wars, and American power, Theodore Roosevelt comes down in American history as a perpetually excitable child. Even late in the twentieth century, his flashing teeth and the flamboyant uniform he had made up for himself as a Rough Rider continued to be fodder for cartoonists. And one incident connected with his name remains, at least by modern standards, worse than juvenile. After a racial clash in 1906 between the town's whites and some segregated black army troops stationed at Brownsville in Texas, Roosevelt, following a report from his war department, made no attempt to distinguish between the guilty and the innocent. Instead, he gave dishonorable discharges to all members of three black companies. In 1972 Congress would do its best to make amends; it granted honorable discharges in memory of the troops. Earlier in his presidency, Roosevelt had made a mild gesture of courtesy that broke with the social practices of the time, casually inviting Booker T. Washington to lunch with him at the White House. For a president then to share a meal with a black American meant something but, as TR's response to the Brownsville incident demonstrates, not a lot.

The president nevertheless also understood the mature uses of power, governmental authority, and diplomacy, and he was charming and clever enough to be an excellent arbitrator. To Portsmouth, New Hampshire, in 1905 he invited representatives of Japan and Russia, then at war. Japan had been firm-

ing its hold on nearby Korea as a prelude to domin-ion over East Asia. Russian activities in the same country and in nearby Manchuria had triggered a war between the two emerging imperial powers. In 1904 Japan's navy destroyed Russia's Far Eastern squadron with a surprise attack, a technique the Japanese would employ with some success thirty-seven years later at Pearl Harbor. Admiral Togo quickly annihilated the rest of Russia's fleet. Though victorious, Japan teetered on bankruptcy. Yet Roosevelt worried that Japan might close the Open Door in China and threaten American impe-rial possessions in the Pacific.

Out of the peace conference came the Treaty of

DINNER GIVEN AT THE WHITE HOUSE BY PRESIDENT ROOSEVELT TO BOOKER T. WASHINGTON, OCTOBER 17th, 1901

Booker T. Washington and Theodore Roosevelt dine at the White House—When Theodore Roosevelt invited Booker T. Washington in 1901, he stirred up a hornet's nest of controversy that continued into the election of 1904. Here in a Republican campaign piece, the meeting is portrayed positively, with TR and Washington pictured under a portrait of Abraham Lincoln, signaling the party's historic commitment to African Americans. Democrats portrayed the meeting in a very different light: their campaign buttons pictured Washington with darker skin and implied that Roosevelt favored "race mingling." (Courtesy, Collection of Janice L. and David J. Frent)

Portsmouth, essentially sealing a Japanese victory. Roosevelt, for all his bluster, had an unusual ability to get along with the proud Japanese nation. At a time when many Americans behaved as though only the white race could be capable of any serious feeling, Roosevelt understood Japan's resentment over American hostility toward Japanese immigrants in California. In 1907 and 1908 he and the Japanese government worked out what is remembered as the Gentlemen's Agreement. The president persuaded the San Francisco school board to drop an order segregating Japanese and other Asian students, and Japan agreed to restrict immigration to the United States. In achieving a civil and courteous solution to a situation brought about by American racial prejudice, Roosevelt displayed faculties of skill and tact. In 1908 Secretary of State Elihu Root gave the president still another diplomatic success. In the Root-Takahira Agreement between Japan and the United States, each promised to abide by existing conditions in the Pacific and not interfere with the possessions of the other in the region. Japan ratified the Open Door policy, and the two nations pledged to protect by peaceful means the independence of China. Japan's interpretation of the agreement as American recognition of Japanese imperial interests in Korea and Manchuria effectively compromised the respect for the sovereignty of China that the pact declared.

In another display of impressive presidential peacemaking diplomacy when France and Germany seemed to be moving toward war over conflicting interests in Morocco, Roosevelt got both to attend a conference at Algeciras, a resort in southern Spain. France and Britain had already worked out an agreement that eventually ripened into an alliance. They settled disputes over territories in Africa by awarding protectorates to each other. The British gained control of Egypt; the French got Morocco. But Germany, too, hungered for a slice of the continents that were now getting quickly divided. Kaiser Wilhelm called for an open door in Morocco and hinted that any delay could bring war with the French. Amid American flattery of each side, the two in 1905 came to an agreement favorable to France. Roosevelt had contributed in an impressive way toward maintaining peace. The French writer André Tardieu wrote favorably: "The United States intervenes . . . in the affairs of the universe. . . . It is seated at the table where the great game is played." For his peacemaking accomplishments in Asia and

Europe, Roosevelt in 1906 received the Nobel Peace Prize, mainly for his arbitration between Japan and Russia.

PROGRESSIVISM AT ODDS WITH ITSELF

Early in 1908 Theodore Roosevelt endorsed compensation laws for injured workers and a tax on inheritances of great wealth. The Inheritance Tax, which became law in 1913, was to receive the approbation of both political parties and two presidents named Roosevelt. President Franklin Roosevelt in 1935 would declare: "the transmission from generation to generation of vast fortunes by will, inheritance or gift is not consistent with the ideals and sentiments of the American people." In the early twenty-first century, Theodore Roosevelt's Republican successors attempted to repeal the tax outright.

In the election of 1908 the Republicans chose as their presidential candidate William Howard Taft, then known to be loyal to Roosevelt and his policies. "If only there were three of you!" TR once exclaimed to his three-hundred-pound secretary of war. Widely defined later as conservative, Taft pursued a careful progressivism that relied on law rather than on dramatic executive action. Even more vigorous than Roosevelt in prosecuting trusts, Taft in bringing legal action against the absorption of Tennessee Coal and Iron by United States Steel provoked the anger of his predecessor, who had assented to the deal. Taft's administration supported legislation enforcing safety standards for railroad workers, a bill requiring railroads to insure their employees against accidents, and a law making it easier for workers to hold employers liable for injuries sustained on the job. Still, at the end of his presidency the United States suffered the highest rate of industrial accidents in the world. The Mann-Elkins Act of 1910 enabled the Interstate Commerce Commission to initiate rate changes and to regulate telephone, telegraph, cable, and similar companies. It also placed the burden of proof on railroads to prove that a rate increase was deserved. The conservationist Taft was as committed as his predecessor to setting aside forestlands. Taft also backed a bill that created the Children's Bureau, to which he appointed as head a veteran labor re-

A man of great girth, President William Howard Taft, it was said, rose from his seat in a streetcar and offered it to three ladies. (Courtesy, National Portrait Gallery, The Smithsonian Institution)

former, Julia Lathrop—the first woman to be made head of a government bureau. Like Roosevelt, he belonged among the legions of Americans who knew that the time had come for an income tax amendment to the Constitution. He also signed the Payne-Aldrich tariff of 1910, a protective measure of a kind embraced by both conservative Republicans and some progressives.

Yet Taft and Roosevelt became enemies. Taft's prosecution of United States Steel for an arrangement that TR had assented to fed the quarrel. More serious was Taft's mishandling of a disagreement between his secretary of the interior Richard A. Ballinger and Roosevelt's friend and chief forester Gifford Pinchot, whom Taft had kept on in his administration. Even though President Taft had compiled a good record in conservation, Pinchot, following the lead of the Interior Department's field worker Louis R. Glavis, accused Ballinger of being too quick to sell public lands and waterpower sites. Taft took the side of Ballinger, eventually dismiss-

ing Pinchot. Roosevelt conferred with Pinchot and Senator Robert La Follette, Taft's worst enemies.

The New Nationalism

While Roosevelt traveled on safari in Africa, a book caught his imagination. Herbert Croly's *The Promise of American Life* called for abandoning the traditional American distrust of economic and governmental consolidation. The future of democracy, Croly claimed, lay in the government's giving direction to the country's growing productive energies. Activist government coordinating and mediating the efforts of the nation's workers and businesses would give capitalism a higher purpose than that of private wealth. In a speech at Osawatomie, Kansas, in 1910, Roosevelt articulated that concept, soon called the New Nationalism. "The national government," he wrote, "belongs to the whole American people, and when the whole American people are interested, that interest can be guarded effectively only by the national government." Rather than dissolve trusts, Roosevelt's ideology would embrace them insofar as under strict federal regulation they gave structure and order to American society. Taft remarked in dismay that the speech "frightened every lawyer in the United States" and began identifying himself as a conservative.

Dollar Diplomacy

Toward Latin America the policies of the Taft administration followed the questionable initiatives of the preceding decade. After some fruitless bargaining with the Chinese government, Washington promoted the nation's economic ambitions in the Western Hemisphere. The idea was for American bankers to invest in Central America in order to promote stable government, if necessary with the aid of military force. To Honduras and Nicaragua Taft's administration sent troops to support political factions friendly to the business interests of the United States. When Nicaragua executed two men caught dynamiting ships in the San Juan River, Taft sent 2,700 marines to "keep order." Under Taft business corporations treated the Caribbean virtually as though their country owned it. The United Fruit Company owned dozens of huge banana plantations in Central America along with railroads that transported the crop to the sea. The American Sugar Refining Company was equally dominant in Cuba.

These companies, of course, wanted governments in power that would protect their economic interests. This aggressive service to the nation's capitalist enterprises, which became known as Dollar Diplomacy, foreshadowed a troubled future for the hemisphere.

Woodrow Wilson, the New Freedom, and the Election of 1912

One Democrat, formerly a president of Princeton University elected governor of New Jersey in 1910, was prepared two years later to take his progressive convictions to the White House. Woodrow Wilson, in 1912 his party's presidential nominee, placed himself in the wing of progressivism that instead of adopting Roosevelt's New Nationalism remained loyal to the idea of trust busting. He elected for what he called the New Freedom, which contemplated the liberation of labor and small business from domination by monopolies. Wilson was a Virginian, a native of a South still nursing resentment toward the national government that had destroyed the Confederacy. His party, deeply rooted in white southern politics, was the logical vehicle for a federal program that instead of consolidating power would dismantle it.

At the 1912 Republican nominating convention, party regulars saw to it that in disputed state delegations the Taft forces were consistently chosen. That assured Taft's renomination. Republicans sharing Roosevelt's convictions, or simply drawn to the compelling drama of the Rough Rider himself, thereupon formed the Progressive Party, selecting Roosevelt as its nominee. From his proclamation to the party's founding convention that he felt as strong as a bull moose in rutting season, the Progressives became known as the Bull Moose Party. The party platform called for woman suffrage, the initiative and the referendum on a state level, and the adoption of a constitutional amendment providing for the direct election of senators. Its social and economic policies included restrictions on child labor, limitation on court injunctions against labor unions, an extensive federal regulation of commerce and industry, and an amendment already under consideration allowing for a federal income tax.

In 1912 as well, a fourth political party made a visible dent. The American public, though generally wary of radical ideas, had not yet been conditioned to shudder at the word "socialism," and in at

PASS PROSPERITY AROUND

On accepting the nomination of the Progressive Party in 1912, Theodore Roosevelt announced "I feel as strong as a Bull Moose. . . ." Here the moose occupies a greater portion of the picture than do TR and his running mate, the progressive California governor, Hiram Johnson. (Courtesy, Collection of Janice L. and David J. Front)

least a few states socialists constituted an important presence. In November, their candidate Eugene V. Debs won over nine hundred thousand votes, slightly under six percent of the nationwide total. Roosevelt got a little more than a fourth of the popular vote, and Taft less than a quarter. Wilson, collecting just under forty-two percent of the vote, captured a huge majority in the Electoral College. The Democrats, having already won the House of Representatives in 1910, now gained control of the Senate.

WOODROW WILSON'S PROGRAM

Wilson, an accomplished orator, brought to the presidency his southern racist background and a stubborn streak characteristic of his father, a Presbyterian minister. From his education, which included a doctorate from Johns Hopkins University, he derived a liking for British institutions, particularly the open debate practiced in the British Parliament. Like Theodore Roosevelt a believer in Anglo-Saxon superiority, he criticized what he termed the mongrel races of southern and eastern Europe. In his inaugural address he proposed reform of the currency and banking system as well as the tariff and regulation of industry. This president, too, was in most of his actions an ardent conservationist.

The New Freedom Becomes a New Centralization

Wilson's most impressive domestic reform he aimed at the "money trust," and he kept Congress in session through the summer of 1913 to obtain it. The Federal Reserve Act established a system of twelve banks, these to be under the control of a Federal Reserve Board, that made for greater flexibility in the issuance of currency and in the supply of bank loans to individuals and businesses. The legislation was not radical except for taking control of currency away from Wall Street, but its high reputation convinced investors in the next decade that it protected the stock market. On a few issues, the new Wilson administration carried out his principle of the New Freedom. In 1913, the president signed the Underwood Tariff, which in lowering rates substituted a measure of free market theory for governmental controls. The Federal Trade Commission, set up in 1914, was given limited powers to halt business practices the FTC found to interfere with fair competition. The Clayton Antitrust Act of the same year increased federal power to break trusts that in theory stifled economic freedom. It held company officials liable for actions. But in general, the administration's policies remained considerably more in line with the concentration of power that Roosevelt advocated than with the dismantling of trusts that Wilson as a presidential candidate had favored.

Ratified in 1913, the Sixteenth Amendment allowing a federal tax scaled to income had Wilson's support and also that of many of his political opponents. To compensate for the shrinking of tariff revenues, Congress enacted the first federal personal income tax. It levied an amount no more than seven percent, and only from the rich. A provision of the 1914 Clayton Act partially exempted unions and farm cooperatives from antitrust prosecution, limited the use of court injunctions against labor actions, and confirmed the right of labor to strike, picket, and boycott. In the same year the Federal Farm Loan Act, working through twelve regional farm boards, provided loans to farmers at low interest rates. The La Follette Seaman's Act of 1915 established better working conditions in the merchant marine. The next year Wilson signed the Adamson Act, setting an eight-hour day for railroad workers. A new law provided a workmen's compensation program for federal employees. And the Wilson administration followed Taft's in legislating for children, a major concern especially among progressive women.

During the progressive period several states enacted legislation setting for women minimum wages and maximum hours of work. And making an exception to the widespread prejudice against pensions, a number of state laws provided limited financial support for mothers who could not get by. Such pensions often brought visits from social workers. Mixing supervision with advice, that practice accorded with the growing belief that professionals could bring expert knowledge to the general public. The Keating-Owen Act of 1916 forbidding the interstate transportation of products of child labor was a major piece of progressive reform: major enough that two years later the Supreme Court in *Hammer* v. *Dagenhart* declared the law to be an unconstitutional expansion of congressional authority over interstate commerce.

Wilson and the Western Hemisphere

By the time Wilson assumed the presidency the United States had accorded itself the right to interfere in the internal affairs of other nations in the Western Hemisphere. Wilson made it clearer. He continued the intervention in Nicaragua; and with the backing of United States troops, Washington essentially governed Haiti and Santo Domingo. Wilson, however, conceived of foreign policy less for its benefits to capitalism than as an exercise in the conduct and teaching of morality. This belief particularly underscored his public pronouncements and his actions toward Mexico.

A dictator, Porfirio Díaz, had ruled Mexico since 1876. When he retired, power fell into the hands of

Pancho Villa, standing third from the right, poses with some of his heavily armed rebel leaders. (Courtesy, Brown Brothers)

Francisco Madero, a man too cautious to give direction to an emerging revolution. Regional leaders, such as Emiliano Zapata and Pancho Villa, assembled armies to the south and north of Mexico City. Investors from the United States worried over government plans to redistribute land, appealed for help, as did the Roman Catholic Church. Taking a moralist's dislike to the subsequent military government of Victoriano Huerta, who had murdered Madero, Wilson explained that the United States would not have dealings with regimes based on "irregular force" rather than law. He evidently failed to consider how very many governments a strict application of that principle would require Washington to shun. A minor incident involving the arrest of sailors who had wandered into a section of Tampico designated off limits to them gave Wilson an excuse to occupy the nearby Mexican port of Veracruz, where streetfighting killed sixty soldiers and some five hundred Mexicans. That sufficiently humiliated and undermined Huerta's government that Venustiano Carranza, another middle-class reformer, took over. But relations between Mexico and Washington continued sour. In 1916 the anti-

clerical Pancho Villa murdered sixteen United States citizens traveling in Mexico. He then raided the New Mexico town of Columbus, killing several more. His apparent objective was to provoke another intervention from the United States that would destabilize Mexico and bring an end to Carranza's regime. Villa got the invasion. United States troops, 6,600 strong, under General John J. Pershing crossed the border and chased Villa's forces around Mexico. About 150,000 National Guard troops sealed off the entire southwestern border. But Carranza did not fall, and early in 1917 Wilson withdrew the troops. His policy toward Mexico had accomplished nothing beyond sowing bad feelings toward the United States.

The Election of 1916

In 1916 Wilson ran for reelection against Charles Evans Hughes, a former governor of New York and an associate justice on the Supreme Court. Hughes had a reform record and a reputation for integrity. But Wilson's policies had made the president popular with labor and with farmers, and his measures gained him the support of progressives on both sides of the old party lines. A central issue in the campaign involved Wilson's effort to distance the United States from the world war that since 1914 had been bloodying the fields of Europe. The Republicans, especially Theodore Roosevelt, urged a stronger stand against what they considered to be Germany's violations at sea of American neutral rights. But Wilson's conciliatory policies appealed to the public. He won, again taking less than a majority of the popular vote.

The president could have looked forward to a second successful term, concentrating on domestic issues and keeping out of the conflict in Europe. That was not to be. Even in his first administration, the war had intruded; in the second it would dominate.

Suggested Readings

Critical overviews of the conservation movement include Samuel P. Hays, *Conservation and the Gospel of Efficiency: The Progressive Conservation Movement, 1890–1920* (1959) and Stephen R. Fox, *The American Conservation Movement: John Muir and His Legacy* (1981). Michael B. Smith's article "The Value of a Tree: Public Debates of John Muir and Gifford Pinchot," *Historian* 60: 4 (1998): 757–778 centers on the clash between preservation and conservation. See also Alfred Runte, *National Parks: The American Experience* (1979).

The field of diplomatic or foreign policy history has undergone sea changes since the 1960s. Today, historians are far more critical of the neo-imperial quest for power that began in the late nineteenth century. General narratives include Ernest R. May, *Imperial Democracy: The Emergence of America as a Great Power* (1961); Robert L. Beisner, *From the Old Diplomacy to the New, 1865–1900* (1986); and Walter LaFeber, *The Cambridge History of Foreign Relations: The Search for Opportunity, 1865–1913* (1993). William Appleman Williams's conclusion that the need to open new frontiers of natural resources and consumer markets abroad fueled American expansionism spurred a debate that continues today. See *The Tragedy of American Diplomacy*, rev. ed. (1962). Two works in this vein are Walter LaFeber, *The New Empire: An Interpretation of American Expansion, 1860–1898* (1963) and Thomas J. McCormick, *China Market: America's Quest for Informal Empire, 1890–1915* (1971). Emily Rosenberg explores the institutional bureaucracy of expansionism in *Spreading the American Dream: American Economic and Cultural Expansion, 1890–1945* (1982).

Renewed interest in the Spanish-American War in recent years promises to add to an already deep historiography. See Philip S. Foner, *The Spanish-Cuban-American War and the Birth of American Imperialism*, 2 vols. (1972). See also David F. Trask, *The War With Spain* (1981); Michael Blow, *A Ship to Remember: The Maine and the Spanish-American War* (1992); H.W. Brands, *Bound to Empire: The United States and the Philippines* (1992); James E. Bradford, *Crucible of Empire: The Spanish-American War and Its Aftermath* (1993); and Joseph Smith, *The Spanish-American War* (1993). William B. Gatewood, Jr. provides a fascinating look at the experience of black servicemen in *"Smoked Yankees": Letters from Negro Soldiers, 1898–1902* (1971). David Healy, *Drive to Power: The United States in the Caribbean, 1898–1917* (1988) unearths American designs on the Caribbean.

One school of thought stresses cultural values, especially on race and gender, as important factors pushing American foreign-policy makers into a more aggressive stance at the turn of the century. The growing obsession with physical and racial fitness is the subject of John Higham, "The Reorientation of American Culture in the 1890's," in John Horace Weiss, ed., *The Origins of Modern Consciousness,* pp. 25–48 (1965). The political impact of changing views on gender and race is the concern of Gail Bederman, *Manliness and Civilization: A Cultural History of Gender and Race in the United States, 1880-1917* (1995) and Kristin L. Hoganson, *Fighting for American Manhood: How Gender Politics Provoked the Spanish-American War and Philippine-American Wars* (1998). For more on the context of racial thinking that informed American neo-imperialism, see these two studies of Darwinist thinking in American culture: Richard Hofstadter, *Social Darwinism in America Thought,* rev. ed. (1955) and Carl N. Degler, *In Search of Human Nature: The Decline and Revival of Darwinism in American Social Thought* (1991). See also the provocative essays in Amy Kaplan and Donald E. Pease, eds., *Cultures of United States Imperialism* (1993). Some opposed American militarism; their story is told in Robert L. Beisner, *Twelve against Empire: The Anti-Imperialists, 1898–1900* (1968)

Michael E. McGerr's *The Decline of Popular Politics: The American North, 1865–1928* (1986) is just one of the epic books written about national politics between 1896 and 1914. President McKinley's political challenges are addressed in Brian P. Damiani, *Advocates of Empire: William McKinley, the Senate, and American Expansion, 1898–1899* (1987). Theodore Roosevelt's larger-than-life persona and accomplishments are the subjects of Edmund Morris, *The Rise of Theodore Roosevelt* (1979); Walter LaFeber, *The Panama Canal* (1978); Richard H. Collin, *Theodore Roosevelt's Caribbean* (1990); Robert V. Friedenberg, *Theodore Roosevelt and the Rhetoric of Militant Decency* (1990); H.W. Brands, *TR: The Last Romantic* (1997). For Taft, see Paolo E. Coletta, *The Presidency of Taft* (1973); Donald R. Anderson, *William Howard Taft* (1973); and Emily Rosenberg, *Financial Missionaries to the World: The Politics and Culture of Dollar Diplomacy, 1900–1930* (1990). For Eugene Debs, see Nick Salvatore, *Eugene V. Debs: Citizen and Socialist* (1982). Arthur Link, *Woodrow Wilson and the Progressive Era* (1954) is a flowing, comprehensive narrative of Wilson.

Childe Hassam, *Allied Flags, Union League Club, 1917.* *(Courtesy, White House Historical Association)*

Of War, Money, Preachers, and Jazz

★

CHAPTER 20

ORDINARY COURAGE ON THE WESTERN FRONT

World War I, stretching from 1914 to 1918, subjected its soldiers to an especially murderous tactic remembered by the phrase "over the top." Periodically officers in one of the various armies would order troops to climb over the edge of their trenches and hurl themselves across open ground toward the enemy lines. Between the two forces might be vicious entanglements of barbed wire through which, before the attack, a few men armed with heavy shears had stealthily cut an opening. The assault itself would occur in the face of deadly, relentless machine gun fire. Waiting to go up the ladder and over the top was an eternity of sickening anticipation.

Arthur Gordon Empey, an American fighting as a volunteer in the British army on the Western front, has left a description of what it was like:

> How I got up that ladder I will never know. . . . I knew I was running, but could feel no motion below the waist. Patches on the ground seemed to float to the rear as if I were on a treadmill and scenery was rushing past me. . . . Men on my right and left would stumble and fall. . . . Then something hit me in the left shoulder and my left side went numb. It felt as if a hot poker was being driven through me. I felt no pain—just a sort of nervous shock. A bayonet had pierced me from the rear. . . . Then a flash of light in front of my eyes and unconsciousness.

Published in 1917 and for a time the most popular book of World War I memoirs by an American, Empey's *Over the Top* remained in print for decades, selling over a million copies, and became a motion picture starring and partly directed by Empey

Over the Top. (Courtesy, Imperial War Museum, London.)

himself. The account presents a ground-level view of the experience of countless troops who went through the war. "Before the charge Tommy"—the popular name for the average British soldier—"is the politest of men," Empey observes. "There is never any pushing or crowding to be first up these ladders."

Empey in his army uniform, jaw set, mouth a thin line, eyes challenging, looks the very model of the cocky young hero that American youth aspired to be in the spring of 1917 when the United States entered the war on the side of Britain and France. Yet Empey and his comrades had been caught up in a carnage in which military commanders repetitively and fruitlessly sent raw human flesh against massively armed entrenchments.

With military thickheadedness, the officers who ordered these assaults employed strategies and tactics that might have made sense a war or two earlier. (A British commander, several wars behind the times, had figured out how it should go: infantry would hold the Germans while cavalry outflanked their lines and hit from behind.) Poison gas, a new horror added to the war arsenal, ate away the lungs, bringing such suffering that the armies in the even bigger Second World War would ban it. From early in the war until 1918, neither side gained much ground along a line about fifty miles east of Paris. Against well-fortified defensive positions reinforced by modern weaponry, an assault meant a patch or two of ground won at a meaningless expense in lives, soon to be matched by an equally senseless attack from the other camp.

In the spring of 1918, Germany modified these methods of slaughter by sending additional mobile units to probe openings and weaknesses in the Allied lines. Benefiting also from the surrender of Russia that year and the release of their troops from the Eastern front, the Germans made significant advances. What stopped them was the infusion of American troops, who just then—a year after the United States declaration of war against Germany—started to enter combat in significant numbers. Having been spared the weariness of four years of unbelievably brutal trench warfare, they arrived fresh and eager. They were also lucky to have for their commander General John (called "Black Jack" for having commanded black troops) Pershing, who had observed the war since its outbreak and independently reached a conclusion similar to that of the Germans. In the deployment of his troops, Pershing would adopt more adroit and rational tactics than the slaughterhouse methods previously used.

For many American soldiers, entering the war late as they did, the experience of battle was brief. As in all wars, some returned maimed; some did not return alive. Yet for many others it counted as a great adventure, the most exciting time of their lives. "There'll never be anything like it in the world again," wrote one war correspondent, "Everything's happening and I'm in it." For European armies the sense of adventure had long since disappeared. All that remained was the hope of survival.

After the war a generation of commentators and novelists who had experienced combat, including Americans spared the very worst, began thinking darkly through what it had all meant. War, they declared, is not noble, not a cause for flag-waving and celebration. Courage consists of the ability to keep sanity and integrity in the face of it: to dissent against the slogans and the passions of the mob.

HISTORICAL EVENTS

1914–1918
World War I

1915
Second Ku Klux Klan founded

1916
Wilson reelected president

1917–1918
United States participation in World War I

1918
Fourteen Points • League of Nations proposed

1919
U.S. troops in Siberia • Treaty of Versailles rejected • over 4,000 strikes • race riots

1920
Warren Harding elected president • Palmer raids • Harlem Renaissance begins • first radio broadcast • *Main Street* by Sinclair Lewis • *Winesburg, Ohio* by Sherwood Anderson

1920–1922
Deep recession

1923
Harding dies • Calvin Coolidge becomes president

1924
Johnson Act of 1924 • Dawes Plan • Coolidge elected president

1925
The Great Gatsby by F. Scott Fitzgerald

1927
Lindbergh makes first solo transatlantic flight to Paris • Radio Act of 1927

1928
Kellogg-Briand Peace Pact • Hoover elected president

1929
Agricultural Marketing Act • Wall Street crashes

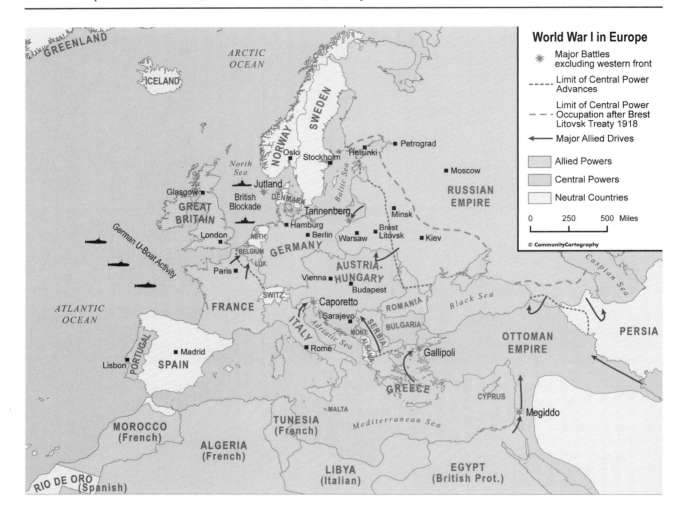

THE EUROPEAN WAR

The war that broke out in August 1914 arrayed the Allied forces of France, Great Britain and its Commonwealth, Russia, Italy, and Romania against the Central Powers of Germany and Austria-Hungary, later to be joined by Turkey and Bulgaria. Japan, in quest of territory in the Far East held by Germany, joined the Allies. Among the war's larger causes were a naval and armaments race between Britain and imperial Germany, animosities between the French and the Germans, and competition for overseas colonies. The immediate occasion was the assassination of the Austrian Archduke Ferdinand by a Serb nationalist in traditionally Serb territory under Austrian control. Russian support for Serbia brought a confrontation between Austria-Hungary and Russia that pulled the other countries into war.

On the Western front, the war soon settled into trench conflict, pitting French and British troops against Germans. In the East, Germany invaded Russia. In southern Europe, Austria battled Italy. British troops fought to deprive Turkey of its empire in the Middle East. None of this in itself bore immediately on the interests of the United States. The presence of the repressive Tsarist Russian Empire on the Allied side constituted an embarrassment to Americans otherwise inclined to sympathize with Britain and France. More directly of concern to Americans was their sea trade with Europe.

Ocean Commerce

Both Germany and the Allies depended on ocean commerce. Each wished to deprive the other of military supplies from neutral nations, especially the

United States. Seizure of such goods accorded with international law, along with the halting and boarding of ships from neutral countries. But these operations brought trouble.

The British held a wide view of what ships they were entitled to halt on the high seas. Although irritating, Americans could put up with it since prior to joining the war they sided on the whole with the British. A massively effective British propaganda machine falsely charging the Germans with atrocities reinforced an American sense of linguistic and cultural kinship with Great Britain. Many Irish Americans, to be sure, felt hostile to Britain, but in this the Irish were not united, and had little power to determine national politics. Overcoming the

NOTICE!

TRAVELLERS intending to embark on the Atlantic voyage are reminded that a state of war exists between Germany and her allies and Great Britain and her allies; that the zone of war includes the waters adjacent to the British Isles; that, in accordance with formal notice given by the Imperial German Government, vessels flying the flag of Great Britain, or of any of her allies, are liable to destruction in those waters and that travellers sailing in the war zone on ships of Great Britain or her allies do so at their own risk.

IMPERIAL GERMAN EMBASSY

WASHINGTON, D. C., APRIL 22, 1915.

Not long before the Lusitania *was torpedoed, the German embassy ran this warning in Washington, DC, newspapers.* (Courtesy, Brown Brothers Photography)

American bias against Germany would have been difficult enough by itself. The technical problems the Germans faced in intercepting commercial vessels bound for all ports made matters infinitely worse for them.

The British navy, enjoying mastery of the ocean, had merely to order merchant ships to stop, board them, and take whatever goods London deemed to be military. The Germans had no such luxury. Driven by the British navy from the surface of the seas, they had to rely in good part on a new weapon, the submarine. But despite their stealth early submarines were frail. Once risen from beneath the waters, they became vulnerable to ramming by an Allied or neutral ship. International law, composed in simpler times, had not contemplated the alternative: torpedoing a ship. That, of course, meant killing a possibly neutral crew and innocent passengers on board. But allowing free passage to commercial ships that might be carrying military goods to the Allies constituted a major threat to the German war effort. And faced with a choice between taking innocent lives and losing a war, no country will find the decision much of a dilemma.

Germany tried to soften the situation. Notices placed by Germans in American newspapers warned civilians of the risks of sailing in British waters on ships flying the flags of Allied nations. Then, on May 7, 1915, two years before the American declaration of war with Germany, occurred a defining event leading to that decision. A German U-boat sank the British passenger liner *Lusitania.* Nearly 1,200 people died, among them 128 Americans. Unknown to the passengers, to the press, and to the American public, the supposedly peaceful *Lusitania* carried munitions to the British. Their explosion, in fact, brought more damage than the German torpedo. Fury at Germany swept the country. President Woodrow Wilson protested so strongly that his secretary of state William Jennings Bryan, a pacifist, resigned. Berlin, needing for the moment at least to keep the United States neutral, ordered its navy to cease attacks on passenger liners.

In 1916 Wilson ran for reelection as the peace candidate. While Congress voted for a partial increase in military forces, some isolationist Republican progressives insisted that the nation should stay out of the self-interested quarrels of Europe. The best American service to the world, they believed, would be to cultivate the country's democratic institutions. Socialists, many of them German Amer-

In this 1916 poster, the Germans are portrayed as violent, invading rapists—nothing less than monsters. (Courtesy, Imperial War Museum, London)

icans, opposed the conflict as a war among capitalists and argued that workers should not be forced into shooting at their fellow workers who lived under a different flag.

In April 1917 came the American declaration of war that Wilson had tried to avoid. The Germans announced their intention to resume unrestricted submarine warfare, and the president thereupon cut diplomatic relations. The subsequent German sinking of the British liner *Laconia* and its torpedoing of three American freighters heightened the crisis. British intelligence officers now revealed that the German foreign minister, Arthur Zimmermann, had sent a telegram to Mexico suggesting an attack against the United States to regain for the Mexicans territories that their neighbor had taken from them

in the 1840s. The fall in 1917 of the harsh Tsarist regime in Russia to a revolution removed one moral obstacle to American engagement. But the United States, Wilson made clear, was not one of the Allies. Wishing to keep his country independent in action and motive, and dreading the prospect of ensnaring it in Europe's tangle of intrigues and animosities, he insisted simply that his nation was only "associated" with its comrades-in-arms.

The Progressive War Effort

Despite the existence within progressivism of an isolationist wing, most progressives lent themselves eagerly to the war effort. From the time of Theodore Roosevelt, many of them had possessed a sense of large national destiny. Such thinking could find in the enterprise of war its most intense application. War also brought a closer coordination between government and private business, and it promised to call on kinds of technical knowledge in which progressives placed much of their faith. So the war in some ways fulfilled a progressive dream: crews of social scientists planning to save resources, direct the workforce, heighten production, organize public opinion.

Among the many new agencies created during this period of enormous wartime expansion in the federal bureaucracy was the Food Administration. Herbert Hoover, the brilliant technician, industrialist, and administrator who served as its chief, stood well within the progressive wing of the Republican Party. Hoover supervised the voluntary rationing of food by Americans eager to be patriotic. "Hoover time," since known as daylight saving time, put the clocks ahead an hour during the warmer months, adding another hour of daylight to increase productivity. Other new federal agencies sprang up to heighten the war effort. The Fuel Administration stimulated coal production. The War Industries Board regulated industrial prices, allocated raw materials, and set industrial priorities, and the War Finance Corporation provided loans to war industries. For many progressives who favored outlawing the manufacture and sale of alcohol, their time had come. As a war measure for conserving grain, a law prohibited the distillation of spirits. In 1917 Congress passed the Eighteenth Amendment forbidding the manufacture, transportation, import and export, and sale of alcohol and sent it to the states for approval.

Labor gained from government policies aimed at avoiding strikes. The War Labor Policies Board guaranteed the right of labor to bargain collectively and established minimum wages for defense industries. The National War Labor Board could arbitrate disputes between labor and management. The Railroad Administration essentially nationalized the country's rails. That was particularly popular with the industry's workers, who after the war were disappointed that the system did not continue. The government wished also to be friendly toward business. But it needed money and the income tax amendment allowed Washington to get it, resulting in a tax taking as much as two-thirds of some of the highest incomes. The most direct form of mobilization, the draft, registered nearly twenty-five million men through the Selective Service Act.

Creating opportunities for a closer ordering of society, the war also revealed the dark side of the progressive impulse. The grimmest effort of the government involved the suppression of dissent. To this purpose, Congress and the Wilson administration instituted a series of repressive measures against antiwar activists. In 1917 Congress at President Wilson's request passed the Espionage Act, prescribing up to twenty years' imprisonment for aiding the enemy or interfering with the draft. The Act empowered the postmaster general to deny access to the mails of any publication deemed to advocate resistance to the law. The Sedition Act of 1918 went even further, allowing the federal government to punish any expression of opinion "disloyal, profane, scurrilous or abusive" toward the government. The actual number of arrests for sedition—some 1,500—is not staggering. More disturbing was the general harassment that government conducted against radicals and religious pacifists. Mob violence against German Americans did not have federal approval, but it contributed to the organized silencing of dissent. Vigilante groups tried amateur spying, denounced radicals and labor leaders, and generally attempted to impose conformity.

The administration meanwhile sought more positive ways to mobilize the public. Liberty drives encouraged patriotic Americans to lend the government money in the form of bonds repayable later during peacetime. Even on urban land, families planted victory gardens with which to feed themselves and thereby release crops for the war effort. George Creel, a Denver journalist with a progressive record, headed the Committee on Public Information. The Committee, enlisting writers and publicists of various kinds, sent speakers around the country and distributed films glorifying the cause of the Allies and the United States. It also suggested to newspapers what they might want to print. Although not coercive, the Committee represented a phase of that total social, political, and psychological organization for combat that would be a characteristic of much modern warfare.

Women Win the Vote

As early as 1869, over two decades before its admission to statehood, the territory of Wyoming had given the vote to women. Shortly afterwards, Utah territory did so. By the time of Wilson's second election, almost half of the western states had granted women the ballot, and east of the Mississippi Illinois allowed them to vote in presidential elections. In 1917 Montana elected Jeannette Rankin to Congress—a pacifist and the first woman to sit in the House of Representatives.

The receptivity of the more newly settled parts of the country to the idea of woman suffrage did not in itself signal a discarding of gender roles. To the contrary: as the presumed carriers of peaceful domestic values, women received an eager welcome in the West. Courtship and marriage civilize a man, so westerners both male and female thought, and the West believed itself to be much in need of civilizing. But that same notion of women as the civilizing sex contributed also to the growth of reform and radical movements among women. In the new century's second decade the effort for a constitutional amendment guaranteeing female suffrage grew apace with the entrance of women into the social work and health professions, and with a peace movement led by radicals such as Jane Addams. Among woman reformers the demand for sexual liberation coexisted with post-Victorian prudery. Thus the suffragist Carrie Chapman Catt insisted in a letter to the birth control advocate, Margaret Sanger, that contraceptives be combined with a call to abstinence from sex. Women, she announced, had been made into "sex slaves," and "merely to make indulgence safe doesn't do enough."

Through a curious twist in events, women made their most effective pitch for the vote not as bearers of civilization and peace but as supporters of the

New York State suffragettes demonstrate for the vote. (Courtesy, Albany Public Library)

war. Before the nation's entry into the conflict, militant suffragists had opposed American involvement. But after the congressional declaration of war, Carrie Catt's National American Woman Suffrage Association argued for a suffrage amendment as an instrument of wartime unity. Under the leadership of Alice Paul, another group of suffragettes meanwhile employed a confrontational tactic in line with those being used in Great Britain. Denouncing Wilson for inaction on the issue, they defied the law, some of them chaining themselves to the fence surrounding the White House and carrying on hunger strikes in prison. Wilson called on Congress to pass an amendment, calling it essential to winning the war. By June 1919 the measure had passed both Houses, and a year later the Nineteenth Amendment, having won ratification by the necessary three-fourths of the states, became a part of the Constitution.

The war chipped away at social and economic barriers. As men went into the military, industry turned to women, who composed about one in four workers in fields contributing to the war. Technology that lightened the demand for physical strength made it possible for some women to work in munitions plants or as machinists. A few became railroad engineers. Demobilization at the end of the war put men back into the jobs women had temporarily filled, but Americans were becoming accustomed to seeing women as coworkers with men.

The Yanks in Battle

In the first year of their entry into the war, relatively few American troops got to Europe and the front lines. The United States, however, financed its European allies with loans. For this purpose the federal government, making use of the recently ratified Sixteenth Amendment allowing heavier income taxes on the wealthy, imposed a massive levy on large personal and corporate incomes. It was another instance of progressive policy applied to the prosecution of war. But American industrial productivity, which would make a major contribution in the Second World War, contributed only marginally to the war effort. The British and the French supplied almost eighty percent of the artillery in use by American troops, and in neither tank nor aircraft production did American industry excel.

Toward the end of the war America's presence on the battlefield became more important. During the summer of 1918 the German offensive, though blunted, continued. Then the infusion of American troops, entering the lines at a rate of about 250,000 a month, tipped the balance toward the Allied side. When a German advance reached Château-Thierry,

A STEALTHIER KILLER: INFLUENZA

On August 28, 1918, eight sailors in Boston sickened with influenza, ordinarily a miserable but short-term illness commonly called the flu. Within a few days, 119 people became sick. On September 8 came the first three deaths in Boston, and the flu appeared at Fort Devens, an army base thirty miles outside the city. Soon the base hospital overflowed with fever-struck soldiers, some of them gasping for air that their lungs could no longer inhale. Bodies began outnumbering available coffins, and one barracks had to be cleared and turned into a morgue. Such a calamity could be expected on the battlefront, not in American cities. But on October 3 Philadelphia, overwhelmed by the illness, shut down all schools, churches, and other public buildings.

Health officials calculated that 2,600 had died from the flu or complications by October 5; in the course of the following week, the epidemic killed upwards of two thousand more. Stories circulated that as the unburied multiplied in Philadelphia, undertakers began refusing to take away the dead of poor families. Some cemetery officials charged for the burial plot and then left the grave digging to the bereaved. And so the illness went, from city to country to continent. In the United States, some people wore gauze masks in public. Baffled doctors tried vaccines containing blood or mucus from flu victims. Some military physicians had troops gargle each day with alcohol or antiseptics. A badly needed draft call was canceled: wherever possible the government had to forego massing men together.

The spread of the lethal flu of 1918 baffled the medical profession. For one thing it attacked a disproportionate number in the strong flush of early adulthood, ordinarily among the least vulnerable age groups. That might be expected of young men packed into army camps. But youth in isolation from crowds also fell victim to the illness. Nor did the flu spread in logical patterns. That it besieged Fort Devens soon after attacking nearby Boston made sense. Yet inexplicably it peaked in Boston the same week as in Bombay, then appeared in Boston's near neighbor, New York City, only three weeks later. Doctors at that time were more willing than they are now to induce volunteers to submit to experimental efforts at infection; sixty-two imprisoned sailors agreed to do so in return for pardons. After spraying the throats of several of them with mucus from victims of the flu, ten talked at close range for five minutes with ten flu patients each of whom coughed five times into the face of the volunteer. With malicious cunning, the virus refused to sicken a single one of the sailors.

Within a few months, the epidemic faded into memory. But in the meantime, nature had mocked mankind's puny efforts at killing. In four years the World War took fifteen million lives, over nine million in combat. The estimated deaths from the epidemic during its brief existence run from twenty to more than a hundred million, and the illness infected about one in five people the world over.

No flu epidemic like the one in 1918 has ever reappeared, but its destructiveness and its defiance of the predictable patterns of infection awakened scientific curiosity. After the disastrous course of the disease, medical specialists fought for years against the ghost of the flu that had killed far more than artillery and poison gas during the war. By the dawn of the twenty-first century, the medical profession had equipped itself with knowledge of viral epidemics, along with means of combating them unavailable to the confused and harried physicians of 1918.

east of Paris, the French army halted it with the aid of American divisions. An attack by United States troops pushed the Germans out of nearby Belleau Wood. By midsummer, the German offensive had ended. In the fall an assault by Allied and American troops sent the Germans reeling. Americans under General Pershing fought in the Argonne forest. Not allowing themselves to be pinned down in trench warfare, they conducted a winning five-week offensive. On November 11, 1918, the Germans submitted to an armistice that amounted to surrender. Over the course of the war, deaths among all combatants together numbered in the millions. The United States had lost over 112,000 men, 48,000 of them in combat and the remainder through sickness.

A Grand Design for Peace

Woodrow Wilson had not intended to be a foreign-policy president. He saw his country as it had

In this cartoon that appeared in 1919, President Wilson is returning from Europe embodied as the League of Nations. Republican isolationists shoot arrows at him from the shore. (Courtesy, Granger Collection)

always seen itself: a new start, a break from the old sinful past, having its own imperfections, to be sure, but free of the evils of ancient lands. When he found himself presiding over a nation apparently fighting less its own war than a European conflict rooted in European rivalries and jealousies, he tried to keep American participation uniquely, separately American. At the war's end, when a continuing involvement in the outside world could no longer be evaded, Wilson attempted to reestablish that world on American terms.

Before the United States went to war against the German kaiser, Wilson had urged the warring nations to accept what he called "peace without victory," a peace, in effect, in which neither side would taste the wretchedness of defeat and begin brooding about a future war of revenge. In a speech before Congress in January 1918, Wilson outlined to his nation at war an ambitious plan, the Fourteen Points, for the reconstruction of the postwar world. He called for open commerce, freedom of the seas, disarmament, self-determination for the peoples of Central and Eastern Europe, and the establishment of a league of nations. The league, as Wilson envisioned it, would commit its members to resisting any aggressor nation.

In 1919 the victorious countries met at Versailles near Paris, site of a magnificent eighteenth-century royal palace, to draw up a peace treaty with the conquered Central Powers. By that time democratic governments had replaced both the German and the Austro-Hungarian emperor. Europe provided three of the four dominant figures at Paris: Prime Minister David Lloyd George of Great Britain, Premier Georges Clemenceau of France, and Italy's Premier Vittorio Orlando. The fourth was Wilson.

The president held a unique position. As a power outside Europe and with no imperial ambitions to pursue, the United States had little interest in favorable territorial settlements or overseas possessions. To this sense of the separateness of the American mission was added Wilson's own stubborn and aloof sense of righteousness. The enthusiasm with which European crowds greeted him as the savior of their continent fortified his conviction of virtue. Determined, moreover, to be untainted by domestic political considerations, Wilson did not, for example, think of taking with him to Europe even a handful of Republicans. Such a gesture might have helped his later dealings with the Senate, under

During the influenza outbreak of 1919, people wore masks in public to protect themselves. About a half a million deaths occurred in the Untied States alone. (Courtesy, National Archives)

Republican control since the 1918 congressional elections.

At the peace conference Wilson worked strenuously. He proved instrumental in working out at the time what seemed a just division of the Austro-Hungarian Empire into the nationalities it had ruled. While the treaty burdened Germany with crippling reparation payments to the European victors for the damage the war had inflicted on them, Wilson resisted the most drastic proposals for shrinking German territory. The conference absorbed his plan for a League of Nations into the Versailles treaty. It also distributed to the Allies "mandates" over former colonies—obligations to govern them until they grew ready for independence. But while the mandate idea reflected good intentions, in practice it added new territories to the British and the French empire.

Wilson next had to get his own country to accept the Treaty of Versailles, which required a favorable vote by two-thirds of the Senate. The powerful head of the Foreign Relations Committee, Republican Senator Henry Cabot Lodge of Massachusetts, could be as stubborn as Wilson. Neither circumstance would necessarily have doomed the treaty in the United States. The matter of central concern for Americans, the provision for a League of Nations to prevent future wars, at first enjoyed great popularity. But initial optimism deteriorated.

Americans of recent immigrant background generally proved hostile to the treaty. German Americans resented the severity of treatment accorded their ancestral homeland. Citizens of Irish descent saw the treaty as advantageous to their old enemy, England. Versailles had given the city of Fiume to the newly created Yugoslavia rather than to Italy, which angered Italian Americans. Groups such as these could not bring the broader public to share their objections, but they could influence the votes of senators from states in which they resided in large numbers. A larger objection to ratification of the League was Article X of its covenant, which would apparently compel the United States to go along any time the League as a whole wanted to make war. That troubled not only isolationists but even citizens and politicians sympathetic to at least a limited American participation in a larger world order. Speaking to that concern, Lodge proposed that the Senate ratify the treaty with reservations maintaining American independence of action.

Wilson would have none of this. Though he did agree to some reservations, he refused to negotiate seriously with Lodge. Instead, he set out on an exhausting cross-country speaking tour to win over public opinion. Desperate to have his League, straining every nerve to increase support for it, Wilson during the later part of his trip suffered a physical breakdown and a stroke that removed him from active politics and statesmanship.

The treaty came before the Senate late in 1919. The first vote considered a version of the treaty that included Lodge's reservations to the League. A majority voted in favor, but Democrats loyal to Wilson joined with isolationists opposed to a treaty in any form, and Lodge's version failed to win the necessary two-thirds. Then in January 1920 came the vote for the original treaty. This time isolationists joined with supporters of Lodge's version, and again the majority for the League fell short of two-thirds.

Thereby hopes for ratification died. So, in the

elections of 1920, evaporated the hopes of Democrats for Congress and the presidency. Ohio's governor James Cox, the Democratic candidate for president, and his running mate Franklin Delano Roosevelt lost the popular vote tally by a margin of almost two to one, and the electoral vote by a greater margin, against the Republican ticket of Senator Warren G. Harding, also of Ohio, and Calvin Coolidge, governor of Massachusetts. In Europe, signatories to the Treaty of Versailles established a League of Nations without American membership. It would turn out to be ineffective. The influence in it of the United States would have depended on domestic political issues.

REDS

It was June 15, 1917. The United States was at war. "Above the hum of conversation and the clicking of the typewriter," declares the anarchist Emma Goldman in her autobiography, "we suddenly heard the heavy stamping of feet on the stairway, and before any one of us had a chance to see what was the matter, a dozen men burst into my office." The leader of the intruders cried, "Emma Goldman, you're under arrest! And so is [Alexander] Berkman." Federal agents and the city's bomb squad had raided the radical journal *Mother Earth* in New York City and detained the two Russian Jewish immigrants for conspiracy to obstruct the wartime draft.

The arrest and subsequent conviction of this famous anarchist pair came after innumerable other brushes with the law. Like the beliefs of the Wobblies, their ideology, so distant from the national consensus, made them objects of suspicion. They rejected all government and property and looked to a time in which individuals would at once prize their freedom and work unselfishly for the common good. Hatred of authority had led Russian anarchists to use violence against it, including assassination.

At the time of the arrest in New York City, California meanwhile attempted to have Berkman extradited to stand trial for involvement in a conspiracy with the iron molder and labor hero Tom Mooney. During a San Francisco parade in July 1916 supporting preparedness for possible war with Germany, the explosion of a bomb had taken several

lives. Mooney and a number of other labor radicals stood convicted. Berkman and Emma Goldman claimed that the bombing had been concocted by California industrialists. The slimness of the evidence against Mooney aroused international protest and President Woodrow Wilson's own doubts led the president to appeal, successfully, to California's governor to commute to a prison term the labor leader's death sentence.

Roots of the Red Scare of 1919

During the nineteenth century, many Americans of older stock had suspected anyone who seemed outside the bounds of what they deemed the national culture or ethos. Roman Catholics, especially of foreign birth or parentage, they viewed as worshippers at a silken, perfumed church submissive to a hierarchy headed by a foreign prince, the Pope. Irish Catholics had the taint of drink, clannishness, and corrupt urban politics. The New Immigrants from Central, Eastern, and Southern Europe who had started to arrive in substantial numbers late in the nineteenth century practiced customs outlandish to rooted citizens. The newer immigrants not in the grip of what Americans presumed to be the reactionary hands of the Roman Church, old-stock Americans feared for bringing the contrary evils of anarchism and the Soviet revolution.

In some ways, earlier American public opinion showed more tolerance of radicalism than it would later in the twentieth century. When Populists in the 1890s called for government ownership of the railroads together with telegraph and telephone services, the general public did not agree, but few reeled in horror. Early in the twentieth century, the Socialist Party gained a modest but respectable political standing. But to conservative Americans the aim of alien radicals and their native comrades appeared to be the destruction of all governmental order. The frenzy of patriotism that swept the nation at war killed the possibility of a leftist alternative in twentieth-century American politics such as had been common in Europe. The presence in the American Socialist Party of many German Americans further eroded whatever degree of tolerance the public had previously accorded socialism.

In November 1917 the Bolsheviks, soon to be

known as Communists, overthrew the provisional democratic regime of Russia that had taken over on the collapse of the Tsarist government. The new rulers in March 1918 signed a peace treaty with Germany, essentially a Russian surrender. This caused a temporary disaster for the Allied powers, permitting Germany now to direct all its resources to the war on the Western front. The more radical Bolshevik leaders of Russia and their refusal to continue the war earned them the loathing of President Wilson and the Allies. In 1919 the United States joined British, French, Czech, and Japanese troops in a brief incursion into Russian Siberia against the Bolsheviks.

Radicals, anarchists, Wobblies on the loose at home, a radical regime in power in Russia: the world, so it appeared to many Americans, faced everywhere the threat of revolution. After the war, some American leftists joined the Third International, a global union of political parties sympathetic to the Communists. The alliance between Communism and a part of the American left would convince many citizens in later decades that the nation's radicalism as a whole had become an arm of a worldwide Communist movement.

Strikes

Adding to the sense of chaos on the march, a series of strikes broke out just after the war, when the shrinking of war industries combined with inflation to worsen the lot of workers. In 1919 about four million walked off their jobs. The American public at the time felt ambivalent about unions. The American Federation of Labor had striven to convince the country that labor believed in American institutions and social stability. But the angry patriotism that the war years had intensified remained alive and alert for enemies, and militant labor unionism looked like one of them.

The most spectacular of the postwar labor disturbances occurred in Seattle, Washington. Early in 1919 city employees, among them streetcar conductors, firefighters, and clerical staff, struck in sympathy with longshoremen. A general strike in the United States was unusual. To insure that the public would not suffer the loss of essential services, the strikers set up a Committee of Fifteen. Its intentions were orderly and respectable, but by its very name sounded revolutionary. Wealthy residents left

In 1919 a steel company poster uses eight different languages to tell its workers to go back to work. Many steelworkers still labored twelve-hour days and six-day weeks. (Courtesy, Historical Society of Western Pennsylvania)

the city; others stockpiled food and fuel. Mayor Ole Hanson called in troops to break the strike. He soon became a highly vocal national opponent of what he perceived to be the Red menace.

Mail Bombs and the Palmer Raids

While Mayor Hanson was on a tour denouncing Bolshevism, a parcel mailed to his office leaked acid, and a secretary exclaimed, accurately, "Good grief, it's a bomb." Reading the newspaper on his way home from work, a postal employee in New York City noticed a description of the package. He rushed back to the main post office, where he had set aside dozens of similar parcels for insufficient postage. Among those to whom the packages had been addressed were Supreme Court justices along with senators favoring immigration restriction. Then an anarchist targeting Wilson's newly appointed attorney general A. Mitchell Palmer stumbled on the stone steps leading to Palmer's front door in the suburbs of Washington, DC, and blew himself up. Judging by the remains, investigators learned that he was an alien anarchist. All these events reinforced a popular image of foreign-born radicals as sinister figures holding a bomb, customarily pictured as a big round bowling-ball object with a rope fuse fixed to it. The image now looked to be coming alive.

Palmer soon unleashed a campaign against the Reds that extended the wartime attack on radicalism. A young clerk named J. Edgar Hoover, borrowed from the Library of Congress, assisted him. By the end of 1919 the government had seized almost 250 aliens, including Emma Goldman and Alexander Berkman. The ship *Buford*, to which they were sent for deportation, quickly became known as the Soviet Ark. The Palmer raids early in January 1920 scooped up four thousand real or suspected aliens and deported about six hundred. The evangelist Billy Sunday wished them all a journey "on ships of stone with masts of lead." Sick and seven months pregnant, the immigrant Sonia Kaross was thrown into a Philadelphia jail with prostitutes who screamed all night for the police to help her. An ambulance came in time to save her life, but not that of her baby.

Credit for keeping the Palmer raids from doing more damage can be given to Louis Post, at the time the acting secretary of labor, whose authority made it possible for him to resist such proceedings. And while George Creel as head of the Committee on Public Information had done much to whip up the wartime fervor, he now joined Post in congressional testimony opposing the Red Scare. The contrast between Post and Palmer indicates the divisions within early twentieth-century progressivism. Post had championed a radical scheme of taxation. Palmer, an advocate of woman's suffrage, labor reform, and the League of Nations, also held impeccable progressive credentials. Beneath his particular conflicts with Post lay a tension between a progressivism that favored an energetic national unity and one more concerned for the rights of individuals.

Other casualties of the Red Scare included a member of the IWW who in November 1919 was lynched in Washington state after a shooting, and five elected Socialists whom the New York State Assembly temporarily banned from their seats early in 1920. But a bomb in Wall Street later that year killing dozens did not revive the Red hunts.

CULTURAL POLITICS OF THE TWENTIES

The 1920s may be the first decade to have a coherent popular identity all its own. Short-skirted young women, speakeasies, and fads of all sorts: the twenties evoke images of cultural experimentation in race, gender, and sex, and all manner of behavior once safely constrained, so most thought, by Victorian propriety. Yet the period began with the Red Scare, an effort to insure that society and politics would stay within limits. And in the years that followed, prohibitionists along with sexual and religious conservatives sought to preserve what they believed to be the foundations of morality. The decade's politics reflected the cultural struggles of the times.

Fundamentalism on the Attack

At the opposite end to the radicals' version of moral and social order stood the fundamentalists, insisting on the literal truth of every declaration in the Bible. Generally associated with a conservative wing of evangelical Protestant churches, fundamentalists abominated Roman Catholicism, which they perceived as a religion alien to American culture and liberty. They also feared many of the teachings of modern science, which they held encouraged religious skepticism.

Especially offensive to fundamentalists was the argument of the British biologist Charles Darwin in *Origin of Species*, published in 1859, and *The Descent of Man*, which appeared in 1874, that the human species has evolved from lower animal forms. This concept they perceived to be in direct opposition to religious faith as put forward in the Bible. Under their influence a few states passed laws forbidding the teaching of evolution in public schools. The best-known test of such legislation occurred in Dayton, Tennessee. There in 1925 John Scopes, a biology teacher, stood trial for violating the state statute, an act done deliberately to provoke a great legal battle on the issue. Presiding over the trial was Judge John Raulston of nearby Gizzards Cove, who described himself as "just a reg'lar mounain'eer jedge" and sat under a sign that said "Read your Bible daily."

Although the Dayton trial has often been portrayed as pitting anti-evolutionist religion against atheistic Darwinism, Scopes's legal team, headed by the great civil libertarian lawyer Clarence Darrow, did not frame the case that way. Scopes had supposedly broken a law prohibiting the teaching of any theory of the origins of humankind that contradicted the account in Scripture. The promoters of the law presumed it to be equivalent to forbidding the teaching of Darwinist biology. But generations of Christian theologians, reading the Genesis account of creation as a symbolic rendering of the mystery of origins, had contended that no conflict existed between Darwinism and Genesis. Darwin himself had remained a practicing Christian. So Scopes's lawyers did not intend to argue that evolution was right and Christianity wrong. They wished only to contend that Scopes, in his presentation of the theory of evolution, had not broken the law. To this end they wanted to call to the stand liberal theologians who believed religion and evolution to be compatible. This would turn the trial into a conflict not between religion and evolution but between conservative and liberal Christianity.

The court did not grant Darrow's team its request. No liberal Christian theologians testified on the stand. The prosecution, on the other hand, called a major spokesman for Christianity who also opposed the concept of evolution: William Jennings Bryan, now retired from the political career that had made him a Democratic Party hero of financially strapped western and southern farmers. Bryan has often been depicted as a clown and bumpkin lured by Darrow into making absurd claims for the literal accuracy of the Bible. He declared his belief, for example, in the biblical story of a great fish swallowing a man named Jonah. The beleaguered Bryan handled himself with little of the rhetorical flair he had employed in the Democratic National Convention of 1896 against eastern bankers he accused of crucifying mankind upon a Cross of Gold. But the Scripture he defended with dogged, unyielding earnestness formed the very morality that had once made him a major force within progressivism. That Bryan himself saw in

Genesis, the first book of the Bible, a poetic concept of the beginnings of the universe—he said the seven days at the Creation could have been geological eras—may have escaped the notice of some of the clever people who mocked him.

Scopes was found guilty and fined, the penalty later set aside on a technicality. For years afterward, fundamentalists succeeded in scaring away high school textbook publishers from covering Darwinism.

Nativists Triumphant

While a main concern of fundamentalism lay in the issue of biblical interpretation, the movement centered within a complex of social and cultural values. Fundamentalists in general associated themselves with older Protestant American ways and with British and Northern European cultures. Many of them disliked the newer immigrants from Eastern and Southern Europe, as well as one Northern European ethnic group of longer standing, Irish Catholics. Enemies of immigration distrusted the newer ethnics because to them newness threatened traditional American stock. The Irish, an older immigrant stream not yet fully assimilated into the socially established American majority, Protestant nativists associated with alcohol and the customs and sociability of the saloon. On the whole, fundamentalists fervently supported prohibition, failing to note the passages in the Bible that speak favorably of wine.

An element of the anti-immigrant movement of the 1920s consisted not of fundamentalists but of upper-class Americans, their notions of British and German racial superiority derived from a facile Darwinism and their highborn taste offended by what they judged the vulgarity of immigrant customs. But fundamentalism, prohibition, and prejudice against immigrant communities united well enough to constitute a recognizable force in American society and politics. Its representatives opposed much that characterized the Jazz Age: provocative skirts, more open sexuality, lavish partying. Sometimes, so it seemed, their anger aimed at the twentieth-century city itself.

In the culture wars of the time, one victory went clearly to the nativists. A temporary law in 1921 restricting immigration gave way to still more severe legislation, the Johnson Act of 1924. That

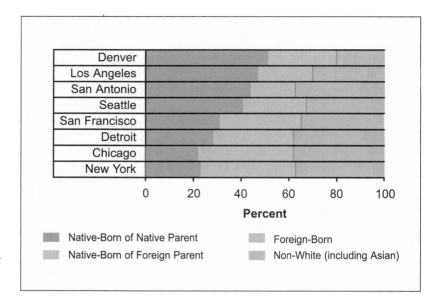

As of the 1920 census, this graph shows the numbers of Americans living in the nation's largest cities who were immigrants or the children of immigrants.

plan shrank immigration from outside the Northwestern European countries that the nativists believed to have contributed the soundest ethnic stock to the American populace. Yet inhabitants of the Western Hemisphere were to be admitted without any restriction by nationality. Farmers in the Southwest profiting from the cheap labor of immigrants from Mexico explains this tolerance toward Caribbean and American continental peoples. The restrictive immigration laws constituted the only large triumph for cultural conservatives. On other issues, conflict was bitter and inconclusive.

The City

Since colonial times, Americans had praised rural virtues and interests. Thomas Jefferson, describing city mobs as sores on the body politic, remains popularly placed in an agrarian tradition honoring the sturdy independent farmer. And whatever their opinion of the countryside and however many labored in factories, Americans still commonly thought of their fellow citizens as tillers of the land. Of the unnamed American patriot who eagerly enlists after the nation's entrance into World War I, a song went:

He was just a gangling country gink,
From away out west where the hoptoads
  wink,
He was six foot three in his stocking feet,

And he kept a-gettin' thinner the more
  he'd eat.

And a musical question about such young men upon their return from Europe was

How're you gonna keep 'em down on the
  farm
After they've seen Paree?

But also, as even these songs illustrate, an attitude fermenting in urban humor derided the rubes and hayseeds of the hinterland. And from the city, meanwhile, seemed to come all the forces of disruption—the speakeasies, the babble of foreign tongues, the fads and newfangled ideas, the fast living. By the 1920s the notion of a divided American culture came to the fore in national life. Still, while the cultural wars of the decade depicted real differences, the conflict cannot be presented as simply between city and country.

Farmers welcomed the new technology emanating from the industrial cities. The most spectacular mechanical achievement of the first years of the century was the automobile. Among the earliest enthusiasts of the Model T were farmers, for whom easy access to the country town had long been a pressing problem. Henry Ford considered himself a product and champion of rural virtues. Farmers, moreover, had long been eager consumers of whatever agricultural machinery they could afford. Rural electrification, only beginning in earnest in the 1920s, soon became vital to the progress of farm life. Farmers, at any rate, had no reason to take less satisfaction than anyone else in American industrialism, then thought to be the wonder of the globe. Certainly Calvin Coolidge, the rural New England representative of modern capitalism in the White House from 1923 to 1929, entirely suited rural evangelical Protestants. And some city dwellers counted among the most vocal fundamentalists, seeing themselves not as defending the countryside alone but as standing by the old Protestant core of city and country alike. On one intensely political issue they agreed with their rural cousins: the evil of alcohol.

Prohibition

He is long, lank, and scowling. On his head rests a stovepipe hat, thin and enormously tall. His coat hangs about a frame that knows no carnal desire. Plainly his only delight is the joy of denying pleasure to others. Such during the twenties was a familiar cartoon personification of prohibition by its enemies, and by implication, of a dank and sour region in the American mind where festered the life-hating morality of the prohibitionists. What relation to American reality did this cartoon figure have?

In the first half of the nineteenth century, agitation for reform of the nation's drinking habits had come from at least two sources. Many Americans of property and social standing immersed themselves in numerous social causes, among them education, mental health, and the abolition of slavery. Such well-bred people commonly assumed that intelligent argument would lead the way to self-restraint and social reform. Early advocates of limiting alcohol consumption called for temperance in its literal meaning—moderation in its use—rather than total abstinence. Other reformers insisted that all alcohol was a curse. Meanwhile, religious revivals called on converts to lead lives of piety, sobriety, and hard work. Revivalists, like the more secular reformers, relied for the most part on persuasion. It was effective. By the middle of the century, the consumption of alcohol had fallen steeply. But some reformers wanted not only moral suasion but also legal action prohibiting the manufacture and sale of alcohol. In 1851 Maine became the first state to pass such a statute. Other states followed.

The formation late in the nineteenth century of the Women's Christian Temperance Union increased the momentum toward prohibition enforced by law. Not long after the WCTU came the Anti-Saloon League. Singling out the saloon for attack reveals much about the concerns of twentieth-century prohibitionists. For the city saloon represented not only alcohol but a whole culture and society surrounding it. It served as a traditional gathering spot for Irish and other incompletely assimilated ethnic groups, a place where workers socialized, sometimes associated with loose women, and engaged in ward politics in back rooms.

Where in all this and in prohibitionist forces early in the twentieth century was the pleasure-loathing figure in a stovepipe hat who was the cartoon caricature in the 1920s? Doubtless he existed in some realm. The temptation to deny to others enjoyments that do not interest you, or do interest you so much they make you fear yourself, is a recognizable human characteristic. But the movement against alcohol also garnered the support of twentieth-century progressivism.

Like much else that falls under the term "progressive," prohibition imposed by Washington meant a radical alteration in the scope of federal power. The Eighteenth Amendment, intended to prevent drinking but forbidding only the manufacture, transportation, and sale of alcohol, stood alone as a constitutional amendment aiming to create a measure of federal control over private lives. Among the distinctive impulses of the progressive period had been social engineering, the effort to put trained professionals to designing solutions for social problems. Social workers could describe the damaging effects of alcohol on impoverished neighborhoods. Efficiency experts argued that modern machine production required of the worker a clearheadedness that earlier working conditions had not called for. In a shoemaker's shop or behind a plow, a moment's inattention would be a small matter; on an assembly line, it could be disastrous. More impassioned progressives denounced the liquor industry for promoting poverty and injustice. Feminists knew what drunken men could do to wives and children.

The Eighteenth Amendment took effect in 1920; and the Volstead Act of that year specified the means of its enforcement. Most Americans assumed the country would go dry and stay that way. In later years, an opposite misconception would appear:

prohibition had done nothing to cut down on the abuse of alcohol. During much of the twenties, consumption of alcohol did decline, and so did the diseases connected with excessive drinking. But prohibition sharpened the line between traditionalists and defenders of cultural change. And a rise in the already established institution of organized crime featured a new breed of highly public gangsters, the most famous being Al Capone with his $25,000 diamond ring and sterling silver toilet seat. The enforcement machinery for prohibition proved expensive and inadequate: two thousand cases of liquor a day slipped in through remote coves and bays of Long Island Sound alone. Later in the 1920s many capitalists, considering among other things that a tax on legal liquor could substitute for a portion of their income tax, began urging repeal of prohibition. The presidential victory in 1932 of the Democrat Franklin D. Roosevelt, who also favored repeal, and the need of the federal government during the Great Depression for sources of revenue doomed the now discredited experiment in banishing alcohol.

Freudianism

The issue of prohibition muddied a cultural conflict larger even than that between wet Catholic immigrant and old-stock Protestant dry. That was the question of what the moral behavior of the individual should be in a time of rapid social change such as the one following the First World War.

Controversy dogged the monumental work of the Viennese physician Sigmund Freud on the causes of mental illness. His shifting of the discussion from the physical basis of neurosis and psychosis to the stresses that society and culture place on the human psyche made his work distinctive. Among the elements that Freud identified is the clash between the sexual drive and the limits society imposes on its expression. Some recent interpreters of Freud have discovered in him a champion of civilization's demands for restraints on cravings, holding that maturity amounts to a hard-won transformation of primitive urges into socially acceptable satisfactions. But Freud did express his displeasure with what he called "prudish America," and many people assumed, his followers eagerly and his opponents with horror, that he was condoning uncontrolled indulgence.

Some prohibitionists would have agreed that lustful desires in general must be crushed, and that law must be enlisted to erase them, no matter what the loss in personal liberty. Among Jazz Age sophisticates, the issue seemed equally clear: Freud had explained that pleasurable appetites are beneficial, and social conventions that curb them endanger mental health. Prohibition, of course, they found to be an expression of an essentially American illness, a neurotic fear of happiness and pleasure. It all went back, some contended, to the grim Puritans of colonial New England—a people, they neglected to observe, who had registered no objection to the moderate use of alcohol.

The Ku Klux Klan

Late in 1915, on Stone Mountain outside Atlanta, a handful of men revived the Klan of Reconstruction days, creating what shortly became a large instrument of racist, antiforeign, and anti-Catholic sentiment in the 1920s. The earlier southern Klan of the post–Civil War era, local outlaws wearing bizarre and ghostly masks and robes of differing colors, had in varying ways harassed newly freed slaves, aiming particularly to keep them from voting. Now the men on Stone Mountain, who warmed themselves wearing sheets of pure white beside a burning cross, reinvented the KKK, calling it the Knights of the Ku Klux Klan and choosing as their head "Colonel" William Simmons. An

The Ku Klux Klan openly paraded the streets of the nation's capital in about 1925. (Courtesy, Library of Congress)

inspiration for the new Klan was D. W. Griffith's silent movie spectacular *The Birth of a Nation*. Released early in 1915 and praised by President Wilson as "history written by lightning," the film was technically innovative but blatantly racist.

An organization that reveled in trappings of mystery and exotic titles, the KKK set its Imperial Wizard over Grand Dragons who commanded at the state level. Then came Great Titans or district commanders, Exalted Cyclops who served as presidents of Klaverns or chapters, Kleagles who acted as recruiters, and other such dignitaries. Klavern meetings included a Kludd, or chaplain. Knights, the common soldiers of the Klan, took oaths of secrecy concerning Klan ritual and activities. But the Kloran, Simmons's authoritative book of Klan practices never to be revealed to the outside world, the author helpfully deposited at the Library of Congress. One pamphlet sent to the Library in the twenties records a possible Klonversation between strangers:

> AYAK? (Are you a Klansman?)
> AKIA. (A Klansman I am.)
> CYKNAR. (Call your Klan number and realm.)
> NO. 1, ATGA. (Number 1, Atlanta, Georgia.)
> KIGY. (Klansman, I greet you.)
> SANBOG. (Strangers are near. Be on guard.)

Such were among the customs of a group that kept a Kalendar in which the seven days of the week took on the names Dark, Deadly, Dismal, Doleful, Desolate, Dreadful, and Desperate; the weeks of the month, Woeful, Weeping, Wailing, Wonderful, and Weird; the twelve months, Bloody, Gloomy, Hideous, Fearful, Furious, Alarming, Terrible, Horrible, Mournful, Sorrowful, Frightful, and Appalling. One man with the initials KKK won automatic membership.

By the early 1920s the organization had evolved from a small fraternity to a large movement with a wide but shapeless program aimed at maintaining native white Protestant power over blacks, Catholics, Jews, and ethnic communities, and at policing the moral behavior of citizens. It drew over forty percent of its membership from Indiana, Ohio, and Illinois. The South and Southwest together contributed a similar proportion. But Klan chapters flourished in every part of the country.

With a membership at its height in 1924 of some four million, the KKK infiltrated both city and country. One estimate locates in urban areas half of its members, most of them recent migrants from the countryside. Spread over many regions, each unit adapting to its locality, the Klan defies consistent description. Torn internally by vicious disputes and competing claims as to who spoke for the official Klan, it had shifting leadership.

The Klan of the 1920s had as much attitude as policies. Unlike its Reconstruction predecessor, which had retained considerable loyalty to the defeated Confederacy, it preached impassioned patriotism to the United States. The new Klan stood, of course, for Protestantism and the superiority of white Northern European stock. It aimed to preserve racial and religious purity, but most of the country was Protestant anyway. Black southerners could hardly be more repressed. The new laws limiting immigration of peoples from outside Western Europe blunted the issue of ethnic diversity.

At times, especially in the South, the Klan overtly menaced. The Klan in Texas tarred and feathered a man suspected of adultery. Sometimes the Klan dabbled in charity, of such kinds as Christmas baskets to poor families, some of them black. It also ran or supported political candidates, but there the issue tended to be the Klan itself rather than any policy it might propose. After the mid-twenties, especially in the wake of a number of sexual and financial scandals, the organization went into a steep decline.

Sprawling, divided, vague in policy, the KKK drew much of its membership from farm and blue-collar workers. Many American men at the time gravitated to fraternal orders offering nothing more than clubby friendship. The KKK suited as well some women attracted to oaths and costumes. Southerners had a regional loyalty founded on race. In one southern town an excitable patron attending a viewing of *The Birth of a Nation* fired a gun at the image on the screen of the lust-maddened black pursuer menacing the innocent flower of white womanhood. For bigotry and raw hatred the Klan provided not only an ideology but a costume, secret signals, and a tacky pomp.

The Jazz Age

The nation that fundamentalists and Klansmen strove to save, on what they thought to be its old

620 • *Chapter 20* OF WAR, MONEY, PREACHERS, AND JAZZ

King Oliver's Creole Jazz Band of the 1920s. (Courtesy, Hogan Jazz Archives, Tulane University)

moral and cultural terms, provided them with compelling evidence that it had embarked on the wrong path. "It was an age of miracles, it was an age of art, it was an age of excess, and it was an age of satire . . . the whole upper tenth of a nation living with the insouciance of grand ducs and the casualness of chorus girls." So F. Scott Fitzgerald in 1931 reminisced in his novel *The Crack Up* about the Jazz Age, as he termed the 1920s, of which he had been so much a public figure and literary chronicler. Trivialized in historical memory as a time of gin flasks and dances that prudish onlookers judged wild and sexual, the twenties brought to American life behavior, tame by today's standards, that at the time seemed either a new sophisticated freedom or a fall from virtue.

Illustrative of the adventurous cultural vigor of the day was a blossoming enterprise, ranging from personal and artistic to political and militant, rooted in a socially marginalized corner of Manhattan.

THE HARLEM RENAISSANCE

"I went up the steps and out into the bright September sunlight," reports the poet Langston Hughes in his autobiography. "Harlem! I stood there, dropped my bags, took a deep breath, and felt happy again." What in the vicinity of this Upper East Side Manhattan subway stop of 1921 so excited a young black midwesterner?

By standards that most white Americans of the time would have expected, little enough. While not yet the congested slum it would become during the Great Depression, Harlem was poor. Many of its once prosperous dwellings were now subdivided into crowded rooms for the black families fleeing an even more wretched existence in the South or emigrating from the West Indies. Among the 73,000 Harlemites in 1920 and close to 200,000 a decade later, little existed in the way of a prosperous middle class. No major industry, with the possible exception of entertainment, gave the district economic vitality. Job discrimination among the area's retail establishments kept residents at lower-paying tasks. Rates of disease associated with poverty were high, as were statistics for crime and drugs. As a neighborhood, Harlem fell in some ways behind black sections of several southern cities. Nor was it the largest northern concentration of blacks. The greatest migration, spurred by emigration northward for factory jobs during World War I, was to Chicago.

A New Pride

An assertive pride at being what the older, black Howard University Professor Alain Locke called a "race capital" gave excitement to Harlem. While blacks owned only a fraction of its businesses, a defiant sense of social and cultural independence, lacking elsewhere among black Americans, animated the community.

A part of that increased self-confidence derived from the fame of black American troops during World War I. After the United States joined the conflict in 1917, Hispanics, American Indians, and African Americans all answered the call, some hoping to win better treatment from their country. Leaders of black opinion, including the formidable W. E. B. Du Bois of the National Association for the Advancement of Colored People, urged that for the moment black Americans put aside their grievances and commit themselves wholly to patriotism. Young black men overlooked such indignities as being placed almost exclusively under white officers or being assigned to labor units, where they had the dangerous job of carrying explosives. Early in 1919 the men of the Harlem regiment marched through Manhattan with honors almost unprecedented for black Americans. The French, by whose side they served, had honored them even more gallantly. Some black soldiers believed their valor would win

Black Belt, *by the African American painter of the Harlem Renaissance, Archibald Moteley, Jr., catches the energies of Harlem.* (Courtesy, Hampton University, Hampton, VA)

for their race a larger acceptance into American citizenship. The race riots that summer in Chicago and elsewhere, incited by whites but encountering an almost unprecedented degree of black counterviolence, sadly responded to that innocent hope.

Pride in Harlem came as well of its belonging to a great cosmopolitan center, New York City. In retrospect it seems unremarkable that Harlem showed itself quick and sassy and in sync with the tempo of northern city life. But at the time it meant a lot to its residents to have escaped the tenant farming or sharecropping or hired labor in the backcountry South, where they lived at the mercy of local police and the bigotry of white neighbors. Instead, they had become streetwise New Yorkers in an intensely self-conscious neighborhood of a northern metropolis. "The New Negro," spoken of by both blacks and whites during the twenties, walked the streets of Harlem. Out of the migration from the South, its lynchings, its casual daily insults, its agriculture devastated by the new cotton-destroying pestilence of the boll weevil, grew a tough city breed of northern African Americans.

An Artistic Flowering

Harlem in the early 1920s entered the first stages of an artistic flowering richer than anything the race had achieved before in this century. The possibilities of a distinctively black music had already been under way. The powerfully intoned blues of Bessie Smith, the more restrained but equally vibrant singing of Ethel Waters, the instrumental jazz of Duke Ellington's band—all this became available by the middle and late twenties to the writers of the Harlem Renaissance. In the years to come, writers and artists would combine with musicians and singers to create for Harlem a cultural energy charged with the rhythms and themes of the black experience. Its exuberance is caught in a line of Bessie Smith's: "Got the world in a jug, got the stopper in my hand."

At one extreme, then, Harlem was a scene of grinding poverty. At the other it offered a gathering place for black artists and intellectuals. The two did not often meet, but there were points of intersection. Speakeasies and jazz cabarets might put into the same room Harlem writers and laboring people. Another Harlem custom arising from poverty but mixing differing social classes was the house-rent party. Advertised informally and offering dancing, alcohol, and such robust country food as Hoppin' Johns made of ham hocks or pig's feet with rice and peas, these parties initially raised rent money for poor tenants. But their frequency made them known to figures of the Harlem Renaissance as well as to the porters and housemaids and truck drivers who made up by far the greater part of the population.

Other participants on the fringe of Harlem life were white patrons of black establishments, or whites who simply came as onlookers. These could be of any variety. Members of the downtown Greenwich Village community of writers and artists might feel some affinity for black Harlem or seek inspiration for their art. Sympathetic white liberals were drawn by conviction. Whites titillated by stereotypical fantasies of African spontaneity and sexuality could hope if not to get some action, at least to watch it. Some black clubs even banned blacks from admission. That way white patrons could have the pleasure of a brief encounter with a black neighborhood without the awkwardness of actually associating with its denizens. Elsewhere venturesome whites and blacks would discard the old taboo against racially mixed dancing.

On another level, the relationship between whites and the black contributors to the Harlem Renaissance became that of publisher or patron to client. In 1926 the white novelist Carl Van Vechten published *Nigger Heaven*, a portrait of the differing social classes of Harlem. The book had a wide but mixed reception. Some black commentators expressed horror at its frank depiction of ghetto life, which they feared would perpetuate a bad image of the race. But the book fascinated much of the white reading public. Van Vechten's novel was instrumental in popularizing Harlem, and he be-

friended Renaissance figures, bringing them into his influential critical and publishing circles. Other white authors and intellectuals similarly served as patrons. Langston Hughes enjoyed the sponsorship of the poet Vachel Lindsay, Zora Neale Hurston of Fannie Hurst, Jean Toomer of Sherwood Anderson, and Claude McKay of the radical Max Eastman. Publishers such as Harcourt Brace, Harper, Boni and Liveright, and Alfred Knopf promoted works out of Harlem.

An American Search for Identity

The Black Renaissance among other things represented a search for identity: a search that in part turned, inevitably, on the issue of color. Many of the figures of the Renaissance were light-skinned. The novelist Jean Toomer, Caucasian in appearance, had for a grandfather the black aristocrat Pinckney Benton Stewart Pinchback, lieutenant governor and briefly governor of Louisiana after the Civil War. Toomer grew up in a black family so white in appearance and standard of living that his racial antecedents did not heavily influence him. Jessie Faucet's fiction examines the issues of a mixed-race middle class, while Wallace Thurman's *The Blacker the Berry* explores color prejudice among blacks. The matter of cultural borrowing posed a question deeper than genetic mixture. Were black customs and art to be considered mostly in their separateness or as variants, like other ethnic heritages, within a larger culture composed of innumerable borrow-

Langston Hughes was a leading member of the Harlem Renaissance. (Courtesy, New York Public Library)

SHARE-CROPPERS
by Langston Hughes

Just a herd of Negros
Driven to the field,
Plowing, planting, hoeing,
To make the cotton yield.

When the cotton's picked
And the work is done
Boss man take the money
And we get none.

Leaves us hungry, ragged
As we were before.
Year by year goes by
And we are nothing more

Than a herd of Negroes
Driven to the field—
Plowing life away
To make the cotton yield.

Cities with Greatest Increase in African American Population, 1910–1920			
City	African American Population, 1920	Increase in African American Pop. Since 1910	
		Number	Percent
Detroit, MI	40,838	35,097	611.3
Cleveland, OH	38,618	26,003	307.8
Chicago, IL	109,458	65,355	148.2
Norfolk, VA	43,392	18,353	73.3
New York, NY	152,467	60,758	66.3
Indianapolis, IN	34,678	12,862	59.0
Philadelphia, PA	134,229	49,770	58.9
St. Louis, MO	69,854	25,894	58.9
Cincinnati, OH	30,079	10,440	53.2
Pittsburgh, PA	37,725	12,102	47.2

ings? The same questions applied to Latino and American Indian cultures that incorporated Anglo-American elements into their work.

Claude McKay, from the Caribbean island of Jamaica, drew heavily on black sources, but he prized education in the British school system there. Countee Cullen insisted on employing longstanding conventions of English-language poetry. But what of blackness itself could black poets and novelists explore? They could use, of course, the experience of being victims of white society. McKay's "If We Must Die," written in the wake of the race riots of 1919, speaks defiance in traditional poetic lines:

> If we must die, let it not be like hogs
> Hunted and penned in an inglorious
>   spot. . . .
> Like men we'll face the murderous,
>   cowardly pack,
> Pressed to the wall, dying, but fighting
>   back!

Or assertion of blackness could be a reference to an ancient past, as in Langston Hughes's majestic "The Negro Speaks of Rivers":

> I've known rivers:
> Ancient, dusky rivers
> My soul has grown deep like the rivers.

Perhaps to have African ancestry could include a poetic treatment of the quality that blacks with increasing pride would later refer to as rhythm.

Black dancers could keep separate rhythms going at once, playing one part of the body against another. The "rhythm of segments," Zora Hurston called it. By the mid-twenties, Langston Hughes deliberately employed musical syncopation in his poem about a black piano player:

> He played that sad raggy tune like a
>   musical fool,
>
> Sweet Blues!
> Coming from a black man's soul.
> Oh, Blues!

In acknowledging the existence of an African beat and pace, would black writers invite stereotyping? Or would they be elevating to the realm of art elements of their folk culture that their parents, along with whites, had scorned or ignored? And if that was legitimate, a black writer might venture further and confront fictionally the flashy, sensual street life of Harlem itself. That risk Claude McKay took in 1928 in *Home to Harlem*.

Divisions in the Black Community

To depict a Harlem of pimps and prostitutes and hoodlums, as McKay did, invited the censure of an older generation of black leaders who favored the more narrowly political rhetoric of the NAACP. W. E. B. Du Bois, the formal product of a more reserved age, feared encouraging racist perceptions of black Americans. Watching warily over the Renaissance, and speaking through the NAACP journal *The Crisis*, Du Bois denounced such works as *Nigger Heaven* and *Home to Harlem*.

Politically opposed to Du Bois but just as committed to a political more than a cultural response to white supremacy was the West Indian Marcus Garvey. For a time early in the 1920s Garvey and his United Negro Improvement Association had the support of countless Harlemites in his campaign for the establishment of a separate black nation in Africa. Garvey and the followers he appointed to be an aristocracy in his projected African homeland encountered an opposition led by black intellectuals and political leftists. His Pan-African movement became tarnished by his contacts with the Ku Klux Klan, with which he shared the ideal of racial separation, and by supposed financial irregularities in his organization. Imprisoned and then deported, he died in Europe in 1951.

A collective portrait of the Harlem Renaissance, then, would show artists struggling to know themselves individually even as they also came to know their own race. Under the pressing economic problems of the Great Depression, that endeavor became secondary to others.

Literatures of Reappraisal

The Harlem Renaissance sustained itself on the distinctiveness of black experience. But it also belongs to a time of artistic flourishing that included both whites brought up on the eastern seaboard and others from the country's interior.

One source of the literature of the postwar decade stemmed from a determination, on the part of highly educated young veterans, to understand both their own encounter of battle and the reasons for the whole mad conflict of World War I itself. In this category falls the work of the young poet who would later sign himself e e cummings. For criticisms a friend made of the war while the two were assigned to an ambulance unit attached to the French military, both received prison sentences. Their detention center was a dumping ground for whoever was too confused, too childlike, too different to fit the demands of governments and armies. *The Enormous Room*, cummings's memoir published in 1922, contrasts the nationally organized insanity of the war to the alleged madness of the prisoners. In the same vein, *Three Soldiers* by John Dos Passos, a novel published in 1921, describes a young man in the American military who finds in the inner life

of artistic sensibility a defense against the regimentation of army life. Such American writings join with a great body of European literature to emerge from the war, exemplified by the work of Henri Barbusse of France, the British war hero turned pacifist Siegfried Sassoon, and from Germany Erich Maria Remarque's great war novel *All Quiet on the Western Front*.

Another motif of the literary twenties arises from the intersection of older rural and village American ways with the young century's new urban culture. The stories that Sherwood Anderson put together in *Winesburg, Ohio*, which appeared in 1920, are a dreamscape of backcountry loneliness and longing that holds its own elusive beauty. The big city offers an escape into a larger, freer world, but a world deprived of the poetry of Winesburg. Better known are the explorations of American society in the novels of Sinclair Lewis, himself a native of a small Minnesota town. *Main Street*, published in 1920, reveals a cutting satire of provincial life, and *Babbitt*, appearing in 1922, is comparably acidic in its portrayal of a businessman in a midwestern city. Both works, however, contain hints of the novelist's critical fondness for his badly flawed but fundamentally well-meaning American inland characters, a fondness that became more explicit in his later fiction. Urban civilization itself gets a harsh evaluation from authors of the period such as Van Wyck Brooks, who found in modern business a war against feeling and spontaneity that he traced back to American rural Puritan traditions.

Still another decision among writers of the era was to embrace some particular component of modern life. That might mean pursuing themes of sensuality and sex, as in the poetry of Edna St. Vincent Millay. Carl Sandburg's poetry, beginning well before the war, celebrates the power of the industrial city of Chicago, finding in it a raw creativity where other commentators detected only repression. Passing from his century to earlier times and back again, William Faulkner explored in brooding fiction a southern heritage of violence and manners, of cruelty and graciousness, haunted by its legacy of slavery. Others also drew on the character of some American region. Robert Frost, in poems that managed to be complex and available to a large public, captured moods of his New England and much of universal human sensibility.

The greatest novel of the 1920s, and one of the finest books ever written by an American author, is

F. Scott Fitzgerald's *The Great Gatsby*. The title is taken by some as a criticism of the materialism of the decade. But Gatsby is great. A man of enormous willfulness wishing to reshape reality itself, he also possesses an exquisite gracefulness; Fitzgerald describes him: "If personality is an unbroken series of successful gestures, then there was something gorgeous about him, some heightened sensitivity to the promises of life. . . . He smiled understandingly—much more than understandingly. It was one of those rare smiles with a quality of eternal reassurance in it, that you may come across four or five times in life. It faced—or seemed to face—the whole external world for an instant, and then concentrate on you with an irresistible prejudice in your favor. It understood you just as far as you wanted to be understood, believed in you as you would like to believe in yourself, and assured

you that it had precisely the impression of you that, at your best, you hoped to convey."

Gatsby's heroic delusion is his exaltation of Daisy Buchanan, his earlier love, into a realm of stainless romance. Daisy in reality is a shallow person: "her voice is full of money," the author says at one point. But the tawdry glitter of her spoiled wealth Gatsby transmutes into an existence unattainably beautiful and free, represented by the green light at the end of Gatsby's pier on the Gold Coast of Long Island Sound. The light reflects the American belief in the country as a land of pure and unending promise; and Daisy is Gatsby's America. What Daisy actually embodies, money, selfish luxury, and corruption, is the reality that mocks Gatsby's fantasy. But there is more than a hint in Fitzgerald's magnificent novel that America will live on, in the soul of the nation's Gatsbys.

Frost, Sandburg, Faulkner, Fitzgerald, members of the Harlem Renaissance, all constitute the familiar figures of the literature of the 1920s. But other writers sought to express different kinds of American experience. Zitkala Sä, a prolific Yankton Sioux writer and activist, and Mourning Dove, an Okanagon laborer, composed some of the first great American Indian literature. Zitkala Sä's short stories and novel *Cogewea* examine from women's perspectives the same kind of tensions surrounding race and culture that had intrigued the Harlem writers. Drawing on a long Hispanic literary tradition, authors detailed the experience of Mexican American citizens and immigrants in the Southwest.

THE AMERICAN ROAD

You've got to get under, get out and get under,
While fixing your little Ford car.

So, more or less, went a popular song early in the Ford era. The elderly man who late in the twentieth century remembered the tune would also recall plummeting down a steep mountain road in his Ford. Though a skilled driver, he had burned out his brakes in the descent. Then he tried to slow his careening car by throwing on one of the gears. It rubbed bare. He tried another, which disintegrated

The Great Gatsby. (Courtesy, Granger Collection)

just about the time he reached the bottom. From a technological point of view, the most interesting part of the story tells of a car shop prudently located at the foot of the mountain in the middle of nowhere that was able to put back into running order an auto that had lost both brakes and gears.

The song and the episode reveal a lot about the presence of millions of cars in the United States by the 1920s. The early Ford, especially after the initiation of the continuously moving assembly line, came to be regarded as a triumph of advanced technology. Yet it could be repaired, up to a point, by anyone who got out and got under. Owners with a minimum knowledge could do much of their own maintenance: clean the spark plugs, tighten the bands, and clear out the carbon. And a rural mechanic could fix major problems using the equivalent of tape and chicken wire. A farmer, declares one of the many Ford jokes of the period, sent the company the tin off his barn roof. Replied the Ford office: "While your car was an exceptionally bad wreck, we should be able to complete repairs and return it by the first of the week." Driving the Model T required skill, or at least alertness. When the driver made a left or right turn, the car's turning wheels snapped completely in the direction desired, as if to say: "Is this what you want?" When the driver fought against the Ford's treachery, it would make a turn in the opposite direction. Struggling with the maliciously over-obedient car and braking to a stop offered a lesson in nerve.

The Assembly Line

Henry Ford's indifference to book learning makes it uncertain how much he may have learned from the efficiency experts. In the lineage of Frederick Winslow Taylor and scientific management, Ford's assistant Clarence W. Avery had read of the latest engineering concepts. Not Ford alone, at any rate, but thinking and experimenting throughout the Ford Motor Company led to the installation at the Highland Park, Michigan, plant in 1913 of a system that incorporated all of the efficiency Taylor had called for.

For some time the factory had been using assembly belts that carried to the workers the car under construction, each laborer repeating some single task as the vehicle presented itself. These lines, however, moved in starts and stops. Then in 1913 came the continuously moving assembly line. Enor-

mous savings in time resulted. For the line to work, however, its speed had to be determined with precision: too slow and time would be wasted; too fast and the work would be flawed. Soon subsidiary conveyor belts fed their partial products into the main trunk, and this made more exacting the problem of minutely determined timing.

Ford wanted workers to be well paid. The enormous profits that came with the assembly line made that easier. In 1914 Ford initiated an astonishing $5 day as the basic wage for male workers on the shop floor. Soon afterward the company extended the wage to women and to the white-collar staff, and set an eight-hour day. At about the same time, Ford ordered that no one be rejected for employment because of a physical handicap. Soon the product was to be a car that most Americans could afford, fulfilling Ford's larger vision of industrialism. Toward the end of the 1920s, the Model T cost as little as $290, reasonable even at the value of dollars of the time.

Ford did not accept the view that tightly controlled factory work degraded workers. His policy, even before 1913, was to employ unskilled workers and train them. The labor itself demanded that the workers pay close and responsible attention. Employees also profited from promotion from one level of skill to another. On the whole, then, the system of work in the Ford Company stressed not mindless obedience but learning, concentration, and advancement. As a spokesman for the American and the global future, Ford made such declarations as that the strict regime of modern industry would

The assembly line at the Ford Motor Company plant in Dearborn, Michigan, in 1928. (Courtesy, Library of Congress)

cut down on heavy drinking. You could not bring a hangover to a relentlessly moving assembly line. Old-fashioned virtues lodged themselves in the newest methods of technology.

Henry Ford and American Culture

From early in the competition among automakers, Ford wished to produce a car that would be not a plaything of the rich but a practical vehicle for the common people. Not only a commoner but a populist, Ford remained close to the thinking of the farmers and laboring folk among whom he had spent his early years. Combined with his method of running the Ford Motor Company, this defines him as a figure of the American culture he did so much both to perpetuate and to transform.

Unlike most manufacturing executives, Ford acted not as a financier but as a worker and technician. In the 1890s, he had built in a shed at the back of his house a primitive forerunner of his automobiles. The folkloric character of that story must be qualified. At the time Ford was no obscure dreamer who happened to make a lucky discovery, but a leading technician in the great business enterprise of Thomas Alva Edison, with the shed itself equipped like an engineering laboratory. Ford admitted that he did not invent the automobile but simply put together the inventions of many predecessors. During the second and third decades of the twentieth century, when Ford led his company to its smashing success, he never abandoned his active role in the technical side of the enterprise. His populism showed in his reluctance to go to Wall Street for financing. He would not put himself at the mercy of distant bankers preoccupied with abstract volumes of profits. The productive rather than the financial component of American industrialism held his allegiance. Ford made no secret of the operations of his factories; whoever wished to do so could tour them.

Yet the close control that Ford maintained over the technical side of his enterprise also kept him from entering fully into the industrial future to which he contributed so much. In the 1920s General Motors under the leadership of Alfred P. Sloan initiated an organizational approach more promising than Ford's. Sloan refused to dictate. To the manager of each branch of GM, including the vigorous Chevrolet division, he gave considerable autonomy, and he encouraged his managers to do the same with their subordinates. GM also had an energetic research department that Sloan, himself the holder of an engineering degree from the Massachusetts Institute of Technology, allowed to pursue its own ideas. Sloan came closer than Ford to coordinating the diverse processes of modern industry.

Ford represented a kind of morality that belonged both to nineteenth-century American traditions and to the aims of reformers in the Progressive Era. He neither drank nor smoked. Soon after his introduction of the eight-hour $5 day, the company established a Sociological Department. Its personnel looked into home conditions among the workers, many of them immigrants, to enforce habits that accorded with Ford's moral convictions; noncompliance brought sanctions. In 1915, at an impressive moment in the history of the Ford enterprise, its founder launched a peace project that captured the most humane hopes of the time. The First World War raged. Ford gathered a number of well-known reformers and peace advocates and sent them to Europe on a mission to persuade the warring parties to negotiate. The project was widely ridiculed. But the peace mission came at the end of a period when some of the most enlightened minds believed that the progress of European and American civilization had made war obsolete.

Speaking for some of the sunnier beliefs of American culture early in the twentieth century, Ford also embodied its closely connected prejudices. Early in the 1920s his *Dearborn Independent* published a series of articles accusing the Jews of causing the ills of the age. Among those listed were provocative short skirts, Hollywood movies, and in general the decadence of the modern world, all of which offended the backcountry morality of much of the American public. Yet in Europe and the United States, persistent anti-Semitism was endorsed by people of wealth and cosmopolitan taste even more strongly than by rural villagers. Later Ford backed some distance away from his bigoted declarations. Whatever Ford's particular variant of the prejudice, it went with a cranky personality, that could be stubbornly resistant to reason, or information that did not accord with his beliefs. That characteristic appeared also in his response to the labor militancy of the Great Depression. Ford used brutal tactics against union organizations: his workers would accept their condition on his terms, not theirs. His was the mentality of a pioneer industrial statesman in many ways uncommonly visionary but, like other visionaries, scarcely able to deal with the world beyond his own perceptions of it.

The New Mobility

The technology that made workers more precise and orderly could bring social disorder, or the fear of it. "The automobile," warned a juvenile judge in Muncie, Indiana, "has become a house of prostitution on wheels." A man and a woman could get into one, drive to a deserted spot, and do everything that overseers of American morals did not want them to do. It is said that long after window shades disappeared from autos, teachers self-appointed to watch over young girls warned: "if he pulls down the shades, watch out." And as the uses of the horse receded, the auto gave mobility to a new generation of bandits.

The automobile changed the relationship between Americans and physical space. The ability to live some distance between home and workplace hastened the growth of suburbs. Sunday drives became a national institution, as did summer cross-country travel. The isolation of the farmhouse and the rural village vanished—or what traces of it remained would give way to the radio and then to television. In the earlier years of the automobile, cabins—forerunners of the full-fledged motel—sprang up as overnight stops for long distance drivers. The famous Route 66 connecting Los Angeles to Chicago became dotted throughout its length with stops where the big bands played. Respectable people spurned the cabins, which seemed so much less substantial than hotels. As late as the 1940s, cautious motorists suffered the inconvenience of driving into the centers of the nearest city of any size to find a hotel for a night's rest. But motels eventually attracted the general public. The car meanwhile had become so accessible that from the drought-devastated Great Plains even some of the poor of the Depression used it in their legendary treks to the promise of California.

Black Americans, Hispanics, Asian Americans, and American Indians all found ways to take advantage of automotive mobility. Migratory workers could cast their net more widely as they searched for jobs. Vegetable farms, a staple of Japanese agricultural work in California, now had motor vehicles to haul their produce to market. In the West, Indian peoples used cars to carry on traditional patterns of movement, reestablishing regular rounds among distant reservation communities. White homesteaders in the West, arriving by train, sometimes expressed surprise at finding newly-opened reservation lands occupied by busy Indians driving new cars, purchased with the proceeds from land sales or leasing. Cars gave people of color the opportunity to move, to escape instances of social oppression, to create economic opportunities, to partake in that certain kind of freedom we have come to associate with the open road.

The automobile brought enormous change to the cities and industry. In the nineteenth century, urban pollution was compounded by the daily mountains of manure, the sewers of urine from horses, the rotted and fly-swarming flesh of the huge beasts worked to death and then left for days in the streets to be carried away. The automobile, though today recognized as a major polluter, freed cities from repulsive odors and dangerous sources of disease. The brutal loads that commerce, with great cruelty, forced upon draft horses passed to unfeeling internal-combustion engines. Automobile manufacture of course became a major industry, spawning car dealerships across the country. For all this, it had a basis in the earlier wagon-and-carriage business. Studebaker, formerly a carriage manufacturer, switched over to autos. Earlier in the twentieth century, carriage makers would simultaneously advertise horse-drawn and motorized vehicles, stressing the handcrafted excellence of each. Soon the trucking industry became a major competitor to railroads, which in the nineteenth century had held majestic sway over long-distance land freight. Subsidiary industries grew: steel for car bodies, petroleum for fuel, rubber for tires, for highways concrete. International competition for oil reserves developed among the many unpredictable consequences of the vehicle that had once born the modest title "the horseless carriage."

INDUSTRY AND POLITICS IN THE JAZZ AGE

At its simplest, the industrial progress symbolized in the engineering imagination of Henry Ford and the organizational genius of Alfred P. Sloan contributed to the character of the Jazz Era the automobile, the radio, and silent movies. Without the auto, the sense of spatial freedom and the opportunities for private meetings and larger social gatherings that became available to the young would have been unimaginable. The new medium of radio brought into the smallest community a cosmopolitan world. Film carried images of freedom, worldly sexual encounter, daring violations of outworn propriety.

Consumerism and International Business

Through the creation of a mass consumer market, business encouraged the pursuit of pleasure. Once advertising had been little more than a modest effort to bring a product to the favorable attention of buyers. It now became a major industry in itself, designed not only to sell a particular good or service but also to encourage potential customers to invest in items they did not really need. Advertising's judgment of the public is captured in the pronouncement of J. Walter Thompson, one of its major figures, that the typical American had the intelligence of a fourteen-year-old. At what other age level, he asked, would you place anyone who could be persuaded to buy a car for the social status or to smoke a pipe and look like a deep thinker? The creation of a widespread system of buying on credit that made the products of industry widely available aided advertising while tempting people to purchase more than they could immediately pay for.

Between the Armistice and the Great Depression of the 1930s prosperity spread unevenly. Postwar inflation coupled with the diminishing of war industries made for at least temporary distress among blue-collar workers, and a recession from 1920 to 1922 brought massive unemployment. Poverty was still widespread. Black and white migrants from the South together formed a pool of badly paid workers. Southern textile mills, locally owned and inefficient, gave wretched pay to their employees, some of them children. Coal miners did dangerous work for unsteady pay. For much of the decade sectors of agriculture were in a slump. Dairy farmers prospered, and vegetable growers benefited from consumers now being taught to be conscious of a healthy diet. Yet when wartime federal price supports for grain growers ceased, many farmers after two decades of prosperity suffered two decades of decline. Mechanization, especially in the form of cheap tractors powered by gasoline, won over farmers who could afford it. Sharecroppers, tenants, and agricultural laborers soon suffered from mechanical changes that made their labor obsolete. Yet real wages for most American workers rose sharply. And by 1928 most American families had electricity in their homes, at a time when industry mass produced irons, vacuum cleaners, washing machines, and other household appliances using electrical energy.

The feelings generated by miracles of technology and the apparently stunning growth of capital cannot be measured. The spectacular success of much of the economy overshadowed the ills that beset some industries, including railroads and shipping. From 1924 until the crash of October 1929, the Wall Street stock market went into a seemingly unending upward streak. "Even when you were broke," F. Scott Fitzgerald would later recall, "you didn't worry about money, because it was in such profusion around you." Money offered glamour. Fitzgerald's hero Jay Gatsby, immersed in romantic fantasy beyond any appetite for wealth in itself, finds magic in the glitter surrounding his unattainable love, Daisy, token of a world of miracles. Fitzgerald omitted from his definition of the Jazz Age nine-tenths of the economy. Black Alabama sharecroppers and white West Virginia miners did not take silver gin flasks to Ivy League football games. But in magazines and movies the upper tenth could tantalize the public at large with glimpses of a life of luxury. The American rich of earlier times had lived in a realm of haughty aloofness, removed from most of the population. In life and even as depicted on the screen, the well-off of the new generation of the twenties appeared with their cars and speakeasies and nightlife to be much like the rest of the public. They were just a bit luckier, just a whisper ahead of where this or next year's salary could take their envious viewers.

Even as business enticed the public to revel in consumer goods, it also urged the opposite value of industriousness. Technocrats wanted a future placed in the hands of scientists and engineers, who could bring to society at large the rationality that governed their material achievements. This idea had some clear affinities to the earlier progressive determination to make scientific and technical rationality an instrument of social reform. But progressivism, as a recognizable movement, had waned with the war. The technocrats of the twenties looked not merely to curing social ills, or to making society more orderly, but to putting technology at the very center of the human enterprise. That went beyond the limits of progressive reform projects, and beyond the objectives of the technical, managerial economy destined to take shape during the New Deal of the 1930s.

Americans saw technological progress as nearly synonymous with business. This gave finance and commerce a natural ascendancy in politics. On the presidential level the prominence of business may be defined as of two kinds. President Warren G. Harding was closer to small-town merchants and chambers of commerce than to corporate managers, and his successor Calvin Coolidge, who was said to have announced that the business of America is business, also had been nurtured in a society of farms and rural villages. As secretary of commerce to Harding and Coolidge and then as president in his own right, the engineer Herbert Hoover more accurately represented an age of giant businesses controlling wondrous new powers of science and machinery. Coolidge and Harding also served that age, but largely as admiring outsiders to it.

Loans the United States made to Allies during the Great War changed the United States from a debtor to a creditor nation. As business boomed following the short depression of the early 1920s, more corporate mergers than ever took place. Then the economic strength that gathered force during the decade pushed outward to the rest of the world, particularly in the form of multinational corporations. International Telephone and Telegraph owned factories throughout Europe and employed more overseas workers than any other American company; the Ford Motor Company followed close behind. The United Fruit Company dominated entire Central American economies, notably Costa Rica. Two decades later Chiquita Banana was to flourish among Americans who learned not to put bananas in the refrigerator. Herbert Hoover worried that the new world economics might deprive the nation's workers of jobs, but that encouraged him to take a major part in securing for the country's businesses access to international trade, investments, and raw materials. The United States was the wonder—and the envy—of the world.

Warren Gamaliel Harding

The genial, honest, hardworking Ohio politician Warren Harding, who entered the White House in 1921, believed in American business partly as an

American but especially because his nature was not to question. He trusted people—excessively, it would turn out. In his call for giving federal courts jurisdiction over prosecutions for lynching, he acted in the best tradition of the Republican Party, at that time still regarded as the party of civil rights. Harding had little interest in Red-hunting, and among the radicals he released from federal confinement was the Socialist leader Eugene V. Debs, who had been imprisoned for antiwar activity. In signing the Sheppard-Towner Act of 1921, which provided federal funding for state programs in prenatal and child health, he demonstrated his receptivity to the activist ideas of others. Harding and Secretary of Commerce Hoover persuaded the steel industry to adopt the eight-hour day. And both favored legislation to end child labor. Harding's cabinet was

Eugene V. Debs, the Socialist Party candidate for president in 1920, won almost a million votes though a prisoner in the Atlanta federal penitentiary. (Courtesy, Brown Bros.)

quite impressive. The greatly respected Charles Evans Hughes, later to be appointed to the United States Supreme Court, became secretary of state. Henry C. Wallace proved a masterful secretary of agriculture. Harding's choice of Hoover for secretary of commerce would make that department a force for mild progressivism within its main role of assisting business to become more cooperative and efficient. The president's signature on the Fordney-McCumber Act, imposing a high protective tariff, indicated his predictable friendliness to industry and commercial farming, which the act protected against cheap imports.

Like a retailer in the midwestern village culture in which he had in fact been reared, Harding was friendly to everyone. Corruption flourished under him not through his connivance but in the absence of any skepticism on his part about people's motives. In return for the leasing of federal oil land in Elk Hills in California and Teapot Dome in Wyoming, Harding's secretary of the interior Albert Fall collected hundreds of thousands of dollars in bribes from the oil businessman Edward Doheny. Fall would eventually become the first cabinet member in American history to be sent to prison. Suspicion also fell on Attorney General Harry Daugherty, but though repeatedly put on trial he was never convicted of any crime. Charles R. Forbes, the head of the Veterans Bureau, sold veterans hospitals' supplies below cost and went to prison for it. These and other misdoings created the most lasting impression of Harding. His death from a heart attack in 1923, brought on in part perhaps

President Harding (right), Henry Ford (left), and Thomas Edison (center). (Courtesy, Brown Bros.)

by this trusting man's discovery of the developing scandals, brought into the White House his vice president, Calvin Coolidge of New England.

Calvin Coolidge

The most publicized act of Coolidge before his presidency and while yet governor of Massachusetts occurred when he called in state troopers to break a police strike in Boston in 1919. Best remembered in that affair is his statement that "there is no right to strike against the public safety by anybody, anywhere, any time." In that time of labor struggles and pervasive fear of radicalism, Coolidge's actions gave him the aura of a defender of the established order against labor agitation. Perhaps he was. His public expression of sympathy with the strikers for their wretched pay has not found its way into the Coolidge legend. Nor has his signing of a good number of progressive laws for Massachusetts, including legislation holding most industries to a forty-eight-hour week.

Coolidge's manner suggested that the country's modern business civilization rested on an older rural American simplicity. During a visit to his native Vermont, he learned that Harding had died. By the light of a kerosene lamp his father, acting in the capacity of a notary public, administered to him the presidential oath. But Coolidge spoke for a business culture at once Puritan in its work ethic and eager to awaken the appetites of consumers.

After the election of 1924, when he defeated a weak Democratic challenger along with the remarkably strong Progressive Party candidate Robert La Follette, Coolidge kept on from Harding's cabinet Secretary of the Treasury Andrew Mellon, a vigorous and over time a successful advocate of reductions in income taxes on the wealthy. But Coolidge was no more a deep-dyed reactionary than Harding. He wanted, for example, a biracial commission to improve race relations. And his administration helped convene the Meriam Commission, which recommended significant improvements in federal policy toward Indians. Secretary of Commerce Hoover also remained from Harding's cabinet. So energetic was the administrator that observers suggested he was trying to be secretary of every other department, Hoover spoke for a Republican progressivism favorable toward business but intent on pushing it toward social responsibility. At Hoover's insistence came regulation of radio, avia-

President Calvin Coolidge fishes while wearing formal clothing. (Courtesy, Brown Bros.)

tion, bird sanctuaries, and pollution in coastal waters. Coolidge's Amherst College classmate and attorney general, Harlan Fiske Stone, ordered the cessation of wiretapping and other forms of spying practiced by some federal agencies.

Welfare Capitalism

Coolidge's presidency came at a time when big business, whatever its realities, was increasingly presenting itself in a way that generally goes by the name "welfare capitalism." The idea that capitalism might act deliberately in the interest of workers and consumers had been germinating for some time. The National Association of Manufacturers, though an enemy to labor unions, supported the idea that equitable wages benefited capitalism, deepening the consumer market that business needed for its own prosperity. For a small number of workers, business began providing life or health insurance or a degree of profit sharing. Presiding over much of this appeared a new kind of manager, trained in a business school to run a business as a profession bringing obligations to employees and the public as well as to stockholders.

These gestures were undoubtedly aimed to undermine labor agitation and other attacks on business. But they also recognized that since big business now controlled much of production and distribution, it constituted an alternative government of the economy, and so bore the responsibilities of that status. Many prewar progressives had believed in cooperation between business and government. But while earlier progressives had wished government to be the senior partner in the enterprise, welfare capitalism now assigned business that position.

However many workers may have benefited from employers persuaded by welfare capitalism, many others continued to encounter casually brutal treatment. In West Virginia and Illinois, dozens of miners died in fights with strikebreakers. Reacting to a

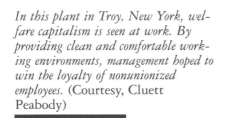

In this plant in Troy, New York, welfare capitalism is seen at work. By providing clean and comfortable working environments, management hoped to win the loyalty of nonunionized employees. (Courtesy, Cluett Peabody)

LUCKY LINDY

The decade produced a genuine American hero.

On May 21, 1927, a single engine plane circled and landed at Le Bourget airport in Paris. Almost immediately some four thousand people engulfed it. What had brought out such a crowd of Frenchmen, a nation not undiscriminating in praise?

Charles Lindbergh was in the tradition of Henry Ford and thousands of other American inventors. For years he had fiddled with planes as he dropped air mail a few hundred feet above Illinois towns on cloudy or stormy nights during the 1920s. The idea struck him of building his own plane and crossing the Atlantic solo to Paris. A firm in San Diego constructed the plane according to his specifications. He flew it to his base of operations in St. Louis and christened it the *Spirit of St. Louis*, earning the approbation and financial support from the city's businessmen who would long cherish his name.

Then Lindbergh moved on to Roosevelt Field in Nassau County just east of New York City. From here he planned to bridge the Atlantic alone. He could not sleep the night before his planned flight, but after checking weather charts Lindbergh climbed into his cockpit around 8:00 a.m. with sandwiches purchased at a local deli in the New York City borough of Queens. Along

with the sandwiches, he took plenty of water to drink and as many extra containers of gasoline as he thought the plane could carry and still take off. It did, narrowly missing some telephone wires at the end of the field. Lindbergh passed over Long Island Sound, Connecticut, and Massachusetts on his way to Nova Scotia. Never before had he flown over a large body of water. As he used more and more fuel, the plane's wings ceased trembling.

The weather unexpectedly turned bad. Heavy rain and turbulent winds buffeted the tiny craft. But after Lindbergh flew over Newfoundland the sky cleared, and he was now alone over the awe-inspiring Atlantic. Night came and he flew with a compass and an altimeter but no way of contacting any other human being. Caught unaware by heavy fog and wintry gusts, he managed to pull up to ten thousand feet. Ice formed on the wings and pulled the plane seaward. Again unexpectedly, the plane emerged under a dome of starlight. Fighting off sleep, Lindbergh passed the midway point. He knew the approximate distance yet to be traveled: only a few weeks earlier he had measured it with a string over a globe in the public library in San Diego.

Twenty-six hours later he spied a land bird and soon Ireland. Descending over a fishing boat, he received no response to his request for directions; but following rocky shores and green fields he came to the English Channel. Then appeared the lights of the Eiffel Tower straight ahead. Thirty-three hours after takeoff Lindbergh stopped his propeller, his plane stilled.

Met at home with ticker-tape parades, "Lucky Lindy" became the country's hero. Supreme Court Justice Charles Evans Hughes announced that the young pilot had "displaced everything that is petty, that is sordid, that is vulgar." Maybe the twenties, an era sometimes entirely conscious of its own exaltation of luxury and wealth, had not banished the old virtues of courage and a becoming modesty. *We,* the title of Lindbergh's autobiography, referred to flier and plane, but it could be taken more broadly to signify a marriage of individualism and modern technology. Perhaps the lesson is that technological advance cannot make the old virtues obsolete, for it needs them for its own maintenance.

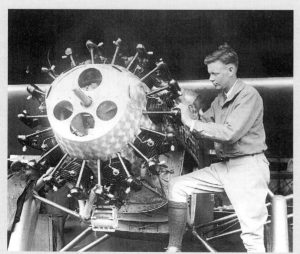

Charles A. Lindbergh and The Spirit of St. Louis. (Courtesy, Library of Congress)

Massachusetts minimum wage law for female building cleaners, the president of Harvard fired these women on the university's staff and replaced them with men. Labor meanwhile became divided against itself. Craft unions within the AFL typically excluded unskilled workers; most unions refused membership to blacks; and much of the labor force supported restriction of immigration.

Prosperity that the country at large enjoyed during much of the decade did not silence politics completely. To child welfare legislation, progressives added a plan to develop a waterpower project at Muscle Shoals on the Tennessee River. In 1924 the venerable Senator Robert M. La Follette of Wisconsin attracted more than sixteen percent of the popular vote as the presidential candidate of the Progressive Party, a combination of Socialists and Republican progressives. That same year, when Congress sharply restricted immigration from nationalities akin to the waves of newcomers earlier in the century, it agreed to give citizenship to American Indians. Congressional legislation also provided low-interest loans to farmers. McNary-Haugen, a plan named after its sponsors, called for federal agricultural price supports to be maintained by purchasing surpluses and selling them abroad. Congress twice passed the bill, only to have it vetoed by Coolidge. As president from 1929 to 1933, Hoover took seriously the farmer's plight. Faithful to his belief in voluntary association, he signed in 1929 an Agricultural Marketing Act setting up a Federal Farm Board empowered to make loans to agricultural cooperatives. These, he hoped, would set production quotas for farmers and create rational ways of marketing their goods. Hoover and Congress set up stabilization corporations that attempted to buy enough wheat and cotton to maintain their value. The appropriations ran out in 1932.

Herbert Hoover and American Business

As an engineer turned administrator of great private concerns, Herbert Hoover had labored to bring professional standards to business administration. The Quaker faith in which he was reared taught an obligation to practice charity and good works. His humanitarian conscience expressed itself in contributing time and personal wealth to a relief project for Belgian victims during World War I. In 1919 Hoover coordinated a massive relief effort for war refugees, and he did the same for the Russian people beset by famine in the early 1920s. Willing to use government spending to combat unemployment, during an economic slump in the early 1920s he proposed speeding up public works projects.

Much in Hoover suggested the practice among Quakers of achieving reasonable consensus through their meetings. Government as he conceived it was to be in part a channel of information and a giver of advice. One of his most important achievements while he was secretary of commerce led to the adoption by industry of common standards of measurement: a success that ranks with the continuously moving assembly line in its importance to advanced industrialism. He wanted business leaders to expand their energies not in shortsighted competition but in cooperative networks. So Hoover also promoted a movement among businesses and industries to form associations within which they could reach voluntary agreements on such policies as the maintenance of high production. An engineering expert who believed in experts of various kinds, the president who came after Coolidge meanwhile organized a series of conferences in which professionals and concerned citizens could address technical issues such as child welfare.

A problem in this approach was that if an enterprise refused to act responsibly on its own or used association, say, as a screen for price-fixing, there was little the government could do. But until the onset of the Great Depression, Hoover's version of benevolent capitalism held some limited promise, although it would be dogged by the tension between making a profit and thinking broadly about community.

Suggested Readings

The management of the war by the European powers and United States's entry are examined in Ian F.W. Beckett, *The Great War, 1914–1918* (2001). The psychological effects of trench warfare is documented in Eric J. Leed, *No Man's Land: Combat and Identity in World War I* (1979). The British government's efforts to draw the United States into the war is a subject of M.L. Sanders and Philip Taylor, *British Propaganda and the First World War, 1914–1918* (1983). On the peace settlement, see Alan Sharp, *The Versailles Settlement: Peacemaking in Paris, 1919* (1991). William G. Pullen, *World War Debts and United States Foreign Policy, 1919–1929* (1987) does a fine job of explaining the complexities and controversies surrounding the war debts issue. On the way the war has been depicted in memory, see Jay Winter, *Sites of Memory, Sites of Mourning: The Great War in European Cultural History* (1995). On American war aims, see Thomas J. Knock, *To End All Wars: Woodrow Wilson and the Quest for a New World Order* (1992) and David M. Esposito *The Legacy of Woodrow Wilson: American War Aims in World War I* (1996). The war and its influence on society and culture are examined in Robert H. Zieger, *America's Great War: World War I and the American Experience* (2000). David S. Foglesong, *America's Secret War against Bolshevism: U.S. Intervention in the Russian Civil War, 1917–1920* (1995), recounts how the United States tried to influence the course of the Russian Revolution. Nancy Bristow, *Making Men Moral: Social Engineering during the Great War* (1996), is a history of the Commission on Training Camp Activities, which was staffed by progressives who hoped to use the military as a model for social reform. Donald Smythe, *Pershing: General of the Armies* (1986) is a biography of the commander of the American Expeditionary Force. The participation of racial and ethnic minorities in the war effort is the subject of Arthur Barbeau and Florette Henri, *The Unknown Soldiers: Black American Troops in World War I* (1974), and Nancy Gentile Ford, *Americans All!: Foreign-born Soldiers in World War I* (2001). Thomas A. Britten, *American Indians in World War I: At Home and at War* (1997), looks at Native Americans. The part played by women in the war is described in Lettie Gavin, *American Women in World War I: They Also Served* (1997). The pandemic of Spanish influenza is most recently analyzed in Gina Kolata, *Flu: The Story of the Great Influenza Pandemic of 1918 and the Search for the Virus that Caused It* (1999).

The standard general survey of the American home front is David M. Kennedy, *Over Here: The First World War and American Society* (1980). On the movement of the South's African Americans into the industrial cities of the North and the use of women in the labor force, see Joe William Trotter, Jr., ed., *The Great Migration in Historical Perspective: New Dimensions of Race, Class, and Gender* (1991); James R. Grossman, *Land of Hope: Chicago, Black Southerners, and the Great Migration* (1989); and Maureen Weiner Greenwald, *Women, War and Work: The Impact of World War I on Women Workers in the United States* (1990). Mark Ellis, *Race, War, and Surveillance: African Americans and the United States Government during World War I* (2001), examines race relations during the war and the demands of African Americans for equal rights. Labor unrest is the subject of Dana Frank, *Purchasing Power: Consumer Organizing, Gender, and the Seattle Labor Movement, 1919–1929* (1994).

David E. Kyvig, *Daily Life in the United States, 1920–1939* (2002) offers a good general view of the twenties with an emphasis on social history. Racial issues are analyzed in Chip Rhodes, *Structures of the Jazz Age: Mass Culture, Progressive Education, and Racial Discourse in American Modernism* (1998). A recent biography of the Lone Eagle and his times is A. Scott Berg, *Lindbergh* (1998). Dorothy M. Brown, *Setting a Course: American Women in the 1920s* (1987) is a good general survey of the subject. Consumer habits and the manipulation of consumer tastes are examined in Susan Strasser, *Satisfaction Guaranteed: The Making of the American Mass Market* (1989); Gary S. Cross, *An All-Consuming Century: Why Commercialism Won in Modern America* (2000); and Martha L. Olney, *Buy Now, Pay Later: Advertising, Credit, and Consumer Durables in the 1920s* (1991). On the expansion of the new industry of advertising that would create a demand for the nation's goods and services, see Jackson Lears, *Fables of Abundance: A Cultural History of Advertising in America* (1994). Stephen Meyer III, *The Five Dollar Day: Labor Management and Social Control in the Ford Motor Company, 1908–1921* (1981) looks at the innovations pioneered by Henry Ford.

The religious culture of the jazz age is studied in Bruce B. Lawrence, *Defenders of God: The Fundamentalist Revolt against the Modern Age* (1989); Joel Carpenter, *Revive Us Again: The Reawaking of American Fundamentalism* (1997); and Edward J. Larson, *Summer for the Gods: The Scopes Trial and America's Continuing Debate over Science and Religion* (1997). Desmond King, *Making Americans: Immigration, Race, and the Origins of the Diverse Democracy* discusses the movement to restrict the flow of immigrants. The reappearance of the Ku Klux Klan in the 1920s has received attention in David M. Chalmers, *Hooded Americanism: A History of the Ku Klux Klan*, 3d ed. (1987) and Nancy MacLean, *Behind the Mark of Chivalry: The Making of the Second Ku Klux Klan* (1994). Kathleen M. Blee, *Women of the Klan: Racism and Gender in the 1920s* (1991) examines the place of women in the Klan and gender issues raised by their membership in the extremist group.

The most prominent race riot is analyzed in James S. Hirsch, *Riot and Remembrance: The Tulsa Race War and Its Legacy* (2002). See Cary D. Wintz, *The Harlem Renaissance* (2003); David Levering Lewis, *When Harlem Was in Vogue* (1981); and Lionel C. Bascom, ed., *A Renaissance in Harlem: Lost Voices of an American Community* (1999).

On Hoover, see David Burner, *Herbert Hoover: A Public Life* (1978); George H. Nash, *The Life of Herbert Hoover: Master of Emergencies, 1917–1918* (1996); and Ellis W. Hawley, ed., *Herbert Hoover as Secretary of Commerce: Studies in New Era Thought and Practice* (1981). David Burner looks at the political culture of the 1920s in *The Politics of Provincialism: The Democratic Party in Transition, 1918–1932* (1967).

Ann Douglas, *Terrible Honesty: Mongrel Manhattan in the 1920s* (1995) examines the influence white and African American authors exerted on each other in the cultural environment of 1920s New York. On Freud, see Nathan G. Hale, Jr., *The Rise and Crisis of Psychoanalysis in the United States: Freud and the Americans, 1917–1985* (1995).

TOP: Tractored Out, Childress County, Texas, 1938. *(Courtesy Library of Congress)*
BOTTOM: Drought Refugee from Oklahoma, Blythe, California, 1936. *(Courtesy Library of Congress)*
Both photographs are by Dorothea Lange.

Hitting Bottom and Climbing Back Up

CHAPTER 21

★

DISASTER ON THE PLAINS

To human observers, animals are uncanny in their ability to sense unseen danger. And so the birds must have seemed on the beautiful sky-blue day of April 14, 1935. That spring afternoon, the air on the Kansas plains had suddenly turned chilly, and the birds flocked together, chirping nervously. Then abruptly the reason for their excitement appeared from the north, a thick black cloud, the more ominous for its total silence. Hours before nightfall, people found themselves groping in the darkness of a dust storm that earned that day the name of Black Sunday.

In its sudden, relentless malice, the wind-borne earth on Black Sunday typified the dust clouds that punished the Great Plains during the 1930s, again and again. But otherwise the storms differed from one to the other. People could feel the dust in varying ways: peppery in the nostrils, or slimy and thick. In the wake of a storm, they had to eat quickly before their food became inedible. In bed, they might have to lie still lest the dust in the sheets be stirred up around them. To protect against the tiny particles that could sift through the smallest openings, families tried sealing the edges of their windows and doors. That could lead to a choking off the oxygen supply inside the homes. Animals too suffered. Dust blinded and confused them or caked their lungs. For a time, pulmonary diseases among human beings increased, baffling scientists who could find no harmful bacteria in the dust. Added to physical sickness was the psychological effect of the storms that hit, one after the other, sometimes without even the warning of the birds as on Black Sunday.

The Great Plains, from Montana and the Dakotas to Texas and New Mexico, became known as the Dust Bowl. But on at least one occasion the dust reached the eastern seaboard. A storm in 1934 that began on May 9 in the northern Plains had by the next day carried the western soil eastward to the skies of Buffalo in New York State. Then it silted Boston, New York, Washington, DC, and Atlanta. Dust from that storm did not stop at the water's edge: it sprinkled ships hundreds of miles off the Atlantic coast.

It was a time, though, when everything about the nation, even its disasters, seemed big enough to boast about. A Texan planned to pay his taxes in Kansas; there, he figured, is where his farm had gone. Prairie dogs, the story went, could now burrow their way up several feet above the ground. One dust storm got so bad that a pilot had to bail out. It took him six hours to dig his way down to earth.

The immediate causes of the dust storms resulted from a combination of heat, drought, and wind. At one time or another during the thirties, much of the nation suffered from lack of rainfall, but on the Great Plains that brought disaster to the region's corn and wheat crops. And as dryness and heat cracked the earth, wind could quickly scoop up the parched loose grains of dirt. It hurled them across flat empty country in billowing masses that could be startlingly beautiful in their rich contrasting folds of dark and light.

Nature had in the human race an unwitting accomplice in the dust storms. For generations Americans had treated their magnificent land with a recklessness that assumed its bounty would never end. Farmers leveled forests to clear fields for agriculture. Livestock sheared grasses that had shielded the ground from the sun's glare and prevented erosion; plows ripped the grass out by the roots. Wind swept freely across a country level to begin with, further flattened by farmers desperate for the money that could be gouged from the earth.

The dust storms themselves worsened the fertility of the Great Plains, blowing away a portion of what remained of the rich soil not leached by farming. Though much of the Plains was spared the storms, the drought seemed to spread everywhere. But it too is insufficient to describe the troubles that moved two and a half million Dust Bowl residents from their farms, most of them to a town or other nearby place or to a neighboring state. A broader explanation lies in the pattern of consolidation of farming, facilitated by modern machinery, that furthered the assault on the land and made it profitable for landowners to throw out their tenants.

The misery of the Great Plains went beyond the farms themselves. That is confirmed by information the government collected about the impoverished migrants from the Plains after 1935: the "Okies" who traveled by whatever means they could to California. That name stuck because the largest single number of them, in the late 1930s seventy-five thousand or a fourth of the whole, came from Oklahoma. Most of the Okies did not even farm. They lived in cities or towns, adding to the farm failure that ravaged the entire region.

The Depression and the Dust Bowl had much in common. As huge and rich as the continent, as wasteful of the materials it worked with as American farming and forestry, the economy itself broke down in the thirties like the agriculture of the Great Plains.

HISTORICAL EVENTS

1929
Agricultural Marketing Act • stock market crashes

1930s
The Great Depression begins • radio shows, movies, games, outdoor camping become widespread throughout decade

1931
Scottsboro boys case

1932
Reconstruction Finance Corporation • Veterans' Bonus Expeditionary Force • Franklin Delano Roosevelt elected president • unemployment rate reaches twenty-five percent

1933
First Hundred Days • Emergency Banking Act • Glass Steagall Act establishes FDIC insuring savings accounts for $5,000 • Tennessee Valley Authority (TVA) • National Industrial Recovery Act (NIRA establishes NRA) • Civilian Conservation Corps (CCC) • Public Works Administration (PWA) • Good Neighbor Policy of reduced tariffs and friendship with Latin America expanded

1934
Indian Reorganization Act • Upton Sinclair runs for governor of California • Securities and Exchange Commission (SEC)

1935
Huey Long organizes Share-Our-Wealth societies • Long is assassinated • Second Hundred Days • Social Security Act • Mexican immigrants returning home reach 500,000 • Supreme Court finds NIRA unconstitutional • Wagner Act (National Labor Relations Board) • Wealth Tax Act • Works Progress Administration (WPA) • Committee for Industrial Organization (CIO) formed, later becoming the Congress of Industrial Organizations

1936
President Roosevelt reelected • Agricultural Adjustment Act (AAA) found unconstitutional • Farm Security Administration

1937
United Auto Workers defeats General Motors in sit-down strike • Roosevelt scheme to pack the Supreme Court defeated

1938
Fair Labor Standards Act and Second Agricultural Adjustment Act passed

1939
John Steinbeck, *The Grapes of Wrath* • 75,000 hear Marian Anderson sing at the Lincoln Memorial

ALL THE WAY DOWN

By 1929 the automobile along with the railroad and the airplane was conquering distance. Possessing a speed beyond the imagining of all previous systems of production, the assembly line could transform steel and glass into the perfect form of a car. Shadows on a silver movie screen blurred the line between reality and dream. And among these marvels of the time, the public gave a special place to Wall Street, which until October 1929 seemed to be generating wealth out of some magic of its own. Why was this, when earnings for a share of stock were not rising rapidly? Stock prices soared because people were buying stocks at high prices on the expectation that others would buy them at even higher prices in hopes that still others would purchase at higher prices still. Investors bought shares paying a fraction of their total price, a practice

Wall Street, October 1929. The mood was dark. (Courtesy, Corbis-Bettmann)

known as buying on margin, assuming that the eventual profit would cover the remainder of the cost.

Most Americans were not at the gambling table. Buying stocks was a game of the rich, along with a part of the middle class with a little extra pocket money to invest. Nor is it fair to dismiss as mere gambling the booming stock market of 1925 through 1929. Wall Street ultimately reflects and sustains the condition of the more solid world of production and exchange. That world, it would turn out, was riddled with problems. Among the most serious was that ordinary citizens lacked the purchasing power to buy indefinitely the goods with which manufacturers flooded the stores. For some time the coal industry had been in a slump. Portions of agriculture struggled with the old problem of overcoming fixed expenses with an income always subject to the fluctuations of the market. Tenants, sharecroppers, and hired hands scraped out a living. Coal miners and southern textile workers would have had difficulty recognizing what was meant by the prosperity of the times. But in an age of technological miracles and, for much of the public, substantial well-being, such weaknesses in the economy could easily be overlooked.

Still, buyers continued to gamble, almost unaware that any drop in confidence would make stocks fall. On October 23 investors lost their nerve. Some unloaded a mass of stocks, others unloaded more, and by the end of the trading day panic had hit Wall Street. Over the next few days the situation appeared to steady. Then on Black Tuesday, October 29, the market collapsed. Stunned and dazed, investors on the exchange floor dumped their holdings. Over $10 billion of invested funds evaporated.

The Crash and the Economy

The rout did not spread immediately throughout the nation's financial institutions. After having plunged by the end of 1929, the *New York Times* average of prices of industrial stocks showed a partial recovery in the first three months of 1930. Even when the market dropped again that spring, many compared the situation to the sharp but brief depression lasting from 1920 to 1922. Surely, they believed, the powerful engine of the economy would not be derailed for long. The elderly Secretary of the Treasury Andrew Mellon could re-

This boy working in a soda parlor is blissfully unaware of the hard times that lay ahead. (Courtesy, Library of Congress)

member more drastic slides. "During the coming year," he said guardedly in 1930, "the country will make steady progress." The shrewd conservative may have simply meant steady progress in letting the air out of the speculative balloon, knowing that the process could take considerable time. As late as January 1931 in his second inaugural address, New York's progressive Democratic governor, Franklin D. Roosevelt, made scant mention of hard times.

The relation between the crash and the Great Depression that followed remains unclear. Many economists today consider the collapse on Wall Street as only one cause of the Depression. Soon after the fall of the stock market, though, the larger economy began its downward slide. In response to President Hoover's pleas, many businesses refrained as long as they could from discharging employees. As a result, many workers received the bad tidings just before Christmas 1930. During the last years of Hoover's presidency, three thousand banks closed their doors, unable to meet their obligations to depositors because borrowers could not keep up their payments on loans. By 1933, gross production nationwide shrank by half. Part of that occurred because the government raised taxes and dried up the money supply instead of pressuring the Federal Reserve Board to increase it. Some small businesses that managed to hang on even built a little equity.

But by the first year of President Franklin Roosevelt's administration, an astonishing one in four Americans was without a job, and unemployment would remain above fifteen percent until 1940.

President Hoover had tried, at least within the scope of his theoretical beliefs, to relieve suffering. His Agricultural Marketing Act of 1929 created a stabilization fund to buy agricultural crops in bad times and hold them off the market until prices rose. Since the Depression quickly became worldwide, little demand for farm products appeared anywhere and the fund, though this was not its purpose, doled out relief to farmers until its appropriations ran out. The Reconstruction Finance Corporation of 1932 provided for a few public works projects, but it mostly tried to rescue large banks hoping that their survival would allow better times to trickle down to the multitudes. Even business tycoons expressed bewilderment. Testifying before congressional committees, some confessed to having not the faintest idea of what had gone wrong. Few ruined investors actually jumped out of windows, as Depression folklore would have it. More often former millionaires stretched on psychiatrists' couches trying to control their panic attacks; some after dinner at home simply sat in their own living rooms in silent despair. Theirs had been a culture, like that of the nation as a whole, in which money measured self-respect and its loss personal failure. Throughout the 1930s Americans would have to find new forms of self-identity, testing and redefining themselves in differing inventive ways.

A few shrewd investors made money by betting that stocks would not soon recover, buying inexpensive "puts" enabling them to collect on future declines. Cautious ones profited from conservative stock portfolios that retained considerable value in the 1930s even though prices of consumer goods sank. From New York City's Upper East Side to San Francisco's old-money Nob Hill, fine imported liquor reflected red or yellow in the light of elegant chandeliers. Sleek fur coats warmed the vanity of their owners even as winter and poverty chilled the bones of the unemployed. Residents of wealthy suburban communities, such as Lake Forest in Illinois, Grosse Point in Michigan, and Scarsdale in New York, were well away from villages—unfairly named Hoovervilles—made up of shacks that sprang up in Manhattan's parks or in a sprawl a hundred miles square outside Oklahoma City.

On the shores of Lake Michigan in 1931 a string

of handsome yachts originally worth a half-million dollars lay at anchor. A man stepped out of a Cadillac and asked their caretaker whether any were for sale. "Are you kidding?" came the response. "They're all for sale." A pair snapped up at a fraction of the original price had their insides gutted of rosewood and oil paintings. They returned to service as rumrunners sailing to the Canadian border to pick up whiskey, pretty women on deck to divert suspicions by the coast guard.

THE DISPOSSESSED

Today photographers would have to look hard to find a simple dwelling with old newspapers tacked to the walls as a barrier against the cold. Fewer grandparents remain to tell how local government distributed relief funds. After endless waiting in sterile public buildings, those seeking help answered embarrassing questions and signed documents. Government workers would then give slips of paper entitling the bearer to some free food. But before receiving funds for shoes or medicine, offi-

cials visited individual homes to verify destitution. Even the thickness of the leather remaining on the soles of a child's shoes had to be measured. It was all a humiliation only a bit less painful than hunger.

Pride lodged in a father's paycheck. When it disappeared, after trudging from one office to another, day after day, failing to find an opening, men lost faith in themselves. Anger turned inward. People wanted not revolution but jobs, some of them giving up when work failed to materialize. With divorces too expensive to be common, and child support and alimony rare, some husbands simply left home, ashamed and despised. Women more often than men either retained respectable positions such as teaching or entered the economy as clerical workers or telephone operators, many taking on jobs previously held by blacks and other minorities who had been dismissed without hesitation as being inferior.

For the poor who had little or no money in savings, a bank's collapse mattered nothing in a direct way. But for Americans of modest means to whom savings were the measure of success and security, a bank collapse could result in psychological as well

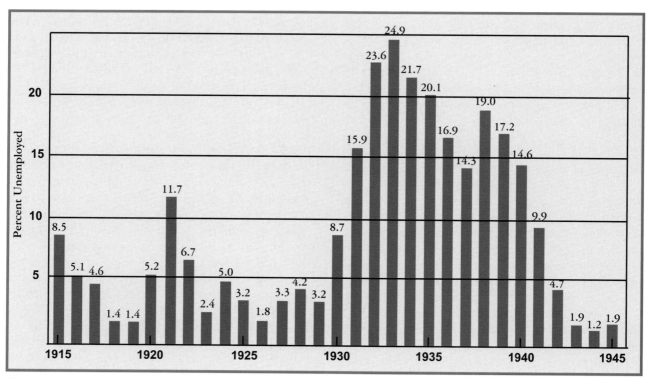

Unemployment, 1915–1945. (Courtesy, *Historical Statistics of the United States,* 1960)

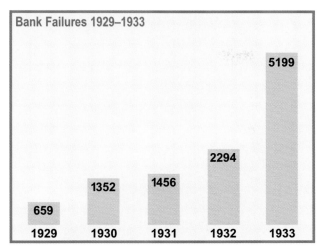

Bank Failures 1929–1933

Year	Failures
1929	659
1930	1352
1931	1456
1932	2294
1933	5199

Bank failures, 1929 through 1933. (Courtesy, C.D. Bremer, *American Bank Failures,* New York: Columbia University Press, 1935)

as economic depression. Long after the passing of the lean years, Americans who had experienced the Depression collected pieces of string, or if they went to a restaurant ordered the cheapest thing on the menu. Hundreds of thousands of people lost their family homesteads, along with their jobs and their dignity. Even if able to keep a house or a simple store, the fear of having it taken away hung over their daily life. People attended foreclosure sales, their pity mixed with curiosity and greed. Family heirlooms might be auctioned for pennies on the dollar. Foreclosures diminished the equation of home and family. As money dried up and lifetime savings vanished, hard drinking and smoking increased.

Drifting

One thing the country did not run out of during the Depression: its great, lonely, beckoning distances. On foot or by rail, sneaking into boxcars when the railroad police were not looking, millions of Americans during the Depression drifted across the continent, adding to the hoboes and migrant workers who had already become a familiar feature of the land. In theory, perhaps, they were searching for a job that they believed had to be waiting for them somewhere in a country so vast. In fact, they traveled because they had no reason not to do so. If no employment lay ahead of them, at least they could flee from the hopelessness at their point of departure. And they could always beg, or steal, or

be fed by a kindly family, or even find an odd job that could earn them a meal or two. Notable among the drifters were adolescents, of both genders. They moved in packs for companionship and mutual protection, gangs forming and parting with the flow of youth.

Included among the travelers with a clearer idea of where they were headed, the Okies, bound for California, believed that in that rich agricultural state there must be work. However they migrated, they are best known for driving beat-up cars, as they do in John Steinbeck's novel *The Grapes of Wrath,* published in 1939. Steinbeck's fictional Joad family, also portrayed in a film starring Henry Fonda, would become as much a legend of the decade as the more factual history of the times.

The drifting portrayed a country physically coming apart. When railroad cars carrying coal slowed down in towns, local people would jump on and off, stealing nuggets to heat their homes. Shifting freight cars accidentally crushed hundreds. People out of work sometimes became criminals of one kind or another, if only by stealing a shirt off a clothesline, milk from a back porch, bread at a grocery store. Hungry people knocked on the rear doors of homes asking for handouts. Local police sometimes treated drifters viciously, fearing that a town's reputation for generosity would draw crowds of the unemployed. Jails filled. Some wealthy families moved away from urban neighborhoods or sent their children to the safety of the remote countryside.

Making Do

Without their possessions, some Americans discovered their creativity. Many who lost everything they had accumulated since their younger days struggled back, as one put it, "by every means known to the human brain." Given up in earlier, more prosperous times, pushcarts filled with fruits or vegetables reappeared. Salesmen swarmed, selling everything from brushes and cosmetics to encyclopedias and Bibles. Junk and scrap metal became comparatively lucrative businesses. One banker accepted a job as a golf caddie. "I had Bach and Beethoven," a musician would recall. "Nothing mattered. I worked in the cathedral of the spirit. . . . Once in the studio a rat ran across my arm and bit me. Luckily a visitor had left a bottle of whiskey. . . . I poured the whiskey over the wound."

The Bonus Army

One group of Americans seeking relief from the Depression was composed of veterans of the First World War. In the summer of 1932 about twenty thousand came to Washington, DC, to demand early payment of a bonus promised for 1945. Accompanied in some cases by their families and placing their main encampment of tents at Anacostia Flats just over a bridge in Maryland, they conducted peaceful demonstrations, hoping that their presence toward itself would make their case. But when police attempted to remove a few of them who had found shelter in condemned buildings on Pennsylvania Avenue, some violence erupted. The city and the federal government feared greater trouble, and considered encampments themselves a nuisance. To General Douglas MacArthur, a highly decorated hero of the war and now chief of staff of the army, President Hoover gave the task of removing the Bonus Army.

Hoover, who the previous December had provided tents, blankets, and other help to six hundred hunger marchers and accepted their petition, did not intend to be inhumane to the Bonus Army, and he gave specific instructions to MacArthur not to enter the family camps on Anacostia Flats. But the orders got to the general too late. His troops proceeded to drive the Bonus Army out of the city with bayonets, sabers, and rifles as well as tear gas. The encampment of families burned their own tents and fled into the countryside.

Hoover—who for a time claimed that a few Communists had threatened the peace—came out of the episode badly. That was mostly the fault of Douglas MacArthur. He had insisted on using the incident for his own self-esteem, preparing for it by encrusting his uniform with his many medals and rendering into a military drama an assault on unarmed veterans and their families. The action was another instance of the egomania that would mar and lessen the career of one of the nation's greatest military commanders.

FDR ENTERS
THE WHITE HOUSE

"My friends, . . ." so Franklin Delano Roosevelt, discarding his cigarette holder and squinting

Franklin Roosevelt. (Courtesy, Franklin D. Roosevelt Library)

through his pince-nez, would begin a speech. One survivor of the Depression years has remembered: "BANG! The moment he addressed his audience with warmth and caring—you were home." After a November landslide victory over Herbert Hoover, by then vastly unpopular for being identified with the Depression, Roosevelt became president on March 4, 1933. Thereafter he would impart to the politics of the day a legendary ability to charm and hearten his public.

The United States has many men and women of wealth and power but almost no aristocracy, no families that held something like the position of Europe's titled nobility. Among the few American localities in which an upper class of that kind could be found—Charleston, New Orleans, Philadelphia, New York City, Boston's Beacon Hill—was the Hudson River Valley of New York State. There a few families comparable to aristocrats stretch back to the brief time when the Dutch possessed the province. As owners of landed estates, they entered the twentieth century still conscious of their ancestry and status. Within their ranks could be found a Dutch name slightly altered to Roosevelt.

Franklin D. Roosevelt, like his relative Theodore Roosevelt, remained very much a man of his class. Acquaintances found him sometimes uncomfortable with people not of his social background. But he was no snob. Snobbery is a vice usually more revealing of the newly rich than of families of long history. Roosevelt took from his upbringing an affable, confident ease of manner, the temper of a self-assured and therefore kindly aristocrat. He spoke to an audience not as a neighbor and fellow worker but as a benign father.

With singular self-control, Roosevelt endured personal affliction. Newspaper photographers never purposely focused on the wheelchair or crutches to which polio had consigned him. But his illness was

In this very unusual picture of Franklin Roosevelt showing his leg braces, he is flanked by his wife and mother. (Courtesy, Franklin D. Roosevelt Library)

well known. Contracting the disease in 1921 after swimming near his vacation home on Campobello Island just north of Maine, Roosevelt had made only slight progress in regaining his mobility. Yet his buoyancy triumphed over his disability and provided for his entire generation a symbol of unconquerable hope. "The only thing we have to fear," Roosevelt declared in his first presidential inaugural address, "is fear itself—nameless, unreasoning, unjustified terror." To combat the Depression he recommended "bold, persistent experimentation." The sweep of that very unspecific phrase made it a more stirring call to action than any clutter of details, however persuasive, would have been.

People far to the left of Roosevelt, their numbers multiplying during the course of the decade, claimed that his program, called the New Deal, merely shuffled the same old deck of cards, stacking them anew against the public. Concerning the president's announcement that one in three Americans lived ill-housed, ill-clothed, and ill-fed, one historian has observed that those figures still remained roughly accurate late in the decade. Temperamentally conservative though rhetorically bold—in the 1932 campaign he advocated reducing governmental expenditures—Roosevelt did greatly want to ease the nation's suffering. Yet many of the more progressive laws associated with his later New Deal came from his advisers, or from Congress, simply getting his assent. The occasional populist vocabulary of this savior of American capitalism confused and enraged conservatives. If haters of FDR cherished class differences, they had little cause for concern. The stretch between wealth and poverty would remain, though with some bettering of the lot of the destitute. But the New Deal did much building: of confidence, of the country's depleted soil, of its cities and dams and roads, of a legislative and administrative structure of welfare and economic security.

The Days of the Alphabet

On FDR's call for "bold, persistent experimentation," he and his Democratic House and Senate made good. During and after a period of unceasing legislative and administrative action at the beginning of his presidency known as the Hundred Days, Washington churned out one relief and recovery agency after another. These and the laws setting

Here is one of FDR's scripts for a radio "fireside chat," this one designed to reassure Americans in 1933.

I want to talk for a few minutes with the people of the United States about banking— with the comparatively few who understand the mechanics of banking but more particularly with the overwhelming majority who use banks for the making of deposits and the drawing of checks. I want to tell you what has been done in the last few days, why it was done, and what the next steps are going to be. . . .

First of all, let me state the simple fact that when you deposit money in a bank the bank does not put the money into a safe deposit vault. It invests your money in many different forms of credit—bonds, commercial paper, mortgages and many other kinds of loans. . . . In other words, the total amount of all the currency in the country is only a small fraction of the total deposits in all of the banks.

What, then, happened during the last few days of February and the first few days of March? Because of undermined confidence on the part of the public, there was a general rush by a large portion of our population to turn bank deposits into currency or gold—a rush so great that the soundest banks could not get enough currency to meet the demand. . . .

By the afternoon of March 3d scarcely a bank in the country was open to do business. . . .

It was then that I issued the proclamation providing for the nationwide bank holiday and this was the first step in the Government's reconstruction of our financial and economic fabric.

The second step was the legislation promptly and patriotically passed by the Congress confirming my proclamation and broadening my power so that it became possible in view of the requirement of time to extend the holiday and lift the ban of that holiday gradually. . . .

The third stage has been the series of regulations permitting the banks to continue their functions to take care of the distribution of food and household necessities and the payment of payrolls. . . .

A question you will ask is this: why are all the banks not to be reopened at the same time? The answer is simple. Your Government does not intend that the history of the past few years shall be repeated. We do not want and will not have another epidemic of bank failures.

As a result, we start tomorrow, Monday, with the opening of banks in the twelve Federal Reserve Bank cities—those banks which on first examination by the treasury have already been found to be all right. This will be followed on Tuesday by the resumption of all their functions by banks already found to be sound in cities where there are recognized clearing houses. . . .

On Wednesday and succeeding days banks in smaller places all through the country will resume business, subject, of course, to the Government's physical ability to complete its survey. . . .

The success of our whole great national program depends, of course, upon the cooperation of the public—on its intelligent support and use of a reliable system. . . .

It has been wonderful to me to catch the note of confidence from all over the country. . . .

Confidence and courage are the essentials of success in carrying out our plan. You people must have faith; you must not be stampeded by rumors or guesses. Let us unite in banishing fear. We have provided the machinery to restore our financial system; it is up to you to support and make it work.

It is your problem no less than it is mine. Together we cannot fail.

(Courtesy, Franklin D. Roosevelt Library)

them up became known by their initials, and in that form identified the New Deal itself.

At the outset of his administration, Roosevelt enforced a five-day bank holiday—a closing of the banks that prevented further panic withdrawals—and the Emergency Banking Relief Act, crafted by holdovers from Hoover's presidency. The effect was emotionally bracing, a return of confidence in banking. In March 1933, stock prices shot up fifteen percent.

An early instance of the New Deal's famous alphabet agencies was the Civilian Conservation Corps, which like many other projects placed work rather than charity at the core of New Deal relief policy. The CCC aimed both to put young men to work and to rescue the country's depleted natural resources. Under the direction of military personnel and high school coaches, formerly unemployed young men reforested land, improved access to national parks, and constructed defenses against erosion.

Harry Hopkins, an adviser to Roosevelt who persuaded him to get as many Americans working as soon as possible under federal programs, had charge of the Federal Emergency Relief Administration.

FERA distributed to states $500 million in relief funds. The states were expected to use the money to institute projects providing jobs. Hopkins also directed the Civil Works Administration. By 1934 the CWA paid localities $4 billion to build schools and playgrounds, clean up parks, paint town halls, lay sewage lines, refurbish hospitals, and construct bridges and libraries, along with about 150,000 outhouses. Though Harold Ickes, the director of the Public Works Administration, acted more cautiously, his PWA would construct a hundred thousand bridges and a half million miles of roads. Still another instance of the determination both to increase the supply of jobs and to build up the country was the Federal Housing Administration. The FHA made loans to middle-income families for home construction and repair, and to save ownership of houses with mortgages in arrears.

The country needed food and clothing for the dispossessed. Yet the New Deal, despite its many efforts to create work and more work, actually paid food and cotton growers not to work: or rather, not to produce. That is what the Agricultural Adjustment Administration, one of the earliest alphabet agencies, set out to do under the leadership of

This wholesome picture shows boys and young men working for the Civilian Conservation Corps. (Courtesy, Forest Service Photo Collection)

Secretary of Agriculture Henry A. Wallace. Its purpose was to cut the supply of farm goods sufficiently to raise their price. The Commodity Credit Corporation resurrected part of Herbert Hoover's Agricultural Marketing Act, while the Federal Farm Board was intended to keep agricultural surpluses off the market. The agricultural program had some success in getting money to farmers. It also unintentionally encouraged big producers to get rid of their tenants and sharecroppers, adding to the unemployment the New Deal had set out to overcome. But in 1936 the Supreme Court, in *United States* v. *Butler*, would declare the AAA an unconstitutional federal exercise of the power to regulate.

One of the most controversial of the early New Deal programs was the National Recovery Administration, established along with the PWA under the National Industrial Recovery Act. The NRA, operating in good part as a voluntary device, permitted a committee of leaders in a particular industry to agree to reasonable schedules of wages and prices. Businesses consenting to abide by these displayed the Blue Eagle poster, in its right claw a machine cog, lightning bolts in its left. Enterprises that joined received the additional enticement of becoming exempt from antitrust laws its program of arranged prices and wages might otherwise violate. General Hugh S. Johnson, the florid leader of the NRA, was rather a blunderbuss who disappeared on alcoholic benders for days.

The NRA aroused major complaints about its turning over to big business inordinate power to develop codes of production. Yet Section 7(a) of the NIRA required participating businesses to recognize unions as bargaining agents. During Hoover's administration and with that much-maligned president's approval, labor had already won the Norris-LaGuardia Act of 1932 limiting the authority of the federal judiciary to issue injunctions prohibiting strikes. The NIRA, further extending the rights of labor, contributed to the enormous growth of unionism in the Depression.

Following a muckraking investigation presided over by the criminal lawyer Clarence Darrow, the NIRA was dead on arrival at the Supreme Court in 1935 in the case of *Schechter Poultry Corporation* v. *United States.* That law the Court declared an unconstitutional delegation to the executive branch of powers reserved to Congress and an interference in commerce within rather than among states. Thereupon a second piece of legislation, the Wagner Act

The NRA Blue Eagle became an emblem of New Deal activism.

of 1935, provided for the protection of unions and collective bargaining between employers and labor earlier provided in the NIRA.

A Second New Deal

In the year of the Wagner Act, a renewed time of New Deal legislation and presidential orders, came the Works Progress Administration, authorized to spend $11 billion on various public works such as constructing airports and hospitals. The agency employed eight million people. Some WPA money went to hiring artists to paint murals on public buildings, to authors to write stories and plays, and otherwise to exercise their talent. Despite attacks by conservatives that it provided a propaganda forum for artists on the left, the program nurtured some of the better-known painters and writers of later times. Under the WPA Roosevelt by executive order set up the National Youth Administration, giving jobs to the young and helping hundreds of thousands to complete college.

And in 1935 came the most important and enduring of New Deal laws, the Social Security Act. Its drafting was in the hands of Secretary of Labor Frances Perkins, the first woman cabinet member and a plainspoken reformer of whom it was said that the Bureau of Standards designed her dresses. The best-known provision of the act required workers and employers to contribute equally to an old-age pension system resembling plans adopted much earlier in Europe. Before that time most Americans had lacked any pension to look to at the time of retirement. Workers labored until they could no longer do so, lost their jobs, or fell back on family or savings. FDR boasted that because recipients contributed their own money "no damn politician can ever scrap my social security program." Many of the unemployed, among them domestic servants and farm laborers, faced initial exclusion. Since then, under the later Republican administration of President Dwight D. Eisenhower, they have gained coverage. A provision of the Social Security Act provided unemployment insurance for workers who during their previous time on the job had built up through required contributions from their employers and themselves a fund to be drawn on during temporary joblessness. Still another part of Social Security gave aid to families with dependent children. Intended especially for widowed mothers, it has become a regular part of the welfare system. To such programs can be added a law passed in 1937,

A poster for the Works Progress Administration, 1938. The WPA, it was hoped, would rebuild workers' self-respect. (Courtesy, New York Public Library)

during Roosevelt's second administration, supplying funds for public housing and for subsidizing the rent payments of impoverished families.

THE MILITANTS

Among federal administrations in the United States, the New Deal stands out because of its efforts to address poverty. But the country's politics operate within many constraints, which include the limits in vision of presidents and legislators themselves. While New Dealers in Washington were busily designing their diverse programs in response to the Great Depression, parts of the American public went beyond the bounds within which wielders of power in the nation's capital operated.

Harlan County, Kentucky

It is hard to imagine that the coal miners in the hills of Harlan County in Kentucky even noticed the coming of the Depression, even harder to believe that it could have made their lives worse. Yet it did, closing down mines and making for some of the nation's highest unemployment. Already a nightmare, Harlan was an environmental disaster, stripped of forests, chewed up with mines, its air thick with coal dust and the smell of burning mineral piles. Poverty, inevitable in an industry that had been ailing for years, only got worse. Company towns were built with little concern for sanitation, and the mine owners extracted rent for their shacks by deducting it from wages. These were usually paid in script, paper exchangeable for goods only at company stores. Miners, in any event, had to buy from these stores. Making purchases elsewhere could get a worker fired. Miners' shacks were subject to search at the will of the police, who acted as the agents of the owners. Evidence of union membership brought dismissal and blacklisting. Union organizers faced beatings or death by deputized gangs, some of them criminals imported from far outside the county.

A few miners dared to fight back. In 1931 a strike in Harlan County turned into a virtual pitched battle, taking the lives of one miner and three deputies. Afterwards came more violence. Bombings and arson followed shootings.

Then, in 1933, section 7(a) of the National

SCREWBALL COMEDY

The movie genre of screwball comedies flourished during the Great Depression. These tales of love disguised as hostility have become lodged in our collective memories. The screwball comedy has no standard rules. One common theme is that the more maddening the relationship, the more chance for an endless romance. As a result of the moralistic Production Code of 1934, many directors and screenwriters had to invent ways to tell stories without depicting any overt sexual content. They devised ingenious narratives to imply but not to depict sexual relations. The absurd and sometimes violent moods of the characters seem a likely response to their frustrations.

Directed by Frank Capra, *It Happened One Night* is a modest, breezy screwball comedy about a seemingly incompatible pair meeting and falling in love on the road. Claudette Colbert plays a runaway heiress angry at her father. Clark Gable plays a reporter who accidentally discovers her. The bright, freewheeling story of the rich girl who finds love and adventure with a commoner sets the tone for much of the screwball genre.

A look back in her life defines the personality of the heroine. In an argument on her father's yacht, he slaps her, and her look of stunned disbelief makes it clear that this is probably the first time she has been disciplined. Her graceful dive from the boat confirms that though a spoiled brat, she possesses style, elegance, and determination. Amid the class and gender uprooting of the Depression era when wealth was under attack, men were out of work, and women had to seek jobs, she will be a real female who stands for privilege, stubborn courage, and helplessness at the same time. A subsequent scene at a bus station reveals that the Depression is in full swing. Colbert waits in a corner trying to avoid prying looks since she knows her father is using his considerable resources to find her. She observes the shuffling underclass of society. Through her eyes viewers feel the rootlessness of jobless people propelled through the grimy station in no particular direction.

The camera pans to Gable in drunken argument on the telephone with his newspaper editor. His use of current American slang identifies him: "That was free verse, you gashouse palooka!" Capra created a portrait of a rebellious reporter as industrious as he is undependable.

At the heart of the relationship between the two, then, is the friction between two classes, two styles of living and thinking. The Depression had solidified class distinctions and made them more apparent. Capra turned a love story into a coy class war that favors the reporter. On a bus trip to New York late in the movie, the heroine is disarmed of her social power, reduced to the level of the other passengers. Gable, though socially beneath her, becomes her protector on the bus.

That role brings gender conflict to the story as well. As the reporter strides toward social equality with the heiress, she in turn reaches gender balance with him. Capra shows her to be craftier than Gable, and Gable more sympathetic than she.

When the couple gets stuck on the road and is forced to hitchhike, Gable launches into a sermon on how to accomplish this task. When his lesson meets failure in the real world, Colbert takes matters into her own hands, or rather legs. She lifts her skirt high to show a passing motorist her limbs, and a car screeches to a halt. Gable is humbled; his companion-antagonist has gained power by exploiting her sexuality, toward which he has been patronizing. This complex commentary on gender relations Capra slips into a light and breezy scene.

In the end, the woman breaks the deadlock. She pulls down the blanket that they use to separate the motel room between them. She confesses her love for Gable, but he does not acknowledge his feelings. He sneaks out to sell the story of her running away from home to his newspaper so he can get what he thinks is

Reginald Marsh, Twenty Cent Movie, *1936.* (Courtesy, Whitney Museum, New York City)

enough money to propose to her. When she awakens in the night she thinks he has fled from her love. When Gable returns and finds that she has left, he believes he has been betrayed. He returns to his world in New York to the news that she is going to be married to a rich playboy.

The costly wedding scene must have awed the Depression era audiences. A longing for the ways of wealth and luxury combined with contempt for overt display of riches is a signature of the screwball comedy. As the momentum of the film moves toward a close and the heroine approaches the altar, her father knows that she and Gable are in love. He also knows that this

everyman will not squander his fortune like the frivolous playboy who awaits her rather indifferently.

Capra's runaway bride scene is still one of the great Depression era images. In the film's last moment, which is not a social but an erotic commentary, the lovers have conquered the barriers of class and gender. The heroine makes the final decision. She chooses adventure and romance over a trivial life of social status. She chooses sex, which Americans of all classes have in common. Yet it is money that in American society gives her the freedom to reject a monied future. The victory over wealth is not quite complete.

Minneapolis police battle striking teamsters in 1934. (Courtesy, Franklin D. Roosevelt Library)

Industrial Recovery Act came to Harlan County, forcing operators there as throughout the nation's coalfields to negotiate with miners. At the head of the United Mine Workers stood John L. Lewis, famous for bushy hair and eyebrows, given to grand theatrical oratory. Lewis spread the claim "The President wants you to join a union." He sent sound trucks through the fields, reinforcing their message with free beer. By the spring of 1934 he had succeeded in unionizing much of the industry. Even the operators of Harlan County were compelled to recognize the UMW.

A New Unionism

The labor violence of the 1930s, of which Harlan County furnished one example, had another manifestation in 1934 around Minneapolis and St. Paul. Businesses there bankrolled the Citizens Alliance, a private army intended to keep labor in its place. When a truckers' union struck for better wages, the Citizens Alliance killed two workers and wounded sixty-seven; two of its own members died. The Teamsters ultimately won recognition of their union. Unrest swept elsewhere in the country through textile districts from New England to the Carolina Piedmont. Half a million workers went on strike. In the South at least eight textile workers

lost their lives, and the union there almost vanished.

The laboring class assumed that FDR was a friend. "Mr. Roosevelt," remarked a North Carolina mill worker, "is the only man we ever had in the White House who would understand that my boss is a sonofabitch." Roosevelt, at least initially, manifested more interest in relief efforts than in unionism. He viewed from a distance the attempt to organize the steel industry in 1935. But labor's forces continued to gain strength, in part because the Depression muted the ethnic rivalries that had gotten in the way of a common working-class consciousness.

The making of a united working class required something like a revival of the dream of the Industrial Workers of the World to organize whole industries, skilled and unskilled labor alike. Within the American Federation of Labor, favoring skilled crafts unions and ordinarily distancing itself from the lowest-paid workers, there existed a few unions with a broader vision. Among these was the United Mine Workers. Coal miners had the distinction of being at once skilled, like other members of the AFL, and brutally exploited like the laborers the Federation generally refused to organize. After the AFL convention of 1935, during which John L. Lewis got into a fistfight with another Federation

General Motors employees stage a successful sit-down strike in Flint, Michigan, during 1937. (Courtesy, Corbis-Bettmann)

chieftain, he and a few others on the left wing of labor formed the Committee for Industrial Organization. Later the CIO broke with the AFL and, keeping its initials, became the Congress of Industrial Organizations.

In Akron, Ohio, in 1936 at the Firestone Rubber Company, workers protesting the firing of some of their number at the plant employed a variant of a tactic common among French unions and used by the IWW early in the century. Instead of picketing at the factory entrances, they sat down at their jobs. After a few days Firestone gave in. Across town at Goodyear, the United Rubber Workers encountered more stubborn resistance. When the police deputized 150 men to clear the factory, ten thousand workers from all over the city confronted the force. Though at the time of the Goodyear strike the United Rubber Workers still held membership in the AFL, the CIO sent representatives to advise and inspirit them. Ultimately Goodyear too surrendered, and the rubber workers switched allegiance to the CIO.

In the automobile industry, an army of three thousand called the Ford Service stalked and beat workers suspected of union sentiments. But autoworkers soon gained a powerful representative: the United Automobile Workers, led by Walter Reuther and affiliated with the CIO. Late in 1937 at the General Motors Fisher Body Plants 1 and 2, industrial unionism further proved its effectiveness.

There, in response to the firing of union members and the speedup of assembly lines, strikers occupied the buildings in another sit-down strike. Those inside usually preserved the company machinery from damage. The Battle of the Running Bulls began when about fifteen policemen— "bulls," in the slang of the era—broke the panels of glass above the factory gate and fired tear gas at the workers. The strikers responded with fire hoses, automobile door hinges, bottles, cans, and stones, driving back the attackers. The police lunged forward again, but the defenders dropped more ammunition: hunks of frozen snow and ice, pieces of pavement. The cops opened fire, wounding several strikers and their sympathizers. Nine of the police were injured, mostly from the missiles thrown from the roof, and the wind blew the tear gas back into their faces. For the duration of the strike women, increasingly energetic supporters of labor rebellion even when they were not part of the workforce involved, conducted pickets and parades outside. Food meanwhile was passed in through the windows; car seats on the assembly line made good beds; morale stayed strong. The new strategy proved far more effective than tramping about the

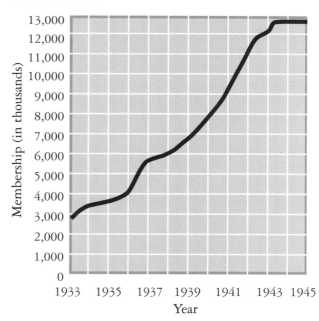

LABOR UNION MEMBERSHIP, 1933–1945

(Courtesy, *Historical Statistics of the United States,* 1960)

picket lines in the cold as the woman supporters and some men had done. After several weeks, the UAW gained a victory that included an agreement by General Motors to recognize the union and negotiate with it.

Mass production was coming back to haunt the industrialists. In causing a snag in its operation, workers could shut down the assembly line, as they did in over five hundred acts of insurgency in 1935. Employers began giving in and recognizing unions. Even United States Steel capitulated, granting a pay hike and an eight-hour day with extra money for overtime.

The Far Left

Almost from its beginning, the Depression had been visible in the clusters of the unemployed waiting outside relief agencies, grouping wistfully at the entrances of factories, sharing misery and warmth at an urban campfire. Such gatherings made dry kindling for anyone who offered anger mixed with hope. And so they were to a body of activists determined to inflame into class warfare the passive despair of the jobless.

In the early years of the Depression, the official membership of the Communist Party in the United States reached a mere eight thousand. Of these, a large number consisted of immigrants still entranced by the Russian Revolution of 1917. The party had not been able to persuade the native-born, or many of foreign birth for that matter, that its cumbersome Marxist-Leninist ideology spoke to American problems. For belief and direction it was expected, like Communist parties throughout the world, to follow orders from the leadership of the Soviet Union, which spoke through an agency known as the Communist International or Comintern. That defined the party as alien to United States politics. Having recently heeded the command of the Comintern to organize labor into a union separate from the AFL, the American Communist Party set out to enlist those groups of stranded unemployed workers.

Some recruits to the party were immensely dedicated. They harangued the jobless out of their discouragement and taught them to form Unemployed Councils. The Councils demanded relief from city governments, not as charity but as what society owed its workers at a time of distress. In several cities the Councils held demonstrations. The party

leadership called for nationwide protests to take place on March 6, 1930. On that day, a total of half a million marched in cities across the country. In New York City the police attacked with clubs and scattered the crowd, thereby providing newspapers with stories that helped the demonstrators.

Few participants in the Unemployed Councils or the demonstrations held official membership in the Communist Party. And in the years to come, countless rank-and-file Communists would leave their party, many of them rejecting its arrogant authoritarianism out of the same independent streak that had made them rebels in the first place. But setting up the Unemployed Councils made the Communist Party in the United States one of the earliest organizations to fight back against the Depression that had stunned much of the nation into immobility.

Radical Farm Unionism in the South

As a small party despised by much of American society and subject to continual legal harassment, the Communists had one advantage: they could afford to take risks, for they had nothing to lose. Their ventures in the South are especially notable. The Democrats, though defining themselves as the friends of the poor, feared to do much for the southern black poor, which might weaken the Democratic Party's important base among the region's whites. Having no considerable base anywhere, the Communists had no such timidity. In fighting ground-level battles for economic and racial justice in the South, among political organizations they were almost alone.

In January 1931 occurred a spontaneous instance of the cooperation that very occasionally brightened the dismal racial history of the South. About five hundred impoverished cotton farmers of both races invaded the little town of England, Arkansas, compelling Red Cross officials there to give them food for their families. The episode had nothing to do with the Communist Party. But Communists in the South, sensing an opportunity and genuinely committed to the unity of the working classes, immediately called for meetings and hunger marches, demanding that merchants and bankers supply relief. Two black organizers formed a sharecropper and farm worker union in the Alabama flatlands.

Throughout that summer white vigilantes broke up union meetings and murdered one of the leaders,

The Farm Security Administration hired Dorothea Lange to take photographs of the American people struggling with the Great Depression of the 1930s. Her technique was to bring an unconcealed camera to transient workers' camps, to the Mississippi delta, and to southern hamlets where people were bound by long, unbroken tradition. Her most famous photo, entitled *Migrant Mother* (see p. 670), was taken at a pea pickers' camp in Nipomo, California. An exhausted mother in a forlorn tent caught her attention. She learned that the crop had failed and that the family was living on a few birds, berries, and scavenged vegetables. The mother could not leave; she had sold the tires from her car. The photograph shows the hurt and sorrow of the Depression, its waste of human resources, the scandal of the selfishness and meanness that left the destitute adrift in the richest of lands.

Dorothea Lange's photography, embodying the spirit of social protest during the thirties, marshaled public sympathy for relief programs and won further appropriations from Congress for that purpose. The pictures that follow are typical of her work.

Dorothea Lange, Family on the Road, *Midwest, c. 1938.* (Courtesy, Library of Congress)

Dorothea Lange, Jobless on Edge of Pea Field, *Imperial Valley, California, 1937.* (Courtesy, Library of Congress)

Dorothea Lange, Hoeing, *near Yazoo City, Mississippi, 1937.* (Courtesy, Library of Congress)

Dorothea Lange, Man Beside Weelbarrow, *San Francisco, 1934.* (Courtesy, Library of Congress)

Dorothea Lange, Family on the Road, *Oklahoma, 1938.* (Courtesy, Library of Congress)

Dorothea Lange, Mother and Children, *on the Road, Tulelake, Siskiyou County, California, 1939.* (Courtesy, Library of Congress)

Dorothea Lange, White Angel Bread Line, *San Francisco, 1932.* (Courtesy, Library of Congress)

Dorothea Lange, Hoe Cutter, *near Anniston, Alabama, 1936.* (Courtesy, Library of Congress)

Dorothea Lange, Ditched, Stalled, and Stranded, *San Joaquin Valley, California, 1935.* (Courtesy, Library of Congress)

Dorothea Lange, Ex-Slave with a Long Memory, *Alabama, 1937.* (Courtesy, Library of Congress)

kicking and shooting the body for hours afterward. A white mob rampaged through the black section of an Alabama town. At the end of 1932 a deputy sheriff attempted to seize the property of an indebted farmer nearby. Armed members of the Share Croppers Union drove him off. In the next few days the police and inflamed whites descended on the local black population in general, bringing protests from a handful of respectable white Alabamans. Thereafter the union grew. At a time of widespread want, the New Deal Agricultural Adjustment Administration made payments to plantation owners to cut production in the interest of raising prices and forced farm workers out of their jobs. Still, during the season for picking cotton when owners felt relatively vulnerable, the union conducted a few strikes among pickers that won some wage increases. Membership in the croppers' union reached eight thousand, a tiny figure and only a fraction of it white. Later in the decade, after further strikes and much brutality against it, the union collapsed. But its combination of Communists and non-Communists had for a time achieved for its era and region a noteworthy defiance.

The Socialists

Another group in the South not quite so despised as the Communists but also excluded from conventional American politics began to distinguish itself for frontline conflict against injustice.

The Socialists, now led by the Presbyterian minister Norman Thomas, like the Communists labeled capitalism the enemy, but rivalry between the two was intense. The Communists, convinced that history would align with the Russian revolution and the Soviet Union, defined all other leftist movements as distractions, knowing or unwitting agents of capitalism. Socialists perceived Communism as a mockery of the socialist ideal of a democratic commonwealth of workers. The two groups differed completely on the value of piecemeal reform. However sincere the Communists appeared in wanting to make things better for the workers they unionized, the leadership believed incremental improvements to be essentially irrelevant. The ultimate purpose of organizing workers was to intensify class warfare in preparation for the time of total revolution. Not so Norman Thomas's Socialists, who wanted to improve and ultimately replace capital-

ism by whatever gradual, reformist methods could work. With this in mind the Socialists accomplished their own brief organizing of a small percentage of the southern poor.

In 1934 in Tyronza, Arkansas, a group of local Socialists and other interested neighbors began holding discussion meetings that ranged from about fifty to 150 people. Norman Thomas opposed the New Deal's Agricultural Adjustment Administration, weighted in favor of large plantation owners against workers. Thomas encouraged the Tyronza Socialists to organize a union. Just outside the town that summer, a black speaker urged an interracial meeting to recognize that the poor, both black and white, had a common interest in fighting the ruling system. The resulting Southern Tenant Farmers Union chose a white president and a black vice president.

After receiving some temporary help from a few AAA administrators, the new union became the object of legal persecution. Southern vigilantes also kicked in, pistol whipping two white radical sympathizers. The union got some support as well from the Communist Party, by custom the enemy of the Socialists, but none from the New Deal. Appeals to the federal administration under Section 7(a) of the National Industrial Recovery Act got nowhere. Washington did not look so kindly on agricultural as on urban and factory unions, which had a degree of practical control over the place and conditions of work. During the cotton-picking season of 1935, a strike by thousands of workers under the sponsorship of the Southern Tenant Farmers Union won a wage concession. And the union received contributions and sympathy from northern liberals. But further violence resulted in the murder of a black unionist. In the end the union essentially collapsed. Yet out of it came a radical farm workers' cooperative very much alive decades afterwards, drawing black activists as committed to labor militancy as to civil rights.

Radical Farm Unionism in California

In the South, radical organizers confronted a system in which even the enemy—the white racists and the plantation owners—fared none too well themselves, common victims to a general stagnation. California, much of its farming given to cotton and fruit production, presented at least a surface glitter of wealth and hope absent in the South. Huge farms with absentee owners, some of them corporations, hinted of a future in which agriculture would be essentially a branch of industry, of planting and harvesting by mass production.

Much of the farm labor of California faced a racism different only in detail from that of the Deep South. By the end of the 1920s, the population in the United States of Mexican birth or ancestry numbered a million and a half. In the California fields also labored Japanese, Filipino, and white workers. Needing labor, the Southwest had benefited from the flow of Mexican migrants. But in the pinched conditions of the Depression, racial hostility led California to employ police raids as a scare tactic to force deportations back to Mexico.

Like southern agricultural labor, California farm workers had little access to the protections that the National Industrial Recovery Act provided to union organizing. Crowded into unsanitary camps provided by the growers or into neighborhoods known as barrios, farm laborers obeyed the growers who had the support of the state and the police. Spontaneous strikes failed. Then in California as in the South, the Communists stepped in.

Communist organizers in California risked only somewhat less danger than in the South. Whether they were breaking laws was irrelevant: the law was whatever the local police and the courts declared it to be. The organizers would hide by day, spread the message to workers at night, and distribute leaflets in the fields. In 1930 they established the beginnings of a union but at the cost of over a hundred workers arrested. Eight of the leaders served jail sentences for illegal organizing.

Participating in a strike among cannery employees, the Communist farm union changed its name to the Cannery and Agricultural Workers Industrial Union. Deputized members of the American Legion and strikebreakers hired by the employers broke the strike. Another insurgency, this time by pea-pickers in response to a cut in wages and aided by the renamed union, collapsed as well.

The farm and cannery union endured, always prepared for violence, such as the fractured skull and broken jaw the police gave one organizer. The membership probably came to no more than two thousand, but many nonmembers accepted its guidance. In the huge California cotton-growing industry, the farm and cannery union planned a strike, including among its demands a wage increase and recognition of the union. And in 1933 between fifteen and twenty thousand workers walked off their jobs. The owners brought in nonunion workers, and the growers had county sheriffs evict families who refused to go back to work. Union activists meanwhile moved by truck from one farm to another, urging the workers to join the strike. Finally the New Deal NRA did intervene, trying to negotiate an agreement on wages though refusing to recognize the union. At one point the suffering of the strikers distressed even the conservative governor of California, who ordered the state administrator of a federal relief agency to get food to them. In the end, the strikers won a wage increase, but the union did not win recognition.

Against the power of the growers and the antagonism of the state authorities, a union tainted by Communism had no chance. In the summer of 1934 raiding parties armed with shotguns and clubs and led by a district attorney invaded union headquarters in Sacramento and made several arrests. The next spring eight of the detainees were convicted, essentially for being members of the union. Two years later appeals reversed the convictions. Meanwhile, however, one of the most combative leaders—the slight, young, impassioned Communist Caroline Decker—had done enough reading in prison to convince her that Communism did not offer the democracy she had sought. She became one more of the radicals whose insurgency had taken them into the party and then back out of it.

NEW DEAL POLITICS AT MIDPOINT

By the mid-1930s the New Deal enjoyed wide popular support and yet was increasingly the target of articulate criticisms coming from well-organized groups. The American Liberty League, speaking for business interests and ideological conservatives opposed to the whole direction of the government under FDR, enlisted members from both major parties. Among their spokesmen was Al Smith, four times the governor of New York, whose earlier brand of progressivism could not stretch to embrace Roosevelt's policies. A collection of individuals more worrisome to New Deal politicians included the radio priest Charles Coughlin, the Louisiana politician Huey Long, and Dr. Francis Townsend, advocate of a scheme of pensions for the elderly. Each commanded a small but enthusiastic segment of the public. Together the three might turn enough otherwise Democratic votes against Roosevelt to give the Republicans the White House in 1936. More immediately, New Deal politicians decided that they needed to take care of the troublesome California gubernatorial candidacy of Upton Sinclair.

Upton Sinclair: California Radical

Sinclair had first drawn the attention of the public with his novel *The Jungle*, a tale of the Chicago stockyards that led FDR's Republican cousin, Theodore Roosevelt, to support legislation regulating the meatpacking industry. A long-time Socialist now living in California, in 1933 Sinclair switched his party registration to Democratic, believing that a major party was now ready to be a vehicle for radicalism. Soon he offered his candidacy for governor of the state, promoting a program he called EPIC, End Poverty in California. The state, as he envisioned its future, would purchase factories closed down by the Depression. These it would give or rent to the poor, who could join in manufacturing goods on their own. California would also purchase and distribute agricultural produce, trading with the factory cooperatives in return for the products of these industrial enterprises. Combining this project with a plan for taxing unused land and with the proceeds setting up communities growing their own food and engaging in manufacture, EPIC imagined a society in which production for personal and communal use might replace capitalist production for profit. EPIC together with Sinclair's forceful presentation of it won him the Democratic nomination.

Rethinking capitalism did not much appeal to New Deal Democrats. They liked capitalism, which they believed they were saving from changes more radical than their programs for patching it up. They also feared the embarrassment of uncovering in the Democratic ranks a principled radical who could frighten away moderate voters. California Democrats unhappy with Sinclair's nomination brokered a deal with the state's Republicans: support New Deal objectives, and the Democratic power brokers would throw the election to the Republican Party.

A heavily orchestrated campaign trashed EPIC. The demolition job included contrived films and other media devices showing the state invaded by bums seeking handouts, and Communists seeking to destroy all that the nation held dear. In the 1934 election for governor, Sinclair still won a solid slice of the California vote, but not enough to win the election.

Long, Coughlin, and Townsend

In isolating Sinclair, the Democrats had rid themselves of a force that might have been a political burden to the New Deal, or possibly an invigorating presence in it. Elated by sweeping midterm election triumphs in 1934 for their party in Congress, the Democrats now had to worry about a triumvirate that might eat into the vote of Roosevelt's presidential candidacy two years hence.

Louisiana's Senator Huey Long's "Share Our Wealth" plan proposed taking away the largest excesses of private wealth and redistributing the money to the masses. Brilliant, energetic, powerful in oratory, gifted in political theater, Long as governor of Louisiana had already promoted reform. For example, he convinced that state's legislature to grant free college schooling to capable students. Unlike other southern governors, Long had established a degree of rapport with his black constituents. "Every man a king, but no one wears a crown" was his slogan. The wealthy, he proclaimed, "were pigs swilling in the trench of luxury."

Father Charles Coughlin of suburban Detroit beamed on the Columbia Broadcasting System a radio program from his church—the Shrine of the Little Flower—attacking Communism, Jews, and Wall Street while promoting inflationary populist programs to help the poor. The conservative Roman Catholic priest rivaled the president in the use of the new medium of radio that directly reached a wide public. With mellifluous tones and irrigating charm, the anti-Semitic Radio Priest won a following that flooded him with more mail than Roosevelt received. Urging his listeners to write to their senators, he was instrumental in defeating a presidential proposal to join the World Court.

Dr. Francis Townsend, the elderly health commissioner of sun-drenched Long Beach, California, proposed two hundred dollars a week for anyone over sixty who voluntarily retired and spent all of the money each week. The idea looked both to helping the aged and to pumping money into the economy.

None of the plans could work. Townsend's scheme would siphon off half the national income. Coughlin's bigotry discredited whatever he urged. Long's plan of distribution could grant to each person a fraction of what he had promised. Yet of the three Long looked to be a possible challenger to FDR in the election of 1936. Introduced to a crowd of Iowa farmers by Milo Reno, a farm leader, Long asked whether they believed in the redistribution of wealth. "Yes," came the answering roar. Afterwards Long boasted, "I could take the state like a whirlwind." His assassination in September 1935—his last words were, "God, don't let me die. I have so much to do"—put an end to the threat. But together such figures as he, Coughlin, and Townsend worried the regular Democrats. Supporters of the agitators included not just the poorest Americans but members of the working class well enough off to have something to lose. The president's Social Security Act of 1935 drew inspiration from Townsend's proposals.

These threats to his reelection, greatly lessened by Long's death, made Roosevelt unbeatable in the election of 1936. He ran as an enemy of irresponsible wealth, denouncing the rich as "economic royalists"; a tax increase on the highest incomes and inheritances reinforced his depiction of the New Deal as the people's program. The Republican candidate Alfred Landon, a former supporter of Theodore Roosevelt's Progressive Party and no rabid enemy to the basic ideas of the New Deal, could get no traction. FDR won nearly sixty-one percent of the popular vote, losing only the states of Maine and Vermont. The Democrats again carried both houses of Congress.

Though the New Deal worked more often to reaffirm American capitalism than to challenge or transform it, it did accomplish a substantial reversal in policy for at least one American social group.

The Indian New Deal

Many American Indians had long been subject to a number of measures designed to destroy their native culture and force Indian people to assimilate. One of these, the Dawes Allotment Act of 1887, broke up communally held reservation lands and distributed them to individual Indians. Under the New Deal, the government repudiated these poli-

cies, setting up instead mechanisms that encouraged tribes to acquire and hold land collectively and to preserve older social and cultural ways. Led by John Collier, the Commissioner of Indian Affairs, Congress enacted the Wheeler-Howard Indian Reorganization Act of 1934. The measure established provisions for the creation of tribal governments, as well as a revolving credit fund and a board promoting the sale of arts and crafts. An Indian branch of the CCC offered employment to many young Indian men.

While the New Deal projects rejected the disastrous allotment and assimilation programs, it brought its own problems. Collier had a romantic vision of harmonious community, which he associated with the pueblos of New Mexico and attempted unsuccessfully to impose on a diverse collection of Native American tribes across the country. Conflicts over the new policy sometimes dangerously split tribal government. Some Indians found Collier's ideas too radical; others disliked the rigid guidelines under which tribal governments were forced to operate. At the same time that Collier's plan abandoned the old-style assimilation, it contradictorily insisted on Indian governments that operated like miniature versions of the American state. Many tribes refused to adopt such governments, preferring forms that incorporated more familiar and local kinds of decision making. Nonetheless, the Indian New Deal, utterly transforming not only federal Indian policy but also the daily lives of native peoples, provided in the tribal bodies a collective political experience that many American Indians would use in future struggles.

Trouble in the Second Term

Triumphant in reelection, Roosevelt had cause to believe that his second administration would move smoothly. On the contrary, it turned out to be probably his most disappointing presidential term.

The rejection of the gubernatorial candidacy of Upton Sinclair in 1934 had displayed the limits of New Deal innovation. A further dip in the economy beginning in 1937 when FDR abruptly cut spending indicated that the government had still not conquered the Great Depression. In 1938 a new Agricultural Adjustment Act passed Congress, one of several attempts by Roosevelt and the national legislature to regulate farm production and raise farm prices. That same year the government appropriated more money for public works projects. The Fair Labor Standards Act of 1938 set for many Americans a floor on wages and a ceiling on hours of work and prohibited the use of child labor in products intended for interstate commerce. But the initiatives of 1938 could not evoke the sense of bold new directions that had attended the earlier days of the Roosevelt presidency.

In 1937 Roosevelt, no longer the harmonizer of conflicting individuals and interests he once had been, reacted rashly to a Supreme Court that seemed determined to halt the New Deal. He offered what became known as the court-packing scheme. When a federal judge or a Supreme Court justice failed to retire or resign within six months after reaching the age of seventy, the president proposed he be authorized to appoint an extra member to the bench. But the Supreme Court enjoyed great respect as a bulwark of law and liberty, and Roosevelt's plan gave him, even to some of his supporters, a power-hungry look. It failed to win approval from Congress, though FDR's loyalists claimed that it helped to scare the Supreme Court into softening its resistance to New Deal programs.

In the midterm elections of 1938, Roosevelt acted also in another way that suggested the arrogance of power. Exercising the informal political pressure that came with the presidency, he attempted, unsuccessfully, to purge from the Democratic Party congressional candidates insufficiently supportive of his policies. That effort contributed to creating a long-lasting liaison between Republicans and conservative Democrats.

The American people rejected President Roosevelt's "court-packing" scheme aimed at obtaining Supreme Court rulings more sympathetic to the New Deal. (Courtesy, Franklin D. Roosevelt Library)

Roosevelt's two terms preceding his nation's entrance into World War II successfully changed the relationship between the federal government and the people. But the New Deal did not envision some large and coherent reconstitution of American society. The enormous help it gave to building the strength of labor through unionization had not been a central objective. And on two counts, the performance of the New Dealers fell far short of forging a social and economic democracy. In agriculture, they largely failed. On the question of racial justice, much of the New Deal at best only offhandedly attempted to reach beyond the thinking of white-supremacist southern Democrats and white Americans in general.

The New Deal and the Farm

Almost alone among political parties, Communists and Socialists addressed the plight of the poorest agricultural workers. Liberal politicians meanwhile concerned themselves with a farm population genuinely distressed but not, like sharecroppers and numerous Hispanic workers, pressed to the far margins of American society.

By the beginning of the Depression, much of American agriculture had already suffered years of hard times. Overexpansion during the First World War had left farmers with land and equipment that, as agricultural prices fell, they could not afford. As the farm failures were shrinking the agricultural population, more efficient machinery was expanding the size of the individual farm. At the start of the twentieth century, over forty percent of the American people had lived on farms; by 1930 only about one in four Americans did so. And the Depression intensified the most dreaded of events for the farmer: foreclosure by a creditor. By 1933, nearly 150,000 farms a year were being foreclosed.

Much of agriculture for decades had operated as a commercial enterprise, an industry like steel making or auto manufacture. But most such farms were still comparatively small units, none able in itself to control any portion of the market. They especially could not control their partner in production, the weather, to which the inhabitants of the Dust Bowl could testify. The Depression accelerated the pressures on the small, market-driven farm that the whole of the modern, urban industrialized economy had made inevitable. Besides being a disaster for Americans who loved working their own land, that meant the decline of an occupation that as late as the 1930s still held a sentimental place in the American consciousness. The family farm traditionally formed the bedrock of American democracy, its members spending their days in productive physical labor and all the while abiding by traditional virtues nurtured by the uncorrupted land.

Agricultural communities have in the land itself a means of survival unavailable to urban areas in distress. During the Depression one county in Iowa burnt corn to heat the courthouse because it was cheaper than coal. For rural neighborhoods in the Upper South that had already converted in good part to mining, simple agriculture helped residents: they could plant and harvest not for commerce but, as in pre-industrial societies, for subsistence. A garden of beans, potatoes, and other sustaining food could feed a family and give it a means of barter with neighbors for tools, firewood, or meat. Families in the hills knew that within a supportive network of friends when alternative means of income such as mines played out, the familiar fields and woods and meadows seemed allies.

Fighting Back

For those facing foreclosure of their land, neighbors might be of immediate assistance. On some occasions a crowd of them would surge onto the grounds of a property to be foreclosed and bid ten cents for a horse, twenty-five cents for a plow, buying them back for the farmer. Sometimes no offers at all were made on the houses, since people who bid soon came to know that they would be dealt with seriously. Agricultural implements and livestock in those cases generally returned to the farm family after the sale. But many did lose their acreage and homes. Mobs in retaliation sometimes dragged foreclosure judges out of court. One judge was carried off to the local fairgrounds, where a rope hung from a stout tree limb. Nothing happened, but reports circulated that he was "never all right" after that and soon retired. A celebrated case had more than a thousand men in fields surrounding the road to a house set to be auctioned, their guns trained on sheriff's deputies assigned to guard a judge. The deputies turned back. In an incident reminiscent of the period preceding the American Revolution, a crowd tarred and feathered another judge. A sheriff's deputy in an adjacent county to

that where the Depression incident occurred had his clothes taken from him, and was left beaten and muddy in a roadside ditch. This prompted the governor to call out the National Guard and round up hundreds of suspects, placing them behind barbed wire.

Crop Restriction in the New Deal

Among many farmers, particularly his fellow Iowans, Milo Reno was a spellbinder of a kind that the Depression spawned across the country. Reno, who in a longstanding rural American tradition did not so much argue politics as preach them, believed in the old virtues and the family farm. He urged a capitalist solution to the troubles of agriculture: to withhold a product from the market, forcing its price to rise. His Farm Holiday movement withheld dairy products.

Reno proposed moderate objectives. For a period in 1932, he persuaded farmers to refrain from taking their goods to market. This would push up prices. His movement also encouraged the government to enact legislation stabilizing farm prices. That would allow farmers to return money into the economy; it would thereupon pass from sector to sector; and everyone would gain.

The movement turned out to be more aggressive than Reno had anticipated. In addition to holding back their own produce, some of his followers began to halt the delivery of food others had grown. In the Midwest, gangs armed with clubs set up roadblocks and scattered nails on the roads. They targeted milk trucks and spilled their contents: this destruction of a commodity associated especially with the feeding of small children met with scant approval. In Iowa, law officers armed with clubs and machine guns faced some twelve hundred or so protesters blocking the highways leading to a produce market. Violence was contained. Yet throughout the nation, fewer than one farmer in ten participated in the Farm Holiday movement. In the wake of the organization's failure, its activists turned to forced blockages of foreclosures.

The Farm Holiday movement and the resistance to foreclosures represented desperate parts of the farm population, but not its most systematically exploited members. Farmers of the sort who followed Milo Reno, losing money on land, gained most of the attention of the New Deal administra-

An African American worker in an Arkansas cotton field during 1938. (Courtesy, Farm Security Administration)

tors because they did not work for anyone, whether southern planters or big California growers. The government could aid them without offending any politically powerful interest.

In paying cooperating farmers not to produce, the New Deal Agricultural Adjustment Act of 1933 enlisted the same remedy that earlier farmers' advocates had proposed. It did not, however, address the most wretched of the agricultural poor. Those Alabama croppers and California migrants whom the New Deal program did not squeeze out of agriculture as it decreased their production might, of course, possibly gain somewhat from the higher prices. And among large commercial farmers, the payments issued by AAA as a reward for not producing served as a boon. But initially the program had an embarrassing run-in with public relations. Beginning in August 1933, it purchased over six million pigs, which it then slaughtered, deliberately destroying tons of meat. The program hunted out especially the larger of the pregnant sows: piglets were considered the market glut of the future. The murder of the piglets horrified Americans who held special affection for infants of any species. And others more capable of hardening their hearts against the nonhuman young could be appalled that in a period of widespread hunger a government program intentionally wasted food. In time, the AAA turned the problems of agricultural produce over to the Federal Emergency Relief Administration.

Another provision of the AAA demonstrated more careful planning. It made refinancing and easy credit available for rescuing farms from foreclosure and farmers from bankruptcy. But this practical and needed law, like the bulk of New Deal politics and legislation, did nothing toward helping sharecroppers, tenants, or migrant workers. After the Supreme Court in 1936 invalidated the first AAA in *United States* v. *Butler* as an unwarranted federal assumption of regulatory power, the government tried the Soil Conservation and Domestic Allotment Act of 1936. The second Agricultural Adjustment Act, passed in 1938, provided forms of farm credit and set up a system of quotas that farmers could approve by voting in favor of them. It was the administration's last effort at regulating farm production.

Noticing the Poorest Farmers

Within New Deal politics and government a handful of efforts tried to look beyond the small business farmers the Democratic Party felt most comfortable with. Some AAA officials, for example, unsuccessfully attempted to find legal protection for tenants against evictions such as members of the Southern Tenant Farmers Union had suffered. Shortly afterward, the president at the request of the Agriculture Department's Rexford Tugwell established the Resettlement Administration, putting Tugwell at its head and giving the agency the task of administering whatever economic aid it could to the rural poor. The RA, however, had neither the authority nor the budget to effect among tenants, croppers, and farm wage laborers the change in power and status that the New Deal brought to industrial workers. The Bankhead-Jones Farm Tenancy Act of 1937 established the Farm Security Administration, which replaced the Resettlement Administration. By empowering tenants and croppers to buy their own farms, the FSA might have maneuvered a genuine social revolution in the rural South. But the underfunded agency reached only a small minority of the rural poor.

The New Deal and the White Migrants

To one segment of the poorest of farm workers, the New Deal responded more swiftly. Refugees to California from the Great Plains differed in several politically favorable respects from migrants of Mexican ancestry. That they descended from British and Northern European stock gave them an advantage. And since they had not always been so poor, their plight could not be dismissed with a political shrug like that of black or Indian or Latino Americans. They are captured in one of the most memorable images of the era: Dorothea Lange's photograph in 1936 of a woman migrant part Indian with white features, her children huddled about her. Her features, lank and careworn, are defined especially by dark eyes shadowed in worry and by a strong set mouth. The black-and-white photo, etching the lines on her face, appears at once ruggedly factual and yet abstract, as though she were born to be a symbol of undefeated suffering. For such as she, the public and the Roosevelt administration readily responded.

The migrants from the Plains needed help immediately, beyond the slow processes of buying land or forming a union. Their worst camps were makeshifts of tin, cardboard, or anything else that might stave off the elements. In 1935, the Federal Emergency Relief Administration together with California authorities built more durable migrant

Dorothea Lange, Migrant Mother. *The woman, working in a California pea pickers' camp at the time, is Florence Thompson, a Cherokee from Oklahoma.* (Courtesy, Library of Congress)

camps with canvas tents and cabins, arrangements for communal cooking, nurseries, first aid stations, and adequate toilet facilities. Temporarily under the Resettlement Administration, the program later came under the Farm Security Administration. By 1941 thirteen stationary federal camps, six mobile camps, and five hundred homes with electricity and running water had been built, all available at low rent. By the end of that year, 45,000 migrants lived in some form of federal shelter.

The Tennessee Valley Authority

On the other side of the continental United States lived another group of much the same ancestry as the Okie migrants. The Tennessee River, looping southward from the state of Tennessee and then twisting north into Kentucky to meet with the Ohio River, creates with its tributaries a great water system through much of the Upper South. The Appalachian hill folk, both small landowners and tenants, were culturally distinct to the point of isolation, separate even from their fellow southerners. Substantial portions of the region had supplied the Civil War with more Union than rebel troops and thereafter voted Republican in defiance of the Democratic solid South. Poor by modern standards, they managed farms that fed them and also supplied a small cash crop to help them get by.

With the stubborn assurance that comes of isolation, many of them followed methods used by their parents and their grandparents before them that greatly injured the land. Often, their plowed rows ran vertically on hillsides, making for massive erosion. They did not rotate crops in a way that would replenish the soil's nutrients. And forests were stripped for immediate use. Generations of such practices had depleted the region's natural productivity.

During the 1920s, the progressive Republican Senator George Norris of Nebraska had argued, unsuccessfully, for the federal development of the Tennessee Valley. In the administration of FDR, the idea was revived, fulfilling itself in the Tennessee Valley Authority of 1933. Although the TVA was not designed solely for the advantage of the rural poor, they were to be its major gainers. It aimed to rescue the valley as a whole from waste, to save and recultivate its resources. Flood control, reforestation, and the redemption of exhausted soil were among its objectives, along with the provision of

Mexican American fruit market during the Depression. (Courtesy, Library of Congress)

electricity for the people of the valley. The building of dams and the flooding of farmlands required removing over thirteen thousand families from their land for low prices set by the government. Within three years of its start, however, the agency was providing nine thousand jobs. TVA manufactured fertilizer, giving it free to demonstration farms that would serve as examples to neighbors. The cheap electricity generated by TVA dams supplied fewer than fifteen percent of the valley's farms, and the agency was a major polluter. Still, that and the agency's other programs, such as flood control, land reclamation, and the providing of expert consultants, made a beginning toward replacing one way of life with another that the region's people in general were happy enough to embrace.

RACE AND THE NEW DEAL

A year before the presidential campaign that took FDR to the White House, a legal saga began that put the issue of white supremacy before the public. On March 25, 1931, a brawl broke out between black and white boxcar drifters on a train passing through the South. In northern Alabama, a posse of white citizens entered the train, seized nine black youths, and took them to Scottsboro, the county seat. The major charge against them was rape, based on testimony given by two white women found in the boxcar with them. While a white crowd gathered outside the jail, the county sheriff acted in a way not usually taken for granted among law officers in the Deep South. He requested National Guard troops to protect the prisoners. The governor obliged.

Just over two weeks after the initial fight, and at the end of two days of trial, eight of the nine received a death sentence, at that time the penalty in Alabama for rape. In many southern newspapers the evidence or lack of it counted for nothing. Black men accused by white women of rape were assumed guilty.

The executions did not take place, and for that some credit goes to the Communist Party. Eager to win converts among black southerners, the Communists denounced the verdicts. They defined the convictions as the work of the ruling classes and organized a defense committee. The publicity the party generated stimulated a nationwide letter-writing campaign to the Alabama government. Non-Communist liberals, notably the American Civil Liberties Union, joined in the protests. The crudeness of the Alabama proceedings also outraged a spectrum of public opinion broad enough to include Hamilton Fish, a wealthy politician widely

THE TUSKEGEE SYPHILIS EXPERIMENT

Beginning in 1932 and lasting until 1970, the United States Public Health Service in conjunction with Alabama's black Tuskegee Institute conducted an experiment entitled the Tuskegee Study of Untreated Syphilis in the Negro Male. The subjects, all black men and all poor, knew neither the title nor the subject of the experiment. The physicians explained to them that it had to do with "bad blood." Of six hundred subjects selected, about four hundred had syphilis. Of this, too, they were not informed.

All through these experimental years, treatment for syphilis existed. At first it was arsenic and mercury; in the 1940s the first antibiotic, penicillin, proved to be effective. But the experiment required that treatment be withheld, so with the exception of a small amount of genuine treatment at the beginning of the process a placebo was substituted. The program also notified local doctors and others who might come into contact with the men that they should not receive medication. The Public Health Service, then, not only withheld treatment itself but insured that the subjects would not get it anywhere else. "So far," boasted a Public Health Service official at one point, "we are keeping the known positive patients from getting treatment." Periodically the program took a sample of fluid from the spinal cord, painfully obtained by an injected needle. The patients, delighted to be a part of a program for which they had received no explanation, trusted their physicians; some brought gifts of homemade cookies or cornbread. As an inducement to the participants, they had been offered free medical care and a small burial fee. Their death, in fact, constituted an important part of the program, for the autopsy allowed a full examination of the effects of the hideous disease. "As I see it," one physician commented, "we have no further interest in these patients until they die."

After forty years, it became obvious to officials connected with the program that it did not even offer the kinds of information that might bring some degree of redemption to the suffering it had induced, and it closed. But the remaining victims received no penicillin until 1972. By then, according to one set of figures, twenty-eight had died of syphilis and a hundred more of complications related to the disease, while forty wives and nineteen newborn children became infected. In 1974 the government settled out of court, paying in all $10 million. At a White House ceremony in 1997, President Clinton offered the survivors an apology.

The Tuskegee program by its own methodology portrayed what a portion of the white administrative and medical establishments thought of the worth of black Americans. But it involved more than racism. Black physicians and administrators participated willingly in the program, convinced that some good could come of it. Ultimately the Tuskegee experiment could itself serve as a psychological study in the ability of the mind to tuck moral considerations off to the side.

---

identified as at the tip of the conservative wing of the Republican Party. A committee embracing among other groups the Communists, the NAACP, and the ACLU fought for the Scottsboro defendants, with ultimate success.

The Supreme Court threw out the first verdicts on the grounds that the Scottsboro boys, as they came to be known, had not had time to prepare an adequate case. A second round of trials and convictions also failed to get by the Court, because blacks had been systematically excluded from the jury. In the course of Alabama's repeated efforts to maintain its racial traditions, it continued to disgrace itself. A doctor who had examined one of the women testified to finding neither the semen nor the live spermatozoa that would have indicated intercourse at the time of the purported crime. Dead sperm suggested that she had engaged in sex sometime before the incident. But that testimony was insufficient to deter the prosecution. At one point Judge James E. Horton of the Alabama circuit court found the evidence against one defendant so shabby that he set aside the verdict and ordered a new trial. His reward for upholding the integrity of the law was defeat for reelection to the court. But after several years Alabama, the object of relentless outrage and contempt across much of the nation and further confronted with one witness's withdrawal of her own claim to have been raped, released the Scottsboro boys.

In all this, as in the organization of Alabama sharecroppers and California migrant workers, the Communists showed a willingness to initiate social justice actions that went beyond the ambitions of American liberals. The Scottsboro campaign, however, differed significantly from labor unionism among the poor. Violence such as Alabama had done to legal procedure, in a nation that congratulated itself on its system of laws, could offend Americans little interested in the black poor. Then, too, a solution to the injustice at Scottsboro was readily available in the appeals to the Supreme Court. So while the Communists showed themselves early champions of the Scottsboro defendants, liberals quickly stepped in to manage the legal appeals. Meanwhile, the determination of the Communists to use the case as propaganda antagonized other supporters of the defendants.

In memory, the Scottsboro case stands as a symbol of the struggle against white supremacy. Equally remarkable is how little noticeable effect it had on the liberal perception of the race question in general. Neatly enclosed within the formalities of court procedures, it was sealed off from the politics of the New Deal.

Discrimination

In 1934 Lorena Hickock traveled throughout the Southwest, reporting to Washington on the successes and failures of FERA programs. White families on relief struggled to make do on $35 a month, she observed, while for blacks and Mexican Americans comparable relief "made possible in many, many cases a *better* standard of living" than they had previously enjoyed. Most New Dealers and local officials working with the poor did not hesitate to maintain customary racial and ethnic distinctions. In Tucson, Arizona, officials divided relief into four

categories—whites, Indians, Hispanic Americans, and Mexican refugees—and set up differential scales for relief payments. Each group would maintain its economic position relative to the others.

Whether to allow discrimination in this way was at the discretion of particular administrators, federal or local. The Civilian Conservation Corps, for example, took in few black youths. Hiring by the Tennessee Valley Authority favored white over black workers. Secretary of the Interior Harold Ickes, head of the Public Works Administration, argued for racial justice in hiring. Harry Hopkins's Works Progress Administration and the National Youth Administration, established under the WPA, were also careful to hire blacks as well as whites. Under Mary Bethune, one of a number of federal officials informally known as the Black Cabinet, the Youth Administration had a Division of Negro Affairs. Her agency over its lifespan employed 300,000 black men and women, which, when compared to the total number of hirings, approached

First Lady Eleanor Roosevelt visits an interracial daycare center in Detroit. (Courtesy, Library of Congress)

the proportion of black to white Americans in general.

One other New Dealer deserves special mention. Eleanor Roosevelt, maritally estranged from her husband but remaining his political companion, gained in her personal distance from FDR the ability to be a separate force. Her newspaper column "My Day" enjoyed a wide circulation. Mrs. Roosevelt, like her husband, was frankly aristocratic. Toward her readers and toward the groups of citizens coping with the Depression whom she liked to visit, she projected the somewhat parental friendliness and concern that mark traditional upper-class breeding. In her early days she had shared prejudices common among Americans. But she had the graciousness of her class at its best, along with the contempt of the well educated for the vulgarity of snobs and bigots. As hard as she could, she strove for a change in customary racial patterns.

Mrs. Roosevelt's best-known gesture her family status made possible. She was a member of the Daughters of the American Revolution. In 1939 the DAR on racial grounds denied the black opera

After the Daughters of the American Revolution denied Marian Anderson the use of Constitution Hall for a concert, Eleanor Roosevelt arranged for her to sing at the Lincoln Memorial. (Courtesy, Library of Congress)

singer Marian Anderson the use of the organization's Constitution Hall in Washington, DC, for an Easter concert. Mrs. Roosevelt thereupon resigned from the Daughters and arranged for the concert to be held at the Lincoln Memorial. It provided a pointed and highly publicized rebuke to white racism.

THE SPIRIT OF THE LAND

Save perhaps in small experiments conducted by the Resettlement Administration in the construction of model communities, the New Deal never contemplated a radical remaking of social institutions. Its refusal to associate itself with Upton Sinclair's EPIC made that clear. What did come out of the Depression years as a distinctive political and literary culture were images of a country both expressing and building a rough-hewn democracy, attempting to perfect the promise made at the nation's beginnings.

Building national confidence became a necessity, for the country's had sagged. Erosion ate away at rich soils. The economy was broken, and with it dreams and projects begun in a better time. So the act of building and rebuilding gave definition to the democratic ideas of the era. The Civilian Conservation Corps put the unemployed into projects of land reclamation. That, construction of dams in the Tennessee Valley, and much else set a democratic people to work on a continent big enough to invite their labors. Industrial unionism, fostered by the CIO, embodied a muscular new union militancy. The literary work promoted by the WPA included artists in the workers' democracy. Poetry and fiction sang of the immensity of the land. Pare Lorentz's *The River*, a poem set in a documentary film about the reclaiming of eroded soils, chants the names of American rivers. Often sentimental and seldom as consciously experimental as the literature that had followed the First World War, the writings of the Depression era capture evocative glimpses of a nation striving to win back its health and strength.

Suggested Readings

On Screwball Comedy: Wes D. Gehring, *Screwball Comedy: A Genre of Madcap Romance* (1986) and Duane Byrge, *Screwball Comedy Films: A History and Filmography 1934–1942* (1991). On the Dust Bowl and migration of displaced farm families, consult Lawrence Svobida, *Farming the Dust Bowl: A First-hand Account from Kansas* (1986); R. Douglas Hurt, *Dust Bowl: An Agricultural and Social History* (1981); Debra McArthur, *The Dust Bowl and the Depression in American History* (2002); Ann Marie Low, *Dust Bowl Diary* (1984); Matthew Paul Bonnifield, *Dust Bowl: Men, Dirt and Depression* (1979); and Charles J. Shindo, *Dust Bowl Migrants in the American Imagination* (1997)

For radical solutions and sharing the wealth, see Forrest Davis, *Huey Long; a Candid Biography* (1935); Suzanne LeVert, *Huey Long: the Kingfish of Louisiana*, (1995); Gerald Meyer, *Vito Marcantonio: Radical Politician* (1989); George Kleinholz, *Battle of Washington, a National Disgrace* (1932); Donald J. Lisio, *President and Protest: Hoover, MacArthur and the Bonus Riots* (2nd ed. 1994); Louis Cantor, *Prologue to the Protest Movement: the Missouri Sharecropper Roadside Demonstration of 1939* (1969); Donald H. Grubbs, *Cry from the Cotton: the Southern Tenant Farmers' Union and the New Deal* (1971);

On the Stock Market, the Crash of 1929, and afterward, consult Louise Gerdes, *The Crash of 1929*, (2002); Bernard C. Beaudreau, *Mass Production, the Stock Market Crash and the Great Depression:The Macroeconomics of Electrification* (1996); Gadis J. Dillon, *The Role of Accounting in the Stock Market Crash of 1929* (1984); Maury Klein, *Rainbow's End: The Crash of 1929* (2001); Thomas Gordon and Max Morgan-Witts, *The Day the Bubble Burst: A Social History of the Wall Street Crash of 1929* (1980); Barrie A. Wigmore, *The Crash and its Aftermath: A History of Securities Markets in the United States* (1985); and Tian Kang Go, *Financial Concentration in the United States during the Great Depression: The Leading New York Banks and the Concentration of Economic Power, 1929–33* (1986);

On President Franklin D. Roosevelt and the New Deal, there are Gary Dean Best, *The Critical Press and the New Deal: The Press versus Presidential Power, 1933–1938*, (1993); Roger Biles, *Memphis in the Great Depression*, (1986); Thomas Biolsi, *Organizing the Lakota: The Political Economy of the New Deal on the Pine Ridge and Rosebud Reservations* (1992); Maxwell H. Bloomfield, *Peaceful Revolution: Constitutional Change and American Culture from Progressivism to the New Deal* (2000); Barbara Blumberg, *The New Deal and the Unemployed* (1979); D.W. Brogan, *The Era of Franklin D. Roosevelt: A Chronicle of the New Deal and Global War* (1977); Melvyn Dubofsky and Stephen Burwood, *Agriculture During the Great Depression*, (1990), *Law and the New Deal* (1990); and *Women and Minorities during the Great Depression* (1990); Mark J. Rozell and William D. Pederson, *FDR and the Modern Presidency: Leadership and Legacy*, (1997); editors of Time-Life Books, *Hard Times, The 30s* (1998); Lawrence E. Gelfand and Robert J. Neymeyer, *New Deal Viewed from 50 Years: Papers Commemorating the Fiftieth Anniversary of the Launching of President Franklin D. Roosevelt's New Deal in 1933* (1984); Otis L. Graham, Jr., *Soviet-American Dialogue on the New Deal* (1989); Louis Adamic, *My America, 1928–1938*, (1976); and Jason Berger, *New Deal for the World: Eleanor Roosevelt and American Foreign Policy* (1981);

On the Congress of Industrial Organizations: Walter Galenson, *The CIO Challenge to the AFL: A History of the American Labor Movement, 1035–1941* (1960); Barbara S. Griffith, *The Crisis of American Labor: Operation Dixie and the Defeat of the CIO* (1988); Walter P. Reuther, *Labor on the March* (1956); Lucy Randolph Mason, *To Win These Rights: A Personal Story of the CIO in the South* (1970); Nelson Lichtenstein, *Labor's War at Home:The CIO in World War II* (2003); Saul David Alinsky, *John L. Lewis, An Unauthorized Biography* (1970); Sidney Fine, *Sit-Down: The General Motors Strike of 1936–1937* (1969); Walter Linder, *Great Flint Sitdown Strike against G.M., 1936–1937* (1969); Benjamin Stolberg, *Story of the CIO*, (1971); and John Raymond Walsh, *C.I.O.: Industrial Unionism in Action* (1937).

For the Scottsboro Boys: Lita Sorenson, *Scottsboro Boys Trial: A Primary Source Account* (2003); Dan T. Carter, *Scottsboro: A Tragedy of the American South* (1979); Allan Knight Chalmers, *They Shall Be Free* (1951); Angelo Herndon, *Four Freed! Five to Go!* (1937); Kwando Mbiassi Kinshasa, *Man from Scottsboro: Clarence Norris and the Infamous 1931 Alabama Rape Trial, in His Own Words* (1997); Clarence Norris, *Last of the Scottsboro Boys: An Autobiography* (1979); Haywood Patterson, *Scottsboro Boy* (1950).

Standing under the big guns of the U.S.S. *Houston*, President Franklin Delano Roosevelt, Commander-in-Chief of the nation's armed forces, reviewed the fleet in San Francisco Bay, July 14, 1938. *(Courtesy, AP/Wide World Photos)*

World War II and Its Prelude

★

CHAPTER 22

BATTLE OF THE
AMERICAN COASTLINE

As World War II broke out in Europe during 1939 and the United States recognized that it might soon become involved, the defense of the Western Hemisphere against possible direct enemy attack preoccupied the military services. The Atlantic and the Caribbean presented problems complicated by the fall of France to the Germans in 1940. Now French possessions in the Caribbean such as the large islands of Martinique and Guadeloupe might become military bases that Germany, enjoying the friendship of the French Vichy government, could hope to use for raids against the Atlantic Coast.

The danger of a full-scale invasion was too slight to require major preparation. More threatening were such possibilities as aerial bombings launched from aircraft carriers. Before the nation's entry into the war, President Franklin Roosevelt was already mapping out a wide portion of the Atlantic as coming within his country's sphere of defense. It stretched as far as Iceland, which the United States was garrisoning. The military also attempted to protect British shipping from the American seacoast halfway across the Atlantic, so much so that in the autumn of 1941 the German navy and ships of the United States were already in an undeclared shooting war.

After the United States went to outright war with Germany and the other Axis nations, Italy and Japan, the feared assaults on the landward side of the eastern seacoast never materialized. A few saboteurs, one group slipping onto Long Island from a submarine, another surfacing in New York harbor, still another detected in the Hudson River near West Point, one in northern Maine, and one outside Jacksonville, Florida, were quickly captured. On the Pacific Coast, defenses included concrete blockhouses and shore guns peppered along California's bluffs and beaches. Japanese ships occasionally shelled the West Coast and sent incendiary bombs in balloons over the Pacific Northwest. Spotters kept alert for enemy planes, and racial prejudice combined with wartime emotions initiated a program for removing Japanese Americans to guarded camps.

But it was the Atlantic outside and just within the country's coastal waters that became, along with the Caribbean and adjacent sea regions, a battle zone. There German submarines picked off merchant ships working the coastal route that carried from countries south of the United States oil, bauxite, and aluminum—materials necessary for war. The Germans were helped by American coastal cities which, not taking the war seriously enough to recognize that it was going on just offshore, remained brightly lighted at night despite the government's efforts to enforce black-outs. The outlines of ships cleanly defined against the lighted coastline made easy targets for the U-boats.

In the first part of 1942 losses near the shore were disastrous. German submarines sank some 285 ships in that year. They destroyed in the Caribbean several British oil tankers and shelled a refinery, seriously disrupting production. About a fifth of the ships working Puerto Rico were lost. An early effort by the American navy was to organize a band of civilian yachtsmen to assist in spotting submarines—an instance of aristocracy at war suggestive of the wealthy young men like John F. Kennedy who commanded the dashing PT boats in the Pacific. Then when a convoy system brought safety to coastal shipping, the German submarines concentrated on merchant ships far out in the Atlantic on their way to Britain, beyond the range of American aircraft that could pick them off when they needed to surface. Adding complexities to their codes that for a time Allied cryptographers could not decipher helped the subs. Again the loss in Allied shipping was heavy. But at the end of 1942 the new German codes had been broken. The Americans were also able to manufacture escorts that included small carriers launching as many as two dozen planes; and the navy in March 1943 added long-range aircraft. Toward the last days of that May, the Germans in effect withdrew from the north Atlantic battle.

The American merchant mariners who guided the Western Hemisphere traffic and then along with the British conducted the Atlantic shipping essential to the survival of Great Britain and the Soviet Union had a special relationship to the war effort. During the war the merchant marine became a regular part of the armed services alongside the army, the navy, and the coast guard. Yet it was not strictly under military discipline: its members were unionized, and up to a point a seaman could decide when and on what ship to sail. The merchant service attracted radicals, appealing to a political rebel's scorn of military obedience or to a desire to fight a workers' war against fascism. The merchant marine suffered one of the heaviest casualty rates among the wartime services. For a time its ships did not even possess guns with which to protect the crew. And the work could be especially harsh. On winter runs between Britain and the Soviet Union, a merchant mariner who grasped a metal railing might find his hand frozen to the object. But for the merchant seamen's want of a strictly military character, members of the other uniformed services widely and incorrectly dismissed their efforts as inferior.

HISTORICAL EVENTS

1921-1922
Washington Naval Conference

1922
World War Foreign Debt Commission

1931
Japanese attack Manchuria

1932
Japanese attack China • Franklin Delano Roosevelt elected president

1935
Neutrality Acts 1935–37, 1939

1936
Hitler marches into the Rhineland • Roosevelt reelected president

1938
Kristallnacht—"the night of broken glass" • Munich Pact

1939
World War II begins in Europe • Stalin signs nonaggression pact with Hitler

1940
Roosevelt reelected president • Germany, Japan, and Italy join as Axis powers

1941
Germany invades Russia • Pearl Harbor

1942
Bataan Death March • Japanese Americans imprisoned • United States victory at Midway in Pacific • Operation Torch begins in North Africa

1943
United States and Britain liberate part of Italy • American victory at Guadalcanal

1944
Operation Overlord opens at Normandy (D Day) • Russians march into Poland • Roosevelt reelected president

1945
Roosevelt, Stalin, and Churchill meet at Yalta • Allies win Battle of the Bulge • Roosevelt dies (April 2) • Harry Truman becomes president • Germany surrenders (May 7) • Atomic bombs dropped on Japan • War ends (August 9)

THE ROOTS OF WORLD WAR II

When President Woodrow Wilson, on the entry of the United States into the First World War, insisted that the nation was not one of the Allies but merely "associated" with them, he had reflected a widespread public sentiment. Even Wilson the internationalist, aiming to project the United States into global events, shared with isolationists a sense that his country was different, untainted by the selfish ambitions and the secret diplomacy of older lands.

Wilsonian ideas persisted in the Republican regime of Warren Harding that followed. The Washington Naval Conference of 1921-22, managed by Secretary of State Charles Evans Hughes, yielded a series of pacts among major powers, limiting the size of their navies and sealing their agreement not to compete with one another for territory in Asia and the Pacific. In a Wilsonian vein, the conference gave the United States a role in the world's future. Equally in that tradition was its objective: not to forge military alliances but to eliminate military competition. Among Republicans who had kept the country out of the League of Nations were several ready to accept the League in modified form. During the twenties, moreover, Republicans began to engage in League conferences. In 1928 Frank Kellogg, Coolidge's secretary of state, for strategic reasons joined over sixty powers as signatories to a pact initially arranged with Aristide Briand of France outlawing war. This ineffective exercise in good will is known as the Kellogg-Briand Pact.

The Coolidge administration, in one more of his country's interventions in Latin America, sent troops to Nicaragua in 1926 to confront Augusto Sandino, who in death became a lasting Nicaraguan hero. And troops from the United States trained a local militia that helped put into power in 1933 the dictator Anastasio Somoza. His corrupt family was to rule and loot Nicaragua for decades. But under Coolidge the United States withdrew troops from Santo Domingo, though continuing to supervise the government's finances. Washington also paid Colombia in effect an indemnity for stealing Panama from that country during Theodore Roosevelt's presidency. J. Reuben Clark of the State Department, requested by Coolidge to define the limits of the Monroe Doctrine, published his findings in 1930 during Hoover's presidency. Reversing the Roosevelt Corollary to the Monroe Doctrine, the Clark Memorandum held that the Doctrine was to resist European intervention in Latin America and did not specify a right of the United States to intrude there. Any number of such intrusions, in fact, have followed in one form or another.

The Debt Problem

During World War I, Americans had made extensive loans to the Allies, money that was necessary to their cause. In the 1920s, paying those loans placed a financial strain upon European borrowers. The readiest means for them to repay was to hold Germany to the huge reparations imposed on that defeated nation. That was disastrous to the German economy, increasing the distress and resentment that would soon lead to Nazism.

In 1922 Congress set up the World War Debt Commission that trimmed the original obligations and the accumulated interest, considering each country's ability to pay. Two years later the Allies adopted the Dawes Plan, drawn up by Commerce Secretary Hoover and Charles Dawes, an American banker, that reduced Germany's indebtedness. Named for another financier, Owen D. Young, the Young Plan of 1928 again softened the burden of reparations. Since none of this was accompanied by a statesmanlike vision of international commerce—the United States along with European countries had protective tariffs—nations had inadequate access to the trade by which they might have made their payments. And the far more radical solution, canceling the reparations and loan payments, was contrary to nationalist feelings and particularly the Republican Party position. The American Smoot-Hawley Tariff raising import duties, reluctantly signed by President Herbert Hoover in 1930, led to retaliatory duties among European nations. International commerce, at a time when desperately needed, was further choked.

In 1931, Hoover arranged a one-year moratorium on debts to the United States. When the moratorium became permanent, at least one economic and diplomatic absurdity of the postwar era had come to an end. Hoover also continued the process of breaking the nation's habit of occupying Latin American countries. A London Naval Conference of 1930 called at his initiative attempted further to reduce naval armaments, an ineffectively earnest last return to the belief in a rational world that the First World War had already mocked.

The Rush for Neutrality

Soon afterward, Hoover faced a foreign crisis that challenged his efforts at world peace. Japan invaded Manchuria in 1931. Hoover and Secretary of State Henry L. Stimson refused to recognize the puppet Manchurian regime established by Japan, a policy that became known as the Hoover-Stimson Doctrine. The League of Nations condemned Japan, but did little else. Japanese aircraft bombed China's largest city, Shanghai, in 1932, but the League had initiated a decade of inaction in face of major aggression that would end in a Second World War.

FDR shaped his foreign policy to treat his country's economic ills. A World Economic Conference of 1933 in London led nowhere. With the aim of making the nation's currency cheaper and thereby effectively lowering the real price of goods so that they would sell better abroad, Roosevelt went off the gold standard that backed paper currency with supplies of gold. Reciprocal trade agreements with Latin American countries provided for negotiated reductions in tariffs. Expanding on Hoover's intentions, Roosevelt also declared what became known as the Good Neighbor Policy, promising to respect the rights of Latin American countries. And when the Mexican government claimed oil lands owned by citizens of the United States, the president, like Coolidge in an earlier such incident, refrained from military intervention. Another initiative, aiming largely to increase markets abroad, was FDR's recognition of the Communist regime in the Soviet Union.

The American public recoiled from issues outside the nation's borders. Accustomed to enjoying their relative immunity to foreign problems and preoccupied with the Depression, Americans in the early thirties were also listening to the claim that the nation's entrance into the First World War had mostly benefited munitions makers and war profiteers. In 1934 Senator Gerald P. Nye of North Dakota became chair of a committee investigating the wealth that the war had brought to the armaments industry. Since war, of course, enriches people who deal in war goods, the Nye committee could not possibly fail to find what it was looking for. And as the committee built up evidence of war profiteering, it was an easy step to conclude that

Some isolationist senators believed in the 1930s that the vast Atlantic Ocean would protect them from the European conflict. (Courtesy, National Archives)

profits had been not simply the effect of the war but the reason for the country's engagement in it.

To insure that the United States would not stumble into future wars, Congress passed a series of neutrality acts that Roosevelt, fast veering toward internationalism, chose not to fight but sometimes ignored. A law passed in 1935 declared that whenever the president proclaimed that a state of war existed anywhere, arms shipments from the United States to either side were to be forbidden. Another act prohibited American banks from lending to warring nations. Legislation in 1937 required that a belligerent buying nonmilitary goods from the United States—the only purchases allowed—must buy not on credit but with cash and must carry away the goods on its own ships. The policy took on the name "cash and carry." But even as Congress tried to seal off the nation from foreign troubles, those problems were mounting.

Nationalism on the March

In Italy, the dictator Benito Mussolini brought to that country an ideology known as fascism. Deriving its name from the fasces—the bundle of sticks bound around an ax that the ancient Romans had used as a symbol of authority—fascism aimed to revive in modern Italy the strengths of Rome. Fascism glorified the state, and expected it to impose on its people a perfect unity. Mussolini cast himself in heroic posture: he is caught on film turning his head so that an adoring crowd could see his square-jawed profile. This vision of national greatness awakened an appetite for conquest and empire, and in 1935 Italy invaded and occupied Ethiopia in northern Africa. The League of Nations called for economic sanctions against Mussolini's regime, but its members declined to enforce them. The League's failure, coupled with its earlier ineffectiveness during the Japanese absorption of Manchuria, made clear its uselessness for keeping the peace.

Japan needed no explicit ideology like fascism. A code of honor called Bushido, prevailing particularly in the armed forces, exalted sacrifice of life in service to the nation and its emperor. The Japanese defined themselves as a people of self-denying virtue. Such a mentality invited military adventure. Japan's great naval victory of 1905 over Russia in the battle of Tsushima Strait, demonstrating that an Asian country had established its place among Western powers, generated enormous national pride and was observed as a yearly holiday. By the late 1930s a Japanese army was carving out a slice of China, and the government was looking to take over Western colonies in Asia rich in raw materials such as French Indochina. In 1937 the Japanese captured Nanking, and in an atrocity so horrible that an official of Nazi Germany tried to aid the victims, the army engaged in a frenzy of rape and murder that left perhaps more than two hundred thousand Chinese dead. Yet even the Japanese sinking of the American gunboat *Panay*, which Japan's army in China suspected of intruding in a Chinese war area, did not shake the conviction of the American public that the United States must stay out of foreign conflicts.

Nazism

Even more threatening than either Italy or Japan was Germany. In the early 1930s the country chose as its leader Adolf Hitler, a powerful speaker with a high-pitched strident voice that conveyed ideological frenzy. Similar to the Italian fascists and the Japanese militarists in elevating national unity, Hitler's National Socialist German Labor Party added a belief in the superiority of the German race. More broadly the Nazis meant the Aryan peoples, inhabiting Germany and dispersed elsewhere in

German youth gather for burning books written by Albert Einstein and Thomas Mann. Were there any book-burning incidents in American history? (Courtesy, UPI Corbis/Bettmann)

northern Europe and in other parts of the world. Poles and other east Europeans, the Nazis insisted, were fit only for slavery; Jews were corrupt and treacherous, and German Jews were declared to be an internal enemy. To restore the power of Germany, regain the lands taken from the nation after the Treaty of Versailles, and ultimately join with Aryans throughout the globe in subjugating or extinguishing inferior people: these were the larger goals of Nazism. Countless nations have had dreams of conquest and glory. What made the Nazis menacing was that, unlike other countries, they actually tried to carry out their fantasies of greatness.

The Nazis waged war on the Jews from the start. In 1935 they passed the Nuremberg Laws, which limited Jewish rights and access to employment. In 1938, when the German government expelled about eighteen thousand Polish Jews, driving them across the border into Poland, a young Jew living in Paris gunned down a German official there. The consequence, orchestrated by the German government, was *Kristallnacht*, the night of broken glass, when the glass from the smashed windows of Jewish establishments sprinkled the streets. Gangs roamed the country looking to attack Jews and their shops, synagogues, and charitable institutions. Twenty thousand Jews were thrown into concentration camps, and decrees robbed them of their property and further restricted their employment. A few nations took in Jewish refugee children. In the United States, Congress and public opinion resisted relaxing immigration laws to admit even the small additional number of twenty thousand Jewish children.

German expansionists, proceeding methodically, in 1936 sent their army into the Rhineland, German territory bordering France that the Treaty of Versailles forbade Germans to rearm. The next year Germany joined Italy in an alliance that became known as the Axis; Japan later became an Axis power. In Spain, Francisco Franco led a rebellion against a republican government that had moved to the left. On his side were conservatives, Catholics, and fascists. The republican forces included Communists, socialists, and anarchists. Germany and Italy both supported Franco, most innovatively in the use of bombings from the air. Though volunteers from outside Spain, such as the Abraham Lincoln Brigade of Americans, served with the republican resistance to Franco and the Soviet Union aided the Communists, the Western powers refrained from rescuing the government. In Spain the Communists meanwhile took to waging war on their anarchist and other leftist comrades, with the intention of dominating the republican side. By 1939 Franco had won. It was a victory at second hand for the Axis, a success for Hitler and Mussolini in extending fascist ideology.

In 1938 Hitler looked eastward. Before an election could take place in Austria on whether to merge with Germany, he swallowed up that country in a bloodless invasion. Then he demanded that Czechoslovakia yield the Sudetenland, a region with a large German population. To forestall a world war, the British Prime Minister Neville Chamberlain flew to Germany, where at Munich he reached an agreement with Hitler to occupy only the Sudetenland and settle future disputes peacefully. But after Chamberlain's announcement that there was now to be "peace in our time," Hitler promptly gobbled up the rest of Czechoslovakia. Next he began making threats against Poland, claiming that until Germans there received justice no peace was possible. It has been the cruel destiny of Chamberlain to be remembered as the appeaser at Munich. Still, as Hitler menaced the Poles, Chamberlain's government guaranteed the independence of Poland—a direct challenge to Germany. Almost immediately, a shift in Soviet foreign policy stunned the West and insured the coming of war.

The Popular Front

Ever since the Bolshevik revolution in 1917, the Communists had been a presence to be reckoned with among Western leftists. In Europe and the United States, small Communist parties adhered slavishly to whatever directive was the latest to come from Moscow. In 1935, Moscow, fearing the growing aggressiveness of Germany, decided to form what it described as a Popular Front against fascism. It directed its parties abroad to present a tolerant and generous face to anyone deemed "progressive." Since American liberals and leftists were independently horrified at Nazi Germany, some of them accepted the Popular Front idea. The strategy was successful enough to give Communism a shaky respectability in some American liberal and intellectual circles. Communists urged American armament to prepare for a stand against Nazi Germany.

Then came a blow that shocked party members along with others who had been impressed for the moment by the Popular Front. In the late summer of 1939 Stalin, having decided that the West would not unite in opposition to Hitler, entered into a nonaggression pact with Germany. The two now cooperated in warmongering. The German army in September 1939 proceeded to seize the western part of Poland; and shortly afterwards, Soviet troops occupied the eastern portion of that nation. In

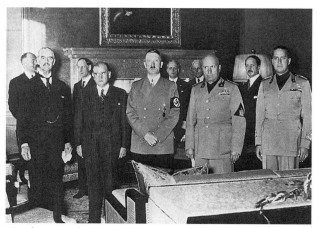

Conferees at the Munich Conference include British Prime Minister Neville Chamberlain (left), Adolf Hitler (third from left), and Benito Mussolini (fourth from left). (Courtesy, UPI)

response, France and Britain declared war on Germany. At the Nazi-Soviet agreement, some American Communists left the party in dazed horror. Others, determined to follow Soviet policy wherever it might lead, switched from calling for rearmament to attacking Roosevelt's policy of building up the military, which might now be used against the Soviet and Nazi armies. When Moscow, wishing to protect the western flank of the Soviet Union, invaded Finland, more Western Communists found reason to turn from Moscow. In the winter of 1939 and 1940, the Finns held out heroically against the Soviet aggressor, but resistance was hopeless. Recoil from Communism was widespread owing to stories of the Spanish Communist repression of independent leftists, disgust at the Soviet pact with the Nazis, and now the plight of Finland. Disillusion with Communism deepened at the report of trials in Moscow during the mid-thirties of old Bolsheviks who had managed to gain the enmity of the Soviet leadership. Torture and the will of Stalin insured that the defendants would be found guilty of crimes against the Soviet state.

The West under Siege

While Hitler together with Stalin was carving up Poland, the German leader gave himself time before attacking Britain and France. For a short while the conflict in the West was a *Sitzkrieg*, a sitting war. After attacking Denmark and then Norway, the Germans in 1940 turned to lightning war, *Blitzkrieg*, against Britain and France. The Maginot Line was a string of fortifications in northern France that were supposed to keep the country protected against Germany. Making good use of the mobility afforded by motorized transport, the Germans simply avoided the Maginot Line. In May 1940, they went north of it, occupying Luxembourg, the Netherlands, and Belgium. Next they turned south on France, which crumbled. About 338,000 British and French troops were evacuated from the French port of Dunkirk in an operation in which British civilians who owned or operated boats crossed the English Channel and helped carry the troops to safety. The north of France, including Paris, then came under German rule. The conquerors left the

Prime Minister Winston Churchill at the ruins of Coventry Cathedral, bombed by the Luftwaffe in October 1941. (Courtesy, British Information Service)

rest of the country to a government they established at the town of Vichy and headed by Marshal Philippe Pétain, a French hero of World War I. Technically neutral, the Vichy regime was essentially in partnership with the Germans.

In Britain, Prime Minister Winston Churchill became remembered as the wartime leader whose grand rhetoric gave meaning to the struggle against the fascists. In 1940 the British alone in the West held out against Germany, inspired by the florid Churchill's grandiloquent vocabulary. "The battle of France had ended," he told Parliament; "the battle of Britain is about to begin." "If we fail, then the whole world . . . will sink into the abyss of a new Dark Age. . . . Let us therefore brace ourselves to our duties, and so bear ourselves that, if the British Empire and its Commonwealth last for a thousand years, men will say, 'This was their finest hour.'" Over their own skies that year, British fighter pilots successfully fought off in the Battle of Britain a German attempt to soften up the island kingdom by bombings. Radio gave drama to the event. The American newsman Edward R. Murrow, whose lank and brooding countenance made him look a good deal like any world-hardened character played by Humphrey Bogart, would frame his broadcasts across the Atlantic with "This . . . is London." The phrase caught perfectly the solemnity of the moment and the unassuming courage of the British people.

The United States Moves Toward War

In the United States, opposition to involvement in outside conflicts remained strong. A curious combination of conservatives and antiwar progressives declared themselves isolationists. Some of the conservatives simply disliked any expenditure of American money to aid foreign governments as they had resisted assistance to the American poor of the Depression; a few were not unsympathetic to Nazi anti-Semitism. The highly respected Charles Lindbergh, the transatlantic flyer, opposed American involvement in the conflict. Beyond the ideological case for isolationism was a general public disinclination to involve the United States in any international conflicts that might bring the country into the war.

As German victories multiplied and Nazi fanaticism became clearer, Roosevelt's efforts to arm against Germany began to get congressional sup-

port. An act passed toward the end of 1939 kept the principle of cash and carry but repealed the prohibition of arms shipments. After the *Blitzkrieg* of 1940, Congress gave FDR appropriations for increases in the military, and the Selective Service Act of 1940, renewed in the summer of 1941, provided for a compulsory draft into the armed forces.

In 1940 Roosevelt, in return for a lease from the British of some naval bases in Newfoundland, Bermuda, and the Caribbean, gave Britain over the protest of isolationists a number of overaged destroyers. These were largely useless, but Roosevelt employed them politically as a way of tightening the American alliance with London. In that year as well the Republicans, themselves swinging away from isolationism, nominated for president Wendell Willkie, a Wall Street lawyer who supported aid to Britain. It was significant of a growing national consensus that Willkie, a former Democrat, accepted in broad outline the New Deal. FDR, breaking with an American tradition, ran for a third presidential term, claiming that in light of the world crisis the country needed continuity of leadership. Public opinion polls indicated that his reelection, though he won a smaller percentage of the popular vote than he had previously captured, was precisely because the public had accepted that need.

The exchange of destroyers for bases had been by presidential order and did not require the consent of Congress. But in March 1941 Roosevelt succeeded in getting from the national legislature a program known as lend-lease; to Britain, starved for cash, the United States would lend war materials rather than selling them. The president also enunciated the "Four Freedoms": freedom of speech and expression, freedom of worship, freedom from want, and freedom from fear. By now, public opinion had moved sufficiently in favor of aid short of entering the war, and the program enjoyed majority support. Moscow, the betrayer of the anti-Nazi Popular Front, in June itself became the victim of betrayal. Germany launched a surprise invasion of the USSR, which along with Britain would then become a recipient of American lend-lease. Immediately, of course, the American Communist Party did another of its nimble turnabouts, abandoning its opposition to rearmament and returning to the anti-fascist militancy of the Popular Front days.

In August 1941 Roosevelt and Churchill, who were working closely together to firm up an alliance, met aboard a ship in the Atlantic Ocean. There they drew up a statement termed the Atlantic Charter, pledging to work for a postwar world free of aggression. They also promised aid to the Soviet Union. And that year the United States entered an undeclared naval war with Germany. Through North Atlantic waters infested with German submarines it escorted merchant ships bound for Britain. During that undeclared war a German U-boat sunk the American destroyer *Reuben James.*

In Asia, Japan was continuing its war in China, opposed by two enemies now in temporary alliance, the anticommunist Chinese government under Chiang Kai-shek and the Communist insurgents led by Mao Zedong. Roosevelt had sent aid to Chiang even at a time when neutrality legislation theoretically prohibited it. Between 1939 and 1941 Washington severed economic relations with Japan, placing an embargo on selling it scrap iron and steel, industrial chemicals, and oil, and freezing Japanese assets in the United States. The fall of the Netherlands and France was a boon to the Japanese, for the Vichy government allowed them into French Indochina, rich in rubber, tin, and tungsten. After fighting off an Allied force, they soon possessed the Dutch West Indies, gaining access to oil they desperately needed. But it was clear that at some point Japan, if it was to gain an Asian and Pacific empire, would have to deal with the United States, the other largest Pacific power.

WAR

On Sunday, December 7, 1941—the sound of that day and date have for a generation possessed a memorable cadence—much of the American Pacific fleet was at Pearl Harbor, along with numerous aircraft. To an enemy bred in naval tradition, it would be particularly tempting that at anchor were all eight of the United States Pacific battleships. A more farsighted foe would have been concerned by the absence at Pearl Harbor of any of the aircraft carriers the United States had consigned to that ocean. The years that followed were to demonstrate that not battleships but carriers, bearing planes that could strike miles beyond sight of the ship itself, would dominate the waters. And from carriers, in fact, the Japanese conducted the surprise air assault by which they hoped to drive the United States out

At Pearl Harbor the Japanese damaged or sank eight battleships, including the U.S.S. Arizona *pictured here.* (Official United States Navy Photograph)

of the Pacific. At the end of the attack, all eight battleships together with ten other vessels were sunk or disabled and about three hundred aircraft were in some state of disrepair. The Japanese killed over 2,300 Americans. President Roosevelt told Congress that December 7 would "live in infamy." Congress declared war on Japan and other Axis powers.

The Japanese leaders knew that in a long war the United States would have the time to bring its industrial potential to overwhelming force against their nation. What they were counting on was that Americans would not fight a long war. Japan believed them a self-indulgent people lacking the will for extended combat. Weakened by Pearl Harbor, they reasoned, the United States would come to an agreement by which the Japanese could rule Asia and the Pacific undisturbed. That was a long and, as it turns out, bad gamble.

Japan Advances

For the moment, though, the Japanese enjoyed enormous success. Within a few weeks they had taken Hong Kong from Britain, and shortly afterward the British colony of Singapore at the top of the Malay Peninsula. Seizing the Netherlands East

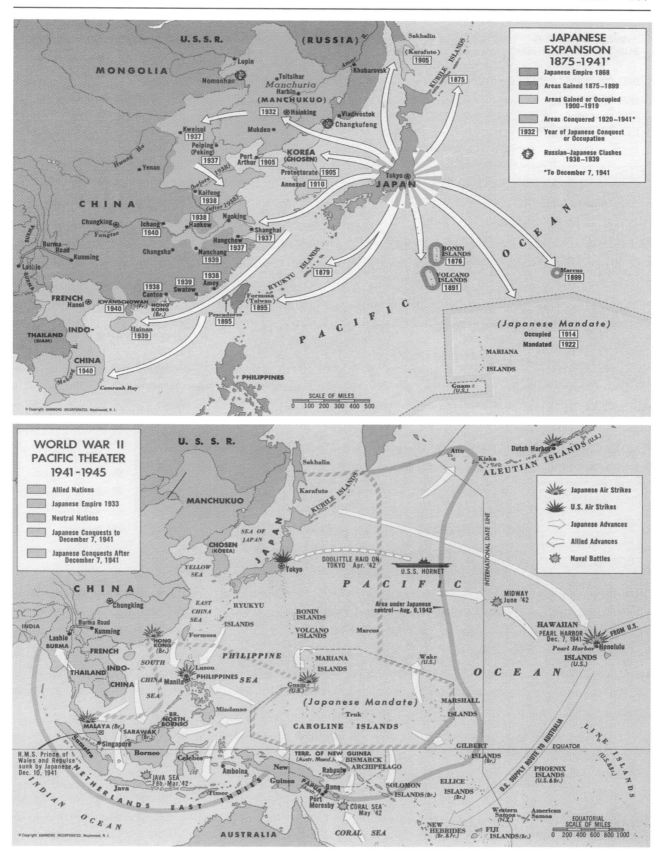

JAPANESE
EXPANSION
1875-1941*

Japanese Empire 1868
Areas Gained 1875–1899
Areas Gained or Occupied 1900–1919
Areas Conquered 1920–1941*
1932 Year of Japanese Conquest or Occupation
Russian-Japanese Clashes 1938–1939
*To December 7, 1941

WORLD WAR II
PACIFIC THEATER
1941-1945

Allied Nations
Japanese Empire 1933
Neutral Nations
Japanese Conquests to December 7, 1941
Japanese Conquests After December 7, 1941

Japanese Air Strikes
U.S. Air Strikes
Japanese Advances
Allied Advances
Naval Battles

Indies, lying between Australia and the Asian mainland, enhanced their strategic position and their oil resources. In May, after months of fighting in the Philippines, they forced the surrender of the last of General Jonathan Wainwright's combined Filipino and American army of eighty thousand. As in their campaign to occupy Singapore, the Japanese by skillful maneuvering had conquered an opposing army larger than their own. Both victors and vanquished in the Philippines were in wretched physical condition. Treating the prisoners with brutal contempt, the Japanese forced survivors on what has become known as the Bataan Death March to imprisonment. Along the long march, examples of Japanese cruelty were casual and spontaneous: using trucks to drag prisoners, bayoneting soldiers who fell exhausted, riding a tank over a fallen soldier and impressing his body into the ground. That the Japanese themselves were low on food and supplies partly explains why the rations provided to the prisoners on the Death March were scanty. General Douglas MacArthur, commander of the defenders at the beginning of the engagement, had meanwhile been pulled out at the orders of FDR, who gave him a larger assignment in the Pacific.

In MacArthur Roosevelt had one of his most brilliant commanders and potentially one of his biggest headaches. As a field officer in the First World War, MacArthur had demonstrated great physical bravery, and he was sincerely committed, in a lofty way, to his troops. But MacArthur had an imperial view of things: he cultivated a look that included sunglasses and a corncob pipe along with the bearing of a Roman patrician. Politicians were much impressed. If MacArthur had chosen to disagree with Roosevelt on any major issue, as he would later do with Truman, the president might have been in political trouble. FDR was careful to stroke his feelings.

The Pacific War Turns

As quickly as their triumphs, fortune turned against the Japanese. In the spring of 1942 the Battle of the Coral Sea, though no clear victory for the American navy, demonstrated that Japan was not unstoppable. There American forces held off a Japanese advance into New Guinea, an East Indies island where Australian troops were fighting. The Coral Sea was also history's first naval battle fought entirely by aircraft launched from carriers: the

ships themselves were 175 miles apart. Then in June came a battle that determined the rest of the Pacific war.

The Japanese had decided to take the American naval base on the island of Midway, located near the center of the Pacific. From there they would have controlled the ocean. But under Admiral Chester Nimitz the Americans, having decoded a part of a Japanese message that they guessed indicated a planned assault on Midway, secretly moved three large aircraft carriers within range. Early in the battle, American dive-bombers attacked the Japanese fruitlessly, one after another shot down. Further waves of planes, however, took out four of Japan's six carriers, while the Americans lost only one. With the addition of another carrier not already at Midway, the United States now had the larger number. Having also lost many aircraft in the battle, the Japanese were henceforth on the defensive. In the following years, American industry was to turn out carriers in numbers the Japanese could not hope to match. In all, the supremacy that carriers now enjoyed in naval warfare revealed, like the swift movements of Allied motorized columns on land, that modern technology was making mobility an enormous ingredient in war.

The War at Home

That the war was a boom time for the workers who maintained those industrial triumphs had become apparent even before the formal entrance of the United States into the conflict. War orders destined for Britain along with general preparedness for combat ended the unemployment of the Depression. After Pearl Harbor, government controls over business increased. During a dispute involving the smaller steel companies known as Little Steel, the National War Labor Board imposed a settlement holding down wages, a formula the government attempted to impose on other industries. Then in return for a wartime pledge not to strike, labor was amply compensated. The Office of Price Administration, or OPA, strove to limit price increases, and the government compelled business to force workers into unions, which as the job market flooded grew significantly. A famous photograph of 1944 shows the crusty executive Sewell L. Avery of Montgomery Ward carried out of his office by troops after he refused to obey the edict. Agricultural labor was in effect exempt from the draft. Rationing,

Save waste fats for explosives

TAKE THEM TO YOUR MEAT DEALER

The Office of War Information used art to tie the home front with the battlefield. Even the simplest acts, so the message went, could contribute to the war effort. (Courtesy, Library of Congress)

keeper showed to a morally outraged father; playing at battle, hordes of invisible enemy troops melting before them; paper troops collecting old newspapers for recycling; the pungent smell of synthetic rubber; the afternoon radio programs, Terry and the Pirates, Jack Armstrong, Hop Harrigan, little bands of heroes taking on diabolical Axis foes; and the songs, "When the Lights Go on Again," "This Is Worth Fighting For," and "When der Führer Says He Is der Master Ace." Air raid wardens walked the safe and quiet streets of residential neighborhoods checking to see that blackout drills were being obeyed. City people found patches of ground on which to plant victory gardens.

Still, in a war fought for the most part thousands of miles away, the country prosecuted it strenuously, with some sacrifice and efficiency mingled with American wastefulness. Lured by jobs or a desire to serve, mastering industrial tasks new to them, and moving by the millions from south to north and from east to west, Americans produced feats of mass production. After Pearl Harbor, Roosevelt called for building sixty thousand planes; he got 300,000. A carrier fleet overwhelmed the Japanese in sheer numbers; war goods provided for the great invasion of Europe and assisted Stalin's huge army. Near war plants, ramshackle housing went up for the workers, while older residents shuddered at the shabby newcomers. Women braved the condescension of male workers and took on jobs in heavy industry, not only because husbands were away and they needed the money but because it was the patriotic thing to do. By day madam is at the Grumann aircraft plant, explains a haughty butler in a *New Yorker* cartoon, but she is not allowed to take calls. Rosie the Riveter, a mythic figure of the era, was not making a statement about women's rights. She took a job because it had to get done. Volunteers in the USO, the United Service Organizations, served gallons of coffee and homelike conversation to troops stationed domestically and abroad, and entertainers from Hollywood and radio gave shows not far from combat zones. The comedian Bob Hope became loosely identified with these productions. Americans did not undergo a fraction of the pain and danger at home that the peoples of Europe and Asia on both sides of the conflict endured. But in the light of how easy it might have been for many citizens to ignore the war entirely, the nation could have done much worse.

Lest it seem that uncoerced Americans were at

enforced by the issuance of government stamps to be yielded at time of the transaction, limited the purchase of food, gasoline, and other items; yet American workers had far more to spend.

In a land that except at its fringes was not a battlefield, the United States provided its soldiers with luxuries such as canned food that were the envy of British soldiers. At home Washington relied on mixtures of regulations, incentives, and propaganda. The military tried to put a premium on war production, but the government attempted to balance consumer goods against defense needs. Among Americans who had no family members in the military, the war was at a comfortable distance. Just inland from the Atlantic shore, children were beginning in perfect safety to store up rich fragments of memory. For them the war might recall counterfeit ration tokens that a morally outraged store-

times uniquely lax in their effort, comparisons with the German performance are in order. Intelligence gathering after the war discovered that for much of the conflict the far more regimented Germans had been sloppier in their production methods and engagement of civilian labor. In 1939 Germans made use of 1,600,000 domestic servants. In September 1944 that figure was only 300,000 lower. Not until the last year or so of the conflict did German industry, under the guidance of the administrator Albert Speer, achieve heroic standards of production. An indication of the predominance of culture over more pressing concerns is that at a time when American industry was turning to women workers, the Nazis were slow to employ their own countrywomen. Work outside the home was not the place for good women of German blood.

Women, Liberation, and Domesticity

Of the many social changes that the Second World War like other wars brought about, the entry of women into previously male occupations seems at first glance to have been a temporary phenomenon. In 1940, only 11.5 million women were employed outside the home, principally single women, widows, and wives from poor families. African American women worked in whatever jobs were available, often domestic service. But after millions of men enlisted in the armed forces, President Roosevelt called for a new attitude in the workplace: "In some communities employers dislike to hire women. In others they are reluctant to hire Negroes. We can no longer afford to indulge such prejudices." And so women and blacks in record numbers went to work in the production of planes, ships, trucks, tanks, armaments, food, clothing, and other supplies that fuel a war. Tales of neglected children became a theme of popular journalism. Yet fully seventy-five percent of women surveyed in 1944 and 1945 expressed a wish to continue in jobs after the war. It is difficult to doubt that with some residue of independence in wartime work by women, some shift in self-perception came with it. But women who took work did so with the understanding that men who had been called from their jobs and sent to combat were promised that upon the coming of peace they could get them back. The most immediate effect of the war on sexual relations was the baby boom, the increase in

Women assembling an aircraft during World War II. (Courtesy, United States Air Force)

(left and right) *Women served as noncombatants in the war itself as WAVES, WAACS, WAFS, and SPARS but also vitally at home by filling jobs normally held by men.* (Courtesy, Library of Congress and Baker Library, Harvard Business School)

childbearing that began not only after but during the conflict, while soldiers waited to go to active service or others returned from it.

Race Relations During the War

White American society was grudging in its concessions to black Americans despite their wartime service. Most black enlistees were put into segregated units and treated with whatever contempt or indifference their white officers displayed. Black sailors whom racism consigned to construction battalions—the CBs or Seabees—might be assigned to labor duties under fire, braving the dangers without recognition. At home, black naval enlistees at Port Chicago in California had the hazardous job of loading bombs onto ships. In 1944, while one such crew was working at top speed into the night, an explosion killed over three hundred people, more than two hundred of them black. Survivors who later refused to go back to work were court-martialed.

The demands of war found a slight tempering of racism and a degree of change. In 1941 the militant A. Philip Randolph, black leader of the Brotherhood of Sleeping Car Porters, threatened to organize a massive march in the nation's capital against racism in the armed services. To avoid a disruptive

demonstration at a time when the country was moving toward war, FDR issued an executive order forbidding discrimination in employment by the government and in defense industries. Businesses got partially around the regulation by giving black employees menial work, but the order did pry open jobs and provided some workers, white as well as black, their first experience of integration. The military later edged away from the blatant racism that confined black enlistees to degrading work under white officers and the elite army air corps and marines accepted some blacks, though in segregated units.

That war industry could, with some lasting effect, widen opportunities both for women and for blacks is illustrated by the story of Fanny Christina Hill. Her tale confirms her sister's observation that "Hitler was the one that got us out of the white folks' kitchen." Fanny Hill, the descendant of slaves and white southerners, began as a domestic servant. Moving to California looking for a better life, she found it in wartime employment at the North American aircraft plant. The work was new to her, and before putting her into a job the plant had her go to a school, where she learned drilling and riveting. Blacks got the most monotonous or backbreaking work, but it usually required enough skill to give a measure of satisfaction. The money was good, up to thirty dollars a week and then some; and Fanny Hill saved the weekly fifty dollars from her husband in the military. Temporarily at the end of the war she lost her job. Yet unlike many women of both races, she was taken back. She along with other blacks was promoted after white workers, but black women were more likely than whites of their gender to stay on after the war, and some acquired a degree of seniority. In the late 1940s, Fanny Hill was able to buy a house in a largely white neighborhood.

Fanny Hill profited from wartime industry. In one respect, though, her experience differed from that of white females. Women of her race expected to work outside the home. There was nothing about entering the labor pool that she could especially identify as liberating. It was the nature of the work, and the pay that went with it, that made war industry an opportunity for her as a woman and as a black American.

Ethnic Tensions

Note that Fanny Hill's journey to prosperity took her not on the traditional path followed by black Americans from south to north, but on a migration from east to west. The West, which had sometimes felt itself an underdeveloped colony, producing food and raw materials for the rest of the nation, boomed during the war, becoming a center for manufacturing, technological experimentation, and military training. From West Coast working cities like Oakland to New Mexico's "Atomic City," Los Alamos, western boom towns drew migrants from across the country and outside its borders. African Americans like Fanny Hill rushed to California, Indian people left reservations for wartime employment and service, and Mexicans crossed the border to work in cities and agricultural fields. The federal government, in fact, sponsored Mexican immigration through the *bracero* program, which sought to fill labor shortages in the agriculture and railroad industries. Between 1942 and 1947, over 300,000 Mexicans helped to bring in crops and maintain railroad lines.

As workers packed together in hastily assembled neighborhoods, western cities became mixing bowls of race and ethnicity. Tension was constant, violence a threat. In 1942, young Mexican American men, many from El Paso and known as *Pachucos* (a slang term referring to that city), migrated to

The Mexican American zoot-suiter wore the costume of his day. (Courtesy, AP, Wide World Photos)

Locations of Japanese American Internment Camps.

"*Exclusion of those of Japanese origin was deemed necessary because of the presence of an unascertained number of disloyal members of the group, most of whom we have no doubt were loyal to this country. It was because we could not reject the finding of the military authorities that it was impossible to bring about an immediate segregation of the disloyal from the loyal. . . .*

Compulsory exclusion of large groups of citizens from their homes, except under circumstances of direct emergency and peril, is inconsistent with our basic governmental institutions. But when under conditions of modern warfare our shores are threatened by hostile forces, the power to protect must be commensurate with the threatened danger: ... To cast this case into outlines of racial prejudice, without reference to the real military dangers which were presented, merely confuses the issue."

Justice Hugo Black,
From the majority opinion of the Supreme Court in Korematsu v. U.S.

Los Angeles. To mark their ethnic distinctiveness, they adopted the zoot suit—floppy pants pegged at the ankle, a long jacket with wide shoulders, and a wide-brimmed hat. The *pachuco* gangs contributed to a rise in crime rates in wartime cities, but sensational newspaper reporting and institutionalized discrimination whipped emotions to a frenzy. And the fashion spread. By 1943, perhaps two out of three Mexican American young men in LA wore zoot suits, although only five percent belonged to gangs. On June 3, 1943, servicemen armed with rocks and sticks swept through the barrio, beating zoot-suiters and tearing the clothes from their backs. Unable to impose order, the police watched helplessly as night after night military personnel surged through the city. It took a full week to impose order and end what had been the city's worst race riot.

Undoubtedly, however, the most widespread instance of racial prejudice resulting from the war was the treatment of California's people of Japanese descent, subject to a program of removal from their homes and internment in relocation camps, most of them inland. Washington acted on the assumption that among the immigrant issei and the American-born nisei loyalty to Japan might be stronger than their ties to the United States. Internment also had

the backing of bigots in California and of interests envious of the commercial success of Japanese vegetable farmers. Forced sales of many Japanese American homes and businesses swelled the holdings of white neighbors. Camp life, often in remote spots like the Arizona desert, made some efforts to provide schooling. The ugliness of the system consisted in its very existence. The policy was an insult to its victims, a statement of their indelibly racial origins, an expression of a prejudice, at least in California, that had traditionally directed itself toward Asians as well as Chicanos. It also permitted theft of property. The son of one merchant would remember that at the time of the war accounts payable became immediately due, while accounts receivable were

Navajo Indians in the Signal Corps sent messages in their native language, which was unknown to the Japanese. (Courtesy, Scribner's Archives)

not collectable. Many of the abandoned homes of the internees were ransacked. In the camps, parents lost their authority and the strong bonds of Japanese American community life were endangered. Two cases, *Hirabayashi* v. *United States*, decided in 1943, and *Korematsu* v. *United States* a year later, came before the Supreme Court that upheld the constitutionality of the program. Toward the end of the war, a government uncomfortable with the whole business ended the internment.

The story has a bittersweet ending. In Europe, a combat unit of Japanese Americans became among the most highly decorated veterans. Unlike the black soldiers who had fought in World War I on the mistaken assumption that their service would bring them wider entrance into American society, Japanese Americans won recognition for their outstanding record. In later years, Congress was to provide restitution to the victims of relocation, many of whom had been robbed of property and certainly of justice. Together with guilt over the internment program, the war may have lessened the prejudice the Japanese had suffered for decades.

Many of the films about World War II presented an image of ethnic reconciliation. A typical movie might put into a combat unit a down-home white southerner, a sensitive Jew from New York, a genial Pole from Minnesota, a street smart Italian from Chicago, a Boston blueblood, and a lank and rangy western cowboy. On some rare occasions, ethnic bonding could embrace racial differences: a black soldier from the South, a Hispanic from Texas, an Asian or American Indian character. Such images have an element of truth to them. American military personnel were, on the average, twenty-six years old, with one year of high school education (a couple of years more than their World War I predecessors) and many were unused to the cosmopolitan world they encountered. In the barracks, recalls one veteran, they replayed the wars of the Reformation, the Civil War, and others of the social and cultural divisions that had multiplied over the course of American history. Out of it all came an increase in mutual acceptance. And while black troops were segregated, American Indian and Latino troops often were not. The famous Thunderbird Division, for example, had a large number of American Indian soldiers. Indian people signed up to serve in numbers proportionally greater than any other racial or ethnic group in the country. The famous Code Talkers, who used Navajo and other native languages as unbreakable codes, worked in integrated units. However far the war may have gone toward making a cosmopolitan nation, it certainly created a sense of expectation among black, Indian, and Hispanic soldiers that they had the right to return to a more tolerant nation at the war's end. That expectation would not take concrete form without concerted political action.

THE ALLIES TAKE THE OFFENSIVE

In the first days of the German invasion of the Soviet Union, the defending army was in disarray, having suffered from an earlier Communist purge of its officers. But Stalin released from prison some of his military experts, and the massive human resources of the USSR were marshaled against the enemy. On their side were the terrible northern winters, for which the Soviet armies were better prepared than were the invaders. At one point the Germans reached sight of the onion domes of Moscow. But the surrender of a German army to Soviet troops at Stalingrad in February 1943 established for the European campaign what Midway had set for the Pacific: the Axis was not going to win. The breaking of the German Atlantic submarine force soon sped the flow of American goods to Britain and the USSR and solidified the Allied position. But while the Axis could no longer realistically hope for victory, the Allies themselves had yet to win. For that, they had essentially two separate wars to fight: against Germany and Italy, and against Japan.

The South Pacific

On the Asian mainland, the Chinese suffered the greatest burden of the Japanese war. Along with Chinese in combat were troops from Great Britain and its colonies together with an American air unit, the Flying Tigers, which flew supplies to the Chinese over the Himalayan Mountains, known as the Hump. On the mainland as well was a separate Chinese force fighting under an American commander, Joseph W. "Vinegar Joe" Stilwell, who urged that Washington cut off aid to the anticommunist Chiang Kai-shek unless he became more aggressive toward the Japanese.

The war in the Pacific fell mostly to the United States, assisted by Australia and New Zealand. It was under two commands. General MacArthur and his army oversaw a region of the southwestern Pacific that included the island of New Guinea

north of Australia, and the Philippines. To Admiral Chester Nimitz and the navy went the Solomon Islands close to New Guinea along with other strategic islands in the Pacific to be taken by marine and army units. As the two armed forces eventually planned their strategy, a major objective was for MacArthur to move northward through New Guinea, while Nimitz took the navy to the nearby Solomon Islands until the two could together seize Rabaul, the center of Japanese operations in the southern Pacific just west of the northern Solomons

The first phase required the navy and its marines, aided by army troops, to dislodge the Japanese from Guadalcanal in the southern Solomons. The battle began just after Midway. It was the first combat for the Americans on Guadalcanal, and both they and the Japanese suffered misery beyond the normal horrors of war. For months the two enemies shared the hot jungle, the Japanese making assaults during which few of them surrendered, the United States soldiers pouring ammunition into the fanatical attackers. During the combat a naval attempt to relieve the Americans failed. It was the worst American naval defeat in history, even as Midway had been the nation's greatest victory on the waters. Supplies for the Americans ran low; for the Japanese, much lower. After another naval relief effort, this time successful, Guadalcanal went to the Americans early in 1943.

The navy, with army as well as marine units, then proceeded north to the Solomon island chain. On that campaign Vice-Admiral "Bull" Halsey established the tactic of leapfrogging. One heavily defended island he simply bypassed to take a more lightly guarded one farther north. In March 1944 the conquest of Bougainville, the northernmost Solomon, was complete. MacArthur meanwhile had battled up to New Guinea. In 1944 Rabaul was open to bombings from American positions not far away, but it was not taken. It too was leapfrogged.

The Mediterranean Campaigns

For the conflict against Japan, China and the Western Allies were not at odds in strategy. But against Germany, the Allies were divided. The Soviet Union did by far most of the fighting, pushing the Germans out of its territory and ultimately invading the Nazi regime from the east. Britain

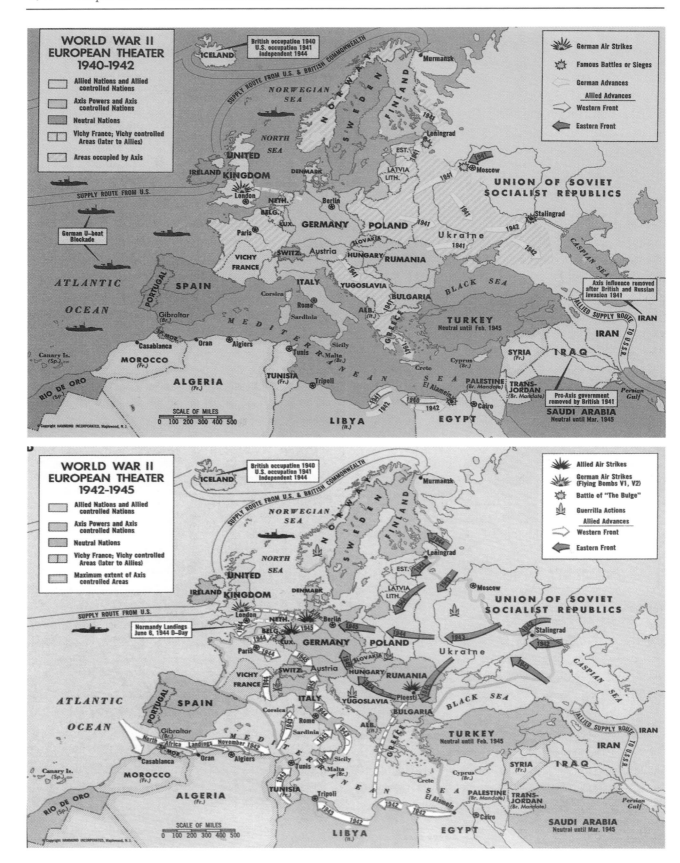

WORLD WAR II
EUROPEAN THEATER
1940-1942

Allied Nations and Allied controlled Nations
Axis Powers and Axis controlled Nations
Neutral Nations
Vichy France; Vichy controlled Areas (later to Allies)
Areas occupied by Axis

German Air Strikes
Famous Battles or Sieges
German Advances
Allied Advances
Western Front
Eastern Front

WORLD WAR II
EUROPEAN THEATER
1942-1945

Allied Nations and Allied controlled Nations
Axis Powers and Axis controlled Nations
Neutral Nations
Vichy France; Vichy controlled Areas (later to Allies)
Maximum extent of Axis controlled Areas

Allied Air Strikes
German Air Strikes (Flying Bombs V1, V2)
Battle of "The Bulge"
Guerrilla Actions
Allied Advances
Western Front
Eastern Front

fought Germany and Italy across North Africa, where the United States joined it. That accomplished, the British and Americans could cross the Mediterranean to take the island of Sicily and then move up the Italian peninsula. As important as the war was there, Stalin thought it a distraction from a major Western assault on Europe. He wanted Britain and the United States to stage a more northerly invasion of Europe that would take pressure off the Soviet effort. Churchill, to the contrary, liked the Mediterranean engagements. It is not hard to define the appeal such a strategy held for him. He remembered the wasted lives in northern Europe during the First World War. Egypt along with the Mediterranean was vital to the protection of the British Empire. A Mediterranean campaign, moreover, would put the Western Allies into Europe's southwestern corner before the Soviet

Union could get there and establish a permanent military presence. But FDR, though like Churchill suspicious of Stalin and a close collaborator with the British prime minister, was increasingly drawn to the strategy of a second front launched by the Western Allies across the English Channel onto the European continent.

Since early in the war, the British had been fighting German and Italian troops in North Africa. From their base in Egypt, they were combating Axis troops from the west under the superb strategist General Erwin Rommel. At Churchill's urging and against the advice of the American military, Roosevelt contributed to an Anglo-American invasion called Operation Torch under an American commander, Dwight D. Eisenhower, to hit Rommel on his west while other British troops pressed on his east. Landing late in 1942 in North Africa, the unseasoned American forces came under fire from troops serving France's Vichy government, which was still collaborating with Germany. An Allied deal with the French fascist vice-admiral Jean Darlan, an enterprise revealing Eisenhower's bent for practicality over ideological purity, neutralized French troops in North Africa. Since this arrangement had been made without the consent of the Vichy regime, Germany thereupon extended its occupation to the part of France previously left to the Vichy collaborators. In the early part of the operation, the American troops were inexperienced and their leadership muddled. But then Eisenhower gave the American field command to the aggressive George C. Patton, a hero of the First World War. A scholar, intellectual, and masterful technician committed to swift motorized warfare, Patton also cultivated the swagger exemplified in his declaration that that the purpose of war is not to die for your country: "it's to make some poor sonofabitch on the other side die for his."

In January 1943, Churchill and Roosevelt met at the North African city of Casablanca. There they agreed to a joint bomber campaign against Germany and to a solid commitment of resources to the Pacific theater, which they had previously treated as secondary to the war with Germany. They also settled on pursuing for the moment not a cross-Channel attack but a further operation in the Mediterranean, a decision that discouraged both Stalin—who wanted a swifter assault on Germany from the west—and the American military, notably the army's chief of staff George C. Marshall, who

One message of this poster by the artist Thomas Hart Benton is that everyone, including artists, could contribute to the war effort. (Courtesy, Library of Congress)

AIR STRIKE ACROSS THE MEDITERRANEAN

From North Africa, now in Allied hands, the United States in August 1943 flew one of its most ambitious bombing raids. The object was to attack an important source of oil for Germany: the refineries of Ploesti in Romania, a nation that together with Hungary and Bulgaria was now an Axis power. The project was an exercise in low-level flying, with improved bombsights promising great accuracy. In training the crews flew so close to the ground that their air drafts blew away the tents of Arab nomads.

Colonel Ellis's description of his fifteen-hour flight unfolds in a flash and roll of scenery that could be a Mediterranean travelogue. The route to Ploesti was a flow of blue sea, mountains, the blue Danube that turned out to be brown, even a costumed Romanian folk festival, the girls waving at the low-cruising bombers. Then the friendly postcard countryside turned hostile, haystacks suddenly transformed into anti-aircraft gun emplacements. Emerging from the smoke of the burning refineries, the crew discovered that the plane had been hit. Flying low, this time because it would be a more difficult target, the ship cut grain and sunflower stalks with its propellers. Once more the scene mingled violence and travelogue innocence: peasant girls waving, German fighters on the attack. Further hits again damaged the American plane, injuring four crew members. The craft, now so low on gas that guns and ammunition had to be thrown out, limped back to Libya, the crew preparing to bail in case the fuel was exhausted. As the gas gauges registered zero, the bomber came into sight of the airfield, where it managed to land by saving just enough hydraulic fluid to control the landing flaps.

It was one of 178 B-24s to have begun the flight. Fifty-nine aircraft were lost en route by crashing or enemy fire; 450 airmen were killed or wounded. The story of the raid on Ploesti was much in the vein of modern warfare: an advanced machine, but in its very complexity highly vulnerable to every kind of malfunction; and a crew that combined sober technical excellence with a primitive urge to survive and win.

thought the Mediterranean operation too slow and cumbersome a procedure. At a press conference, Roosevelt singly made a further pronouncement; he called for the unconditional surrender of the Axis powers.

Committed to remaining in the Mediterranean, the Allies in July 1943 invaded the Italian island of Sicily, landing troops from Britain, Canada, and the United States, the last led by Patton. In Sicily Patton got into trouble in a way that revealed his temperament: he slapped a soldier recovering from battle fatigue, calling him a coward. But when he was directing his brand of aggression against a real foe rather than an invalid, he was unsurpassed as a commander, as he would prove not only in Sicily but in the later days of the war.

That August the Sicilian campaign succeeded, but over a hundred thousand German and Italian troops managed to retreat to the Italian mainland. Churchill called for an invasion of Italy that would remove it from the war. Insisting in return for a cross-Channel invasion to begin the following spring, Stalin agreed. Hitler poured additional troops into Italy, turning that country from a confederate to a partially occupied country. The Allied troops then invaded Italy from Sicily. In September 1943, Mussolini having already been dismissed from the premiership by the king of Italy, the Italian government turned from an Axis to an Allied power. That same month a British and United States force commanded by an American, Mark Clark, landed at Salerno on Italy's west coast, where the attackers were pinned down and almost ejected. At Monte Cassino nearby, German defenders held out for months against Allied forces from the south. In the course of the battle there, bombers destroyed an old monastery on the mistaken assumption that it was a German fortification. During the frustrating assault on Monte Cassino, the Allies tried another western landing, at Anzio, north of the German lines. It too stalled. In May, Polish and French Moroccan troops—France's African posses-

American planes rolled off the assembly lines in unparalled numbers. (Courtesy UPI/Corbis-Bettmann)

sions were now in the war against the Axis—broke Monte Cassino. The Germans, making use of Italy's mountainous and river-sliced terrain, then retreated to another line farther up the peninsula. In June, General Clark took Rome.

At the end of 1943 FDR, Churchill, and Stalin met at Teheran in Iran. There the Western leaders got to see close up the master of the Soviet Union, whose manner of a blunt and shrewd peasant made him a rather likeable front for a harsh regime. At Teheran, the second front Stalin craved and Churchill shunned was agreed upon for the spring of 1944. FDR implicitly consented to move the boundaries of Poland westward, allowing the Soviet Union possession of a slice of the Polish east, and giving Stalin a sphere of influence in the Baltic. Stalin agreed to enter the war against Japan after the defeat of Germany.

Overlord

Ever since 1943 American planes based in Britain had bombed Germany, already under bomber attack from the Royal Air Force. Some of these assaults brought horrendous losses in planes and personnel, but new United States fighter planes

inflicted devastation on the Luftwaffe, the German air force. The American preference was for hitting military reserves. As a means of undermining the enemy's will to fight, the British came sooner to the concept of terror bombing of civilian populations. By the end of the war, American moral scruples on the subject would also fade. Attacking civilians has since become embedded in military practice, and this despite evidence from Germany and more recent engagements indicating that the effect on the determination of peoples subject to such bombings is limited. Research by American intelligence officers after the war indicated that the bombings had not been a miracle weapon. Following destruction of aircraft plants, for example, Germany actually increased its production for the Luftwaffe.

At the approach of the day for Overlord, as the invasion of the coast of France in Normandy was named, American ground troops in Britain had grown to nearly two million. Added to them and the British as troops available to back up or participate in a landing in Europe were three Canadian divisions, a division of French soldiers opposed to Vichy, other units of exile Poles, Czechs, and Hungarians. Preparing to resist an invasion but not knowing where it would occur was a German command jointly held by Rommel and Gerd von Rund-stedt. On June 6, D Day, the Western Allies unleashed their might on the continent. The British and Canadians, landing to the north of the United States force, quickly established themselves ashore.

At Omaha Beach the going was more difficult for the Americans. In the landing crafts on a cold, cloudy dawn were packed boys, most of whom had never seen battle. They were laden with assault jackets that might contain a variety of equipment including grenades, pills for motion sickness, and blocks of TNT; a web belt containing entrenching tools and similar items; and, of course, weapons and ammunition. All in all, they were burdened with as much as sixty-eight pounds, most of which they might never use.

Troops had trained for a year for a siege that was supposed to move in precisely timed waves, each unit heading for a specific part of the beach. But weather and sea did not accommodate. Splashing ashore was bad enough, though the pull of the tide shoreward helped in a clumsy way. One veteran would remember that at the first burst of firing he scrunched down, his outstretched arms pressing against the sands and holding his head above water. As he scrambled onto the beach, there was no semblance of discipline and purpose; he found himself amidst a litter of wrecked machines along with the dead and wounded, while dark figures moved toward the bluff they were supposed to storm. He

could not even find the unit he commanded. A single German rifle company, he concludes, would have cleared that section of the beach. Rangers scaled a nearby cliff, a heroic and costly effort that gained little advantage. Soldiers not wounded, their emotions blunted or confused, did manage to climb the bluffs, probably as much on their individual initiative as from any military organization, and because there was nothing else to do. As more and more troops landed, the German defenders were pushed back by weight of numbers.

The story of Omaha Beach gives a glimpse of war as telling as the bombing raid on Ploesti. In the one case, the operation was orderly and precise. The airmen, held compactly together within their craft and flying in formation, were able to put skills to answering such problems as: what do you do when you are low on gas and hydraulic fluid? In the other, the fortunes of battle and weather dictated disorder through which victory found its awkward way. The Americans at Omaha Beach were lucky that an enemy confused by an assault at an unexpected point—Hitler insisted on thinking it secondary—was in equal disarray. But the raid on Ploesti and the landing at Omaha Beach had one thing in common. Ultimately they were fought not by a perfectly geared army but by individuals, in one instance thinking their way through the technical demands of aircraft, in the other blundering their way to the top of the bluffs at Normandy.

The D Day Landing established a second front—Italy had been the first—in Western Europe, the French province of Normandy. Germans shelled the men from the high cliffs, killing many even before they reached the beach. (Courtesy, UPI/Bettmann Archives)

THE MAN WHO WON THE WAR

An interesting sidelight to the story of D Day can be discovered in the work of Andrew Jackson Higgins. During the 1930s, Higgins developed a shallow-draft boat he called the *Eureka* to suit the needs of Louisiana trappers, oilmen, and lumbermen, who worked in the state's many bayous. Eventually, his impressive boat design attracted business from the Army Corps of Engineers, the Biological Survey, and later, of course, the United States navy. With later modifications the *Eureka* proved be an ideal boat for amphibious assaults critical to the D-Day invasion and in the shallow waters leading up to Pacific islands. In order to get his boat appreciated by the navy, however, Higgins had to fight the stubborn naval bureaucracy who wanted nothing to do with this hard-drinking Irishman; he had been aptly named for the hot-tempered president Old Hickory. Eventually the navy reluctantly awarded him many contracts for his designs, which became landing crafts called LCVPs, LCPs, LCPLs, and LCMs. Without Higgins's designs and his company's mass production of them, higher Allied casualties would have resulted. Higgins Industries, based in New Orleans, produced 20,094 boats for the Allied cause. Supreme Allied Commander Dwight D. Eisenhower called Higgins "the man who won the war for us."

The Western Allies Advance

In the months to come the experience of the single American soldier, like that of soldiers on all sides during most of the war, was in small operations that appeared to have no relation to broader goals. It was generally a matter of fighting for a patch of terrain, a street, a building. The war put itself together out of an infinity of personal decisions and acts.

Not making the mistake that had occurred at Anzio of tightening a beachhead and falling into a defensive posture, the invaders at Normandy intended to rush forward. The problem, unnoticed even in aerial photographs taken before the landing, was the Norman countryside, overgrown with natural fencing known as hedgerows. From thick embankments grew masses of shrubbery and trees that in some cases arched across the paths between them. The German military had been trained in hedgerow defense; to the Allies, that peculiarity of the Norman landscape came as a nasty surprise.

A fast advance would have been impossible. The defenses had to be taken one by one, on an average perhaps of two hedgerows a day, the Allied troops teaching themselves what their commanders had not prepared them for. American tanks, inferior in construction to their German counterparts but churned out in greater numbers, provided an opportunity. The Allies invented one device after another. Credit for one inventive tool goes to a sergeant, a former Chicago cab driver who thought up and then was put in charge of constructing a hedgerow slicer recycled from iron used in a German roadblock. Young men who back home had worked in service stations and repair shops put damaged Sherman tanks back together with whatever materials they could assemble; hopelessly wrecked tanks were stripped for parts. From their own damaged machines the Germans simply walked away. The whole effort was an undertaking in the American manner, a project by a sleepless and innovative work crew.

Nearly two months after the start of the landing, the Allies had broken through hedgerow country. Except for the natural Norman terrain, that would have been the story more than a month before. In the race eastward, the mobility provided by motorized units allowed encirclement of enemy positions and proved, like the Pacific carrier fleets, that speed, reach, and conquest of distance were essential to modern war. That, together with the combined size of the Allied armies and the sheer quantity of American war goods, made it impossible for the Germans to hold a line. The enemy also had to cope with a smaller Allied invasion in the south of France. The German troops in France meanwhile were being punished by air attacks, as was their homeland itself. Allied aircraft were taking possession of the German skies, and besides disrupting transportation systems by the end of 1944 they would take out enough fuel supplies essentially to ground the Luftwaffe.

On August 25, 1944, Paris was liberated and General Charles de Gaulle, leader of the Free French troops that had assembled in North Africa, installed a government. France was now fully won by the Allies. That same month, another capital was not so lucky. Soviet troops had pushed into Poland. As they approached Warsaw, an uprising of the Polish resistance to the Nazis broke out. Moscow, calculating that it did not want in Poland an independent leadership, held back its army and allowed the Germans to crush the resistance movement.

At home, Roosevelt had a far-reaching political victory. This time selecting as his vice-presidential running mate Senator Harry Truman from Missouri—Henry Wallace, his vice president since 1941, had been for some Democratic Party leaders too radical—FDR inadvertently prepared for Truman to extend his party's leadership into the postwar era. In the meantime, Roosevelt faced in the election of 1944 Thomas E. Dewey, governor of New York. Dewey, who as a district attorney had built a reputation for aggressive prosecution of organized crime, was known for integrity. The charismatic FDR, though his popularity had waned, had enough of it left to beat his politically lackluster opponent.

Hitler was now further enraged by an attempt on his life by several of his officers. On July 20, a colonel planted a bomb underneath a table where the Führer was holding a conference. In the aftermath several officers were executed, and Rommel, who had not been directly involved but was known to have turned against Hitler, took his own life. The plot touches on one of the most disturbing questions in the Allied conduct of the war. For some time, a conspiracy against the Nazi government had been operating among officers who knew that Hitler was leading them to disaster. Germans appalled by Nazism joined them. Allied leaders knew of the conspiracy: they even used the military information it supplied them. Yet they refused to cooperate with the rebels in plans that would have overthrown Hitler while leaving Germany intact. Were the Allies more interested in crushing Germany as a potentially troublesome power in the future than they were in an early overthrow of

Nazism, a regime that for every day of its continued existence would torture and kill? Britain and the United States were aware of the campaign of genocide against the Jews and for military reasons refused to act on the knowledge. (The public revelation, which might have put pressure on Germany to halt its policy of extermination, would have revealed to Berlin that the Allies had broken German codes.) The moral priorities of the Western Allies remain unclear.

That autumn the flight of the German army halted at the Siegfried Line, which Germany had established at the edge of its territory west of the Rhine River. Germans constructed a formidable war zone of concrete fortifications, minefields, barbed wire, and other devices. Especially clever was the practice of establishing defenses not outside towns but within them, where buildings provided additional means of resistance. Once more the Allies had to invent offensive maneuvers. Street

Der Führer—Adolf Hitler. (Courtesy, Scribner's Archives)

fighting, they discovered, required blasting defended buildings with mortar, artillery, and bombings, then rushing the torn walls. They learned also not to make the mistake of bunching up their infantry. And the wise course was not to try quick major assaults but to take buildings one at a time.

Hitler still nurtured hopes of achieving at least a satisfactory peace with the Allies. Belgium's thick Ardennes forest, where one of the last battles of the First World War had drawn American troops, lay between the British army and the American, which was to the south. On December 16, 1944, Hitler sent tank divisions through the forest. His objective was to sever the tenuous Allied supply route. The Battle of the Bulge, named for the swelling German lines, took the Allies by surprise. Many Americans and British were taken prisoner; others fled, not an unreasonable act when lines of defense became untenable. Slowing the German advance were tiny and stubborn units that held some piece of ground, some small line of defense. When the Germans demanded surrender from the American Brigadier General Anthony C. McAuliffe at Bastogne, he gave the famous reply "Nuts." The German advance ran out of fuel, and by the middle of January the Battle of the Bulge was over.

In the fighting during the last months of 1944 and the first of 1945, arms fire and shelling describe only part of the story. There was trench foot, the illness of that notably cold winter that led to disabling or at times amputation of a foot. Preventing it required daily massaging. Then there was the trick of digging foxholes through hard-frozen ground. When pickaxes failed, soldiers used explosives to loosen frozen earth. Some soldiers on both sides violated the rules of war and humanity by taking deliberate aim at medical corpsmen in the enemy lines responding to the cries of casualties. Huddled close to the ground against relentless German shelling, one soldier took refuge in a "Hail Mary" repeated endlessly through the night.

In the Soviet city of Yalta in February 1945, FDR, Churchill, and Stalin, their nations now known as the Big Three, met once again. Stalin renewed his promise to enter the war against Japan after Germany's conquest, but made major demands. The permanent partition of Germany did not get Roosevelt's assent, though the transfer of a wealth of German industrial material to the USSR did. For the proposed United Nations, the Soviet leader got an extra seat on the General Council for each of two Soviet republics, Ukraine and Byelorussia or White Russia. An agreement essentially to allow the USSR to have a Polish government friendly to it was to be for years a matter of controversy. Conservatives have repeatedly accused Roosevelt of leftist sympathies that led him to sell out to Stalin, more particularly to betray Poland. Actually, the president was distressed over the situation, but in no military or diplomatic position to dislodge the Soviet army from Eastern Europe.

By the time of Yalta the Soviet army had entered eastern Germany. The Americans held a portion of Germany that lay west of the Rhine River. The United States air force, now reconciled to the policy of attacking civilian populations, was bombing Berlin and several days later setting off a firestorm in the historic city of Dresden. The army meanwhile found a bridge over the Rhine that the Germans had not destroyed in their retreat. Making use of it, the troops plunged into the German heartland. In April, the Soviet army captured Berlin. Hitler, holed in a bunker, committed suicide. Germany unconditionally surrendered in early May. A few days earlier, Italian anti-fascist partisans had hanged the deposed dictator Mussolini.

Combat Ends in the Pacific

The leader of an American participation in the victory was not there to enjoy it. On April 12, at the rest center Warm Springs in Georgia, the ailing president had died. His vice president Truman was now in office.

Though it was the attack on Pearl Harbor that brought the United States into World War II, Washington had put most of its resources into the European war, thinking that Germany more than Japan held the world's fate in question. Yet Japanese and American troops fought each other with a savagery beyond that between the Western Allies and the European fascists. Many Americans, conditioned by racist thinking, viewed the Japanese as beneath human decency or feeling. In engagements with the Americans, Japanese dug into tunnels would take their own lives or allow themselves to be scorched by flamethrowers or blown up by grenades rather than surrender. That was not only because surrender was considered dishonorable, but because they expected upon capture by the Americans to be tortured or killed. Japanese who become prisoners ceased to have the identity of servants of the emperor and were so willing to obey their new masters as to astonish the American troops guarding them.

After an amphibious landing in the summer of 1944 in which a hundred thousand marine and army forces took the island of Saipan from its thirty thousand Japanese defenders, hundreds of Japanese civilians hurled themselves off a seaside cliff. Horrified, the Americans, abandoning any abstract hatred they had nurtured toward the Japanese, pled through interpreters for the despondent and terrified civilians to stop.

MacArthur's command and that of the navy, having worked together in the fight to subdue Rabaul, now took their separate courses. The navy set itself to capturing islands en route toward Japan. It also hungered for a single decisive battle with the Japanese navy. MacArthur meanwhile was planning after the retaking of New Guinea to capture the Philippines, and thereby to redeem his pledge, "I shall return."

A string of islands, including Tarawa in November 1943 and Kwajalein, Eniwetok, and Saipan in the first half of 1944, fell to the navy and the ground troops it conveyed, while it bombed into destruction the Japanese base on Truk. Admiral Spruance at the battle for Saipan veered off to clash with an enemy fleet elsewhere in the wider Marianas island cluster. In the engagement coldly called the Marianas Turkey Shoot, the trained American fighters, taking on inexperienced Japanese—the most expert of their pilots were dead—shot down over three hundred Japanese aircraft while losing less than a tenth that number. Some, however, ran out of fuel on the long flight back to Spruance's carriers. American submarines sank two carriers and American planes a third. Losing three carriers, about 480 aircraft, and many pilots, the Japanese navy was nearly incapacitated for any further air war. The island campaign proceeded on the well-worn tactical assumption that attackers must outnumber defenders. While there were more enemy than American troops in the Pacific, the navy generally at any one time could concentrate an assault force larger than the opponent. It was the same maneuver by sea that the Japanese in taking the Philippines from the Filipino and American troops had used against an army larger than theirs.

Strategic and political considerations existed for retaking the Philippines. Japan, hurting badly for oil, was getting a trickle from the Netherlands East Indies channeled mainly through the Philippines.

SECOND WORLD WAR CASUALTIES

Country	Battle Deaths	Wounded
Canada	32,714	53,145
France	201,568	400,000
Germany	3,250,000	7,250,000
Italy	149,496	66,716
USSR.	6,115,000	14,012,000
Australia	26,976	180,864
Japan	1,270,000	140,000
New Zealand	11,625	17,000
United Kingdom	357,116	369,267
United States	291,357	670,846

Source: *Information Please Almanac* (Boston: Houghton Mifflin Co., 1988)

A return to the island cluster could also avenge an American humiliation. Yet influential strategists supported their own form of leapfrogging: bypass the Philippines, let the conquerors there sit helpless, and go more directly for Japan. Hugely figuring into the equation was MacArthur himself. Commitment to the Filipinos, a wish to return to the possession from which he had been ejected: for whatever combination of reasons, he craved recapturing the islands.

For the Philippines campaign, MacArthur and the navy again had to work together. After an American landing in October on Leyte, one of the Philippine Islands, MacArthur was photographed wading ashore, where he announced his return. During the culminating naval engagement of the Pacific war, the Battle of Leyte Gulf, the Japanese unleashed their last spectacular weapon of the war. In kamikaze attacks, pilots took off from land and consciously ending their lives smashed into American ships. The land war for the Philippines went on until the end of March 1945, especially brutal warfare in which, in the street fighting for Manila alone, a hundred thousand Filipino civilians died.

Two further land battles waged by the naval command marked the last months of the Second World War. The islands of Iwo Jima and Okinawa, that last considered by the Japanese to be part of their national territory, lay on the route to Japan.

Out of the fight for Iwo Jima came a famous photograph of marines raising the American flag on Mount Suribachi. The struggle for Okinawa, stretching from April through most of June 1945, took the lives of all but seven thousand of the original 77,000 Japanese, together with over 7,600 Americans on land and nearly five thousand sailors killed by kamikaze attacks. More than a hundred thousand Okinawan civilians died.

The Bomb

Several Japanese statesmen were now recognizing that their country would have to accept a defeat of one kind or another. But the powerful military wing of the government found the idea insupportable. As the Japanese were considering their plight, the Americans worried about the terrible cost in lives of an invasion of the country. An inconclusive meeting at the Berlin suburb of Potsdam in July brought together Truman, Churchill, and Stalin in a further attempt to solidify a postwar world. Out of it came the Potsdam Proclamation, signed by Truman and Churchill and by Nationalist China's Chiang Kai-shek, who signed on by wire. It demanded the unconditional surrender of Japanese forces. But how could the Japanese, dedicated to the belief that surrender is disgrace, be induced to submit without an invasion? The answer came in the successful completion of an enterprise called the Manhattan Project that the American government had been conducting in secret: the unleashing of the explosive power of the atom, an object of research also of a few Nazi scientists.

The project that built the bomb involved a vast coordination of activities. One community developed especially for work on it was at Oak Ridge, Tennessee. Another was on a military post at Los Alamos, New Mexico. Letters that Phyllis Fisher, wife of a scientist at Los Alamos, wrote to her parents describe a futuristic scientific community, its members well treated but caged, restricted in their movements, their families scarcely aware of what it was all about.

Phyllis Fisher's letters repeat that she cannot tell her parents her location. But what she describes is security that is both tight and absurd. At one checkpoint, cars were permitted to go through without passes. Pedestrians, to the contrary, had to have a pass. On her way back to her home, Mrs. Fisher's car died just outside the checkpoint. Hav-

ing forgotten her pass, she was stopped by the military police, who could see her car. Then, again in sight of the MPs, she hitched a ride and was let through. Even in the midst of a project gathering much of the most advanced scientific knowledge in history, security remained as close and as primitive as in a backward dictatorship.

After some questionings over the moral legitimacy of using atomic weapons, the United States administration had decided before the Potsdam meeting that if the Japanese continued unwilling to accept unconditional surrender, the weapon would be employed. On August 6 an atom bomb destroyed the Japanese city of Hiroshima, killing fifty thousand people at the moment and by burns and radiation another hundred thousand within a few days. On August 8 the USSR declared war on Japan. Still the Japanese military held out for a conditional surrender with provisions that there be no military occupation, that they conduct their own disarmament, and that trials for war crimes be carried out by Japanese courts. Then came the additional atomic bombing of Nagasaki. As terrible as were the atomic explosions, they were in the same magnitude as a conventional air attack on Tokyo that March that had destroyed a fourth of the city and killed 130,000. After Nagasaki the emperor Hirohito intervened, declaring his acceptance of the surrender. The same code of honor that made surrender so shameful also required obedience to the will of the emperor. Some Japanese military officers attacked the imperial palace to halt the public issuance of the emperor's recorded statement of surrender, but on August 15 the recording was broadcast in the archaic Japanese language of the court, almost indecipherable to the people who heard it. The terms worked out amounted not quite to unconditional surrender: the emperor and the Japanese government were to remain, though under the ultimate authority of an Allied Supreme Commander. But the war was over.

THE WORLD THE WAR CREATED

The defeat of the Axis powers was a victory far greater than that of 1918, and brought its due measure of rejoicing. But the world was a more solemn place than that which had emerged from World War I. That the Soviet Union, a regime per-

At the top is pictured the results of the British firebombing of Dresden, Germany. The 5,824,000 pounds of bombs killed an estimated 60,000 people. At the bottom is shown Hiroshima, where one bomb weighing 20,000 pounds killed many more. (Courtesy, UPI/Corbis-Bettmann)

haps as brutal as Nazi Germany, was among the victors and in a position to press its will upon much of the territory liberated from the Nazis was soon to turn triumph into gloom. At the war's end came the appalling public revelation of Nazi death camps into which Jews had been herded. The stacked bodies, the skeletal, blankly staring survivors raised questions about human nature that preoccupy theologians, philosophers, and social scientists to this day. The camps made dubious the moral level of the Allies, who had known of them but made no effort to save victims by destroying railroad track leading to them. And to humankind, which would have gotten it eventually anyway, the war gave the nuclear bomb, and images of its ravaged, burned, still living Japanese victims, their bodies carrying radiation that would sicken the infected years later. Emerging from the conflict, then, were problems of longer reach than the difficulties of winning it.

Just after the dropping of the bomb on Hiroshima, Phyllis Fisher had the startling experience of hearing the name of Los Alamos over the radio, of knowing that her secret location was now public, and she was free to speak. Equally astonishing to her was hearing the gloating of the commentators as they described the incineration of a city. Soon afterwards came the news of Nagasaki, an act that horrified her for its pointlessness. An indirect participant of sorts at the project for developing atomic weaponry, she was among the first Americans to recoil from the consequences.

Suggested Readings

The causes and conduct of World War II are treated in Gerhard L. Weinberg's *A World at Arms* (1994); John Keegan's *The Second World War* (1990); Martin Gilbert, *The Second World War* (1989); and Richard Overy's *Why the Allies Won* (1997). On American diplomacy during the war see Robert Dallek, *Franklin D. Roosevelt and American Foreign Policy, 1932–1945* (1979) and Gaddis Smith, *American Diplomacy during the Second World War* (2nd ed., 1985). Other works include David Reynolds, *From Munich to Pearl Harbor* (2001) and Williamson Murray and Allan R. Millett, *A War to be Won* (2000). For the war in the Asian Pacific see Akira Iriye, *The Origins of the Second World War in Asia and the Pacific* (1987) and Michael A. Barnhart, *Japan Prepares for Total War* (2001).

Stanley G. Payne's *A History of Fascism, 1914–1945* (1995) is a broad survey and Ian Kershaw's two-volume biography, *Hitler: 1889-1936: Hubris* (1999) and *Hitler: 1936–1945: Nemesis* (2000) is exhaustive. Detlev J. K. Peukert, *Inside Nazi Germany* (1987) helps to explain the support Nazism received from ordinary Germans. See Alexander De Grand, *Italian Fascism* (3rd ed., 2000); Hugh Thomas's *The Spanish Civil War*, 3d ed. (1977); Robert C. Tucker, *Stalin in Power: The Revolution from Above, 1928–1941* (1990); and Herbert P. Bix, *Hirohito and the Making of Modern Japan* (2000).

On Jews under the Nazis, there are Martin Gilbert, *The Holocaust* (1985) and Raul Hilberg, *The Destruction of the European Jews* (rev. ed., 1985). Daniel Jonah Goldhagen's *Hitler's Willing Executioners: Ordinary Germans and the Holocaust* (1996) claims that most Germans supported the murderous suppression of the Jews. United States policy is treated in David Wyman, *The Abandonment of the Jews.* William B. Rubinstein, *The Myth of Rescue* (1997) defends the policies of the Allies toward the Holocaust.

Opposition to American involvement in the war is examined in Wayne S. Cole, *Roosevelt and the Isolationists, 1932–1945* (1983). See also Cynthia Eller, *Conscientious Objectors and the Second World War* (1991); Glen Jeansonne, *Women of the Far Right* (1996); and Rachel Waltner Goosen, *Women against the Good War* (1998).

Histories by John Ellis, *Brute Force: Allied Strategy and Tactics in the Second World War* (1990) and Nathan Miller, *War at Sea* (1995) examine various military campaigns. Gerald F. Linderman, *The World Within War* (1997) studies the American soldier.

On Roosevelt's leadership see Warren Kimball, *The Juggler* (1991). See Carlo D'Este, *Eisenhower* (2002); Geoffrey Perret, *Eisenhower* (1999); Michael Schaller, *Douglas MacArthur* (1989); and volumes two and three of Forrest C. Pogue's biography of George C. Marshall.

Combat in the European Theater is the subject of Peter Schrivers, *The Crash of Ruin* (1998) and Russell V. Weigley, *Eisenhower's Lieutenants* (1989).

Gordon W. Prange has dealt with the Japanese attack on Pearl Harbor in several books. On the war in the Far East that followed the attack, see Akira Iriye, *Power and Culture: The American War with Japan* (1985); John Dower, *War without Mercy* (1987); and Harry A. Gailey, *The War in the Pacific* (1995). Japanese atrocities in China are studied in Iris Chang's *The Rape of Nanking* (1997).

Richard Rhodes's *The Making of the Atomic Bomb* (1986) is highly technical; see Robert S. Norris, *Racing for the Bomb* (2002). Historians have staked out a variety of positions on the use of the bomb: J. Samuel Walker, *Prompt and Utter Destruction* (1997); Ronald Takaki, *Hiroshima* (1995); and Gar Alperowitz, *The Decision to Use the Bomb* (1995).

On the homefront see John W. Jeffries, *Wartime America* (1996); Michael C. C. Adams, *The Best War Ever* (1994); and Richard Polenberg, *War and Society* (1972). On workers and labor issues, James B. Atleson, *Labor and the Wartime State* (1998); George Lipstiz, *Rainbow at Midnight*, rev. ed. (1994); and Nelson Lichtenstein, *Labor's War at Home* (1982).

Issues of race and ethnicity are dealt with in Ronald Takaki, *Double Victory* (2000); Neil A. Wynn, *The Afro-American and the Second World War*, rev. ed. (1993); Alison R. Bernstein, *American Indians and World War II* (1991); and Beth Bailey and David Farber, *The First Strange Place* (1992). Frank Füredi's *The Silent War* (1998) sees a race war. See also Dominic J. Capeci, Jr. and Martha Wilkerson, *Layered Violence: The Detroit Rioters of 1943* (1991); Robert L. Allen, *The Port Chicago Mutiny* (1989); Mauricio Mazon, *The Zoot-Suit Riots* (1984); and Roger Daniels, *Concentration Camps U.S.A.: Japanese Americans and World War II* (1989).

On women and the war see Sherna Berger Gluck, *Rosie the Riveter Revisited* (1988). See also Allan Bérubé's *Coming Out Under Fire: The History of Gay Men and Women in World War Two* (1990) and John Costello's *Virtue Under Fire: How World War II Changed Our Social and Sexual Attitudes* (1985).

George H. Roeder Jr., *The Censored War: American Visual Experience during World War Two* (1993), deals in part with the censorship of newsreels. Frank A. Warren, *Noble Extractions* (1999), describes the relationship between the government and intellectuals during the war. See also Richard W. Steele's *Free Speech and the Good War* (1999)

On treatment of the Axis states after the war and on postwar agreements, consult Remi Nadeau, *Stalin, Churchill, and Roosevelt Divide Europe* (1990); Michael Schaller, *The American Occupation of Japan* (1985); John Dower, *Embracing Defeat: Japan in the Wake of World War II* (2000); Gary B. Ostrower, *The United States and the United Nations* (1998); and Randall B. Woods and Howard Jones, *Dawning of the Cold War* (1991).

Scene from the movie *Invasion of the Body Snatchers.* *(Courtesy, Movie Stills, Inc.)*

Warm Hearths and a Cold War

23

SLEEP NO MORE

At the beginning of *Invasion of the Body Snatchers*, a movie released in 1956, Dr. Miles Bennell and his friend Becky sense something wrong in their California town of Santa Mira. Many of its inhabitants, appearing outwardly as they had always been, seemed somehow not the same. When the couple late at night discover duplicates of their own bodies being formed out of large seedpods, they realize that some monstrous and mysterious invading force is transforming Santa Mira. And they discover that they cannot turn to the police, who have already become pod people.

The thought of being remade by a vampire's bite or a werewolf attack into something terribly unlike your former self has long sent shivers of pleasurable horror through the spines of moviegoers. Vampires like Dracula are cruel, cunning, and hungry for blood; werewolves at every turn of the full moon change into ferocious beasts. But it is the special evil of the pod people to have no cravings at all. They still reason, speak, and move about, but with no purpose save that of making the entire human race into likenesses of their passionless selves. Having no emotions makes life so much better, they explain with a kindness peculiar in being free of all emotion, than to have to live with human dreams and fears and passions. It is that absence that the diminishing number of fully human inhabitants had detected from the beginning, without being able to define it. The full horror of that state unfolds when Miles, briefly separated from Becky in their flight, returns and kisses her. Becky's lifeless kiss reveals that she, too, is now a pod.

Miles, now completely alone, tries to warn the world, even as truckloads of pods pass by going down a California highway. The movie ends with a suggestion that his warning has gotten through.

As a combination of horror and science fiction, *Invasion of the Body Snatchers* works brilliantly on its own. It is stark, economical, and chilling. But at the time of the film's release, the Cold War with the Soviet Union dominated much of American thinking, and some critics detected in *Body Snatchers* a symbolic expression of the public's idea of Communist subversion. Anyone, so went a popular notion, your neighbor, your children's social studies teacher, the town librarian, could be a Communist. Such people would not openly argue for Communism; they would work to implant alien ideas in unguarded minds. They might offhandedly draw attention to some social injustice, or casually recommend a book on race, or raise some doubt about the wisdom of nuclear armament. The pod people are similar. "There's no difference you can actually see," observes one character, but at every moment they wait to take over their trusting, unsuspecting victims—victims most vulnerable when asleep, just like Americans asleep to the Communist menace. In their absence of feeling, the pods closely resemble the Communists as popularly portrayed: coldly indifferent to every passion of freedom, patriotism, love of family, loyalty to friends. Some critics believe that the movie represents the producer's own idea of the Communist threat; others, that it mocks the public's paranoid notions of subversion.

HISTORICAL EVENTS

1945
United Nations founded • Potsdam Conference

1946
George F. Kennan proposes containment policy

1947
Truman Doctrine • National Security Act • Marshall Plan • Taft-Hartley Act

1948
Truman elected president • Berlin Airlift

1949
China becomes Communist

1950
National Security Council Report No. 68 • Senator Joseph R. McCarthy alleges Communist influence in government • Korean War (1950–1953)

1952
Dwight D. Eisenhower elected president

1954
Communist Control Act

1956
Hungarian Revolution • Eisenhower reelected

1957
Sputnik I and II

Body Snatchers, then, belongs to the social history of the Cold War. And as science fiction it also expresses its era, particularly the fascination among moviegoers for an artistic form that seemed to bespeak the scientific wonders of the century.

THE BEGINNINGS OF THE COLD WAR

During World War II, Joseph Stalin and the Western leaders had never been at ease with each another. Stalin chafed at the time it took for Britain and the United States to open a second front in northern Europe, which finally came with the Normandy invasion of June 1944. Until then the ill-equipped Soviet army sustained enormous losses carrying the burden of the European land war. By the war's end, the USSR had lost as many as fourteen million combat troops; the American dead numbered 292,131. The West in turn had every reason to detest the savagely repressive Soviet regime. In allowing Moscow to decide which anti-Nazi leaders would govern Poland after the defeat of Germany, London and Washington yielded to necessity, not to trust.

The United Nations General Assembly, New York. Completed in 1952. (Courtesy, United Nations)

Postwar public opinion toward Communism in the United States became uncompromisingly hostile. Roman Catholics especially loathed it for its animosity toward religion. Stalin himself had been a butcher of his own people during the 1930s, killing as many as a million for disloyalty. In a few years much of the American labor movement would be clearing its leadership of Communists and their sympathizers. The West, so many believed, must learn from its dealings with Nazism. When Hitler came to power, Western leaders had expected his more fanatical pronouncements to soften as he dealt with the responsibilities of government. Instead, he turned out to mean everything lethal he had ever said, and more. This time, Western leaders resolved, they would not make the same mistake. Communist ideology pronounced death upon all systems but its own. The West would take that seriously, and prepare to resist. Scholars since have interpreted Moscow's foreign policy as more defensive than expansionist, reflecting fear of an invasion from the West akin to Germany's in two world wars, and building around itself a belt of Communist satellite states for protection. Nonetheless, the USSR would sometimes behave with an apparent ruthlessness that suggested its existence endangered the world.

The United Nations

Briefly, very briefly, a wish for postwar cooperation flickered between Moscow and the West. In the spring of 1945 the Soviet Union joined with Western leaders at San Francisco in devising a charter for the United Nations. Delegates from all countries would make up its General Assembly. But greater power would rest in a Security Council of fifteen members, with permanent seats held by the United States, Britain, France, the Soviet Union, and China, along with ten other nations, each elected for two-year terms. At the insistence of the Soviet Union, the five permanent nations each possessed a veto over all decisions of the council. UN agencies performing humane services soon included the World Health Organization, or WHO, and the United Nations Educational, Scientific, and Cultural Organization, or UNESCO. Though the UN could not compel members to back its decisions, its military actions over the years would win considerable support. In addition to assisting a number of peacekeeping missions, UN member nations contributed to two major wars: Korea, from 1950 to 1953, and the Gulf War in 1991. The United Nations, it was hoped, might serve as a forum for the settlement of issues between the USSR and the West. But decades of military standoff, together with real war in Korea and Vietnam, would preclude meaningful peace between Communist regimes and the West.

Origins of Containment

Moscow's longstanding determination to impose puppet governments on the Poles and other East European peoples close to the Soviet Union, together with a general climate of distrust between the USSR and the West, banished hopes for postwar stability. In 1946 George F. Kennan, an American diplomatic official in the Soviet Union, argued in a famous telegram to Washington that the Soviet Union was fixed on an implacable course of hostility to the West. In an article the next year under the name "X," he articulated a policy that came to be known as containment. Kennan did not blame Soviet behavior on Communist fanaticism alone; he recognized that Russia's suspicion of the outside world also contributed. But he insisted that Moscow's antagonism to the West would not soon fade and that aggression could be expected whenever the Soviet Union could get away with it. Soviet ambitions, then, must be met by a strategy of deft countermoves. Just after Kennan's long telegram, Winston Churchill in a speech in Fulton, Missouri, contributed a familiar phrase to the Cold War vocabulary. An Iron Curtain, he said, had descended across the face of Europe, cutting off the Communist from the non-Communist world. The image was apt: the cranking could be heard in the click of rifles and the stomp of boot heels across Eastern Europe.

In 1947 President Truman put containment into practice. At that time the Soviet Union was pressuring its neighbor Turkey for joint control of the passage between the Black Sea and the Mediterranean, while in Greece Communist and anticommunist forces engaged in civil war. The president advanced a policy, soon to be called the Truman Doctrine, of defending free peoples against foreign or internal threats. Congress, though dominated by Republicans, granted economic and military aid to Greece and Turkey. In the same year, the national legislature passed the National Security Act, which reorganized the military services under a new Department of Defense. The act also established the National Security Council and created the Central Intelligence Agency, granting it authority to gather information and otherwise to operate quietly in foreign countries in pursuit of American policy. The CIA has since earned a reputation for engaging in outlandish operations in support of right-wing regimes. Initially, however, it included academic liberals who saw the war against Communism as a new phase of the conflict with totalitarianism that FDR had waged against the Axis powers.

The Marshall Plan and the Berlin Airlift

After the National Security Act, Truman won from Congress one of the most remarkable foreign policy programs in the nation's history. Drafted by George C. Marshall, the World War II general now secretary of state, the Marshall Plan of 1947 detailed an extensive program of financial aid to Europe. An effort to relieve suffering, it also contemplated a reborn Europe that could be a vigorous trading partner with the United States. Most urgently it aimed to keep Communist parties in France and Italy from gaining governmental power.

In 1948 came the first direct test of wills between Moscow and the West. On February 25, Communists staged a successful coup d'état in Czechoslovakia, convincing many in the world of the Soviet Union's aggressive designs. Within six weeks the Congress responded with seventeen billion dollars of Marshall Plan aid to Western Europe. Then came crisis with Germany.

The Potsdam Conference of 1945 had carved up defeated Germany into four zones of control, putting the eastern zone under Soviet military occupation. France, Britain, and the United States each controlled a zone in western Germany. Berlin was similarly divided, the eastern part of the city being assigned to Soviet jurisdiction. The western zones of Berlin quickly united, as did the western portions of Germany as a whole. All of Berlin lay within the part of Germany given to the Soviet Union, with the provision that the Western Allies could travel by land to the city. Stalin, having decided to force the Western powers to leave Berlin, cut off their land routes through eastern Germany. Three years

German children wait for candy bars to be dropped in handkerchief parachutes by Lieutenant Gale S. Halvorsen of Garland, UT, approaching Tempelhof Airport during the Berlin Airlift, October 4, 1948. (Courtesy, AP/Wide World Photos)

after the end of World War II the West now faced a stark choice: to let the Communists get away with absorbing the city, or smash through to West Berlin with ground forces risking another major war. Britain, France, and the United States embarked on an imaginative third course, the Berlin Airlift that flew supplies into the city. C-47s swooped low as they came in to land, their crews even dropping candy to children waiting in the fields beneath. The airlift proved a spectacular success. At first thought to be possible for only a short time, or perhaps to face attack by Soviet aircraft, it went on month after month, until the Communists gave up, having met with unexpected Western resistance. They reopened ground traffic to Berlin.

The Blocs Harden

The Soviet Union, through intrigue and force, had by 1948 imposed satellite regimes on Poland, Hungary, Bulgaria, Romania, and Czechoslovakia. Together with eastern Germany, they formed a Communist bloc in Eastern Europe, later entering with the USSR into the Warsaw Pact. In 1949 the West had formed the North Atlantic Treaty Organization, consisting of Northern European and North American nations. The NATO military alliance obliged all members to come to the assistance of any signatory attacked by a "foreign nation." Everyone knew of course which foreign power NATO had in mind. That same year, the frontiers of confrontation hardened further. The Soviet detonation of an atomic bomb shocked the Western powers who then reeled in 1949 at the Communist conquest of China and the retreat of Chiang Kai-shek's government to the offshore island of Taiwan.

Truman and his new secretary of state, the iron-willed Dean Acheson, dug in for a hard fight against the Communists. In 1950 the National Security Council issued a report, the famous NSC-68, defining the USSR as an irreconcilable enemy and arguing for massive defense expenditures. The atmosphere in Washington led the Truman administration to give vast sums to France to finance an attempt to regain its colonial empire in French Indochina, which included Vietnam. Truman aimed to strengthen France against Communism in Europe, but the policy of aiding colonialism in Asia came back to haunt future administrations.

Cold War Liberalism and Its Critics

In devising military, economic, and diplomatic counterattacks against the Communist bloc, the Truman administration was responding to what it saw as practical dangers at pressure points throughout the world. Communists made entirely clear their wish to impose their ideology on the world, or as they would say, to liberate the world from capitalism. The Soviet Union could back away from risk, as it demonstrated during the Berlin Airlift. But policy makers in the United States and Western Europe saw no reason to interpret caution on the part of Moscow as evidence that Communists would let the world alone. Prudence required the West to assume that the Soviet Union would remain an enemy, yielding in the face of Western resolve but always ready to strike when opportunity appeared.

Behind these specific reasons for the Cold War strategies of Truman's presidency lay a mentality among Democratic liberals and the liberal wing of

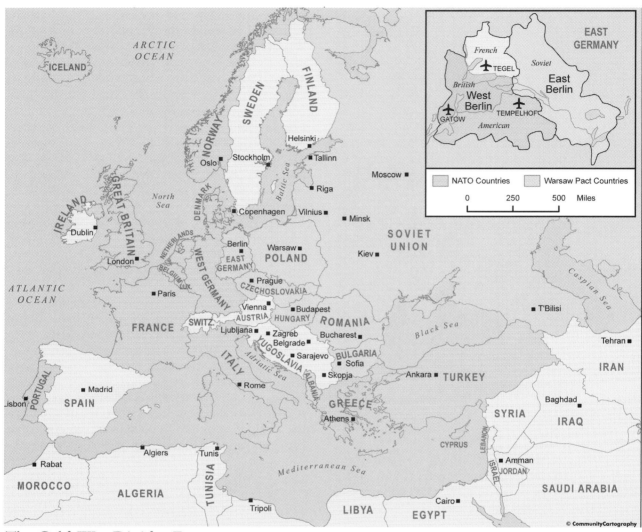

The Cold War Divides Europe

the Republican Party, stretching back to a time before the Soviet Union even existed.

Theodore Roosevelt had been the first American president to imagine for the United States a large and ceaselessly active engagement in the outside world. The Republican Roosevelt's idea has been long regarded as a simple, power-flexing imperialism. More significantly, he wanted the United States to have a presence abroad worthy of the country's size, wealth, and political values. A complement to Roosevelt's idea of his country's place in the world was the more missionary spirit of the Democratic President Woodrow Wilson. Immunized from the sins of the Old World, he believed, the United States would be a force for

good throughout the globe. Having overcome his hesitancy to bring the nation into the squabbles of Europe, Wilson became so eager to make the United States a leader among nations that recent interventionist policies can be traced to Wilsonian internationalism. Theodore Roosevelt's Democratic cousin Franklin—shrewd and cheerfully manipulative, much more skilled than the icy moralist Wilson in the business of swaps and secret deals—slowly brought the United States fully into the tangle of global politics.

By the end of World War II, then, the country led by President Truman had assumed the role of a major world power. Much of the public embraced the fact, enormously proud of the American contribution to the Allied victory and convinced that feats of strength and generosity would define the nation's future. The project of resisting Communism seemed exactly fitted to the country's responsibilities abroad. Truman's foreign policy nevertheless had two clearly distinguishable sets of critics.

On one side stood conservatives, most of them Republican and some of them isolationists. Resistant like right-wingers in general to government spending, most isolationists considered aid to other nations for whatever purposes, even the containment of Communism, to be just another New Deal giveaway of American tax dollars. Truman's internationalism also required alliances, and Republicans hated to surrender any particle of American freedom to act independently. Isolationists were especially hostile to the United Nations, which they thought of as a world government in the making, a subordination of American interests to the needs of other countries. Yet at the same time, many Republicans argued that the programs liberals had devised for stopping Communism were too weak. The Communist bloc must not simply be prevented from expanding; it should be crushed. Any diplomatic arrangement with the Soviet Union aiming to temper the conflict or keep it from turning violent was a sellout.

How did conservatives, especially isolationists, resolve the contradiction between defeating Communism and neither spending the money nor entering the alliances needed for doing so? They did not, because they could not. Soon the politics of conservative Republicans dissolved into a huge campaign at home in search of Communists and fellow travelers, the term for Communist sympathizers. The initiative seemed just right: it was inexpensive and entailed no diplomatic complications. In short, it was an enormously satisfying outlet for anticommunist and antiliberal fury.

At the other end of the political spectrum were radicals who accused liberal internationalists not of weakness but of seeking to submit the globe to American capitalism. American Communists, of course, believed this. And even many radicals who detested Communism as a mockery of the socialist ideal could not bring themselves to put any trust in the anticommunist alliance of capitalist nations.

Still, some socialists, anarchists, and others on the left preferred waging the Cold War even on Truman's terms to allowing expansion of a repres-

sive Communist system. Walter Reuther, the militant leader of the United Automobile Workers, wanted assurance that the worldwide struggle against Communism would be for democracy and not for wealth and privilege. In time the National Association for the Advancement of Colored People came fully to endorse the Cold War methods waged by Truman liberals. Yet the NAACP urged the United States to cleanse itself of the white supremacy that weakened the Western claim of acting in the defense of freedom. Other critics of American institutions had little hope that liberalism would ever willingly accept a fundamental redistribution of political and economic power. But hating Communism even more than they detested capitalism, they accepted in effect the formula: stop Communism first; then construct a better future than the liberal wing of American capitalism offered.

THE POP CULTURE OF ANTICOMMUNISM

"Fight the Red Menace," urges the slogan at the bottom of a set of bubblegum cards put out in 1951 under the title "Children's Crusade Against Communism." A typical card describes on one side the attempt by the Soviet authorities to prevent the peoples of the USSR from hearing the Voice of America, a regular radio program beamed worldwide by the State Department. The other side pictures a family under arrest, the father seized by a brutal policeman, the mother holding a baby while a little girl huddles at her side. Maybe, the card suggests, a trusted friend turned in the family for listening to the Voice; anyone may spy for the secret police.

The naive and simplistic character of the Children's Crusade makes it easy to forget that the card contained more than a little truth. Communist governments did suppress information from both within and outside their countries, and people who questioned authority were in danger of betrayal by friends and associates. But what might have been a plain American resistance to Communism transformed itself into something approaching hysteria. It invaded popular culture in movies, stories, and comics, portraying the evil seeping westward from the Soviet Union and featuring depraved and power-hungry agents of the Communist conspiracy,

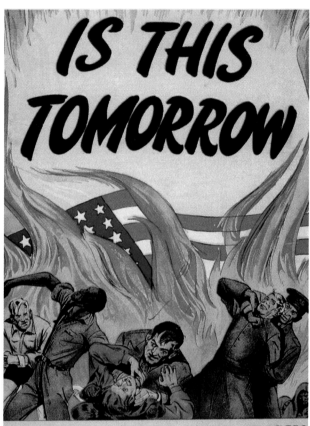

IS THIS TOMORROW

AMERICA UNDER COMMUNISM!

This comic book, widely circulated by church groups, depicted the United States during the final apocalyptic Communist takeover. (Courtesy, Michael Barson Collection / Past Perfect)

aided by beautiful temptresses luring the innocent into its web. "Her beauty," announced an advertisement for the 1949 film *I Married a Communist*, "served a mob of terror whose one mission is to destroy!"

Among Americans on the political right, some of them quick to assume that Communism, democratic socialism, and even the mild measures of the New Deal all constituted a worldwide drift toward totalitarianism, the anti-Soviet religion came easily. But angry anticommunism embraced a far larger part of the American population than the fantasies on the right could have reached. The suggestion of a long future of armed preparation for conflicts with the Soviet government invited an ideology of total war and brought a bracing sense of high purpose and national unity. Then too, the Communists had

their own ideology, wide in its foundations and presented with an aggressive arrogance that baited opponents into an equally uncompromising creed. To the ideology of Marxism, prominent former Communists brought a passion all their own. Having once thought that Karl Marx defined reality and the Soviet Union embodied the future, they now in their disillusionment proclaimed an anticommunism as all-encompassing as their old pro-Communist beliefs.

Government Watchdogs and the Hollywood Ten

The government did not force the Communists into manipulative secrecy. By preference they operated not by open persuasion but by drawing well-meaning citizens into "fronts," organizations hiding their Communist leadership and claiming to promote some virtuous cause like peace or racial progress. In its deviousness Communism seemed an insidious, hidden infection of the mind, to be combated by the antibody of spotless patriotism.

The conservative House Un-American Activities Committee, or HUAC, furthered this perception of Communism. In 1947, HUAC investigated what it thought to be Communist infiltration of Hollywood, the same Hollywood that would soon be turning out films warning of the Communist conspiracy. Some members of the film industry who refused to answer questions asked by the committee did so on the grounds of the Constitution's Fifth Amendment, which prohibits the government from forcing people to testify against themselves. These the committee had no legal way to punish. Ten others, however, including writers of note, refused to appeal to the Fifth Amendment. They based their silence instead on the argument that the committee's snooping masqueraded an effort to frighten the film industry away from independent thinking. The Hollywood Ten, along with over two hundred other movie notables, were thereupon blacklisted by the industry: that is, put on lists of people not to be employed. The Ten were singled out and cited for criminal contempt of Congress. HUAC succeeded in planting more firmly within the public mind the conviction that Communism had invaded the country's major institutions.

Under President Truman, the executive branch of the federal government also went Red-hunting. On the assumption that Communists working for the government would act to subvert it, the president issued executive orders establishing boards to investigate federal employees for evidence that they might endanger the national security. Workers might be a risk if homosexual and therefore subject to blackmail or if affiliated with any organization on the attorney general's list of groups found to be fascist, Communist, or otherwise subversive.

In retrospect, the process Truman put in motion seems excessive. For employees with access to military or diplomatic secrets, an investigative process was in order. For the rest, whose attempt to undermine the government could not have gone much beyond stealing thumbtacks, their presence could have safely been tolerated. The loyalty program injured federal workers who had done no more than ignorantly join front groups controlled by hidden Communists. Thousands of homosexuals were summarily fired. And the hunt for subversives added to a public mood of suspicion spreading like an angry rash. Truman himself, architect of the loyalty program as well as the American armed standoff with the USSR, soon came under attack not only for carelessness about security risks in government but for being soft on Communism in general.

The Trials

In 1948, the Truman administration prosecuted eleven leaders of the Communist party for violation of the Smith Act of 1940, which made it a crime to advocate the overthrow of the government by force. In itself, the act came close to violating the First Amendment protection of freedom of speech. But the eleven Communists faced trial and conviction not especially for what they had said or done as individuals but for being members of a party that apparently taught armed revolution. The Supreme Court, in any case, upheld the legality of the convictions. The government then went after other members of the party. A federal trial in 1951 convicted and sentenced to death two radicals, Julius and Ethel Rosenberg, for conspiracy to commit espionage as members of a spy ring that had attempted to provide the Soviet Union with atomic secrets. Documents recently opened in Moscow suggest that at least Julius was guilty. They were electrocuted at Sing Sing prison. In 1954 Congress passed the Communist Control Act prohibiting party members from being political candidates for public office. Within a few years the Communist

Julius and perhaps Ethel Rosenberg, according to Soviet documents released in the 1990s (the Verona Project), attempted to pass atomic secrets to the enemy. At Sing Sing prison in Ossining, New York, they died in the electric chair on June 19, 1953. (Courtesy, Michael Barson Collection / Past Perfect)

Party, broken both by governmental prosecutions and by the moral and intellectual absurdity of its service to the Soviet Union, had dwindled to perhaps five thousand, a good many of them agents of the FBI.

More divisive at the time was a legal battle between two remarkable men, Whittaker Chambers and Alger Hiss, before HUAC and later in federal criminal court. Chambers as he tells his story in his powerful autobiography, *Witness*, had endured a brooding, introspective childhood. Knowing the wretchedness not of poverty—he came from a modestly well-to-do if eccentric family—but of inner, self-isolating doubt and torment, he quickly responded to an ideology that promised a better world for the masses. As a Communist he took its creed and its hopes deep into his troubled soul. *Witness* presents a world of secret meetings in darkened corners, among Communists or ex-Communists who knew the subtleties of Marxism and the horrors of the European past.

In time Chambers concluded that the party in which he had sought mercy toward the world was merciless, an expression of the century's spiritual death rather than a way out of it. He turned to the Quaker faith, embracing its simple piety though not its pacifism. He also became passionately anticommunist. In 1948 Chambers spoke before HUAC about Communist infiltration of the government: the title *Witness* refers both to giving legal testimony and to the Quaker concept of the obligation to witness to truth. Chambers accused among others Alger Hiss, first of being a Communist agent within the State Department and then of spying.

Chambers represented one kind of twentieth-century temperament: rootless, deprived of traditional beliefs and certainties, questing for meaning through politics and ideology. Hiss provided another kind of representative figure. Slim with chiseled features, elegant, aristocratic, he was a walking contrast to the rumpled Chambers and an embodiment of liberal urbanity. His accuser, though a noted writer for *Time*, could never shed his air of lonely outsider. Hiss, enjoying the privilege of an education at Johns Hopkins and at Harvard Law School, had from the first been successful and admired. A clerk at the Supreme Court, he went on to work at the State Department and to accompany FDR to Yalta, resigning to direct the prestigious Carnegie Endowment. Hiss belonged to the Washington crowd as much as Chambers remained alienated from it.

When Hiss, called before HUAC, denied Chambers's claims, liberals gathered to his side, and not only liberals but the essentially conservative secretary of state, Dean Acheson. Liberals, no friends to Communists, actively prosecuted the Cold War against Moscow at a time when right-wingers were still reluctant to contribute American resources to

Alger Hiss, convicted of perjury, was suspected of being a spy for the Soviet Union during the 1930s and 1940s. (Courtesy, Scribner's Archives)

Whittaker Chambers testifies against Alger Hiss before the House Un-American Activities Committee, August, 1948. (Courtesy, UPI)

resisting Communist expansion. Many liberals sided with Hiss simply because he appeared to exemplify liberalism at its best: so well educated, so articulate, so much a part of the eastern foreign policy elite. Such people, liberals thought, could not possibly be Communists. Some opponents of Chambers used his homosexuality to discredit him. In those days, liberals shared the widespread homophobia that later liberal generations have renounced.

An aggressively ambitious young World War II veteran, Richard Nixon of California, served on HUAC. Nixon's pursuit of the accusations against Hiss would catapult him from statewide into national prominence. HUAC and Nixon could do nothing independently to Hiss except question him. But he could be prosecuted in federal court if it could be shown he lied under oath. Accordingly, Hiss faced trial for perjury. Chambers told his story in court and backed it up with evidence he had kept in a hollowed-out pumpkin on his Maryland farm. Following a mistrial, Hiss, convicted in 1950, went to prison.

Conservatives took to Chambers as a hero in the fight against Communism. Yet he never fully became one of them. The hatred of suffering and cruelty that had sent him into the Communist Party and then out of it made it impossible for him to accept the ruthless economics of the political right. He remained an outsider.

TRUMAN AT HOME

On assuming the presidency at Roosevelt's death, Truman had the good fortune to inherit the popular politics that FDR had brought to the Democratic Party. Simultaneously he had the bad fortune to be a living contrast in background and manner to a president who remained a singularly revered figure.

Born into an old family and old money, FDR embodied the model of an aristocrat or as close to one as the United States can produce. In an early contest for office in New York State, one of his handlers had found it necessary to tell him not to campaign wearing the outfit then favored by men of wealth when they went horseback riding. But combined with his promotion of the economically egalitarian policies of the New Deal, FDR's background worked in his favor, giving him the aura of fatherly sponsor of programs for the relief of suffering. In his backstage political maneuvering, he could be brutal in destroying an opponent. But Roosevelt's public air of easy confidence, appropriate to a gentleman of good background, suggested that he would never do anything cheap and vulgar. The public loved it; liberal intellectuals loved it even more.

Truman stood in harsh contrast to FDR. Though personally honest, the new president was known for having launched his career with the support of a corrupt Missouri political machine. His folksy manner would later serve him well—a public charmed by patrician grace can also warm to a language of streets and shirtsleeves—but at the beginning of his presidency it did not please Washington insiders. One observer would remember being disturbed by the sight of the new president walking into a meeting. FDR had seemed less confined to a wheelchair than rooted in it, fixed and solid as the presidency itself. A president who walked: such a leader now appeared severed from substance and authority.

Labor at War's End

Organized labor, its growth spurred by the struggles and successes of the Depression years, had gained further during the war, when the need for rapid, massive production gave the workforce an advantage. But a great number of brief walkouts, notably in 1944, broke wartime union pledges against strikes. Then, as peace brought with it a sudden decline in the demand for workers, more serious strikes broke out in one industry after another. This became Truman's first domestic crisis.

A railroad strike posed one of the greatest threats, for early in 1946 it could have paralyzed much of the nation's business and industry. In late May an enraged Truman, after unsuccessfully urging rail union leaders not to go through with it, went before the House of Representatives. Enthusiastically welcomed, he called for a law authorizing the president to draft workers whenever a strike threatened to create a national emergency. In the midst of his speech he received word that the union leaders had agreed to the settlement he proposed, and Truman upon announcing it to his audience again received applause. He had a moment of triumph, but it carried distinct political risks.

That same year Truman took on one of the best-known labor leaders of the time. Beloved of the coal miners and despised by much of the public at large,

PAUL ROBESON

Few Americans have packed such breadth of accomplishment into one lifetime as Paul Leroy Robeson: college football all-star, Columbia Law School graduate, star of Broadway shows and movies, acclaimed folk and operatic singer, civil rights activist at home and campaigner for freedom of people around the world. He spoke, wrote, and sang in more than twenty languages. In May 1942, Robeson received a citation from the Secretary of the Treasury for "distinguished and patriotic services to our country," while the House Un-American Activities Committee (HUAC) placed him on its list of presumed communists. In spirit, both descriptions may have been true.

Paul Robeson was born in 1898 to a distinguished family in Princeton, New Jersey. The Reverend William Drew Robeson, escaped from slavery in North Carolina at age fifteen, served as minister of Witherspoon Street Presbyterian Church for twenty years. In 1901, accusations that he promoted "unrest and dissatisfaction" by speaking against injustice ended his ministry there. In 1906, he became a minister in the African Methodist Episcopal Zion Church; Paul's

Paul Leroy Robeson. (Courtesy, Library of Congress)

older brother Ben later served as pastor of Mother Zion church in Harlem.

At seventeen, Paul won a four-year scholarship to Rutgers. In spite of racist attacks during try-outs and practice, his 6'7" 190- pound frame and unrelenting determination got him on the varsity team his freshman year. He played on the 1917 All-American college team, won fifteen varsity letters in football, baseball, basketball, and track, and was elected to every honor society on campus, including Phi Beta Kappa his junior year. He was chosen for the Cap and Skull Society and as valedictorian delivered the commencement speech for his graduating class.

At Columbia Law School, Paul Robeson's classmates included William O. Douglas, in later years a Supreme Court justice, and Thomas E. Dewey, a future governor of New York. He supported himself through law school playing professional football for the Akron Pros and Milwaukee Badgers. A brief stint in law with the New York firm of Stotesbury and Miner ended the first time Robeson buzzed for a stenographer, who said "I never take dictation from a nigger." Recognizing that he would never actually appear in court, for the firm's wealthy white clients would fear prejudice against their case from the judge or jury, he left the practice of law.

The playwright Eugene O'Neill cast Robeson in 1924 as the lead of *All God's Chillun Got Wings*. He went on to acclaimed roles in *The Emperor Jones*, *Show Boat*, and *Porgy and Bess*. He had lead movie roles in a film production of O'Neill's *The Emperor Jones*, *King Solomon's Mines*, *Jericho* (filmed in Egypt), *Sanders of the River*, *Tales of Manhattan*, and *Song of Freedom*. Trying to overcome racial stereotypes, he was repeatedly disappointed by the final cut of the movies. The only movie he remained proud of was *Proud Valley*, in which he plays an unemployed American seaman seeking work in the coal mines of southern Wales.

Robeson's best-known stage role was the lead in Shakespeare's *Othello*. The actor had discovered that Othello was played in England in the 1500's and early 1600's by Africans, as Shakespeare intended. Robeson first appeared in a six-week run in 1930 in London, telling a reporter it was the most fulfilling role of his career. He appeared as Othello in the United States in 1942, and won a Donaldson Award (the equivalent of the Tony today) in 1944. In 1943, the production opened on Broadway for a record year-long run, then went on a seven month tour of forty-five cities around the United States.

Paul Robeson's musical partnership with pianist Lawrence Brown began in 1922 and lasted for nearly forty years. Beginning with performances of traditional spirituals and gospel music, they added folk songs from around the world, labor movement anthems, themes from Broadway musicals, and classical pieces. In 1945, Robeson and Brown were an acclaimed feature of the first interracial USO tour, playing for troops stationed in Germany, France, and Czechoslovakia. Their last tour together, through Australia and New Zealand, was in 1960.

In December 1934 the distinguished film director Sergei Eisenstein had invited Robeson to visit the Soviet Union. Warmly received by government officials, enthusiastically welcomed by concert audiences, seeing no signs of racial prejudice, Robeson remarked that "Here for the first time in my life, I walk in full human dignity." He and Lawrence Brown returned to do a concert at the Moscow Conservatory in December 1936. In 1937 Robeson decided to leave England for Spain, where supporters of the elected republican government were resisting a civil war begun by army officers under Generalissimo Francisco Franco. Enduring bombing of Spanish cities by the fascist air force, and artillery salvos from enemy lines, Paul toured the republican battlefront giving concerts and encouraging the troops, including over a thousand American volunteers in the Abraham Lincoln Brigades.

CBS radio featured Robeson in a November 3, 1939, broadcast introducing the nation to Earl Robinson and John LaTouche's ten-minute long "Ballad for Americans." This stirring tribute to the aspirations that had launched the infant United States, and the diversity of peoples and occupations that built it, was enthusiastically embraced by Americans struggling to come out of the Great Depression and witnessing the start of a world war. Paul Robeson's warm baritone carried the lyrics into homes across the nation.

Robeson opposed Britain, France, and the United States in their worldwide campaign after World War II against Communism, thinking it to be a cover for a British and French attempt to retake colonial possessions in Africa and Asia with American support. In 1949, arriving in Moscow for a concert tour, he found many Jewish friends from previous visits in prison or murdered. At a packed Moscow concert, Robeson sang in Yiddish the song of the Warsaw Ghetto resistance, *Zog Nit Kaynmal*.

In 1945, Robeson had received the Springarn Medal, the NAACP's highest honor. By 1951, the NAACP leaders Roy Wilkins and Walter White were denouncing him for his sympathies with Communism. In 1949, anticommunist hysteria made Peekskill, NY, site of three successful Robeson concerts, into a battleground. Announcement of a fourth concert turned out the local Veterans of Foreign Wars, American Legion, and St. Joseph's Catholic High School to protest, throwing rocks at car windows, dragging concertgoers out of their cars, and beating them; uniformed police officers looked the other way. A second concert was more successful, members of the United Electrical Workers Union, Longshoremen's union, and Fur and Leather Workers union providing security. But another riot along the road home produced more casualties. Robeson was driven out on the floor of an automobile, covered with a blanket, with union security guards covering him. In 1952 Robeson accepted the Stalin Peace Prize. Proud to serve as director of the Civil Rights Congress, labeled a "Communist front" by the Attorney General, Robeson presented a CRC petition to the six-year-old United Nations, charging the United States with genocide against African-Americans. Robeson led a delegation to ask President Truman for anti-lynching legislation, receiving a short and unsympathetic response.

From 1948 to 1958, Robeson was blacklisted from the American stage. Audiences in many other countries demanded that he come sing, but the State Department revoked his passport in 1950. A "Let Paul Robeson Sing" campaign flooded the State Department with petitions and letters from Britain and other countries.

Robeson died in 1976 at the age of seventy-eight.

the maverick John L. Lewis had not refrained, even during wartime, from putting the interests of miners above broader national concerns. That coal workers did a particularly dangerous and dirty job in an industry that traditionally had exploited them ruthlessly is a partial explanation. Lewis's United Mine Workers conducted a strike and got a settlement. But then, later that year, he decided that he did not like the terms and called out the miners once more—at a time when, typically for Lewis's brazenness, winter was approaching and a coal strike raised the prospect that millions of families might go without fuel. Truman got a court injunction against the strike. Lewis initially ignored it, but when a huge fine was slapped on the UMW and another on Lewis himself, the combative leader did something unusual: he asked for negotiations. When Truman refused, Lewis did something even more unusual: he backed away, calling off the strike. The green and politically fragile president had faced down one of the nation's most formidable labor leaders.

In spite of Truman's success with labor unrest, the troubles of that year put his party in danger.

The Democrats, so closely identified with organized labor, suffered from the confrontations. Truman, then, faced the wrath not only of labor but of its enemies. In the midterm elections of 1946, just a few weeks before the end of the clash with Lewis, an increasingly conservative public turned Congress over to the Republicans.

That victory, combined with the presence in the national legislature of southern Democrats who worked with conservative Republicans, ultimately redeemed Truman with labor, making him the champion of organized workers in their war with the newly elected body. In 1947 Congress passed the Taft-Hartley Act, which placed restrictions on union activity. It allowed the president to impose an eighty-day cooling-off period before a strike that might endanger the national interest could go forward. It forbade secondary boycotts, in which if a company is deemed hostile to labor, workers in other firms will refuse to handle goods related to it. The act also prohibited the closed shop, a company agreement to hire only workers unionized at the time of hiring; and it allowed states to forbid the union shop, which requires workers to join the rel-

A labor strike protesting cuts in wages, Los Angeles, 1946. (Courtesy, AP/Wide World Photos)

evant union after hiring. Labor leaders perceived Taft-Hartley as a devastating blow. Truman vetoed it but Congress passed it over his veto. Truman's resistance to the legislation readmitted him to the New Deal coalition, if he had ever been expelled from it.

Most of organized labor thrived in the postwar years. The Taft-Hartley Act was not actually a union-buster: it left intact the basic protections of union organizing and collective bargaining between labor and management. And the remarkable wave of prosperity that came shortly after postwar readjustment to peace eased tensions between unions and management. For the most part, unionized workers in major industries benefited greatly from the good times. In the years after the temporary agitation awakened by Taft-Hartley, a neat pattern was established. A strike or the threat of one would bring a rise in wages, which management then passed on to consumers by a compensating increase in prices. Organized labor returned to what it had essentially been from the beginning: workers within a capitalist enterprise withholding their product from the market until it got the right price. And white unionized workers continued to resist major recruitment of blacks, Hispanics, and women.

Truman Liberalism

Against the Republican Congress, sitting from 1947 to 1949 and containing a powerful bloc of Republicans and southern Democrats able to kill liberal legislation, the liberal in Truman found full expression. His portrayal of what he called the "do-nothing Eightieth Congress" helped him to reawaken an alliance among groups that in depression times had gathered within the Democratic Party. His fight against Taft-Hartley was especially helpful. Truman's recognition of the Jewish state of Israel, which accorded with widespread American popular sympathy for the Jews as victims of Nazism, appealed particularly to the Jewish vote, strongly supportive of the Democrats during the New Deal.

Two elements of the New Deal coalition the president could not reconcile. The allegiance of the old white Democratic solid South had been reconfirmed by New Deal measures for agriculture and the poor. But white southerners would not tolerate concessions to the northern black electorate now shifted

from the Republican Party to the Democratic. That had been no problem for FDR. The switch in party loyalty of black northerners—few southern blacks could vote—did not come of any New Deal enthusiasm for civil rights. Roosevelt's administration had been shamefully willing to tolerate racism in its own programs. Black attraction to the Democratic Party resulted rather from some friendly rhetoric together with New Deal relief programs that African Americans benefited from along with the white poor. But now Truman turned to work for the justice that his mind and conscience dictated in spite of his own racist instincts historians have discovered in his private correspondence. A final split came when Commerce Secretary Henry A. Wallace questioned the need for such a hard-line policy toward the Soviet Union. Truman fired him, and he ran for president on a third party ticket in 1948.

In 1946, the new president had failed to get legislation he sought making permanent the wartime Fair Employment Practices Commission, a body with limited authority to promote an end to racial discrimination in businesses awarded government contracts. But he did appoint a committee that in 1947 issued a report, "To Secure These Rights," proposing a remarkable range of new racial policies. These included the outlawing of discrimination in employment, interstate transportation, and public accommodations; federal protections of voting rights; and an executive order ending racism in the federal government. Truman asked Congress for some of the measures the committee had called for. He did not press the matter, knowing that southern members would effectively block passage. Yet he had sufficiently identified himself and his party with civil rights. After the Democratic National Convention of 1948, with his hesitant backing, added a strong civil rights plank to the party platform, a number of southern Democrats broke away to form the rebel States' Rights Party, or Dixiecrats. As though in defiant response, Truman by executive order declared an end to discrimination in the civil service and to segregation in the armed forces.

Southern insurrection notwithstanding, Truman had recharged much of the New Deal coalition. In the presidential contest with Thomas E. Dewey, the moderate Republican governor of New York State, polls predicted Truman would lose. Yet he achieved one of the greatest upsets of American political history, pulling out a narrow victory. The result can partially be attributed to a triumph of style: Tru-

President Harry Truman on his whistle-stop campaign at Bridgeport, CT, in October 1948. At the top is the sheet music for his campaign theme song, "I'm just wild about Harry." (Courtesy, Truman Presidential Library. Sheet music: Collection of Janice L. and David J. Frent)

man's scrappy populism against Dewey's reserved and colorless manner. Truman's whistle-stop campaign, his train halting at small towns as well as cities so he could preach from the caboose his fiery denunciations of Republicans and privilege, had reinvigorated the substance of working and middle-class liberalism.

What made the 1948 presidential victory all the more remarkable was that Truman survived not just one but two rebellions within Democratic ranks. Dixiecrats, putting up the conservative Strom Thurmond of South Carolina, endangered Democratic control of the solid South and actually won

four states in that region. To Truman's left, a Progressive Party headed by Henry A. Wallace and opposing the hardening Western confrontation with the Soviet Union threatened to draw away enough Democratic votes to throw New York State to Dewey. A wartime vice president under FDR, Wallace was no Communist. But he retained the vanishing wish for a livable peace between Moscow and the West. In a talk in Madison Square Garden before an audience of Communists and their friends, he proposed a friendlier policy toward the USSR. Across the nation Cold War liberals and conservatives alike recoiled. Yet the audience, still entranced by Communism, took offense at Wallace's description of the Soviet Union as repressive. Wallace was to become in a few years a confirmed cold warrior himself.

Now president in his own right rather than simply the successor to a deceased chief executive, Truman proposed an extension of the New Deal that he called the Fair Deal. From a Congress that had now passed back to Democratic control he had reason to expect cooperation. He argued, of course, for the repeal of Taft-Hartley. Other proposals included federal aid to education, civil rights legislation, development of public power, a program boosting prices of farm products, the instituting of national health insurance, and a heavier income tax on the wealthy. Some of the president's proposals carried: an expansion of public housing funded by the government, the widening of Social Security, and a hike in the minimum wage. But much of the Fair Deal failed to get past even the Democratic Congress, in which southern conservatives headed important committees. Among Truman's signal failures was his plan for federally supported health insurance, opposed by the American Medical Association as "socialized medicine."

THE ERA OF McCARTHY AND KOREA

Events in the year 1950 took the Cold War further along two disastrous courses. At home, the Red Scare instigated by HUAC and the government security program got into the hands of one of the most effective demagogues in the nation's history. In Asia, the United States extended Cold War policy already developed in Europe, and in the years to come most of the blood drawn in that conflict would be shed in Asia.

Joe McCarthy

On February 9, 1950, Joseph R. McCarthy, the junior Republican senator from Wisconsin, spoke to a women's club in Wheeling, West Virginia. McCarthy, a Catholic and a marine air veteran of the Pacific campaign in World War II, had hitherto been relatively unknown. But he was a political street brawler, and he now put his instincts to use.

He announced to the meeting that he had a list of 205 State Department employees who had been identified to the secretary of state as Communists but remained at work in his department.

No one ever got to see that list. Nor did the press get a clear sense of the basis for McCarthy's claims for the other lists that from time to time he brandished. He did name some individuals, although without evidence. But evidence really did not matter too much because McCarthy's followers operated for reasons essentially emotional. McCarthy himself

Senator Joseph R. McCarthy (Republican, Wisconsin) issued frequent charges claiming that Communists infested the Washington bureaucracy. In retrospect, McCarthy's claims seem irresponsible and even silly, but they cost over a thousand people their jobs in the United States government. A handful of American Communists did work for the Soviet Union, but almost none had access to important materials and McCarthy's charges resulted in no convictions. (Courtesy, Hank Walker. LIFE MAGAZINE, Time Warner Inc.)

"Communists always appear before the public as 'Progressives.' Yesterday they were 'Twentieth Century Americans,' last week they were 'defenders of all civil liberties,' tonight they may be 'honest, simple trades unionists.' They are 'liberals' at breakfast, 'defenders of world peace' in the afternoon, and 'the voice of the people' in the evening. These artful dodges and ingenious dissimilations obviously make it difficult for the average trusting citizen to keep up with every new Communist swindle and con game. . . . Many newspapers and other publicity media have secret Communists on their staffs who regularly slip in a neat hypodermic full of Moscow virus."

James G. O'Neill
"How You Can Fight Communism"
American Legion Magazine, August, 1948

perpetually lied. He lived on the edge of his own emotions, convinced of his rightness.

Hatred of Communism alone did not make a McCarthyite. Nor did conservatism suffice. The conservative Democrat Millard Tydings of Maryland headed a Senate committee in 1950 that found McCarthy's charges to be out of line, and for his resistance to his colleague Tydings met slander and defeat in his next election. The kind of conservatism, quite common at the time, that stresses careful procedure had little tolerance for the bullying vulgarity of a McCarthy. He appealed to a highly partisan segment of the public that seethed with suspicious resentment at what it took to be the power and snobbery of liberals, New Dealers, and the foreign policy elite. Many Republicans, of course, found McCarthy useful, for while he had perhaps the backing of only a minority of Americans, that minority was sizable and passionate.

For four years, from 1950 to 1954, McCarthy steadily made headlines. When the Republicans took control of the Senate in 1953, they gave him the chairmanship of a subcommittee that he employed to investigate subversion in the government. In 1954, however, he overreached himself when he raised charges of disloyalty in the army. Attacking the highly decorated General Ralph Zwicker for failing to provide information in a supposed case of subversion, he declared Zwicker unfit to wear his uniform. At about the same time Edward R. Murrow, famous for his broadcasts from Britain early in World War II and in the 1950s director of his own news program, presented a devastating television exposé of McCarthy simply by showing film clips of the senator in action. There followed a televised Senate committee investigation of McCarthy's charges against the army, in which the senator looked so bad before a nationwide viewing public that he lost his credibility. Eventually the Senate officially censured him. But by then his political power had vanished.

The larger effect of McCarthy's charges of subversion is as difficult to pin down as the charges themselves. He certainly intensified the Red Scare that occurred during his years of prominence. Having already threatened Hollywood, the scare was now shifted to public schools and universities. In the early fifties and for years afterwards, any open dissent from hard-line Cold War policy became politically risky. Here, though, the influence of McCarthy is to be questioned. The idea that every Communist is exactly like every other, that no Communist is motivated by any social or patriotic concern outside of the pursuit of absolute domination, had taken root itself in the American consciousness. And for that, considerable responsibility rested not on the McCarthy camp but on its liberal enemies who had purged the government of alleged subversives. McCarthyism further poisoned an already deeply sickened political culture.

Korea

At the end of World War II the Soviet Union had for a time occupied the northern part of the Korean peninsula, a concession given in return for Moscow's last minute entry into the conflict against Japan. The United States kept temporary control of southern Korea. This division of Korea being arbitrary and the South Koreans occasionally threatening the north, the Communists there decided to unify the country by force. On June 25, 1950, North Korea launched an invasion of the southern half of the country. North Korea's well-trained and tough army caught South Korea unprepared.

President Truman swiftly committed the Amer-

ican military to the defense of President Syngman
Rhee's southern regime. He put in charge of the
American forces General Douglas MacArthur, who
as head of the postwar American occupation of
Japan had been essentially a benevolent despot, dismantling Japanese militarism and preparing the
country for democratic institutions. Truman acted
in Korea without a congressional declaration of war.
The authority he soon received came not from Congress but from the United Nations—from which
the Soviet Union, then boycotting the organization,
was temporarily absent—acting in its vaguely defined role of peacekeeper. The United States provided most of the Western Allied troops that supported the South Korean military.

The American army, diminished in size after
World War II, needed new recruits in Korea who
would have to get much of their training in combat.
Before long the United Nations forces had been
driven back into a narrow patch of territory at the
southern end of the peninsula. But then MacArthur,
as head of all the UN troops, achieved one of the
grand strokes of his brilliant though erratic career.
After making a surprise landing on September 15
at the port of Inchon on the western coast of South
Korea, the UN forces sliced eastward, cutting off
the North Korean troops. They nearly destroyed
the Communist army, a portion of it fleeing northward.

At this point the United Nations, only a few
months into the war, could claim victory. Had a
decision then been made to stop, the United States
could have savored one of the sweetest triumphs in
its history, saving the South Koreans from a regime
far more brutal than their president Syngman
Rhee's, corrupt and dictatorial though it was. Mac-
Arthur, his prestige now enormously enhanced,
convinced himself that his forces could go north,
smash the Communists completely, and unify
Korea. The Truman administration, now committed to fighting Communism wherever feasible,
agreed to the venture. And so the UN forces crossed
over the thirty-eighth parallel, the dividing line
between North and South Korea.

For a time, the new phase of the war went well
with the North Koreans unable to resist the Allied
advance. Yet toward the end of October 1950, some
Chinese soldiers began to appear among prisoners
taken by the UN. MacArthur maintained his insistence that China would remain out of the conflict.
Then the Allied armies, continuing their offensive,

*While supreme commander of United Nations forces in
Korea, Douglas MacArthur was fired by his boss, President Harry Truman, for failing to obey orders. That the
president is Commander-in-Chief of the armed forces had
not fully gotten through to MacArthur.* (Courtesy, Carl
Mydens, LIFE MAGAZINE, Time Warner Inc.)

approached the Yalu River dividing China from
Korea. Hundreds of thousands of Chinese poured
across the river and overwhelmed the UN forces,
sending them spinning southward in savage wintry
weather.

For retreating troops to regroup and steady
themselves is an enormous task. It means, among
other things, overcoming a mentality of panic and
defeat. By January 1951 that had happened. Much
of the credit goes to a lesser-known American commander, Matthew Ridgway (anyone in the vicinity
of the grandiose MacArthur was likely to be less
known). Ridgway ceaselessly worked the front
lines, going from unit to unsteady unit, earning a
reputation for being one of his country's outstand-

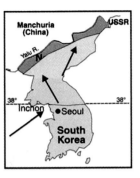

| June 25, 1950 | Sept. 14, 1950 | Nov. 25, 1950 | July 27, 1953 |

Military advances, withdrawals, and stalemate during the Korean War, 1950–1953.

ing battlefield officers. One unit of marines, temporarily cut off in the north, fought its way back through enemy lines, adding one more feat to the corps' list of famed exploits. Once more the UN took the offensive, eventually establishing a position roughly tracing the former border between the two Koreas.

MacArthur, meanwhile, had been demanding afresh the freedom to wage a more extensive war. His pronouncements defied Truman's orders not to make public statements at odds with the policy of the administration. Finally, in April 1951 an exasperated Truman removed MacArthur from command. The public turned furiously against the president and upon the general's return to the United States treated him as a hero. His speech to Congress blossomed into a great national event, his words repeated over and over that evening. "Old soldiers never die," the general had announced, recalling the words of an army song, "they just fade away." The awe with which the public repeated the line made it clear that MacArthur, at least, had not yet faded.

Already convinced that it was soft on Communism and perhaps weakened by enemy subversion, enemies of Truman's administration saw the dismissal of MacArthur as proof of their worst suspicions. In conjunction with the McCarthyite furies of the time, the passionate public embrace of MacArthur represented an especially heated moment in American popular and political culture.

After its first volatile year, the Korean War dragged on, the deaths on both sides unredeemed by significant gains to either. The fighting itself stopped soon after the inauguration of the Republican Dwight D. Eisenhower as president in 1953.

By its end it had taken close to 34,000 American lives and far more among the Koreans. It brought terrible, widespread death and devastation to Korean civilians. Both Communists and South Koreans practiced brutalities on prisoners. Technically the war did not end in 1953. Into the twenty-first century there would be a continuing truce, but distrust on the part of the North Korea and the West prevented a permanent accommodation. In a demilitarized zone between the parties, a rich vegetation and animal life have reappeared, undisturbed by war and other human intrusions. During Eisenhower's two administrations attention would return to domestic issues; that president made a remarkable record of avoiding foreign entanglements.

A CONFORMIST SOCIETY?

The sociologist David Riesman and his associates in 1948 published *The Lonely Crowd*, a study of American society, or essentially the white middle classes that many academics identified with the nation at large. Typical of the nineteenth century, claimed the authors, had been a mentality they defined as "inner-directed." Individuals in an inner-directed society pursue firmly determined goals demanding work and singleness of purpose. By the mid-twentieth century, according to *The Lonely Crowd*, the more common state of mind was "other-directed." People of this temperament center their lives not in career ambitions but in their relations with others, and this makes them remarkably susceptible to external influences. Adolescents, for example, define themselves by the taste they share in pop stars and favorite records. Riesman described the square-jawed, clear-eyed, granite-hewn Victorian American as not necessarily agreeable or even moral: inner direction, in fact, could encourage cold ruthlessness. Nor were such people predictably independent: their pursuit of the money or prestige prized by an inner-directed culture might be completely unthinking and dependent on what the people around them defined as respectable objectives. But readers quickly perceived *The Lonely Crowd* as describing the collapse of the American character.

Later evaluations of American postwar culture were still more pessimistic. William Whyte's *The Organization Man*, for example, deplored the dominance of corporations. They had learned to manage and pacify labor instead of clashing with it, to take care of their young executives and administrators, to nurture agreement rather than punish dissent. The organization in Whyte's description encourages a comfortable mediocrity destructive of character.

The Suburbs

Neither David Riesman nor William Whyte centered on the phenomenon that perhaps above all others became the main object of social criticism in these years. Fascinating yet troubling were the suburbs that sprawled around the major cities especially after the war, their growth assisted by government loans, new methods of housing construction, and the automobile. The result? A general loosening of ties to urban neighborhoods, village homes, and family farmsteads.

Unlike older communities outside major cities, the new suburbs did not draw only on the more affluent classes. They represented a mass movement, and by 1960 embraced about a third of the American people, many of them families of veterans who had qualified for government mortgages. Among the most inexpensive suburbs were the Levittowns built by William J. Levitt on Long Island and elsewhere, their houses constructed cheaply, quickly, but well, according to blueprints that made them seem nearly indistinguishable from one another.

To the thinking of social critics or social snobs, the Levittowns embodied bland uniformity. The suburbs differed from the big city with its variety of business and residential sections, its ethnic communities, its enormous energy—and its crime rates, an important concern influencing the shift of the middle classes to the suburbs. And in at least one respect the suburbs did take on the sameness their critics attributed to them: their residents were almost all white. That was partly because black Americans in general had less money with which to buy even the least expensive homes and in larger part because builders, private lenders, and even the government's loan programs practiced racial discrimination.

The suburbs harmed the cities by draining them of well-to-do residents once relied on as a source of tax revenues. By day suburbanites could commute

Built by William Levitt, a Long Island developer, this suburban housing project in Levittown, Pennsylvania, dates to 1949. The homes, though lacking in privacy and—by today's standards—spaciousness, fulfilled the dreams of many newly-married couples. (Courtesy Van Bucher/Photo Researchers)

to the city to work. But in the evening they fled by auto or commuter train to their quiet and comfortable homes, having exploited the city for their own advantage.

Home and Children

The growth of the suburbs necessarily meant tearing apart old neighborhoods and social customs and family connections. Yet suburbia presented a contradiction: it associated itself with a national celebration during the 1950s, virtually an ideology, of family and children. The time of the Baby Boom, which had actually begun a decade earlier, burst into full visibility—an increase in childbearing along with a determination to bring up children in just the right way. Marrying earlier, couples began having children at a younger age and more of them, often three or four. The Baby Boom resulted chiefly from the return of veterans of World War II, eager to begin the family life that war had postponed. Postwar prosperity now supplemented by veterans' benefits made it easier to rear children.

The years of the Baby Boom came with an intensely held attitude toward family and offspring. Although the calculated spacing of children had gone on in Western Europe and America for centuries, the norm had been for marriage, sex, and children—or sex, marriage, and children—to take their natural course. But in an age of technical and scientific method, family building and child raising became defined as planned acts, to be done with the aid of modern medicine and psychology.

The suburbs, for their defenders, seemed the appropriate place for the focused, carefully considered raising of children. The mother expected to remain at home, but not as a traditional upholder of feminine tasks and virtues. Advocates of modern domesticity called her a professional, an efficient operator of stoves and vacuum cleaners and washing machines, a student of proper diet. And during the 1950s clerical and other white-collar workers came to outnumber for the first time the traditional labor force. Although the father as the breadwinner returned from the city in the evening, calling out the "Hi, honey, I'm home" so often satirized today as a mantra of this bygone age, he would often participate fully in the activities of homemaking. This included sharing responsibilities with his wife, such as policing the children's studies or, without any threat to his status, perhaps donning an apron for

dishwashing. The upbringing of children usually incorporated the very latest in psychological and sociological findings. The experts dictated how to avoid too little or too much mothering, how to instruct children in right and wrong, and distinguished between adequate and inadequate discipline. Dr. Benjamin Spock, the arbiter of proper parenting, is widely remembered as a folk figure of the age.

The ethos of suburbia, family, and scientific childrearing supposedly frustrated and isolated the lives of the postwar Baby Boomers. The mentality that required a household of father, mother, and a couple of children or more is sometimes perceived as reinforcing the sterile sameness and conformity of suburban housing and the hypnosis of television. But it may make just as much sense to discover in midcentury family practices a desirable intensification of privacy and intimacy. Unlike her nine-

Most working women after World War II held low-paying jobs, often as telephone operators, secretaries, or waitresses. (Courtesy, AP/Wide World Photos)

teenth-century grandmother, moreover, the wife and homemaker was expected to be an enthusiastic bedmate. It served to solidify the marriage, it brought more children, and besides, new scientific research questioned older notions of female sexual passivity. Nor did women retreat from the workforce. The ideology of homemaking to the contrary, the proportion of woman wage earners rose in the fifties, constituting one in three married females, albeit most in clerical and other low-paying jobs. As for the children of the Boom, the extraordinary ability to question the established social and political order that some of them displayed in the later, heated years of civil rights and Vietnam, suggests that whatever they were trained to do, it was not a life of brainless conformity.

Television

Brainless conformity: that has been the common charge made against television during and after the 1950s. TV as its enemies have seen it turns millions into passive consumers disengaged from what they are watching. Observers during the 1950s worried that television absorbed an excessive portion of the attention of children, reducing the time they spent reading. Newton Minow, head of the Federal Communications Commission during John F. Kennedy's presidency in the early 1960s, called television "a vast wasteland."

Television reproduced older entertainment forms—the variety show, for example, and the newsreel—but it quickly moved to develop its own genres, notably the situation comedy or sitcom, which derived from radio comedy dramas. Programs like *The Adventures of Ozzie and Harriet* and *I Love Lucy* helped frame the portrait of family life being shaped in the decade. Lucy and her husband Ricky Ricardo frequently test familiar assumptions about the relationship between home and work, labor and child tending, men and women, with Lucy often envious of Rick's show business career. In the episode "Job Switching," the two, along with sidekicks Ethel and Fred, confidently trade men's work

A HOUSEWIFE OF THE 1950s

Joy Wilmer recounts her early years of marriage and motherhood and her struggle to accommodate herself to what Betty Friedan has termed the "feminine mystique."

"I felt totally fulfilled, totally happy. We were the perfect couple—Ted was supportive of me and I was supportive of him and we never argued. Well, we didn't know how. We'd had no experience with conflict. Everything was fine. I had my next child sixteen months after the first. The second child was neither exactly planned nor unplanned. I didn't really intend to get pregnant again, but on the other hand, we weren't using birth control because, after all, we already had *one.* . . .

After the second baby, that was the first time I can remember conflict, feelings of being trapped, wondering what I was doing with my life. These weren't very distinct feelings, not like I wonder if this is the right man for me. Just uncomfortable feelings. At some point I expressed some of these feelings, in a very tentative way, to Ted and he said, 'Well, if you feel that way, maybe we should get a divorce.' I was terrified. The idea of divorce was inconceivable. I never mentioned the subject again.

At the same time, I got such pleasure, real physiological pleasure from my children—from playing with them, feeding them, watching them develop. Then we moved and Ted went into general practice, and at about the same time I had another child. I became his secretary, his nurse, and I was also handling the children, keeping them out of his hair. And of course, we were also establishing our identity as the doctor and his wife, so there was a lot of socializing. It was a busy time.

What amazes me now is that it never occurred to me not to do this. His career was just my life. There came a time when I felt I didn't have the strength for all this and I started breaking down. I can remember going into the shower and screaming—in the shower so that no one could hear me. Even then I didn't have conscious thoughts of 'I hate this life'—I didn't think there was anything objectively wrong with the way I was living, just that I couldn't take it any more."

and feminine domesticity, only to find that women really do belong in the home and men on the job. Also intriguing about the series is the birth to the ethnically mixed couple of a son, Little Rickey. *Father Knows Best*, *Leave It to Beaver*, and *The Dick Van Dyke Show*, among many programs throughout the 1950s and 1960s, conveyed similar values. And Americans of that time tended to watch television differently from the way today's viewers do. They often clustered as families at specific times to watch specific programs, much as their parents had gathered together to listen to favorite radio shows. Early television was often about families watching families.

From radio, TV derived its method of paying for itself. After waging a strenuous campaign over how radio would finance its programming, advertisers had won out; television quickly adopted their system of sponsorship by commercials. And sponsorships that worked for radio would be applied directly to television. Beckoning, enticing, and nagging its viewers to buy for pleasure, fun, and luxury, advertisers appeared determined to sell to the postwar public not this or that product alone but consumption itself as a way of life. Yet these dramas of hard-working parents dedicating themselves to the upbringing of their lovably mischievous children told—like the police stories such as *Dragnet*—of a world more earnest and purposeful than pleasure-seeking. And so as the television screen might shift from a suburban living-room scene to a liquid detergent commercial and back again, the ad carried a message that went beyond its celebration of soap. It implicitly proclaimed that wise consumption builds a solid base for a society of middle-class virtues. Or so the advertisements hinted, even as they also promised a life of effortless luxury.

Rocket Cars

Over time, the cars of the 1950s increasingly seemed in motion, even as they sat on the showroom floor. Front ends tilted forward as if the hood were bypassing the wheel just as fins and rocketlike protrusions on the rear suggested that the car wanted to participate in the Cold War's space race. The chrome content increased markedly as well, so that eventually automobiles took on the look of shiny silver spacecraft. They became as much social statements as conveniences. For more settled generations, they said "money"; for young men on the prowl, they spoke of flash and style; for teenagers, they proclaimed a futuristic brand of power and speed. Each year new models emerged. Advertisers encouraged the purchase of new cars not on the basis of significant changes in performance, but through innovations in style alone.

Aiding the growth of the suburbs and benefiting from their expansion, spreading as well to city streets and the backcountry, the gas-guzzling American car of the 1950s even overshadowed television as the emblem of the era. By 1960 four in five American families owned a car or, in a few cases, more than one. Along with cars came hamburger stands, drive-in movies, and other manifestations of an automobile culture especially popular among adolescents. Much that the new plastic dishes called Tupperware embodied at midcentury had an opposite in automobiles: flash and glitter as opposed to usefulness, quickly changing models in contrast to the durability of Tupperware's designs.

Detroit and its advertising agencies relied in the 1950s on various appeals to vanity and self-assertion. Toward the end of the decade, though, the appeal faded, possibly because buyers began to sense that if every other car on the road is a clutter of fins and silver strips, one more of them could have little to say. Whatever the explanation, buyers started calling for smaller cars that offered economy and could fit into parking spaces. Sensible foreign cars such as the Volkswagen soon invaded the domestic market. Detroit, some of its leaders hiding their contempt for consumers they saw as seeking dowdy cheapness and practicality when they could be purchasing glamorous excess, began producing smaller models. In time the advertising industry would catch on to the inverse snobbery that allowed a Volkswagen owner silently to proclaim, "I know who I am: I don't need my car to do my speaking for me."

Buyers who did not go in for economy began choosing finless autos built for compact muscularity. But beyond their changes in style, automobiles had established themselves during the decade as icons of a separate youth subculture embracing cars, and set to music. Elvis Presley marked his success with the purchase of a pink Cadillac.

Rock' n' Roll

In 1955 appeared a movie, *The Blackboard Jungle*, and in its sound track a song, "Rock Around the Clock," performed by Bill Haley and the Comets.

TUPPERWARE AND THE STATUS OF WOMEN

Mingling invitations to pleasure with calls to virtue, television commercials suited American postwar prosperity. Even the anticommunism that became a part of the American creed fused with materialism. The parade of consumer goods was perceived as a triumphal contrast to Communist backwardness. Among the mixtures of moral conviction and consumerism, none was more remarkable than the making and selling of Tupperware.

Earl Tupper, living in rural New Hampshire and hard-pressed for cash, was self-taught, a correspondence school student, and an inventor. In accord with the legend of Yankee enterprise, he believed in the social value of his inventions, which aimed at fixing simple problems of everyday living. Early in his life, for example, he devised a cover for the rumble seat that used to pull out from the back of automobiles. That idea vanished with the disappearance of rumble seats. After various kinds of employment that included tree surgery, Tupper by arrangement with the Du Pont chemical company began making from plastic his astonishingly plain and serviceable kitchen goods. Plastic in its cheaper forms was a flimsy, unreliable material. But Tupper used a higher grade, and its clean and smooth surface seemed particularly suitable for storing food.

Tupper did not completely avoid ornamentation but his products became known for stark simplicity of design. A moralist, he denounced excess and luxury, and his kitchen products presented a statement of unpretentious usability. Yet simplicity and efficiency, when visibly embodied in modern products at their best, some art critics have perceived as capturing a kind of beauty. A number of Tupper's designs are on display at the Museum of Modern Art.

The Tupper enterprise, then, mated old-fashioned backcountry Yankee inventiveness to the advanced possibilities of the chemical industry, its chaste cups and containers casting silent judgment on the chrome and neon wastefulness of the United States in the 1950s. Tupper also had ideas of salesmanship that gave consumption moral meaning. He believed in advertising not as enticement but as information available for rational, well-planned living. But Tupper's attempt to sell his wares conventionally through advertising and store display had limited success. The enormous popularity of Tupperware owed instead to a device that he did not invent: the Tupperware party, which in the 1950s became the means of selling his products. The scheme of the parties belonged to Brownie Wise, a single mother and an especially successful mover of Tupper's goods. In 1951 she became a vice president of his company, in charge of Tupper Home Parties.

At a Tupperware party, a homemaker would invite a group of neighbors to an informal social gathering centering in a dealer, commonly also a neighbor, who showed and demonstrated the company's wares. The parties quickly became a female domain. The events were associated with the suburbs, where women who stayed at home could quickly assemble, eager to add to the inventory in their new houses. But Tupperware parties were also held in black and Hispanic neighborhoods, and eventually they would spread to foreign countries.

Tupperware parties generated enormous enthusiasm. The inspirational Brownie Wise led women across the country to want to earn some extra money. And becoming a part of the sales force took them into a world of excitement, material plenty, and communal effort. They believed in the product—rightly so—and even the shyest learned to believe in themselves as part of a far-reaching project. Brownie Wise had a frank appetite for rich material goods, the more so if they bore her favorite color—pink. And the splendor that radiated from her lavish Florida estate and from a palatial meeting center, also in Florida, added to the feeling of vastness, daring, and profit in the Tupperware venture.

Loving material things, Brownie Wise also enjoyed giving them away. The annual Tupperware Homecomings—the term suggests the sense of the sales force as a collegiate or family community—featured awards as well as seminars and speeches. The 1954 Homecoming asked Tupperware women to go on a treasure hunt, following clues to buried watches, rings, even a toy automobile that could be traded for the real thing. So far was the mentality of Brownie Wise from that of Tupper that before the end of the decade he had in effect fired her. But her enthusiastic salesmanship and her embrace of luxury represented self-confident, productive, cheerful living that blended with an American strain drawing in part on religious sources. As instructors in the many uses of Tupperware, women shared a form of knowledge that belonged to

their own daily living. Earlier in the century, ambitious women had claimed that their gender equipped them for the nurturing but professional role of social worker or health provider. Now once again an activity appeared that provided some women a distinctively female point of intersection between the private and the public sphere.

The action takes place in the high school of a poor urban neighborhood, not a suburb. Its story has since become a convention: troubled angry youth (one of them black, which for its time was something of an advance) won over by a tough but caring teacher. The song, short on words and memorable for a hard ragged beat, was an important part of the story. The most redeemable of the students, the viewers understand, will go on to adult lives of work and respectability; the song signifies the youthful world of sex and violence that for a time they inhabit. The music is rooted deep in American social history.

Early in the twentieth century, Memphis, Tennessee, a rough-and-tumble town on the Mississippi River, had been the destination for rural black southerners seeking a better existence. Blacks gathered around Beale Street and its surroundings, and the neighborhood became rowdy and rich in the culture, the pleasures, and the music of the black South. In Memphis blues developed into a sophisticated urban artistic form. By midcentury the city vibrated with the music of both races, hillbilly, popular, gospel, and blues.

In 1948 WDIA transformed itself into an early assertively black radio station, presenting over the airwaves gospel, blues, and a newer energetic variant since known as rhythm and blues. Recognizing that the city's mixture of musical strains attracted an interracial audience, the program "Red, Hot and Blue" began ranging all the way from black gospel to white country. White adolescents not only invited African American bands to play at their parties but attended musical revues at a local black theater, though made to sit in roped-off white sections.

Sam Phillips, an enthusiast for the music coming out of Memphis who founded Sun Records, looked

for one thing: "If I could find a white man who had the Negro sound, the Negro feel," he said, "I could make a billion dollars." In Elvis Presley he found that man, his first recording pairing with the free flying blues "That's All Right," written by the black bluesman Arthur Crudup, and the bluegrass classic "Blue Moon of Kentucky" by Bill Monroe, a white singer. Like Elvis, lots of southern whites could sing black for fun. Accounts of the session that produced "That's All Right" emphasize the moment in which Presley shifted from just goofing around to realizing that black style provided the critical element in his personal synthesis of country, gospel, and blues. Black writers of Presley's music never received much compensation. Elvis, the best known performer to cross the racial line, stood along with rock 'n' roll in a long history of social mixing, a history that starkly contrasted with the legal and political prohibitions meant to keep the races apart.

When Sam Phillips helped Elvis Presley pull together pop-gospel, R and B, hillbilly and blues, he combined Memphis's musical forms to jump the color line. Rock 'n' roll was born. That the country singer Johnny Cash was another Sun discovery reveals the breadth of musical innovation happening in Memphis. Carl Perkins's "Blue Suede Shoes," cut at Sun Records in 1956, scored a hit in the pop, R and B, and hillbilly listings. No longer a single genre, the music was self-procreating in ever-new varieties.

By the mid-fifties black performers of rock 'n' roll, among them Fats Domino and Chuck Berry, began playing before general audiences, while whites put out their own versions of the music. As much for its pulse as for its lyrics, the music quickly came to represent among friends and opponents alike adolescent energies on the loose. At the same time,

Chuck Berry. (Courtesy, AP Photo/Mark Duncan)

Elvis Presley. (Courtesy, AP Photo)

more sedately romantic songs targeted the same age group. Elvis, his fame certified when he appeared on the Ed Sullivan television show in 1956, bridged these two types of music. To the rhythms of rock 'n' roll, he added hip movements that shocked the preservers of morality. But in personal style and manner he was hopelessly clean. Such songs as "Love Me Tender" and "Don't Say Don't" put him among the more sentimental performers of his day. Dick Clark's popular television program *American Bandstand* also assisted in bringing rock together with tamer music; all of it aimed at the increasingly affluent young.

The Crossing of Racial Boundaries

In the last years of the 1950s, Berry Gordy, Jr., developed his own vision of musical race crossing, founding Motown Records in an effort to reach out not only to black listeners but to the white audiences who followed Presley and others. Stylistically appealing and efficient as an automobile assembly line, Motown came to be a smash success, far beyond the scope of Sun Records. And Gordy's Detroit sound would furnish the soundtrack for white Americans for decades to come.

Rock 'n' roll, whatever its social composition, provided the music; juvenile delinquency, a major obsession for older Americans worried about the

young, set the theme; Detroit supplied the mobile chrome and grillwork. Teenage Americans heard repeatedly that they belonged to a special, separate group, whether urban tough, suburban spoiled or, with the young actor James Dean, troubled and lost amid adults incapable of understanding them. In that last perception of themselves they could turn as well to Holden Caulfield, the troubled prep school boy betrayed by peers and grownups in J. D. Salinger's *Catcher in the Rye*. Published in 1951, before the youth culture was fully defined, it has continued to be one of the most important novels in defining an adolescent sensibility.

Cracking the Barriers

Active discontent with white supremacy came of experiences of the Second World War. Black veterans returned home with a new expectation of equality. Many had toured the world, been accorded a measure of respect, fought for this country, watched friends die for it. Taking advantage of the postwar GI Bill of Rights, which enabled a few to acquire a college education, a new generation of leaders arose ready to challenge the social status quo.

Segregation of black southerners took such forms as separate water fountains, restrooms, schools, and restaurants; rules forced blacks to give up seats to white bus riders; restrictions abounded on voting, housing, and work; hostility appeared in signs proclaiming "No dogs or niggers." Unknown to most black and white Americans were other signs around the country that read "No dogs or Indians" or "No dogs or Mexicans." And while American minority groups have rarely formed effective coalitions in struggling against these conditions, they have waged parallel battles.

Following the war, Mexican American veterans organized the GI Forum, which began as an effort to lobby for veterans' rights and soon changed into an organization committed to political and social reform, particularly in schools and police brutality cases. The Latino organization LULAC, founded in 1929 and standing for League of United Latin American Citizens, had long been active in legal work. In *Mendez* v. *Westminster School District*, a Supreme Court case decided in 1946, and *Delgado* v. *Bastrop Independent School District*, which came in 1948, six years before the more celebrated *Brown* v. *Board of Education*, Hispanics won victories. In both, the Court declared unconstitutional the educational segregation of Mexican children. But not until another series of decisions in the 1970s did the courts rule that ethnic separation, such as Latinos had endured, can be as damaging as racial segregation.

American Indians confronted additional problems. The very experience of wartime integration led some in the national legislature to push the assimilationist agenda with a new insistence. Indians had done well in the war, the argument went, and a campaign to resettle them from rural reservations to urban work would allow the government to shed obligations to Indian tribes that formal treaties had obliged it to honor. Termination and relocation, the names of the resulting programs, aimed to end the tribal governments established during the New Deal. However well-meaning, termination threatened standing conditions under which Native Americans had arranged their lives. Indian leaders, mobilizing in both tribal settings and the National Congress of American Indians, spent much of the later 1950s fighting them off.

All this points to the complicated state of racial relations in the postwar United States. Latinos and blacks fought for equal rights and access to American institutions, while most Indian people fought against assimilation into those very institutions. At the same time, some whites began experimenting in the crossing of boundaries at once racial and cultural. One such group Norman Mailer described as "looking for action with a black man's code to fit their facts." He spoke of a movement of literary and cultural rebels who became known by the label Beat Generation.

The Beats

The term "Beat" has been taken to signify the state of being beaten down and driven to rebellion by the dead conformity of American society, and at the same time to refer to the beatific vision sought by mystics. It also suggests the beat of jazz. In drugs, jazz, and experimenting with new forms of writing, the Beats sought to expand the boundaries of consciousness. In the practice of Asian philosophy and mysticism, they pursued higher spiritual awareness or reunion with a cosmos from which they believed humankind had succeeded in alienating itself. Severed from conventional society, the Beats responded to primal American energies and experiences: big modern cities, or the endless spaces of the continent.

Jack Kerouac's semi-autobiographical novel *On the Road,* which did much to popularize the Beats, takes its inspiration from the open land. Published in 1957, *On the Road* narrates a lyrical account of trips, internal consciousness trips drug-induced and jazz-inspired, but mostly road trips with the narrator's crazy friend Dean Moriarty at the wheel, Dean's rantings a kind of poetry. Allen Ginsberg, a homosexual openly defiant of sexual conventions and a pacifist hostile to all institutions of power, capitalist and Communist, in 1956 contributed his long poem "Howl" that sings of the mad visionaries of the movement. Kerouac's writings drew on the vast backcounty; Ginsberg and his work were rooted in the American city. His poem "Sunflower Sutra" finds in a tough, soot-covered sunflower growing beside rusting iron a symbol of life that gains dignity from the discarded metal.

In the fifties the Beat style attracted followers on college campuses and elsewhere. In coffeehouses scattered across the country, musicians played jazz or folk music and poets chanted improvised verse. And as far as the Beats stood from the adolescent society—they were a decade or so older—inevitably there would be intersections. Perhaps most notable in kinship to the Beats was the figure of James

Beat poet Allen Ginsberg. (Courtesy, UPI / Corbis-Bettmann)

Dean, who in life and on the screen embodied pained and questing youth: a *Rebel Without a Cause*, as his best-known film was titled.

THE EISENHOWER ERA

President Dwight D. Eisenhower presided for two terms over the unstable peace that followed the end of the Korean War. Given to finding workable compromises in place of political confrontations, unwilling to sound too vigorously the alarms about international Communism that had become a staple of right-wing rhetoric, Eisenhower gave much of the era a calm that has come to be associated with his name.

The age took some of its tone as well from a new kind of religiosity that reflected in part a reaction against the militant atheism of the Communists. A celebration of material abundance, an outpouring of consumerism, and a contented churchgoing religion abided comfortably together. The Roman Catholic Bishop Fulton Sheen, an electrifying television speaker, had a gaze startlingly piercing and insistent, as though his eyes called his viewers to truth. More typical was the Protestant minister Norman Vincent Peale, whose soothing version of Christianity seemed eminently compatible with worldly success and tranquillity.

Worries still abounded about the decline in

James Dean posing for the movie Rebel Without a Cause. (Courtesy, Movie Still Archives)

738 • Chapter 23   Warm Hearths and a Cold War

American character and morality. Studies by the professor of zoology Alfred Kinsey on the sexual behavior of men and women distressed the prudish. Warnings spread about the effect of sexually graphic comic books on the morals of the young. And concern continued over the possible connection between rock music and juvenile delinquency. But all this coexisted with a secure conviction that overall the nation's spiritual health remained sound.

A Moderate Republicanism

The first important popular vote that Eisenhower faced came not in the general election of 1952 but in the Republican presidential primaries that preceded it. Eisenhower competed for his party's nomination with Robert A. Taft, the highly respected head of the conservative and isolationist wing of the party. One reason that Eisenhower, who basically disliked politics, entered the race in the first place was his fear of an isolationist gaining the presidency. The struggle, then, was for the soul of the Republican Party. Yet however sharp and important the ideological issues, the primary campaigns revolved about clashing personalities. Eisenhower's popularity and personal amiability had their perfect foil in Taft's frigid integrity. The general's unwillingness to be a dynamic campaigner made him seem fatherly and statesmanlike; Taft's equally great reserve came out as cold aloofness. Predictably, the general won the nomination.

To Americans who considered winning wars a national birthright, the Truman administration was unable to explain why the country could not win the Korean War. Burdened by the war, the Democrats twice nominated, in 1952 and 1956, a candidate personally admirable in many ways but politically hopeless. Adlai Stevenson, governor of Illinois, was intelligent, thoughtful, witty, and except in his hesitancy to address the issue of civil rights, an apparent embodiment of the liberal intellectual in politics. In 1960, in the candidacy of John F. Kennedy, the formula would work. The year 1952 was not yet the right time.

That November Eisenhower garnered over fifty-five percent of the popular vote. His presidency would end the bitter conflicts of the preceding few years. His political management of the office made it clear that the New Deal, which he had no intention of overturning, was firmly lodged in the country's institutional structure. It also became clear

that Cold War policy would follow the lines laid down by the Democrats. Both realities angered the right wing of the Republican Party, which became frustrated with the president in a way that the Democrats would not begin to match. Never pushing government beyond what the public would easily tolerate, Ike initiated few new programs. But he supported measures in the liberal vein, among them increasing the number of people eligible for Social Security benefits. He added to the presidential cabinet a Department of Health, Education, and Welfare, and in a mild contribution to social change appointed as its first secretary a woman, Oveta Culp Hobby.

The Cold War at Home and Abroad

To be his secretary of state, Eisenhower chose John Foster Dulles. A rigid moralist, Dulles defined Communism as irredeemably evil. Leftist regimes he considered to be manipulated by Communists, natural allies to that ideology, or simply bad in themselves. In 1953 the Central Intelligence Agency arranged a coup in Iran that removed the nationalist premier Mohammed Mossadegh, replacing him with a royal family more cooperative toward American interests. The intervention insured a flow of Iranian oil to the West. The following year the CIA, with the approval of the administration, maneuvered the overthrow in Guatemala of a progressive government, and in its place would come a succession of regimes, many of them brutally repressive internally but friendly to capitalism and to Washington.

During Eisenhower's presidency, however, the Soviet Union and the United States moved closer to accommodation than had seemed imaginable in the Truman years. The calmer relations began with a truce that the Republican administration arranged in 1953 with the Communist forces in Korea. No better than anything Truman could have achieved, it nonetheless stopped the killing. Thereafter Washington set on a course aimed at stabilizing the world.

An Uneasy Peace

Behind Eisenhower's thinking lay the assumption that nuclear weapons could by themselves insure the peace. His administration adopted a policy it called the "New Look," which involved build-

President Dwight D. Eisenhower. (Courtesy, Eisenhower Presidential Library)

Governor Adlai E. Stevenson of Illinois, the Democratic candidate for president in 1952 and 1956. (Courtesy, Scribner's Archives)

ing up an arsenal of nuclear bombs and a capability for delivering them. This, the idea went, would deter any major Communist aggression. The New Look allowed Eisenhower to work for cutbacks in conventional military spending, which suited his craving for economy in government. He once observed, in language to be expected more from a liberal than from a conservative, that every weapon means money stolen from the cold and the hungry. And the New Look, despite the horrifying images it evoked of a world devastated by nuclear war, seemed at the time a force for stability. It implied that there need be no more Koreas, no rushed military deployment from one flash point to another to resist a Communist invasion or insurgency.

During the Eisenhower presidency, intervention in Guatemala provided an instance of the Washington practice of letting clients in Latin America do the killing and the repressing there. In 1954 and into the next year the mainland Chinese Communists shelled the offshore islands of Quemoy and

Matsu, held by the anticommunist Chinese who had fled to Taiwan. Eisenhower pledged to protect the exile regime against a direct Communist attack, but resisted demands for a war on the mainland Chinese. In the same year Eisenhower made his wisest decision: he remained out of the conflict between French and native forces in Vietnam. Even though Vice President Nixon and Secretary of State Dulles pleaded with him to lend air support to the failing French forces at the battle of Dienbienphu, Eisenhower would not do so. He would not allow the United States to risk another land war in Asia. He preferred conciliation to confrontation. In the autumn of 1956, following a partially successful uprising in Poland against Communist rule, Hungarians rose in rebellion against their country's virtual occupation by the Soviet Union. Soviet tanks and troops crushed the insurrection. While the rebels pleaded over radio for Western aid and refugees streamed across the Hungarian border, the anticommunist world watched furious and grieving, but passive. That same autumn, Israeli, British, and French troops invaded Egypt to secure the Suez Canal against control by the Egyptian nationalist regime of Gamal Abdel Nasser. But in a session at the United Nations, Washington actually joined with the USSR in condemning the action, and the invaders withdrew. Eisenhower stationed American troops in Lebanon to quell a civil disturbance threatening Western interests, but the intervention was short, surgical, and safe.

Civil Defense and the Bomb

As terrible as an atomic war would have been in the 1950s, the tonnage of the bombs and the sophistication of planes did not make survival unthinkable. Federal and local authorities therefore instituted air-raid drills for saving lives during a possible nuclear attack. Occasionally sirens in one city or town would test the warning system. Schoolchildren trained to fall down, pull clothing over exposed skin, and thereby prepare for the flash following an atomic explosion—searing, and yet so brief that a simple cloth would supposedly exhaust its heat before human skin had been burned. A song instructed Americans to "duck and cover," and film footage showed how a child could flatten for safety. A flurry of underground bomb-shelter construction took place on private residences. Citizens could follow government advice on what to store there and how long to wait after a nuclear attack before people could safely emerge. The bomb-shelter fad led to unpleasant discussions about whether a family that had built one could in good conscience exclude intruders seeking to stay alive.

Especially harrowing to the imagination was not the bomb blast itself but the radioactivity, silent and invisible as it seeps through the air. In the movie *Rocketship XM*, released in 1950, a space crew landing on Mars discovers a civilization destroyed by atomic warfare, its ruins still saturated with radioactivity. *THEM!*, a 1954 film, portrays ants made enormous by mutation from atomic testing. The surface of earth in the 1956 production *World Without End*, set in 2508 after an atomic war, is covered with monstrosities, great spiderlike creatures and other fearsome mutations that have driven normal human beings underground. The Japanese film industry had a peculiar fascination for the effects of atomic war, understandable in light of Hiroshima and Nagasaki. The best-known product is

the monster Godzilla, revived by atomic testing and endowed with radioactive breath.

Making Peace

In July 1955 world leaders met at Geneva, among them Premier Nikolai Bulganin and the Soviet Communist Party secretary Nikita Khrushchev representing a new government in the USSR following the death of Joseph Stalin in 1953. The gathering proved remarkable for its lack of hostility. There President Eisenhower offered his open-skies proposal: the USSR and the United States each would open its skies to aerial photography from the other and thereby lessen any suspicion of a planned surprise attack. France and Britain endorsed the idea, but the Soviet leadership rejected it. The proposal was more notable than the rejection, and the meeting ended so amicably that for a time commentators referred to a "spirit of Geneva."

More startling yet was a speech that Khrushchev made in February 1956 to the Twentieth Congress of the Soviet Communist Party. Given in secret but leaked to the world, the talk denounced the murders and the general criminality of the era presided over by Stalin. Khrushchev called for a saner leadership structure and suggested that a shooting war between Communism and capitalism might not be inevitable. Khrushchev said he preferred a war of ideas. Yet any notion that the USSR might be moving into a period of worldwide cooperation evaporated late that year when Moscow brutally crushed the Hungarian uprising. But the speech, together with Khrushchev's firm grip on power, made it plain that the worst horrors of Communism in its early years in power were ending. Thereafter, the USSR would be ruled by a repressive but not a pathologically murderous regime.

Together Geneva and Khrushchev's speech ushered in a time remembered by the phrase "peaceful coexistence." Tensions lessened, but far from completely. In 1957 the Soviet Union humiliated the United States by launching the first two satellites to circle the earth, Sputnik and Sputnik II. The second satellite, weighing over half a ton, carried a little pioneer of space exploration, the dog Laika. Instruments attached to this first earth creature in space could communicate information about the effects of space travel on life forms. Demonstrating that the USSR could construct a missile with enough thrust to make possible the launching of

Children in an elementary school during the Korean War "duck and cover" to dodge the effects of a possible atomic bomb. (Courtesy, UPI/Corbis-Bettmann)

nuclear warheads against Western targets, Sputnik humbled Americans convinced until then of their scientific and technical superiority. The West had been assuming that nuclear strikes could come only from conventional bombers; now it appeared that they might come from missiles, possibly delivered from space itself. Though in missile development the Soviet Union appeared to be ahead of the West, Sputnik did not make the Cold War more directly confrontational. But it caused panic nonetheless. Renewed efforts went into America's own space program, and in 1958 the National Defense Education Act provided graduate fellowships for study in American universities.

In the summer of 1959, Vice President Nixon toured the Soviet Union, crowds gathering to catch a glimpse of him. At a display of the kitchen of an American home set up in Moscow, Nixon engaged in a debate with Khrushchev, arguing for the greater ability of American capitalism to turn out consumer goods. Quickly called the kitchen debate, it boosted the visibility of Eisenhower's vice president. Nixon's defiance of a Latin American mob that attacked his car while he was on a trip a year before had already given him a public image for toughness, enabling him to emerge from the obscurity that went with being second in office to the popular Eisenhower.

In September the Soviet leader visited the United States. For the most part it was a friendly occasion, though marked with flashes of temper and boasting on the part of the blunt and earthy Khrushchev. The trip ended with a meeting at Camp David, the presidential retreat in Maryland.

The exchange went cordially enough to make for talk of a "spirit of Camp David."

Yet the final public relations between the Soviet and the American leader went sour. In 1960 the Soviet military shot down deep within the USSR an American U-2 spy plane flown by Francis Gary Powers. The United States had long been secretly conducting such flights, fearing the inadequacy of other means of gathering information about military activities in the Soviet Union. Powers, convicted of spying, later gained release. Khrushchev reacted angrily to the event, abruptly leaving a summit meeting in Paris and putting Eisenhower in the awkward position of having to travel home empty-handed and rebuffed.

END OF AN ERA

Eisenhower's final years in office were not his best. Along with the U-2 incident, Sputnik and Moscow's successful launching of a moon rocket unsettled Americans. A series of recessions questioned the ability of a Republican administration to manage the economy. In the midterm elections of 1958 the Democrats, already in control of both houses of Congress, dealt the Republicans a smashing defeat. Fidel Castro's guerrilla movement in 1959 overthrew a repressive government friendly to the United States and set up an oppressive regime of another kind, though more attentive to problems of poverty and illiteracy. Washington and Castro quickly adopted a mutual dislike, and Castro

"We annually spend on military security more than the net income of all United States corporations.

This conjunction of an immense military establishment and a large arms industry is new in the American experience. The total influence— economic, political, even spiritual—is felt in every city, every State house, every office of the Federal government. We recognize the imperative need for this development. Yet we must not fail to comprehend its grave implications . . .

In the councils of government, we must guard against the acquisition of unwarranted influence, whether sought or unsought, by the military-industrial complex. The potential for the disastrous rise of misplaced power exists and will persist.

We must never let the weight of this combination endanger our liberties or democratic processes. . . . I confess that I lay down my official responsibilities in this field with a definite sense of disappointment."

President Dwight D. Eisenhower
Farewell Address, 1961

turned to Moscow for support. Beyond these particular setbacks a broadening attack developed among Democrats and social commentators on the Republican administration for allowing the nation's energies to go torpid. Education, said the critics, lacked rigor; students were becoming soft and lazy. Democrats claimed that the Republicans had allowed the development of a missile gap, an excess of Soviet over American nuclear missile power. The Democrats were essentially accusing the Republicans of being insufficiently militant cold warriors.

The benign elderly president could have taken that last as a compliment. He had never found much good in activity for its own sake. Against the insistence that the country have more and better weapons, he once observed that since the United States had the ability to destroy an enemy, any further destructive power would be pointless. Eisenhower, not some leftist Democrat, made the first explicit public warnings about the military-industrial complex, a system of mutual self-interest between the military and the industries that produce for it. During Eisenhower's tenure his avoidance of confrontation had made for some major failings: a hesitancy to stop McCarthy and an inability to see that black Americans deserved more than counsels of patience. But his dislike of bold adventure left the country, at least for a while, at peace of a kind.

Suggested Readings

A broad view of the conduct of the Cold War is David Reynolds's *One World Divisible: A Global History since 1945* (2000). Deborah Welch Larson offers a psychological portrait of the antagonism in *Anatomy of Mistrust: U.S.-Soviet Relations during the Cold War* (1997), and John Lewis Gaddis, *The Long Peace: Inquiries into the History of the Cold War* (1987) emphasizes that the nuclear stalemate between the Soviet Union and the United States resulted in a long period of peace and stability. Martin Walker's *The Cold War: A History* (1994) is a comprehensive study that claims neither side won the Cold War. William Curti Wohlforth in *The Elusive Balance: Power and Perceptions during the Cold War* (1933) compares the Soviet Union's assumptions about the balance of power with those of the United States. Walter LaFeber, *America, Russia, and the Cold War, 1945–1996*, 8th ed. (1997) attributes the Cold War to American efforts to expand the capitalist free market. H. W. Brands in *The Devil We Knew: Americans and the Cold War* (1993) believes that both sides to the conflict share responsibility for the Cold War. Lynn Boyd Hinds and Theodore Otto Windt, Jr., *The Cold War as Rhetoric: The Beginnings, 1945–1950* (1991) and Martin J. Medhurst, et al., *Cold War Rhetoric: Strategy, Metaphor, and Ideology* (1990) are postmodernist interpretations of the Cold War that view it principally as a problem in language and political communication. Louis J. Halle, a former member of the State Department, claims in *The Cold War as History* (1991) that the United States sought to preserve the balance of power in Europe as a response to Soviet incursions into Eastern Europe.

Other recent general histories of Cold War foreign policy include Fraser J. Harbutt, *The Cold War Era* (2002); Ronald E. Powaski, *The Cold War: the United States and the Soviet Union, 1917–1991* (1998); S. J. Ball, *The Cold War: An International History, 1947-1991* (1998); Ralph B. Levering, *The Cold War: A Post-Cold War History* (1994); and John F. N. Bradley, *War and Peace since 1945: A History of Soviet-Western Relations* (1989). See also David S. Painter, *The Cold War: An International History* (1999); Joseph

Smith, *The Cold War, 1945–1991*, 2nd ed. (1998); and John W. Mason, *The Cold War, 1945-1991* (1996).

On the origins of the Cold War, Thomas J. McCormick, *America's Half-Century: United States Foreign Policy in the Cold War* (1989) is a good example of revisionist historiography. McCormick sets the Cold War in the context of what he sees as the naturally expansionist nature of Western capitalism. Thomas G. Paterson, *On Every Front: The Making and Unmaking of the Cold War*, Rev. ed. (1992) is also a good introduction to Cold War revisionist history. Paterson's study offers a temperate assessment that locates the conflict in the failures in leadership in both the Soviet Union and the United States. Daniel Yergin, *Shattered Peace: The Origins of the Cold War and the National Security State* (1977) also indicts both contestants. Melvyn P. Leffler, *The Specter of Communism: The United States and the Origins of the Cold War, 1917–1953* (1994) claims that American policymakers failed to understand the Soviet concerns for national security. James L. Gormly, *From Potsdam to the Cold War: Big Three Diplomacy, 1945–1947* (1990) recognizes that both superpowers had legitimate interests in the postwar world, but blames the United States for exaggerating the differences with Moscow. Randall B. Woods and Howard Jones, *Dawning of the Cold War: The United States' Quest for Order* (1991) argues that the United States was responding to a genuine threat from the Soviet Union.

Among studies that focus on President Truman's diplomatic policies are Michael J. Hogan, *A Cross of Iron: Harry S Truman and the Origins of the National Security State, 1945–1954* (1998), which by and large favors Truman's handling of national security issues, and Melvyn P. Leffler, *A Preponderance of Power: National Security, the Truman Administration and the Cold War* (1992), a revisionist history that is critical of Truman's policies and believes that had the United States been more understanding of Soviet security interests the Cold War might have been avoided. See also Arnold A. Offner's *Another Such Victory: President Truman and the Cold War, 1945–1953* (2002), which offers a critical view of Truman's foreign policy.

On nuclear strategy between the United States and the Soviet Union, see David Holloway, who examines Soviet nuclear thinking in two studies, *The Soviet Union and the Arms Race*, 2nd ed. (1984) and *Stalin and the Bomb: The Soviet Union and Atomic Energy, 1939–1956* (1994). Patrick Glynn, *Closing Pandora's Box: Arms Races, Arms Control, and the History of the Cold War* (1992) argues that American military strength had the effect of deterring aggression. Soviet strategy is described in Vojtech Mastny, *The Cold War and Soviet Insecurity: The Stalin Years* (1996), which relies heavily on the recently opened Soviet archives to support the claim that the Cold War was the consequence of Stalin's excessive insecurity. The United States policy of containment is best articulated by George F. Kennan, who published his thinking under the pseudonym "X" in a long article, "The sources of Soviet Conduct," for the journal *Foreign Affairs* (July,1947): 566–582. Kennan reflects on the Cold War and his years in the Foreign Service in two volumes of autobiography, *Memoirs* (1967-72), and in a later account of global politics, *At a Century's Ending: Reflections, 1982–1995* (1996). Secretary of State Dean Acheson has told his own story in a brilliant memoir, *Present at the Creation: My Years in the State Department* (1969). Acheson has attracted a number of biographers, most recently James Chace, *Acheson: The Secretary of State Who Created the American World* (1998).

See also Walter Isaacson and Evan Thomas, *The Wise Men: Six Friends and the World they Made: Acheson, Bohlen, Harriman, Kennan, Lovett, McCloy* (1986).

The story of the Berlin Blockade is described by Thomas Parrish, *Berlin in the Balance 1945-1949: The Blockade, the Airlift, the First Major Battle of the Cold War* (1999). For the origins of NATO, see Don Cook, *Forging the Alliance: NATO 1945–1950* (1989). The United Nations and its origins are discussed in Townsend Hoopes and Douglas Brinkley, *FDR and the Creation of the U.N.* (1997).

Communism in the United States is the topic of Robbie Lieberman's *the Strangest Dream: Communism, Anticommunism, and the U.S. Peace Movement, 1945–1963* (2000), and Kate Weigand, *Red Feminism: American Communism and the Making of Women's Liberation* (2001). David Caute's *The Great Fear: The Anti-Communist Purge under Truman and Eisenhower* (1978) gives a comprehensive study of the anticommunist crusade in the United States. Richard Gid Powers, *Not without Honor: The History of American Anticommunism* (1995) is a history of the conservatives who contributed so much to the crusade and find that, despite the presence of some fanatics, the anticommunist movement was necessary and successful, an important force contributing to Communism's ultimate collapse. Concerning the prosecution of the Communist leadership in the U.S., see Stanley I. Kutler, *The American Inquisition: Justice and Injustice in the Cold War* (1982); Ronald Radosh and Joyce Milton, *The Rosenberg File*, 2nd ed. (1997); and Allen Weinstein, *Perjury: The Hiss-Chambers Case*, Updated ed. (1997). Whitaker Chambers, Hiss's accuser presents the trial and the background in his own story in the brilliantly written *Witness* (1952), and Sam Tanenhaus, *Whittaker Chambers: A Biography* (1997), chronicles the life of this complex and tragic figure.

For a general solid study of the Marshall Plan, see Michael J. Hogan, *The Marshall Plan: America, Britain, and the Reconstruction of Western Europe, 1947–1952* (1987). And on party politics during the late 1940s, see Gary A. Donaldson, *Truman Defeats Dewey* (1999). The McCarthy era in the early 1950s is studied in Ellen Schrecker, *Many Are the Crimes: McCarthyism in America* (1998), and in David M. Oshinsky, *A Conspiracy So Immense: The World of Joe McCarthy* (1983), which is a first-class biography of the man and the atmosphere of suspicion and fear that he helped to create.

Bruce Cumings has written a massive two-volume study of *The Origins of the Korean War: Liberation and the Emergence of Separate Regimes, 1945–1947*, Vol. 1 (1981) and Vol. 2, *The Origins of the Korean War: The Roaring of the Cataract, 1947–1950* (1990). William Stueck in two works, *Rethinkng the Korean War: A New Diplomatic and Strategic History* (2002) and *The Korean War: An International History* (1995), describes the diplomatic history surrounding the war. Stueck fixes responsibility for the war with Moscow, which sponsored and supported the North Korean Communists.

The Eisenhower presidency is examined in Chester J. Pach, Jr. and Elmo Richardson, *The Presidency of Dwight D. Eisenhower*, Rev. ed. (1994). The essays in Richard H. Immerman, ed., *John Foster Dulles and the Diplomacy of the Cold War* (1989) debate the virtues and wrongs of Secretary of State Dulles's policymaking. How containment led to intervention is the subject of David L. Anderson, *Trapped by Success: The Eisenhower Administration and Vietnam, 1953–1961* (1991).

Here Anne Moody and her friends are abused at the Woolworth's lunch counter in Jackson, Mississippi, in 1963. Moody's popular book about her experience is entitled *Coming of Age in Mississippi.* *(Courtesy, State Historical Society of Wisconsin)*

Politics Takes to the Streets

CHAPTER

24

★

COMING OF AGE IN MISSISSIPPI

Early in the morning of May 28, 1963, three students from Mississippi's black Tougaloo College, two of them women, sat down in the white section of a Woolworth's lunch counter in the state capital of Jackson. Soon the manager turned off the lights at the counter and roped the area. For the better part of an hour the three sat unserved in the darkened space, from which the waitress had retreated. The police waited outside Woolworth's, sufficiently law-abiding to obey a court injunction against arresting the three demonstrators but not enough to protect them.

By early afternoon a crowd of whites had gathered, and for a few minutes they contented themselves with taunts. The three students could ignore these. Then a group of white men rushed them. After the sole male student, Memphis Norman, had been thrown to the floor, Anne Moody and Pearlina Lewis were knocked off their seats, but got right back on them. Norman meanwhile was being stomped as he lay bleeding on the floor. A plainclothes policeman arrested both the battered Norman and, remarkably for Mississippi, his segregationist attacker—both, in the thinking of the lawman, having disturbed the peace. The swelling white mob added its opinions to the mayhem: "bitch," "whore," "go back to Russia," "sheeeyiiit." A crowd-pleasing young blonde swirled forward, dumped mustard on the unmoving students, received the applause of the onlookers, and then faded back into the crowd.

The harassment continued as the wrath of the mob found more to feed on. Two white women stepped forward and sat down at the counter, along with a white man and three male black students. Then Pearlina Lewis and one of the new recruits, Joan Trumpauer, were dragged by the hair toward the doors but broke free and ran back to the counter. A white boy hit one of the seated black male students on the head with a metal object. The victim, dazed, fell to the floor, then regained consciousness and pulled himself back onto his seat. Another white boy brought down his brass-knuckled hands on the white male demonstrator, John Salter, and then spray-painted words of hate on the backs of the impassive men and women at the counter. People at the rear of the crowd now hurled ashtrays, napkin holders, and bottles of ketchup. Only closing the store ended the mounting violence, which had been punctuated throughout by the flash of news cameras.

The episode represented a particular character of the civil rights movement that made it one of the most distinctive political and social events in the nation's history. Nonviolent resistance to injustice had recurred in the American past. Religious pacifists who went to prison for refusing to support the American participation in the First World War were notable contributors to a tradition of nonviolent disobedience. But never before had the spirituality of nonviolent action so closely allied itself with a practical technique of social change. It was perfectly fitted to the rights movement. Nonviolence amounted to a statement of peace and reconciliation against the violence of white supremacy. Its habit of studied calm was a way of saying that emotions, including the passions of racism and the anger of the victims of racism, could be brought under control. And its contrast to the stupid and self-defeating conduct of the white mobs enabled whites previously indifferent to race issues to see that a time of change was arriving.

Amid all the ugliness confronting Anne Moody and her fellow demonstrators came moments of redeeming civility. During the first relatively quiet forty-five minutes, one young white woman at the counter did not flee with the other customers but quite deliberately finished her breakfast before leaving. And a middle-aged white customer walked up to the three seated African American students and excused herself, saying that she would have liked to stay but her husband was waiting. In such small gestures lay the possibility of an alternative racial future.

HISTORICAL EVENTS

1954
Brown v. *Board of Education of Topeka, Kansas*

1955
Montgomery bus boycott

1956
Allen Ginsberg reads "Howl"

1957
Jack Kerouac publishes *On the Road* • Little Rock's Central High School is desegregated

1960
John F. Kennedy elected president • Greensboro sit-ins

1961
Bay of Pigs • Alliance for Progress • Berlin Wall • Freedom Rides

1962
Cuban Missile Crisis

1963
March on Washington • Test Ban Treaty • Kennedy is assassinated • Lyndon Johnson becomes president

1964
Civil Rights Act of 1964 • Economic Opportunity Act • Johnson elected president • Freedom Summer

1965
Voting Rights Act • Medicare and Medicaid • Water Quality Act • Malcolm X assassinated • Great Society Program initiated: Elementary and Secondary School Act, Head Start, Job Corps, and other programs

THE CIVIL RIGHTS MOVEMENT

The demonstrators at Woolworth's had been practicing a discipline known as nonviolence involving open but peaceful defiance of an institution or social custom, risking arrest or the violence of a mob and refraining from giving way either to fear or to anger. Nonviolence therefore requires a steady mastery of the emotions of its practitioners: it tests inward strength to face outer evils.

In the United States nonviolence has a history going back at least to Henry David Thoreau, who in 1846 spent a night in a local Massachusetts jail to protest the war with Mexico. He had refused to pay a state tax that he saw as aiding a war for the sake of southerners hungry for territory in which to extend slaveholding. Thoreau's form of nonviolence goes by the name of civil disobedience. The most well known advocate of civil disobedience in the first part of the twentieth century was Mohandas

Gandhi, who in his opposition to British rule in India drew on strains of nonviolence in Indian spirituality. In leading a march of his countrymen to the sea to draw salt from it, for example, Gandhi defied a tax imposed by the British. Nonviolence may also be exercised in support of law, as it was among black southerners who in attempting to register to vote braved the anger of local authorities who themselves were violating the Constitution.

An event in 1954 from which the modern civil rights movement is often dated involved no demonstrations, no police or troops, and relatively little publicity. It occurred in the near-seclusion of courtrooms and had many precedents. Oliver Brown, a black Methodist minister, sued the school board of Topeka, Kansas, for ordering his nine-year-old daughter to attend a segregated public school miles from her home when an all-white school stood just down the street. Brown's attorneys argued that school segregation contradicted the Fourteenth Amendment of the Constitution, which bars indi-

Practically everything was segregated in the South before 1955. (Courtesy, Corbis-Bettman)

vidual states from denying equality to any of their citizens on the basis of race. Brown's opponents in the Supreme Court case *Brown* v. *Board of Education of Topeka, Kansas,* drew on the standard known as "separate but equal" established in the Court's 1896 decision *Plessy* v. *Ferguson*. The Court had then ruled that if segregated facilities imposed by a state offered equal facilities, the Fourteenth Amendment had not been violated. Lawyers hired by the National Association of Colored People, the NAACP, argued that segregated schools purposely imposed a badge of inferiority on the black race. This time the Supreme Court sided with African Americans and in 1954 overturned *Plessy*.

The Montgomery Bus Boycott

The *Brown* decision inspired a bus boycott started by blacks a year later in Montgomery, Alabama. If segregation in schools imposed by a

state on blacks amounted to an unconstitutional denial of their equality, then so, too, did segregation on city buses. On Thursday, December 1, 1955, Rosa Parks, a seamstress in a Montgomery department store and also the secretary of the local NAACP, was arrested for refusing to obey a driver's command to yield her seat to a white person.

Rosa Parks's decision that Thursday afternoon was unplanned. But what followed had long been contemplated in Montgomery. White bus drivers, possessing the authority to rearrange passengers for the sake of enforcing a complicated form of segregated seating, had usually been quick to insure that no black could be seated while a white person stood. Waiting for an opportunity to challenge the system, activists within Montgomery's black community found it in the treatment of the militant but eminently respectable Rosa Parks. That evening, Montgomery's black residents waited uneasily, talking in clusters on the streets, phoning one another, uncer-

Mrs. Rosa Parks seated almost alone at the front of a city bus, Montgomery, Alabama, December 1956. (Courtesy, UPI/Bettmann)

tain about what to do in response to an affront that an earlier generation might have assumed to be a tolerable incident in their continuing subjugation. But on Friday, leaflets prepared by a black women's organization appeared throughout the city, calling on all black people to boycott the buses on Monday. That same women's council met with the city's black ministers, a powerful force in their community. The planners also organized a system of voluntary carpooling, which included following the regular bus routes and picking up those walking. Jo Ann Robinson, leading the woman's contingent vital to the movement, was a forerunner to the activism among women in the politics of the 1960s.

The Monday boycott extended into a yearlong operation. The Reverend Martin Luther King, Jr., previously a moderate and little noticed local black minister, became its chief spokesman. King, the son of a middle-class Atlanta minister, had attended a local black college and then went north to earn his doctorate at Boston University. Now the young pastor fused the practice of nonviolence with the Christian spirituality of much of the black South. By walking to work or organizing car pools whose drivers faced police and other white harassment, the participants gave the boycott a dignity that defined it as a central early episode in the civil rights movement. Later, nonviolence would enter as well into the antiwar movement of the Vietnam years and other causes.

While the boycott continued, its leadership argued in the courts. The *Brown* decision implied that Montgomery's segregated buses violated the Fourteenth Amendment. In the closing days of 1956, a federal district court agreed. Similar demonstrations, meanwhile, sprang up in a dozen other southern cities. King, widely heralded for his leadership of the Montgomery resistance, became the most prominent figure in the formation of the Southern Christian Leadership Conference in 1957. Composed largely of male Protestant ministers, the

Students jeer Elizabeth Eckford, one of the earliest black students to arrive to register at Little Rock's Central High School in 1956. (Courtesy, Corbis-Bettmann)

SCLC formed a social and political elite within the black community. Young black activists and some women would soon challenge that elite.

Little Rock, Greensboro, and the Freedom Rides

A federal court ordered the public schools of Little Rock, Arkansas, to integrate beginning with the 1957 school year. To prevent the enrollment of black students at Central High School, Governor Orval Faubus called out the state's National Guard, contending that he must ward off public disorder. His action encouraged, to his satisfaction, the very passions he pretended to thwart. In response to a mob that gathered in front of Central High, President Eisenhower acted as a law-abiding conservative and trumped Governor Faubus. He put the Arkansas National Guard under federal authority and ordered it to protect the handful of black students entering the school. He also sent regular army troops to Little Rock. Under the shelter of

military protection these young blacks braved the taunts and howls of the whites and attended class. The federal courts overturned Faubus's effort to close the schools.

Little Rock differed fundamentally from the other racial confrontations of the 1950s in bringing to the support of civil rights not only the federal courts but the nation's armed forces. For the first time since the end of Reconstruction, a president had deployed soldiers in defense of racial justice. After eight decades of near total neglect of the South's flagrant violation of the country's fundamental law, federal troops overrode the will of a southern governor. White supremacists reacted in horror. To the civil rights movement, it offered the prospect that the federal government might someday be persuaded to become a full ally. Little Rock contributed to a national awareness that at last white supremacy was under serious siege.

One of the most impressive examples of nonviolent action occurred at another Woolworth's three years before Anne Moody's ordeal in Jackson,

The North Carolina Agricultural and Technical school demonstrators at the Greensboro, North Carolina, lunch counter in 1960 were religious and some later supported the Vietnam War. For days they endured verbal and sometimes physical abuse. (Courtesy, Greensboro News and Record)

This Greyhound bus, carrying the first Freedom Riders into Alabama, was set afire by a mob outside Anniston in May 1961. (Courtesy, AP Photo/str)

Mississippi. On Monday, February 1, 1960, four young black men formed a circle outside the Woolworth's in Greensboro, North Carolina, and recited the Lord's Prayer. After sitting unserved at the lunch counter reserved for whites, they had left the store at its normal closing time. These students at a local black agricultural and technical college had acted on a plan, hatched in a dorm room the night before, to challenge racial patterns in Greensboro, a relatively progressive city within a white-supremacist state. The event was notable for being spontaneous and local.

The demonstration caught on. By Wednesday, more than sixty people attended; on Friday, over three hundred, and the sit-in, this new form of civil disobedience, spread to dozens of southern cities. The speed with which they multiplied showed that the demand for equality had become important within much of the black population of the South and a small part of the white.

By 1961 the Congress of Racial Equality, or CORE, an interracial civil rights group dating back to World War II, inaugurated a campaign initially involving eight black and eight white students who would ride on interstate buses to challenge segregation in bus terminals in the Deep South. After leaving Washington, DC, and encountering little resistance in the Upper South, the group known as Freedom Riders faced at Anniston, Alabama, a mob that beat several of them with clubs and set their bus afire. In the heavily segregated industrial city of Birmingham, Alabama, police stood by while Klansmen clubbed the riders. A contingent daring to continue on to Montgomery was attacked once

again, along with a white Justice Department official. Some riders braved the journey all the way to Mississippi. By arrangement between officials of that state and the timid Justice Department headed by President John F. Kennedy's brother Robert, the last few riders to Jackson continued without incident, but officials there arrested them upon the Kennedy administration's promise not to interfere if their safety was guaranteed. Refusing release on bail, the detained students remained imprisoned for weeks. Washington, though it withheld the protection the riders believed the federal government owed them, imposed through the Interstate Commerce Commission an effective ban on segregation in interstate travel. Conducting campaigns in Albany, Georgia, in 1961 and 1962, the civil rights movement sustained only a modest momentum. Laurie Pritchett, the Albany police chief, arrested demonstrators but remained sufficiently respectful and restrained in his treatment of them to avoid contributing to the growing national impression of the South as a land of police thugs and primitive whites.

Federal Troops Go South Again: James Meredith at Ole Miss

In 1962 came a defining moment for the extension of civil rights. As the fall semester opened at the University of Mississippi, James Meredith with the backing of a court order attempted to break the barrier there against admission of black students. Six years before, Autherine Lucy had made a similar daring invasion of the Deep South when she enrolled at the University of Alabama, but a student riot forced her to withdraw. And a year before Meredith's action Charlayne Hunter, who later as Charlayne Hunter-Gault became an anchorwoman on a national television station, overturned the race barrier at the University of Georgia. Now Meredith intended to crack open a university in the state most closely identified with southern white-supremacist militancy. In a night of campus violence that resulted in two deaths, federal marshals held off a mob, the air thick with stones, insults, and tear gas, while Governor Ross Barnett gave his implicit support to the racists. As the plight of the marshals in their attempt to restrain the white attacks became desperate, federal troops sent by President Kennedy entered the campus and restored order. Meredith succeeded in entering the school that students affectionately call Ole Miss. Once again the federal government, prodded by events rather than initiating them, had been brought to fulfill its duty to enforce a court ruling.

In 1963 Vivian Malone and James Hood achieved the victory at the University of Alabama that had eluded Autherine Lucy. There Governor George Wallace squeezed as much drama out of the event as he could. In a widely publicized symbolic gesture, he stood in a doorway to a building of the university. He blocked nothing: anyone needing to enter could have walked around him. But the stance added to his pronouncement: "Segregation now, segregation tomorrow, segregation forever" and solid-ified his leadership position among white racist forces. Segregation, at least as the governor's supporters had known it, was already passing into a deservedly discredited history. In time Wallace, like almost all southerners, himself would abandon it.

Birmingham

The confrontation at the University of Alabama came at a moment when the civil rights movement was waging within that state its largest citywide campaign in Birmingham. During 1963, the Reverend Fred Shuttlesworth had begun an effort to get the city's stores to hire black clerks, and tensions ran high in the heavily segregated city. "Bull" Connor, the police commissioner with a nickname expressive of his personality, acted the part of villain in a bad movie. Demonstrators endured mass arrests, police dogs, cattle prods, and fire hoses powerful enough to strip the bark off a tree from a hundred yards away. Martin Luther King wrote while in prison his "Letter from a Birmingham Jail," one of the best-known documents of the civil rights movement. Responding to local white religious leaders who had urged caution, King argued the need to act now rather than continue to acquiesce in injustice, and spoke for nonviolence as an alternative to the black violence that might otherwise erupt in response to white bigotry.

King and Shuttlesworth found in Birmingham an ally they had not expected. The city's business

Firemen turn powerful hoses on civil rights demonstrators in Birmingham, Alabama, in 1963. (Courtesy, Charles Moore/Black Star)

leaders had at least a commercial sense lacking in the racist rabble. Under pressure from the Kennedy administration and recognizing that the disturbances threatened to keep respectable corporations like IBM away from the city, they negotiated agreements to hire some blacks in downtown department stores. But on September 15, 1963, the bombing of a black Sunday school killed four little girls and left a reminder that racism was deeply engrained.

Events in Birmingham and the defiant effort to keep the University of Alabama segregated pushed the hitherto cautious Kennedy administration toward stronger action against white bigotry. In a June 1963 speech, televised across the nation, the president called for passage of a federal law barring segregation in public places. And that August came a glorious celebration for the civil rights forces. A march to Washington, DC, at the inspiration of the elderly black labor leader A. Philip Randolph gathered a quarter of a million people of both races to

LETTER FROM BIRMINGHAM CITY JAIL

by the Reverend Martin Luther King, Jr.

King's attack on white moderates who counseled patience is a classic.

My dear fellow clergymen, while confined here in the Birmingham City Jail, I came across your recent statement calling our present activities "unwise and untimely." Seldom, if ever, do I pause to answer criticism of my work and ideas. If I sought to answer all of the criticisms that cross my desk, my secretaries would be engaged in little else in the course of the day and I would have no time for constructive work. But since I feel that you are men of genuine good will and your criticisms are sincerely set forth, I would like to answer your statement in what I hope will be patient and reasonable terms. . . .

You deplore the demonstrations that are presently taking place in Birmingham. But I am sorry that your statement did not express a similar concern for the conditions that brought the demonstrations into being. I am sure that each of you would want to go beyond the superficial social analyst who looks merely at effects, and does not grapple with underlying causes. I would not hesitate to say that it is unfortunate that so-called demonstrations are taking place in Birmingham at this time, but I would say in more emphatic terms that it is even more unfortunate that the white power structure of this city left the Negro community with no other alternative.

In any nonviolent campaign there are four basic steps: (1) collection of the facts to determine whether injustices are alive; (2) negotiation; (3) self-purification; and (4) direct action. We have gone through all of these steps in Birmingham. There can be no gainsaying of the fact that racial injustice engulfs this community. Birmingham is probably the most thoroughly segregated city in the United States. Its ugly record of police brutality is known in every section of this country. Its unjust treatment of Negroes in the courts is a notorious reality. There have been more unsolved bombings of Negro homes and churches in Birmingham than any city in this nation. These are the hard, brutal, and unbelievable facts. On the basis of these conditions Negro leaders sought to negotiate with the city fathers. But the political leaders consistently refused to engage in good faith negotiation.

Then came the opportunity last September to talk with some of the leaders of the economic community. In these negotiating sessions certain promises were made by the merchants—such as the promise to remove the humiliating racial signs from the stores. On the basis of these promises Reverend [Fred] Shuttlesworth and the leaders of the Alabama Christian Movement for Human Rights agreed to call a moratorium on any type of demonstrations. As the weeks and months unfolded we realized that we were victims of a broken promise. The signs remained. As in so many experiences of the past, we were confronted with blasted hopes, and the dark shadow of a deep disappointment settled upon us. So we had no alternative except that of preparing for direct action, whereby we would present our very bodies as means of laying our case before the conscience of the local and national community. . . .

The March on Washington, August, 1963. (Courtesy, R.W. Kelley, LIFE magazine @ Time, Inc.)

demand an end to segregation. King gave his most famous speech, "I Have a Dream," envisioning a future of racial harmony. The Civil Rights Act of 1964, passed after Kennedy's assassination the previous November, outlawed discrimination in employment and in restaurants, hotels, and other places of public accommodation involved in interstate commerce.

Selma, Alabama

Early in 1965, the police in Selma, Alabama, took up whips and clubs to disperse marchers campaigning for voter registration. In the course of the demonstrations a state trooper killed a young black church deacon, Jimmy Lee Jackson, and thugs murdered James Reeb, a white minister. In response, King called for a march from Selma to the state capital of Alabama. On March 7, later known as Bloody Sunday, state troopers with tear gas and clubs halted the march at Selma's Edmund Pettus Bridge and continued to attack the demonstrators after they scattered. Television viewers across the nation saw film clips of Alabama troopers, who like other southern mobs of the time, both uniformed

and civilian, so acted as unintentionally to engender support for the civil rights movement.

Though preaching elsewhere on Bloody Sunday, King shortly afterwards led a second march that succeeded in crossing the bridge, then turned back in the presence of police and a federal court order prohibiting him from marching. By this time, some young activists had begun expressing impatience with King's leadership, which they thought overly conciliatory. Then on March 21 protesters, their safety assured by a court order and by federal troops ordered into the state by President Johnson, began a third and triumphal march from Selma to Montgomery. On this occasion many northerners along with Hollywood celebrities joined in making it a national event. But in the course of it, Klansmen murdered Viola Liuzzo, a Detroit housewife, as she rode in a car along the marchers' route. The trek from Selma to Montgomery enacted one of the last great moments in the interracial quest for a color-free society.

The march inspired the Voting Rights Act of 1965, a victory that sent federal registrars deep into the South, hastening the process of black registration and voting. The Twenty-fourth Amendment to

In what may have been the last large comparatively peaceful event of the civil rights era, marchers from Selma to Montgomery, Alabama, join in singing freedom songs. As a direct result of the march, Congress passed the Voting Rights Act of 1965. (Courtesy, Bob Adelman/ Magnum Photos, Inc.).

BLACK VOTER REGISTRATION			
	1960	1966	Percent Increase
Alabama	66,000	250,000	278.8
Arkansas	73,000	115,000	57.5
Florida	183,000	303,000	65.6
Georgia	180,000	300,000	66.7
Louisiana	159,000	243,000	52.8
Mississippi	22,000	175,000	695.4
North Carolina	210,000	282,000	34.3
South Carolina	58,000	191,000	229.3
Tennessee	185,000	225,000	21.6
Texas	227,000	400,000	76.2
Virginia	100,000	205,000	105.0

Source: U.S. Bureau of the Census, Statistical Abstract of the United State: 1982–83 (103d edition) Washington, DC, 1982.

the Constitution, ratified in 1964, prohibited in federal elections the imposition of a poll tax, a device that had kept black Americans, Indians, Latinos, and poor whites from using the ballot. By the late 1960s black southerners and Latinos in the Southwest were winning local elective offices and voter registration rose sharply.

A CATHOLIC WAR HERO BECAMES PRESIDENT

John F. Kennedy, the new young president, announced in his inaugural address on January 20, 1961, that Americans were ready to "pay any price, bear any burden, meet any hardship." Civil rights activists had already shown that readiness, and in the Freedom Rides would demonstrate it again later

that same year. But John F. Kennedy was not thinking of the civil rights movment. Nor was civil rights on the minds of most of the people to whom he spoke—predominantly white, mostly well-off, conscious of being in a triumphant age of technology, science, and production. His address called for the country to stand firm amid the costs and dangers of a world still in the grip of the Cold War.

The Young Hero

The youngest president elected in American history, born into an Irish Catholic family of established wealth, was educated to break out of the social ghetto to which Catholics had long been consigned. John's mother Rose, the daughter of Mayor John "Honey Fitz" Fitzgerald of Boston, personified the well-to-do, lace-curtain Irish who had left behind the shanty Irish of the nineteenth-century immigrations. John's rough-hewn father Joe added a fortune to the wealth he had inherited. In the Catholic community, the future president John Kennedy would represent manners, learning, social ease, physical grace, and, of course, money—almost everything Americans hold to be aristocratic.

John—familiarly known as Jack—and his brothers grew up in the shadow of their father's ambition to break into Boston's old-money Massachusetts Protestant society of English descent. To that end, he sent his eldest sons to Harvard, having already initiated them in the culture of the upper classes, including the sport of sailing. Meanwhile Jack, subject to many childhood illnesses, had developed a mentality not unknown among sick children: a preoccupation with inner strength and courage. Jack's senior thesis at Harvard, an examination of Britain's failure to prepare to confront Hitler, was published as *Why England Slept* and widely distributed by his father.

During World War II, Jack gained through his father's influence a commission in the navy from which his multiple physical problems, such as a bad back injured from playing sports in college, should have excluded him. At that time the aristocracy served its country by participating in war rather than use its money to avoid doing so. Kennedy commanded one of the navy's most colorful if ineffective weapons, a light and mobile PT boat, providing the dash and daring appropriate to an upper-

President John F. Kennedy. (Courtesy, John F. Kennedy Presidential Library)

class young man trained in sailing. Assigned to the Pacific theater of the war, Jack committed a major blunder—getting his craft rammed and split by a Japanese destroyer—but more than redeemed himself by swimming to an island towing an injured crewman and then swimming farther to get help for his men.

The Politician

In the following years Jack Kennedy, first elected to represent Massachusetts as a Democratic member of the House of Representatives and then as a senator, became notable less for any one political creed than for what he represented: a veteran, handsome, rich, and in later years married to a beautiful woman, self-contained in a way that may have resulted from his ailing, bookish childhood. After an unsuccessful attempt to become the Democratic vice–presidential candidate in 1956, he won his party's presidential nomination in 1960, with a Texan, Senator Lyndon Johnson, as his running mate for regional balance. Neither the fight in the primaries for the nomination nor the general election contest between Kennedy and the Republican candidate, Richard Nixon, presented extensive ideological differences. The most significant social consequence of Kennedy's election was that he had broken the cultural barrier against having a Catholic president.

The absence of a clear ideological profile for JFK did not contradict his significance for liberals. In 1960 the liberal wing of the Democratic Party, more so than the Republicans, called for bold economic growth and an aggressive prosecution of the Cold War. In the Eisenhower era, these liberals mistakenly claimed that the Soviet Union possessed more missiles than the United States—the missile gap. Investment in science and technology and a more rigorous education would prepare the country's youth for a difficult international future. All this made Kennedy the ideal liberal candidate. He also was a certified intellectual: publishing a serious book testified to that. An appearance of strength and vigor—his chronic ill health was little known to the public—combined with his war record to reassure the pubic that here stood an appropriate leader for an era of trial and national renewal. That was the tone of the inaugural, with its curious call to will and sacrifice at a time with no specific global challenge on the horizon.

KENNEDY'S FOREIGN POLICY: RECKLESS OR CAUTIOUS?

John F. Kennedy inspired idealism in young people. His inaugural address had urged them to "ask not what your country can do for you but what you can do for your country." Much of the speech, however, concentrated on foreign policy and articulated Cold War themes: "Let every nation know," he orated, "whether it wishes us well or ill, that we shall pay any price . . . support any friend, oppose any foe to assure the survival and the success of liberty. This much we pledge—and more." How did these words play out in the new administration's actual conduct of foreign policy?

The first major act of foreign policy during Kennedy's administration had been prepared earlier by the Central Intelligence Agency at the end of the 1950s. Determined to overthrow Cuba's repressive regime of Fidel Castro that cooperated with Moscow even as it acted to improve the lives of Cubans, the CIA under President Eisenhower had secretly trained an invasion force and planned an attack that it hoped would spark a national uprising. The enterprise was predicated on the conviction, widely held in the United States, that wherever Communism reigned the people were eager to overthrow it. When Kennedy came into office, he had little choice but to approve the project's continuation. The troops landed in April 1961 at the Bay of Pigs, a singularly ill-advised spot, shallow and dotted with coral reefs inhospitable to landing craft. The place was familiar to Castro as one of his favorite fishing spots. The Cuban army quickly triumphed. Kennedy decided, wisely, neither to rescue the soldiers with air support nor to invade Cuba. But as the flap in the Caribbean subsided, a more menacing situation developed in Europe.

The Berlin Wall

For years the status of Germany had been held in suspension. West Berlin, a self-governing part of West Germany under the protection of NATO troops, was connected with it by air and a highway passing through the eastern zone of Germany. The immediate problem for the Soviet Union bloc of nations resulted from an exodus of professionals from East Germany into West Berlin, in such numbers as to endanger the economy of East Germany

and therefore of the Communist bloc in general. West Berlin amounted to major trouble for Moscow.

At a conference of the major powers in Vienna in June 1961, the Soviet leader Nikita Khrushchev threatened that without a satisfactory arrangement for the whole area, Moscow would sign a separate peace treaty with East Germany. That endangered the separate status of West Berlin. But President Kennedy was committed to protecting West Berlin from Communist rule, and Khrushchev and Kennedy sparred inconclusively over the issue. Kennedy, known for his cool detachment, appeared agitated, for he had recently injured a chronically painful back, and may have conveyed to the Soviet premier a mistaken impression of weakness.

Moscow's concerns had substance, but the West had a genuine dedication to freedom in West Berlin. To allow its citizens to be dependent on the good will of the Communist East German republic would have been a betrayal of everything the anti-communist West claimed to stand for. From Moscow's standpoint, however, Germany, as the country that had invaded Russia in two world wars, remained a threat. The Soviet Union saw its European satellite nations as a shield, and it wanted to keep Germany divided, the eastern part Communist and subservient. The flood of professionals and technicians fleeing Communist rule to West Berlin, moreover, also worried the NATO

East Germans quickly constructed the Berlin Wall in August 1961. President Kennedy accepted the wall rather than risk nuclear war. The wall, a symbol of the Cold War, came down in 1989. (Courtesy, Corbis-Bettmann)

countries, fearful that a panicked Soviet Union might in some way bring on nuclear war. Kennedy's reaction compounded strength with restraint in a way that liberal cold warriors of the Kennedy years approved.

As a show of force, Kennedy announced an increase in draft quotas and put reserve troops on alert. In response, the Communists in August 1962 began restricting movement from East to West Berlin and started building a wall to halt further migration. Kennedy then dispatched a token number of troops to the western part of the city. He also sent to Berlin his vice president, Lyndon Johnson, with General Lucius Clay, who in 1948 had directed the airlift that thwarted Moscow's earlier effort to isolate the city of Berlin. In October a standoff in the city between Soviet and American tanks ended when the Communist tanks backed away. But despite sincere expressions of outrage from the West at the construction of the Berlin Wall, Kennedy and the anticommunist alliance recognized the reasons for it and acquiesced in them.

The result remained unsatisfactory, but bearable. Moscow established East Germany as a nominally independent state, and the wall that denied East Germans the freedom to travel to West Germany and freedom remained. West Berlin survived free and connected to West Germany by air and roadway, the Soviet and German Communists recognizing that any interference there would be unacceptably risky.

The Cuban Missile Crisis

Fear of risk, however, did not completely govern Soviet policy. The USSR, a year after the muddled resolution of the German question, brought the world to its most dangerous moment. The occasion was Cuba, the time the summer and fall of 1962.

The failed Bay of Pigs invasion had convinced both Castro and Khrushchev that the United States would continue to target the island republic. They were right. The Kennedy administration became obsessed with Fidel Castro, to the extent of running a secret CIA campaign, called Operation Mongoose, with the goal of taking out the dictator one way or another. Castro responded by seeking suppport from the Soviet Union. Moscow obliged, beginning the installation in Cuba of nuclear missiles aimed at the United States.

The exact purpose for which the missiles were intended remains unclear. The West and the Soviet bloc each had ample atomic weapons and delivery systems to devastate the other. The presence of Soviet submarines armed with nuclear missiles already situated near the East Coast of the United States made the Cuban missiles a virtually meaningless addition. Khrushchev, however dedicated a Communist, had revealed the crimes of the Stalinist era and worked to modify the harshness of the Soviet system. Possibly he saw the Cuban venture as a way of pacifying the hardline Soviet military. At the same time the missiles would sufficiently dramatize the Soviet presence in Cuba, discouraging further aggression against the island by the United States.

When an American spy flight over Cuba early in the autumn of 1962 discovered the missile emplacements, the Kennedy administration faced the grimmest moment of the Cold War. To decide simply that the missiles in Cuba, only some ninety miles from Florida, posed no more of a threat than missiles the West had already placed close to the borders of the USSR would be politically unacceptable to Washington. The Soviet Union's action now boldly placed itself in the Western Hemisphere, which the United States for more than half a century had held to be its exclusive sphere of influence. By unspoken agreement, the West had accepted Eastern Europe as being within Moscow's sphere. That mutual understanding met a condition for keeping the Cold War safely cold. Now the Soviet Union seemed to be undermining one of the main pillars of the balance between the two blocs. For the United States to do nothing might invite Khrushchev to attempt other provocative steps, and then others, beyond the point at which peace would remain possible.

The president swiftly assembled a group of advisers designated by the crisp name ExComm, and pondered a range of options. At one extreme were the joint chiefs of staff, who recommended that the military destroy the missile sites; at the other was Adlai Stevenson, Kennedy's ambassador to the United Nations, who wished merely to bring the matter before its General Assembly. The administration took a middle course and settled on a military blockade of Cuba, to be described by the milder word "quarantine," to keep Soviet ships from carrying further missile parts to the island. The act would be sufficiently confrontational to let the USSR know it had gone beyond acceptable bounds. It would also make clear that unless Khruschchev came to some agreement further military action would be forthcoming.

On Monday, October 12, 1962, a television address by Kennedy informed the American public of the presence of the missiles and of the quarantine. For the next few days, the world did not know whether it would soon be pulling itself out of nuclear wreckage. The American navy allowed an unarmed Soviet ship to go through quarantine waters. Then on Wednesday, a Russian vessel carrying missile equipment turned back, a silent acknowledgment of Soviet respect for the blockade. Meanwhile, Washington and Moscow carried on secret deliberations with more prudence than might have been thought possible. In an intricate negotiation betweeen Robert Kennedy and the Soviet ambassador, Khrushchev agreed to dismantle the missile bases while the United States pledged to remove obsolete missiles in Turkey and to forego any planned invasion of Cuba. On Sunday, October 18, the world learned that the day, and the next, and the foreseeable future would not bring the worst of world wars.

A welcome outcome of the affair was a slight relaxation of relations between the Soviet Union and the West. Kennedy and Khrushchev developed something like a friendship; they had been through much together. They also achieved the first major modification of the Cold War, the Test Ban Treaty of 1963 prohibiting the testing above ground of nuclear weapons. With the help of moderately conservative Republican legislative leaders and over the opposition of Americans hostile to any reconciliation with the Soviet Union, the treaty won the necessary vote of two-thirds of the Senate.

The missile crisis stamped for the future an image of Kennedy. The mixture of firmness and caution he then exhibited seemed to be what the circumstances demanded.

Symbols of the Kennedy Era

A venture in which the Kennedy style found expression was a program for Latin America called the Alliance for Progress. Devised in the wake of the Bay of Pigs, it combined economic and military aid with some ineffective attempts at getting dictatorial regimes in that region to consider serious land and political reform. Another foreign policy idea, the Peace Corps, turned out to be among the

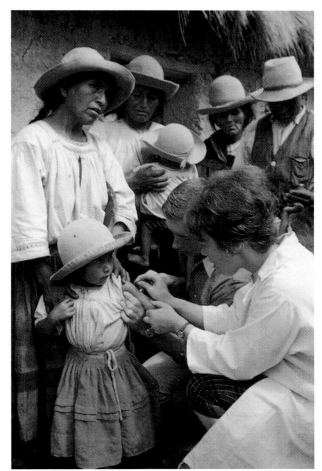

The Peace Corps, representing the best of Kennedy's New Frontier, drew many thousands of idealistic young Americans. These volunteers are vaccinating children in Bolivia. (Courtesy, David S. Boyer/National Geographic Society Image Collection)

most attractive programs of Kennedy's presidency. The Corps, made up of volunteers, went to underdeveloped areas of the globe to assist in making improvements as modest as a village well or a new schoolhouse. Despite having no age limits, the Corps especially appealed to young people attracted by the Kennedy aura. A military counterpart to the Peace Corps was the Special Forces, popularly known as the Green Berets. Trained as a military elite, its members were skilled in counterguerrilla fighting but intended also to make friends among the people in disputed areas. Together the Alliance for Progress, the Peace Corps, and the Green Berets constituted an effort to respond in a practical way to the ideological appeal of Communism in impoverished parts of the world.

Kennedy also placed his impress on an ambitious space program. The Eisenhower administration, responding to the Soviet launching of Sputnik and Sputnik II, had established the National Aeronautics and Space Administration, or NASA. In 1961, just after the Soviet Union propelled the first human being into orbit around the earth, Kennedy received congressional approval for expanded funding on space ventures: he projected landing an American on the moon before the decade's end. The next year a capsule manned by John Glenn orbited the earth. And in July 1969 while a spacecraft from the Apollo program containing Mike Collins circled the moon, a smaller vehicle landed, and from it stepped Neil Armstrong and Edwin Aldrin in pressurized suits. The mission of Apollo 13 failed in 1970 after the space vehicle exploded shortly after taking off, but various subsequent manned and unmanned vehicles explored the solar system.

THE NEW FRONTIER

The term New Frontier embodied the spirit of the Kennedy administration. The purpose of Kennedy liberals seemed not much more definite than to restart a nation that they claimed had stalled. On the frontier of racial justice the Kennedy brothers at first acted mildly, initiating hardly any significant advance in civil rights. Even Robert Kennedy, the more aggressive of the two brothers, as attorney general worried more about safety and public order than about the need for social change. A reason given for caution was that the Freedom Rides of 1961 came at the time of the Berlin crisis, when the administration wished for unity at home. And the Democratic Party itself, which in the past had relied on the white South as its mainstay, remained uneasy about pressing racial issues. But the president meanwhile was becoming interested in the closely related subject of poverty.

Poverty Rediscovered

During the New Deal, when the Great Depression had impoverished millions of Americans, poverty reigned as a major political issue. Once the worst of the depression had passed, poverty nearly vanished from political discussion. Among liberals who a few years earlier would have been angry

This book influenced presidents Kennedy and Johnson.

defenders of migrants or sharecroppers, the assumption became widespread that federal programs now met everyone's basic needs. And the economy, even while lagging in the late 1950s, seemed to promise unending growth. The most visible social criticism fixed on neither race nor poverty. It centered rather on that typical American as presented in social commentary, white, middle-class, and trapped in a sterile suburbia or in a corporate structure promising wealth at the expense of independent thought and action. Then came a cluster of studies, the best known being Michael Harrington's *The Other America*, published in 1952, that revealed the existence of poverty in a nation that had virtually forgotten about it.

The new commentaries proceeded in part on an insight attributable especially to Harrington: the poor were now invisible to the rest of the country, hidden in the hills of Appalachia or in ghettoes, barrios, or otherwise isolated corners of the national culture. Their presence was further masked by a peculiar result of American productivity. The poor wore clothing that made them look little different from the rest of the population. And social scientists were beginning to discover other facts. In addition to including large numbers of the elderly, their ranks were heavily black, Hispanic, or American Indian, people widely expected to be poor and therefore ignored or unnoticed. For the first time since the Depression, educated Americans contemplated images of poor Appalachian whites, hands gnarled and faces creased with age and hardship. Or more farsighted liberals might glimpse poverty the New Deal had scarcely noticed, Hispanic migrants picking California grapes and dismissible at the wave of an employer's hand, or black adolescents in slums that offered drugs in place of hope. Above all, poverty also came to be understood as a state of mind breeding upon itself, passing from generation to generation an ingrained pessimism unable to see the point of schooling and ambition and a life of effort directed to a purpose.

The New Frontier Responds

The Kennedy forces defined themselves as doers, their shirtsleeves rolled up, their resolve set, directing the vast energies of their country toward the conquest of first one problem and then another. Poverty was a beginning problem in their crusade. In the thriving United States of the later twentieth century it had no place or logic. The resources of technical innovation and university research for which Kennedy liberals felt an affinity seemed exactly fit to combat it. And as the heirs of the New Deal, which had made the widest assault on economic distress ever undertaken in the nation's history, the Democrats could assume a mandate to confront the issue.

A major Kennedy administration strategy aimed not specifically at poverty but at the whole economy was a tax cut on personal and corporate income, intended to stimulate business and industry. Signed into law early in 1964, it typified the liberalism of the time. Tax reduction, of course, pleased wealth and business, and many liberals then eagerly allied with the major institutions of power and production. Once Kennedy did clash with business. That happened when United States Steel in 1962 announced a price hike by the larger producers that went counter to a previous understand-

ing between the government and this group known as Big Steel. The president publicly denounced the steel executives. The administration also threatened antitrust action, a tax audit, and a switch in government contracts to steel corporations that had not yet raised prices. The offending companies backed down.

Typical of Kennedy's attack on poverty was his Manpower Development Act, a program providing training in job skills for the impoverished. The goal belonged to a liberalism rooted in the New Deal, which had looked to construct a commonwealth of workers rather than create an underclass dependent on welfare payments. It also responded to a problem that the New Deal had not faced: a high-tech economy that appeared to exclude from employment people unacquainted with the new skills. The Manpower Act, along with job training, anticipated the more ambitious Great Society programs of the administration of President Lyndon Johnson. And by that time, the issue of poverty had become inextricable from that of civil rights, until then considered a separate question.

An Elusive Legacy

By the late months of 1963, the Kennedy style had nearly completed its evolution into a Kennedy policy. Internationally it amounted to a balance of force and prudence that had brought the first easing of the Cold War's intensity. Kennedy delivered a speech at American University that year calling for an end to the Cold War. In domestic programs it initiated a mild revival of New Deal activism updated to a more technically advanced society and cautiously adding a concern for civil rights that had been the most shameful absence in earlier Democratic liberalism. Only toward Vietnam did the administration seem to lack any clear direction. Kennedy would not have time to find one. On November 22, 1963, as the president rode in a motorcade through Dallas, Texas, a rootless and brooding young man named Lee Harvey Oswald shot him with a rifle. That forces behind Oswald were involved is doubtful but cannot be disproved: a few days later while under arrest Oswald in turn was assassinated by Jack Ruby, a prominent businessman having underworld connections. The mystery surrounding the whole affair, and the conspiracy theories that have continued to swirl around it, have aided in keeping sharp the memory of that black November day.

President Lyndon B. Johnson, standing next to Jacqueline Kennedy, takes the oath of office following the assassination of John F. Kennedy. (Courtesy, Library of Congress)

The civil rights movement embodied passion; the Kennedy style evoked coolness. The rights movement was grounded in the spiritual fervor of evangelical religion; Kennedy liberals felt at home with the more impersonal demands of education, science, and technology. The two mentalities were never at ease with each other, and by the end of Kennedy's tenure civil rights leaders increasingly wondered what they could expect of an administration seemingly so committed to rules and procedures. Their troubled relationship lay at the root of much of the social and political strife of the later decade.

A NEW LEFT

In the 1950s, a polite formality characterized American college campuses. Much of the faculty considered itself liberal. That meant despising the Red-hunts of the McCarthy period, aimed in part against universities. It directed snobbery toward President Eisenhower, a member of the moderate wing of the Republican Party but, university faculty concluded, hopelessly average. Campus discussions centered on whether Americans were becom-

ing conformists in a culture surrendering to a bland consumerism. But few academic liberals seriously questioned the distribution of power and wealth within American society. The policies of the New Deal and the Truman administration they assumed to have taken care of much of the problem; expanding prosperity they supposed would do the rest. Liberal faculty members might have endorsed progress on civil rights, but race was not a hot topic. And the universities happily cooperated in confronting Communism, especially when they received federal grants for weapons research to defend what was defined as the free world.

Yet as a center of free critical inquiry, the campus spawned ideas and groups that went beyond its own tame liberalism. In 1960 when the antiquated Red-hunting House Un-American Activities Committee held hearings in San Francisco to look into whatever the members might think to be subversion, students at the University of California at Berkeley attempted to disrupt the proceedings. Some the police arrested, and against others they directed water hoses, washing them down the steps outside the building in which the House committee was meeting. And at the time that students at Berkeley and the University of Wisconsin progressed toward developing a critical politics, the most notable student organization of the coming years was about to come into being: Students for a Democratic Society, or SDS.

SDS

The origins of SDS, a group at the forefront of what would soon be called the New Left, lay squarely within the staunchly anticommunist Old Left that SDS would later reject. In the spring of 1962, in Port Huron, Michigan, at a park owned by the United Automobile Workers, a number of student groups assembled, SDS prominent among them. There, after much free-flowing discussion, a document emerged known as the Port Huron Statement. This founding manifesto gained SDS a distinctive identity. In the face of a culture they judged to be corrupted by advertising and money-making, the rebels envisioned a future in which citizens would join in controlling the various institutions that shaped their daily lives. Soon the concept came to be widely known as participatory democracy.

One of the arguments in the Port Huron Statement, however, led to major trouble with the traditional American left. While making clear its opposition to Communism, the manifesto accused the West as well as Moscow of perpetuating the Cold War. That was too much for the old anticommunist radicals. Before long, relations between them and their offspring broke off. It was the first of the decade's conflicts between generations.

Students in Rebellion

At its formation, SDS was an organization of students but not about students. Its concerns lay in the world beyond the campus. But as the 1964 fall semester began at Berkeley, events pressed the inseparability of the university from the larger world.

Berkeley was a part of the statewide University of California system, of which the Chancellor was the liberal Quaker Clark Kerr. But as the semester opened the university administration, to please conservatives among the regents who controlled the state's higher education system, approved a ban against solicitations on campus for political causes. The prohibition applied to such activities as setting up tables and passing out political literature to students.

In an earlier time when universities acted with

Mario Savio uses a bullhorn to talk to demonstrators occupying Sproul Hall at the University of California. These students drew their tactics of nonviolent resistance from Martin Luther King's earlier practice of it in the South. (Courtesy AP/Wide World Photos)

parental authority and students expected them to do so, the revised policy might have gone unnoticed. By the mid-sixties, though, political activism animated major campuses. Among the impassioned at Berkeley was Mario Savio, fresh from civil rights work in Mississippi. Savio became a leader among students of all political persuasions, including conservatives, who protested the university ban. After recruitment for the civil rights movement occurred in defiance of the new regulations, students blocked passage of a police car in which a protester was being held. Savio, courteously removing his shoes so as not to damage the vehicle, climbed on top of it and spoke to the students with a megaphone. Soon afterwards an organization calling itself the Free Speech Movement, or FSM, came into being to coordinate the insurrection.

That autumn and into the next year, Berkeley students waged war with their administration. Suspended students had their punishments debated between administrators and faculty. Folksingers such as Joan Baez, in this decade of the sixties that seemed set to a sound track, entertained the rebels. On December 2, students occupied Sproul Hall, a major administration building, and the police took hours in the middle of the night to clear it since some students used the civil-disobedience tactic of letting their bodies go limp, making it difficult for officers to carry them out. Hundreds went to jail for trespassing. Faculty protested the presence of the police on campus, and some posted bail for the arrested students. On December 8 the faculty senate with some significant dissent supported the FSM, and graduate students called off a strike that had shut down Berkeley, where, as in other large universities, faculty cannot ordinarily complete their teaching responsibilities without the aid of graduate assistants. Within weeks the regents essentially agreed to the students' demands. Tables and soliciting would be allowed on campus.

The Free Speech Movement won the point that a university should foster political discussion and argument and allow students to organize and collect money for causes outside the campus. The FSM was arguing for participatory democracy among students, as radicals were also calling for it in the workplace and pressing for it in Mississippi. The Berkeley movement, exemplified in the thoughtfulness and civility of Savio, distinguishes itself from some forms of student activism that came afterwards. And when a few months later some students

demanded the right to yell obscenities, in the Filthy Speech Movement, as it became called, Savio repudiated the development; his Free Speech Movement stood for serious and intelligent debate.

SNCC

At the time of SDS's formation another of the most important forces in shaping student opinion during the sixties had already appeared. Ella Baker, a critic of the clerical domination of the Southern Christian Leadership Conference, founded in 1960 an organization that she planned as a more democratic force for civil rights. It adopted the name the Student Nonviolent Coordinating Committee, or SNCC.

SNCC advocated the principle that SDS was discovering for itself. In a democracy citizens not only vote for good policies but also act for them. When black southern sharecroppers in Mississippi came

Bob Moses of the Student Nonviolent Coordinating Committee (SNCC) exercised quiet but influential leadership over his organization. He insisted that white college students be allowed by SNCC to aid in registering black voters in 1963 and 1964. (Courtesy, Robert Moses)

together to demand the right to vote, the act of making the demand embodied the freedom and equality they sought. SNCC had a few leaders, notably the northern black intellectual Robert Parris Moses. But its ideal was to be as close to leaderless as possible. In meetings Moses often stood in the back of the room, almost silent, not giving directions except to facilitate discussion.

In Mississippi a small band of black activists soon began the dangerous task of organizing the poorest of their brothers and sisters to vote. A few white Mississippians joined their ranks as well, breaking with the system that had worked in their favor. One of the bravest of the black activists, Mrs. Fannie Lou Hamer, could remember when her mother had been so poor that the patchings and repatchings of her clothes made them heavy to wear. When the owner of the land that Mrs. Hamer and her husband worked on learned that she was trying to register to vote, he evicted her. Arrested on trumped-up charges, she was beaten by black inmates on orders from the white police. She went to work for SNCC.

SNCC gave the Mississippi activists their loosely constructed organization, and religion, particularly the vision of Martin Luther King, gave many of them their model of the future, a community based in faith. The phrase "Do your own thing," subsequently so trivialized by the media, as originally used in the Mississippi movement meant: "Your courage and commitment have been tested; we know you are one of us; work with us in any way that seems fitting to you."

Mississippi's black poor, denied access to decent schooling, needed to be educated for the examination required of voter registrants. "Freedom schools" therefore became an essential part of the movement. Black Mississippians who raised the courage needed for attempting to register, and went equipped with the necessary literacy and information, would more than likely be turned down anyway on one technicality or another. A typical question would read, "Write and copy in the space below Section ____ of the Constitution of Mississippi." The registrar designated the section—any one of 285. Then the applicant would be asked to write a reasonable interpretation of that particular section: the registrar, of course, judged the answer. Black voter registration, which the Kennedy administration encouraged, was particularly threatening to white supremacy, for it would mean not merely the overturning of social custom but acquiring black political strength. And the greater the threat to white Mississippi, the greater the danger for civil rights activists. But for black Mississippians the attempt to register became enormously important. Just to make the attempt meant overthrowing the whole psychology of inferiority and discovering their personal and collective power.

While the voter registration campaign took place in the countryside, Medgar Evers of the NAACP was directing in the state capital of Jackson a strategy of boycotts and civil disobedience that led to hundreds of arrests. In June 1963 the defiant Evers was gunned down in his driveway, becoming one of many revered black martyrs to white racism.

A separate vote that Mississippi civil rights

workers conducted that summer—apart from the official white supremacist Democratic Party primary—garnered at least eighty thousand votes for candidates for governor and lieutenant governor. The process contributed to the formation of the Mississippi Freedom Democratic Party, which sought to represent the state's black community along with a band of whites, among them the Reverend Edwin King. The campaign enlisted the services of some white college students from out of state. Its success encouraged a plan for a larger project in the summer of 1964. For the project, organizers enlisted a thousand college students from the North, most of them white. That brought into the movement young privileged whites alien to the life of black Mississippians and unseasoned in the toil and danger that had been the lot of long-term activists. But they would add needed numbers and involve wealthy and powerful sectors of the white North. When affluent white youth from northern elite colleges, the sons and daughters of the favored classes, entered the struggle, the national media were forced to give to Mississippi an attention they had never paid to black southerners.

Freedom Summer

In the spring of 1964 at a midwestern college gathered as idealistic a group of Americans as has ever congregated at a single spot. In orientation sessions conducted by veterans of the Mississippi battleground, they came to understand the conditions under which they must be prepared to act in that state, calmly, patiently, and in the face of fear. All this was brought home to them when the announcement came that three rights workers in Mississippi, the black southerner James Chaney and the white northerners Michael Schwerner and Andrew Goodman, had disappeared. Northern media concentrated on the disappearance, for unlike the killing of some obscure black Mississippian this case threatened the children of the well-to-do. The three, murdered by Klansmen, were found that summer buried in an earthen dam. Years later some Klansmen served brief prison sentences for the crimes.

Freedom Summer of 1964 in Mississippi, reinforced by the presence of the northern white volunteers, carried out another vote among blacks, this time for delegates to the Democratic National Convention to be held in August. At the conven-

tion, held in Atlantic City, New Jersey, the nomination of Lyndon Johnson to head the Democratic presidential ticket was assured. His election in November also approached near certainty. Yet one issue at Atlantic City made the party leaders uneasy. The Freedom Democratic delegates claimed that as a slate chosen in a vote that had excluded no race, they had the moral right to represent Mississippi rather than the official delegation picked in a primary banning most blacks. The new party therefore demanded official recognition. But the national Democrats, nervous about losing white votes in a fading Democratic solid South, maneuvered the Freedom Democrats to the side, offering them only nominal representation. That this gesture did not satisfy the Freedom Democrats perplexed the party's Democratic leaders, who were revealing themselves to be willing to compromise even deeply moral questions.

Johnson got his nomination, and in November his election. But his deference to the white-supremacist Mississippi Democrats did not save that state for him. It along with only five other states cast electoral votes for the very conservative presidential nominee, Republican Barry Goldwater. The effect of the party's treatment of the Freedom Democrats was disastrous. Up to August 1964 black activists and an increasingly radical portion of their white allies had clung to the hope that Washington and the liberals would eventually throw full support to their cause. Effectively excluded, the Freedom Democrats went home from Atlantic City embittered. Black militants already moved toward full separation from whites. That resulted in rejection even of the white radicals who themselves had become deeply alienated from white society and politics.

BLACK POWER

Among the black militants who now parted from their white allies appeared competing vocabularies and ideologies. These varied from genial presentations of black culture to efforts at establishing separate political bodies excluding whites, and in some cases creeds exalting violence. Chicano activists began using similar kinds of language, as did Native Americans, who started questioning their commitment to working within the American political system. But Black Power figured most prominently in public discourse.

Malcolm X

In black urban neighborhoods the Nation of Islam, popularly known as the Black Muslims, under the leadership of the Reverend Elijah Muhammad had long been drawing recruits. The Black Muslims professed a devotion to the great Islamic faith. But their religious conduct was very much of their own devising. They combined with a severe code of personal morality a claim that the

Malcolm X was a powerful black leader who moved from preaching separatism and violence through most of his influential leadership years to renouncing these values toward the end of his life. He was assassinated by other members of the Black Muslims in 1965. (Courtesy, Black Star)

white race is inherently evil, a concept totally alien to Islam. A more positive side to the Black Muslims has been their effort to bolster pride and hope within the black community.

A close associate of Elijah Muhammad and an eloquent recruiter in Harlem for the Nation of Islam, Malcolm X had been born Malcolm Little. After his turn to racial ideology, he shed the family name presumably imposed by whites on his ancestors. A former petty criminal, he could understand the alienation of impoverished black youth. Self-taught in prison, he possessed the initiative and intelligence appropriate to a leader. Malcolm X for most of his career espoused an antiwhite rhetoric laced with denunciations of Jews. Eventually, however, he began to drift away from the Nation and its racial teachings. A pilgrimage in 1964 to Mecca, for traditional Muslims worldwide the holiest of shrines, introduced him to an Islam that embraced people of all races and preached universal harmony. That experience and a personal falling out with Elijah Muhammad turned Malcolm against the Black Muslim leader. By the mid-sixties he was preaching his own brand of black militancy, still arguing on practical grounds for exclusively black organizations but abandoning his earlier condemnation of whites. In February 1965 he was shot and killed at a Harlem rally, an act for which three Black Muslims were tried and convicted. After his death, Malcolm X gained a major place among black activists of his time and since.

From Civil Rights to Separatism

In 1966 James Meredith, whose enrollment at the University of Mississippi in 1962 had integrated that institution, was shot and wounded as he walked across that state in a lone protest against racism. In response, African Americans staged in June a march through Mississippi. Like other demonstrations, it included whites as well as blacks. But unlike others, it extended to white participants at best a qualified welcome. During the event, reporters seized on a phrase, "black power," associated particularly with Stokely Carmichael, a young immigrant from the Caribbean and veteran of SNCC's Mississippi campaign. Carmichael had led the chant "black power" to roadside supporters as he continued the march across Mississippi. The slogan marked the end of a civil rights movement defined by interracial activism.

Not long after Malcolm began to temper his views, Carmichael (later adopting the African name Kwame Touré) took an opposite course. The practice of civil disobedience, the enlistment of whites in the cause, the eagerness for integration—all no longer won his assent. Such tactics, he decided, amounted to consorting with the enemy, and he believed it threatened to dull the combative pride that blacks needed for the struggle. Unlike leaders of other exploited groups who sought immediate practical solutions to problems, Carmicheal indicted an entire white history. Yet friendships with whites, including those who disagreed with him, that he was to maintain throughout his life contradicted the ferocity of some of his statements. His remarks about what Black Power amounted to also tended to be contradictory. Sometimes he would present it as the rejection of Western civilization, at other times a simple matter of political organizing among blacks to win practical concessions. The Black Power movement, at any rate, succeeded in expelling whites from SNCC and CORE in the later sixties. Soon afterwards, SNCC disbanded and CORE's membership dwindled almost to extinction.

The Black Panthers

Relations between white police and young black men had long been a flashpoint for racial trouble. The Black Panther Party for Self Defense, formed in Oakland, California, in 1966 by Huey Newton and Bobby Seale, began to monitor the activities of the police. On Oakland's streets, heavily armed Panthers patrolled, watching for police misconduct. In keeping with the organization's paramilitary character, some Panthers adopted a uniform consisting of black trousers, powder-blue shirts, and black leather jackets. One armed group appeared on the floor of the California state legislature in Sacramento and read a list of demands. A few shootouts added to the reputation of the party for violence. In 1967 Newton was wounded during an exchange of gunfire in which a patrolman was killed. Upon his arrest, a national campaign to free him won the support of several white celebrities. His trial was never completed, and two years later Newton was released from prison on a technicality.

The Panthers, as they organized in cities nationwide, designated for black people a distinct and separate role in what they considered as an ongoing

world revolution. But they did not adopt the posture of animosity to whites that some other Black Power advocates favored. They accepted revolutionary whites as allies. Panthers also engaged in more peaceful activities, notably providing breakfast for hungry children in black neighborhoods. Yet their reputation for violence made them a regular target for the police. And the Federal Bureau of Investigation waged against them a campaign that included infiltration and legal harassment, tactics that the FBI used as well toward the American Indian Movement and the Chicano activists. By the early 1970s, the Black Panther organizations were disintegrating.

MARGINALIZED PEOPLES STAKE THEIR CLAIMS

For black Americans, Little Rock in 1957 had foreshadowed an era of federal intervention on behalf of civil rights. Toward Indian people, Washington took just the opposite course during the 1950s, withdrawing services that had been guaranteed, in many cases, by treaties that ceded land to the federal government. Among the first tribes to have government support terminated were the Klamaths of Oregon and the Menominees of Wisconsin, their lands reduced from protected reservation to state or county jurisdiction, their resources opened to exploitation, and their people often pushed into the cities. President Eisenhower had hesitated to sign the legislation, noting that it lacked the required Indian consent and that it reflected an "un-Christian spirit."

American Indians responded. There were similarities in status and conduct between the black elites who founded the SCLC and the native political leadership that formed the National Congress of American Indians. The NCAI worked as a pan-Indian lobbying organization, fighting the disintegration of Indian culture at the national level and supporting tribes in their own struggles. Churches, associations, and urban centers created local opportunities for Indians to forge political bonds that went beyond their own tribes. By 1961, when five hundred young Indians from over a hundred tribes gathered for the American Indian Chicago Conference, native people were primed like black Americans to fight for their rights. And although the dissolution policy would not be formally repudiated until the Nixon administration, a concerted campaign of protest and challenge ended the program by the early 1960s.

Among American Indians the maintenance of separate institutions constituted not a sudden angry ideological response to white racism but an allegiance to traditions of tribal integrity, at times aided by the federal government. A sense of a common Indian ancestry and history grew alongside loyalty to a tribe and to an extent replaced that loyalty. By the late 1960s some Indian militants had borrowed the spirit of confrontation that infused white and black radicalism. Beginning in 1969, a group of Indians making little of their differing tribal heritages occupied the abandoned former prison island of Alcatraz in San Francisco, asserting the right a nineteenth-century treaty had given Native Amerians to settle on federal land. The act was both symbolic and peaceful. For two years the federal government, which held jurisdiction over the island, allowed the Indians to stay, and the removal of those remaining in 1971 required no pitched battle. But for over two months in 1973 members of AIM, the American Indian Movement, conducted an armed occupation of Wounded Knee in South Dakota, site of a historic army massacre of Indians in 1890. The action signified protest against repeated violations of treaties with Indians. In the course of the standoff between AIM and federal agents, one Indian was killed.

Racial and ethnic groups, of course, had issues in common: access to equal and substantial education, an end to discrimination in labor, housing, and voting, eliminating police brutality and the casual, everyday violence that enforced white privilege. But while the civil rights struggles of black Americans concentrated on the inequalities of segregation, the battles of Native Americans spoke for the preservation of either tribal or pan-Indian integrity. Mexican Americans and Mexican immigrants had their own distinctive concerns, closely related to their particular status of surplus labor. Last hired and first fired, repatriated to Mexico dur-

Wounded Knee, South Dakota, is the site of a massacre of Teton Sioux by American soldiers in 1890. In 1973 armed members of the American Indian Movement seized the village, now part of a Sioux reservation, and occupied it for over two months pressing their demands for reform in federal Indian policy. (Courtesy, Michael Abramson/Black Star)

ing depressions, imported back to the United States when laborers were scarce, Mexican workers formed the underpinnings of the nation's agriculture and with it much of the industrial economy. Harvesting the massive farm produce of California and the Southwest for pennies a day, they held down the cost of food enough to support low-end wage workers in other industries. And by filling labor needs in railroading and industry, they allowed capitalists command of the labor market. Many of the brutal social conditions experienced by Latino people, then, directly linked to work

While earlier reformers in the Latino LULAC and the Mexican American GI Forum had addressed the familiar issues of segregation and schooling, a new group of leaders including César Chávez, Dolores Huerta, and Gil Padilla banded together to demand better wages and conditions for workers in the fields. In 1962 Chávez began organizing his

César Chávez found inspiration in the tactics of the nonviolent civil rights movement; here in 1965 he led striking grape pickers with the words "God Is Beside You on the Picket Line."

National Farm Workers Association; by 1965, he had over 1,700 members, as well as the support of churches and some national unions. The ending of the *bracero* program in 1964—which beginning in 1942 had legally invited Mexicans across the border to work during farm harvests—came at the expense of impoverished Mexicans who now had to slip illegally into the country seeking jobs. But abolition of the program also weakened the ability of the landowners to control the labor market, which they had done by importing workers as need arose. Now the year-round workers at Chávez's base in Delano, California, could more readily conduct strikes and boycotts, forcing local grape growers to provide better wages and working conditions. In 1966, Chicanos formed the United Farm Workers, which initiated a boycott campaign against several growers. Adopting Martin Luther King's tactics of nonviolence and enlisting support from the Roman Catholic Church, Chávez gained considerable national support. Sympathetic Americans across the nation refrained from buying table grapes. And although the United States military in Vietnam made up for slack sales, many growers eventually signed contracts with the union, which turned next to the lettuce industry.

Among Latinos, movements asserted ethnic values and solidarity. Formed in the early 1960s, La Alianza under the leadership of Reies López Tijerina demanded that the federal government honor land rights of which Latino inhabitants of territory conquered from Mexico had been defrauded. The Alianza occupied national forests. In an attempted citizen's arrest of a district attorney, López Tijerina engaged in a running gun battle with the authorities. During the Poor People's Campaign of 1968, a massive demonstration in Washington, DC, that set up a tent city and for several days protested against the conditions of poverty, he confronted black militants among the organizers. He threatened to pull the Chicano participants out of the campaign unless they were treated as equals. An interest in Hispanic artistic and theatrical expression had grown, along with a call among young Brown Berets for Hispanic studies programs in colleges.

Boycotts were particularly successful when the stakes revolved around the economies of producing and consuming. Lobbying, such as that conducted by the National Congress of American Indians, worked best for political issues. Legal challenges, such as *Brown* v. *Board of Education*, were effective when issues could be framed in judicial terms. But each group had also to confront and change social attitudes and cultural beliefs to win over white sympathizers. And for that goal, perhaps no strategy was more effective than that of nonviolence, ordinarily associated with the black struggle for civil rights but employed by other movements as well.

Combating Poverty

By late 1964, before the steep American intensification of the war in Vietnam, antiwar sentiment, already strong in SDS, now dominated many college campuses. But at least part of its membership was prepared to work with the government and other American institutions. Accepting a grant from the United Auto Workers in 1964, a number of SDS activists embarked on an Economic Research and Action Project. In the spirit of the Johnson administration's recently announced social programs for the poor, ERAP workers went into impoverished urban neighborhoods with the intention of organizing the residents to take control of the forces that shaped their lives. The project represented another attempt at creating participatory democracy. It soon faltered. As a college elite, student members of SDS could not effectively become part of the poverty culture that they intended to activate. Still, the effort was significant for indicating that the labor movement, an administration in the legacy of the New Deal, and a portion of SDS could for the moment agree on a common idea of social progress.

During the 1930s, President Lyndon Johnson had been director of the Texas state division of Franklin Roosevelt's National Youth Administration. A rugged, aggressive New Deal liberalism was in his blood and bone. At the same time he possessed a fondness for big business. That combination came naturally to liberals who liked large projects and were prepared to use a range of institutions to accomplish them. Johnson craved the combats and triumphs of politics. Upon his assumption of the presidency, he defined the most ambitious objectives he could think of. He spoke of shaping a Great Society. What this would consist of he did not immediately clarify, yet it was supposed to be a matter not only of physical but of cultural progress. Inseparable from the attainment of the Great Society was the War on Poverty. Johnson was sin-

cere about that. In his youth he had seen and been moved by the existence of poverty in rural Texas. He also committed his administration to civil rights. Liberals of Johnson's persuasion knew that for black Americans, their poverty figured as both result and cause of white racism.

Central to Johnson's attack on poverty was the Economic Opportunity Act that he pushed through Congress in 1964. For head of the agency, he appointed the former Peace Corps director, Sargent Shriver, who was related by marriage to the Kennedys. Under the terms of the Act, an array of programs materialized. A Job Corps brought young people into camps where they would be taught skills and if necessary given a basic education. A Community Action Program gave money to neighborhood and Indian reservation groups that were to use it for education and training. Volunteers in Service to America, or VISTA, was essentially a domestic Peace Corps. Other funds were allocated

President Lyndon Johnson's War on Poverty included regions of Appalachia as well as urban ghettoes. (Courtesy, Corbis-Bettman)

to develop small business. Shriver added Legal Services, a program supplying free legal help to the poor. And in 1965 he started one of the most attractive projects, Head Start, which provided very young children of the poor with preschooling, helping them catch up with offspring of the more affluent classes. Much of the War on Poverty—including the training camps of the Job Corps that threw together young southern whites and black ghetto kids—posed difficulties that made the poverty program an easy political target for enemies of the administration. Federal funding of community action groups, some of them militant and confrontational, became vulnerable to attack. But the problems born of the War on Poverty were predictable of an enterprise so huge and sprawling.

Another of Johnson's major achievements was the medical program that President Kennedy had envisioned. Medicare, providing medical services for the elderly, passed through Congress, and to it was attached Medicaid for the poor. The plan—far short of a scheme of national health insurance and yet opposed by the American Medical Association—broke through the barriers that had previously defeated federal efforts to provide health insurance for all Americans. The Elementary and Secondary Education Act of 1965 supplied funding especially to school districts serving the poor. And

even as late as 1968, a president then weakened both by the war in Vietnam and by growing white resistance in the North to civil rights programs retained sufficient political clout to enact funds for housing construction, though few of the units built went to the poor. Still more remarkable was the passage that same year, with some Republican help, of a law banning discrimination in the financing, sale, and rental of a sizable portion of the nation's housing.

Many of Johnson's programs, among them Medicare, student college loans, consumer protection, and funds for housing construction, particularly benefited the middle class. The National Endowment for the Arts and a similar Endowment for the Humanities, along with the Corporation for Public Broadcasting, the well-to-do considered to be especially their province.

During his presidency, then, President Johnson accomplished, in part by sheer force of will, a mass of legislation comparable to that produced by President Roosevelt. By the end of Johnson's presidential years, much of the labor movement had turned more conservative while SDS and SNCC were spinning toward an imitation of third-world radicalism. Yet Johnson could look back on a presidency that had sustained the legacy of the New Deal.

Suggested Readings

General works on the 1960s include David Farber, *The Age of Great Dreams: America in the 1960s* (1994); David Chalmers, *And the Crooked Places Made Straight: The Struggle for Social Change in the 1960s* (1991); David Steigerwald, *The Sixties and the End of Modern America* (1995); David Burner, *Making Peace with the 60s* (1995); Maurice Isserman and Todd Gitlan, *The Sixties* (1988); Taylor Branch, *Parting the Waters: America in the King Years 1954–63* (1988) and *Pillar of Fire: America in the King Years 1963–63* (1998); Robert Weisbrot, *Freedom Bound: A History of America's Civil Rights Movement* (1990); Harvard Sitkoff, *The Struggle for Black Equality, 1954–1992*, rev. ed. (1993); Aldon D. Morris, *The Origins of the Civil Rights Movement: Black Communities Organizing for Change* (1984); and Fred Powledge, *Free at Last? The Civil Rights Movement and the People Who Made It* (1991).

More specific studies of groups and issues, such as Black Power, in the period, both pro and con, are William L. Van

Deburg's *New Day in Babylon: The Black Power Movement and American Cultures, 1965–1975* (1992); Hugh Pearson's *Shadow of the Panther: Huey Newton and the Price of Black Power in America* (1994); and Yohuru Williams', *Black Politics/White Power* (2000). On the earlier Beat culture, which anticipated the counterculture that developed in the sixties, see Steven Watson, *The Birth of the Beat Generation, 1944-1960* (1995), and John Arthur Maynard, *Venice West: The Beat Generation in Southern California* (1991). Books on the student movment, particularly at Berkeley and Columbia, include the detailed study by W. J. Rorabaugh, *Berkeley at War: The 1960s* (1989) and that by a student at Columbia, James Kunen, in the period entitled *The Strawberry Statement: Notes of a College Revolutionary* (1969; reprinted in 1994). The origins of the women's movement is captured in Sara Evans' *Personal Politics: The Roots of Women's Liberation in the Civil Rights Movement and the New Left* (1980). On the liberalism prevalent during much of the decade, see Allen Matusow, *The Unravelling of America: A History of Liberalism in the 1960s* (1984). In Dan T. Carter, *The Politics of Rage* (1995) the shift to a new, conservative politics in America is explored. The events that took place during the Democratic National Convention in 1968 are depicted in David Farber's *Chicago '68* (1988). Studies of John F. Kenney include W. J. Rorabaugh, *Kennedy and the Promise of the Sixties* (2002) and David Burner, *John F. Kennedy and a New Generation* (1988; rev. ed. 2003). Lyndon Johnson and the Great Society are examined in Robert Dallek, *Lone Star Rising*: *Lyndon Johnson and His Times 1908–1960* (1991) and *Flawed Giant*: *Lyndon Johnson and His Times 1961–1973* (1998); and Irwin Unger and Debi Unger, *LBJ*: *A Life* (1999).

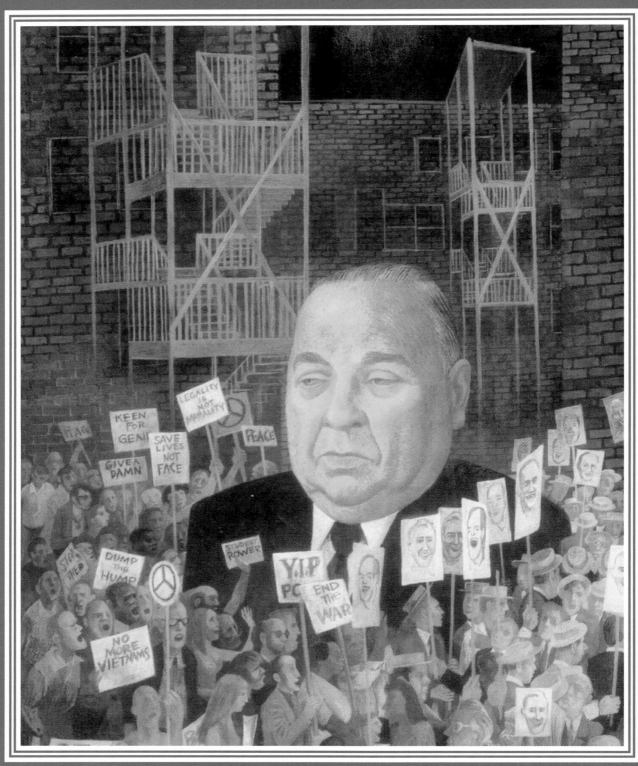

Bernard Perlin, *Mayor Richard Daley.* 1968. *(Courtesy, Library of Congress)*

Vietnam— The Longest War

CHAPTER 25

CHICAGO, 1968

A hot Chicago August greeted the delegates to the Democratic National Convention, assembled to choose a presidential candidate. The arrival of thousands of demonstrators from all over the country, there to protest the Democratic Party's continued support for the Vietnam War, promised clashes to match the weather. How did trouble start? Did a hippie protester taunt beyond endurance an overworked policeman? Or perhaps a lawman drunk on war-inflamed patriotism took the initiative, cracking a demonstrator on the skull. In any event, the violence on the streets, characterized by a national investigating panel as a police riot, is more vividly remembered than the convention itself.

The city of Chicago, a wide clustering of ethnic groups from Central and Eastern Europe as well as Ireland, had also become in the time of World War I a gathering place for blacks from the South and hillbillies from the southern mountain states, both fleeing stagnant economies and seeking larger opportunities. Chicago has also long been unashamed of its urban machine politics. From the Great Depression at least into the 1960s, the Democratic Party offered blue-collar groups in this city and others a promise of concrete aid and economic benefit, especially in thanks for voter loyalty. The system is practical, even if it lacks a larger vision of politics.

In 1968 Chicago, now led by Mayor Richard Daley, was still in the hands of a Democratic machine dating back to the New Deal. His constituents of the old Democratic and urban sort did not quickly embrace the African Americans and politically involved college students who were finding favor with some of the most vocal liberals of the 1960s. While Daley did oppose the war in Vietnam, the flamboyant behavior of much of the peace movement had no appeal for him. Nor did it appeal to his police.

What has been characterized as a "police riot" happened at the 1968 Democratic National Convention in Chicago. The twenty thousand law enforcement officers included federal army troops carrying flamethrowers and bazookas. (Courtesy, Corbis-Bettmann)

Under no circumstances could the Democratic Convention of 1968 have been orderly in Chicago. The party was badly split. With President Johnson out of the running, Democratic politicos backed his vice president Hubert Humphrey. His opponent, Minnesota's Senator Eugene McCarthy, his dry, skeptical manner a contrast to the style of Democratic regulars, wanted the war scaled down until peace could be achieved. Many visitors to Chicago, however, came uninvited. Several thousand peace activists descended on the city. The most highly visible demonstrators were a contingent of cultural rebels, some of them drawn by the Yippies, or Youth International Party, founded by Abbie Hoffman and Jerry Rubin. The "Party" in the title was supposed to be in the sense of "let's party."

The streets outside the convention filled with assorted antiwar demonstrators. At some point, nerves cracked. After provocations from a number of protesters, cops whose purpose had been simply to keep the crowds orderly began wading into them. But since the angriest police were prepared to see a radical in anyone who simply looked young or collegiate, bystanders became victims as well. Tear gas that burned unprotected eyes filled the air. Many activists within the peace movement and its civil rights predecessors had become seasoned veterans of protest, so the crowds were not completely defenseless. Among them circulated paramedics who had anticipated such an emergency and went to work treating the gassed and injured. On television screens nationwide, a domestic war was broadcast.

On the floor of the convention hall, Senator Abraham Ribicoff of Connecticut compared the Chicago police to Hitler's gestapo. Mayor Daley screamed at him. The noise from the convention floor drowned out his voice, but the TV cameras revealed his lips as they clearly pronounced a common two-word obscenity. Amidst the turmoil, the convention nominated Hubert Humphrey for president.

HISTORICAL EVENTS

1945
Ho Chi Minh declares Vietnam's independence

1954
Dien Bien Phu falls to Ho's forces

1960
Student Nonviolent Coordinating Committee (SNCC) is formed

1962
Students for a Democratic Society (SDS) is formed

1963
Buddhists begin strong protests against Saigon regime • Premier Diem is deposed and assassinated

1964
Gulf of Tonkin Resolution • Lyndon Johnson elected president

1965
"Rolling Thunder" • first antiwar demonstration (University of Michigan)

1967
500,000 American troops in Vietnam • 200,000 rally against the war

1968
Tet offensive • slaughter at My Lai • The Reverend Martin Luther King, Jr., and Robert Kennedy assassinated • the Soviet Union invades Czechoslovakia • Richard Nixon elected president

1969
Days of Rage in Chicago • People's Park at Berkeley is demolished • Apollo 11 lands on moon

1970
Invasion of Cambodia • four protesting students killed at Kent State University in Ohio by national guardsmen

1973
American troops leave Vietnam

1974
Nixon reelected president

THE COURSE
OF A DISASTROUS WAR

President Lyndon Johnson's ambitious Great Society policies would have made the era memorable on its own. Had his administration confined itself to such programs, his presidency would almost certainly be defined as a success. Instead it has come to be identified more closely with the war in Vietnam, a horror and ultimately a debacle. An argument once popular among some conservatives asserts that more troops, more bombs, and more money could have won the American war in Vietnam. The claim fails to suggest anything we could possibly have done to the Vietnamese that we refrained from doing or anything that they could not respond to with assistance from their allies. What happened in this little country, about the size of the state of Maryland, halfway around the world?

Background

A sketch of the encounter between Vietnam and the West might begin in the middle nineteenth century. France, seeking like other European nations to acquire an empire, imposed imperialist rule on Indochina, which included the separate Southeast Asian countries of Vietnam, Cambodia, and Laos. During World War II, Indochina came under Japanese control. At the end of the war, liberated France aimed to take back its Asian empire. In its effort, it faced a unique mixture of Communism and Vietnamese nationalism fused in the leadership of Ho Chi Minh.

A Marxist educated in France, a wisp of a man, frail and gaunt with a goatee, Ho prized French culture even as he fought against French imperialism. Just after the war, when the future of Vietnam and the rest of Indochina remained unsettled, he and his fellow nationalists declared that their movement constituted the legitimate Vietnamese government. Ho courted the United States, offering a naval base and using in a Vietnamese declaration of independence passages from Thomas Jefferson's American Declaration of 1776. President Franklin Roosevelt had desired an end to the various European empires in Africa and Asia. The defeat of the Axis powers in 1945 was supposed to bring with it an age of the democratic and egalitarian values that Allied propaganda had proclaimed during the war. But

Ho Chi Minh, longtime Communist leader of Vietnam. (Courtesy, AP/Wide World Photos)

the United States under FDR's successor, President Harry Truman, wanted even more to keep the friendship of France, a country indispensable to an anticommunist alliance of Western European nations. Recognizing the authority of Ho's revolutionary government would have protected it against the effort of the French to reestablish their empire and thereby threaten American relations with France. So Truman rejected Ho's overtures. In the long stretch, no one profited from that decision: not the French, who were freed to wage an exhausting and fruitless war; not the Americans, as events would demonstrate; and certainly not the Vietnamese or their Cambodian and Laotian neighbors.

So the French returned to Southeast Asia, their army supported in large measure by the United States treasury. For Vietnam they set up a nominally independent government headed by an emperor who preferred Paris nightlife to performing the mockery of rule the French had provided for him. At one point, officials attempting to drag him back to his duties in Vietnam had to chase him throughout France: like process servers, in one description, running down a fugitive from the courts. For eight years Ho's troops battled the French and their Vietnamese allies. In 1954 French and colonial forces at the remote outpost of Dien Bien Phu came under siege from Ho Chi Minh's guerrilla fighters. The system of defenses the French had set up there was supposed to be impregnable. The revolutionary troops, however, succeeded in hauling devastating artillery through jungle the French thought to be impenetrable, and it pounded relentlessly at the stubborn defenders. At the news of the fort's crumbling, the French assembly stood silent in tribute to the conquered troops. Certain that the recent stalemate in the Korean War demonstrated the risk of using ground troops in Asia, former general Dwight D. Eisenhower, elected president of the United States in 1952, had rejected proposals to intervene at Dien Bien Phu on the side of France. But he also articulated the domino theory: if one Asian country fell to the Communists, a chain of Communist victories would follow.

Washington Supports South Vietnam

The fall of Dien Bien Phu to Ho Chi Minh in 1954 ended the French cause. It did so not by creating a militarily irreversible situation, but simply by making clear that any further effort on the part of the French would not be worth the effort. Later that year in Geneva, Switzerland, France and the various Vietnamese parties to the conflict along with the Soviet Union agreed to a brief and temporary division of the country, giving Ho's forces control of the north with its capital at Hanoi and establishing an anticommunist government in the southern Saigon City. Nationwide elections scheduled in two years were supposed to unify the country. Washington, however, had not signed on to the Geneva accords and ignored them, instead supplying military aid to the new South Vietnamese president Ngo Dinh Diem. The appointment of Diem, a dedicated Roman Catholic who had lived in a monastery, ran counter to a simple fact: Vietnam was ninety percent Buddhist. Diem, of course, refused to hold the elections scheduled for 1956 since Ho Chi Minh would no doubt have won. In that time of unqualified anticommunism, a coalition in the United States ranging from Catholics to political conservatives and to democratic socialists lob-

Premier Ngo Dinh Diem of South Vietnam was as fervent a Roman Catholic as he was an anticommunist. Supported by the United States, he ruled South Vietnam from 1954 until his assassination in 1963. (Courtesy, SUNY at New Paltz Library)

bied for continued American aid to the South Vietnamese forces. By the early 1960s, Ho's regime in the north centered in Hanoi was infiltrating into territory under Diem's rule thousands of former South Vietnamese who had gone north after the Geneva Accords.

Involvement Deepens

President John F. Kennedy, like Eisenhower before him, refused to make an all-out commitment. No less a figure than the World War II hero General Douglas MacArthur advised him not to get involved in a land war in Vietnam. "MacArthur made a hell of an impression on the President," so noted Maxwell Taylor, Kennedy's chairman of the Joint Chiefs of Staff. "Whenever he'd get this military advice [to escalate the war] he'd say, 'Well, now, you gentlemen, you go back and convince General MacArthur, then I'll be convinced.'" Hesitant but captive to the prevailing Cold War con-

First Buddhist monk to protest the South Vietnam government by setting himself afire, 1963. (Courtesy, AP/Wide World Photos)

viction that saw every form of Communism as an enemy, Kennedy took several incremental measures to resist it. In a vain effort to shore up the South Vietnamese government, Kennedy sent more and more American advisers there. Eisenhower had already dispatched about nine hundred. Each time you send more, Kennedy said, was like taking a drink: the effect wears off and you have to have another. Here as in the Berlin standoff and the Cuban missile crisis, he evidently had little of the imperial, crisis-seeking mentality attributed to him by critics who search for an explanation for the expanded Vietnam War. Yet by November 1963, the American advisers and other support forces in Vietnam numbered sixteen thousand. During the Kennedy years Ho Chi Minh saw Kennedy's poker stakes and raised him, sending more men down mountain roads to aid their comrades in the south.

Supporting South Vietnam was complicated by the nature of its incompetent and corrupt regime. As though he did not have enough of a challenge in opposing Communist insurgents, Diem saw in the Buddhist majority an obstacle to the full prosecution of the war against Communism. At times he set up barbed wire fences around Buddhist pagodas. Toward the end of his regime, a protesting Buddhist monk named Thich Quang Duc struck back by soaking his body with five gallons of gasoline and setting himself afire. Other Buddhist self-immolations followed. Diem's Catholic sister-in-law, Madame Nhu, observed that she would be willing to provide the gasoline for the next barbecue.

Opinions are divided about whether Kennedy, had he lived beyond November 1963, would have attempted to withdraw from Vietnam after 1964. Though he made public statements to the contrary and his cabinet supported the war, he told several friends he would do so. His assassination in the fall of 1963 has left that question unanswered. Meanwhile, however, the problem of Diem was solved. In a coup secretly encouraged by Washington, South Vietnamese army generals removed the premier from office and, against Washington's wishes, killed him. In the next fourteen months South Vietnam's leadership would change hands seven times.

Edging Toward Full War

In August 1964 gunboats in the Gulf of Tonkin off the North Vietnamese coast were reported to have attacked the American destroyer *Maddox*. What really happened is unclear; the Americans may have fired first. But in looking for further freedom in action toward Vietnam, President Lyndon Johnson, who after Kennedy's death succeeded him in the White House, requested and obtained from Congress the Gulf of Tonkin Resolution, essentially authorizing him to act toward that country in whatever way he judged appropriate. Johnson's landslide election to the presidency over Barry Goldwater in the fall voting seemed to ratify the congressional decision. After that heady encouragement this master manipulator of others, and perhaps of himself, had few of Eisenhower's and Kennedy's doubts

GULF OF TONKIN RESOLUTION, AUGUST 7, 1964

This resolution, which passed the Senate with only two dissenting votes and the House of Representatives with no members in opposition, gave President Johnson legal cover for his subsequent escalation of the American presence in Vietnam. The occasion for it was the military clash between the United States and North Vietnam that had just taken place in the Gulf.

To promote the maintenance of international peace and security in southeast Asia.

Whereas naval units of the Communist regime in Vietnam, in violation of the principles of the Charter of the United Nations and of international law, have deliberately and repeatedly attacked United States naval vessels lawfully present in international waters and have thereby created a serious threat to international peace; and

Whereas these attacks are part of a deliberate and systematic campaign of aggression that the Communist regime in North Vietnam has been waging against its neighbors and the nations joined with them in the collective defense of their freedom; and

Whereas the United States is assisting the peoples of southeast Asia to protect their freedom and has no territorial, military or political ambitions in that area, but desires only that these peoples should be left in peace to work out their own destinies in their own way: Now, therefore, be it

Resolved by the Senate and House of Representatives of the United States of America in Congress assembled, That the Congress approves and supports the determination of the President, as Commander in Chief, to take all necessary measures to repel any armed attack against the forces of the United States and to prevent further aggression. . . .

---

about the need for unlimited commitment. He listened to other viewpoints, he worried about how to win the war, but having been molded in Cold War politics he could not bring himself to turn back.

Urged on by Secretary of State Dean Rusk and Secretary of Defense Robert McNamara, Johnson comfortably embraced the idea of a monolithic Communist conspiracy that would advance wherever upon the globe it found an opportunity. Most of the nation, including the *New York Times*, agreed. David Halberstam, later the author of a book critical of the war, wrote in the paper as late as 1965: "Vietnam is a strategic country in the area. It is perhaps one of only five or six nations that is truly vital to U.S. interests." The tortured President Johnson, most responsible for taking his country on a course disastrous for it and far more so for the Vietnamese, would have doubts about the war, but he never swerved from his goal of achieving a noncommunist South Vietnam.

Full Metal Jacket: 1965–1967

Full war came in 1965. "We are faced here with a seriously deteriorating situation," declared Maxwell Taylor, by then Johnson's ambassador to Saigon. "To take no action now," his cable in January of that year warned, "is to accept defeat in the fairly near future." The Vietcong then began a series of effective guerrilla attacks on American bases, notably near Pleiku in February. Goaded by his advisers and the new aggressiveness on the part of the foe, Johnson authorized Rolling Thunder, a program of continuous bombing sorties against North Vietnam. At this time came also the first massive increase in draft calls, and tens of thousands of volunteers and draftees went unquestioningly to serve their country. In April 1965 pilots flew 3,600 sorties against North Vietnam. Johnson greatly expanded the use of chemicals to denude jungle areas where the Vietcong operated. Defoliants turned into mud hundreds of thousands of acres of jungle and rice paddies. Eventually, twenty percent of the land of South Vietnam would be tainted with dangerous chemicals.

All this carnage was supposed to convince North Vietnam that its attempt to reunite the country would be too costly in lives lost, property destroyed, city and countryside alike ruined. Secretary of State Dean Rusk spoke of twisting the enemy's testicles until Hanoi would cry out for relief. The administration conceived a gradually escalated war, pressure to be exerted in stages until the Vietcong met their breaking point. General William West-

"Grunts"—the ordinary ground soldiers in Vietnam.
(Courtesy, Robert F. Martin)

plete with miniskirted stewardesses and free liquor. The Defense Department distributed to fresh American recruits comic books that portrayed the enemy as part of a Communist effort to conquer the world and the Vietcong as bloodthirsty warriors who tortured and killed innocent South Vietnamese. That the Vietcong were indeed brutal gave American propaganda enough believability to cover its more preposterous claim that the enemy was not acting for internal Vietnamese reasons but were puppets of China or the Soviet Union. Every six months ordinary American soldiers, the "grunts," got a break for rest and recreation—vacations in air-conditioned luxury hotels in Asia with their wives flown in to see them. Americans built in Vietnam twenty-six hospitals, 2,500 miles of paved roads, 1,300 commercial generators, and others on floating barges. Forty army ice cream plants were constructed, and thousands of cold storage lockers assured fresh fruits, vegetables, meat, and dairy

moreland, the American commander, agreed except that he urged a faster intensification of the pressure. No matter that the foe increasingly inhabited networks of tunnels immune from attack by air. Bombings could crush North Vietnam's industrial infrastructure. Then the enemy would simply have to capitulate.

But for Ho Chi Minh this was total war on home territory. The American bombing of North Vietnam, meant to break the people's will, instead reinforced it. American resolve, Ho calculated, would weaken in a conflict in which no interest vital to the United States was involved. The "numbers of dead American boys," he observed, "will steadily increase. Their mothers will want to know why." While many more enemy troops were killed than Americans, both Ho and his commanding general Vo Nguyen Giap avoided large battles where the Americans would have the advantage.

More and more American troops were dispatched to Vietnam to fight. The American command asked in June 1965 for 150,000 and got them. By 1968 General Westmoreland had 542,000 and wanted more. Some arrived on commercial airliners com-

President Lyndon Johnson on his ranch in Texas.
(Courtesy, AP/Wide World Photos)

products. Post exchanges afforded air-conditioned movies, bowling, beer, Cokes, hot dogs, hamburgers, French fries, sundaes, candy—and plenty of ice. The amenities of home appeared everywhere the military could place them. The Vietcong seemed oddly able to survive without ice cream.

Losing Hearts and Minds

Almost from the outset American soldiers found that the enemy Vietcong were impossible to distinguish from South Vietnamese civilians. From the air, of course, identification was irrelevant. Bombs, rockets, and napalm, an incendiary jelly made by the Dow Chemical Company that fastened to human skin and burned, fell on Vietcong and peasants alike. Villages were destroyed; noncombatants died, children along with adults; many of the survivors turned to the rebels. Under Premier Diem millions of South Vietnamese peasants had already

been forced at gunpoint to abandon their ancestral villages to be confined in safe hamlets, so that any who remained could be presumed to be Vietcong and killed. American bombing hastened the process of driving out peasants from their old homes. The Americans failed to recognize that the village was the heart and soul of Vietnamese life, its nearby mud fields producing its rice, its hallowed ground containing the bones of ancestors. The war destroyed those ancient ways and communities and killed 400,000 civilians. American friendly fire, bombs or bullets accidentally killing bystanders or peasants who had not sympathized with the Vietcong, injured another million. American suspicions of all Vietnamese heightened, and for reasons that the United States itself was responsible for.

With a naiveté all the more cruel for its sincere intent, the liberal administration in Washington waging the war convinced itself that it was fighting for a more democratic Vietnam. For the belief that

The United States entered the longest war in its history to prevent Communist North Vietnam from taking over noncommunist South Vietnam. The Ho Chi Minh Trail was a system of roads the North Vietnamese used as a supply route for the Vietcong, or Communist rebels, in South Vietnam. (Courtesy, Brandywine Press)

Communism was not the way of freedom, Johnson and his supporters had ample evidence. Most appealing of all to liberals was the concept of a counterinsurgency war waged by United States advisers and elite fighting units in conjunction with the ARVN troops of the Saigon regime. Acting more like guerrillas than like conventional frontline troops, such forces would strike deftly at the enemy, sparing civilian casualties and enlisting peasants in the anticommunist cause. A strategy of this kind, enlisting advanced technical skills and training and putting Americans to fighting side by side with a third-world population rather than against it, would have been in the Kennedy legacy. The Special Forces, or Green Berets, established under Kennedy, were schooled in that kind of conflict. Liberals had even hoped for a time that the fortified hamlets, liberated from the oppressive landowner system of South Vietnam, would provide a social democratic alternative to Communism. They envisioned their becoming self-defending communities, running their own lives while Saigon and the Western troops provided education, medicine, technology. But Washington had neither the ability nor the will to transform Vietnam from the outside. And far from winning the hearts and minds of the Vietnamese, the United States accepted new and brutal South Vietnamese leaders who succeeded Diem. Nguyen Cao Ky, who walked with a swagger, publicly proclaimed his admiration for Hitler. Nguyen Van Thieu adored Mussolini. So Vietnam burned while well-meaning liberals dreamed the idealistic visions born of World War II.

Carried along by the stubbornness of Cold War thinking, the conflict continued into 1966 and 1967. The Johnson forces increased their punishing air raids, confident that these would bring negotiations. They did not. American bombs could not prevent twelve thousand trucks from coming down the mountainous Ho Chi Minh Trail every few days. It was not one simple backwoods trail but as many as ten separate good roads. Bridges were reconstructed within days of having been bombed; makeshift pontoon structures brought out at night got vehicles across streams and rivers after American planes bombed bridges. Industry shifted from the cities to the countryside, even to jungles, mountains, and caves. Neither side would abandon its goals: for the United States, a stable, independent South Vietnam; for North Vietnam, a reunited country. Which side would cave in first was debated

throughout the world. Prime Minister Harold Wilson of Britain told Johnson that his war would lead nowhere. Charles de Gaulle of France, his own country's experience behind him, was savagely blunt: "The United States cannot win this war. No matter how far they push it in the future, they will lose it." Only a few countries, notably South Korea, contributed troops to the American effort. Everyone else waited for the inevitable.

The Antiwar Movement

One of the earliest demonstrations of opposition to American involvement in Vietnam took the form of teach-ins, held on or off university campuses, discussions at which opponents would give factual and moral arguments for withdrawal. Following the first teach-in at the University of Michigan, another in Berkeley in May 1965 lasted for thirty-six hours. Twenty thousand students and teachers attended. A month earlier, at the initiative of Students for a Democratic Society, twenty-five thousand people

Not all marchers opposed the war: "hardhats" march in support of war, New York City, 1970. (Courtesy, Charles Gatewood)

THE DRAFT

The Eisenhower administration, by requiring every American male to register at his local draft board when he turned eighteen, had created conditions for later resentment. Beginning in the 1950s, a set of classifications determined the degree of eligibility for the draft. The category 1-A brought a high probability of conscription. The most serious health problems, or homosexuality, would result in a 4-F exemption. Married men and workers in industries deemed essential to national defense had little or no reason to expect being called up. The most questionable category, at least so it would later appear, was 2-S, renewable by the applicant every year and intended to enable students to continue their education through college and graduate school.

On paper the category 2-S meant not exemption from the draft but deferment from one year to the next. A provision that whoever applied for this classification would continue eligible for the draft beyond the usual cut-off age of twenty-six and remain so until thirty-four seemed a hedge against a student's deliberately stretching his studies beyond the age he could be drafted. But not until the massive American involvement in Vietnam would draft boards begin inducting ex-students whose time of eligibility had lengthened beyond the age of twenty-six.

The rationale for providing 2-S deferments was that to be strong in the face of the Communist foe the country needed as many well-educated people as possible. That went well with the American faith in education. But the ability to turn student deferment into permanent exemption demonstrated that even in a theoretically egalitarian republic, money and the right upbringing offer an infinity of advantages. Well-to-do parents could buy their children private-school education, or at any rate live in neighborhoods with public schools geared to college entrance. Such families could also pay college and graduate tuition and in other ways support their offspring throughout their higher education. It took a war in Vietnam years after the installing of the system to expose a fundamental reality of American democracy: the poor and unquestioning patriots fought; the affluent studied or partied or, to do them credit, protested.

While the Johnson administration conducted its war, a sizable antiwar campaign was developing, especially within the baby boomer generation on college campuses. The students were not cowards acting out of fear of being drafted and sent to battle, for they were exempt as long as they remained in school. But the draft angered Americans of less privileged classes. It was they or their brothers or sons—poor mountain whites, urban ethnic families, black and Hispanic Americans—who made up the bulk of the military. And Americans sympathetic to the war or waiting anxiously for letters from their sons in Vietnam resented students who enjoyed the extended years in college that their country provided them. And in the antiwar movement that soon developed, the students, so it seemed, were mocking everything American. The accusation was unfair. Essentially a white, middle-class, moral generation raised on the idealism of John Kennedy and the civil rights movement, the students particularly observed that the Vietnamese were a nonwhite people. The conflict in Vietnam, they thought, simply extended to Asia the racial war that white American society had for centuries waged against a colored race within its own borders. The antiwar students had a conscience and acted on it. But the resentment was inevitable.

had demonstrated in Washington, DC, and six months later outside the White House thirty thousand protested the war. During 1967 the antiwar forces launched yet more massive demonstrations. In April of that year the Mobe, the Mobilization to End the War in Vietnam, called out opponents nationwide. In San Francisco alone more than sixty-five thousand marchers assembled, and in New York City Martin Luther King participated at a similar gathering. At Sheep Meadow in New York's Central Park burning draft cards illuminated the night. During a demonstration that October in the nation's capital, a few thousand strayed off to the area surrounding the Pentagon. Some of them, refusing military orders to withdraw, were beaten or teargassed. And in the Moratorium, the great demonstration of October 1969, perhaps three-fourths of a million protesters went to Washington.

The nonviolence of the earlier civil rights movement had employed as one of its expressions civil disobedience, the refusal to obey a law deemed to be immoral. Burning selective service cards or sending them back to the draft board extended civil disobedience into the antiwar years. Nonviolent lawbreaking, by the very fact of its peacefulness, made a strong symbolic statement against war. In the demonstrations of April 1967, about 150 young men in New York had burned their draft cards. In October of that year during the Resistance, as civil disobedience to the draft was called, youth in several cities burned them or turned them in. Such nonviolent actions involved no aggression; the young man who destroyed or mailed in his card merely seceded from the war effort. But draft resistance also took other and more assertive forms.

An example is the action in mid-October 1967 in Oakland, California. There protesters, some of them beaten by the police, attempted to block the streets leading to the city's draft induction center. A few days later thousands gathered, some dragging parked cars onto streets they wished to block. As police moved on protesters at one intersection, groups of them moved to another. For hours they kept at their activity. Like the card-burners, they did not practice violence against individuals. But they did place physical obstacles in the path of traffic. In May 1968 occurred another instance of nonviolent force. At Catonsville, Maryland, the Catholic priests Daniel and Philip Berrigan raided the office of the draft board, pouring animal blood over selective service records.

The Berrigans represented a small but determined contingent of Christian and Jewish clergy who resisted the war. Prominent among them was William Sloan Coffin, a Protestant chaplain at Yale. At the end of World War II, Coffin as a military intelligence officer in Europe had declined to interfere as the American army forced back into the hands of the Soviet Union a group of Russian defectors who had served in the German army. After the war, Coffin worked for a time in the newly formed Central Intelligence Agency. He did so for the most

				N. Vietnamese & Vietcong Battle Deaths (estimated)

The Escalating War in Vietnam
1960–1968

Year	U.S. Troops	U.S. Battle Deaths	S. Vietnamese Battle Deaths	N. Vietnamese & Vietcong Battle Deaths (estimated)
1961	3,164	11	(three-year	12,000
1962	11,326	31	total =	21,000
1963	16,263	78	13,985)	21,000
1964	23,310	147	7,457	17,000
1965	184,000	1,369	11,403	35,382
1966	385,000	5,008	11,953	55,524
1967	486,000	9,378	12,716	88,104
1968	536,000	14,589	27,915	181,149

progressive of reasons: he wanted to be part of the effort to stop Soviet totalitarianism. And in those days, the CIA attracted academics and liberals who looked to it as encouraging socialist and social-democratic movements abroad as a counterforce to Communism. Then when the Vietnam war expanded, Coffin determined that this time he would not again cooperate with governmental injustice as he had cooperated in the betrayal of the Russian prisoners. He apparently thought of the resistance as a way of compensating for that moment in his own past.

It was inevitable that supporters of the war, particularly conservatives, would denounce the peace movement as unpatriotic and soft on Communism. But even before 1968, the antiwar forces were to be strengthened by the addition of peace advocates invulnerable to such charges. Some Vietnam veterans themselves joined the antiwar marches, a number ready to tell of atrocities on the part of battle-maddened soldiers.

Turning Point: 1968

Polls taken during the summer of 1967 indicated that for the first time less than half of the public was supporting the war. In San Antonio, President Johnson offered to stop bombing North Vietnam and even suggested that the Vietcong be allowed to participate in a postwar government. Toward the end of the year Johnson decided that maintaining public support would require a great victory. He thought it would come at Khe Sanh, located in a western province near neighboring Laos. The Vietcong massed forty thousand troops around the outpost. In the White House situation room Johnson built a scale model of the town so he could follow the predicted battle hour by hour. He expected it to be another Dien Bien Phu, only this time victory would go to the West.

Johnson got it wrong. The Vietcong were preparing to attack all right, but not at all where he expected. As American troops readied to fight at Khe Sanh, Communist forces massed, eighty-four thousand strong, for what became known as the Tet Offensive, launched on January 31, 1968. More than half of South Vietnam's troops were on holiday celebrating the Vietnamese New Year. Striking simultaneously in thirty-six provincial capitals, enemy troops even managed to blast their way onto

Brigadier General Nguyen Ngo Loan of South Vietnam executes a Vietcong suspect in 1968. (Courtesy, AP/Wide World Photos)

the grounds of the American embassy in Saigon. The Vietcong temporarily captured much of the city of Hué, near the border of North Vietnam, massacring inhabitants suspected of cooperating with the South Vietnamese government. One of the war's most spectacular pieces of photojournalism took place the following day. A South Vietnamese officer in broad daylight encountered a Vietcong prisoner being escorted in the street. He walked up to the prisoner, placed a gun to his temple, and blew his brains out. An Associated Press photographer captured the incident, and NBC News filmed the entire clip for its nightly news. The breaching of the American embassy and the point-blank shooting of the prisoner became defining incidents of the Tet Offensive.

Who won Tet? The Communist offensive was broken, and with enormous losses to the attackers. General Westmoreland claimed a great victory, and had he possessed the authority to carry through against the Vietcong it might have been just that. But countless Americans, their patience with the war already worn thin, had another view of it. Now the evening television news suggested that far from being near exhaustion, the Vietcong had been able to mount an astonishingly broad attack on over thirty cities throughout South Vietnam. President

Johnson, like Westmoreland seeing a victory in Tet, had said too often that the end of the war was just around the corner. Perhaps he was right this time. But his countrymen wanted out.

The American Public Wavers

Up to a point Americans will support whatever war their nation is involved in, and with no questions asked so long as the public is persuaded that the national interest will gain. Most politicians will do the same, because they share the popular sentiment or at least respond to it. At the start of the American escalation of the war in 1965, the public had been behind the effort, along with most of Congress. Liberals backed it as an expression of the Cold War strategy of resisting every territorial spread of Communism. Conservatives endorsed it out of a reflexive anticommunism. Even in the colleges, opposition was confined to uncommonly informed or politically sensitive students and faculty.

By 1966, however, public figures who in no way shared the styles of the campus antiwar movement started raising questions. From retirement Matthew Ridgway, an outstanding battlefield general who had steadied the American lines in the Korean war after the Allied retreat from the Chinese, advocated a switch to defensive positions. Senators J. William Fulbright of Arkansas, George McGovern of South Dakota, and Eugene McCarthy of Minnesota called for some means of scaling down the war. In 1967 a group of intellectuals invited to the White House used the occasion to denounce the conflict. Johnson complained that they had done everything "but piss in the punchbowl." By that year even some members of the administration itself were wavering. In public Secretary of Defense Robert McNamara came across as a steely technocrat, reducing the fighting to numbers of Communist dead and able to show by frigid arithmetic that the Allied forces were sure to win. Privately, he agonized over the war, recognizing the Vietnamese not as numbers but as human victims of bombs and napalm in a war he had presented antiseptically as charts and figures and position papers. He resigned in 1967, not long after General Westmoreland told him it would take five years to achieve victory.

The liberals were beginning to doubt. Doubt was at once a liberal virtue and a liberal burden. From the late 1940s onward, the Cold War had been an enterprise more of liberals than of conservatives, who at the beginning did not want to pay for a global strategy of containment. But while conservatives were initially less dedicated than liberals to doing anything about the spread of Communism, they also demonstrated less awareness of the infinite diversities of social revolution outside the borders of the United States. In their eyes, every leftist regime or revolution was in the service of a monolithic Communist conspiracy, and Communism was Communism, all Communism was evil, and that was that. After the earliest years of the Cold War, liberals showed more inclination to recognize distinctions between one kind of Communism and

Presidential candidate Senator Eugene D. McCarthy of Minnesota, campaigning in 1968, greets students in Tallahassee, Florida. (Courtesy, UPI/ Bettmann)

another, between Communism and local peasant radicalism, and between both and struggles for national liberation. Some liberals, then, knew that what called itself Communism in Vietnam might be different from Communism in Beijing, or Moscow, or Cuba. And if so, why were we fighting the Vietcong? On the other hand, if we did not fight them, would not Communist totalitarianism spread throughout Southeast Asia? And could we surrender to the Communists the limited freedom that the South Vietnamese enjoyed, however compromised under the corrupt rule provided by Saigon? What about the anticommunist Vietnamese who had fought on, assured that the United States would back them up? Could we walk away and leave them to the mercies of the Communists? Such dilemmas tortured liberals, including liberals who had begun by defending Johnson's widening of the conflict in Vietnam.

Presidential Politics in Turmoil

In March 1968, Johnson received a shock. It had been taken for granted that as the occupant of the White House, he would win his party's nomination for reelection. But in the Democratic presidential primary in New Hampshire, he won a popular vote barely larger than that of Senator Eugene McCarthy, who had entered the campaign to challenge the administration's policy in Vietnam.

McCarthy was a Roman Catholic intellectual, spare in manner, understated, in no way fitting the model of a vote-getting politician. Then there were his enthusiastic young college troopers: the Children's Crusade, so their efforts were termed, the phrase taken from a medieval crusade that had sent children against Muslim forces. Knowing the hostility that beards and long hair and other hippie styles in the antiwar movement awakened in much of the public, McCarthy's forces had been careful to insure that whoever among them might encounter the voters directly would be impeccably neat and conventional in dress and manner. It is unclear what the vote for McCarthy in New Hampshire meant— some of it came from Democratic supporters of the war dissatisfied with its failure to bring quicker success—but the result was bad news for Johnson. A president who could muster only a slight majority of the vote in an early primary within his own party did not look like a promising candidate for the general election against the Republicans.

Senator Robert F. Kennedy of New York, running for the Democratic nomination in 1968, inspired strong passions among his followers and had a broad constituency among African Americans and Roman Catholics. (Courtesy, Steve Schapiro/Black Star)

Then came another shock. Robert Kennedy, now a senator from his adopted state of New York, appraised the meaning of New Hampshire and announced his own candidacy for the Democratic presidential nomination. His act looked to be pure opportunism, a desire to profit from the revolt McCarthy had started. But Kennedy may also have been thinking that for the sake of the Democratic Party, the nomination ought to go to someone with more combativeness and wider appeal than McCarthy possessed. Kennedy shared McCarthy's Catholic faith, but little else. In contrast to the Minnesota senator with his air of slightly amused detachment, Kennedy breathed aggressive determination. McCarthy seemed almost disconnected from the political process; Kennedy, who craved winning, was all politics. As the primary campaigns progressed, McCarthy might yawn himself out of the whole vulgar business. Kennedy, so Johnson must have known, would be sure to attack and keep attacking. And he had the asset of being brother to Jack Kennedy, more popular in death than in life.

On March 31, 1968, the president appeared on television. He announced a tempering of the war in Vietnam. He would cut back on the bombing of North Vietnam, and not increase the numbers of American troops. Then he made a startling announcement: in the interest of national unity, he would not be a candidate for his party's presidential nomination.

The simplest explanation for Johnson's decision was his own political weakness, made clearer by polling among Wisconsin Democrats. But the president had been thinking, even before New Hampshire, that he was now too controversial a figure to be an effective national leader. His announcement, at any rate, was a political triumph for the peace movement, and a moral triumph for Eugene McCarthy.

The Democratic Party now had three potential presidential nominees: McCarthy, Kennedy, and Johnson's vice president Hubert Humphrey, who upon the president's withdrawal had stepped in as champion of administration policy. Each represented a segment of the electorate. McCarthy had a following among liberal suburbanites together with faculty and students. Humphrey, a latter-day New Dealer, could divide with Kennedy the Democratic black, blue-collar, and Hispanic vote. But Kennedy could add widespread support among minority groups and because he called for finding some way out of the war, a large portion of politically involved youth to the left of Humphrey's partisans. In the primaries that followed, Humphrey garnered delegates from states chosen by the traditional Democratic politicos, and Kennedy defeated McCarthy in two popular primaries but lost in Oregon, where suburban liberals swung the vote to McCarthy. Then in California Kennedy, on June 5, at the moment of his narrow but important win there, fell to a Palestinian assassin acting on his own and angry at what he saw to be Kennedy's association with Israel.

Humphrey versus Nixon

The most memorable events of the Democratic Convention in Chicago that August took place in the streets. But the meeting did choose Humphrey, who had collected delegates from states in which they were chosen not by a popular vote but by party operatives. In Humphrey the Democrats had a lineal descendant of the New Deal. He believed in the kinds of energetic governmental programs that his party had promoted for years. In a normal election that would win him nearly unanimous support among liberals and people who considered themselves progressives. But now many such people had come to see government as hopelessly subservient to capitalism and the military. It was also liberal of Humphrey to be a supporter of a war that issued logically from the global anticommunism shaped in the Truman administration. But what made Humphrey a good Democrat distanced him not only from the left but from a growing segment of American liberalism.

Against Humphrey the Republicans nominated Richard Nixon, who had lost a presidential contest to John F. Kennedy in 1960. A politician who managed to make enemies of the press, Nixon actually was something of a moderate in domestic policy. But his stiffly conventional manner defined him as a social conservative, an exact opposite to everything that much of the public detested in the campus and off-campus radicals.

That the antiwar forces were as alienated from Humphrey as from Nixon did not reconcile conservatives to the Democratic candidate. By now, a significant portion of the electorate identified Democrats with liberalism and liberalism with radicalism, and radicalism with drugs and anti-Americanism. Humphrey became the victim of that equation. Such voters had also come to associate the Democrats, and the antiwar forces, with concessions to black militants and campus radicals. At the same time, Nixon's implied promise somehow to extricate the country from Vietnam helped him with middle-class and blue-collar Americans who simply wanted an end to the war. The third-party candidacy of the Alabama Democrat George Wallace, then an enemy to the civil rights movement, attracted votes from two components of the traditional Democratic coalition: working-class whites and, of course, white southerners. But these votes in Wallace's absence might have gone to Nixon or perhaps not have been cast at all. As the election neared and Humphrey spoke more of peace and distanced himself from Johnson, he did better in the polls. During the last few days, Humphrey, for fear of offending Johnson, refused to indicate that new peace proposals were being made, and the Republicans succeeded in prevailing on the South Vietnamese to keep these a secret. In November, Nixon was the winner, Humphrey a fairly close competitor in the popular vote, and Wallace a respectable third. It was the end of eight years of Democratic presidencies that had established a tenuous alliance with civil rights forces but splintered the party disastrously.

Vietnamization

By the time Nixon came to the presidency in January 1969, in Paris peace talks were already in place between Hanoi and the United States. It had become clear that the Saigon government and its American allies were not going to crush the Vietcong or the North Vietnamese troops fighting at their side. Nor could the North Vietnamese win a military triumph against the United States as they had against France. Saigon wanted the unattainable, a victory over North Vietnam. Nixon, wishing to come as close to winning the war as was possible, encouraged the South Vietnamese. More American casualties occurred in 1969, after his inauguration, than in any other year, and about half of the 58,000 soldiers who died in the conflict did so after he became president.

Ultimately the administration undertook what came to be called Vietnamization, a process of bringing home American troops and turning the ground conflict over to the South Vietnamese. As it became apparent among American foot soldiers that their job was coming to a close, they began their own separate withdrawal from a war that their countrymen had abandoned. Some openly refused to fight; some wore peace symbols; drug use became common.

Cambodia and My Lai

Washington, however, set about waging one last ground offensive. From bases within Vietnam's neighbor Cambodia, the foe had been slipping troops into and out of South Vietnam. Cambodia's president Sihanouk, a prince by birth who had surrendered his throne to become a democratic politician, kept his country neutral. Early in 1970, however, a right-wing coup with CIA support overthrew his regime. In April, a South Vietnamese and

American force invaded Cambodia to wipe out the Communist bases; bombs rained down from the air again. At a time when the war was losing all meaning, the operation looked like a pointless extension of the killing. Throughout the United States, college students turned from studying to protesting. During a confrontation with protesters at Kent State University in Ohio, tense National Guardsmen fired a nervous volley and four students died. "Soldiers are gunning us down," sang the group Crosby, Stills, Nash, and Young of the four dead in Ohio; the country appeared to be at war with its students. Yet the guardsmen were of the same age as the demonstrators they had suddenly found themselves facing. In an unrelated incident a few days later that further divided the country, two students at Mississippi's African American Jackson State University died from police gunfire.

At the same time, the nation was trying to come to terms with another horror: the massacre on March 16, 1968, by American troops of civilians, men, women, and children, at a village called My Lai. The event did more to form a worldwide impression of the American forces than the restraint of countless other American troops since the beginning of the intervention. Before attacking My Lai, suspected of being an enemy stronghold, Company C or Charlie Company of Task force Barker received a briefing reminding the men of previous casualties they had suffered at the hands of the Vietcong.

One of the four dead students at Kent State University in Ohio, killed by a nervous National Guardsman. (Courtesy, AP/Wide World)

TESTIMONY BEFORE CONGRESS OF ROBERT T'SOUVAS

Q: Have you ever heard of Pinkville?

A: Yes. As far as I remember Pinkville consisted of My Lai (4), My Lai (5), and My Lai (6), and maybe some other hamlets. The Pinkville area was mostly our area of operation, to my knowledge.

Q: Is there one operation in the Pinkville area that stands out in your mind?

A: Yes. In March 1968 we went on an operation to My Lai (4) which is in the Pinkville area. This area stands out in my mind because there was so many women, children, and men killed.

I do not remember the name of my Platoon Leader or my Platoon Sergeant. After we got out of the helicopters, we organized. As soon as I got out the helicopter threw a smoke bomb and I and my Squad were told to look for the Viet Cong in the vicinity where the helicopter had dropped the smoke bomb. Names are hard to remember and I do not know at this time who the soldiers were that accompanied me. We searched for the Viet Cong, but we could not find them until the helicopter radioed and hovered at a certain spot right over the Viet Cong. Personnel in our Company went to the busy area and found a weapon. I do not know if they found the Viet Cong. I was there with my machine gun. After this my Platoon moved into the hamlet and we went on search and destroy missions. I seen people shot that didn't have weapons. I've seen the hootches [simple houses] burn, animals killed—just like saying going to Seoul and start burning hootches and shooting—a massacre wherein innocent people were being killed, hootches being burned, everything destroyed. They had no weapons and we were told that they were VC sympathizers. To come right to the point, we carried out our orders to the very point—Search and Destroy. In my mind, that covered the whole situation.

Q: How many people do you think were shot by C Company in My Lai (4)?

A: This is hard to say—from my personal observation I would say 80 that I have seen myself.

Q: What did the people that you saw shot consist of?

A: Women, men, children and animals.

Q: Did you at any time receive hostile fire?

A: I was told that we were fired upon, but I myself did not receive direct fire.

Q: Were there still any people living in the Hamlet when you came through?

A: When we got there there was still people alive in the hamlet and the Company was shooting them, however, when we left the hamlet there was still some people alive.

Q: Did you see a trail in the village with a pile of dead women and children?

A: I seen dead women, children and men in groups and scattered on the trails and the rice paddies. I seen people running and just innocently being shot.

Q: Did you shoot 2 wounded children laying on the trail outside of My Lai (4)?

A: I opened up on people that were running. I do not remember that I shot at 2 children that were laying down on the trail. However, I do remember I did shoot a girl that was sitting there amongst 5 or more people, sitting there completely torn apart. She was screaming. I felt just as if it was my mother dying. I shot her to get her out of her misery. She was around 15. This happened inside the hamlet. However, I do not remember about the 2 children laying on the trail. I also shot 5 wounded villagers because they did not give them medical aid. They refused to give them medical aid. . . .

Q: Was the combat assault on My Lai (4) different than any of the others you were on?

A: Yes, I never heard anything so stupid as to search and destroy and to kill all those people.

Q: Is there anything else you would like to say?

A: I wanted to talk about this for a long time—and am glad now that it is off my chest—it is wrong. Even before it was investigated, I wanted to write about it to my Senator, but I didn't know how to go about it. This is all that I know about the incident. It is such a long time ago and it is hard to remember the exact sequence of events and I am not too good a map reader and I will not be able to draw a sketch of the hamlet and show how we went through the hamlet.

Some of the dead at My Lai, 1968.
(Courtesy, United States Army)

Finding no hostile forces, they nevertheless fired on the old men, women, and children who remained in the hamlet, killing somewhere between one and four hundred. Rapes preceded several of the killings. A coverup of the event lasted for just one year when Ronald L. Ridenhour, a former infantryman who had heard about it, wrote a letter to Congress that forced an investigation.

Much of the country reacted with shame. But many Americans, either discouraged by the war or angry at the opposition to it, made heroes of the murderers. Americans conscious of the complexities of the problem Vietnam presented knew that guerrillas do not obey the international rules of warfare and often control areas through deliberate terror. The massacre that the Vietcong had carried out at Hué is testimony to that. The effort to eliminate guerrillas from a population within which anyone might be a friend, an enemy, or simply a peasant who wants to be left alone, invites episodes of indiscriminate killing of civilians. One United States pacification effort in a Mekong Delta province in 1969, for example, produced an official body count of eleven thousand Vietcong killed. That only 745 weapons were captured makes it likely that a great many of those dead, if the number has not been grossly exaggerated, were noncombatants. A few who put themselves at personal risk to save Vietnamese lives at My Lai later received official military commendation for their maintenance of a soldier's honor.

The congressional investigation of My Lai, led by the distinguished General William R. Peers, re-sulted in the conviction of only one man, Lieutenant William Calley. Convicted of the deaths of at least twenty-two people and sentenced to life in prison, Calley in 1974 received a parole from President Nixon. When hearing that, General Peers told reporters: "To think that out of all those men, only one, Lieutenant William Calley, was brought to justice. And now, he is practically a hero. It's a tragedy." "After the shooting," recalls Nyugen Bat, a hamlet chief at My Lai who was not a Vietcong before the massacre, "all other villagers became Communists."

In 1972 Nixon, hoping as always to bring about a favorable end to the war, now ordered a heavy bombing of North Vietnam and the mining of its harbors. And at the end of the year, he sent especially massive air raids against Hanoi and the port city Haiphong. But in late January 1973 Nixon, having won reelection by an overwhelming margin the previous November, entered with Saigon, Hanoi, and the Vietcong into the Paris peace accords. Essentially they stipulated that the Communist insurgency and the Saigon government each would hold on to whatever territory in South Vietnam it then possessed. The United States finally was out of the war. When the agreement broke down and North Vietnam in 1975 was on the verge of a total victory, Congress refused to authorize any further aid to the besieged Saigon regime. As the days of that government ended, terrified South Vietnamese crowded outside the American embassy hoping for passage to the United States. The American military did what it could, packing into helicopters

794 • *Chapter 25* VIETNAM: THE LONGEST WAR

as many Vietnamese as would fit, while others clutched in panic at the copters. The scenes of rout carried in the media were for Americans at home their last significant glimpse of Vietnam. With the collapse of Saigon, the two parts of the country were reunited under the Communist government at Hanoi.

A STYLE AND POLITICS OF REJECTION

The radicals of the early sixties, most clearly represented in the newly formed SDS and SNCC before its Black Power years, had approached authority skeptically, critically, but were prepared to see signs that authority was listening or reforming itself. SNCC distrusted Washington but wanted federal intervention against southern racist institutions; the Free Speech Movement at Berkeley attacked the policies of the university yet above all wanted Berkeley to survive as a free campus. The complexity of attitudes at Berkeley is revealed in the relations between the students and the university president Clark Kerr. During the 1964 strike at that school, the activists had identified Kerr with the administration. But when the state university system later removed him for his leniency toward campus activists, students rallied to his support. He had tried, they knew, to stand between them and the state's reactionaries.

By the late sixties, the mood even of nonviolent opponents of the government's policies had changed. The great majority of them did continue to work through established institutions, notably by supporting the candidacies of Robert Kennedy or Eugene McCarthy. Yet by now power itself had come to seem the enemy—all power in government, capitalism, and large private institutions, even the pervasive power of customs. Perhaps, thought some radicals, society should dissolve itself into anarchist communes. Others wanted to use power to smash power, and dreamed fantasies of armed revolution.

The Student Left in Search of Identity

As the war increasingly alienated the student activists from American society as a whole, some student rebels came to define the university itself as an arm of the capitalist and imperialist enemy. Not simply its administrative structure but the content of its courses and even its rules of civility some radicals thought to be at best irrelevant. The discovery of the involvement of some faculty in weapons development deepened the sense of academia as pervasively corrupt. Yet the campus continued to be a forum for dissident ideas. And while ready to call in the police against disturbances, administrators had toward young insurrectionists a degree of solicitude absent in the rest of society. Faculty too had concern for their students and a degree of sympathy for the expression of angry ideologies. University rebels for their part could recognize that the campus was the most congenial public space for publicizing ideas they perceived as revolutionary.

For a moment in 1967, some members of Students for a Democratic Society offered a solution of sorts to a central problem for student radicals: if you are already among the most privileged Americans, how can you identify with the oppressed? Students, the SDS theorists decided, belonged to a new working class. They trained to become the professionals, the artists, the technicians and scientists whom capitalist society intended to use for its own purposes. They were being educated to be exploited: not by poverty or miserable working conditions—to the contrary, they could look forward to a comfortable future—but by being compelled to corrupt their work for the advantage of capitalist imperialism. As radicals, they must refuse to serve the foe.

Among the strikes and other actions that students directed against their colleges and universities late in the decade, the most widely publicized came at Columbia University in the spring of 1968. One demand of the activists was that Columbia withdraw from the Institute for Defense Analysis, a group of universities engaging in research into weapons systems. The university thereupon did withdraw, though its president kept his own membership in the IDA. Another incendiary issue involved a university gymnasium, then under construction on a hill overlooking Harlem that appeared to be a physical invasion of the nearby black ghetto. Under the leadership of Mark Rudd, SDS occupied Low Library, where the university administration had its offices. Black students took over Hamilton Hall. After several days Columbia called in the police. The African American students left peacefully and in good order. The police instead went brutally after the white radicals and a few young faculty members.

Columbia University protesters proclaim REVOLUTION. New York City police invaded the campus and bloodied the students, who opposed military research and the construction of a gymasium on a hill between Morningside Heights and Harlem. (Courtesy, Steve Schapiro/Black Star)

In 1969 Cornell University was subject to an episode that marked a fitting climax to the student radicalism of the time. African American students there demanded a black studies program under racially separatist direction. They also insisted on the university's dropping disciplinary action against some of their number for disruptive incidents. Several dozen of them armed themselves and seized a building. Though they ended that occupation, they announced that Cornell had better submit to them or face the consequences. Cornell gave in to the demands of the black militants.

The Chicago Eight

In that same year, a federal trial in Chicago provided an epilogue to the violence at the previous year's national Democratic Convention. Eight defendants—and then seven since a black militant among them succeeded in getting his case handled separately—had been accused essentially of inciting a riot. Among them were Jerry Rubin and Abbie Hoffman. The two gave the affair much of its color. At one point the Jewish Hoffman addressed the judge, also named Hoffman, in Yiddish, chastising him for working for the *goyim*, the Gentiles. When

Daley entered the courtroom, Hoffman offered to duke it out with him. The mayor, perhaps in his Chicago background as earthy as Hoffman in his, broke out laughing. Earnest reporters of various political persuasions tried to make much of the trial. The jury, more modest and practical in its intentions, failed to find the defendants guilty.

The Prague Spring

In 1968, remembered as the year that the student movement crested, rebellion had seemed worldwide. In France, strikes by students and workers, a coalition of a kind unknown in the United States during the era, brought down the administration of Charles de Gaulle. China fell victim to the Cultural Revolution, an attempt by the regime of Mao Zedong to revive the original Communist uprising. Young Chinese, orchestrated by the government, rampaged through the country attacking teachers, administrators, and any others who by one reasoning or another could be labeled reactionary. In Czechoslovakia, meanwhile, genuine insurrection was in progress. Alexander Dubček, a Communist who was also a sincere reformer committed to freeing the country of its oppressive apparatus, headed a faction that provided a time of openness and public debate known as the Prague Spring. Moscow, however, would have none of it. Claiming to be acting on behalf of the Czech regime, Soviet and other Eastern bloc troops that summer invaded the country and repressed the freedom Dubček and like-minded reformers had initiated.

SDS Turned Inward

That militancy had become its own purpose grew increasingly apparent when in the last days of SDS the group split into two factions, each concerned more with revolutionary purity than with events in the larger world. The National Office identified with third-world revolutionists. Against the National Office was Progressive Labor, which rejected drugs, beards, and promiscuity, and sought a more traditional Marxist alliance with blue-collar workers. Progressive Labor went in for sobriety, the National Office for sex and marijuana.

As SDS disintegrated, adherents of the National Office formed Weatherman, taking the term from a verse by the folk singer Bob Dylan ("you don't need a weatherman to know which way the wind blows"). The Weathermen endorsed revolutionary violence. In Chicago in October 1969, about five hundred of them enacted their theatrical form of it. During their four Days of Rage, they rampaged through the city trashing property. In 1970, in a New York City townhouse that a group of revolutionists had been using for making bombs, an accidental explosion killed two occupants.

The Counterculture

The SDS founded early in the 60s stressed the achievement of identity earned by thought and action. SNCC in its earlier days worked for the liberation of black Mississippians from their bondage to white racism. But as events unfolded during the 1960s, the idea of self-fulfillment among the young became increasingly associated with sensual experience, especially of drugs and sex. Angry at the war in Vietnam, moreover, some radicals concluded that a life-hating repression in American society might be to blame for it all: war, racism, the greed and selfishness of wealth. Could it even be that technology itself, substituting for green living nature, was the ultimate enemy to life? In Vietnam, at any rate, the technology of war was demonstrably set on exterminating life. The hatred of power that turned the later SDS to visions of revolution took other radicals on an opposite course. Going beyond the

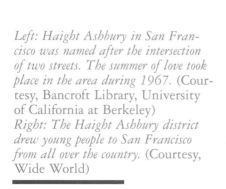

Left: Haight Ashbury in San Francisco was named after the intersection of two streets. The summer of love took place in the area during 1967. (Courtesy, Bancroft Library, University of California at Berkeley)
Right: The Haight Ashbury district drew young people to San Francisco from all over the country. (Courtesy, Wide World)

idea of participatory democracy, they imagined a society dissolved into anarchist communes. Out of such considerations came the phenomenon of the sixties known today as the counterculture.

The counterculture had antecedents. As recently as the Eisenhower era, the Beats had shaped their own culture, gathering in communities in Greenwich Village, San Francisco, and elsewhere, drawn to folk music or experimental jazz. Among the Beat poets, Allen Ginsberg articulated a rebellion against a modern culture imbued at once with war and with spiritual death—"Moloch," he named it—and carried his protest straight through into the antiwar movement of the Vietnam years. Then there was the music of the sixties—folk, rock, blues, together with traditional instruments mating with electronic sound—that entered into the student communes and the festivals of the counterculture.

In the mid-1960s a bus painted in Day-Glo colors and equipped with a stereo set blasting rock music sped across the country, filled with proto-hippies calling themselves the Merry Pranksters. One young woman went by the name of Stark Naked. The destination sign on the front of the bus read simply FARTHER. At the wheel was Neal Cassady, already a legendary figure as the model for the innocent rogue Dean Moriarty in Jack Kerouac's beat novel of 1957, *On the Road.* Whatever the counterculture and its hippie members may later have thought about the evils of modern technology, the road-devouring Pranksters were all automotive gears and service stations combining with enormous distances to express a distinctive American energy. In 1967 the hippie Summer of Love centered in San Francisco's Haight Ashbury district. "If you're going to San Francisco," advised a popular song, "you're sure to meet some gentle people there." The streets of that city were bright with flowers and peasant skirts, flowing with long hair, alive with music and couples and communes. And drugs. By the end of the summer, drug hustlers came out the winners, while some formerly sheltered middle-class children were trying to mend bodies and minds wrecked with chemicals.

Woodstock

Though the counterculture had roots in the dissenting movements of the period, it is often described as antipolitical. And certainly the irreverent spirit of the counterculture went against every kind of political or ideological solemnity. But the Yippies and their founders Hoffman and Rubin, as far from solemnity as any group of jesters could be, put their form of rebellion to political uses, or at least to a commentary on the absurdities of capitalism and its politics. At one point, some of this crew managed to throw a bunch of dollar bills onto the floor of the New York Stock Exchange. Traders, of course, scrambled for them. The presence of Yippies at the 1968 Chicago convention announced that if serious politics could lead to the Vietnam War, politics had better not be taken seriously.

In San Francisco in 1967, cultural radicals calling themselves the Diggers exercised direct political action: they liberated private property, stealing food from stores and distributing it free. They also passed out marijuana. Their program was named in honor of the Digger sect in seventeenth-century England, which had asserted the rights of all people to dig in the earth wherever they are and take its

Woodstock, 1969. (Courtesy, Photograph by Ken Heyman)

goods by their own labor. At Berkeley in 1969, students and neighbors defying conventions of private property constructed on some land owned by the university a People's Park. Shortly, the university prevailed. The park's gardens were bulldozed, and police together with Governor Ronald Reagan's California National Guard removed the occupants.

In the summer of 1969 the counterculture crested publicly at the Woodstock festival in upstate New York. Hundreds of thousands of young people came to hear the Jefferson Airplane, Country Joe and the Fish, Jimi Hendrix, and others, endured rain and mud, and went home feeling joyful and transformed. Woodstock was followed not long afterward by another rock festival, this time in Altamont, California. Its organizers hired as its security forces some motorcycle outlaws. After violence broke out that included the beating death of a spectator, Altamont became known as sealing the end of countercultural peace and love, dreamed of at Woodstock only a few months earlier.

Most distinctive of the cultural radicals, though, were their more intimate and festive activities, some of these enacted in the belief that beyond the reach of everyday consciousness lies a realm of ecstasy and revelation. The counterculture became most clearly defined by its communes, small groups of men and women sharing an apartment or a farmhouse, and by its experimentation with drugs and its practice of farming or handicrafts. In the kneading of clay, the stretch of thread, the press of a knife along wood grain, the young dropouts could receive in their brains and fingers an experience more fulfilling than any drug could offer. Most communes did not last. But the counterculture along with civil rights and antiwar activism lingered, contributing to new movements for gay liberation, women's liberation, and environmental protection. As they grew older, the countercultural radicals brought their experience with them as they entered law, politics, journalism, and in come cases business. In time, some of them would discover in computer technology a skill combining independence with the most advanced technical knowledge, and so leading the way from the rebellious 1960s to the high-tech decades to come.

Suggested Readings

Analyses of the war in Vietnam include James S. Olson and Randy Roberts, *Where the Domino Fell, America and Vietnam, 1945 to 1990* (1991); Marilyn B. Young, *The Vietnam Wars, 1945–1990* (1991); Neil Sheehan, *The Bright and Shining Lie: John Paul Vann and America in Vietnam* (1988); and Guenter Lewy, *America in Vietnam* (1978). A broad survey of South Vietnam during this period is Anthony James Joes' *The War for South Vietnam, 1954–1975* (1989).

Vietnam's history and culture are included in Milton E. Osborne's *Southeast Asia: An Introductory History*, 5th ed. (1991). The role of French colonialism in Vietnam is studied in David G. Marr, *Vietnam, 1945: The Quest for Power* (1995). and explorations of events in Vietnam during the 1950s include Edward G. Lansdale, *In the Midst of Wars* (1972) and J. Lawton Collins, *Lightning Joe: An Autobiography* (1979).

Among the recent monographs on the Vietnam War are Robert Buzzanco, *Masters of Deceit* (1997); Marita Sturkan, *Tangled Memories* (1997); Arnold A. Isaacs, *Vietnam Shadows: The War, Its Ghosts, and Its Legacy* (1997); Fred Turner, *Echoes of Combat: The Vietnam War in American Memory* (1996); Karen Gottschang Turner with Phan Tham Hao, *Even the Women Must Fight* (1998); Keith Beattie, *The Scar that Binds: American Culture and the Vietnam War* (1998); and Jerry Lembeke, *The Spitting Image: Image, Memory, and the Legacy of Vietnam* (1998).

American presidential policies in Southeast Asia are examined in an anthology edited by David L. Anderson, *Shadow on the White House: Presidents and the Vietnam War, 1945–1975* (1993); Lloyd C. Gardner, *Approaching Vietnam: From World War II through Dienbienphu, 1941–1954* (1988); and David L. Anderson, *Trapped by Success: The Eisenhower Administration and Vietnam, 1953–1961* (1991). See also the memoir of Dean Rusk, who served as an adviser to President Kennedy: *As I Saw It: The Memoirs of Dean Rusk* (1990). A three-volume biography on Lyndon Johnson by Robert A. Caro includes much on that president's policy in Vietnam: *The Years of Lyndon Johnson: The Path to Power* (1982); *The Years of Lyndon Johnson: Means of Ascent* (1990); and *The Years of Lyndon Johnson: Master of the Senate* (2002). Other studies that examine the role of presidential advisers include Walter Isaacson and Evan Thomas, *the Wise Men: Six Friends and the World They Made* (1986); David Di Leo, *George Ball, Vietnam, and the Rethinking of Containment* (1991); and Robert McNamara, *In Retrospect: The Tragedy and Lessons of Vietnam* (1995).

Studies that argue for or against American policy in Vietnam are Lewis Walt, *Strange War, Strange Strategy: A General's Report on Vietnam* (1970); William Colby and James McCargar, *Lost Victory: A Firsthand Account of America's Sixteen-Year Involvement in Vietnam* (1989); Eric M. Bergerud, *The Dynamics of Defeat: The Vietnam War in Hau*

Nghia Province (1990); Raphael Littauer and Norman Uphoff, eds., *The Air War in Indochina;* Jack Broughton, *Going Downtown: The War against Hanoi and Washington* (1988); James C. Thompson, *Rolling Thunder: Understanding Policy and Program Failure* (1980); Mark Clodfelter, *The Limits of Air Power: The American Bombing of North Vietnam* (1989); and Earl H. Tilford, Jr., *Crosswinds: The Air Force's Setup in Vietnam* (1993). The best source of documentary material remains the Pentagon Papers, and a good introduction to their content is in an introduction by Neil Sheehan and others, *The Pentagon Papers as Published by the New York Times* (1971).

Among the many oral histories of those who fought in the war are Al Santoli, *Everything We Had: An Oral History of the Vietnam War by Thirty-three American Soldiers Who Fought It* (1981); Mark Baker, *Nam: The Vietnam War in the Words of the Men and Women Who Fought There* (1981); Harry Maurer, *Strange Ground: Americans in Vietnam, 1945–1975, An Oral History* (1989); Otto J. Lehrack, *No Shining Armor: The Marines at War in Vietnam, An Oral History* (1992); and Eric M. Bergerud, *Red Thunder, Tropic Lightning: The World of a Combat Division in Vietnam* (1993). A collection of oral histories from people in South Vietnam is in Don Luce and John Sommer, *Vietnam: The Unheard Voices* (1969).

For studies that view the Vietnam experience from the perspective of minorities and women, see Robert W. Mullen, *Blacks in Vietnam* (1981) and Lynda Van Devanter, *Home before Morning: The Story of an Army Nurse in Vietnam* (1983).

Interviews collected from among North Vietnamese officials and former Vietcong members appear in David Canoff and Doan Van Toai's *Portrait of the Enemy* (1986). An examination of the Tet offensive is in Dan Oberdorfer, *Tet!* (1971) and his *Tet: The Turning Point of the War* (1983); James R. Arnold, *Tet Offensive: 1968, the Final Turning Point in Vietnam* (1990). See also Keith W. Nolan, *Battle for Hue: Tet, 1968* (1983). The battle at Dienbienphu is described in

Jules Roy's, *The Battle of Dien Bien Phu* (1965) and in Bernard Fall's *Hell in a Very Small Place: The Siege of Dien Bien Phu* (1966). See also Robert Pisor, *The End of the Line: The Siege of Khe Sanh* (1982).

Among the many studies that describe and analyze antiwar movement are Nancy Zaroulis and Gerald Sullivan, *Who Spoke Up? American Protest against the War in Vietnam, 1963–1975* (1984); Charles DeBenedetti and Charles Chatfield, *An American Ordeal: The Antiwar Movement of the Vietnam Era* (1990); Tom Wells, *The War Within: America's Battle over Vietnam* (1994); and Melvin Small and William D. Hoover, eds., *Give Peace a Chance: Exploring the Vietnam Antiwar Movement* (1992).

For the process of disengagement of Vietnam by Henry Kissinger, Secretary of State under Presidents Nixon and Ford, see *The White House Years* (1979) and *Years of Upheaval* (1982). Works on Kissinger and his role in political strategy in the last years of the war include Robert D. Schulzinger, *Henry Kissinger: Doctor of Diplomacy* (1989); Roger Morris, *Uncertain Greatness: Henry Kissinger and American Foreign Policy* (1977); and Seyom Brown, *The Crisis of Power: An Interpretation of United States Foreign Policy during the Kissinger Years* (1979). Other studies of the final years of the conflict include Gareth Porter, *A Peace Denied: The United States, Vietnam, and the Paris Agreement* (1975) and P. Edward Haley, *Congress and the Fall of South Vietnam and Cambodia* (1982).

Specific analyses of the aftermath of United States. bombing in Cambodia include Marie Alexandrine Martin, *Cambodia: A Shattered Society*, trans. Mark W. McLeod (1994); Ben Kiernan, *How Pol Pot Came to Power* (1987); and William Shawcross, *Sideshow: Kissinger, Nixon, and the Destruction of Cambodia* (1979). See also David P. Chandler, *A History of Cambodia* (1983). A study of Laos and the communist infiltration there is in MacAlister Brown and Joseph J. Zasloff, *Apprentice Revolutionaries: The Communist Movement in Laos, 1930–1985* (1986).

Richard Nixon in disgrace leaves the White House following his resignation over the Watergate scandal. *(Courtesy, Library of Congress)*

Testing the Reach of Power

CHAPTER 26

WATERGATE

G. Gordon Liddy is, by his self-presentation, a man of will: *Will* is the title he gives to his autobiographical account of Watergate. Gun lover, war lover, for a time FBI agent, Liddy craved a world of risk and danger, secret operations, outlaw missions on behalf of right-wing anticommunist causes. To toughen his will, for years he subjected his left hand and forearm to greater and greater burns: his gun hand he would not damage. He also had a peculiar fascination for Nazi terms and strategies. One of the plans Liddy presented to the Committee to Reelect the President, the presumably crack political team working for President Nixon, involved kidnapping and temporarily detaining antiwar activists who might try to disrupt the 1972 Republican Convention. He called it *Nacht und Nebel*, night and fog, a phrase Nazi storm troopers had adopted for some of their tactics. Yet Liddy showed no evidence of Hitler's racism, and in prison he would apply his legal training on behalf of black convicts. Hugely confident of his ability at dashing intrigue, in action he was a blunderer, quickly ensnared in his own theatrical top-secret schemes. Liddy profiled the kind of operative Nixon loyalists recruited in the war they intended to wage on the national Democratic Party.

On large national issues, Richard Nixon acted beyond his own resentments. Breaking with assumptions that had dictated the course of the Cold War for over two decades, he initiated a measure of accommodation with China and the Soviet Union. But gnawing at his soul was an obsession with supposed foes of his presidency. Nixon's closest political tacticians saw in Liddy, correctly, a good soldier of the cause and, mistakenly, someone who might be efficient at it. They managed to get him appointed to an office in the White House commissioned, vaguely, to attend to matters of security, with the understanding from the outset that the office would be used for forays against the Democrats.

The Committee to Reelect the President—an unfortunate title lending itself to being rendered as CREEP—teemed with secret aggressions, planned or executed, against the Democrats. Of the people who clustered at CREEP, Liddy was the most interestingly deranged. Another major figure, E. Howard Hunt, had worked behind the lines in China as an agent of the Office of Strategic Services during World War II. Hunt afterwards joined the Central Intelligence Agency, the successor to the OSS. At the CIA he conducted covert operations overseas. Another member of CREEP was James McCord, also formerly of the CIA. The first acting director of the committee was Jeb Stuart Magruder, a young businessman standing in for Attorney General John Mitchell. As ultimate supervisor of the committee, Mitchell heard the ideas Liddy came up with from time to time. At one point Liddy surpassed himself: he suggested hiring drug-zonked hippies to do a pee-in at the Miami Democratic Convention headquarters of George McGovern, the leading candidate for that party's nomination. This got Mitchell's abrupt veto: he was slated to occupy these same quarters when the Republicans also met in Miami.

The first assignment that came to Liddy and Hunt preceded their direct involvement in CREEP. In June 1971, the *New York Times* began publishing government documents revealing the process of decision-making that had taken the nation ever deeper into Vietnam. Their revelation was the work of Daniel Ellsberg, a former director of a program in Vietnam but now a passionate opponent of the conflict. The Pentagon had been collecting them for eventual release, so the theft and publication of the documents amounted to a technical rather than a serious breach of security. But the Nixon White House had to act against Ellsberg and the *Times*, the more so since materials would come out bearing on the Nixon years. Legal action included prosecution of Ellsberg and an attempt to secure an injunction against publication of further installments of what were called the Pentagon Papers. But the Nixon people also wished to discredit the culprit. Liddy, always on hand with a novel idea, proposed that at a dinner party Ellsberg's soup be spiked with LSD. Assisted by some refugees from Castro's Cuba, Liddy carried out the more ambitious if less imaginative project of breaking into the Beverly Hills office of Ellsberg's psychiatrist, where they sought unsuccessfully to find damaging information about the patient.

It says much about Liddy's thinking and the conspiratorial mentality of the Nixon people he served that subsequent proposals he made to CREEP went by code names suggestive of military operations. Most important, as it turns out, was Operation Opal, which required planting electronic listening bugs in Democratic National Committee headquarters at Washington's luxury Watergate apartment complex. Approval of that idea, ultimately under Magruder's command, began the downfall of Nixon's presidency.

In preparation for the break-in at the Watergate, McCord in May 1972 rented a room at a nearby motel serving as a lookout post for an assistant assigned to spot any police who might endanger the burglars at their work and to warn them by walkie-talkie. Into a hotel close by moved Liddy, Hunt, and a team of Cuban Americans. After a couple of failed attempts to get into the Democratic suite, during the second of which the burglars discovered that they did not have a proper tool for picking the lock, they did get in and planted electronic eavesdropping equipment.

But the bugs were defective. One did not transmit anything; from the other came a trickle of words that told the spy team next to nothing. Magruder now ordered another entry, this time mainly to photograph records containing information the Democrats might have on the Nixon forces.

On June 16, McCord entered the Watergate building and taped open the latches of several stairwell doors for use in a possible emergency dash from the stairs to a corridor. An odd precaution, it put the spies at risk of discovery and would provide only a second or two extra escape time: from the inside the doors opened without a key anyway. More sensibly, McCord taped the garage-level stairwell, which the burglars would need to open from the outside. Soon after midnight, he and four companions tried to slip into the Watergate by means of that last door. They discovered that its tape had been removed; that meant that they would have to tamper with a lock. It also meant that someone, perhaps a guard, had spotted their presence. But after going back to the hotel room occupied by Hunt and Liddy and receiving instructions to press on, McCord and two others returned to find that the lock had been successfully picked. They went in, one of them making the peculiar decision to retape the garage-level door. It proved a reckless act, for the tape would provide one more indication of a burglary.

And so it did. The same guard who had removed the original tape found the door newly taped and called the police, who began searching the building. The team meanwhile, having once again failed to pick the lock to the DNC offices, had forced the door open.

Liddy's lookout placed in sight of the Democratic headquarters now saw two casually dressed men just outside the DNC offices. By walkie-talkie he called Liddy, asking how their people were clothed. They were in suits, replied Liddy. The lookout reported the alarming news. Again by portable transmitter, Liddy ordered the team to abandon the DNC.

It was too late. The police found the intruders crouched behind desks. Hunt and Liddy, realizing that one of their men had the key to their hotel room, stopped listening and gathered what they could for a quick getaway. In their haste, however, they failed to empty the room.

Even more disastrous was James McCord, who gave the police information. As a member of CREEP, unlike the other burglars, McCord compromised the whole organization. Thus originated the set of revelations that history remembers by the name Watergate.

At the time, the incident itself received scant public notice. Before Judge John Sirica's grand jury the defendants pleaded guilty, which eliminated public exposure through a lengthy trial. From the beginning, however, both CREEP and the White House had been in an uproar. The guilty plea of McCord and his friends got Nixon out of reach before his connections would be fully explored. But Nixon's people—with the president's knowledge—had been using hush money to keep the burglars quiet; and that, while solving immediate dangers, created future ones. The payoffs might themselves be discovered. McCord, who would go to jail after his conviction, became furious at what he saw to be his superiors' desertion of him. Several months later, in March 1973, Judge Sirica received a shocking letter from him asserting that White House staff had been involved and telling of the hush money. Thereupon a Senate committee headed by the respected Sam Ervin, a Democrat from North Carolina, began a wide-ranging investigation into the conduct of Nixon's staff. The story

MEMORANDUM TO: Mr. William O. Bittman
FROM: Dorothy Hunt
SUBJECT: Accounting of Monies Received

In July, I received and paid out the following amounts:

$5,000	Bail money for Frank Sturgis
$15,000	Income replacement James McCord
$12,000	Bail at $4,000 each for Messrs. Barker, Martinez and Gonzalez
$6,000	Income replacement for Mr. Barker
$4,000	Income replacement for Mr. Sturgis
$30,000	Income replacement for Mr. Hunt and Mrs. Hunt
$3,000	Income replacement for Mr. Martinez
$3,000	Income replacement for Mr. Gonzalez
$10,000	Under table bail money for Mr. Barker

(Note: Income replacement was for a period of July-Nov.)

In August, I gave Mr. Barker a total of $3,000 for expenses of travel for himself and others and for telephone expenses, and for interest paid on pawning of wife's jewelry.

In other words, I received a total of $88,000 and have paid out $91,000 (using the final $3,000 from my own funds).

After Mrs. E. Howard Hunt was killed in an airplane crash, it was discovered that she had been carrying $100,000 in cash contributed by Richard Nixon's bankers. (Courtesy, Stanley I. Kutler, *Watergate,* St. James, NY: Brandywine Press, 1997)

started unraveling. Conscience or fear led Magruder and John Dean, a White House lawyer and another supervisor of Liddy, to talk to investigators. The trial of Ellsberg added to the troubles of CREEP. The revelation of the attempted burglary of his psychiatrist's office was good for Ellsberg, forcing a mistrial. But it was bad for the White House team that had conducted the burglary, now known as the plumbers—they fixed leaks.

On April 30, 1973, Nixon had announced the resignation of John Erlichman and H. R. Haldeman, two powerful members of his White House staff. His statement praised them and gave no clear reason for their departure. But the implication was that whatever problems had existed within the White House, the resignations would end them and the American people could now turn their attention elsewhere. In May televised hearings of Senator Sam Ervin's committee would begin. Meanwhile Carl Bernstein and Robert Woodward, reporters for the *Washington Post*, began publishing everything they could about Watergate and its implications, including reports leaked by members of the FBI.

For the open position of attorney general following Mitchell's resignation, Nixon nominated Elliot Richardson, a New Englander of integrity and political standing. As the Senate considered confirmation, Richardson agreed to appoint a special prosecutor to look into White House misdeeds. Once confirmed, he chose Archibald Cox, a distinguished Harvard law professor. Soon after, a witness before Ervin's committee inadvertently revealed that the White House customarily taped conversations between the president and his staff. The practice, which had preceded the Nixon administration, was intended to leave a record for historians of the presidency. But now the tapes promised to be a prosecutor's dream: to be able to listen into the conversations of possible felons discussing their crimes.

Cox demanded that the White House turn over a number of tapes to Judge Sirica's grand jury, still assembled for investigation of the Watergate burglary. The president refused and ordered Richardson to fire Cox. Rather than do so, Richardson resigned. In October 1973 Solicitor General Robert Bork, now appointed acting attorney general, did fire the special prosecutor. This Saturday Night Massacre, as it quickly came to be called, made the White House look even worse.

Soon the House of Representatives began considering resolutions calling for Nixon's impeachment, an action that would empower the Senate by a vote of two-thirds to remove the president from office. Then the White House released the tapes. One of them contained a "smoking gun," in the terminology that attended Watergate, an offer by the president himself to find money to buy the burglars' silence. The tapes revealed a president so boldly running a lawless executive branch that the House Judiciary Committee on a bipartisan vote recommended articles of impeachment to the full House. The Supreme Court ruled that Nixon had to turn over yet other tapes. These newest transcripts revealed that he had participated in an effort to conceal information about the conduct of his staff: in effect, that he too had obstructed justice by using the CIA to thwart the FBI initiative. Now Republican opposition to impeachment collapsed.

The call for impeachment never reached the full House. On August 8, 1974, Nixon resigned. The drama had ended.

Historical Events

1963
The Feminine Mystique by Betty Friedan
• *Gideon* v. *Wainwright*

1965
National Organization for Women (NOW) formed

1966
Miranda v. *Arizona*

1967
Six-day War in Middle East

1968
Nixon elected president

1970
César Chávez's United Farm Workers win contract from California grape growers

1971
Pentagon Papers

1972
President Nixon visits China • Watergate break-in • Nixon reelected president • La Raza Unida formed

1973
American Psychiatric Association revokes definition of homosexuality as mental disorder • seizure of Wounded Knee battlefield by American Indian Movement • Yom Kippur War • OPEC oil embargo begins

1974
Gerald Ford becomes president after Nixon resigns

1975
Cambodia seizes *Mayaguez*

1976
Jimmy Carter elected president

1978
Regents of the University of California v. *Bakke*

1979
Ayatollah Khomeini seizes American embassy in Tehran, Iran • Soviet Union invades Afghanistan

1980
Ronald Reagan elected president and Republicans win control of Senate

1983
Strategic Defense Initiative (SDI or Star Wars) proposed

1984
Reagan reelected president

1987
Iran-Contra hearings

1988
George Herbert Bush elected president

1989
Berlin wall torn down

1990
Iraq invades Kuwait

1991
Desert Shield ends January 15 • Desert Storm begins • Anita Hill accuses Supreme Court nominee Clarence Thomas of sexual harassment

STRANDS OF IDENTITY

As late as the 1960s it was possible to discern within the Democratic Party a coalition sustained since the New Deal including labor, urban ethnic groups, and much of the white South, with the addition of recently enfranchised black southerners. But that last addition, logically completing part of the Democratic politics of the New Deal, complicated the coalition. White southerners, even though their racial views were softening a bit, began to move away from the Democrats. So did some union members in the North, among whom racism was common. The peace wing of the Democratic Party and the growing visibility of feminists and advocates of a strengthened and sometimes separate representation in politics for one or another minority—identity politics, it has come to be called—cast over the party a new public face and a problem.

Identity politics presents legislators with a quandary. Conventional interest-group politics addresses people on the basis of economics: farmer, retailer, steelworker, teacher; or locality: city, country, South. The newer militancies seek to define individuals according to biological imperative, sexual preference, ethnic ancestry, or upbringing. And they do so, at least in part, recognizing that people will be so identified whether they wish to be or not. Politicians, along with the new militants themselves, have had to decide how to reconcile that perception with the concept of justice as operating on impersonal standards of equality. The civil rights movement of the 1950s and 1960s raised the question, but a corollary movement—a new feminism—did so even more urgently.

The Women's Movement

In 1963 Betty Friedan published *The Feminine Mystique*, an attack on society's consignment of women to what she described as the constraining and psychologically crippling role of housewife. That same year the report of the Kennedy administration's Presidential Commission on the Status of Women appeared. It cataloged injustices women faced in the workplace as well as in such matters as property laws. At a time when the civil rights movement had made equal justice for everyone a major national issue, the question of sexual discrimination deserved to be addressed.

The Civil Rights Act of 1964, originally targeting racial discrimination, added the word "sex" as another grounds for banning discrimination. This was partly the result of a miscalculation by a southern representative who, hoping that the inclusion of the word would kill the whole bill, had joined with northern supporters of women's rights in endorsing the addition. Both houses passed the bill as amended, and President Lyndon Johnson signed it into law.

The formation two years later of the National Organization for Women, with Betty Friedan as its president, gave the women's movement a wider voice. Opening its membership to both genders, NOW argued that the prevailing system of relations worked injustices on men as well as women. Among the range of reforms for which NOW worked was the passage of an equal-rights amendment to the Constitution, prohibiting sexual discrimination by federal or state governments. The organization also called for an end to legal restrictions on abortion.

Soon afterwards, some women adopted the confrontational style then popular. In 1969 a group calling itself the Redstockings characterized men in general as oppressors; their subjugation of females had been "the oldest, most basic form of domination." Inequality between the sexes they deemed the basis of capitalism, imperialism, and racism. It must therefore be uprooted along with all customary forms and relations between the sexes. A few feminists held lesbianism to be the only appropriate female orientation. Perhaps in some future social and cultural transformation, radical feminists thought, women and men will join in true partnership; meanwhile, sisterhood is powerful and must take its own path.

Among the reasons for this angry turn by at least some feminists should be counted the experience of female civil rights and antiwar workers. Having absorbed the egalitarian ideals of these movements, women activists expected to be treated, and respected, as the fully equal companions of male activists. Instead, they often found themselves assigned the task of coffee maker or typist or supplier of sexual recreation for the male front-line soldiers of social change. Women began forming consciousness-raising groups: small gatherings at which they aired their frustrations and the sense of inferiority instilled in them by a patriarchal social order. Such experiences could uncover many problems involv-

A state criminal abortion statute of the current Texas type, that excerpts from criminality only a *life saving* procedure on behalf of the mother, without regard to pregnancy stage and without recognition of the other interests involved, is violative of the Due Process Clause of the Fourteenth Amendment.

(a) For the stage prior to approximately the end of the first trimester, the abortion decision, and its effectuation must be left to the medical judgment of the pregnant woman's attending physician.

(b) For the stage subsequent to approximately the end of the first trimester, the State, in promoting its interest in the health of the mother, may, if it chooses, regulate the abortion procedure in ways that are reasonably related to maternal health.

(c) For the stage subsequent to viability the State, in promoting its interest in the potentiality of human life, may, if it chooses, regulate, and even prescribe, abortion except where it is necessary, in appropriate medical judgment, for the preservation of the life or health of the mother.

Source, Roe v. *Wade, 410 U.S. 113, 1973*

able by merely economic or other political measures, and many women now discovered in active bonding with other women a strengthened female identity, a resource and means of support. Feminists addressed the violence to spouses and children when men abandon pregnant women; shelters established for abused women revealed another wayward tendency of some men.

One issue identified with almost all parts of the women's movement has long made for intense controversy: abortion. *Roe* v. *Wade*, a Supreme Court decision of 1973, held that abortion assisted by a willing physician is a woman's absolute right during the first three months of pregnancy and a presumable right during the second trimester if not beyond. In response, a right-to-life movement, widely if not exclusively among social conservatives and Roman Catholics, argued to the contrary that

the fetus has a meaningful life that must be protected.

Gay and Lesbian Liberation

Over much of the twentieth century, conservatives and liberals alike have expressed widespread hostility to homosexuality. During the McCarthy period, liberals spread accurate but, most would say today, morally irrelevant stories about the senator's staff. But with the more general widening of sexual freedom during the 1960s, prejudice against homosexuality made little sense. The call that the civil rights movement made to abandon prejudice and hatred encouraged a growing public rejection of discrimination against homosexuals and lesbians.

The birth of the modern gay liberation movement is often traced to an incident at the Stonewall Inn, a gay bar in New York City's Greenwich Village. In 1969 police raided Stonewall, expecting customers to flee or submit to arrest. Instead, they and other gays in the area, spurred by the growing pride expressed by other groups, fought the police. This act of assertion by members of a previously scorned population evoked among many gays a will to confront discrimination publicly. In 1973 the American Psychiatric Association officially revoked its longstanding definition of homosexuality as a mental disorder. Considerable evidence that biology largely determines sexual preference has buttressed the view that homosexuality occurs naturally and is as morally neutral an orientation as heterosexuality.

In the early 1980s the gay community was struck a devastating blow with the appearance among many of its members of the deadly affliction known as AIDS—acquired immune deficiency syndrome, brought by the virus HIV after years of dormancy. The ravages of AIDS have led to widely supported demands for governmental funding for treatment and research. Combating AIDS, communicable by sharing the needles used in drug abuse as well as sexual encounters, has given gay activism added purpose and energy.

A Newer New Immigration

The census of 1990 counted Asians by birth or ancestry—Chinese, Japanese, Korean, Vietnamese, or others—as together constituting three percent of the population of the United States. Since then, these new groups have been steadily gaining visibility, in movie and TV drama, as newscasters, on the nation's campuses. The soaring immigration of Asians has been enabled by the Immigration and Naturalization Act of 1965, which eliminated restrictions that legislation early in the century had placed on certain social and ethnic groups from the Old World. Until the McCarran Act of 1952, in fact, immigrants from Asia were almost excluded altogether.

The same census revealed that Hispanics born in Spanish-speaking countries in the Western Hemisphere, or descended from families of such origin, made up nine percent of the country's population. A near synonym is "Latino," though that term includes as well people with roots in Portuguese-speaking Brazil. Much of the nation's Hispanic population is of mixed European and pre-Columbian American strains. The largest number, known as Chicanos—shortening of "Mexicano"—is concentrated in California as well as Texas and elsewhere in the Southwest. Other Latinos came from Central America or the Caribbean. And Puerto Ricans, citizens of the United States by birth, have added two million to the mainland population of Hispanics. Cuban Americans cluster in Florida. Hispanics of varying backgrounds also live in large cities such as New York.

The 1965 law imposed a limit of twenty thousand immigrants a year from each country outside the Western Hemisphere. The new law placed limitations for the first time on people immigrating to the United States from the Americas, restricting them to 120,000 a year. An amendment in 1976 placed a limit of twenty thousand per country with the exception of Cuba. Recognizing the repressiveness of Cuba's essentially Communist regime, Congress made an exception and allowed Cuban refugees to enter the United States in unlimited numbers. Within the national quotas set by recent laws, immigrants possessing desirable skills or having family members already in the United States are granted preference. Overriding all this, though, are waves of immigrants who enter the United States illegally and lead a precarious underlife here.

Hispanic Activism

From almost the moment in the nineteenth century when the United States took control of territory won during the Mexican War, Chicanos have suffered from poverty and ethnic prejudice, to-gether with illegal or questionable seizure of their lands. In responding to the liberation politics of the 1960s, they could draw on the resources of a community already in place. Asserting cultural power was nearly indistinguishable from seeking economic and political progress.

Soon after the Second World War, Chicano veterans and other Hispanics in the Southwest had organized to fight discrimination. Then, in 1963, the ethnically Mexican majority in Crystal City, Texas, won control of the city council, establishing a new political presence. That year Reyes López Tijerina founded the Alianza. La Raza Unida, formed in Texas in 1972 and led by José Angel Gutierrez, also sought political organization.

Of all forms of Hispanic activism, the greatest national attention went not to an assertively ethnic

In 1972 Mexican Americans formed La Raza Unida to further Chicano causes. (Courtesy, Sally Andersen-Bruce, Museum of American Political Life, University of Hartford, West Hartford, CT)

movement but to César Chávez's United Farm Workers. By 1970 the well-established UFW had brought half the grape growers to terms. The union went on to organize the lettuce pickers. Though the UFW had few expressly cultural concerns, the numerical dominance of Chicanos in the organization, the widespread use of Spanish among them, and the status of outsider that they suffered both as migrants and as Hispanics led naturally to a melding of political, economic, and cultural expression.

Indian Activism

The diverse peoples who today generally are defined under the terms American Indians, Indian peoples, or Native Americans have had an extraordinarily shifting set of relations with the federal government. At one time or another, European Americans have perceived them as altogether outside civilization, as separable into civilized and wild, as internal nations, or simply as Americans of particular cultures.

During the sixties and afterwards, Indian activists inspired by the civil rights movement fought at once for economic betterment and for the assertion of American Indian culture. The peaceful occu-

An American Indian Movement protest lasting over two months at the site of the Battle of Wounded Knee in South Dakota. (Courtesy, Library of Congress)

pation of Alcatraz Prison and the armed seizure of the Wounded Knee battlefield encompassed both objectives. A continuing demand called for the return of lost tribal lands. The National Indian Youth Council worked for the preservation of the rights of Indians as a separate people. Legislation passed in 1974 gave to tribes additional control over federal programs on their lands. Other laws returned territory to Alaskan Eskimos and Indians, and tribes in Maine received some reparations for lost territories. Compensation went also to the Lakota Sioux for the Black Hills of South Dakota, which had been taken from their ancestors in the 1870s.

Affirmative Action

A controversial policy of the federal and state governments is affirmative action. It allows practices in employment and college admission that in some degree favor women, blacks, and members of ethnic groups previously victimized by prejudice. The original intent of affirmative action did not propose perpetual special entitlement to women and minorities, but aimed rather at breaking down surviving patterns of discrimination. Once the old practices had been overcome, the belief went, affirmative action would disappear. The problem, or so claim opponents of the policy, is that in seeking to end preferential hiring of whites, men, and other customarily privileged Americans, it has bestowed continuing and permanent preferential status on newly assertive groups.

The clearest problem is constitutional. Suppose the federal government hires or a state college admits a Hispanic solely on the grounds of ethnicity, thereby excluding another applicant. In that event, the kind of discrimination that the Supreme Court in its earlier civil-rights rulings has held to be unconstitutional would seem to have occurred. In 1978 the Court held in *Regents of the University of California* v. *Bakke* that the university's affirmative action policy for admission to its medical school had unlawfully discriminated against a white applicant. But even in its ruling in *Bakke* the Court by no means eliminated race, gender, or ethnic origin as a consideration that could be taken into account. Affirmative action programs continue to exist in one form or another. And the policy promises to be politically volatile, as recently demonstrated by referenda in California, Texas, and Georgia in which voters approved of measures prohibiting all consideration of race or gender by the state government in hiring, contracting, or university admissions.

In 1968, the politics of racial and sexual identity had as yet little visibility within the Democratic Party on the level of presidential campaigning. But by 1972 many delegates to its national convention were in effect apportioned on the basis of just such criteria. The Republicans meanwhile began picking up, with the help of Richard Nixon, many once safely Democratic votes from groups like white southerners and northern blue-collar workers.

ARRANGING GLOBAL POWER

Failure in Vietnam did not result in any significant American withdrawal from other engagements worldwide. Nixon and his foreign policy adviser and then secretary of state, Henry Kissinger, had a passion for the global management of power—more so, perhaps, than their predecessors. But they now looked for subtler ways to wield the nation's might. To that end Nixon began a process of détente, of a lessening of hostilities between the United States and the Communist world.

Since the late 1940s, American foreign policy had been founded on the presupposition of a general, pervasive conflict between the Communist and the non-Communist world. The existence of non-aligned nations came to complicate that view, as did the rupture between China and Moscow from the 1960s onward and awareness that the Communist regime in the USSR was less brutal than it had been under Stalin. But the essential attitudes of the Cold War had changed little. They included on the part of the West the moral assumption that Communism in all its forms brought such misery to its people and expressed ideas so alien to Western values that the anticommunist alliance must be its uncompromising foe. And every extension of territory under Communist rule threatened to make for greater danger to the rest of the world, offsetting the balance of power. These two beliefs had sent the United States into Vietnam. Nixon and Kissinger shared in the anticommunism that had shaped American thinking for the previous thirty years. But how to arrange balances of power around the globe interested the administration more than ideology.

By the 1970s China and the Soviet Union had grown hostile toward each other. While Moscow had learned to temper its revolutionary fervor, China under Mao Zedong and Chou En-lai directed the Cultural Revolution, turning mobs into the streets seeking to purge supposed enemies of the Revolution. And long since, the USSR and the anticommunist Western alliance had established such nuclear missile capacity that neither could expect to win, or survive, a major war against the other. The globe, then, contained three major power blocs: China; the Soviet Union and the countries it dominated in eastern Europe; and a military and diplomatic partnership between the United States and other anticommunist nations. None of the three had any fondness for the other two; yet none stood to gain from a war. Kissinger and Nixon projected a world of carefully arranged balances among the blocs.

For a beginning, Kissinger journeyed secretly to China, and in 1972 Nixon, to the horror of his right-wing supporters, openly visited that country.

President Nixon surprised the entire world by his trip to China in February 1972. (Courtesy, Library of Congress)

Thus began a process of diplomatic acknowledgment of Communist China that had previously been unthinkable to American policy-makers. In 1972 as well, Nixon extended a friendly diplomatic gesture to the Soviet Union. So long as Beijing and Moscow each needed assurances that Washington would not swing its economic and possibly its military support to the other, each could be counted on to seek some accommodation with the United States. A tricornered world would be safer for everyone to live in, so reasoned Nixon and Kissinger, and that world they sought to establish.

The Nixon administration at the same time prepared to tolerate or encourage anticommunist governments, even totalitarian ones, if that meant satisfactory arrangements of power. The administration used the Central Intelligence Agency, for example, to bring about the overthrow of Salvador Allende's leftist government in Chile. A right-wing military coup there against Allende during Nixon's second administration installed a government under General Augusto Pinochet that soon developed a reputation for torture of dissenters.

NIXON AND MIDDLE AMERICA

Beneath the stiff and starched surface of Richard Nixon, the public image that appealed to his conservative constituency, worked an agile, driven mind that fashioned policy to his tastes. Nixon's transformation of American power in the world appealed neither to militantly anticommunist conservatives nor to liberals concerned with human rights. In domestic policy he proved equally a surprise. Far friendlier to welfare programs than his liberal opponents expected, he nonetheless attempted to recast thinking about welfare. And he as well as his inner circle had an appetite for the authority of the presidency that broke sharply with an earlier twentieth-century conservatism. In reaction to Franklin D. Roosevelt, Republicans had learned to fear the presidential branch of government. In contrast, the Nixon people were enraptured with it, to the point of wanting special uniforms for the presidential guard. The global strategy that envisioned worldwide dispositions of power arranged by the leaders of huge nations fit with his grandiose sense of the presidency. In the end, the inflated conception of the executive office that possessed both Nixon and his staff would become his undoing.

What Nixon called the New Federalism—a plan to share federal revenues by returning some funds to the states to be used as they saw fit—appealed to conservatives who wished to shrink the national government. Yet in his presidency, spending on such projects as housing for the poor grew, and rules were enacted to safeguard the health and safety of employees in industry. Nixon chose the first day of 1970 to sign the National Environmental Policy Act. Declaring the need to establish "harmony between man and his environment," the law set up a Council on Environmental Quality and required of future building projects a statement of their effect on the environment. The Endangered Species Act of 1973 aimed to protect animal and plant species threatened by extinction.

In response to a condition eventually named "stagflation"—an odd combining of inflation and economic stagnation—Nixon imposed a temporary freeze on wages and prices. Such drastic governmental regulation of the economy affronted every conservative instinct. An especially notable proposal that failed under the sponsorship of the Nixon administration would have given poor families direct governmental payments, these to decrease as the breadwinners received more income at work, but at a rate less sharp than a recipient's income grew. The intent of the plan was to encourage work and shrink a welfare system that conservatives thought to be sustaining a culture of dependence.

Nixon cast his public appeal to people he called Middle Americans. That meant middle in being physically inland from the liberal seacoasts, middle in being middle-class, middle in representing the average American—neither black, nor poor, nor otherwise at the margins for which conservatives had little interest. Nixon pitched his programs to Middle Americans in a vague cultural way, and it was splendid politics. But he did not act so meanly as his rhetoric would suggest. He believed that everyone, black or white, who was not a Middle American should become one.

The Supreme Court

Nixon determined to shape a Supreme Court less committed to introducing social considerations into its rulings than the Court presided over by Chief Justice Earl Warren, who died in 1974. Yet the

Court's best-known decision, the *Brown* case desegregating public schools, had won by the late sixties the approval even of conservatives. Other judgments, too, of the Warren Court eventually became solidly entrenched in the legal system. Among these is a 1963 decision, *Gideon* v. *Wainwright*, requiring that when a defendant in a criminal trial is unable to afford an attorney, the state must provide one. Another ruling three years later, *Miranda* v. *Arizona*, held that anyone placed under arrest must be informed of basic rights, such as the right not to make self-incriminating statments. Upon Warren's retirement in 1969, Nixon appointed to be chief justice a conservative, Warren Burger. During his first term the president added three more justices he expected to vote likewise.

The Democratic Party in Transformation

By 1972 Democrats who had supported Johnson's conduct of the war in Vietnam lost control of the party's national machinery. The party now increasingly represented black civil rights activists, antiwar forces, and the women's and gay liberation movements. This regrouping the Democratic presidential campaign of 1972 made clear. As a World War II hero the party's nominee, Senator George McGovern of South Dakota, might have provided connections to the older New Deal Democratic coalition. But the McGovern delegates chiefly represented youth, peace-movement, black, feminist, and other groups that neither liked nor were liked by traditional members of the Democratic coalition. The popularity Nixon had gained during his first term, together with the widespread impression that Democrats now scorned values of the American majority, assured the president an enormous victory in the election of 1972.

He was not to enjoy his triumph for long. Welcoming home American airmen captured during the Vietnam War and released as stipulated by the peace settlement gave the president a moment's celebration. But Watergate dominated his second administration. The man who succeeded him in the White House after his resignation from the presidency was not Spiro Agnew, Nixon's vice president. Agnew had resigned in October 1973 after the discovery that he had received bribes while governor of Maryland as well as during his vice presidency. Nixon, acting under a newly conferred constitutional power, had appointed in his place Gerald

Ford of Michigan, a politician of uncommonly plain integrity. So Ford in August 1974 took over the presidency from Nixon.

GERALD FORD'S TROUBLED PRESIDENCY

Ford tried to put the Watergate affair behind him by pardoning Nixon of any crimes the former president might have committed. The Vietnam War had now turned wholly into an internal conflict. Ford had only to confront its aftermath. Just after Hanoi's victory in 1975 came triumph for the Cambodian Communists, known as the Khmer Rouge forces. A unit of Khmer Rouge seized the American merchant ship *Mayaguez* and detained its crew. Ford sent a sizable naval and marine force to the region, gaining the crew's release. His last

President Gerald Ford pardoned Richard Nixon for his crimes committed during the course of the Watergate scandal. (Courtesy, Library of Congress)

major action bearing on the war admitted refugees fleeing the Communists who had triumphed throughout Indochina.

The spirit of liberation, the sense of possibility grown limitless that gave hope to the black and feminist and antiwar movements in their early days, took energy from an expansive economy. But spending on Vietnam unaccompanied by tax increases invited inflation. Then in October 1973 on Yom Kippur, the Jewish High Holy Day of repentance for sin, Arab forces attacked Israel. At first the Egyptians pushed the Jewish state out of part of the Sinai Peninsula it had won in a 1967 conflict. Israel's counterattack regained some of the disputed territory, but after several days the United States persuaded Israel to settle for a truce that divided the Sinai with Egypt. Angered at friends of Israel, especially the United States, Arab nations imposed an oil embargo that lasted for several months. The long lines at gasoline service stations in the United States gave the country a new sense of limits. The embargo, coupled with a decision by OPEC, the Organization of Petroleum Exporting Countries, to raise the price of oil, drove energy costs high enough to turn an already inflated United States economy into a fever zone.

In 1975 President Ford met with Soviet premier Leonid Brezhnev in Helsinki, Finland. Pledging to recognize European boundaries set after World War II, he gained from Brezhnev and other Communist leaders an agreement to respect human rights. The Communist regimes had no intention of permitting freedom and plurality within their borders. Ford knew this, and the Russians must have known that he knew it. But the agreement extended the slight softening of relations between the two countries that Nixon had begun.

By 1976, when Ford faced the coming presidential election, the federal government in general had lost standing. Watergate, the disastrous war in Vietnam, the flagging economy, a general antagonism to Washington as a dictator of ideas alien to much of the country: all that made it advantageous to select a Washington outsider to run for office.

The claim of outsider in the election of 1976 came from the Democratic candidate for the presidency. Governor Jimmy Carter of Georgia as an evangelical Christian presented a species foreign both to liberals and to the Republican establishment. A white southerner, he was also a committed liberal on racial matters. Having held only one electoral office, the governorship of Georgia, kept him

distant from Washington politics. Carrying much of the South, where he added to a portion of the white electorate a massive support from blacks, Carter also garnered enough northern votes to gain a narrow victory over Ford.

JIMMY CARTER: GOVERNING BY PRECEPT

As president, Carter attempted to govern by moral principle. That demonstrated how far outside he was, not only from Washington but from much of the country at large.

The Energy Crisis and Deregulation

Burdened by the cost of petroleum, the economy continued to tumble. Carter proposed conserving the use of energy. Urging carpooling and the lowering of home thermostats, he also called for taxes that would discourage the purchase of gas-guzzling cars and gave tax credits to promote home insulation. For the long haul, Carter wanted programs for developing alternative energy sources.

Carter got little of what he asked for. Despite waiting in long lines for gas, the public was not interested in cutting its use of energy, voluntarily or otherwise, and the automobile and oil industries disliked the idea of having themselves taxed. An accident in a nuclear power plant in 1979 at Three Mile Island in Pennsylvania raised the danger of radioactive leakage. In a two-week drama widely publicized by the media, neighboring areas were evacuated while engineers struggled to shut down the plant.

Carter assumed that energy conservation, both voluntary and encouraged by law, would appeal to the public. But what had begun as Henry Ford's modest offering of the Model T to workers and farmers was now an addiction, and for employees separated from their workplace and lacking public transportation, a necessity.

Another policy of the Carter administration called for removing some of the regulations that the government had imposed on prices and other practices of various industries. Designed to promote competition that would stimulate economic activity and bring down costs to consumers, deregulation sailed through Congress. Republicans, opposed in general to governmental controls, joined Dem-

American motorists during 1973 and 1974 faced gasoline shortages for the first time since World War II. (Courtesy, Tony Korody/Sygma)

ocrats in supporting it. And the public, not being asked to do anything like make sacrifices, had no objection to it. Among the industries deregulated were trucking and the airlines. Congress also removed a number of rules on banks, allowing them wider discretion in making loans. Deregulating the banks and other financial institutions made possible some of the reckless greed of the following, more economically boisterous decade.

Carter's Foreign Policy

Carter achieved one important triumph in foreign policy. In 1978 at the presidential retreat of Camp David in Maryland, he met with the Egyptian president Anwar Sadat and Israel's Prime Minister Menachem Begin. For years the two countries had quarreled about the Six Day War of 1967 when Israelis occupied Jordanian, Egyptian, and Syrian territories. Many Israelis particularly wanted to hold permanently such areas as the west bank of the Jordan River, including East Jerusalem, the Arab section of Jerusalem controlled by Jordan before the Six Day War. Building on important work Henry Kissinger had accomplished during the Nixon administration, Carter managed to get the two hostile leaders to agree to an arrangement whereby Israel would relinquish to Egypt the portion of the Sinai Peninsula it still held and Egypt would recognize the existence of Israel. After some months, the Camp David Accords resulted in a peace treaty that Begin and Sadat signed at the White House. For the first time, Israel and an Arab country were at full peace.

In keeping with efforts of his Republican predecessors to ease relations with the Communist world, the Democrat Jimmy Carter aimed at achieving a new Strategic Arms Limitation Treaty, or SALT. Nixon and the Soviet premier Brezhnev had signed a treaty known as SALT I, limiting the number of future nuclear missiles. Carter and Brezhnev worked out SALT II, providing for further restrictions. But when the Soviet Union invaded Afghanistan in 1979 to prevent that officially Marxist country from falling to Islamic rebels, Carter asked the Senate to postpone ratification. Anger at Moscow's occupation of Afghanistan also prompted Carter to impose restrictions on grain shipments to the USSR, provide military aid to the Afghan rebels, and institute an American boycott of the Olympics to be held in Moscow. No one so determinedly moral had occupied the presidency since Woodrow Wilson.

Iran

Ever since the Central Intelligence Agency helped overthrow the Iranian nationalist prime minister in 1953, Iran had been governed by a shah, or king, friendly to Washington and granting the United States generous oil concessions. Though the shah made some efforts to improve the lot of his people, his regime seemed to Iranian patriots an American domination of their country. Muslim fundamentalists, committed to a literal reading of the Koran, also looked on the West in general and the United States in particular as decadent and an enemy to Islamic virtue. In 1979 Muslim nationalists overthrew the shah, and the Ayatollah Khomini, religious leader of the country's Shiite branch of Islam, came to power. The Ayatollah

President Carter called the Ayatollah Khomeini of Iran a "crazy man." (Courtesy, Library of Congress)

detested Western and American ways. His government countenanced a mob seizure of the United States embassy in Tehran. For a year the embassy staff was held hostage, its captors demanding the return to Iran of the shah, who had fled to receive medical treatment in the United States. Carter refused, and his government took over Iranian assets in the United States. Except for a failed attempt in the spring of 1980 to rescue the hostages by helicopter, Carter remained steady and unmoving in his public posture toward Iran. Negotiations brought release of the captives on the day that Carter left office. In return, Iranian assets in the United States were released.

Human Rights under Carter

Nowhere did Carter show more resolve to commit American policy to moral principles than in his dedication to human rights. In his inaugural ad-

dress he declared that the country's foreign policy must be consistent in its commitment to them; Congress had already attempted to prohibit the executive branch from extending aid to countries that abused them. Genuinely committed to the issue, Carter established a human rights office in the State Department to monitor violations abroad.

The Soviet Union, correctly reckoning that the policy amounted to condemnation of abuses there, took offense. American advocates of a foreign policy devoted wholly to questions of power also acted with outrage. Concern for human rights would mean, they feared, an end of support to military regimes that employed torture and death squads but remained friendly to Washington.

A lasting monument to a foreign policy grounded in moral conviction was Carter's conclusion of a treaty with Panama that would turn over the Canal Zone to that country in 1999. The treaty enlisted the support of some conservatives who recognized its statesmanship and its contribution to good relations with Latin America, but it stood among the most unpopular acts of a president who remained a genuine outsider.

RONALD REAGAN: THE SUNSHINE PRESIDENT

The Sunbelt

The United States once contained a number of regions that Americans could recognize by name and identity, by folkways and accent. These areas included New England, the middle Atlantic, the mountain South, the Deep South, the Middle West, the Rocky Mountains, and the Pacific. Shrewdness, hard work, and spareness of words characterized New Englanders; many white southerners might be expected to speak romantically of the Lost Cause of the Confederacy. Identification by these sections has not disappeared; but cutting through several of the customary regions is another, often called the Sunbelt. Stretching along the most southern part of the continental states from Florida through California, it has become known for its ability to attract northerners and, on the Pacific Coast, immigrants from Mexico, Asia, and the Pacific islands. Population growth in the Sunbelt has increased its representation in the House of Representatives. Though California in particular continues to be home to liberal and left as well as right-wing movements, much of the Sunbelt would acquire during the 1980s a reputation for conservatism. That is especially because of its identification with the politics of Ronald Reagan, a former movie star and beginning in 1966 governor of California.

The Election of 1980

By the time Carter and his vice president Walter Mondale came up for reelection in 1980, the economy and the Iranian hostage crisis had soured the nation against the Democrats. The call to trim the uses of energy, delivered with the crisp air of vigor of a John Kennedy, could have cast about the presidency an aura of drama and purpose. But Carter's delivery came in a tone at once lecturish and gloomy.

To run against Carter, the Republicans chose a politically perfect opposite. Ronald Reagan beamed innocent assurance that his country could effortlessly do anything. No turning down thermostats and no cutting back on pleasure driving marked his cheery vision. And he benefited from the same distrust of Washington that had worked in the previous presidential election for Carter. Reagan could also identify with the hostility toward Washington among those who opposed big government in general. In November, Reagan and his running mate George Bush, a naval air hero of World War II and a former director of the CIA, won slightly over half of the popular vote and an overwhelming majority of the electoral vote.

Reagan's Supporters

Among the supporters who gathered around Reagan were economic supply-siders, tax-cutters with an argument more sophisticated than appeals to pure selfishness. Lowering taxes, they claimed, would stimulate economic activity. That would generate business growth and thereby so widen the tax base that the government, though taxing a smaller percentage of the nation's wealth, would end up with more total revenue. It characterized Reagan-era optimism: the so-called Laffler curve marking what Reaganites claimed to be the most productive points of taxation originated as a scribble on a cocktail napkin. In having their taxes cut in 1982, taxpayers would virtually be performing a

patriotic duty, contributing to productivity, indirectly pouring money into Washington, and perhaps even providing funds for social programs.

Another major argument of the Reagan politics declared that the country had been declining in strength and prestige. The CIA, missing the steady disintegration of the Soviet economy and society, overestimated the power of the USSR. This President Reagan played up though at little expense in taxation—he borrowed the money—and none in risky ventures. In the process, he made Americans feel good, which set the tenor of much of his presidency.

Adding to support for Reagan was the Christian conservative right, evangelical Protestants who maintained a literal interpretation of the words of Scripture and believed that family life was under assault from liberals. The Christian right along with conservative Catholics fused with the market ideology of Reaganism religious sensibilities not at odds with capitalism.

Deficit Economics

Since the days of the New Deal, liberal Democrats had endorsed the principle of deficit spending as put forth by the British economist John Maynard Keynes. The theory, in brief, holds that in spending beyond its tax receipts, and going into debt, governments can stimulate economic growth. Balancing the books either through massive taxation or by strict governmental economy, Keynesianism held, can hinder growth. Most conservatives, keeping to a belief in frugality, predictably opposed deficit spending. Between the two remedies for it, heavy taxation or cutbacks in social services, they preferred cutbacks. They hated taxation, and they had little liking for the services provided by the welfare state.

Yet early in their tenure the Reagan economists adopted deficit financing. They cut taxes on the wealthy, increased military spending, and borrowed. The administration in 1981 sliced deeply into such programs as food stamps for low-income families and free school lunches for poor children. Neither spending on the military nor any application of supply-side theory resulted in expanding the economy and therefore enriching the tax base sufficiently to hold down the growth in the national debt. Enough loyalty to the doctrine of restrained budgets remained among congressional conservatives to produce the Gramm-Rudman Act of 1985, which decreed at least an attempt at yearly budget balancing. But by the end of Reagan's second term an administration that had denounced liberal extravagance left a hugely expanded deficit.

Reaganomics also entailed releasing previously protected natural resources. James Watt, Reagan's first secretary of the interior, allowed offshore drilling for oil and gas, increased strip-mining that leaves behind an ugly and toxic landscape, and otherwise encouraged industrial exploitation of resources. Watt's policies stayed much in keeping with the Reagan approach, not only because they transferred land and resources from public to private hands but because they expressed a preference for large-scale production and quick profit-taking.

PATCO

The attitude on the part of Reagan conservatism toward unions, a long-standing component of the country's liberal coalition, was revealed when the members of the Professional Air Traffic Controllers' Organization (PATCO) went on strike for higher wages and for relief from the stress to which their job subjected them. The president fired them for violating the pledge against strikes that the con-

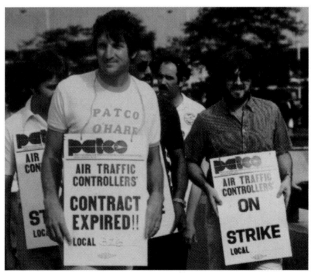

Although the Professional Air Traffic Controllers' Organization (PATCO) had supported President Reagan during the election of 1980, he fired striking air traffic controllers and refused to hire them back when the strike collapsed. (Courtesy, Bettmann Archives)

trollers, like other federal employees, had been required to sign as a condition of working for the government. PATCO was one of the handful of unions that had endorsed Reagan in 1980. Soon unions found that the National Labor Relations Board and the Department of Labor were demonstrating a new sympathy for the self-interest of employers.

STANDING TALL

In foreign policy, the greatest emotional concern for the administration was over the global stature of the United States. The failure in Vietnam, the frustration of the Iran hostage crisis, the distress among conservatives at the waning of the anticommunist fervor of the Cold War made for a sour mood within much of the public that Reaganites longed to address. Their foreign policy reflected the need for Americans to regain pride in themselves. Throughout the eight years of the Reagan presidency, the public would be treated to displays of national pride.

Nuclear Weapons

The Reagan White House sought to increase the nation's capacity to wage nuclear war. At the end of Eisenhower's presidency, liberals had erroneously convinced themselves that the USSR had forged ahead of the United States in missile development. Now the conservatives began to warn of a shift toward Moscow in the balance of power. With Russian industry and society deteriorating, the possibility of the Soviet Union mastering the world with its missile arsenal became preposterous. But Reaganites pushed the Strategic Defense Initiative, or SDI, labeled by some Star Wars after a science-fiction movie of the time. Announced in 1983 and not extensively pursued, SDI was designed to be a system of missiles able to detect and shoot down enemy missiles so effectively that the nation would emerge unharmed.

The administration in practice had little of the fanaticism about nuclear war that some of its policies and the statements of its supporters suggested. Despite the determination to build up the arsenal of nuclear weapons, for example, Reagan did not seriously contemplate its use. An ample supply of intercontinental ballistic missiles could simply add to the American collection of international bargaining chips that Washington could offer to eliminate in exchange for a reduction in Moscow's store of weapons. And for SDI, whatever its feasibility, Reagan had intentions greater than the provision of a nuclear shield behind which the United States could dominate the world. Recognizing how nervous American contemplation of the idea made the USSR, Reagan offered to share American technology with Moscow. That held out the inviting if unlikely prospect of rendering harmless the entire supply of the world's nuclear weapons.

Confrontation and then Détente

In theory, the Reagan administration dedicated itself to unrelenting conflict with Communism in all its manifestations—Soviet, Chinese, Southeast Asian. Liberals of the Truman era had been architects of the Cold War. Jimmy Carter's declarations of human rights had been aimed against Communist as well as right-wing repression. But by the end of the Vietnam War, liberals began to view Communism as simply one more evil in a world filled with massive social problems. Among Reagan's supporters, to the contrary, the Soviet Union was, as the president called it, "an evil empire" and the "focus of evil" of the era. Communism symbolized more than repressiveness: it was anti-capitalist; and Reaganites appointed themselves the purest champions of capitalism.

The administration held to that view when the Russians shot down, in 1983, a Korean civilian airliner that had accidentally wandered into Soviet territory. The event, however discreditable to the USSR, was not intended to set off an international incident. No country could wish to portray itself as the cold-hearted killer of innocent passengers. But the president chose to view the act as deliberate.

Yet in its apparently uncompromising anticommunism, the Reagan White House policy turned out to be far more complex than its public posturing would indicate. Moved perhaps by its habitual unwillingness to place demands on the American public—in this case farmers—the administration lifted the grain embargo that Carter had imposed on the USSR after the invasion of Afghanistan. Reagan's weapons policy embodied a pattern of saber rattling and offers to engage in mutual disarmament. He even moved toward closer relations with Communist China. And later during his tenure,

when Mikhail Gorbachev became general secretary of the Communist Party in the USSR, the president would demonstrate an astonishing willingness to engage, even to trust, a Communist who was also a reformer.

Human Rights under Reagan

Jeane Kirkpatrick, a scholar and Reagan's ambassador to the United Nations, made much of a distinction between totalitarian and authoritarian states. Authoritarian regimes, by her definition, merely enforce existing arrangements of power, status, and wealth, while totalitarian regimes aim at total control of the minds of their people. Dr. Kirkpatrick also accused liberals of practicing a double standard, attacking right-wing authoritarian governments while apologizing for the wrongdoings of totalitarian movements to the left.

The distinction made some sense but failed to note that conservatives as well as liberals employ double standards. Conservatives habitually complained of the brutality of Communist regimes while shrugging at brutality within regimes on the right. Conservatives much admired Professor Kirkpatrick's work, and incorporated it into their pronouncements on foreign policy. Carter's single standard on human rights they rejected for getting in the way of support for military regimes.

And so the Reagan administration supported the infamous military dictatorships of El Salvador and Guatemala in Central America despite their known use of torture, death squads, and what is called "disappearance." Leftist enemies of the state would vanish, the government afterwards announcing its distress and its ignorance of what had happened to them. In Guatemala especially, the military waged war on sectors of the native Indian population. As Salvadorans and Guatemalans fled from civil war, the administration refused to acknowledge their requests for refugee status that United States law granted to individuals with a well-founded fear of political persecution in their home countries.

Nicaragua presented a special problem. In 1979 a repressive government headed by Anastasio Somoza fell to a popular revolution by the Sandinistas, who called for distribution of land to impoverished peasants and other reforms. Yet the Sandanistas also engaged in their own repression of dissenters. Against them arose in the early 1980s another insurgency group called the Contras, gathering people of differing leftist and right-wing persuasions. The Reagan administration, convinced that the Sandinistas were slipping military supplies to revolutionists elsewhere in Central America, wanted to get military assistance to the Contras. But the Democratic-controlled House of Representatives attached to appropriation bills amendments prohibiting such aid. The administration's attempt to get around the restriction would later bring scandal to the White House.

Once again, though, Reagan showed himself not quite so insensitive as liberals thought. Aware of wretched poverty in Central America and the brutality of right-wing forces, he hoped to bring the government of El Salvador to consider some land redistribution and other reforms. Washington provided aid to the Salvadoran presidential candidacy of José Napoleón Duarte, a relatively moderate candidate whose election in 1984 brought a measure of restraint upon the savagery of the country's far right. When a reformist government came to power in Guatemala, the president expressed genuine pleasure in the event.

Lebanon and Grenada

To Lebanon, a country bordering on Israel and wracked by internal turmoil, Reagan sent American servicemen to help keep order. In 1983 a truck carrying explosives managed to break into a marine barracks, killing 241 American soldiers. Reagan, interested more in symbols than in uses of force and stricken by the deaths, essentially pulled out of the country. Soon afterwards there occurred in the Caribbean an event expressive of the militant anticommunist policy side of the American president. A coup on the island republic of Grenada installed a Marxist government friendly to Cuba. Claiming that medical students from the United States on the island needed protection, Reagan ordered an invasion that ousted the government, apparently with the support of the islanders. The incursion, though of no geopolitical importance, pushed the Lebanon disaster into the shadows and gave evidence of an American resolve reawakened.

Morning in America: The Election of 1984

In 1984 the Democrats nominated as their presidential candidate Walter Mondale of Minnesota, formerly Carter's vice president. As his running mate Mondale chose Representative Geraldine Ferraro of New York, the first woman to attain such a rank in a major party. The Democratic primaries also had been notable for the presence of the Reverend Jesse Jackson, the first serious black candidate for president. Reagan, presiding over an economy robustly recovering from a slump earlier in his administration and conveying a happy assurance in his country's good fortune, made him an unbeatable opponent. His heroic recovery from an assassination attempt increased his popularity. Reagan's presidency, his supporters rejoiced, had made it once again "morning in America." The Democrats, though soliciting the identity groups that they had sought since 1972, lacked a core of beliefs and a major, predictable coalition of constituencies such as they had enjoyed in the days of FDR, Truman, and Lyndon Johnson. Reagan won the popular and electoral victory overwhelmingly.

The president's second term in office, however, did not progress so comfortably as his first. Almost halfway into it began the public revelations of a set of secret international maneuvers that came to be known collectively as Iran-Contra.

The End of the Cold War

In the mid-1980s Mikhail Gorbachev, now the leader of the USSR, embarked on a program that involved both *glasnost*, or openness of critical discussion, and *perestroika*, restructuring the system so that it would allow more individual initiative. Gorbachev recognized that a rigid and repressive bureaucracy had stymied the Soviet Union.

Yet Gorbachev faced two kinds of enemies. In the USSR he had to confront Communists committed to one-party rule and the suppression of dissent. In the United States, anticommunists considered him at best an enigma, one who seemed to be at war with his ideology. He appeared nearly as shocking to their ideological sensibilities, which held Communism to be a seamless evil, as he was to the beliefs of ideologues in the Soviet Union who thought Communism to be a seamless good. For Gorbachev to achieve anything in the USSR, he needed ample international respectability and stature to fortify him against foes at home. The American president helped him.

Reagan, often ridiculed by liberals for his simplicity and naiveté, discarded much of his rigid ideology and followed his feelings, which were sound.

IRAN-CONTRA

Marine Lieutenant Colonel Oliver North could have posed for a military recruitment poster. His hand raised to take the witness oath before a televised joint congressional committee, he looked slightly upward, his face conveying the sincerity of a cub scout reciting a creed. The events that he had been called to testify to in the summer of 1987 implicated him in one of the most contradictory, bizarre, and ultimately embarrassing plots ever hatched by the White House, for which he had acted as a secret agent.

Even more in foreign than in domestic policy, the presidency of Ronald Reagan presented itself as operating on ideological grounds. Like every other executive branch from Truman's onward, it staunchly proclaimed itself anticommunist, but also acted more quickly than previous administrations to identify all leftist governments and uprisings with Communism. And even more emphatically than its predecessors, both liberal and conservative, it willingly backed repressive right-wing movements and regimes that would stifle the left. The determination to appear strong, clashing with an unwillingness to demand any actual endurance on the part of the American people, collided with the complexities of a real world beyond the nation's borders. All this produced the scheme that would put Colonel North before a congressional inquiry.

The Middle East presented a continuing problem. Iran fell into the hands of a radical Muslim regime that governed by mob rule. Iran and Iraq went to war over border territory. In Lebanon, a Muslim faction loyal to the Iranian regime was holding a number of Americans captive. Restoring working relations with Iran, a major producer of oil and a force for stability in the Middle East, served the American interest. It might also get the hostages freed. But any gesture of friendship toward Muslim radicals would betray the Reagan presidency's posture of toughness.

Central America posed a dilemma of another sort. There the Reagan administration knew exactly what it wanted: an end to rebellions of the left in El Salvador and Guatemala and the toppling of the leftist Sandinista government of Nicaragua. And it knew how to get what it wanted: support the military in Guatemala and El Salvador and an anti-Sandinista insurgency, collectively called the Contras, in Nicaragua. Reagan could point out that the Sandinistas were imposing their own forms of repression. But his policies went counter to the human-rights advocacy that had partially guided the Carter presidency, and the fairly liberal Democratic Congress refused to cooperate, instead passing a set of measures together known as the Boland Amendment, prohibiting military aid to the Contras.

In both Central America and the Middle East, the Reagan administration's efforts were blocked: in the one case by the Boland Amendment, on the other by the necessity of avoiding any open trafficking with Iran. So a clique within the administration took the logically alternate course: secrecy. The conspirators included the CIA director William Casey, the national security advisers Robert McFarlane and Admiral John Poindexter, and McFarlane's aide Oliver North.

To gain some leverage with the Iranians, Washington secretly arranged the sale of missiles they could use in their desperate war with Iraq. In return, Iran would use its influence to free the Americans held captive in Lebanon. On that part of the deal, the administration was badly taken; only two hostages were freed, and during negotiations two more Americans became captive. Later Iran would brag of fooling the United States into yielding weapons. With equal stealth, the administration conspirators raised money for the Contras from other foreign governments, including Israel and the white supremacist regime in South Africa, as well as from wealthy conservative Americans. Money from the sale of missiles to Iran also went to the Contras. In all these dealings, Colonel North did much of the legwork, operating out of an office in the White House itself, scuttling back and forth among the various foreign parties.

Where did the president fit into all this scheming? It may never be known. In November 1986, a Lebanese paper published the story of arms for hostages; quite possibly the Iranian government had leaked the affair. Reagan's early reaction was to appoint a commission to report

Marine Lieutenant Colonel Oliver North destroyed official documents and lied to Congress about the Iran-Contra affair. Yet the voters of Virginia almost elected him to the Senate. (Courtesy, Library of Congress)

then admitted, that it had been intended as a trade for hostages, calling it a humane undertaking. In testimony before Congress, North and Poindexter both claimed to have kept Reagan from knowing about the illegal Contra end of the plot. White House supporters, now anxious in other cases to portray their leader as stern and unyielding, were happy with the public image of him as gentle, detached from the ugly details of governing, naively incapable of trickery. That curious political wrinkle helped to shelter Reagan from scrutiny, even as his administration was temporarily scarred.

During the course of the revelations, the CIA director Casey died. North, although initially convicted of obstructing justice and Poindexter of perjury and other charges, later emerged with all charges overturned. Many on the American political right embraced North as a patriot and hero. He later narrowly lost a contest for the Senate from Virginia. Passing beyond the scandal, Reagan more than survived, not as the unbending anticommunist his supporters wished him to be but as a statesman of more breadth and shrewdness than could have been expected. He struck amicable relations with the Soviet reformer Mikhail Gorbachev: for a conservative, an act of ideological heresy. And the two successfully negotiated the end of the Cold War.

on the whole business. John Tower, a Republican senator from Texas, headed the investigation. The commission's findings separated the president from direct involvement in the whole business. As to the arms deal: Reagan first denied, and

He liked Gorbachev, who apparently liked him. The two held a series of meetings. In 1987 Gorbachev came to the United States, where he charmed the American public and worked out with Reagan a treaty pledging each nation to destroy a number of nuclear missiles. Modest in itself, the agreement along with the American reception of Gorbachev and his undermining of the monolithic power of the Soviet Communist Party meant the passing of the Cold War.

Society in the Reagan Era

The country during Reagan's second term in office will be remembered for quick wealth and extravagant spending by the fortunate beneficiaries of a booming economy. It left a legacy of the growth

in numbers not simply of the rich but of a class marginalized even within the traditional poor: the underclass, it was termed.

Of these there numbered some ten million. Unemployment (which dropped among the working class in general), mental illness, homelessness, or drug addiction drove them into deep poverty. Cutbacks in social programs spread. But the creation of the underclass cannot be laid entirely at the president's door. For one thing, the breaking of social and communal bonds that religious conservatives complained of was a reality. Monied conservative allies contributed to that breakdown by attacking the ethic of public responsibility for welfare that had inspired the New Deal and other twentieth-century political movements. Liberals also may have added to the problem. Opposed to the forced

President Ronald Reagan to his surprise found that Mikhail Gorbachev believed that large corporations dominated the American government. The two men liked each other, and their two countries became more friends than enemies. (Courtesy, Library of Congress)

confinement of the mentally ill on civil liberties grounds, they managed to win legal policies sending into the misery of the streets people who could have profited from treatment. Even one of the genuine blessings of modern science, the development of drugs for the control of mental illness, added to homelessness by releasing from mental wards people who did not take the medication they required to get by.

In contrast, the extravagances of Wall Street, plagued during the era by cheating scandals, along

PERCENTAGE SHARE OF AGGREGATE FAMILY INCOME, 1980–1998			
	1980	1992	1998
Top 5 Percent	15.3%	17.6%	19.5%
Highest Fifth	41.6	44.6	48.0
Fourth Fifth	24.3	24.0	
Third Fifth	17.5	16.5	
Second Fifth	11.6	10.5	
Lowest Fifth	5.1	4.4	

Source: U.S. Bureau of the Census, Current Population Reports: Consumer Incomes, Series P-60, Nos. 167 and 184, 1990, 1993. U.S. federal data compiled by Ed Royce, Rollins College.

with the rise of a trendy class known as yuppies, "young urban professionals," can be traced in part to the Reagan era. In place of the moral scolding of the Carter era, some of Reagan's supporters substituted a celebration of wealth. They went so far as to imply that the quest for wealth meshed with the good of the country, for it was the only reliable stimulus to work and production.

The money grabbing and the buying habits of the yuppies came in part simply from an economy fired up by the deficit spending of the administration. In boom times, whether Democrats or Republicans run the government, fast money in all its self-indulgent display will make its appearance. And the deregulation movement of the Carter presidency started the spiral that lifted the restrictions that would have made the ambitious responsible for them.

THE PRESIDENCY OF GEORGE HERBERT BUSH

As presidential candidate to succeed Reagan, the Republicans in 1988 selected his vice president, George Bush. For his running mate, Bush chose a conservative young senator, J. Danforth Quayle of Indiana. The Democrats chose for their presidential

To appease conservatives, President Bush pledged "no new taxes," and when he had to compromise on the issue he lost believability among them. (Courtesy, Library of Congress)

nominee Michael Dukakis, a successful governor of Massachusetts.

The Republicans still benefited from the glow of Reagan's popularity. But taking no chances, they waged an aggressive campaign, screening racist television commercials about Dukakis's furlough from prison of a black criminal who then raped a white woman. They endeavored to pin on the Democratic Party their customary accusation of softness on crime. But they also knew that the wide publicity they gave to the affair would flow into the white-racist corners of American politics.

Such campaign tactics Dukakis could not handle. The Democrats had little in the way of a unifying vision, and he could not on his own generate a sense of the urgent necessity for a Democratic victory. At one point in a televised debate with Bush, an African American reporter asked Dukakis whether he would seek revenge if his wife were victim of a brutal crime. He denied the justice of acting individually out of passion: an answer so maddeningly liberal as to invite the political harm it brought him. Dukakis stood in the tradition of Ford and Carter: a man of decency and integrity made for better things than the grubby business of presiden-

tial politics. He was spared. Bush won with a low voter turnout.

The World in 1989

In 1989, the revolution that Gorbachev began within Communism spread until very little of the old repressiveness remained. Throughout Eastern Europe, peoples who now knew the Soviet Union would not intervene overturned their Communist regimes, and for the most part peacefully. Most Russians and Eastern Europeans, in fact, seemed happy enough to abandon their lifeless system.

The Solidarity labor movement in Poland, which had carried on a steady resistance under Communism, prevailed. Hungary and Bulgaria freed themselves. Czechoslovakia underwent what came to be called the Velvet Revolution, a remarkably civil affair of successful street demonstrations against the regime. Much of the inspiration came from the Czech playwright Vaclav Havel, one of a number of Central European intellectuals, among them the human rights advocate Andrei Sakharov in the Soviet Union, who in face of official harassment had kept alive the idea of personal and political freedom. East Germany embodied a remarkable case. Russia, afraid of the power of a unified non-Communist Germany, might intervene if the East German regime was overturned. It did not. By the end of 1989 the wall keeping East Berliners from fleeing west had been torn down. The next year, the two Germanies united. In 1990 there occurred in Romania the bloodiest of the revolutions against European Communism. There the dictator Nicolae Ceausescu was overthrown and executed; for several days fighting raged between his followers and the revolutionists.

A year later the Union of Soviet Socialist Republics was no more. The Baltic states of Latvia, Estonia, and Lithuania withdrew from the USSR, and after an unsuccessful countercoup by Communists within Russia itself, the entire Soviet Union gave way to a loose Commonwealth of Independent States. Boris Yeltsin, a Communist turned anticommunist, now was president. And the Communist Party not only held no power but was shunned virtually as an illegal organization.

Tiananmen Square

In China, the madness of the Cultural Revolution had long since given way to more mundane repression allowing only a few tiny openings to freedom. In the spring of 1989 students and others calling for a greater measure of liberty gathered in Beijing, congregating in the city's Tiananmen Square. For a few weeks, while the government acted with a restraint new to Chinese Communism, Western governments and journalists watched the drama with nervous fascination. But the Communists there chose not to open up China as Gorbachev had opened the USSR. When the protesters refused to disband, the military government massacred thousands. Afterward, China continued in a peculiar condition combining essentially free-market economics with a claim to Communist ideology reinforced with much, though not total, suppression of dissent.

Central America

Events in Europe and in China proceeded without direct involvement on the part of the Bush administration. Though not the major field of ideological conflict that the Reagan presidency had made of it, Central America drew Bush's considerable attention.

Manuel Noriega, military ruler of Panama, in 1989 annulled an election that the opposition had apparently won. In this case, the violation of human rights coincided with another concern in Washington, Noriega's involvement in the drug trade. At the end of 1989 and into the new year, Bush conducted an invasion of Panama that flushed out the military dictator. Taken to Florida, Noriega was convicted in 1992 under a United States law against drug trafficking.

Meanwhile the situation in Nicaragua took a surprising turn. After several Central American governments arranged a truce there between the Sandinista government and the Contras, the Sandinistas in 1990 risked a free election, sure that they would win. They did not. Violeta Barrios de Chamorro, a former Sandinista disillusioned at the regime's turn to repression, prevailed. Washington, the Sandinistas, and journalists observing Nicaragua were equally astonished.

Notable is the good will that the Bush administration had extended toward the electoral process in Nicaragua, even when it was widely assumed that the Sandinistas would win. Some of Bush's people made a point of emphasizing the difference between his administration and that of his predecessor,

insisting that the harsher days of the Reagan era were over. And in 1992 to Washington's pleasure, the warring sides in El Salvador came to an agreement. The rebels disarmed and consented to operate as a peaceful opposition; the government dismantled much of its repressive apparatus and agreed to land reform.

Iraq

Iraq's strongman Saddam Hussein, recently the victor in a war with Iran, invaded in 1990 the tiny Arab principality of Kuwait, claiming that it was historically Iraqi. The incursion amounted to a blatant violation of another country's sovereignty. Saudi Arabia and other states on the Arabian Peninsula expressed alarm for their own safety. Israel saw a strong enemy on the march. The West reacted with genuine horror at the brutality. But its deeper concern betrayed so much self-interest that conservatives barely tried to hide it: fear of Iraqi domination of much of the world's oil supply.

With the United States in the lead, the United

Saddam Hussein of Iraq. (Courtesy, AP/Wide World Photos)

Nations Security Council immediately condemned the invasion and called for a world economic boycott of Iraq. Bush, with the consent of Saudi Arabia, also immediately began Operation Desert Shield, a military defense against the southward expansion of Iraq. In the following months, Bush worked to build an international alliance against Saddam. The UN Security Council authorized force against Iraq if that nation did not leave Kuwait.

After bitter debate between Republicans and many reluctant Democrats, Congress granted Bush authorization to use force. Two days after the Allied coalition's January 15 deadline for withdrawing from Kuwait, Desert Shield changed to Desert Storm. By now the buildup included troops from Britain, France, Egypt, Syria, and Saudi Arabia, as well as the United States. An American general, Norman Schwarzkopf, took immediate command of the coalition forces. Colin Powell, the first African American chairman of the Joint Chiefs of Staff, oversaw the progress of the war.

For about a month, the coalition troops did not

During the Gulf War women for the first time served in combat-support positions. Eleven died and two became prisoners of war. (Courtesy, Corbis-Bettmann)

actively engage the Iraqi ground forces. Instead they subjected Iraq and its military to relentless bombings and missile assaults. Iraq, hoping to arouse feeling against Israel, tried feeble missile attacks to goad the Israelis into retaliation. Accepting the protection of the United States, Israel refused to take the bait. Then in February, the ground war began. Demoralized by air attacks beyond human endurance, Iraq's troops crumbled. Within a few days, Kuwait had been liberated and Iraq invaded. When Bush declared a cease-fire, 100,000 Iraqi troops had been killed. Enemy fire took less than two hundred coalition lives, most of these American.

Western oil was safe. So were the Kuwaitis. But the Kurds of northern Iraq, who during the war had rebelled in expectation of help from the Western coalition, were abandoned, no longer revelant to the geopolitical considerations that had governed the whole operation. The Iraqi military, released from the war, turned on them with vicious success.

The Passive Community of Television

An ugly underside of the war was its portrayal on television. Americans watched the war with unabashed pride in their country's devastation of the enemy: a nation of Rambos sitting in comfort in front of their television sets.

Since its early days, TV has had its communities of viewers, people aware not only of privately watching their own screens but also of being part of a viewing public. Everyone old enough to remember *I Love Lucy* assumes that others in the same age cohort will understand an allusion, say, to Fred and Ethel, as a younger generation will be familiar with the family of Tony Soprano. At times the watchers experience an intensity, sensing that others are also taking part: grief at the funeral of John Kennedy, horror at the segregationist mobs as white supremacy thrashed about in trapped fury. Such events recall the families gathered at their radios during the 1930s, collectively drawing hope from FDR's fireside chats. The TV screening of the Gulf War, however, provided another kind of collective event: the ability to sit, watch, enjoy, and even applaud, while violence and death take place in the real world. The experience led Americans to believe they could in the future wage push-button wars while lounging in the safety of their living room couches.

The fleeing Iraqi army set fire to the oil fields of Kuwait; the flames continued for months. (Courtesy, U.S. Army)

Bush at Home

Bush's domestic program had little definition. In general he considered himself committed to the conservatism practiced by his predecessor. The Reagan administration, determined to change the character of the Supreme Court, had appointed three conservatives: Sandra Day O'Connor, the first woman to receive the post; Antonin Scalia; and Anthony M. Kennedy. Bush appointed two more. At his senate hearings David H. Souter encountered no significant congressional resistance. Bush's other choice, the African American Clarence Thomas, a conservative opposed to affirmative action, brought the president more trouble. During congressional hearings a young black law professor, Anita Hill, accused Thomas of sexual harassment. In the autumn of 1991, both Thomas and Ms. Hill gave widely televised testimony before the Senate Judiciary Committee considering the appointment. Thomas narrowly won Senate confirmation.

On education and the environment, two subjects in which Bush had expressed interest, little action took place. No significant plan to improve educa-

tion appeared. Nor did Bush propose any comprehensive program for the environment. Most of his appointees to the Environmental Protection Agency favored conservation of one kind or another. But aside from a brief disturbance when in 1989 the tanker *Exxon Valdez* struck a reef and spilled thousands of gallons of oil into Alaskan waters, the environment did not command the attention either of the administration or of the public.

From Desert Storm, Bush emerged with soaring popularity. But his political fortunes surprisingly did not endure. His ill-considered pledge "Read my lips: No new taxes" melted away when with considerable courage he uttered the politically damaging confession that new taxes would be necessary. In a complex compromise with the Democratic Congress, he endorsed late in 1991 a tax bill somewhat stiffer on the wealthy, besides raising taxes on cigarettes, gasoline, and beer. And during his administration, the economic boom fed by Reagan's deficit-spending tactics collapsed. As he moved toward the election of 1992, Bush's favor with the public had declined.

ANITA HILL TESTIFIES

"After a brief discussion of work, he would turn the conversation to a discussion of sexual matters. His conversations were very vivid.

He spoke about acts that he had seen in pornographic films involving such matters as women having sex with animals, and films showing group sex or rape scenes. He talked about pornographic materials depicting individuals with large penises, or large breasts involved in various sex acts.

On several occasions Thomas told me graphically of his own sexual prowess. Because I was extremely uncomfortable talking about sex with him at all, and particularly in such a

Law school professor Anita Hill accused Bush's Supreme Court nominee, Clarence Thomas, of boorish sexual harassment. (Courtesy, Liaison Agency, Inc.)

graphic way, I told him that I did not want to talk about these subjects. I would also try to change the subject to education matters or to nonsexual personal matters, such as his background or his beliefs. My efforts to change the subject were rarely successful.

Throughout the period of these conversations, he also from time to time asked me for social engagements. My reactions to these conversations was to avoid them by limiting opportunities for us to engage in extended conversations. This was difficult because at the time, I was his only assistant at the Office of Education or Office for Civil Rights.

During the latter part of my time at the Department of Education, the social pressures and any conversation of his offensive behavior ended. I began both to believe and hope that our working relationship could be a proper, cordial, and professional one.

When Judge Thomas was made chair of the EEOC, I needed to face the question of whether to go with him. I was asked to do so and I did. The work, itself, was interesting, and at that time, it appeared that the sexual overtures, which had so troubled me, had ended."

The conservative President Bush shrewdly chose a black conservative, Clarence Thomas, for the Supreme Court. (Courtesy, Liaison Agency, Inc.)

Suggested Readings

On the Watergate affair and Richard M. Nixon, see Stanley I. Kutler, *The Wars of Watergate* (1995); Leon Friedman and William F. Levantrosser, *Watergate and Afterward: The Legacy of Richard M. Nixon* (1992); Philip B. Kurland, *Watergate and the American Political Process* (1975); and Heron Marquez, *Richard Nixon* (1999). For American relations with China after President Nixon's visit there: James Mann, *About Face: A History of America's Curious Relationship with China from Nixon to Clinton* (1999); Anne Collins Walker, *China Calls: Paving the Way for Nixon's Historic Journey to China* (1993); and Shia-ling Liu, *U.S. Foreign Policy Toward Communist China in the 1970's: The Misadventures of Presidents Nixon, Ford and Carter* (1988).

Several biographies are simply entitled *Jimmy Carter*, including those by Hugh Sidey (1979), Kerry Acker (2002), Paul Joseph (1998), Charles Mercer (1977), Tim O'Shei (2002), Anne Schraff (1998), and Ed Slavin (1989); consult also Peter G. Bourne, *Jimmy Carter: A Comprehensive Biography from Plains to Postpresidency* (1997) and Edwin C. Hargrove, *Jimmy Carter as President: Leadership and the Politics of the Public Good* (1988).

On wars in the Middle East several good books are called *The Yom Kippur War.* Among the authors are Peter Allen (1982), A.J. Barket (1974), and the insightful team of the London Sunday Times (1975). See also Shmuel Bar, *Yom Kippur War in the Eyes of the Arabs* (1986); M.M. Salehi, *Insurgency Through Culture and Religion: The Islamic Revolution in Iran* (1988); Ofira Seliktar, *Failing the Crystal Ball Test: The Carter Administration and the Fundamentalist Revolution in Iran* (2000); Anthony H. Cordesman, *Iran-Iraq War and Western Security* (1987); Robert E. Hunter, *U.S. Policy and the Iran-Iraq War* (1984); Stanley A. Reshon, *The Political Psychology of the Gulf War: Leaders, Publics and the Process of Conflict* (1993); Peter Rowe, *The Gulf War 1990–91 in International and English Law* (1993); John Bulloch and Harvey Morris, *The Gulf War: Its Origins, History and Consequences* (1991); and Thomas Houlahan, *Gulf War: The Complete History* (1999).

For Ronald Reagan's presidency, see Arthur M. Schlesinger, Jr., The *Election of 1980 and the Administration of Ronald Reagan* (2002); Elton Rayback, *Not So Free to Choose: The Political Economy of Milton Friedman* (1987); Morris H. Morley, *Crisis and Confrontation: Ronald Reagan's Foreign Policy* (1988); Friends of the Earth, *Ronald Reagan and the American Environment* (1982); Robert Dallek, *Ronald Reagan: The Politics of Symbolism* (1999); and Michael Deaver, *A Different Drummer: My Thirty Years with Ronald Reagan* (2001).

On American-Soviet relations in the 1980s, Lester R. Brown, *U.S. and Soviet Agriculture: The Shifting Balance of Power* (1982); Zbigniew Brzezinski, *Game Plan: A Geostrategic Framework for the Conduct of the U.S.-Soviet Contest* (1986); Robert F. Byrnes, *U.S. Policy toward Eastern Europe and the Soviet Union* (1989); Audrey Kurth Cronin, *U.S. Responses to Soviet "New Thinking"* (1990); Michael Arthur Ledeen, *Superpower Dilemmas: The U.S. and the U.S.S.R. at Century's End,* (1992); and John Lenczowski, *Soviet Perceptions of U.S. Foreign Policy: A Study of Ideology, Power and Consensus* (1982). On United States relations with Latin America in the 1970s and 1980s: Tomás Borge, *The Patient Impatience: From Boyhood to Guerrilla: A Personal Narrative of Nicaragua's Struggle for Liberation* (1992); Violeta Barrios de Chamorro's autobiography, *Dreams of the Heart* (1996); Donald Clark Hodges, *Intellectual Foundations of the Nicaraguan Revolution* (1986); Lynn Horton, *Peasants In Arms: War and Peace in the Mountains of Nicaragua, 1979–1994* (1998); Adam Jones, *Beyond the Barricades: Nicaragua and the Struggle for the Sandinista Press* (2002); Robert Kagan, *Twilight Struggle: American Power and Nicaragua, 1977–1990* (1996); Joan Kruckewitt, *Death of Ben Linder: The Story of a North American in Sandinista Nicaragua* (1999); Alejandro Martinez Cuenca, *Sandinista Economics in Practice: An Insider's Critical Reflections* (1992); Matilde Zimmerman, *Sandinista: Carlos Fonseca and the Nicaraguan Revolution* (2001); David S. Behar, *Invasion: The American Destruction of the Noriega regime in Panama* (1990); Juan E. Méndez, *Laws of War and the Conduct of the Panama Invasion* (1990); and Nicholas E. Reynolds, *Just Cause: Marine Operations in Panama 1988–1990* (1996).

Rodney King. *(Courtesy, AP/ Wide World Photos)*

New Alignments and a New War

CHAPTER 27

RODNEY KING

In Los Angeles, wracked with violence from street gangs involved in the dangerous drug business, relations between police and black youth had been particularly bad. The police were quick to suspect gatherings of young black males, who grew accustomed to being questioned on the slightest excuse. Black adults were not immune. On March 3, 1991, a group of white law officers, after chasing Rodney King as a robbery suspect, pulled him from his car. On the assumption that he was resisting, they mauled him without noticing an observer videotaping them. Four policemen were tried in a largely white suburb: the defense had argued that in the angry mood engendered by the incident, the city itself could not guarantee a fair verdict. On April 29, 1992, the suburban jury after considerable deliberation freed all of the defendants.

In response young blacks in Los Angeles rioted, looting and burning stores in their neighborhoods and assaulting whites, while Rodney King himself went on television and made a halting plea for calm. A group beat a white truck driver unconscious until some black onlookers braved the mob to rescue him. A second videotaping, which caught the assailants in this act, aided in bringing them to trial. They as well as King's attackers, later retried on new charges, were in time convicted.

Both the police who beat Rodney King and the mobs who reacted as they did were acting out of passions deeply embedded in the country's racial history. But actions and passions can be controlled, and the Los Angeles police force promised to rein in its own members and pay more attention to relations with the black community.

HISTORICAL EVENTS

1992
William Jefferson Clinton becomes president

1993
North American Free Trade Agreement (NAFTA) becomes law • Branch Davidians die in Waco, Texas

1994
Republicans win House of Representatives after proposing a "Contract with America"

1995
Dayton, Ohio, agreement proclaims a cease-fire in Bosnia • Oklahoma City bombing

1996
Clinton reelected

1998
House impeachment of Clinton • Wye Conference lessens Israeli-Palestinian tensions

1999
Clinton not convicted of impeachment charges in Senate

2000
George W. Bush becomes president in disputed election • Slobodan Milosevic is driven from power in Serbia

2001
Bush rejects Kyoto global warming treaty and signs repeal of inheritance tax set to end in 2011 • September 11: World Trade Center buildings destroyed by terrorists

2002
Middle East crisis • Collapse of Enron and WorldCom corporations • Republicans gain control of both houses of Congress in off-term elections • Economic recovery delayed

BILL CLINTON: THE FIRST FOUR YEARS

The Rodney King event bore a reminder of the nation's old division over race. Population changes were meanwhile in progress that, if the word "race" even applies, pointed to a new racial and ethnic composition of the country.

Beyond Race and Borders

Until recently, American society acted on the assumption that races could be easily defined: white, black, red, and yellow, with perhaps a brown contingent in the Pacific. None of the races, of course, had exactly the color assigned to it. "Negro," the Spanish and Portuguese term for *black*, meant a person of strongly sub-Saharan African features. Few African Americans approach that description. The color of American Indians is not red; nor are Asians yellow; and Caucasians, by one scheme of categorizing, are "pink." The use of terms designating strong, clearly distinct colors stressed the notion of separate races, a biology of skin tone.

The swelling of immigrant populations from mainland Asia, the Pacific islands, and the Western Hemisphere, coupled with the increased political visibility of Hispanics and other communities, has complicated the concept of race. The distinctions in ethnic background between Chinese and Koreans, between Filipinos and Vietnamese, give the lie to any notion of an undifferentiated Asian or "yellow" influx. And what category can be assigned to immigrants from India, dark-skinned but as Caucasian as any "white" American? Or in what race can Salvadorans or Chicanos, mating European and pre-Columbian American stock, be classified? They are

New immigrants taking the oath of citizenship. (Courtesy, © 1996 Andrew Holbrooke)

collectively termed Hispanic. But is that a race or an ethnicity?

Among minorities of longer background in the United States, categories too need rethinking. Do Native Americans constitute a separate race? Then what of the distinctions they make among themselves by ancestry: Cherokee, Oglala, and the various other groups that have continued their own identities despite the Euro-American perception of them solely as American Indian? And in the 2000 census, some Americans who by white-supremacist tradition would have been defined simply as "Negro" have listed their background more accurately as mixed. That renews an older practice in census data of including such categories as "mulatto." But "mulatto" sounded like freezing into a sub-race the individuals so described. The newer self-chosen identification of separate strands of ancestry gives due recognition to uniqueness of background.

The diversity of ethnic groupings challenges not only the idea of race as the white majority once maintained it but older assumptions about the composition of the American populace. It was once very simple. "Whites" constituted the majority. Other peoples were expected to adjust to that and be grateful for any acknowledgment that the Caucasian American populace made of their social and legal rights. But at some point in the first half of the twenty-first century, Euro-Americans will no longer be the nation's majority, though they will continue to outnumber any other single population.

The census of 2000 discovered a virtual equality in numbers between African Americans and Hispanics. The nation has become a patchwork of ethnicities and, if the word means anything, races.

Poverty and misery attended immigrants as they had haunted the dumbbell-tenement dwellings on New York City's Lower East Side a century ago, or the refugees from southern and western Ireland who fled the potato famine of the 1840s. Undocumented Hispanics, having little recourse to the law, became tempting targets of abuse at the hands of employers. But a substantial portion of the recent newcomers does not conform in economic and educational status to the earlier waves of immigrants. Nurses from the Philippines and the West Indies, Chinese computer technicians, engineers and physicians from India: these are a small sampling of the professionals who make up a goodly number among the newly arrived.

One thing common to the great migrations at both ends of the twentieth century is a web of connections between the United States and the land of birth. Friends and relatives already settled here have provided information about their new homeland and offered a temporary place to stay and work in accord with immigration laws. And from the successful in the new country has flowed money to family members in the old. At the turn of the twenty-first century, migration from Mexico and Central America to the West Coast of the United States and back again has created a Hispanic cultural and political community across borders. A new channel of communication, email, provides links between immigrants with some financial means and their friends in the homelands. The new president elected in 1992 was to preside over a country of borders increasingly permeable, with streams of culture flowing from and to it.

The Internet

Within the United States, the same electronic means of communication were altering the way people talked to one another, and connected themselves with the nation and the world in general, at low cost, or even no cost. By email long conversations became common. Words displayed on a cold screen reported the most powerful emotions silently. The internet also allowed an individual alone in front of a computer to receive instant news, information, and misinformation from across the planet. For scholars the search engines would provide extraordinary opportunities: for looking up facts, for getting access to documents, and for finding and ordering books on-line. Simple word processing made far easier the mechanics of composition, though not at all easier the questions of precision and style. On-line research provides access to information, but does not assure its accuracy.

As inspiration for creating desktop computers, Bill Gates drew on a $397 computer game Altara, named from a planet in the television series *Star Trek*. He was only twenty years old when he teamed with a school friend to write software, instructions to convert electrical signals into letters and numbers, using an early version of the Intel chip. That the two inventors could do so is an illustration of the truth that advanced technology, often thought to replace skill with mechanized routine, offers its own kinds of independent workmanship.

Calling for Citizen Participation

Social critics worried about whether home computers in producing a nation of isolated individuals, substituting private for public activities, can point to the drop in the percentage of Americans who vote. Two candidates for the presidency in 1992 attempted to revive the public sphere that voting data showed to be in decline. They were William Jefferson Clinton for the Democrats and Ross Perot, a millionaire maverick running as the choice of his

own Reform Party on a program for controlling the federal deficit. In this election year they shared a hope that the new media technologies might work to create a continuing conversation embracing the public, the politicians, and the government. Clinton hit on the idea of "televised town meetings," suggested by the village democracy of colonial New England, consisting of nationally aired gatherings of citizens who would ask him questions. The aim of the town meetings, of course, was to get Clinton elected. Still, it secondarily made an attempt to create an ongoing participatory democracy that the very size of the country appears to make impossible. To promote his candidacy, Perot appeared on television screens across the country with easily understandable graphs and charts.

The New Democrats

Clinton's climb to the presidency had begun when as governor of Arkansas he became the chairman of a group calling itself the Democratic Leadership Council. Fearing that the party's diverse interest groups had become too strident to be politically effective, the Council attempted to relocate it closer to the political center. Clinton wanted to free the party of its identification with policies of "tax-and-spend," a term the Republicans had been using effectively to deride the Democrats for over-financing allegedly wasteful federal programs.

During the 1992 primaries, Clinton emerged as the Democrat most likely to bring healing unity to his fragmented party. He presented to the wider public the same inclusiveness that he had preached among the Democrats. Black Americans had grown used to seeing the Democrats as the party of civil rights, and Clinton was supremely comfortable with them. Feminists found Clinton congenial to their views. His running mate Al Gore of Tennessee, who came from a political family, had served briefly in Vietnam as an army newspaperman.

President George Bush, the hero of the Gulf War, a year earlier had looked unbeatable. Now as head of the Republican Party in power he labored under a failing economy, a courageous but politically disastrous reversal of his pledge to reject new taxes, and an opponent who radiated a personal warmth the president lacked. The November result of the presidential campaign reflected not much more than the nation's unfocused desire for some kind of change. Clinton, the winner in the Electoral

College, received forty-three percent of the popular vote, Bush thirty-eight percent, and Perot the remainder. Clinton profited from the women's vote, a strong source of future support for Democrats. More blacks, women, Asian Americans, and Hispanics gained House seats than ever before; and five women won in the Senate.

The Early Clinton Days

The social liberalism that constituted part of Clinton's strategy and ideology included a determination to appoint women to administrative posts. For attorney general he selected Janet Reno, and as his second secretary of state Madeleine Albright.

Statue of Bill Clinton playing the saxophone. Bill Potts of Denver made this carving on wood. (Courtesy, National Archives)

Over the opposition of conservatives and the military establishment, he gained a partial opening in the armed services for gays and lesbians. The formula, known as "don't ask, don't tell," stipulated that no recruits could be asked about their sexual orientation, but any enlistees who by statement or behavior reveal themselves to be gay could be dismissed. Neither side has found it to be satisfactory; its significance lies rather in its very hesitant contribution to cracking prejudices about sexual preference.

Clinton wanted simultaneously to institute modest advances in social programs and to hold down taxes. But he quickly discovered, like Bush, that the federal government could not operate without money. Clinton, moreover, projected cutting into the huge national debt the Republicans had built up. The president endangered his political standing by proposing a fresh set of taxes, including a heightening of the levy on gasoline. These awakened the anger of a public primed by the antitax rhetoric of Leadership Council Democrats as well as conservative Republicans. Soon widely unpopular, Clinton's presidency in its early days had a look of failure. He did get through a small tax increase on the wealthiest, together with a gas tax and some funding for job training. In a presidency that was destined to go from crisis to crisis, the semi-victory gave him a respite. Then Clinton in 1993 won his first unclouded triumph, steering through both Houses the North American Free Trade Agreement, or NAFTA, which completed the process of bringing Mexico together with Canada into a free-trade zone.

The issue of NAFTA reveals a new alignment in American politics. In an earlier day much of big business, to protect profits, could be expected to support high tariffs, on this issue agreeing with large labor unions. The shrinking of the world through technology and communications has brought business to reverse itself. Seeking labor pools in countries with a docile, low-paid workforce, capital is now eager for free-trade arrangements. Most unions remain opposed to them. But to its old objection to competition with cheap foreign labor, union leadership now sometimes adds the argument that trade agreements failing to ensure justice in impoverished nations will amount to collaboration with repression there. In the absence of provisions requiring recognition of unions abroad, so labor and environmental groups argue, free trade merely supplies capital with a worldwide supply of underpaid workers laboring under unhealthful conditions, in time including the labor force in the United States. The Democratic Party, still seeking a labor constituency even while it courted newer groups, therefore supplied much of the opposition to NAFTA. But Republicans in the national legislature gave Clinton the necessary margin of support.

Late in 1993 Clinton began what would become the most ambitious program of his entire tenure. A commission headed by his wife, Hillary Rodham Clinton, started work devising a comprehensive program of health coverage. After half a year of congressional investigation, during which the medical establishment and other opponents shrewdly attacked the proposal as massively bureaucratic and expensive, chance of passage disappeared.

A Republican Victory in 1994

For about forty years, the Democrats controlled the lower House, weakened only by divisions within the party. The year 1994 was different. For a long time an unfocused hostility to Washington, strengthened by Democratic as well as Republican

A powerful HMO lobby group, the Health Insurance Association of America, paid ten million dollars for ads to defeat Hillary Clinton's universal health care bill during her husband's first year in office. (Courtesy, Goddard-Clausen/First Tuesday)

House Minority Whip Newt Gingrich and other Republican House members sign a "Contract with America" before making gains for their party in the 1994 elections. (Courtesy, AP/Wide World Photos)

denunciations of "big government," had become a part of the political culture. Newt Gingrich of Georgia, Republican minority leader in the House, circulated a Contract with America pledging its signers to work for a conservative government. In November Congress went Republican, the House of Representatives being particularly noted for a contingent of vigorous young conservatives such as Gingrich.

That autumn the Clinton administration had only one success: the downfall in Haiti of a brutal government against which the United Nations, with much support from Washington, had imposed a trade embargo. That triumph has since been much lessened by the continuation of economic and social misery in Haiti.

The Balkans

For decades the Communist state of Yugoslavia had held peacefully together a cluster of nations and peoples in the Balkan region of southeastern Europe. With the crumbling of Communism, Yugoslavia fell apart. Serbia, under the leadership of Slobodan Milosevic, aimed to create from the wreckage a larger Serb nation. To that end, ethnic Serb localities in Croatia and Bosnia began a rebellion against the states containing them. In Bosnia, they turned to expelling or in some cases massacring Muslims in their vicinity: ethnic cleansing, it was called. The worst bloodshed in Europe since

World War II had begun. In the course of it, Serbs turned against Muslims and Croats, and Croats against Muslims. Most generally, Muslims were the victims; but they held murderers within their ranks as well.

Western Europe and the United States feared that the fighting would endanger the frail peace that prevailed over much of the world. Many Europeans and Americans expressed genuine horror over the suffering of the innocent. A Western embargo on arms shipments to the region, intended to control the fighting, unintentionally aided the Serbs. From Russia, which culturally identified with them, they could get equipment they needed, keeping arms from the Muslims.

Eventually bombing raids by NATO indicated to the Serbs that the UN and Washington might get serious. In the autumn of 1995, Clinton brought to Dayton, Ohio, representatives of the factions in Bosnia who agreed to a cease-fire to be monitored by a NATO peacekeeping force. The troops included American soldiers.

A Reversal of Political Fortunes?

The newly elected Republican Congress assumed that it had the public's mandate to demolish much of the structure of Democratic programs. Conservative legislators were mistaken. The midterm elections had expressed no more than a fleeting irritation at a president who appeared to provide no coherent leadership. When toward the end of 1995 Clinton refused to sign an appropriations bill that he thought to be stingy, the government partially shut down. National parks and museums closed; some Social Security and Medicare checks were delayed. The public blamed not the president but Congress, which quickly retreated from its posture of ideological confrontation.

Thereafter the White House and the Republican legislature became more cooperative. Liberals won a rise in the minimum wage. In 1996 conservatives won a reform of the welfare system. Restricting to five years an individual's total lifetime receipt of welfare, the law required of many recipients that they look for work and after two years get off the program. Early indications showed that the new system was operating well rather than cruelly for those on the rolls, turning welfare clients into wage-workers. But the plan had come into being just as the economy as a whole revived and began provid-

Young William Clinton greets President John F. Kennedy. (Courtesy, Arnie Sachs/Consolidated News Pictures/ Liaison International)

ing jobs. Whether in hard times it would go from benign to harsh had yet to be discovered. Liberals meanwhile consoled themselves that except in its arbitrary cutoff provisions, it was not contrary to the spirit of the New Deal but within it. The Democratic liberals of the 1930s had preferred providing work to handing out a dole.

THE SECOND TERM

The election year 1996 offered little to stir popular emotions. The Republicans, having overplayed their congressional conquests of two years before, had struggled to overcome their appearance of vindictiveness, and were now vying with the Democrats to occupy the bland political center. By this time the Democrats had on their side a reviving economy and a president grown popular, if not for his private image then for his official performance. Possible scandal attached to the Clintons in Arkansas concerning a failed real estate and banking scheme known as Whitewater. More immediately, questions arose concerning the acceptance of funds for the 1996 Democratic presidential campaign from Chinese officials.

(from left to right) Democratic vice-presidential nominee in 1992 and 1996 and presidential nominee in 2000 Al Gore of Tennessee, his wife Tipper Gore, Bill Clinton, and Hillary Clinton. (Courtesy, AP/Wide World Photos)

Robert Dole of Kansas, who resigned from the Senate to run, received the Republican Party's endorsement. His running mate Jack Kemp was known for urging that conservatives develop policies friendly to the poor. As a badly wounded hero of World War II benefiting from the GI Bill of Rights, Dole knew the good that government could do for the disadvantaged; he did not buy into right-wing hatred of the welfare state. But his glum manner played badly against Clinton's geniality. The president, running with Al Gore once more, remained the candidate of African Americans and women as well as portions of the high-tech business community.

Collecting a majority in the Electoral College, Clinton again came out with less than fifty percent of the popular vote. Dole split the remainder with a vote for Perot much less than that third party's share in 1992. The Republicans managed to keep control of the Senate along with the House of Representatives, although the majority they had won in 1994 shrank. The election indicated that the middling course that Clinton was following by choice, and the humbled congressional Republicans by necessity, had become satisfactory to an American public that sent only half of its eligible electorate to the polls. Young people especially exhibited a lack of interest in politics.

Trouble Ahead for Clinton

In the course of his political career, Clinton had gotten the label The Comeback Kid. During his second administration he continued to display his remarkable facility for getting into trouble and then limping out of it.

The first months were relatively calm politically. A Congress friendly to big tobacco rejected a settlement against tobacco companies for damage to the nation's health and for concealing information about the dangers of smoking. But an amazingly robust economy made possible a significant achievement to which both Congress and the White House were parties: an agreement on balancing the budget. Then in January 1998 unraveled a scandal about the president that dominated national politics for about a year. During his presidency Clinton had carried on an affair of sorts with a young White House intern, Monica Lewinsky.

Had the discovery gone no further, it would have done nothing worse than to show Clinton to be a male politician on the prowl. But Republicans and the media slathered for details, while the White House scrambled to hide as many of them as it could, and the incident grew and grew.

Impeachment and Trial

Kenneth Starr as an independent counsel appointed by the government was carrying on a long grand jury investigation of the Clintons' role in the Whitewater scheme. Starr got authority to probe into whether the effort to stifle the sexual scandal might involve any illegal concealment of facts related to Whitewater. Neither presidents nor ordinary people can be prosecuted for cheating on their marriage. Lying under oath or tampering with evidence, about sex or anything else, is another matter. At the time, Clinton confronted a sexual harassment suit brought by another woman, Paula Jones, for an advance he had allegedly made to her while governor of Arkansas. Seeking to establish a pattern of behavior on the part of Clinton, Paula Jones had both the president and Ms. Lewinsky called as witnesses, and under oath the two denied having a sexual liaison. Clinton twice addressed the public on the matter. In his first statement, he announced that he had not had "sexual relations" with Ms. Lewinsky. (Clinton, interpreting sexual relations as referring only to the act of intercourse, may have reasoned from his legal training that he was being technically accurate.) Clinton's later address to the nation admitted to an "inappropriate" relationship.

In September 1998, Starr delivered to the lower House a lengthy report containing information that, he proposed, might be grounds for that body's impeachment of the president; that is, for having him called before the Senate for judgment. Made public, the report created a blood-feast for the media and Republicans. And on December 19, after months of deliberation, the House voted along party lines to impeach the president. One article charged Clinton with perjury in his White House testimony to the grand jury; the other accused him of obstruction of justice. Impeachment by the House had assigned the president's fate to the Senate, which by a vote of two-thirds majority could remove him from office.

For weeks the Senate met essentially as a court presided over by William Rehnquist, Chief Justice of the Supreme Court. Questions of fact clashed with questions of politics. The issue, pared down, was this: should a wayward husband be expelled from the presidency after he had lied under oath and obstructed justice to protect his public image? Were his sins and probable crimes grievous enough to warrant the Senate's wounding the office of chief executive? Public opinion polls answered in the negative. That, on February 12, 1999, was also the answer of the Senate. On the question of perjury, the count totaled fifty-five to forty-five, a majority but not by the two-thirds necessary for Clinton's removal; on that of obstructing justice, the vote split evenly. The Clinton presidency had been saved.

New Life in the Clinton Administration

While Clinton by his extramarital behavior was damaging himself, he managed otherwise a more than creditable job of being president. For the present, he had wide public backing.

As early as 1993 Clinton had succeeded in advancing the process initiated by his Republican predecessors of what seemed to be reconciliation between Israelis and Palestinians. With nudging from Washington, Israel and the Palestinian Liberation Organization headed by Yasser Arafat arrived at an agreement. The Israelis granted the Arabs

some autonomy in portions of the Gaza Strip and the West Bank; the PLO in effect recognized the existence of Israel and foreswore terrorism. In October 1998 the two parties met at the Wye Conference Center in Maryland and somewhat broadened the accord. From the end of 2000, however, clashes between Israelis and Palestinians that in the next year worsened would endanger the whole process, but for a time more progress had been made than in earlier days had seemed possible.

In the November 1998 elections, while politicians and the press were continuing to mine the Monica Lewinsky scandal, the Republicans received one of their worst surprises in years. At a time when voter hostility to taxes and government no longer prevailed, the GOP had little to say. The Democratic Party gained five seats in the House of Representatives, leaving the Republicans with the slenderest of majorities. In itself the vote, which drew only about thirty-six percent of the eligible electorate and a much smaller percentage of the young, would have meant nothing more than that the parties looked to be about equally popular. What stunned political observers is that the result went against an almost unbreakable pattern: in midterm congressional elections, the party in possession of the White House is supposed to lose seats, not break even or advance. Not since 1934, at a time when the presidency of FDR was widely supported, had anything comparable happened.

After elections disappointing to them, Republicans forced the resignation of their once popular speaker of the House, Newt Gingrich. The failure of the new Senate early the next year to remove Clinton from the presidency completed the subduing of the Republican assault on his administration.

In the spring of 1999, Clinton committed one of the acts of political courage that, like his fight for tax hikes in 1993, contrasted to his often eager accommodation to public opinion.

In its province of Kosovo, Serbia initiated an especially brutal war against the inhabitants while the Kosovo Liberation Army sought national freedom for the largely Muslim region. After efforts on the part of Washington failed to arrange a settlement between the KLA and Serbia's Milosevic, the United States led the North Atlantic Treaty Organization in a bombing campaign on Serbia and Kosovo. The Serbs meanwhile heightened the war until it appeared that by torture, expulsion, and death they were pursuing the ethnic cleansing that they had practiced in Bosnia: their object, to make Kosovo overwhelmingly Serb. The bombing had for a time the support of the American public, which usually endorses any war the country conducts. In this case, moreover, the horrible stories of torture, and the sight of Kosovars (a term usually confined to the Muslims in the province) huddled in refugee camps, gave the war a humanitarian turn. But American bombings that killed civilians in Serbia proper unsettled even proponents of the war. And a conflict that aimed for the good of people other than Americans and seemed to have no cash value for the United States brought out a predictably selfish streak.

But Clinton persisted. After a short campaign that brought no combat deaths to American and other NATO troops, the Serbs withdrew their army. Thereafter the United Nations gave authority to NATO to send peacekeeping forces into Kosovo, still nominally belonging to Serbia. Refugees returned from camps outside the province of Kosovo while others, displaced but still in the province, went back to their homes. Troops from the United States and other NATO nations along with a force from Russia, which had sympathized with the Serbs

President Bill Clinton visits American troops in Bosnia. (Courtesy, Peterson/Gamma Liaison)

as ethnic cousins, worked to keep restraints on the more vicious elements among Serbs and Muslims.

In the autumn of 2000 a majority within Serbia itself, a country isolated from much of the rest of the globe and suffering from economic sanctions, voted Milosevic out of office and when he stalled, drove him from power. The following year the Serb government, seeking to improve relations with other nations around the world, turned him over to a world court empowered to try accused perpetrators of atrocities. The breaking of the politician widely blamed for having begun the whole campaign of Serb conquest, from Croatia to Bosnia to Kosovo, gave some hope that the future of the Balkans might be better than their heart sickening recent past.

CRIME AND ITS PUNISHMENT

For policing the Balkans, the United States like its allies found the confidence to intervene. But at home Americans for years had been preoccupied with domestic crime.

Yet an FBI report released in 2000 recorded a drop of twenty-one percent since 1990 in the number of violent crimes, and of nineteen percent in crimes against property. The reasons eluded observers. A popular explanation contends that adolescent males and young men, the age and gender segment that is quickest to turn to crime, now made up a smaller portion of the whole population. That jobs were plentiful could also reduce the incidence of lawbreaking. Poverty and unemployment can quicken not only theft but acts of violence spawned by frustration. Or did a toughening in the criminal justice system account for the growing safety of the nation's streets?

That more rigorous sentencing prevailed is clear enough. One of the most astonishing social phenomena of the late twentieth century can be seen in the staggering increase in the size of the federal and state prison population. In 1977 fewer than 200,000 were confined; by the end of 1998 the figure stood at an astonishing 1.82 million. Figures for 1990 put the United States ahead of all other countries in rates of imprisonment, its two closest rivals being white supremacist South Africa and a Soviet Union just awakening to freedom.

One reason for the swelling of the ranks of the

A teenage boy in a Texas jail. Nineteen of twenty prison inmates were male, and the majority of these African American. Most had been convicted on drug charges. (Courtesy, Bob Daemmrich/The Image Works)

imprisoned was an increasingly widely adopted policy on the state level of lengthening sentences for repeat offenders. At its most severe, the practice is known as "three strikes and you're out." Criminologists have observed that a large portion of crime reflects the work of a fairly small number of hardened felons. To the extent that this holds true, removing a single violent male repeater from the streets could eliminate many savage crimes. That is especially so if the convict is released after aging beyond the years when men are most apt to be physically aggressive.

Policies on the order of three-strikes nevertheless explain only a part of the rise in the inmate population. One estimate claims that in 1992 less than one-third of admissions to state prisons resulted from violent crimes. Much of the growth nationwide in imprisonment resulted from a determination on the part of the federal and state governments to smash the drug trade. That involved incarceration of young people whose only crime was against themselves, and small-time pushers whose only injury was to their willing customers. The

CRIME PAYS: PRIVATE PRISONS

"Crime pays," announces the title of an analysis put out in the late 1990s by the stockbrokerage firm Paine Webber. The report refers to private prisons, a growth industry listed and popular on Wall Street that attended the state and federal crackdown on lawbreaking.

That private industry could make money from imprisonment has precedents in the American past. In the nineteenth century, inmate labor and even the partial administering of prisons had been hired out from time to time to private contractors. The renting, essentially, of ex-slaves who had run up against the southern justice system made for a continuation of servitude after the Civil War. But by the later twentieth century, the open exploitation of prison gang labor such as the states of the former Confederacy had practiced was no longer acceptable to the public. The engagement of business enterprise in the prison system acquired a less visible presence.

In the late 1990s eighty thousand inmates lived in private prisons that supplemented regular federal and state incarceration. The theory, nourished by the ideology of Ronald Reagan's era, holds that private enterprise can be depended on to be more efficient than federal or state bureaucracy. Prisons owned by businesses could expect sympathetic treatment from politicians who approved of them as exemplars of free-market economics. A further ground of friendship between private prisons and government was the presence of former public officials on the boards of prison corporations.

courts crammed the prisons, particularly with non-violent black and Latino drug abusers.

The narcotics trade begets violence of several sorts, but attacking it was pressing a whole class of users more deeply into a violent criminal underworld. And convicts often reenter society coarsened by their experience rather than reformed. On any day in the early nineties one in three young black men was either in prison or in some other state of legal supervision such as parole or probation.

Violence

As crime in its conventional form declined, while politicians continued to behave as though controlling it required heroic measures, other unexpected sorts of social violence erupted.

As startling as the event was at the time, the bombing of the World Trade Center in February 1993 in which five people died had connections to political and cultural conditions brewing abroad. For that act five Muslim fanatics were convicted, people of a kind who for decades had directed their hatred against Americans. The bombing was noteworthy only in taking place within the United States rather than elsewhere. But the incidents of violence that stood out in the 1990s were characterized by bizarre motives, cultish expressions of rage or alienation taken out on others.

In August 1992, the summer before Clinton's election, the FBI had laid siege to Randy Weaver, who was living with his family in a cabin outside Ruby Ridge, Idaho. Weaver, a right-winger steaming with fury at the government, had been accused of illegally selling arms. In a shoot-out, one of Weaver's sons along with a federal agent was killed and another law officer wounded. Supporters gathered at the scene to jeer at the authorities, who had built a road up to his cabin capable of moving in tanks. Later Weaver's wife was shot and killed, her baby in her arms. Weaver surrendered, but the whole affair had been so badly handled that he got a light sentence for arms dealing.

In Waco, Texas, a gathering of fundamentalist Christians known as the Branch Davidians lived in a commune led by David Koresh, a preacher with extraordinary power over his followers. At one point, for example, he announced that husbands in the community no longer were to have sexual access to their wives, who instead would have intercourse with him. That the men accepted the remarkable arrangement, which Koresh claimed to find in Scripture, indicates the force of his personality. Rumors of child abuse spread; the commune was also storing up arms. Federal authorities thereupon put the compound under siege. A gunfight took the lives of four federal officers and six Branch Davidians. On April 19, 1993, open war broke out. The compound went up in flames, and Koresh together

with eighty-six of his followers died, some of them children. To this day, the ultimate intentions of the cult, if any, remain obscure. But for bands of armed paramilitary forces found here and there in the American backcountry and calling themselves militias, Waco as well as Ruby Ridge became legendary.

The Militia

The private military bands found their legal justification in the reference to militias in the Second Amendment to the Constitution, and the same Amendment told them that they had a right to bear arms. Their larger purpose was to defend whatever they believed to remain of traditional American liberties and culture, under threat from a perceived ultraliberal Washington or a wider world plot. At least for a time, rumor had it that the global conspiracy could be spotted by the presence of unmarked black helicopters. Included among targets of militia hostility are gun laws, taxation, and environmental regulations, all supposed to be invasions of property, locality, and the individual. Some militias make relatively mild claims. Typical of one of them is a North Carolina organization that calls itself the unorganized militia, to distinguish itself from the National Guard. Its bylaws present it as lacking racial or other prejudices; its object, as the North Carolinians defined it, is simply to defend liberty. Much of the movement identifies with old-stock white American blood strains, which members think to be in danger of losing out to alien racial and ethnic intruders.

Timothy McVeigh, a veteran of the Gulf War, was a drifter attracted to the mystique of guns and militias. Like others on the far right, he defined the federal government as the enemy. On the second anniversary of the attack on the Branch Davidian commune, a bomb destroyed the federal building in Oklahoma City. After days of searching by volunteers from across the country, much of it through remains that might at any moment collapse further, the final count of the dead was 168, among them children at a day-care center. Though well planned, the bombing left enough evidence to be traceable to McVeigh and a friend. Convicted of murder, McVeigh was executed in the summer of 2001.

McVeigh was a resentful outsider. To accuse the militias of complicity in his act, or of sympathy with it, is wrong. But the bombing took place in 1995, at a time when some Republicans thought that the country's political future lay fairly far to the right. A few of them fished a bit to see whether the militia movement might have something to offer them. Republicans in Congress suggested investigating Ruby Ridge and Waco for evidence of governmental—for which read "liberal"—wrongdoing. (Even the Republican administration of the elder George Bush, when Ruby Ridge happened, could be assumed to be infiltrated by liberals.) But the public in general had nothing but loathing for the murders in Oklahoma City, and soon relegated the event to the desperate, bitter madness of Timothy McVeigh.

A final act of violence defines the peculiar lonely darkness of a certain kind of cult mentality. At Columbine High School in Littleton, Colorado, two students formed a comradeship aloof from their schoolmates. On April 20, 1999, they entered school weighed down with guns and bombs. There they killed twelve students and a teacher, afterwards taking their own lives.

These incidents of violence set observers to look for explanations. The availability of guns was blamed, and a slim majority of Americans want one form or another of gun control. But guns have always been easy to get. Violence on TV draws the wrath of both liberals and conservatives; but television violence went along with a drop, rather than an increase, in assault and murder in real life. Rather than look into the reaches of the human mind where violence originates, advocates of gun control have proposed a shorter route: make the enactment of violence more difficult; put guns out of the reach of young people.

Millennial Questioning

Era by era, Americans have asked themselves what their country was becoming. In the late 1990s, the question was conditioned by concerns over the failings of American education and by uncertainty about the country's role in the world.

The Alfred P. Murrah Federal Building following an explosion Wednesday, April 19, 1995, in downtown Oklahoma City. The devastation included the killing of 168 people. (Courtesy, AP/ Photo/David Longstrath)

The United States, came the refrain, had become the world's only superpower. In earlier times when it was not, it had assigned itself clearer and greater tasks, foremost among them that of partner in the alliance against the fascist and then the Communist powers. At a time of rapidly falling crime rates, Americans also puzzled at a series of shootings lacking the motives of common crime and suggesting that society was losing its ability to hold individuals to rational behavior. Some of these acts were racial in motive. Disgruntled employees account for others. Particularly disturbing was a growing number of gun incidents such as that at Columbine.

As Clinton's presidency neared its end, questions about the nation's future took their tone from a trick of numbers. According to the Gregorian calendar, the third millennium was at hand.

A millennium, of course, is an arbitrary mathematical construct, governed by the decimal system. But as the year 2000 approached—a neater figure than 2001, which mathematicians hold to be the right year for designating a change in millennia—imaginations were powerfully affected. Some people predicted the end of the world. A hitch in the numerical systems of computers worldwide suggested a more mundane disaster. Computers fixed continuously to register month, day, and year carried only the final two digits of the year. The digits 93, for example, meant the year 1993. But there was no provision for 00. Some experts feared that at the moment those digits were supposed to appear, computers across the globe would break down. The danger became known as Y2K: the year two thousand. An army of technicians went about repairing the problem. Yet the possibility existed that in anticipation of a computer failure, or the world's end, groups of fanatics might try to topple whatever remained of social and political order.

On the day that from time zone to time zone would become 2000, television viewers could witness the New Year's celebrations hourly as one zone after another turned to January 1. Computers did not crash; the world did not end.

THE DISPUTED ELECTION OF 2000

The election year 2000 promised little controversy. Enjoying several years of prosperity, the public concerned itself with few issues. Republicans and Democrats together were crowding to the political center. Democrats refrained from pushing any major redistribution of wealth or social privilege; Republicans prepared no plan to demolish the welfare state. Clinton's private behavior embarrassed the Democrats and worked in the Republicans' favor.

The Democrats

In the Democratic primaries, Clinton's vice president Al Gore had the support of the party establishment. Bill Bradley, an ex-senator from New Jersey, ran in a few primaries, but having neither the visibility of Gore nor the backing of the party's leaders, he soon withdrew. Gore glided through the primary process. After his nomination he chose Joseph Lieberman, a conservative Connecticut senator, as his vice-presidential candidate. Lieberman added to the ticket his reputation for strict morality, an antidote to the trouble that the memory of Clinton's conduct might heap on the Democratic ticket. An Orthodox Jew who keeps to the rituals of his faith, refusing during the Jewish Sabbath, for example, to drive a car, Lieberman had been one of the few Democratic legislators publicly to condemn Clinton's sexual behavior.

The Republicans

The Republican primaries generated more energy. The leading contender was George W. Bush, governor of Texas and a son of former President George H. Bush. He faced a formidable challenger in Senator John McCain of Arizona, who pressed for some reforms that might be expected more of Democrats than of Republicans. He favored federal legislation placing limits on large contributions to political campaigns falling under the category of soft money. Such a measure would cut more of such funding given to the Republican Party than to the Democrats. Conservatives disapproved out of a conviction that spending money on campaigns represents an act of free speech and is therefore protected by the Constitution.

Long something of a maverick among Republicans, McCain urged a policy the United States eventually adopted, the opening of diplomatic relations with Communist Vietnam. That could have exposed him to the charge of being soft on Communism. But as a naval pilot who fought in Vietnam, where he was captured and held for years in a Hanoi prison and tortured, he was immune to any such accusation. His war hero background, in stark contrast to that of George W. Bush, allowed him to stake out new territory in Republican presidential politics.

Bush, whose general strategy was to present himself as a moderate, saved his candidacy with a play for the vote of the far right. In South Carolina he spoke at Bob Jones University, known for religious fundamentalism, for anti-Catholic and anti-Jewish websites, and for prohibiting interracial dating, a policy it eventually abandoned. Bush carried the South Carolina Republican primary, and despite McCain's subsequent victory in Michigan, the governor went on to win the nomination. As his vice-presidential running mate, Bush chose Richard Cheney, the elder Bush's secretary of defense and, judging by his previous voting record in Congress, one of the most pronounced conservatives in American politics.

A Campaign in Search of Issues

In campaign speeches and in a series of debates, the two candidates defined few differences in policy. Gore called for giving patients effective power to sue their health maintenance organizations when these refused to cover costs of necessary treatments. He also promised to keep untouched in a "lock box" the federal revenues designated for pensions and other benefits under Social Security. Bush proposed allowing people during their working years to invest in the stock market a portion of the funds that would otherwise go into their Social Security taxes. The argument here accorded with a difference between the two parties: Republicans have long had closer ties to Wall Street.

Beyond these issues, however, the campaign took its character from a contrast of personalities. Al Gore had a reputation for dullness so marked that he made fun of it himself, telling Al Gore jokes. He seemed so wooden, he said, because he suffered from Dutch elm disease. During one television debate with Bush, he added to his public image the look of intellectual arrogance, sighing with pained boredom at the Republican candidate's remarks. The networks, by breaking a rule against directing the camera on the candidate not speaking, contributed to Gore's self-inflicted injury. Bush labored under a reputation for being embarrassingly ignorant. Here the debates helped him. Any respectable effort would have blunted the insistence among Democrats that he was not intellectually up to the job of president, and his performance appeared to most viewers to be adequate.

In the contest were two other visible candidacies. Since Nixon's presidency, Patrick Buchanan had been a spokesman for an older Republican conservatism—one isolationist and hostile to free trade and immigration. For decades mainline conservatism had abandoned the concept of protective tariffs, perceiving foreign lands as ripe for American economic opportunity. Buchanan instead considered them a threat to the nation's domestic economy. By 2000 his political clout had weakened, but he managed to capture the nomination of Ross Perot's Reform Party. While Buchanan might seize a sliver of the Republican vote, the GOP had little reason to fear that he could garner enough support to throw the election to Gore. The Democrats, however, had every reason to fear Ralph Nader, running as the candidate of the Green Party.

For years a Green political movement had thrived in Western Europe, centering on protecting the environment from the ravages of industrialism. In the United States, environmentalists had been politically active as well, though a nationally visible Green Party has appeared only recently. American environmentalists oppose such specific assaults on nature as massive timber cutting, industrial pollution of air and rivers, and drilling for oil on public lands in Alaska and elsewhere. A minority calls for a wholly new human relationship with nature, including the dismantling of modern technology and the relearning of older ways of living with the land. Nader earned his reputation fighting for legislative restrictions on dangerous or unhealthy consumer goods. Such issues led him to oppose chemical pollutants in the environment, for example, well before the emergence of a large and politically recognizable national Green movement. Environmental concerns also figure prominently within Democratic liberalism. That and Nader's embrace of advanced welfare programs raised the danger for the Democrats that he could take enough votes from Gore in one or more states and throw the election to Bush. Polls heightened that fear by showing that neither of the two major candidates held a clear lead, especially as the election drew near. Nader's presence posed for a few political activists a dilemma. Should they go for Nader, on the certainty of his defeat and the risk of electing Bush over the moderate, liberal Gore? In that case, the only reason for supporting Nader would have been the possibility of building a left politics that might influence the Democrats in an unknown and uncertain future. That millions did vote for Nader subjected them to charges that in throwing the vote to Bush they aided their worst fear: national policies of environmental destruction.

An Election Searching for Closure

Ordinarily presidential contests are settled on election night, or the following morning. For hours on November 7 as the votes were being counted, it appeared that things would go about as they do every four years. In the popular tally, Bush went into an early lead that he soon lost. The large, swing states of Michigan and Pennsylvania falling to Gore meant that the Democratic candidate's capture of Florida would likely make him the winner whatever the outcome of the popular tally. For much of the course of the night's counting, Gore appeared to have taken Florida and therefore the national presidential election, but twice most of the networks put Florida into the undecided column. By Wednesday morning it became clear that this could be one of the few presidential elections in which the raw vote nationwide might not square with the final and determining electoral results.

In the middle of the night, some newscasters had temporarily awarded the election to Bush. But then they announced second thoughts just as Gore was traveling by car to give a speech conceding the election. Gore telephoned Bush from his car and indicated that he would have to turn back to await the final results since the networks had declared the

election undecided. In the popular vote nationwide Gore's lead over Bush would climb to more than half a million votes: a triumph of sorts for him but, again, not the deciding vote in the Electoral College. That depended on Florida.

And for weeks afterward, so it remained. That is not only because the recounting went slowly, but because controversies arose over what ballots should be considered valid. The practice in Florida had been to discard computer card ballots not cleanly punched through. Florida law, to the contrary, required that in close elections every ballot be examined closely for indications of the voter's intention. Vote counters in normally Democratic neighborhoods in Florida had gone with custom and against the law, rejecting many ballots partially but not completely perforated. A ballot in one predominantly Democratic county added to the confusion. The uneven layout of the names of Gore and Buchanan on the cardboard ballots there had led a sizable number of Jewish voters accidentally to mark the Reform Party candidate, who has been associated with hostility to Israel. And the largest numbers of votes thrown out occurred in counties with large populations of African American and Hispanic voters. That Jeb Bush, the governor of Florida, was the presidential candidate Bush's brother deepened the question of whether the vote counting would proceed fairly, given that his secretary of state, Katherine Harris, had the task of certifying the vote.

Democratic and Republican lawyers went to state and federal court. Florida's Democratic Supreme Court allowed the Democrats a partial recount in a few Democratic-leaning counties, and by December 12 Bush's statewide lead shrank to 318 votes. Had the Democratic lawyers been wiser, requesting a statewide recount and demanding that ballots from the military be counted according to strict legal standards, they would, according to Katherine Harris's statement two years later, have won the election. Amid the confusion and stalemate, the federal Supreme Court, by a majority of five conservatives appointed by Republicans to four members considered moderate or liberal, ordered that the recounting stop. According to the majority opinion of Justice Sandra Day O'Connor, Bush was president-elect. Nader took over two percent of the roughly hundred million ballots cast. Voters for Nader resoundingly told pollsters that their second choice had been Gore. Had the Green candidate not run,

POPULAR VOTE ELECTION OF 2000	
George W. Bush (R)	50,465,169
Albert Gore (D)	50,996,062
Ralph Nader (I)	2,529,871
Patrick Buchanan (I)	323,950

Supreme Court Justice Sandra Day O'Connor wrote the five-to-four majority opinion deciding the election of 2000 in favor of President George W. Bush. (Courtesy, AP/ Wide World Photos)

Gore would have been indisputably the president-elect.

A Divided Government

The closeness of the presidential election had its likeness in the composition of the new Congress. The lower House remained Republican by a few seats. In the Senate, each party had fifty members. But since Vice President Cheney, as president of the Senate, could cast the deciding vote in case of a tie, Republicans took control there too. That party organized the Senate under the majority leader Trent Lott of Mississippi. Then in May 2001, the moderate Republican Senator James Jeffords of Vermont announced that he was leaving a party he had found to be increasingly abrasive and extreme. Thereafter he would vote as an independent. That made the Democrats the controlling party and Tom Daschle of South Dakota majority leader.

For a time before the departure of Jeffords, Bush and his fellow Republicans had been able to run the country without the help of the Democrats. They triumphed when the Senate confirmed Bush's ap-

pointment of John Ashcroft of Missouri, a declared staunch social conservative, to the office of attorney general. The greatest success of the Republicans came when they pushed through a tax schedule lowering rates especially for the wealthiest taxpayers and also programming a gradual abolition over ten years of the inheritance tax—an eighty-year-old tax supported by Republican progressives like Theodore Roosevelt and William Howard Taft. Since the government would lose trillions in tax dollars as a result, liberals predicted the law would result in the creation of dynasties of the rich, the weakening of the middle class's economic position, and the undermining of the Social Security program. The legislation also included an immediate rebate over the summer of 2001 for each taxpayer of about $300. The Republicans justified the tax cuts on the grounds that the nation appeared so prosperous, and the federal surplus so large, that the government could afford the drop in taxes. Soon, however, the economic bubble collapsed— as boom times invariably have—and the federal budget amassed large deficits.

Vermont's Senator James M. Jeffords. (Courtesy, United States Senate)

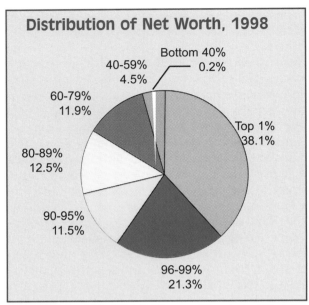

Source: Edward N. Wolff, "Recent Trends in Wealth Ownership, 1983–1998," April 2000.

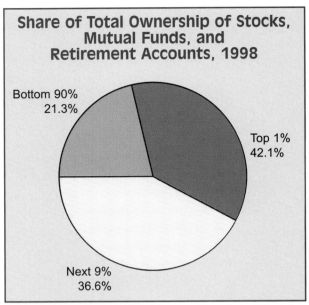

Source: Edward N. Wolff, "Recent Trends in Wealth Ownership, 1983–1998," April 2000.

Bush also rejected, in a manner foreign nations considered cavalier and arrogant, his country's participation in discussions at Kyoto in Japan where the world's industrial nations were shaping a treaty requiring the signers to keep down the level of industrial emissions spewed into the air. The gases, forming a barrier in the atmosphere against the escape of heat from the earth, threatened a "greenhouse effect," as it is called. In the opinion of all but a few climatologists, the globe would warm to an extent injurious to agriculture and to low-lying areas such as islands, which would become exposed to floods from the melting of ice in colder regions. Adding to his ignoring the concerns of environmentalists, Bush announced an intention to allow drilling for oil in several locations, notably a wildlife preserve in Alaska that had previously been protected from exploitation. Waiting to drill in the protected lands were companies such as Exxon, already infamous for the spilling on Alaska's shores of crude oil from the tanker *Valdez*.

The aggressive conservatism of the administration's first months, sharply opposite to the moderate program the presidential candidate had promised the electorate, ran into major trouble. Senator Jeffords's break with the party jolted Republicans. Bush's disregard for environmental considerations encountered considerable public skepticism. Tax cuts always are supposed to be good politics, but Americans showed considerable doubt. A proposal to which Bush expressed deep commitment—allowing religious institutions to have a part in social programs—raised objections bearing on the

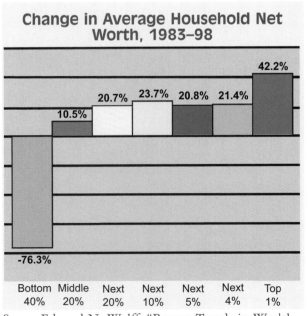

Source: Edward N. Wolff, "Recent Trends in Wealth Ownership, 1983–1998," April 2000.

Constitution's First Amendment provision for the separation of church and state. Secular liberals feared that the plan would give organized religion too much power within government; religious conservatives warned that it would give government too much power over religion. A more immediate concern arose over whether under Bush's program money would go to religious organizations that discriminate among potential staff members or intended recipients. Devising rules for preventing a host of such perceived dangers stumped the scheme's supporters.

A WORLD OF HATE?

On September 10, 2001, the issues of the preceding months seemed destined to rule American politics for the immediate future. And the retreat of the economy along with the stock market for the previous eighteen months promised trouble for Bush and the Republicans. The next morning, the world that those issues inhabited seemed swept into some distant past.

Resentment at the United States for decades had simmered, and at times exploded, within the Muslim nations, Arab, Iranian, and beyond. The hostage crisis toward the end of Carter's presidency illustrates it. Part of the hostility comes from observing a sometimes flagrant American prosperity and comfort that, to the sight of the world's poor, Americans appear to flaunt with a naive expectation that all of it is their birthright. Another source of antagonism derives from American support of Israel. A continuing trade embargo led by the United States against Iraq had been aimed at removing that country's ruler Saddam Hussein. But though the embargo exempted medicine and other goods necessary for the sustenance of life, it further impoverished that already poor country and caused the death of an indeterminate number of Iraqi children. And beyond such tangible grounds for hatred of the United States exists a fanatical form of the Muslim religion that sees all Western culture as decadent and Americans as the degenerate and arrogant embodiment of it. This religious strain argued that all things Western must be destroyed in order that the values of Islam could prevail.

In anger at the United States, terrorists in August 1998 bombed American embassies in the African republics of Kenya and Tanzania. A total of 224 died and over 4,500 were injured, the great majority Africans in the vicinity. In essentially ineffectual gestures of retaliation, President Clinton ordered an air strike on a pharmaceutical plant in Sudan supposedly connected with the bombings and another raid on a suspected terrorist training camp in Afghanistan. Then on October 12, 2000, a ship loaded with explosives pulled alongside and detonated a hole in the USS *Cole*, an American naval vessel docked in Yemen on the Arabian Peninsula, killing seventeen naval personnel. Evidence for both the attacks pointed to a terrorist network called al-Qaeda financed largely by Osama bin Laden, a wealthy Saudi living in Afghanistan, a country governed by a fundamentalist Muslim party calling itself the Taliban—"the students."

A New Kind of War

On September 11, 2001, nineteen Muslims armed only with small but deadly cutting tools got easily through airport checkpoints in the eastern United States. Traveling in four groups, each boarded a plane heavily fueled for transcontinental flight. In all cases one or more of the Muslims, with some training in piloting a plane, took over the cockpit while others held the passengers at bay. Two of the planes were then flown, with cold determination, into the twin towers of the World Trade Center in downtown Manhattan, one to each tower. Another smashed into the Pentagon. A fourth went down in the Pennsylvania countryside. Indications are that passengers there knew that their hijackers were going on another suicide mission that would take more lives, possibly an attack on the White House or the Capitol. Cell phone conversations from passengers and sounds from the voice box recovered from the plane suggest that they resisted the hijackers, knowing that this would probably hasten their own deaths but save the lives of intended victims.

For weeks police, firefighters, and other rescue workers threw themselves into the dangerous job of at first evacuating and later digging through the ruins of the World Trade Center in hopes of finding victims alive. The work proved so dangerous, in fact, that hundreds of them had died in the first hours as the buildings collapsed. Rudy Giuliani,

(above left) Hijacked United Airlines flight #175 flies toward the south tower of the World Trade Center just seconds before slamming into it at 9:03 a.m., September 11, 2001. The plane exploded on impact, drenching the tower with burning fuel. (above right) The north tower had already been hit at 8:47 a.m. by hijacked American Airlines flight #11. (bottom) In the background are remains of a section of the Pentagon, also hit by a hijacked plane; in the foreground are Defense Secretary Donald Rumsfeld and President George W. Bush. (Courtesy, AP/Wide World Photos)

the feisty mayor of New York, distinguished himself by his continual presence and reassuring bearing at the scene of the disaster. Residents in the city and elsewhere lined up to donate blood. New Yorkers discovered hidden reserves of civility in themselves. Rubble, dust, and smoke marked the site of the twin towers, a landmark that for the murder and heroism and compassion that attended it would be for a long time the city's chief monument.

In all, the number of deaths from the planes, the Pentagon, and the World Trade Center was finally estimated at roughly three thousand. A country angry and puzzled that it could invite such hatred looked to a president who, hitherto not having distinguished himself as a public presence, now presented a dignity worthy of the times. Amid an outburst of hatred against Arab Americans and foreigners who looked the least Middle Eastern, President Bush called for sanity. In a demonstration of solidarity with Muslims in the United States he met with members of their community. The president declared, in effect, that a state of war existed, and promised military action. Against terrorists hidden and operating across national boundaries the response would have to be devised with little experience to draw on. The administration also sought a number of new security measures, among them widened authority for wiretapping and surveillance, and authorization indefinitely to detain immigrants, that disturbed civil libertarians, including some conservative Republicans. Over non-citizens President Bush even proposed exercising military tribunals, depriving them of public counsel and allowing conviction and execution by only a two-thirds vote.

The response among Americans to foreigners in their midst varied. To counter the outbreaks of hatred, some citizens went out of the way to express friendship toward people of Middle Eastern birth or background. As a symbolic gesture of patriotism— facing an enemy almost impossible to identify or locate, symbols were about all that was available— Americans displayed the flag on their homes, cars, and lapels. Polls registered a huge surge in the popularity of President Bush. Public opinion also specifically endorsed a willingness to forego some civil liberties for the sake of greater police surveillance of potential terrorism. Yet majorities also claimed to reject any suppression of unpopular anti-war activism. Americans found themselves forced to think through some of the beliefs that were sup-

These scenes are of New York City on September 11, 2001. (Courtesy, AP/Wide World Photos)

posed to be foundations of the country's political and social life.

Fashioning a Response

After the attack on the World Trade Center and the Pentagon, much of Washington's foreign policy was dictated by the nation's war on the bin Laden group, al-Qaeda, to which President Bush gave a more ambitious term: the war on terrorism. For a time the United States, benefiting from sympathy over September 11, had the pleasant and unusual experience of being liked by much of the world. The administration, recognizing that it could not pursue a global war on terror all by itself, added to the good feeling by briefly modifying, in manner if not in substance, its practice of unilateralism. The word had come into use to refer to a habit, illustrated particularly by Washington's dismissal of the treaty discussions at Kyoto, of acting alone in foreign policy without much concern for what any other country might have to say about things. Over Afghanistan and al-Qaeda, President Bush consulted with European leaders. In persuading General Pervez Musharraf, president of Afghanistan's neighbor Pakistan, to abandon his friendship for the Taliban and turn his troops against al-Qaeda units sheltered in fundamentalist Muslim regions of Pakistan, Washington scored an important diplomatic success.

After a few days of futile negotiation with the Taliban demanding that bin Laden be turned over to the United States, the administration decided that it must invade Afghanistan. In a corner of that country, a combination of fighters known as the Northern Alliance had already held out against the Taliban regime ever since its beginning. Other groups, some of them detestable warlords, also united against the equally detestable Taliban. Traditional rivalries in a nation badly fragmented into armed tribes reinforced hostility to the rulers and their cruel lunacies. The presence of al-Qaeda members from Arab and other lands, behaving like foreign overlords of a subject people, deepened the anger of the regime's opponents. When small elite units from Britain, Canada, the United States, and other nations entered the war, they essentially supplemented the anti-Taliban Afghans, supplying air power and, when necessary, ground troops trained for special conditions such as mountain combat. At the same time, Washington reached out to the Afghan people, seeing them as victims of a fanatic despotism and knowing that ultimately it would be Afghans rather than western troops who must win the war against the Taliban and its foreign al-Qaeda supporters.

At home, the discovery that someone was sending through the mails a powder containing anthrax bacteria brought new fears. The mailings of a bacteria causing a highly lethal illness indicated either private malice or possibly another phase of the terrorism of September 11. Anthrax appeared in letters to elected government figures, mostly Democrats, and briefly in October caused the closing of the Capitol and legislative office buildings to be inspected for traces of the powder. Still, the nature of the incidents suggested a single individual or a small group, enjoying the excitement or nursing some lonely paranoid resentment. A few people fell ill, beginning with a woman in Florida who succumbed to the disease, and when two employees in the main post office in Washington, DC, died of it, that building also was shut down until such time as investigators could determine that the danger had passed.

Collapse of the Taliban

When the United States and other Western nations determined to go into Afghanistan, they had no idea what to expect. In a conflict during the 1980s, Afghans had worn down an occupying army from the Soviet Union. Had the Western coalition acted the part of invaders, their fate would almost certainly have been that of the Soviet forces. But as partners of the opponents of the Taliban, the Western troops had a better reception. Some observers still projected a long, exhausting war against Taliban and al-Qaeda forces dug into mountainous regions that the Soviet army had been unable to take in years of bitter fighting.

Aided by air support from the Western coalition, the Northern Alliance troops pressed southward, meanwhile persuading one local leader after another to join in throwing out a government that had little of charm to begin with. The bargaining had a multiplying effect: the more local factions joined the uprising, the quicker still others agreed to join. When the anti-Taliban combined force, itself a ruthless crew who killed their opponents mercilessly, entered Kabul, crowds in the liberated city celebrated the small important freedoms that had come to them. Music was again acceptable; men who had been forced to wear the long beards required by the Taliban trimmed them; even a kite was hoisted. Women still had to be cautious. In parts of the Muslim world not just religious fanatics demanded their subordination. But the more daring women shed some of the covering the Taliban had demanded.

There were still the mountains. The Tora Bora mountain range in eastern Afghanistan had provided a fortress against the Soviet army, and it might similarly serve the Taliban and al-Qaeda. A network of caves and tunnels built during that ear-

Osama bin Laden. (Courtesy, Library of Congress)

lier war was now even more intricate. And the defenders were highly determined fundamentalist Muslim militants, who might hold out for years. But air strikes beginning on November 30, combined with attacks by Afghan fighters and some assistance from Western units, made the mountains inhospitable territory for the enemy. A major setback was realized, however, when many of the defenders escaped, including their leaders, apparently among them bin Laden himself.

By the end of 2001, Afghanistan had established an interim government headed by the engaging and aristocratic Hamid Karzai. His government set out to reverse the horrors of the Taliban, promising, for example, to bring women into politics. Later a Loya Jirga, a gathering traditional in Afghanistan in which leaders of various tribes agree upon matters of state, patched together a government that might reconcile the feuds of an incessantly divided country. Karzai remained at the head of it. As of late fall 2002 it continued a shaky existence.

In March 2002 Western and Afghan troops undertook the task, like that in the Tora Bora range, of dislodging al-Qaeda from another portion of the country. This time the Shah-e-Kot Valley was targeted. Americans gave the assault the name Anaconda. Like the similarly named strategy of the Union during the Civil War, it projected surrounding the enemy and crushing it as the Anaconda snake kills. The assault did rid the valley of al-Qaeda, but again it failed effectively to close off escape routes. It appears that much of the al-Qaeda force evaded the allies, possibly slipping across the border into the rugged portion of western Pakistan where Islamic fundamentalism remains popular and the Pakistani army finds it difficult to operate. Pakistanis as a whole were divided. While the government supported the war against al-Qaeda and went after members wherever it could, the population included militants who considered themselves at war with the West and with all religions outside Islam. An act of which they boasted was the kidnapping of an American Jewish journalist, Daniel Pearl. The terrorists had a liking for putting their exploits on tape, and a filming of their murder of Pearl by knife gave them particular pride.

In the course of a war, the unplanned deaths of civilians becomes both inevitable and a horror. In Afghanistan misdirected American bombings brought a number of such killings, among them an air attack on a convoy carrying tribal representatives to the Loya Jirga and the bombing of a pre-wedding party. The incidents typically brought an initial justification from the American command: either the attack was legitimate and the enemy had been scattered among the civilians, or the military had acted on good information provided by presumably friendly informants. The quickness of the American military to go automatically defensive, later backing off into halfway admissions that a mistake had been made, did more to injure than help the image the United States wished to maintain in Afghanistan. In the terrible misfortunes of war, meanwhile, anti-Taliban fighters and Westerners fell to instances of what is called "friendly fire." In one of these, a stray bombing killed four Canadian troops.

CONTROVERSIES AT MIDTERM

From early on, the Bush administration gained a reputation for being divided on foreign policy. Secretary of State Colin Powell, who had experienced combat in Vietnam, urged caution in turning to military responses to crises and favored discussion with foreign nations. Vice President Cheney repeatedly spoke for an aggressive foreign policy dictated by the will of the United States and involving minimal consultation with other countries. Especially complicated was the case of Saudi Arabia. There the government resided in a royal family that both supported Islamic fundamentalism and knew itself to be despised by fundamentalists who believed it to be insufficiently strict and lax toward the West. Needing the cooperation of the authorities in Islamic nations, the Bush administration decided for the most part to overlook the authoritarian character of the governments with which it dealt. But the question of how to manage foreign policy endured: should the United States act completely on its own wishes whenever it could, or did the policy of Secretary of State Powell make more sense?

On domestic issues, Bush took somewhat more care to make friends. A unilateral foreign policy, with excursions into cooperativeness, seemed feasible; but dealing at home with a Congress in which the Senate was in Democratic hands and the lower House delicately balanced between parties required

conciliation. Sticking essentially to a policy of market conservatism, Bush nonetheless tempered his aggressiveness on such matters as his plan for partial privatizing of Social Security and his opposition to federal regulation of campaign finances, which he reluctantly signed into law.

A New Crisis in the Mideast

In the Six Days' War of 1967 between Jews and Arabs, the Israelis had occupied Gaza, a patch of land bordering southwestern Israel and belonging to Egypt, and the Jordanian kingdom's West Bank between the Jordan River and the Jewish state. After many years in which the future of the conquered territories remained uncertain, an agreement worked out in Oslo, Norway, between the Israelis and representatives of the people of the territories and signed in 1993 established a Palestinian Authority. Headed by Yasser Arafat, the former leader of an anti-Israeli guerrilla force, the Author-

Yasser Arafat, leader of the Palestinian Authority. (Courtesy, AP/Wide World Photos)

ity was given partial governing power over those lands in preparation for turning them into an independent state. But many Palestinians wanted the Israeli occupation to end immediately, and insisted that all of Israel itself must become once again Palestinian. A faction of Israelis meanwhile has held that the territories, as part of ancient Israel, belong to the Jews, and to insure that they do, some of them established further settlements in the West Bank. Jerusalem, a city holy to Jews and Muslims as well as to Christians, remains a particular flashpoint. Eastern Jerusalem is part of the West Bank; the western part of the city belongs to the Israelis. Most Palestinians are Muslim, and they, along with much of the population in other Islamic countries, see all of Jerusalem as a Muslim city. Hardliners among the Israelis claim the city for Judaism. For Jerusalem, the conquered territories, and Israel itself, religion both Muslim and Jewish as well as nationalism both Palestinian and Israeli insured that the compromises of the Oslo Agreement would be under constant siege.

Beginning in late winter and continuing into the spring of 2002, hostility erupted into a string of suicide bombings. Palestinians carrying hidden explosives blew themselves up in the midst of Israelis. Israel's prime minister Ariel Sharon held Arafat's Palestinian Authority to be accountable at least for not stopping the bombings, and possibly for being behind them. Pressed by Sharon, Arafat had to fear also the wrath of Palestinian fanatics dissatisfied with the idea of a two-state solution and insisting that Palestine prevail over Israel. Arafat had to negotiate the delicate politics of the situation; he also wanted to stay alive. Although he criticized the killings of civilians, he did so not forcefully and repeatedly, leaving his real sentiments unclear. Sharon, at any rate, decided that the Palestinian Authority was carrying on a war with Israel. Israeli troops responded by military incursions into the West Bank in actions that included what war inevitably brings: disruption of civilian lives and the unintended killing of bystanders. For a time Israeli troops surrounded Arafat's headquarters. The worst incidents occurred in fighting in April between Palestinians and the Israeli army at the Jenin refugee camp on the West Bank. Human Rights Watch, which investigates rights violations throughout the world, entered the camp shortly afterwards. After combing through accounts of wit-

Prime Minister Ariel Sharon of Israel. (Courtesy, AP/ Wide World Photos)

nesses, it concluded in a report issued early in May that it could document twenty-two civilian deaths, some of them deliberate. The group noted finding instances in which the troops had used civilians as human shields. Human Rights Watch, however, made it clear that it had no convincing evidence to support Palestinian assertions that the Israelis had massacred hundreds of inhabitants. Amid the invasion of the conquered territories, some Israeli reservists refused to serve, believing Sharon's response to go beyond Israel's justifiable determination to stop the suicide murders.

President Bush tried cautious intervention. The trouble made it harder for him to be on good terms with Muslim governments antagonistic to Israel who identified Washington with the Jewish state. Bush tried to persuade Sharon to try a more conciliatory policy toward the Palestinians. The response he got was vague. But violence on both sides gradually diminished, though unaccompanied by the

slightest hint of how to solve the deep and enduring conflict between Israelis and Palestinians.

Enron

A few weeks after the suicide attacks in Israel,
there erupted a business scandal so large as to compete with news of the war against al Qaeda. One
major corporation in particular, its surfaces glisten-
ing with a look of success and big money, began
falling apart, and scattered among the wreckage lay
evidence of major corruption.

The huge Enron enterprise, operating out of
Houston, Texas, had made a fortune out of electrical energy: or rather, out of owning stock in various
companies that actually produce energy. But by the
later months of 2001, some company executives
along with members of their accounting firm Arthur Andersen knew that Enron was close to bankruptcy. Ethics and the law alike require a corporation to make accurate publication of its profits and
losses. Enron and its auditing agency instead doc-
tored the figures, hoping to keep actual and potential investors confident in the company's prospects.
At the last moment before the collapse, executives
dumped their holdings and walked away with
swollen bank accounts. Employees, proud of the
prestigious corporation and trusting it, lost much of
their retirement savings, for Enron had urged them
to buy shares and in face of its troubles gave them
no more warning than it gave the larger public.

To deception and lawbreaking, Enron had added
betrayal.

The revelations made public in 2002 outraged
not only Democrats and liberals but, as least as
measured by their heated rhetoric, conservatives
and Republicans who generally are more permissive
toward the doings of big business. The callousness
of Enron could anger people of every political persuasion; and the company's behavior threatened to
discredit Wall Street capitalism. Congress considered ways of preventing further such abuses. Called
to testify before congressional hearings, the Enron
executives Kenneth Lay and Jeffrey Skilling invoked their Fifth Amendment right against giving
self-incriminating testimony. It was their privilege,
but it further blackened the public image of the
corporation. The Arthur Anderson firm, which had
contributed to Enron's effort at deception and later
was discovered to have destroyed documents indicating its involvement, shared in the humiliation.
Clients fled from it, a Houston jury convicted it of
obstructing justice, and the giant firm went into
bankruptcy.

Following the exposure of Enron, other companies suffered public disgrace at evidence that they
too had put out false claims of profit. WorldCom, a
huge concern that existed in large part for the purpose of holding stock in other corporations, caused
a particular stir when in July, after declarations of
its financial soundness, it, too, declared bankruptcy.

The ill effect of September 11 on the economy

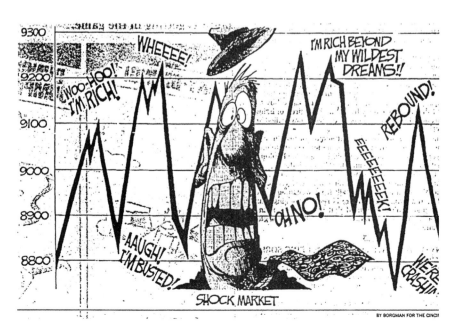

*As this political cartoon illustrates,
the stock market has in recent years
gyrated wildly.* (Courtesy, King
Features Syndicate)

had been significant. Enron and subsequent exposures cut deeper still. It is common practice for corporations to evade laws governing such matters as air pollution, or to be opportunistic in their treatment, for example, of cheap labor in countries outside the United States to which their holdings extend. But they are not expected to steal from investors, who expect profits. Scandal sent buyers running from all Wall Street stocks, many of them overvalued on account of their meteoric rise from 1995 to 1999. At the time of the Enron revelations, more than half of the American population belonged to families with some stockholdings, however modest. When the stock market, during the summer of 2002, dropped sharply, crisis visited middle-class savers. People of modest means who, like the Enron workers, had committed their future to the success of investment capitalism faced possible loss of security for their retirement years.

The Question of Iraq

For much of his presidency, Bush had prepared for some action, which might be a military invasion, that could topple Saddam Hussein. There was moral reason enough for wanting Iraq to be rid of him, as there has been legitimate moral reason for removing any number of rulers both of countries at odds with the United States and of nations friendly to Washington. The repressiveness of Saddam's rule was never in question. But Bush and the members of his administration most supportive of his preoccupation with removing Saddam centered their case in the claim that the Iraqi dictator continues to develop nuclear or biochemical weapons of mass destruction that he could use or give to terrorists.

As the defeated opponent of the United Nations in the Gulf War of 1991, Iraq was obliged by that world body to forego such weapons and to open up the country to inspections insuring that it was doing so. But a mechanism established by the UN for inspecting Iraq's weaponry ran up against the regime's evasive resistance. The issue brought out a fundamental question within the Bush presidency concerning how much consultation Washington, in its various interactions with the rest of the world, should have with foreign nations. Having gotten a reputation for arrogance in its dealings with other countries, the administration acquiesced in a new round of inspections by the United Nations before it began a war on its own. Late in 2002 UN inves-

Saddam Hussein of Iraq was suspected of stockpiling chemical, biological, and possibly nuclear weapons. Fear of what he might do with them reopened the thorny question of whether a democracy is ever justified in making a preemptive strike. (Courtesy, AP/Wide World Photos)

tigators were in Iraq amid disputes over how much cooperation they were getting there and Washington's insistence that they were getting none. The administration, having the support of Britain's Labour Party prime minister Tony Blair, was meanwhile casting about for other allies and especially for Middle Eastern countries willing to allow the United States to base invasion forces in their territory. When at the end of the year North Korea too indicated that it would go ahead with a program of developing nuclear weapons, the question of how much political and diplomatic energy Washington should invest in containing Iraq became further complicated.

The Elections of 2002

Going into the midterm congressional elections of 2002, the Democrats held a margin of one vote over the Republicans in the Senate, and the Republicans a slender majority in the lower House. President Bush deployed his popularity in support of

Republican candidates, and almost certainly because of that the Republicans regained the Senate, though by a majority only of fifty-one to forty-nine, the independent Jeffords voting with the Democrats, while the party slightly widened its lead in the House. It was a signal triumph for Bush, not only because it demonstrated his political power but because the Republicans now held both branches of the national legislature. His victory was slightly dampened a few weeks later when in Louisiana in a run-off election the Democratic senatorial incumbent Mary Landrieu retained her seat, essentially by campaigning on a local economic issue. Wishing to bring the autumn success to a smashing conclusion, the president and his party had pressed hard to defeat the moderate Democrat, who was in great part a supporter of the policies of the White House.

Shortly afterwards, the Republicans embarrassed themselves. Senator Strom Thurmond of South Carolina had been in 1948 the presidential candidate of the white-supremacist Dixiecrats, a temporary breakaway movement by southern Democrats who resented their national party's sympathy for civil rights. In late autumn 2002 Thurmond celebrated his hundredth birthday. At the festivities the Senate majority leader Trent Lott of Mississippi, like the South Carolinian a Democrat turned Republican, spoke favorably of Thurmond's Dixiecrat effort, referring vaguely to "problems" in the nation's recent history that Thurmond's election would have prevented. The remark tainted the Republicans. Their recent successes in the South over the past decades were founded in their having become, in contradiction to their earlier history, the party less favorable to black social and political aspirations. Yet they aim to present themselves as inclusive of the hopes of all citizens. Demographics indicate that the present Republican base in white males, especially rural and small-town, will soon not be sufficient for electoral victory; so reaching out to minorities makes political sense. Lott's words seemed to reveal an ugly underside to Republican politics, a stage whisper to white racists that their home is in the GOP.

A combination of strategy and principle drove Republicans, from Bush downward, to condemn Lott's comments. The hapless senator made several apologies, defining his remarks as an effort to offer some genial birthday flattery to an old man. The discovery that two decades ago he had said much the same thing of Thurmond deepened his difficulties. His position hopeless, he resigned as prospective Republican majority leader, and by the end of December his colleagues had chosen Senator Bill Frist of Tennessee, a surgeon especially interested in issues of health care.

Suggested Readings

Whether the civic disturbance in Los Angeles in 1992 should be labeled a "riot" or an "uprising" is the subject of ongoing debate among activists and academics. See Nancy Abelmann, *Korean Americans and the Los Angeles Riots* (1995) and Robert Cooding-Williams, eds., *Reading Rodney King, Reading Urban Uprising* (1993). Many consider California's ethnically and racially diverse coastal cities to be harbingers of future demographic trends in the United States. For more on California, see Leland T. Saito, *Race and Politics: Asian Americans, Latinos, and Whites in a Los Angeles Suburb* (1998) and Kent Ono, *Shifting Borders: Rhetoric, Immigration, and California's Proposition 187* (2002).

On the politics and economics of United States policy regarding its southern border, see Peter Andreas, *Border Games: Policing the U.S.-Mexico Divide* (2000) and Eva Bertram et al., *Drug War Politics: The Price of Denial* (1996). For overviews of the "Fourth Wave" of immigration, consult Desmond S. King, *Making Americans: Immigration, Race, and the Origins of the Diverse Democracy* (2000), and

Daniel J. Tichenor, *Dividing Lines: The Politics of Immigration Control in America* (2002). The resurgence of Native-American self-identification since the 1970s is explained in Joane Nagel, *American Indian Ethnic Renewal: Red Power and the Resurgence of Identity and Culture* (1996).

Multiculturalism is too often unfairly ridiculed or thoughtlessly defended. Sophisticated treatments can be found in David A. Hollinger, *Postethnic America: Beyond Multiculturalism* (1995); Joseph T. Rhea, *Race Pride and the American Identity* (1997); and Nathan Glazer, *We Are All Multiculturalists Now* (1997). Elisabeth Lasch-Quinn's *Race Experts: How Racial Etiquette, Sensitivity Training, and New Age Therapy Hijacked the Civil Rights Revolution* (2001) is a thought-provoking polemic. Cultural historians have been debating the effects of mass media on traditional notions of community for many decades. The rise of the Internet has spurred new research into this subject, such as Patricia M. Wallace, *The Psychology of the Internet* (1999). Sociologist Robert Putnam's *Bowling Alone: The Collapse and Revival of*

American Community (2000) puzzles over the causes and consequences of the decline of traditional forms of civic engagement like the PTA.

A concise and solid history of the American presidency through Bill Clinton can be found in Michael A. Genovese, *The Power Of The American Presidency, 1789–2000* (2000). Clinton's presidency, like the man himself, was rife with paradox and is contentiously debated. Some of the keenest insights into Clinton's election and his turbulent administration can be found in Bob Woodward, *The Agenda: Inside the Clinton White House* (1994); David Maraniss, *First in His Class: A Biography of Bill Clinton* (1995); Theda Skocpol, *Boomerang: Clinton's Health Security Effort and the Turn against Government in U.S. Politics* (1996); Jacob S. Hacker, *The Road to Nowhere: The Genesis of President Clinton's Plan for Health Security* (1997); Haynes B. Johnson, *The Best of Times: America in the Clinton Years* (2001); and Joe Klein, *The Natural: The Misunderstood Presidency of Bill Clinton* (2002). Kenneth Baer, *Reinventing Democrats: The Politics of Liberalism from Reagan to Clinton* (2000) and John B. Judis, *The Emerging Democratic Majority* (2002) assess the Democratic Party's fortunes in the Clinton era and thereafter. Clinton was a brilliant campaigner; but he was often criticized for conducting a perpetual campaign while in office. For more on Clinton's political techniques and style, see Jack W. Germond and Jules Wicover, *Mad as Hell: Revolt at the Ballot Box* (1993); Dick Morris, *Behind the Oval Office: Winning the Presidency in the Nineties* (1997); and James B. Stewart, *Blood Sport: The President and His Adversaries* (1996).

Clinton's shift to the political center was nowhere clearer than in his stance on free trade. Frederick W. Mayer, *Interpreting NAFTA: The Science and Art of Political Analysis* (1998) looks more closely at the North American context. For the confusion besetting American foreign policy after the fall of its perennial enemy, the Soviet Union, see Michael Hogan, ed., *The End of the Cold War: Its Meaning and Implications* (1992) and David Halberstam, *War in a Time of Peace: Bush, Clinton, and the Generals* (2001). Prominent conservatives spelled out their plan for unseating the Democrats in 1994 and reforming government in Newt Gingrich, *Quotations from Speaker Newt* (1995) and Ed Gillespie and Bob Schellhas, *Contract With America* (1994). Charles O. Jones, *Clinton and Congress, 1993–1996: Risk,*

Restoration, and Reelection (1999) offers a more dispassionate analysis of the "Republican Revolution" of 1994, while Justin B. Watson, *The Christian Coalition* (2000) and Karen Armstrong, *The Battle for God* (2000) explore the goals and strategies of the Christian fundamentalists whose campaigning helped bring Republicans to power. Clinton's congressional opponents stepped up their assault during the Monica Lewinsky scandal, the consequences of which are addressed in two anthologies: Mark Rozell and Clyde Wilcox, eds., *The Clinton Scandal and the Future of American Government* (2000) and Leonard Kaplan and Beverly Moran, eds., *Aftermath: The Clinton Impeachment and the Presidency in the Age of Political Spectacle* (2001).

Charles H. Logan, *Private Prisons: Cons and Pros* (1990) is a good introduction to a growing phenomenon. For more on the Waco and Ruby Ridge fiascos, and the militia movement's bloody response, see Stuart A. Wright, ed., *Armageddon in Waco: Critical Perspectives on the Branch Davidian Conflict* (1995); Kenneth Stern, *A Force upon the Plain: The American Militia Movement and the Politics of Hate* (1996); Mark S. Hamm, *Apocalypse in Oklahoma: Waco and Ruby Ridge Revenged* (1997); and Lou Michel, *American Terrorist: Timothy McVeigh and the Oklahoma City Bombing* (2001). Prophecy belief at the turn of the century is dealt with in Marth F. Lee, ed., *Millennial Visions: Essays on Twentieth-Century Millenarianism* (2000); Jayne S. Docherty, *Learning Lessons from Waco: When the Parties Bring their Gods to the Negotiation Table* (2001); and James D. Faubion, *The Shadows and Lights of Waco: Millennialism Today* (2001).

Abner Greene, *Understanding the 2000 Election: A Guide to the Legal Battles that Decided the Presidency* (2001); Jeffrey Toobin, *Too Close to Call: The Thirty-Six-Day Battle to Decide the 2000 Election* (2001); and Bruce Ackerman, ed., *Bush v. Gore: The Question of Legitimacy* (2002) explore the twists of that famous event. For more on John McCain's maverick run for the presidency, see Elizabeth Drew, *Citizen McCain* (2002).

For more on the Bush presidency and its many domestic and foreign policy challenges after the terrorist attacks of September 2001, see Frank Bruni, *Ambling into History: The Unlikely Odyssey of George W. Bush* (2002); Thomas L. Friedman, *Longitudes and Attitudes: Exploring the World after September 11* (2002); and Daniel Benjamin and Steven Simon, *The Age of Sacred Terror* (2002).

Clearcutting. *(Courtesy, American Heritage)*

The End of Nature?

CHAPTER

28

In 1989 Bill McKibben, a writer on the environment, published *The End of Nature*, a bleak commentary on the greenhouse effect. Most climate scientists have decided that the accumulation high above the earth of carbon dioxide emitted into the air from factories and cars is forming a layer in the atmosphere that traps beneath it the heat from the sun, as the glass in a greenhouse captures and preserves the sun's warmth. The results are not yet predictable. Some low lying lands including entire thickly populated islands will disappear within this century if glaciers continue to melt at the present rate. A number of regions may actually benefit from global warming that will increase their growing season. But the near certainty that the presently unknowable changes will be great, raising the sea level and turning into deserts or steaming jungles portions of the earth that are now temperate, has worried environmental scientists. McKibben, however, does not stop there. For a world inhabited by species altered by genetic engineering, he foresees the end of nature that the book title announces. The sun will still shine and breezes will yet freshen the air of springtime, but the breezes will stir in response to atmospheric conditions of human making. Nature as an independent foundation of human life, apart from us, to be counted on in its rough weather and its balmy days, its life forms obedient to forces uncontrolled or only lightly modified by human activity, is going to disappear. And McKibben laments its passing not only for the possible dangers but for the loss in itself.

It may be questioned whether the winds and tides, the hot spells and blizzards of the future will be so much a product of human activity that they can no longer belong to something that is now called nature. In any event, though, McKibben's book can be read as a way of looking backward through American history. In a few early generations, the European settlement of New England transformed northerly deep forests into cleared land. When farmers left the region, trees grew again but numerous species had been lost.

From then to now, much of American history has been a vast project of reshaping nature. Dramatically bad effects had been visible to

Americans before the recent work of environmentalists included the Dust Bowl and the scars left by strip mining. A spectacularly good effect, the enormous productivity of American agriculture, is easily overlooked, taken as a given. But for evil or good, the American experience of the land has assumed various forms that reflect the nation's culture and values.

*   *   *

The Puritans, already conditioned by their religion to see the world around them as a place to be conquered, its wildness to be subdued along with their own sins, encountered surroundings that would not yield to them without a struggle. Bitter winters, rocky soil, the menace of Indians (who, not unreasonably, saw them to be a menace) required vigilance and continuous work. That is so particularly because enterprising New Englanders looked on their environment not simply as a region to be lived in, as did Native Americans, but as an occasion for the development of crafts and industry, for the rum and lumber production, and for commercial farming. Yet by the end of the seventeenth century, New Englanders had built around their village life and their industrious farms a solid and healthy existence. Settlement in Virginia tells a different story. For the first days of the colonial experience there, a mania for producing tobacco as a cash crop proceeded with little concern for shaping a comfortable relationship with the earth, and not much more for the lives of the workers. Virginia therefore took longer than New England to have a population long-lived enough to sustain its own growth without constant immigration.

Virginia, though, did produce at the end of the colonial period and the early years of the republic a writer who had a more generous idea of the land. Thomas Jefferson hoped that the inland would offer plots on which farming could engage the great bulk of the population. Land as Jefferson conceived it is simply a place for communion with nature. It supplies private property, and therefore will keep its owners independent and fit for republican citizenship; and it is the material basis for the nurturing of daily industry appropriate to a virtuous citizen. The unexplored inland had particular meaning for Jefferson the figure of the Enlightenment. It would be a vast scientific laboratory, to be investigated for its plants and animals and climate. The land, then, was to serve multiple purposes: as a source of beauty and refreshment such as the view that Jefferson's home at Monticello offered; as a foundation of republican virtue; and as a stimulus to the enlightened scientific intellect.

In the first half of the nineteenth century, New England produced writers who saw in human and outer nature not the grim field for conquest that Puritans had perceived there but an unending source of truth and renewal. The Transcendentalists as they were called, exemplified by the essayist Ralph Waldo Emerson, perceived all of existence as the expression of a single spirit. Mind and nature are therefore identical: gaze on a sun-drenched field and you see the light that floods your own soul; contemplate the darkened sky of a storm and you find the mysteries that dwell within you. Contemporary to the Transcendentalists though not necessarily sharing their intellectual persuasion was the Hudson River school of artists, so named for their paintings of that prized stretch of New York State, though much of their work was taken from other scenes. At a time when territory was moving westward, they caught patches of the wilderness that remained, portraying it in powerful images of wide fields, shadowed woods, and rugged mountain terrain, dwellings suited for the cosmic spirit that Transcendentalists thought to find there.

The New England writers were drawn to the abolitionist and other reform activities of their day, convinced that the triumph of freedom, justice, and general well-being will bring the perfection that is already latent within the world spirit and seeking fulfillment. But one of them, Henry David Thoreau, held at least partially aloof from the reformist movements, though committed to the struggle against slavery. From 1845 to 1847 he lived much of the time in a hut at Walden Pond outside Concord, Massachusetts. He was not quite the hermit he has been depicted, but his effort was to discover how an individual might live alone, free both from commercial entanglements and from trivial needs and desires. His relations with nature were complex. He looked to simplify his desires by the aid of nature. Yet he remained somewhat distant from it, a respectful observer. He studied the detail of nature with a sharp, scientific inquisitiveness somewhat at variance with the Transcendentalist passion for nature in its broad strokes. He also sought patterns there: the leaf design, for example, that he found not only in tree leaves but in feathers, in the human hand, in the spread of rivulets as water trickles down hillsides. Careful reading he spoke of as being among the highest enterprises. Thoreau would read books with the same precision with which he examined the natural phenomena of Walden Pond. In him a love of the wild united with the scholarly mind of New England.

The Republican administration that fought a civil war for the preservation of the Union, and ultimately for emancipation, envisioned a more centralized nation and economy. To that purpose it defined for the lands of the West a more worldly future than the Transcendentalists had given to nature. The Homestead Act, ultimately an unsatisfactory means to the settlement of the West, granted a plot of federal holdings to any farmer willing to work it. Homesteaders were supposed to furnish a market for the manufactures of the East in return for the produce of their fields. The Homestead Act contemplated an additional advantage in accordance with Republican antislavery sympathies. It was to people the West with free farmers in place of the slave-worked plantations that southerners had hoped for. The Jeffersonian ideal of a nation of virtuous tillers of the earth mated with a practical scheme for the benefit of an industrial as well as agricultural economy.

The West did fill up, but not mainly by reason of the Homestead Act. Among the instruments of settlement were generous sales by railroad companies of plots carved from the huge chunks of the West the federal government had given them. Railroad executives knew they could profit more from a thicker population than from land prices. The dream of a hard-working but tranquil agrarian West, however, did not materialize, at least to the extent antislavery forces had imagined. The West became a place of lust-filled assaults on the land and its resources. Grasslands chewed up and trampled by cattle ranching, ores gouged from the earth by quick-profit mining operations, soils raided and torn by farmers desperate to keep on top of debt: all this defines much of far-western settlement.

Still, the West offered one generous vision that differed from the Jeffersonian. Its huge productivity became, for such as the twentieth-century Chicago poet Carl Sandburg, the twin and reflection of powerful cities and their industry. Sandburg's Chicago, in all its crudeness, he caught in images of its placement at the edge of midwestern prairies. The nation, then, is seen for what it has been in other ideas of the land: soil and minerals and technology joined in a vast building project.

It is very much in the American spirit that the conservationist movements at the turn of the twentieth century and the environmentalism of more recent times have engaged in their own gigantic building enterprise: putting nature back together by such efforts as the New Deal Civilian Conservation Corps, and constructing legal defenses against further raids against land and resources. And for this they have employed much the same tools of scientific inquiry that industrialism and postindustrial computer technology have employed in covering nature over with factories and cities, power plants, and the invisible webs of the Internet. But many of them attempt to infuse their work and its results with a respectful perception of climate and landscape that earlier generations of Americans were much lacking. So an examination of environmentalism and the ills it addresses can serve as an epilogue to the story of the American encounter with the land up to the present.

The Wilderness

"[W]ithin a hundred miles of southern Oregon there are two million acres of wilderness, national parks, and national monuments," declared an executive of a northwestern timber company in the 1990s. He saw no reason for setting aside any more lands for protection: "How," he wanted to know, "can any one person see two million acres of wilderness?" It was against just such reasoning that new groups of environmental activists mobilized.

In the summer of 1982 about five hundred members of an organization calling itself Earth First! gathered in a basin of the Gros Ventre range in Wyoming, a magnificent region threatened by oil drilling. Under the slogan OMDB (Over My Dead Body) they pulled up survey stakes, destroyed oil company equipment, and blockaded the access route to the site. The protest led not to a predictable dismissal of the protesters as hippy freaks but to an investigation by the Interior Department and afterwards to the rescue of Gros Ventre, which Congress designated a wilderness. In like spirit was David Foreman, a member of the Wilderness Society who had turned from conventional lobbying to environmental radicalism. His *Ecodefense: A Field Guide to Monkeywrenching* describes ways of peacefully sabotaging equipment employed by companies attacking the environment.

Gros Ventre and Foreman's book were part of a worldwide guerrilla movement by backpackers out of the later 1960s, but its method and thinking go back to earlier strains of anarchism. Its members did not even have to act in concert. A single ecological warrior alone in the woods could do some serious damage—slashing the tires on an un-guarded tractor or burning earthmoving equipment—and quickly be gone, a freely acting member of a world cooperative.

Environmental militants have employed differing tactics. A pro-tester dumped industrial waste in the office of steel executives. Another dressed in a bear costume and chained himself to a newly opened restau-rant in Yellowstone on a spot that had been a habitat for grizzlies. Some activists have engaged in violence. Earth First! to the contrary favored informing the businesses being targeted so that workers would not be injured. Together, though, such activists represent the farthest reach of environmentalism. The Oregon timber executive, puzzled at why all that wilderness was needed, does not quite embody their opposite. Other entrepreneurs go further and want commercial exploitation of lands already protected from development. The twenty-first century administration of President George W. Bush embraces that goal.

As radical environmentalists demonstrate, the concern for the preservation of nature that distinguished the presidency of Theodore Roosevelt is gaining an aggressive edge. Conservation, the management of natural resources for human ends, clashed predictably with timber barons and others eager to exploit nature quickly for profit. Now, how-ever, many defenders of nature reject the very idea of conservation as embodied in Gifford Pinchot's insistence on "the greatest good for the greatest number for the longest period of time." They speak instead for a sensibility centered less on the human than on the natural, an attitude that recoils from any more than the most sparing disruption of nature. Conservation, such new environmentalists are convinced, embodies sim-ply a more subtle assault upon nature than crudely greed-driven capi-talists wish to carry out. Conservation as its environmental opponents see and fear it aims at nothing short of a more effective rationing of nat-ural resources that are nonetheless destined to be ultimately chewed up in the machinery of modern production.

Aldo Leopold

In John Muir, today's environmentalists possess an ancestor. Nearly a century ago, that feisty Scotsman defended California's Hetch Hetchy Valley against the successful effort, backed by Theodore Roo-sevelt's conservationist ally Gifford Pinchot, to have the valley flooded and its water channeled to supply San Francisco. A more extensive case against all ambitious and large-scale uses of nature came from Aldo Leopold, whose writings continued until about midcentury, not long before the awakening of a combative environmentalism.

As supervisor in 1912 of the Carson National Forest in the South-west, Leopold zealously enforced regulations limiting but not extin-guishing the grazing rights of sheep ranchers on federal lands. Under his direction, the partly denuded range began to recover. That accorded with the idea of land conservation for human use. But over time, Leopold's feeling toward nature took a different course. The change in him, one of his many essays explains, came after he joined with com-panions in shooting a wolf. There, in the wilderness of the Colorado mountains, he saw in her dying, green-burning eyes a life that had its own meaning and right. In 1935 he joined in founding the Wilderness Society, devoted to preserving lands in their wild state. For years he was a professor of game management at the University of Wisconsin.

Leopold's best-known book is *A Sand County Almanac*, published in 1949, a year after his death. Human beings, the work reasons, are no more or less than members of an interdependent community of nature. They are obliged to act modestly and cooperatively toward the other members, each of which has its own claim to existence. That is a long way from Gifford Pinchot and the drowning of Hetch Hetchy Valley.

Landscape and Modern War

Leopold's ideas, in his time an eccentric position even among defenders of nature, would soon have an unwelcome ally. The war in Vietnam demonstrated how far modern technology could go in destroying all life, human and otherwise. Earlier twentieth-century conflicts had already done much the same. British officers in the First World War, educated in pastoral poetry, recoiled at the sight of landscapes turned to mud and trenches and wire. The atomic bombs that ended the second war subjected the Japanese to the recognition that not only their cities but their fragile beloved landscape could one day be scorched and evaporated, a demonstration that nature was no longer a permanent, nurturing ground of their culture. Vietnam, calling into being a counterculture that fled from machines to the pursuits of agriculture and crafts, made for further proof that nothing green and living, and certainly not human life itself, was safe from devastation.

Modern weaponry, then, looms over the landscape environmentalists contemplate, like the mushroom cloud of nuclear war that is the background for a cartoonist's depiction of a world at risk. Few of the many forms of recent environmental thought, however, demonize the science and technology that make such weapons of war possible. More typically, environmental activity of one kind or another has risen in response to some particular problem as it becomes increasingly noticeable. And in seeking a remedy, environmentalists strenuously pursue the methods and findings of scientists working in biology and climate. In so doing they treat as an object of technical study the nature they also revere as having a mystery beyond human understanding and manipulation. Environmentalists usually seek refined and sophisticated ways of doing things: as an example, the capture of energy through solar screens. Established manufacturing and mining industries have been the technological reactionaries, keeping to existing methods and equipment as long as these remain profitable while balking at investing in technologies that might pursue the same goals with less environmental damage.

Ecology

An instance of late twentieth-century environmentalism was an effort to protect the Everglades of Florida and other wetlands. The concern for the wetlands depends on a knowledge of their contribution to their surroundings, in such ways as purifying water and sponging up its excess, which might otherwise swell into floods. That recognition of the

interlacings that make up natural systems—ecologies, they are called—
is essential to modern environmentalists who embrace nature as an
organic whole. Sound and useful knowledge of an ecology requires a
commitment to rigorous scientific investigation. And the defense of
swampland, a part of nature that earlier opinion had held to be worthy
only of being drained, was in the spirit of recent environmentalist thinking. Public pressure led several states in the late 1960s and early seven-
ties to enact protective legislation against intrusion into wetlands. But
as federal law was weakened by challenges from property rights advocates in the courts, their conversion into agricultural lands and building
sites was to be an increasing reality.

Pine barrens, swamps, deserts: such places once considered
grotesques of nature have won, like the wetlands, a high status among
ecological activists. They became the equivalents of the endangered
species that legislation adopted during the Nixon presidency put under
federal protection.

Among ecosystems more quickly recognizable than swamps for
their majesty, as well as their use, are rivers and the life they sustain.
During the 1930s the Tennessee Valley Authority built dams on the
Tennessee River as part of an effort to develop the region it drains. Dams
produce electricity and reduce flooding, but they may also back up
rivers into dry beds and streams broken in their flowing, endangering
fish that can thrive only in free flow. In 1986 a new law contemplated
such effects along with recreational value in renewing federal licenses for
their operation. Wild salmon, a greatly prized fish, have found an enemy
in hydroelectric dams in the Northwest. Their turbines chop up the fish,
and their interruption of free flow has kept salmon from swimming
upstream to spawn. Fish ladders or sluices built around dams are
intended to allow a return of the old travel upstream. In the Little Butte
River in Oregon, carefully placed tree trunks created pools in which, the
planners hoped, fish can spawn. And where the river crosses federal
lands, foresters planted trees along the bank providing shade and, once
they have grown, logs for forming pools. Yet such attempts have done
little toward overcoming the physical obstacles that dams create, which
are often accompanied by other environmental problems—warmer
water, for example, or increased levels of mud and silt. As an alternative,
a few dams are scheduled to be removed.

Insidious Enemies

Science, instructing environmentalists in the sponge effect of wetlands and the proper spawning habitat for salmon, also yields a treasury
of information on the invisible forces of microbes and chemicals as they
interconnect with their surroundings.

Rachel Carson's *Silent Spring*, published in 1961 and invaluable in
motivating environmental activism ever since, imagines a spring
silenced by pesticides such as DDT that kill bird populations. The book
embodies the awareness, later much intensified, of the unanticipated
ways by which supposedly useful inventions victimize nature and
human beings. A similar recognition has contributed to laws beginning
in the later 1960s insuring clean water and air, initially as part of Pres-

ident Lyndon Johnson's pursuit of a Great Society. Pollution, biologists know, destroys not only human health but ecologies: carbon monoxide kills vegetation; factory wastes dumped into the rivers kill fish. In the 1970s investigators began defining what is known as acid rain: the bombardment of water, soil, and ecological systems by chemicals released in the air from industrial processes and then captured in rain, sleet, and snow. Acid rain, blown eastward from the Middle West, has killed fish in lakes throughout New York and New England, and some lakes themselves are considered dead.

Greenpeace

The observance of Earth Day, first celebrated in 1970, reflects an ecological consciousness that had been growing since World War Two. Earth Day serves as a convenient marker of a shift in American attitudes, from an interest in production and management of resources to a centering on preservation and recreational consumption of natural landscapes, and a concern for the effects of production on human health. At the same time, a shift in the social dynamics underlying conservation is traceable, from an elite group of managers, trained under Pinchot and later empowered by the New Deal, to a far broader, popular engagement in environmental issues. In 1971, for example, nearly a decade before Earth First! came into existence, an organization that under the name Greenpeace would call up an international army of environmental militants prepared to take on the range of forces destructive of nature. The group's members have made nonviolent war on both the weapons of military conflict and the technologies that rip into natural systems. Best known for conducting campaigns from small ocean-going vessels, they have staged actions employing the techniques of civil disobedience associated with Gandhi and Martin Luther King. They have sailed in the path of whaling ships, blockaded Russian logging operations, and otherwise placed their bodies and their principles in the way of whatever they think to be at war upon life, human, animal, or vegetable. Greenpeace has managed to occupy a place alongside its more conservative allies in defense of nature, including John Muir's Sierra Club and the Wilderness Society.

Outside the two parties, meanwhile, ecological activism has spread to several political initiatives collectively known as the Green movement. The movement began in Europe, perhaps most strongly in Germany, near the twentieth century's end. In the United States separatist Green parties have been too weak to accomplish their goals and, by draining support from more broadly based alternatives, may even subvert them.

The Risks to Health

It does not take an ecological militant to be concerned with the health hazards of industrial byproducts. During the 1970s two spectacular events dramatized how great these might be. A community in New York State lay sprawled over the site of the uncompleted Love Canal, earlier used as a dumping ground for chemical waste and then filled in. Seepage of waste from the ground, discovered in 1977, convinced the authorities that for the indefinite future the spot must be treated as uninhabitable; the residents were evacuated. Then, in the early spring of 1979, engineers hurriedly shut down the nuclear power plant at Three Mile Island, Pennsylvania, which seemed at the point of a meltdown that would have released radiation over the surrounding area. For nearly a week until the plant was fully secure, Three Mile Island was a major news story. Love Canal and Three Mile Island made clear what harm highly concentrated industrial materials could do to whole populations.

The public meanwhile was becoming increasingly aware of less sensational but more insidious harm from air-borne pollutants and from chemical processes to which workers in a particular industry might be exposed. Debra Davis spent her earliest years in a Pennsylvania steel town. On October 26, 1948, a cold front in the area caught the industrial gases that ordinarily would have dissipated in air. Residents sickened, and some died. At the time, the incident was dismissed as the work of a mysterious fog. But as a health researcher, Dr. Davis knows better. *When Smoke Ran Like Water*, published in 2002, is her account of the painstaking statistical studies by which investigators map out the prevalence of certain industrial conditions and correlate them with people who come down with lung or other illnesses, possibly years after removing from the noxious environment. Her own struggles and the combats of other health experts with industries that hire scientists to disprove such studies (sometimes the researchers so hired end up by confirming the conclusions of the original inquiries) make for quiet drama, as the two sides fight to shape government policy.

Battles Local and Global

In the 1980s and nineties the environmental issue grew especially combative in the Northwest. Logging companies lusted after old-growth timber on federal lands, trees that had not been artificially planted, some of them having stood for centuries. Environmentalists insisted that forests of that kind are invaluable and irreplaceable, only in part because they are habitats for such species as the disappearing spotted owl. Enlisting the aid of scientists who demonstrated the richness of the ecology that cutting would destroy, they succeeded in halting logging operations. Sealing a triumph already achieved in the courts was President Clinton's decision in 1994 to set aside a vast acreage of northwestern old-growth federal forest.

Saving the Northwest forests required only a decision by proper authorities. On other questions undertaken by nature activists, nothing more could be promised than a continuing struggle. Toxic waste, for example, is a problem that will continue with the march of industry and population growth. No one decree will eliminate it: Green activists and ordinary citizens are set to fight, city ordinance by federal law by executive decree, to halt its spread. The preservation of the Amazon rain forests from logging operations joins environmentalists from the United States with like-minded activists from around the world. The leaves of these forests release a good portion of the world's oxygen; their diminishing would affect the atmosphere. Meanwhile, the Indian peoples of the region are losing out. Their governments have ravaged their homelands in cooperation with industry, and the Indians themselves, needing firewood and the money from selling timber, have been compelled to join in the destruction. Still, both the governments and the Indians of the Amazon could make a case against any lecturing from Europe and North America. Developing nations point to the history of the United States and other countries that built their prosperity through similar kinds of destructive environmental extraction. Why, they ask, should they not be allowed to pursue prosperity through similar means? Such nations also point out that the United States and other developed nations are the world's most notorious consumers of environmental resources. Why should developed nations continue to consume, while refusing others the right to produce?

Stopping the industrial extraction of the natural riches of a region as vast as the Amazon come up against major corporate interests, but for that very reason the contending parties can be clearly defined and policies outlined for the protection of nature. In environmental summits in Rio de Janeiro, Kyoto, and Montreal, nations established goals and processes for dealing with environmental problems. The Montreal Protocols, for example, which aimed to reduce the chlorofluorocarbons responsible for destroying the earth's protective ozone, have been markedly successful. In Rio, developing nations agreed to institute environmental protections in exchange for economic support from developed countries. That support has been notably absent. And while several European nations have followed the Kyoto Accords and successfully reduced carbon emissions, the United States and other nations have opted for volunteerism and research leading to further research preparing the way for still further research. While the research continues, the carbon continues to be released.

Yet perhaps the greatest of all tasks for environmentalists would be far more subtle and many times more difficult: to deal not only with production, but with habits of consumption that have become deeply ingrained. How to persuade the public to accept some small modifications in daily living, such as turning off electric lights and appliances not in use, that had become foreign to American standards of comfort? How to create a market for cars efficient in energy? Or to convince consumers of the virtues of similarly efficient compact florescent light bulbs? These are challenges involving the complexities of culture and behavior, rather than the negotiations and positions found in diplomacy, politics, and economics.

Any quick-profit capitalist ought to share with the most militant ecowarrior an alertness to the world's energy supplies and other natural resources. The rise of oil prices in 1973 along with a power crisis in California that in 2001 required rolling blackouts—the crisis now appears to have been engineered by the infamous corporate giant Enron—have brought home some hard facts. Yet capitalists, at least in the old productive and extractive industries, have what they think to be a solution: rip open some further oil or coal reserve. And if that runs out? Rip open more. Thus the Sagebrush Rebellion among cattle and timber interests during the Ronald Reagan years demanded that the government turn over western lands that were under federal protection. Lately the presidential administration of the younger George W. Bush made it one of its first objectives to release for oil drilling an Alaskan wilderness that Bush's predecessor Clinton had tried to shelter. Recently public lands have been opened to drilling for oil or mining for minerals or timbering and snowmobiling. In seeking to appropriate natural resources, some conservatives appeal to the ethos of property rights: that individuals have an unlimited right to use land or mineral resources as their property, regardless of the consequences for the community or society in which they live.

At the other pole of the debate over energy preservation may be found a very few ecological activists who reject outright the whole of the consumerist argument. Every convenience provided by the modern world is a liability, so they hold: not since the days of a simple existence by foraging and primitively small-scale agriculture has the good life been available. That would eliminate the whole question of what to do when oil and other energy resources employed by modern industry are depleted. They would not be used at all.

Most environmental activists stay far short of that. If they dislike automobiles (overlooking the suffering to which draft animals were vulnerable before the coming of the internal combustion machine), they like bicycles, a product of nineteenth-century industry and much refined in the twentieth. Environmental advocates are drawn to electronic technologies, which bear lightly on their surroundings. Computers, when employed by workers applying their advanced skills independent of large corporations, offer much in common with ecological science setting the investigator to self-motivated study of a patch of nature. Environmental activists favor methods of drawing on alternate sources of energy. Prominent among these is the sun, which flings out such abundance of presently unused energy that it is for practical purposes incapable of being exhausted by human projects.

Still, the idea of a life more sparing of resources attracts even some liberals who are not closely identified with environmental activism. During a period of soaring oil prices in the 1970s President Jimmy Carter, addressing only the practical need for preserving energy resources, was of this mind when on television he urged Americans to turn down the heat a couple of degrees. He even wore a sweater, for the enlightenment of Americans unacquainted with the garment. And what he got, in part for proposing a course of mild austerity was Ronald Reagan.

Contrasting virtuous environmentalists to self-indulgent exploiters puts the case too simply. Opponents of logging have more recently come to recognize that together with the preservation of forests must come consideration for employment, and President Clinton provided funds to be used in retraining lumber workers for other jobs. Upper-middle class residents of carefully preserved communities resist the invasion of their homes and open spaces by low-income housing. But whatever the genuine advantages of preserving gracious old corners of a city or alternating suburban tracts with land preserves, the gain goes to residents with the money to enjoy them.

A New Consciousness of Environment

Questions relating to the environment promise increasingly to influence future political alignments. The Clinton presidency sustained an alliance between Democrats and environmentalists that had defined itself at least from the time when the two found common cause against the Reagan administration. Clinton's successor, the younger George Bush, has solidified the partnership between Republicans and the extractive industries. Beyond specific political quarrels is a change, slow and halting, in the consciousness that Americans hold of nature.

Earlier American generations of European ancestry had shot to extinction the vast flocks of passenger pigeons that once swept the skies. They sent rich soils in rivulets down the slopes of the Tennessee Valley. They stripped western plains of trees and grass, leaving the ground naked to the sun's pounding; and it thereupon became the Dust Bowl. To the mining and manufacturing industries, to western bonanza farms and cattle ranches, and later to agribusiness, they consigned great portions of the country's natural heritage. Perhaps developers, too, loved their huge sprawling land, even thinking that their mammoth raids upon it were acceptable expressions of its own stretch and power.

That way of associating with nature has fitted much of the nation's real success. The abundance that could be wrung from the resource-rich land of North America allowed the United States to flourish in ways that other countries had not done. Spain, France, Britain, Germany, Japan and others sought to build overseas empires, in part to give them access to resources. The United States, for much of its early history, confined its imperial practices to North America itself. It found there all the resources it could possibly use. The nation's rise to a position of global dominance in the twentieth century, however, has been marked by a staggering increase in our consumption of resources and a growing dependence on the environments of other nations. Environmental, economic, and political activities go closely together. This has never been so clear as in the last thirty years, as, for example, American dependence on foreign oil—we have for all practical purposes outstripped North America's petroleum abundance—creates a delicate global infrastructure in which national aspirations, terrorism, trade, and diplomacy are constantly mingled. The future presents a series of equally daunting challenges around water, food, health, and the myriad forms of pollution and waste.

Long before and long after the moment of first contact, indigenous people in North America confronted the problems inherent in their own environmental practices and they figured out ways of using the land in sustainable terms. Sometimes that meant abandoning villages and towns. Sometimes it meant seasonal migrations, or a self-imposed limit to the number of days for fishing or the time of year for hunting. Always it meant coming to some kind of understanding of the ecological connectedness of life. Nor have European settlers been unable to muster intimate and understanding relationships with the land. European

Americans who live by directly producing from the land may acquire some feeling for it, even if they are often unable to change they ways in which they farm, ranch, mine, or log.

When Bill McKibben warns of the death of nature, he mourns the loss of a nature that is outside of human control. But between nature and humankind no clear and absolute line of demarcation can be traced. Ecology and economy have the same root word—*oikos*, referring to the household—and they have always been partners in the world human beings make for themselves. The environmentalist concerns of recent years have been efforts to figure out ways to honor that partnership, to learn respect for the self-sustaining land, and to do so not simply within national boundaries, but in awareness of the place of the American land in the earth as a single entity, its peoples inseparably joined in tending the earth's goods.

Suggested Readings

On ecology in general, see Bill McKibben, *The End of Nature* (1990); Tom Griffiths and Libby Robin, *Ecology and Empire: Environmental History of Settler Societies* (1997); Mark Sagoff, *Ecology and Law: Science's Dilemma in the Courtroom* (1987); Leonardo Boff, *Ecology and Liberation: A New Paradigm* (1995); Lincoln Allison, *Ecology and Utility: The Philosophical Dilemmas of Planetary Management* (1991); Eugene P. Odum, *Ecology: A Bridge Between Science and Society* (1997); John Bellamy Foster, *Ecology Against Capitalism* (2002); Bruce L. Gardner, *American Agriculture in the Twentieth Century: How It Flourished and What It Cost* (2002); Melvin A. Bernarde, *Our Precarious Habitat* (1989); Clive Ponting, *A Green History of the World: The Environment and the Collapse of Great Civilizations* (1992); Charles H. Southwick, *Global Ecology in Human Perspective* (1996); and Stewart Udall, *The Quiet Crisis and the Next Generation* (1988).

On specific regional ecologies: Aldo Leopold, *A Sand County Almanac* (1949); Barbara McMartin, *Hides, Hemlocks and Adirondack History* (1992); Peter C. Welsh, *Jacks, Jobbers and Kings: Logging the Adirondacks, 1850–1950* (1995); David McCally, *Everglades: An Environmental History* (1999); John C. Gifford, *Everglades and Other Essays Relating to Southern Florida* (1912); Daniel Blaustein, *Everglades and the Gulf Coast* (1999); Thomas E. Lodge, *The Everglades Handbook: Understanding the Ecosystem* (1998); Anthony B. Anderson, *Alternatives to Deforestation: Steps toward Sustainable Use of the Amazon Rain Forest* (1990); Augusta Dwyer, *Into the Amazon: The Struggle for the Rain Forest* (1990); Susanna Hecht and Alexander Cockburn, *Fate of the Forest: Developers, Destroyers and Defenders of the Amazon* (1989); Goulding, Smith and Mahar, *Floods of Fortune: Ecology and Economy along the Amazon* (1996); Mary Reeves Bell, *Sagebrush Rebellion* (1999); William Coons, *Sagebrush Rebellion: Legitimate Assertion of State's Rights or Retrograde Land Grab?* (1981); and Stewart Udall, *The Forgotten Founders: Rethinking the History of the Old West* (2002).

Greenhouse Effect is the title of several books, including studies by Harold W. Bernard, Jr. (1980), Kathlyn Gay (1986), Jack C. Harris (1990), Darlene R. Stille (1990), Eric Stokes (1983), and Sharon Elaine Thompson (1992); see also Lydia Dotto, *Ethical Choices and Global Greenhouse Warming* (1993); Mohamed Suliman, *Greenhouse Effect and Its Impact on Africa* (1990); Edwin Kindeman, *Greenhouse Effect and Its Impact on Industry* (1990); Geoffrey Palmer, *Greenhouse Effect and Its Relevance to the Pacific Basin* (1988); and Rebecca L. Johnson, *Greenhouse Effect: Life in a Warmer Planet* (1993).

Wilderness Preservation is the topic of Howard Zahniser, *Where Wilderness Preservation Began: Adirondack Writings of Howard Zahniser* (1992); Michael Frome, *Battle for the Wilderness* (1997); Roderick Nash, *Wilderness and the American Mind* (1982); Dyan Zaslowsky and T.H. Watkins, *These American Lands: Parks, Wilderness and the Public Lands* (1994); Richard West Sellars, *Preserving Nature in the National Parks* (1997); and Marc Reisner, *Cadillac Desert* (1993).

Air and water pollution are the subjects of Rachel Carson, *Silent Spring* (1962); Stanley E. Degler, *Federal Pollution Control Programs: Water, Air and Solid Wastes* (1971); David F. Paulsen and Robert B. Denhardt, *Pollution and Public Policy* (1973); Dorothy E. Shuttlesworth, *Clean Air, Sparkling Water: The Fight against Pollution* (1968); David Pimentel, *Ecological Effects of Pesticides on Non-Target Species* (1971); Shirley A. Briggs, *Silent Spring: The View from 1987* (1987); B.J. Alloway and D.C. Ayres, *Chemical Principles of Environmental Pollution* (1993); Harold Crooks, *Giants of Garbage: The Rise of the Global Waste Industry and the Politics of Pollution Control* (1993); Andrew Farmer, *Managing Environmental Pollution* (1997); Curtis Moore, *Green Gold: Japan, Germany, the United States, and the Race for Environmental Technology* (1994); and Frank R. Spellman, *The Science of Environmental Pollution* (1999).

Chemical warfare during the Vietnam War is discussed in John Cookson and Judith Nottingham, *A New Perspective on War: Chemical and Biological Warfare, a Study with Special Reference to Vietnam* (1968); Barry Weisberg, *Ecocide in Indochina: The Ecology of War* (1970); Paul Frederick Cecil,

Herbicidal Warfare: the Ranch Hand Project in Vietnam (1986); and Bo Bengtsson, *Ecological Effects of Chemical Warfare and Bombing in Vietnam* (1976).

Books on environmental disasters include Therese De Angelis, *Three Mile Island* (2002); Susie Derkins, *Meltdown at Three Mile Island* (2002); Joseph Gerald Drazan, *Three Mile Island—A Preliminary Checklist* (1981); Lois Marie Gibbs, *Love Canal: My Story* (1982); Adeline Levine, *Love Canal: Science, Politics and People* (1982); and Jonathan Lash, *A Season of Spoils: The Reagan Administration's Attack on The Environment* (1984).

On the Civilian Conservation Corps, see Philip M. Conti, *The Civilian Conservation Corps: Salvaging Boys and other Treasures* (1998); John A. Salmond, *The Civilian Conservation Corps, 1933–1942, a New Deal Case Study* (1967); John C. Paige, *The Civilian Conservation Corps and the National Park Service (1933–1942)* (1985); James Eugene Potts, *Civilian Conservation Corps, Bear Valley, 1933–1936* (1979); and Marlys Rudeen, *The Civilian Conservation Corps Camp Newspapers: A Guide* (1991).

Studies of environmental advocacy organizations include Michael Harold Brown and John May, *The Greenpeace Story* (1991); Michael P. Cohen, *The History of the Sierra Club,* (1988); Tom Turner, *Sierra Club: 100 Years of Protecting Nature* (1991); Martha F. Lee, *Earth First!: Environmental Apocalypse* (1995); Derek Wall, *Earth First! and the Anti-Roads Movement: Radical Environmentalism and Comparative Social Movements* (1999); and David Foreman, *Ecodefense: A Field Guide to Monkeywrenching* (1993).

Some important biographies are *John Muir* by David and Patricia Armentrout, Herbert F. Smith (1965); Frederick W. Turner, *John Muir: from Scotland to the Sierra* (1997);

Doherty Kiernan, *Marjory Stoneman Douglas: Guardian of the Glades* (2002); Steven C. Schulte, *Wayne Aspinall and the Shaping of the American West* (2002); Char Miller, *Gifford Pinchot and The Making of Modern Environmentalism* (2001); Virginia Cornell, *Defender of the Dunes: The Kathleen Goddard Jones Story* (2001); Della A. Yannuzzi, *Aldo Leopold: Protector of the Wild* (2002); David Lowenthal, *George Perkins Marsh, Prophet of Conservation* (2000); Andrew Revkin, *The Burning Season: The Murder of Chico Mendez and The Fight for The Amazon Rain Forest* (1990); and Cecil Andrus, *Cecil Andrus: Politics Western Style* (1998).

Among books on alternative energy sources are Mark E. Hazen, *Alternative Energy* (1996); Dohn Riley and Mark McLaughlin, *Turning the Corner: Energy Solutions for the 21st Century* (2001); Paul Rosenberg, *Alternative Energy Handbook* (1993); A.L. Walton and E.H. Warren, Jr., *The Solar Alternative: An Economic Perspective* (1982); Bill Yanda, *Rads, Ergs and Cheeseburgers: Guide to Energy and the Environment* (1991); Diane Gibson, *Solar Power* (2000); Thomas E. Drennan, *Solar Power and Climate Change Policy in Developing Countries* (1993); Susan Jones, *Solar Power of the Future: New Ways of Turning Sunlight Into Energy* (2002); and Winter Sizmann and Vant-Hull, *Solar Power Plants: Fundamentals, Technology, Systems, Economics* (1991).

An important environmental historian is Donald Wooster, *Dust Bowl: The Southern Plains in the 1930s* (1979), *Rivers of Empire; Water, Aridity and the Growth of the American West* (1985); *Under Western Skies: Nature and History in the American West* (1992); *An Unsettled Country: Changing Landscapes of the American West;* and *A River Running West: The Life of John Wesley Powell* (2000).

APPENDIX

The Declaration of Independence

When in the Course of human events, it becomes necessary for one people to dissolve the political bands which have connected them with another, and to assume among the Powers of the earth, the separate and equal station to which the Laws of Nature and of Nature's God entitle them, a decent respect to the opinions of mankind requires that they should declare the causes which impel them to the separation.

We hold these truths to be self-evident, that all men are created equal, that they are endowed by their Creator with certain unalienable Rights, that among these are Life, Liberty and the pursuit of Happiness. That to secure these rights, Governments are instituted among Men, deriving their just powers from the consent of the governed, That whenever any Form of Government becomes destructive of these ends, it is the Right of the People to alter or to abolish it, and to institute new Government, laying its foundation on such principles and organizing its powers in such form, as to them shall seem most likely to effect their Safety and Happiness. Prudence, indeed, will dictate that Governments long established should not be changed for light and transient causes; and accordingly all experience hath shown, that mankind are more disposed to suffer, while evils are sufferable, than to right themselves by abolishing the forms to which they are accustomed. When a long train of abuses and usurpations, pursuing invariably the same Object evinces a design to reduce them under absolute Despotism, it is their right, it is their duty, to throw off such Government, and to provide new Guards for their future security.—Such has been the patient sufferance of these Colonies; and such is now the necessity which constrains them to alter their former Systems of Government. The history of the present King of Great Britain is a history of repeated injuries and usurpations, all having in direct object the establishment of an absolute Tyranny over these States. To prove this, let Facts be submitted to a candid world.

He has refused his Assent to Laws, the most wholesome and necessary for the public good.

He has forbidden his Governors to pass Laws of immediate and pressing importance, unless suspended in their operation till his Assent should be obtained; and when so suspended, he has utterly neglected to attend to them.

He has refused to pass other Laws for the accommodation of large districts of people, unless those people would relinquish the right of Representation in the Legislature, a right inestimable to them and formidable to tyrants only.

He has dissolved Representative Houses repeatedly, for opposing with manly firmness his invasions on the rights of the people.

He has refused for a long time, after such dissolutions, to cause others to be elected; whereby the Legislative Powers, incapable of Annihilation, have returned to the People at large for their exercise; the State remaining in the mean time exposed to all the dangers of invasion from without, and convulsions within.

He has endeavoured to prevent the population of these States; for that purpose obstructing the Laws of Naturalization of Foreigners; refusing to pass others to encourage their migration hither, and raising the conditions of new Appropriations of Lands.

He has obstructed the Administration of Justice, by refusing his Assent to Laws for establishing Judiciary Powers.

He has made Judges dependent on his Will alone, for the tenure of their offices, and the amount and payment of their salaries.

He has erected a multitude of New Offices, and sent hither swarms of Officers to harass our People, and eat out their substance.

He has kept among us, in times of peace, Standing Armies without the Consent of our legislature.

He has affected to render the Military independent of and superior to the Civil Power.

He has combined with others to subject us to a jurisdiction foreign to our constitution, and unacknowledged by our laws; giving his Assent to their acts of pretended legislation:

For quartering large bodies of armed troops among us:

For protecting them, by a mock Trial, from Punishment for any Murders which they should commit on the Inhabitants of these States:

For cutting off our Trade with all parts of the world:

For imposing taxes on us without our Consent:

For depriving us in many cases, of the benefits of Trial by Jury:

For transporting us beyond Seas to be tried for pretended offences:

For abolishing the free System of English Laws in a neighbouring Province, establishing therein an Arbitrary government, and enlarging its Boundaries so as to render it at once an example and fit instrument for introducing the same absolute rule into these Colonies:

For taking away our Charters, abolishing our most valuable Laws, and altering fundamentally the Forms of our Governments:

For suspending our own Legislature, and declaring themselves invested with Power to legislate for us in all cases whatsoever.

He has abdicated Government here, by declaring us out of his Protection and waging War against us.

He has plundered our seas, ravaged our Coasts, burnt our towns, and destroyed the lives of our people.

He is at this time transporting large armies of foreign mercenaries to compleat the works of death, desolation and tyranny, already begun with circumstances of Cruelty & perfidy scarcely paralleled in the most barbarous ages, and totally unworthy the Head of a civilized nation.

He has constrained our fellow Citizens taken Captive on the high Seas to bear Arms against their Country, to become the executioners of their friends and Brethren, or to fall themselves by their Hands.

He has excited domestic insurrections amongst us, and has endeavoured to bring on the inhabitants of our frontiers, the merciless Indian Savages, whose known rule of warfare, is an undistinguished destruction of all ages, sexes and conditions.

In every stage of these Oppressions We have Petitioned for Redress in the most humble terms: Our repeated Petitions have been answered only by repeated injury. A Prince, whose character is thus marked by every act which may define a Tyrant, is unfit to be the ruler of a free People.

Nor have We been wanting in attention to our British brethren. We have warned them from time to time of attempts by their legislature to extend an unwarrantable jurisdiction over us. We have reminded them of the circumstances of our emigration and settlement here. We have appealed to their native justice and magnanimity, and we have conjured them by the ties of our common kindred to disavow these usurpations, which, would inevitably interrupt our connections and correspondence. They too have been deaf to the voice of justice and of consanguinity. We must, therefore, acquiesce in the necessity, which denounces our Separation, and hold them, as we hold the rest of mankind, Enemies in War, in Peace Friends.

We, therefore, the Representatives of the United States of America, in General Congress, Assembled, appealing to the Supreme Judge of the world for the rectitude of our intentions, do, in the Name, and by Authority of the good People of these Colonies, solemnly publish and declare, That these United Colonies are, and of Right ought to be Free and Independent States; that they are Absolved from all Allegiance to the British Crown, and that all political connection between them and the State of Great Britain, is and ought to be totally dissolved; and that as Free and Independent States, they have full Power to levy War, conclude Peace, contract Alliances, establish Commerce, and to do all other Acts and Things which Independent States may of right do. And for the support of this Declaration, with a firm reliance on the Protection of Divine Providence, we mutually pledge to each other our Lives, our Fortunes and our sacred Honor.

The Constitution of the United States

We the people of the United States, in Order to form a more perfect Union, establish Justice, insure domestic Tranquility, provide for the common defense, promote the general Welfare, and secure the Blessings of Liberty to ourselves and our Posterity, do ordain and establish this CONSTITUTION for the United States of America.

ARTICLE I

Section 1. All legislative Powers herein granted shall be vested in a Congress of the United States which shall consist of a Senate and House of Representatives.

Section 2. The House of Representatives shall be composed of Members chosen every second Year by the People of the several States, and the Electors in each State shall have the Qualifications requisite for Electors of the most numerous Branch of the State Legislature.

No Person shall be a Representative who shall not have attained to the Age of twenty-five Years, and been seven Years a Citizen of the United States, and who shall not, when elected, be an inhabitant of that State in which he shall be chosen.

Representatives and direct Taxes shall be apportioned among the several States which may be included within this Union, according to their respective Numbers, which shall be determined by adding to the whole Number of free Persons, including those bound to Service for a Term of Years and excluding Indians not taxed, three fifths of all other Persons. The actual Enumeration shall be made within three Years after the first Meeting of the Congress of the United States, and within every subsequent Term of ten Years, in such Manner as they shall by Law direct. The Number of Representatives shall not exceed one for every thirty Thousand, but each State shall have at Least one Representative; and until such enumeration shall be made, the State of New Hampshire shall be entitled to chuse three, Massachusetts eight, Rhode-Island and Providence Plantations one, Connecticut five, New-York six, New Jersey four, Pennsylvania eight, Delaware one, Maryland six, Virginia ten, North Carolina five, South Carolina five, and Georgia three.

When vacancies happen in the Representation from any State, the Executive Authority thereof shall issue Writs of Election to fill such Vacancies.

The House of Representatives shall chuse their Speaker and other Officers; and shall have the sole Power of Impeachment.

Section 3. The Senate of the United States shall be composed of two Senators from each State, chosen by the Legislature thereof, for six Years; and each Senator shall have one Vote.

Immediately after they shall be assembled in Consequence of the first Election, they shall be divided as equally as may be into three Classes. The Seats of the Senators of the first Class shall be vacated at the Expiration of the second Year, of the second Class at the Expiration of the fourth Year, and of the third Class at the Expiration of the sixth Year, so that one-third may be chosen every second Year; and if Vacancies happen by Resignation, or otherwise, during the Recess of the Legislature of any State, the Executive thereof may make temporary Appointments until the next Meeting of the Legislature, which shall then fill such Vacancies.

No Person shall be a Senator who shall not have attained to the Age of thirty Years, and been nine Years a Citizen of the United States, and who shall not, when elected, be an Inhabitant of that State in which he shall be chosen.

The Vice President of the United States shall be President of the Senate, but shall have no vote, unless they be equally divided.

The Senate shall chuse their other Officers, and also a President pro tempore, in the absence of the Vice President, or when he shall exercise the Office of the President of the United States.

The Senate shall have the sole Power to try all Impeachments. When sitting for that purpose, they shall be on Oath or Affirmation. When the President of the United States is tried, the Chief Justice shall preside: And no person shall be convicted without the Concurrence of two thirds of the Members present.

Judgment in Cases of Impeachment shall not extend further than to removal from Office, and disqualification to hold and enjoy an Office of honor, Trust, or Profit under the United States: but the Party convicted shall nevertheless be liable and subject to Indictment, Trial, Judgment, and Punishment, according to Law.

Section 4. The Times, Places and Manner of holding Elections for Senators and Representatives, shall be prescribed in each state by the Legislature thereof; but the Congress may at any time by Law make or alter such Regulations, except as to the Places of Chusing Senators.

The Congress shall assemble at least once in every Year, and such Meeting shall be on the first Monday in December, unless they shall by Law appoint a different Day.

Section 5. Each House shall be the Judge of the Elections, Returns and Qualifications of its own Members, and a Majority of each shall constitute a Quorum to do Business from day to day, and may be authorized to compel the Attendance of absent Members, in such Manner, and under such Penalties, as each House may provide.

Each House may determine the Rules of its Proceedings, punish its Members for disorderly Behavior, and, with the Concurrence of two thirds, expel a Member.

Each House shall keep a Journal of its Proceedings, and from time to time publish the same, excepting such Parts as may in their Judgment require Secrecy; and the Yeas and Nays of the Members of either House on any question shall, at the Desire of one fifth of those Present, be entered on the Journal.

Neither House, during the Session of Congress, shall, without the Consent of the other, adjourn for more than three days, nor to any other Place than that in which the two Houses shall be sitting.

Section 6. The Senators and Representatives shall receive a Compensation for their Services, to be ascertained by Law, and paid out of the Treasury of the United States. They shall in all Cases, except Treason, Felony, and Breach of the Peace, be privileged from Arrest during their Attendance at the Session of their respective Houses, and in going to and returning from the same; and for any Speech or Debate in either House, they shall not be questioned in any other Place.

No Senator or Representative shall, during the Time for which he was elected, be appointed to any civil Office under the Authority of the United States, which shall have been created, or the Emoluments whereof shall have been encreased during such time; and no Person holding any Office under the United States shall be a Member of either House during his continuance in Office.

Section 7. All Bills for raising Revenue shall originate in the House of Representatives; but the Senate may propose or concur with Amendments as on other bills.

Every Bill which shall have passed the House of Representatives and the Senate, shall, before it become a Law, be presented to the President of the United States. If he approve he shall sign it, but if not he shall return it, with his Objections, to that House in which it shall have originated, who shall enter the Objections at large on their Journal, and proceed to reconsider it. If after such Reconsideration two thirds of that House shall agree to pass the bill, it shall be sent, together with the objections, to the other House, by which it shall likewise be reconsidered, and if approved by two thirds of that House, it shall become a Law. But in all such Cases the Votes of both Houses shall be determined by Yeas and Nays, and the Names of the Persons voting for and against the Bill shall be entered on the Journal of each House respectively. If any Bill shall not be returned by the President within ten Days (Sundays excepted) after it shall have been presented to him, the Same shall be a Law, in like Manner as if he had signed it, unless the Congress by their Adjournment prevent its Return, in which Case it shall not be a Law.

Every Order, Resolution, or Vote to which the Concurrence of the Senate and House of Representatives may be necessary (except on a question of Adjournment) shall be presented to the President of the United States; and before the Same shall take Effect, shall be approved by him, or being disapproved by him, shall be repassed by two thirds of the Senate and House of Representatives, according to the Rules and Limitations prescribed in the Case of a Bill.

Section 8. The Congress shall have Power To lay and collect Taxes, Duties, Imposts and Excises, to pay the Debts and provide for the common Defence and general Welfare of the United States; but all Duties, Imposts and Excises shall be uniform throughout the United States;

To borrow money on the credit of the United States;

To regulate Commerce with foreign Nations, and among the several States, and with the Indian Tribes;

To establish an uniform Rule of Naturalization, and uniform Laws on the subject of Bankruptcies throughout the United States;

To coin Money, regulate the Value thereof, and of foreign Coin, and fix the Standard of Weights and Measures;

To provide for the Punishment of counterfeiting the Securities and current Coin of the United States;

To establish Post Offices and Post Roads;

To promote the Progress of Science and useful Arts, by securing for limited Times to Authors and Inventors the exclusive Right to their respective Writings and Discoveries;

To constitute Tribunals inferior to the Supreme Court;

To define and punish Piracies and Felonies committed on the high Seas, and Offences against the Law of Nations;

To declare War, grant Letters of Marque and Reprisal, and make Rules concerning Captures on Land and Water;

To raise and support Armies, but no Appropriation of Money to that Use shall be for a longer Term than two Years;

To provide and maintain a Navy;

To make Rules for the Government and Regulation of the land and naval forces;

To provide for calling forth the Militia to execute the Laws of the Union, suppress Insurrections and repel Invasions;

To provide for organizing, arming, and disciplining the Militia, and for governing such Part of them as may be employed in the Service of the United States, reserving to the States respectively, the Appointment of the Officers, and the Authority of training the Militia according to the discipline prescribed by Congress;

To exercise exclusive Legislation in all Cases whatsoever, over such District (not exceeding ten Miles square) as may, by Cession of particular States, and the acceptance of Congress, become the Seat of Government of the United States, and to exercise like Authority over all Places purchased by the Consent of the Legislature of the States in which the Same shall be, for the Erection of Forts, Magazines, Arsenals, dock-Yards, and other needful Buildings—And

To make all Laws which shall be necessary and proper for carrying into Execution the foregoing Powers, and all other Powers vested by this Constitution in the Government of the United States, or in any Department or Officer thereof.

Section 9. The Migration or Importation of such Persons as any of the States now existing shall think proper to admit, shall not be prohibited by the Congress prior to the Year one thousand eight hundred and eight, but a tax or duty may be imposed on such Importation, not exceeding ten dollars for each Person.

The privilege of the Writ of Habeas Corpus shall not be suspended, unless when in Cases of Rebellion or Invasion the public Safety may require it.

No Bill of Attainder or ex post facto Law shall be passed.

No Capitation, or other direct, Tax shall be laid unless in Proportion to the Census or Enumeration herein before directed to be taken.

No Tax or Duty shall be laid on Articles exported from any State.

No Preference shall be given by any Regulation of Revenue to the Ports of one State over those of another: nor shall Vessels bound to, or from, one State, be obliged to enter, clear, or pay Duties in another.

No Money shall be drawn from the Treasury, but in Consequence of Appropriations made by Law; and a regular Statement and Account of the Receipts and Expenditures of all public Money shall be published from time to time.

No Title of Nobility shall be granted by the United States: And no Person holding any Office of Profit or Trust under them, shall, without the Consent of the Congress, accept of any present, Emolument, Office, or Title, of any kind whatever, from any King, Prince, or foreign State.

Section 10.   No State shall enter any Treaty, Alliance, or Confederation; grant Letters of Marque and Reprisal; coin Money; emit Bills of Credit; make any Thing but gold and silver Coin a Tender in Payment of Debts; pass any Bill of Attainder, ex post facto Law, or Law impairing the Obligation of Contracts, or grant any Title of Nobility.

No State shall, without the Consent of the Congress, lay any Imposts or Duties on Imports or Exports, except what may be absolutely necessary for executing its inspection Laws: and the net Produce of all Duties and Imposts, laid by any State on Imports or Exports, shall be for the Use of the Treasury of the United States; and all such Laws shall be subject to the Revision and Control of the Congress.

No State shall, without the Consent of Congress, lay any duty of Tonnage, keep Troops, or Ships of War in time of Peace, enter into any Agreement or Compact with another State, or with a foreign Power, or engage in War, unless actually invaded, or in such imminent Danger as will not admit of delay.

ARTICLE II

Section 1.   The executive Power shall be vested in a President of the United States of America. He shall hold his Office during the Term of four years,

and, together with the Vice-President, chosen for the same Term, be elected, as follows:

Each State shall appoint, in such Manner as the Legislature thereof may direct, a Number of Electors, equal to the whole Number of Senators and Representatives to which the State may be entitled in the Congress; but no Senator or Representative, or Person holding an Office of Trust or Profit under the United States, shall be appointed an Elector.

The Electors shall meet in their respective States, and vote by Ballot for two persons, of whom one at least shall not be an Inhabitant of the same State with themselves. And they shall make a List of all the Persons voted for, and of the Number of Votes for each; which List they shall sign and certify, and transmit sealed to the Seat of the Government of the United States, directed to the President of the Senate. The President of the Senate shall, in the Presence of the Senate and House of Representatives, open all the Certificates, and the Votes shall then be counted. The Person having the greatest Number of Votes shall be the President, if such Number be a Majority of the whole Number of Electors appointed; and if there be more than one who have such Majority, and have an equal Number of Votes, then the House of Representatives shall immediately chuse by Ballot one of them for President; and if no Person have a Majority, then from the five highest on the List the said House shall in like Manner chuse the President. But in chusing the President, the Votes shall be taken by States, the Representation from each State having one Vote; a quorum for this Purpose shall consist of a Member or Members from two-thirds of the States, and a Majority of all the States shall be necessary to a Choice. In every Case, after the Choice of the President, the Person having the greatest Number of Votes of the Electors shall be the Vice President. But if there should remain two or more who have equal votes, the Senate shall chuse from them by Ballot the Vice-President.

The Congress may determine the Time of chusing the Electors, and the Day on which they shall give their Votes; which Day shall be the same throughout the United States.

No person except a natural-born Citizen, or a Citizen of the United States, at the time of the Adoption of this Constitution, shall be eligible to the Office of President; neither shall any Person be eligible to that Office who shall not have attained to the Age of thirty-five years, and been fourteen Years a Resident within the United States.

In Case of the Removal of the President from Office, or of his Death, Resignation, or Inability to discharge the Powers and Duties of the said Office, the same shall devolve on the Vice-President, and the Congress may by Law provide for the Case of Removal, Death, Resignation, or Inability, both of the President and Vice-President, declaring what Officer shall then act as President, and such Officer shall act accordingly, until the disability be removed, or a President shall be elected.

The President shall, at stated Times, receive for his Services a Compensation, which shall neither be increased nor diminished during the Period for which he shall have been elected, and he shall not receive within that Period any other Emolument from the United States, or any of them.

Before he enters on the execution of his Office, he shall take the following Oath or Affirmation:— "I do solemnly swear (or affirm) that I will faithfully execute the Office of President of the United States, and will, to the best of my Ability, preserve, protect, and defend the Constitution of the United States."

Section 2. The President shall be Commander in Chief of the Army and Navy of the United States, and of the Militia of the several States, when called into the actual Service of the United States; he may require the Opinion, in writing, of the principal Officer in each of the executive Departments, upon any subject relating to the Duties of their respective Offices, and he shall have Power to Grant Reprieves and Pardons for Offences against the United States, except in Cases of Impeachment.

He shall have Power, by and with the Advice and Consent of the Senate, to make Treaties, provided two thirds of the Senators present concur; and he shall nominate, and by and with the Advice and Consent of the Senate, shall appoint Ambassadors, other public Ministers and Counsuls, Judges of the Supreme Court, and all other Officers of the United States, whose Appointments are herein otherwise provided for, and which shall be established by Law: but the Congress may by Law vest the Appointments of such inferior Officers, as they think proper, in the President alone, in the Courts of Law, or in the Heads of Departments.

The President shall have Power to fill up all Vacancies that may happen during the Recess of the Senate, by granting Commissions which shall expire at the End of their next Session.

Section 3. He shall from time to time give to the Congress Information of the State of the Union, and recommend to their Consideration such Measures as he shall judge necessary and expedient; he may, on extraordinary occasions, convene both

Houses, or either of them, and in Case of Disagreement between them, with respect to the Time of Adjournment, he may adjourn them to such Time as he shall think proper; he shall receive Ambassadors and other public Ministers; he shall take Care that the Laws be faithfully executed, and shall Commission all the Officers of the United States

Section 4. The President, Vice President and all civil Officers of the United States, shall be removed from Office on Impeachment for, and Conviction of, Treason, Bribery, or other high Crimes and Misdemeanors.

ARTICLE III

Section 1. The judicial Power of the United States, shall be vested in one supreme Court, and in such inferior Courts as the Congress may from time to time ordain and establish. The Judges, both of the supreme and inferior Courts, shall hold their Offices during good Behavior, and shall, at stated Times, receive for their Services, a compensation, which shall not be diminished during their Continuance in Office.

Section 2. The judicial Power shall extend to all Cases, in Law and Equity, arising under this constitution, the Laws of the United States, and treaties made, or which shall be made, under their Authority;—to all Cases affecting ambassadors, other public ministers and consuls;—to all cases of admiralty and maritime Jurisdiction;—to Controversies to which the United States shall be a Party;—to Controversies between two or more States;—between a State and Citizens of another State;—between Citizens of different States,—between Citizens of the same State claiming Lands under Grants of different States, and between a State, or the Citizens thereof, and foreign States, Citizens or Subjects.

In all Cases affecting Ambassadors, other public Ministers and Consuls, and those in which a State shall be Party, the supreme Court shall have original Jurisdiction. In all the other Cases before mentioned, the supreme Court shall have appellate Jurisdiction, both as to Law and Fact, with such Exception, and under such Regulations as the Congress shall make.

The trial of all Crimes, except in Cases of Impeachment, shall be by Jury; and such Trial shall be held in the State where the said Crimes shall have been committed; but when not committed within any State, the Trial shall be at such Place or Places as the Congress may by Law have directed.

Section 3. Treason against the United States, shall consist only in levying War against them, or in adhering to their Enemies, giving them Aid and Comfort. No Person shall be convicted of Treason unless on the Testimony of two Witnesses to the same overt Act, or on Confession in open Court.

The Congress shall have power to declare the Punishment of Treason, but no Attainder of Treason shall work Corruption of Blood, or Forfeiture except during the Life of the Person attainted.

ARTICLE IV

Section 1. Full Faith and Credit shall be given in each State to the public Acts, Records, and judicial Proceedings of every other State. And the Congress may by general laws prescribe the Manner in which such Acts, Records and Proceedings shall be proved, and the Effect thereof.

Section 2. The Citizens of each State shall be entitled to all Privileges and Immunities of Citizens in the several States.

A Person charged in any State with Treason, Felony, or other Crime, who shall flee from Justice, and be found in another State, shall on demand of the executive Authority of the State from which he fled, be delivered up, to be removed to the State having Jurisdiction of the crime.

No Person held to Service or Labour in one State, under the Laws thereof, escaping into another, shall, in Consequence of any Law or Regulation therein, be discharged from such Service or Labour, but shall be delivered up on Claim of the Party to whom such Service or Labour may be due.

Section 3. New States may be admitted by the Congress into this Union; but no new State shall be formed or erected within the Jurisdiction of any other State; nor any State be formed by the Junction of two or more States, or parts of States, without the Consent of the Legislatures of the States concerned as well as of the Congress.

The Congress shall have Power to dispose of and make all needful Rules and Regulations respecting the Territory or other Property belonging to the United States; and nothing in this constitution shall be so construed as to Prejudice any Claims of the United States, or of any particular State.

Section 4. The United States shall guarantee to every State in this Union a Republican Form of Government, and shall protect each of them against Invasion; and on Application of the Legis-

lature, or the Executive (when the Legislature cannot be convened) against domestic Violence.

ARTICLE V

The Congress, whenever two-thirds of both Houses shall deem it necessary, shall propose Amendments to this Constitution, or, on the Application of the Legislatures of two-thirds of the several States, shall call a Convention for proposing Amendments, which, in either Case, shall be valid to all Intents and Purposes, as part of this Constitution, when ratified by the Legislatures of three-fourths of the several States, or by Conventions in three-fourths thereof, as the one or the other Mode of Ratification may be proposed by the Congress; Provided that no Amendment which may be made prior to the Year One thousand eight hundred and eight shall in any Manner affect the first and fourth Clauses in the Ninth Section of the first Article; and that no State, without its Consent, shall be deprived of its equal Suffrage in the Senate.

ARTICLE VI

Debts contracted and Engagements entered into, before the Adoption of this Constitution, shall be as valid against the United States under this Constitution, as under the Confederation.

This Constitution, and the Laws of the United States which shall be made in Pursuance thereof; and the Treaties made, or which shall be made, under the Authority of the United States, shall be the supreme Law of the Land; and the Judges in every State shall be bound thereby, any Thing in the Constitution of Laws of any State to the Contrary notwithstanding.

The Senators and Representatives before mentioned, and the Members of the several State Legislatures, and all executive and judicial Officers, both of the United States and of the several States, shall be bound by Oath or Affirmation to support this Constitution; but no religious Test shall ever be required as a qualification to any Office or public Trust under the United States.

ARTICLE VII

The Ratification of the Conventions of nine States shall be sufficient for the Establishment of this Constitution between the States so ratifying the same.

Done in Convention by the Unanimous Consent of the States present the Seventeenth Day of September in the Year of our Lord one thousand seven hundred and Eighty seven, and of the Independence of the United States of America the Twelfth. In Witness whereof We have hereunto subscribed our names.

Signed by
George Washington
Presidt and Deputy from Virginia
(and thirty-eight others)

Articles in Addition to, and Amendment of, the Constitution of the United States of America. Proposed by Congress, and Ratified by the Legislatures of the Several States, Pursuant to the Fifth Article of the Original Constitution.

AMENDMENT I [1791]

Congress shall make no law respecting an establishment of religion, or prohibiting the free exercise thereof; or abridging the freedom of speech, or of the press; or the right of the people peaceably to assemble, and to petition the Government for a redress of grievances.

AMENDMENT II [1791]

A well regulated Militia, being necessary to the security of a free State, the right of the people to keep and bear Arms, shall not be infringed.

AMENDMENT III [1791]

No Soldier shall, in time of peace be quartered in any house, without the consent of the Owner, nor in time of war, but in a manner to be prescribed by law.

AMENDMENT IV [1791]

The right of the people to be secure in their persons, houses, papers, and effects, against unreasonable searches and seizures, shall not be violated, and no Warrants shall issue, but upon probable cause, supported by Oath or affirmation, and particularly describing the place to be searched, and the persons or things to be seized.

AMENDMENT V [1791]

No person shall be held to answer for a capital or otherwise infamous crime, unless on a presentment or indictment of a Grand Jury, except in cases arising in the land or naval forces, or in the Militia, when in actual service in time of war or public danger; nor shall any person be subject for the same offence to be twice put in jeopardy of life or limb; nor shall be compelled in any criminal case to be a witness against himself, nor be de-

prived of life, liberty, or property, without due process of law; nor shall private property be taken for public use, without just compensation.

AMENDMENT VI [1791]

In all criminal prosecutions, the accused shall enjoy the right to a speedy and public trial, by an impartial jury of the State and district wherein the crime shall have been committed, which district shall have been previously ascertained by law, and to be informed of the nature and cause of the accusation; to be confronted with the witnesses against him; to have compulsory process for obtaining witnesses in his favor, and to have the Assistance of Counsel for his defence.

AMENDMENT VII [1791]

In suits at common law, where the value in controversy shall exceed twenty dollars, the right of trial by jury shall be preserved, and no fact tried by a jury, shall be otherwise reexamined in any Court of the United States, than according to the rules of the common law.

AMENDMENT VIII [1791]

Excessive bail shall not be required, nor excessive fines imposed, nor cruel and unusual punishments inflicted.

AMENDMENT IX [1791]

The enumeration in the Constitution, of certain rights, shall not be construed to deny or disparage others retained by the people.

AMENDMENT X [1791]

The powers not delegated to the United States by the Constitution, nor prohibited by it to the States, are reserved to the States respectively, or to the people.

AMENDMENT XI [1798]

The Judicial power of the United States shall not be construed to extend to any suit in law or equity, commenced or prosecuted against one of the United States by Citizens of another State, or by Citizens or Subjects of any Foreign State.

AMENDMENT XII [1804]

The Electors shall meet in their respective States and vote by ballot for President and Vice-President, one of whom, at least, shall not be an inhabitant of the same State with themselves; they shall name in their ballots the person voted for as President, and in distinct ballots the person voted for as Vice-President, and they shall make distinct lists of all persons voted for as President, and of all persons voted for as Vice-President, and of the number of votes for each, which lists they shall sign and certify, and transmit sealed to the seat of the government of the United States, directed to the President of the Senate;—The President of the Senate shall, in the presence of the Senate and House of Representatives, open all the certificates and the votes shall then be counted;—The person having the greatest number of votes for President, shall be the President, if such number by a majority of the whole number of Electors appointed; and if no person have such majority, then from the persons having the highest numbers not exceeding three on the list of those voted for as President, the House of Representatives shall choose immediately, by ballot, the President. But in choosing the President, the votes shall be taken by states, the representation from each state having one vote; a quorum for this purpose shall consist of a member or members from two-thirds of the states, and a majority of all the states shall be necessary to a choice. And if the House of Representatives shall not choose a President whenever the right of choice shall devolve upon them, before the fourth day of March next following, then the Vice-President shall act as President, as in the case of the death or other constitutional disability of the President.—The person having the greatest number of votes as Vice-President, shall be the Vice-President, if such number be a majority of the whole number of Electors appointed, and if no person have a majority, then from the two highest numbers on the list, the Senate shall choose the Vice-President; a quorum for the purpose shall consist of two-thirds of the whole number of Senators, and a majority of the whole number shall be necessary to a choice. But no person constitutionally ineligible to the office of President shall be eligible to that of Vice-President of the United States.

AMENDMENT XIII [1865]

Section 1.   Neither slavery nor involuntary servitude, except as a punishment for crime whereof the party shall have been duly convicted, shall exist within the United States, or any place subject to their jurisdiction.

Section 2.   Congress shall have power to enforce this article by appropriate legislation.

.AMENDMENT XIV [1868]

Section 1.   All persons born or naturalized in the United States, and subject to the jurisdiction thereof, are citizens of the United States and of the State wherein they reside. No State shall make or enforce any law which shall abridge the privileges or immunities of citizens of the United States; nor shall any State deprive any person of life, liberty, or property, without due process of law; nor deny to any person within its jurisdiction the equal protection of the laws.

Section 2.   Representatives shall be apportioned among the several States according to their respective numbers, counting the whole number of persons in each State, excluding Indians not taxed. But when the right to vote at any election for the choice of electors for President and Vice-President of the United States, Representatives in Congress, the Executive and Judicial officers of a State, or the members of the Legislature thereof, is denied to any of the male inhabitants of such State, being twenty-one years of age, and citizens of the United States, or in any way abridged, except for participation in rebellion, or other crime, the basis of representation therein shall be reduced in the proportion which the number of such male citizens shall bear to the whole number of male citizens twenty-one years of age in such State.

Section 3.   No person shall be a Senator or Representative in Congress, or elector of President and Vice-President, or hold any office, civil or military, under the United States, or under any State, who, having previously taken an oath, as a member of Congress, or as an officer of the United States, or as a member of any State legislature, or as an executive or judicial officer of any State, to support the Constitution of the United States, shall have engaged in insurrection or rebellion against the same, or given aid or comfort to the enemies thereof. But Congress may by a vote of two-thirds of each House, remove such disability.

Section 4.   The validity of the public debt of the United States, authorized by law, including debts incurred for payment of pensions and bounties for services in suppressing insurrection or rebellion, shall not be questioned. But neither the United States nor any State shall assume or pay any debt or obligation incurred in aid of insurrection or rebellion against the United States or any claim for the loss or emancipation of any slave; but all such debts, obligations, and claims shall be held illegal and void.

Section 5. The Congress shall have the power to enforce, by appropriate legislation, the provisions of this article.

AMENDMENT XV [1870]

Section 1. The right of citizens of the United States to vote shall not be denied or abridged by the United States or by any State on account of race, color, or previous condition of servitude—

Section 2. The Congress shall have power to enforce this article by appropriate legislation.

AMENDMENT XVI [1913]

The Congress shall have power to lay and collect taxes on incomes, from whatever source derived, without apportionment among the several States, and without regard to any census or enumeration.

AMENDMENT XVII [1913]

The Senate of the United States shall be composed of two Senators from each State, elected by the people thereof, for six years; and each Senator shall have one vote. The electors in each State shall have the qualifications requisite for electors of the most numerous branch of the State legislature.

When vacancies happen in the representation of any State in the Senate, the executive authority of such State shall issue writs of election to fill such vacancies: *Provided,* That the legislature of any State may empower the executive thereof to make temporary appointments until the people fill the vacancies by election as the legislature may direct.

This amendment shall not be so construed as to affect the election or term of any Senator chosen before it becomes valid as part of the Constitution.

AMENDMENT XVIII [1919]

Section 1. After one year from the ratification of this article the manufacture, sale, or transportation of intoxicating liquors within, the importation thereof into, or the exportation thereof from the United States and all territory subject to the jurisdiction thereof for beverage purposes is hereby prohibited.

Section 2. The Congress and the several States shall have concurrent power to enforce this article by appropriate legislation.

Section 3. This article shall be inoperative unless it shall have been ratified as an amendment to the Constitution by the legislatures of the several States, as provided in the Constitution, within seven years from the date of the submission hereof to the States by the Congress.

AMENDMENT XIX [1920]

The right of citizens of the United States to vote shall not be denied or abridged by the United States or by any State on account of sex.

Congress shall have power to enforce this article by appropriate legislation.

AMENDMENT XX [1933]

Section 1. The terms of the President and Vice-President shall end at noon on the 20th day of January, and the terms of Senators and Representatives at noon on the 3d day of January, of the years in which such terms would have ended if this article had not been ratified; and the terms of their successors shall then begin.

Section 2. The Congress shall assemble at least once in every year, and such meeting shall begin at noon on the 3d day of January, unless they shall by law appoint a different day.

Section 3. If, at the time fixed for the beginning of the term of the President, the President elect shall have died, the Vice-President elect shall become President. If a President shall not have been chosen before the time fixed for the beginning of his term, or if the President elect shall have failed to qualify, then the Vice-President until a President shall have qualified; and the Congress may by law provide for the case wherein neither a President elect nor a Vice-President elect shall have qualified, declaring who shall then act as President, or the manner in which one who is to act shall be selected, and such person shall act accordingly until a President or Vice-President shall have qualified.

Section 4. The Congress may by law provide for the case of the death of any of the persons from whom the House of Representatives may choose a President whenever the right of choice shall have devolved upon them, and for the case of the death of any of the persons from whom the Senate may choose a Vice-President whenever the right of choice shall have devolved upon them.

Section 5. Sections 1 and 2 shall take effect on the 15th day of October following the ratification of this article.

Section 6. This article shall be inoperative unless it shall have been ratified as an amendment to the Constitution by the legislatures of three-fourths of the several States within seven years from the date of its submission.

AMENDMENT XXI [1933]

Section 1. The eighteenth article of amendment to the Constitution of the United States is hereby repealed.

Section 2. The transportation or importation into any State, Territory, or possession of the United States for delivery or use therein of intoxicating liquors, in violation of the laws thereof, is hereby prohibited.

Section 3. This article shall be inoperative unless it shall have been ratified as an amendment to the Constitution by conventions in the several States, as provided in the Constitution, within seven years from the date of the submission hereof to the States by the Congress.

AMENDMENT XXII [1951]

No person shall be elected to the office of the President more than twice, and no person who has held the office of President, or acted as President, for more than two years of a term to which some other person was elected President shall be elected to the office of the President more than once.

But this Article shall not apply to any person holding the office of President when this Article was proposed by the Congress, and shall not prevent any person who may be holding the office of President, or acting as President, during the term within which this Article becomes operative from holding the office of President or acting as President during the remainder of such term.

AMENDMENT XXIII [1961]

Section 1. The District constituting the seat of Government of the United States shall appoint in such manner as the Congress may direct:

A number of electors of President and Vice President equal to the whole number of Senators and Representatives in Congress to which the District would be entitled if it were a State, but in no event more than the least populous State; they shall be in addition to those appointed by the States, but they shall be considered, for the purposes of the election of President and Vice President, to be electors appointed by a State; and they shall meet in the District and perform such duties as provided by the twelfth article of amendment.

Section 2. The Congress shall have power to enforce this article by appropriate legislation.

AMENDMENT XXIV [1964]

Section 1. The right of citizens of the United States to vote in any primary or other election for President or Vice President, for electors for President or Vice President, or for Senator or Representative in Congress, shall not be denied or abridged by the United States or any State by reason of failure to pay any poll tax or other tax.

Section 2. The Congress shall have the power to enforce this article by appropriate legislation.

AMENDMENT XXV [1967]

Section 1. In case of the removal of the President from office or his death or resignation, the Vice President shall become President.

Section 2. Whenever there is a vacancy in the office of the Vice President, the President shall nominate a Vice President who shall take the office upon confirmation by a majority vote of both houses of Congress.

Section 3. Whenever the President transmits to the President pro tempore of the Senate and the Speaker of the House of Representatives his written declaration that he is unable to discharge the powers and duties of his office, and until he transmits to them a written declaration to the contrary, such powers and duties shall be discharged by the Vice President as Acting President.

Section 4. Whenever the Vice President and a majority of either the principal officers of the executive departments, or of such other body as Congress may by law provide, transmit to the President pro tempore of the Senate and the Speaker of the House of Representatives their written declaration that the President is unable to discharge the powers and duties of his office, the Vice President shall immediately assume the powers and duties of the office as Acting President.

Thereafter, when the President transmits to the President pro tempore of the Senate and the Speaker of the House of Representatives his written declaration that no inability exists, he shall resume the powers and duties of his office unless the Vice President and a majority of either the principal officers of the executive departments, or of such other body as Congress may by law provide, transmit within four days to the President pro tempore of the Senate and the Speaker of the House of Representatives their written declaration that the President is unable to discharge the powers and duties of his office. Thereupon Congress shall decide the issue, assembling within 48 hours for that purpose if not in session. If the Congress, within 21 days after receipt of the latter written declaration, or, if Congress is not in session, within 21 days after

Congress is required to assemble, determines by two-thirds vote of both houses that the President is unable to discharge the powers and duties of his office, the Vice President shall continue to discharge the same as Acting President; otherwise, the President shall resume the powers and duties of his office.

AMENDMENT XXVI [1971]

Section 1. The right of citizens of the United States, who are eighteen years of age or older, to vote shall not be denied or abridged by the United States or by any State on account of age.

Section 2. The Congress shall have power to enforce this article by appropriate legislation.

AMENDMENT XXVII [1992]

No law, varying the compensation for the services of the Senators and Representatives, shall take effect, until an election of Representatives shall have intervened.

Admission of States to the Union

1	Delaware	Dec. 7, 1787	26	Michigan	Jan. 26, 1837
2	Pennsylvania	Dec. 12, 1787	27	Florida	Mar. 3, 1845
3	New Jersey	Dec. 18, 1787	28	Texas	Dec. 29, 1845
4	Georgia	Jan. 2, 1788	29	Iowa	Dec. 28, 1846
5	Connecticut	Jan. 9, 1788	30	Wisconsin	May 29, 1848
6	Massachusetts	Feb. 6, 1788	31	California	Sept. 9, 1850
7	Maryland	Apr. 28, 1788	32	Minnesota	May 11, 1858
8	South Carolina	May 23, 1788	33	Oregon	Feb. 14, 1859
9	New Hampshire	June 21, 1788	34	Kansas	Jan. 29, 1861
10	Virginia	June 25, 1788	35	West Virginia	June 19, 1863
11	New York	July 26, 1788	36	Nevada	Oct. 31, 1864
12	North Carolina	Nov. 21, 1789	37	Nebraska	Mar. 1, 1867
13	Rhode Island	May 29, 1790	38	Colorado	Aug. 1, 1876
14	Vermont	Mar. 4, 1791	39	North Dakota	Nov. 2, 1889
15	Kentucky	June 1, 1792	40	South Dakota	Nov. 2, 1889
16	Tennessee	June 1, 1796	41	Montana	Nov. 8, 1889
17	Ohio	Mar. 1, 1803	42	Washington	Nov. 11, 1889
18	Louisiana	Apr. 30, 1812	43	Idaho	July 3, 1890
19	Indiana	Dec. 11, 1816	44	Wyoming	July 10, 1890
20	Mississippi	Dec. 10, 1817	45	Utah	Jan. 4, 1896
21	Illinois	Dec. 3, 1818	46	Oklahoma	Nov. 16, 1907
22	Alabama	Dec. 14, 1819	47	New Mexico	Jan. 6, 1912
23	Maine	Mar. 15, 1820	48	Arizona	Feb. 14, 1912
24	Missouri	Aug. 10, 1821	49	Alaska	Jan. 3, 1959
25	Arkansas	June 15, 1836	50	Hawaii	Aug. 21, 1959

Population of the United States, 1790–1990

YEAR	NUMBER OF STATES	POPULATION	PERCENT INCREASE
1790	13	3,929,214	
1800	16	5,308,483	35.1
1810	17	7,239,881	36.4
1820	23	9,638,453	33.1
1830	24	12,866,020	33.5
1840	26	17,069,453	32.7
1850	31	23,191,876	35.9
1860	33	31,443,321	35.6
1870	37	39,818,449	26.6
1880	38	50,155,783	26.0
1890	44	62,947,714	25.5
1900	45	75,994,575	20.7
1910	46	91,972,266	21.0
1920	48	105,710,620	14.9
1930	48	122,775,046	16.1
1940	48	131,669,275	7.2
1950	48	150,697,361	14.5
1960	50	179,323,175	19.0
1970	50	203,235,298	13.3
1980	50	226,504,825	11.4
1990	50	249,632,692	10.2
2000	50	281,421,906	12.7

The Vice Presidents and the Cabinet

SECRETARY OF STATE
(1789–   )

Thomas Jefferson	1789	Daniel Webster	1850	Elihu Root	1905
Edmund Randolph	1794	Edward Everett	1852	Robert Bacon	1909
Timothy Pickering	1795	William L. Marcy	1853	Philander C. Knox	1909
John Marshall	1800	Lewis Cass	1857	William J. Bryan	1913
James Madison	1801	Jeremiah S. Black	1860	Robert Lansing	1915
Robert Smith	1809	William H. Seward	1861	Bainbridge Colby	1920
James Monroe	1811	E. B. Washburne	1869	Charles E. Hughes	1921
John Q. Adams	1817	Hamilton Fish	1869	Frank B. Kellogg	1925
Henry Clay	1825	William M. Evarts	1877	Henry L. Stimson	1929
Martin Van Buren	1829	James G. Blaine	1881	Cordell Hull	1933
Edward Livingston	1831	F. T. Frelinghuysen	1881	E. R. Stettinius, Jr.	1944
Louis McLane	1833	Thomas F. Bayard	1885	James F. Byrnes	1945
John Forsyth	1834	James G. Blaine	1889	George C. Marshall	1947
Daniel Webster	1841	John W. Foster	1892	Dean Acheson	1949
Hugh S. Legaré	1843	Walter Q. Gresham	1893	John Foster Dulles	1953
Abel P. Upshur	1843	Richard Olney	1895	Christian A. Herter	1959
John C. Calhoun	1844	John Sherman	1897	Dean Rusk	1961
James Buchanan	1845	William R. Day	1897	William P. Rogers	1969
John M. Clayton	1849	John Hay	1898	Henry A. Kissinger	1973

Cyrus Vance	1977
Edmund Muskie	1979
Alexander M. Haig, Jr.	1981
George Shultz	1982
James A. Baker, III	1989
Warren Christopher	1993
Madeleine K. Albright	1997
Colin Powell	2001

SECRETARY OF THE TREASURY (1789–   )

Alexander Hamilton	1789
Oliver Wolcott	1795
Samuel Dexter	1801
Albert Gallatin	1801
G. W. Campbell	1814
A. J. Dallas	1814
William H. Crawford	1816
Richard Rush	1825
Samuel D. Ingham	1829
Louis McLane	1831
William J. Duane	1833
Roger B. Taney	1833
Levi Woodbury	1834
Thomas Ewing	1841
Walter Forward	1841
John C. Spencer	1843
George M. Bibb	1844
Robert J. Walker	1845
William M. Meredith	1849
Thomas Corwin	1850
James Guthrie	1853
Howell Cobb	1857
Philip F. Thomas	1860
John A. Dix	1861
Salmon P. Chase	1861
Wm. P. Fessenden	1864
Hugh McCulloch	1865
George S. Boutwell	1869
William A. Richardson	1873
Benjamin H. Bristow	1874
Lot M. Morrill	1876
John Sherman	1877
William Windom	1881
Charles J. Folger	1881
Walter Q. Gresham	1884
Hugh McCulloch	1884
Daniel Manning	1885
Charles S. Fairchild	1887
William Windom	1889
Charles Foster	1891
John G. Carlisle	1893
Lyman J. Gage	1897
Leslie M. Shaw	1902
George B. Cortelyou	1907

Franklin MacVeagh	1909
William G. McAdoo	1913
Carter Glass	1918
David F. Houston	1920
Andrew W. Mellon	1921
Ogden L. Mills	1932
William H. Woodin	1933
Henry Morgenthau, Jr.	1934
Fred M. Vinson	1945
John W. Snyder	1946
George M. Humphrey	1953
Robert B. Anderson	1957
C. Douglas Dillon	1961
Henry H. Fowler	1965
David M. Kennedy	1969
John B. Connally	1970
George P. Shultz	1972
William E. Simon	1974
W. Michael Blumenthal	1977
G. William Miller	1979
Donald T. Regan	1981
James A. Baker, III	1985
Nicholas Brady	1988
Lloyd Bentsen	1993
Robert Rubin	1995
Lawrence H. Summers	1999
Paul O'Neill	2001
John W. Snow	2003

SECRETARY OF WAR (1789–1947)

Henry Knox	1789
Timothy Pickering	1795
James McHenry	1796
John Marshall	1800
Samuel Dexter	1800
Roger Griswold	1801
Henry Dearborn	1801
William Eustis	1809
John Armstrong	1813
James Monroe	1814
William H. Crawford	1815
Isaac Shelby	1817
George Graham	1817
John C. Calhoun	1817
James Barbour	1825
Peter B. Porter	1828
John H. Eaton	1829
Lewis Cass	1831
Benjamin F. Butler	1837
Joel R. Poinsett	1837
John Bell	1841
John McLean	1841
John C. Spencer	1841
James M. Porter	1843
William Wilkins	1844

William L. Marcy	1845
George W. Crawford	1849
Charles M. Conrad	1850
Jefferson Davis	1853
John B. Floyd	1857
Joseph Holt	1861
Simon Cameron	1861
Edwin M. Stanton	1862
Ulysses S. Grant	1867
Lorenzo Thomas	1868
John M. Schofield	1868
John A. Rawlins	1869
William T. Sherman	1869
William W. Belknap	1869
Alphonso Taft	1876
James D. Cameron	1876
George W. McCrary	1877
Alexander Ramsey	1879
Robert T. Lincoln	1881
William C. Endicott	1885
Redfield Proctor	1889
Stephen B. Elkins	1891
Daniel S. Lamont	1893
Russell A. Alger	1897
Elihu Root	1899
William H. Taft	1904
Luke E. Wright	1908
J. M. Dickinson	1909
Henry L. Stimson	1911
L. M. Garrison	1913
Newton D. Baker	1916
John W. Weeks	1921
Dwight F. Davis	1925
James W. Good	1929
Patrick J. Hurley	1929
George H. Dern	1933
H. A. Woodring	1936
Henry L. Stimson	1940
Robert P. Patterson	1945
Kenneth C. Royall	1947

SECRETARY OF THE NAVY (1798–1947)

Benjamin Stoddert	1798
Robert Smith	1801
Paul Hamilton	1809
William Jones	1813
B. W. Crowninshield	1814
Smith Thompson	1818
S. L. Southard	1823
John Branch	1829
Levi Woodbury	1831
Mahlon Dickerson	1834
James K. Paulding	1838
George E. Badger	1841

Abel P. Upshur	1841	Frank Carlucci	1988	Hubert Work	1922
David Henshaw	1843	Richard Cheney	1989	Harry S. New	1923
Thomas W. Gilmer	1844	Leslie Aspin, Jr.	1993	Walter F. Brown	1929
John Y. Mason	1844	William Perry	1994	James A. Farley	1933
George Bancroft	1845	William Cohen	1997	Frank C. Walker	1940
John Y. Mason	1846	Donald Rumsfeld	2001	Robert E. Hannegan	1945
William B. Preston	1849			J. M. Donaldson	1947
William A. Graham	1850			A. E. Summerfield	1953
John P. Kennedy	1852	**POSTMASTER GENERAL**		J. Edward Day	1961
James C. Dobbin	1853	(1789–1970)		John A. Gronouski	1963
Isaac Toucey	1857	Samuel Osgood	1789	Lawrence F. O'Brien	1965
Gideon Welles	1861	Timothy Pickering	1791	W. Marvin Watson	1968
Adolph E. Borie	1869	Joseph Habersham	1795	Winton M. Blount	1969
George M. Robeson	1869	Gideon Granger	1801		
R. W. Thompson	1877	Return J. Meigs, Jr.	1814		
Nathan Goff, Jr.	1881	John McLean	1823	**ATTORNEY GENERAL**	
William H. Hunt	1881	William T. Barry	1829	(1789–)	
William E. Chandler	1881	Amos Kendall	1835	Edmund Randolph	1789
William C. Whitney	1885	John M. Niles	1840	William Bradford	1794
Benjamin F. Tracy	1889	Francis Granger	1841	Charles Lee	1795
Hilary A. Herbert	1893	Charles A. Wickliffe	1841	Theophilus Parsons	1801
John D. Long	1897	Cave Johnson	1845	Levi Lincoln	1801
William H. Moody	1902	Jacob Collamer	1849	Robert Smith	1805
Paul Morton	1904	Nathan K. Hall	1850	John Breckinridge	1805
Charles J. Bonaparte	1905	Samuel D. Hubbard	1852	Caesar A. Rodney	1807
Victor H. Metcalf	1907	James Campbell	1853	William Pinkney	1811
T. H. Newberry	1908	Aaron V. Brown	1857	Richard Rush	1814
George von L. Meyer	1909	Joseph Holt	1859	William Wirt	1817
Josephus Daniels	1913	Horatio King	1861	John M. Berrien	1829
Edwin Denby	1921	Montgomery Blair	1861	Roger B. Taney	1831
Curtis D. Wilbur	1924	William Dennison	1864	Benjamin F. Butler	1833
Charles F. Adams	1929	Alexander W. Randall	1866	Felix Grundy	1838
Claude A. Swanson	1933	John A. J. Creswell	1869	Henry D. Gilpin	1840
Charles Edison	1940	James W. Marshall	1874	John J. Crittenden	1841
Frank Knox	1940	Marshall Jewell	1874	Hugh S. Legaré	1841
James V. Forrestal	1945	James N. Tyner	1876	John Nelson	1843
		David M. Key	1877	John Y. Mason	1845
		Horace Maynard	1880	Nathan Clifford	1846
		Thomas L. James	1881	Isaac Toucey	1848
SECRETARY OF DEFENSE		Timothy O. Howe	1881	Reverdy Johnson	1849
(1747–)		Walter Q. Gresham	1883	John J. Crittenden	1850
James V. Forrestal	1947	Frank Hatton	1884	Caleb Cushing	1853
Louis A. Johnson	1949	William F. Vilas	1885	Jeremiah S. Black	1857
George C. Marshall	1950	Don M. Dickinson	1888	Edwin M. Stanton	1860
Robert A. Lovett	1951	John Wanamaker	1889	Edward Bates	1861
Charles E. Wilson	1953	Wilson S. Bissell	1893	Titian J. Coffey	1863
Neil H. McElroy	1957	William L. Wilson	1895	James Speed	1864
Thomas S. Gates, Jr.	1959	James A. Gary	1897	Henry Stanbery	1866
Robert S. McNamara	1961	Charles E. Smith	1898	William M. Evarts	1868
Clark M. Clifford	1968	Henry C. Payne	1902	Ebenezer R. Hoar	1869
Melvin R. Laird	1969	Robert J. Wynne	1904	Amos T. Ackerman	1870
Elliot L. Richardson	1973	George B. Cortelyou	1905	George H. Williams	1871
James R. Schlesinger	1973	George von L. Meyer	1907	Edwards Pierrepont	1875
Donald Rumsfeld	1974	F. H. Hitchcock	1909	Alphonso Taft	1876
Harold Brown	1977	Albert S. Burleson	1913	Charles Devens	1877
Caspar Weinberger	1981	Will H. Hays	1921	Wayne MacVeagh	1881

Benjamin H. Brewster	1881
A. H. Garland	1885
William H. H. Miller	1889
Richard Olney	1893
Judson Harmon	1895
Joseph McKenna	1897
John W. Griggs	1897
Philander C. Knox	1901
William H. Moody	1904
Charles J. Bonaparte	1907
G. W. Wickersham	1909
J. C. McReynolds	1913
Thomas W. Gregory	1914
A. Mitchell Palmer	1919
H. M. Daugherty	1921
Harlan F. Stone	1924
John G. Sargent	1925
William D. Mitchell	1929
H. S. Cummings	1933
Frank Murphy	1939
Robert H. Jackson	1940
Francis Biddle	1941
Tom C. Clark	1945
J. H. McGrath	1949
J. P. McGranery	1952
H. Brownell, Jr.	1953
William P. Rogers	1957
Robert F. Kennedy	1961
Nicholas Katzenbach	1964
Ramsey Clark	1967
John N. Mitchell	1969
Richard G. Kleindienst	1972
Elliot L. Richardson	1973
William Saxbe	1974
Edward H. Levi	1974
Griffin B. Bell	1977
Benjamin R. Civiletti	1979
William French Smith	1981
Edwin A. Meese, III	1985
Richard Thornburgh	1988
William P. Barr	1992
Janet Reno	1993
John Ashcroft	2001

SECRETARY OF THE INTERIOR (1849–)

Thomas Ewing	1849
T. M. T. McKennan	1850
Alexander H. H. Stuart	1850
Robert McClelland	1853
Jacob Thompson	1857
Caleb B. Smith	1861
John P. Usher	1863
James Harlan	1865
O. H. Browning	1866
Jacob D. Cox	1869

Columbus Delano	1870
Zachariah Chandler	1875
Carl Schurz	1877
Samuel J. Kirkwood	1881
Henry M. Teller	1881
L. Q. C. Lamar	1885
William F. Vilas	1888
John W. Noble	1889
Hoke Smith	1893
David R. Francis	1896
Cornelius N. Bliss	1897
E. A. Hitchcock	1899
James R. Garfield	1907
R. A. Ballinger	1909
Walter L. Fisher	1911
Franklin K. Lane	1913
John B. Payne	1920
Albert B. Fall	1921
Hubert Work	1923
Roy O. West	1928
Ray L. Wilbur	1929
Harold L. Ickes	1933
Julius A. Krug	1946
Oscar L. Chapman	1949
Douglas McKay	1953
Fred A. Seaton	1956
Steward L. Udall	1961
Walter J. Hickel	1969
Rogers C. B. Morton	1971
Thomas S. Kleppe	1975
Cecil D. Andrus	1977
James G. Watt	1981
William P. Clark, Jr.	1983
Donald P. Hodel	1985
Manuel Lujan	1989
Bruce Babbit	1993
Gale Norton	2001

SECRETARY OF AGRICULTURE (1889–)

Norman J. Colman	1889
Jeremiah M. Rusk	1889
J. Sterling Morton	1893
James Wilson	1897
David F. Houston	1913
Edwin T. Meredith	1920
Henry C. Wallace	1921
Howard M. Gore	1924
William M. Jardine	1925
Arthur M. Hyde	1929
Henry A. Wallace	1933
Claude R. Wickard	1940
Clinton P. Anderson	1945
Charles F. Brannan	1948
Ezra Taft Benson	1953
Orville L. Freeman	1961

Clifford M. Hardin	1969
Earl L. Butz	1971
John A. Knebel	1976
Bob Bergland	1977
John R. Block	1981
Richard E. Lyng	1986
Clayton Yeutter	1989
Edward Madigan	1991
Mike Espy	1993
Dan Glickman	1995
Ann M. Veneman	2001

SECRETARY OF COMMERCE AND LABOR (1903–1913)

George B. Cortelyou	1903
Victor H. Metcalf	1904
Oscar S. Straus	1906
Charles Nagel	1909

SECRETARY OF COMMERCE (1913–)

William C. Redfield	1913
Joshua W. Alexander	1919
Herbert Hoover	1921
William F. Whiting	1928
Robert P. Lamont	1929
Roy D. Chapin	1932
Daniel C. Roper	1933
Henry L. Hopkins	1939
Jesse Jones	1940
Henry A. Wallace	1945
W. A. Harriman	1946
Charles Sawyer	1948
Sinclair Weeks	1953
Lewis L. Strauss	1958
F. H. Mueller	1959
Luther Hodges	1961
John T. Connor	1965
A. B. Trowbridge	1967
C. R. Smith	1968
Maurice H. Stans	1969
Peter G. Peterson	1972
Frederick B. Dent	1973
Elliot L. Richardson	1974
Juanita M. Kreps	1977
Philip M. Klutznick	1979
Malcolm Baldridge	1981
C. William Verity, Jr.	1987
Robert Mosbacher	1989
Ronald H. Brown	1993
Mickey Kantor	1996
William Daley	1997
Norman Y. Minela	2000
Don Evans	2001

SECRETARY OF LABOR
(1913–   )

William B. Wilson	1913
James J. Davis	1921
William N. Doak	1930
Frances Perkins	1933
L. B. Schwellenbach	1945
Maurice J. Tobin	1948
Martin P. Durkin	1953
James P. Mitchell	1953
Arthur J. Goldberg	1961
W. Willard Wirtz	1962
George P. Schultz	1969
James D. Hodgson	1970
Peter J. Brennan	1974
John T. Dunlop	1975
W. J. Usery, Jr.	1976
Ray Marshall	1977
Raymond J. Donovan	1981
Elizabeth Dole	1990
Lynn Martin	1991
Robert B. Reich	1993
Alexis Herman	1997
Elaine Chao	2001

SECRETARY OF HEALTH, EDUCATION, AND WELFARE
(1953–1979)

Oveta Culp Hobby	1953
Marion B. Folsom	1955
Arthur S. Flemming	1958
Abraham A. Ribicoff	1961
Anthony J. Celebrezze	1962
John W. Gardner	1965
Wilbur J. Cohen	1968
Robert H. Finch	1969
Elliot L. Richardson	1970
Caspar W. Weinberger	1973
Forrest D. Matthews	1974
Joseph A. Califano, Jr.	1977

SECRETARY OF HEALTH AND HUMAN SERVICES
(1979–   )

Patricia R. Harris	1979
Richard S. Schweiker	1981
Margaret Heckler	1983
Otis R. Bowen	1985
Louis W. Sullivan	1989
Donna E. Shalala	1993
Tommy Thompson	2001

SECRETARY OF HOUSING AND URBAN DEVELOPMENT
(1966–   )

Robert C. Weaver	1966
George W. Romney	1969
James T. Lynn	1973
Carla Anderson Hills	1974
Patricia Harris	1977
Moon Landrieu	1979
Samuel R. Pierce, Jr.	1981
Jack Kemp	1989
Henry G. Cisneros	1993
Andrew Cuomo	1997
Mel Martinez	2001

SECRETARY OF ENERGY
(1977–   )

James R. Schlesinger	1977
Charles W. Duncan, Jr.	1979
James B. Edwards	1981
Donald Hodel	1982
John S. Herrington	1985
James Watkins	1989
Hazel R. O'Leary	1993
Frederico Peña	1997
Bill Richardson	1998
Spencer Abraham	2001

SECRETARY OF TRANSPORTATION
(1967–   )

Alan S. Boyd	1967
John A. Volpe	1969
Claude S. Brinegar	1973
William T. Coleman	1975
Brock Adams	1977
Neil E. Goldschmidt	1979
Andrew L. Lewis, Jr.	1981
Elizabeth Dole	1983
James L. Burnley, IV	1987
Samuel Skinner	1989
Frederico Peña	1993
Rodney Slater	1997
Norman Y. Mineta	2001

SECRETARY OF EDUCATION (1979–   )

Shirley M. Hufstedler	1979
Terrel Bell	1981
William J. Bennett	1985
Lauro F. Cavozos	1988
Lamar Alexander	1991
Richard W. Riley	1993
Rod Paige	2001

SECRETARY OF VETERANS AFFAIRS
(1989–   )

Edward Derwinski	1989
Jesse Brown	1993
Togo D. West, Jr.	1998
Anthony Principi	2001

VICE PRESIDENT

John Adams	1789–97
Thomas Jefferson	1797–1801
Aaron Burr	1801–05
George Clinton	1805–13
Elbridge Gerry	1813–17
Daniel D. Tompkins	1817–25
John C. Calhoun	1825–33
Martin Van Buren	1833–37
Richard M. Johnson	1837–41
John Tyler	1841
George M. Dallas	1845–49
Millard Fillmore	1849–50
William R. King	1853–57
John C. Breckinridge	1857–61
Hannibal Hamlin	1861–65
Andrew Johnson	1865
Schuyler Colfax	1869–73
Henry Wilson	1873–77
William A. Wheeler	1877–81
Chester A. Arthur	1881
Thomas A. Hendricks	1885–89
Levi P. Morton	1889–93
Adlai E. Stevenson	1893–97
Garret A. Hobart	1897–1901
Theodore Roosevelt	1901
Charles W. Fairbanks	1905–09
James S. Sherman	1909–13
Thomas R. Marshall	1913–21
Calvin Coolidge	1921–23
Charles G. Dawes	1925–29
Charles Curtis	1929–33
John Nance Garner	1933–41
Henry A. Wallace	1941–45
Harry S Truman	1945
Alben W. Barkley	1949–53
Richard M. Nixon	1953–61
Lyndon B. Johnson	1961–63
Hubert H. Humphrey	1965–69
Spiro T. Agnew	1969–73
Gerald R. Ford	1973–74
Nelson A. Rockefeller	1974–77
Walter F. Mondale	1977–81
George Bush	1981–89
J. Danforth Quayle	1989–93
Al Gore	1993–00
Richard B. Cheney	2001–

Presidential Elections, 1789–2000

Year	Candidates	Party	Popular Vote		Electoral Vote
1789	**George Washington**				69
	John Adams				34
	Others				35
1792	**George Washington**				132
	John Adams				77
	George Clinton				50
	Others				5
1796	**John Adams**	Federalist			71
	Thomas Jefferson	Democratic-Republican			68
	Thomas Pinckney	Federalist			59
	Aaron Burr	Democratic-Republican			30
	Others				48
1800	**Thomas Jefferson**	Democratic-Republican			73
	Aaron Burr	Democratic-Republican			73
	John Adams	Federalist			65
	Charles C. Pinckney	Federalist			64
1804	**Thomas Jefferson**	Democratic-Republican			162
	Charles C. Pinckney	Federalist			14
1808	**James Madison**	Democratic-Republican			122
	Charles C. Pinckney	Federalist			47
	George Clinton	Independent-Republican			6
1812	**James Madison**	Democratic-Republican			128
	DeWitt Clinton	Federalist			89
1816	**James Monroe**	Democratic-Republican			183
	Rufus King	Federalist			34
1820	**James Monroe**	Democratic-Republican			231
	John Quincy Adams	Independent-Republican			1
1824	**John Quincy Adams**	Democratic-Republican	113,122	(30.9%)	84
	Andrew Jackson	Democratic-Republican	151,271	(41.3%)	99
	Henry Clay	Democratic-Republican	47,531	(12.9%)	37
	William H. Crawford	Democratic-Republican	40,856	(11.1%)	41
1828	**Andrew Jackson**	Democratic	642,553	(55.9%)	178
	John Quincy Adams	National Republican	500,897	(43.6%)	83
1832	**Andrew Jackson**	Democratic	701,780	(54.2%)	219
	Henry Clay	National Republican	484,205	(37.4%)	49
	William Wirt	Anti-Masonic	100,715	(7.7%)	7
1836	**Martin Van Buren**	Democratic	763,176	(50.8%)	170
	William H. Harrison	Whig	550,816	(36.6%)	73
	Hugh L. White	Whig	146,107	(9.7%)	26
	Daniel Webster	Whig	41,201	(2.7%)	14
1840	**William H. Harrison** **(John Tyler,** 1841)	Whig	1,275,390	(52.8%)	234
	Martin Van Buren	Democratic	1,128,854	(46.8%)	60

Year	Candidates	Party	Popular Vote		Electoral Vote
1844	**James K. Polk**	Democratic	1,339,494	(49.5%)	170
	Henry Clay	Whig	1,300,004	(48.0%)	105
	James G. Birney	Liberty	62,103	(2.3%)	
1848	**Zachary Taylor**	Whig	1,361,393	(47.2%)	163
	(Millard Fillmore, 1850)				
	Lewis Cass	Democratic	1,223,460	(42.4%)	127
	Martin Van Buren	Free Soil	291,501	(10.1%)	
1852	**Franklin Pierce**	Democratic	1,607,510	(50.8%)	254
	Winfield Scott	Whig	1,386,942	(43.8%)	42
1856	**James Buchanan**	Democratic	1,836,072	(45.2%)	174
	John C. Frémont	Republican	1,342,345	(33.1%)	114
	Millard Fillmore	American	873,053	(21.5%)	8
1860	**Abraham Lincoln**	Republican	1,865,908	(39.8%)	180
	Stephen A. Douglas	Democratic	1,382,202	(29.4%)	12
	John C. Breckinridge	Democratic	848,019	(18.0%)	72
	John Bell	Constitutional Union	591,901	(12.6%)	39
1864	**Abraham Lincoln**	Republican	2,218,388	(55.0%)	212
	(Andrew Johnson, 1865)				
	George B. McClellan	Democratic	1,812,807	(44.9%)	21
1868	**Ulysses S. Grant**	Republican	3,013,650	(52.6%)	214
	Horatio Seymour	Democratic	2,708,744	(47.3%)	80
1872	**Ulysses S. Grant**	Republican	3,598,235	(55.6%)	286
	Horace Greeley	Democratic	2,834,761	(43.8%)	66
1876	**Rutherford B. Hayes**	Republican	4,034,311	(47.9%)	185
	Samuel J. Tilden	Democratic	4,288,546	(50.0%)	184
1880	**James A. Garfield**	Republican	4,446,158	(48.2%)	214
	(Chester A. Arthur, 1881)				
	Winfield S. Hancock	Democratic	4,444,260	(48.2%)	155
	James B. Weaver	Greenback-Labor	305,997	(3.3%)	
1884	**Grover Cleveland**	Democratic	4,874,621	(48.5%)	219
	James G. Blaine	Republican	4,848,936	(48.2%)	182
	Benjamin F. Butler	Greenback-Labor	175,096	(1.7%)	
1888	**Benjamin Harrison**	Republican	5,443,892	(47.8%)	233
	Grover Cleveland	Democratic	5,534,488	(48.6%)	168
1892	**Grover Cleveland**	Democratic	5,551,883	(46.0%)	277
	Benjamin Harrison	Republican	5,179,244	(42.9%)	145
	James B. Weaver	People's	1,024,280	(8.5%)	22
1896	**William McKinley**	Republican	7,108,480	(51.0%)	271
	William J. Bryan	Democratic; Populist	6,511,495	(46.7%)	176
1900	**William McKinley**	Republican	7,218,039	(51.6%)	292
	(Theodore Roosevelt, 1901)				
	William J. Bryan	Democratic; Populist	6,358,345	(45.5%)	155

Year	Candidates	Party	Popular Vote		Electoral Vote
1904	**Theodore Roosevelt**	Republican	7,626,593	(56.4%)	336
	Alton B. Parker	Democratic	5,082,898	(37.6%)	140
	Eugene V. Debs	Socialist	402,489	(2.9%)	
1908	**William H. Taft**	Republican	7,676,258	(51.5%)	321
	William J. Bryan	Democratic	6,406,801	(43.0%)	162
	Eugene V. Debs	Socialist	420,380	(2.8%)	
1912	**Woodrow Wilson**	Democratic	6,293,152	(41.8%)	435
	Theodore Roosevelt	Progressive	4,119,207	(27.3%)	88
	William H. Taft	Republican	3,486,383	(23.1%)	8
	Eugene V. Debs	Socialist	900,369	(5.9%)	
1916	**Woodrow Wilson**	Democratic	9,126,300	(49.2%)	277
	Charles E. Hughes	Republican	8,546,789	(46.1%)	254
1920	**Warren G. Harding** **(Calvin Coolidge,** 1923)	Republican	16,133,314	(60.3%)	404
	James M. Cox	Democratic	9,140,884	(34.1%)	127
	Eugene V. Debs	Socialist	913,664	(3.4%)	
1924	**Calvin Coolidge**	Republican	15,717,553	(54.0%)	382
	John W. Davis	Democratic	8,386,169	(28.8%)	136
	Robert M. La Follette	Progressive	4,814,050	(16.5%)	13
1928	**Herbert C. Hoover**	Republican	21,411,991	(58.2%)	444
	Alfred E. Smith	Democratic	15,000,185	(40.7%)	87
1932	**Franklin D. Roosevelt**	Democratic	22,825,016	(57.4%)	472
	Herbert C. Hoover	Republican	15,758,397	(39.6%)	59
	Norman Thomas	Socialist	883,990	(2.2%)	
1936	**Franklin D. Roosevelt**	Democratic	27,747,636	(60.7%)	523
	Alfred M. Landon	Republican	16,679,543	(36.5%)	8
	William Lemke	Union	892,492	(1.9%)	
1940	**Franklin D. Roosevelt**	Democratic	27,263,448	(54.7%)	449
	Wendell L. Willkie	Republican	22,336,260	(44.8%)	82
1944	**Franklin D. Roosevelt** **(Harry S Truman,** 1945)	Democratic	25,611,936	(53.3%)	432
	Thomas E. Dewey	Republican	22,013,372	(45.8%)	99
1948	**Harry S Truman**	Democratic	24,105,587	(49.5%)	303
	Thomas E. Dewey	Republican	21,970,017	(45.1%)	189
	J. Strom Thurmond	States' Rights	1,169,134	(2.4%)	39
	Henry A. Wallace	Progressive	1,157,057	(2.3%)	
1952	**Dwight D. Eisenhower**	Republican	33,936,137	(55.1%)	442
	Adlai E. Stevenson	Democratic	27,314,649	(44.3%)	89
1956	**Dwight D. Eisenhower**	Republican	35,585,245	(57.3%)	457
	Adlai F. Stevenson	Democratic	26,030,172	(41.9%)	73
1960	**John F. Kennedy** **(Lyndon B. Johnson,** 1963)	Democratic	34,221,344	(49.7%)	303
	Richard M. Nixon	Republican	34,106,671	(49.5%)	219

Year	Candidates	Party	Popular Vote		Electoral Vote
1964	**Lyndon B. Johnson**	Democratic	43,126,584	(61.0%)	486
	Barry M. Goldwater	Republican	27,177,838	(38.4%)	52
1968	**Richard M. Nixon**	Republican	31,783,148	(43.4%)	301
	Hubert H. Humphrey	Democratic	31,274,503	(42.7%)	191
	George C. Wallace	Amer. Independent	9,901,151	(13.5%)	46
1972	**Richard M. Nixon**	Republican	47,170,179	(60.6%)	520
	George S. McGovern	Democratic	29,171,791	(37.5%)	17
1974	**Gerald R. Ford**	Republican	Appointed on August 9, 1974, as President after the resignation of Richard M. Nixon.		
1976	**Jimmy Carter**	Democratic	40,828,587	(50.1%)	297
	Gerald R. Ford	Republican	39,147,613	(48.0%)	240
1980	**Ronald Reagan**	Republican	43,899,248	(50.7%)	489
	Jimmy Carter	Democratic	35,481,435	(41.0%)	49
	John Anderson	Independent	5,719,437	(6.6%)	
	Ed Clark	Libertarian	920,859	(1.0%)	
1984	**Ronald Reagan**	Republican	54,451,521	(58.8%)	525
	Walter F. Mondale	Democratic	37,565,334	(40.5%)	13
1988	**George H. Bush**	Republican	47,946,422	(54.0%)	426
	Michael S. Dukakis	Democratic	41,016,429	(46.0%)	112
1992	**Bill Clinton**	Democratic	43,682,624	(43.2%)	378
	George H. Bush	Republican	38,117,331	(37.7%)	168
	H. Ross Perot	Independent	19,217,212	(19.0%)	0
1996	**Bill Clinton**	Democratic	45,628,667	(49.9%)	379
	Robert Dole	Republican	37,869,435	(41.5%)	159
	H. Ross Perot	Independent	7,874,283	(8.6%)	0
2000	**George W. Bush**	Republican	50,465,169	(47.9%)	271
	Albert Gore	Democrat	50,996,062	(48.4%)	266
	Ralph Nader	Independent	2,529,871	(2.1%)	0
	Patrick Buchanan	Independent	323,950	(.4%)	0

INDEX

A

capitalism—*(continued)*
    economy, 835–836; Reagan cham-
      pioned, 819; seeking a higher pur-
      pose for, 595
Capitalist System, Pyramid of the, 486
Capitol, burned in War of 1812, 248;
      presidential inaugurations, 225, 349
Capone, Al, 618
Capra, Frank, 650
caravela redonda, 14–15
caravels, 34
carbon dioxide pollution, 861
carbon monoxide pollution, 868
Carey, Matthew, 260
caribou hunters, 19–20
Carlisle Commission, 166
Carlisle School, 528
Carmichael, Stokely, 767–768
Carnegie, Andrew, 518–520, 584, 589
Carnegie Endowment, 718
Carnegie Institute of Technology, 520
Carolina colony, 95. *See also* North Car-
    olina; South Carolina
Caroline, 364
carpetbaggers, 469
Carranza, Venustiano, 598
cars. *See* automobile
Carson, Kit, 385
Carson, Rachel, 867
Carson National Forest, 865
Carter, President James E., 814–816,
    871
Carteret, Sir George, 90
Cartier, Jacques, 52–53
Cartwright, Peter, 328
Casablanca meeting (WW II), 697
Casals, Pablo, 586
Casey, William (CIA dir., Reagan),
    821–822
Cash, Johnny, 734
Cass, Sen. Lewis (MI), 388–389
Castlereagh, Robert, 257
Castro, Fidel, 584, 742, 757–759
Castro, José, (gov. California), 384
Catawba Indians, 124–125
Catcher in the Rye, 735
Catlin, George, 503
Catt, Carrie Chapman, 560, 607–608
cattle ranching, 43, 95, 490–491, 514,
    863
cavaliers, English Civil War, 81
Cayuga, 24, 176
Ceaucescu, Nicolai, 824
Cedar Creek, Battle of, 444
census bureau, 508
Centennial Exposition of 1876, 483–484
Central America, immigration from,
    833; independence from Spain,
    258; United Fruit dominated, 630
Central Intelligence Agency (CIA),
    agency created, 712; assassination

attempts, Castro, 758; Cambodian
    govt. overthrown, 791; Chilean
    govt. overthrown, 812; Cuba inva-
    sion, 757; George Bush director,
    817; Guatemala govt. overthrown,
    738; Iran-Contra, 821–822; Iranian
    govt. overthrown, 738, 815; liberals
    attracted to, 786–787; overesti-
    mated USSR, 817; used to thwart
    FBI, 806; Watergate, 802, 806
Chaco Canyon, 23
chain stores, 522, 568
Chamberlain, Col. Joshua Lawrence,
    437
Chamberlain, Neville, 683
Chambers, Whittaker, 717–721
Chamorro, Violeta Barrios de, 825
Champlain, Samuel de, 54
Chancellorsville, Battle of, 437
Chaney, James, 766
Channing, Rev. William Ellery, 326,
    333, 383
Chapultepec, Battle of (1847), 385–386
Chardon, Francis, 4
Charles I, King of England, 74, 90, 81,
    145
Charles II, King of England, 81, 90–92
Charles Town, SC. *See* Charleston, SC
Charles V, King of Spain, 58
Charleston and Hamburg Line, 292
Charleston, SC, in American Revolu-
    tion, 170, 173; Civil War begins at,
    423; competition with New York,
    292; embargo of 1807, 240; port in
    1800, 227–228; slave revolt, 3, 266
Charlot, 532
Chase, Salmon P., rep. OH, 405; sec. of
    treas. (Lincoln), 431, 435
Chase, Samuel (Sup. Ct. justice), 231
Château-Thierry battle, 608, 610
Chattanooga, Battle for, 440
Chauncey, Isaac, 245, 247–248
Chautauqua, 566
Chávez, César, 770, 810
Cheney, Vice President Richard, 847,
    854
Cherokee, 20, 227, 355–356, 833;
    attacked in South Carolina, 133;
    support for British in Am. Rev.,
    177; written language and constitu-
    tion, 231–232
Cherokee Nation v. *Georgia*, 355
Chesapeake (USS), 239–240, 244, 247
Chesapeake and Ohio Canal, 291
Chesapeake Bay colonies, 66–67, 69–11
Chesnut, Mary, 415
Cheves, Langdon, 260
Cheyenne, Battle of Little Big Horn,
    484; defeats in 1877, 484; devas-
    tated, 497, 499
Chiang Kai–shek, 686, 695, 705, 713

Chicago, African American migration
    to, 620; Democratic convention
    1968, 775–777, 790; fugitive slave
    law denounced, 396; immigration
    to, 553; as industrial center, 490;
    labor in, 549–551; meatpacking
    industry, 516, 566; neighborhoods,
    551; and poetry of Carl Sandburg,
    624, 864; race riots 1919, 621; ten-
    ements created in, 526; World's
    Fair of 1893, 513–515
Chicago Eight trial, 795
Chickamauga Creek, Battle of, 440
Chickasaw, 227, 231–232, 235, 355
Chicken, Captain George, 124
chicken pox, 31
Chicora, 46
Chief Joseph (Nez Percé), 498–499
child labor, 295, 522–523, 526, 566,
    588–589, 591, 596, 597, 667
childhood diseases, 31–32
children, colonial New England, 82;
    criminal law, 588; job safety laws,
    588; suburbs and, 730–731
Children's Bureau, 594–595
"Children's Crusade Against Commu-
    nism," 715
China, communists win civil war, 713;
    creation story, 2; Cultural Revolu-
    tion in, 795; empire of, 9–10; and
    free-market economics, 825; ice
    exported to, 254; immigration from,
    398, 832–833, 495, 525, 554,
    808–809; Japanese invasion of,
    682; Kissinger visit 1972, 811–812;
    Korean War entry, 727–728; navy
    in 1492, 9; Nixon's accommodation
    with, 801, 811–812; under Open
    Door Policy, 584–585; Tiananmen
    Square protests, 824–825; trade
    routes to Italy 1200s, 29; trade with
    U.S., first treaty, 382; U.S. agree-
    ments with Japan, 594; U.S. policy
    toward communists, 739; Western
    exploitation, 585; in WW II, 695
chinampas, 44
Chinese Americans, building transconti-
    nental railroad, 488; fraternal
    organization, 556; industrial
    employment, 525; as laborers, 3;
    legal discrimination against, 398,
    499, 506; and prostitution, 4; riots
    against, 488
Chinese Exclusion Act of 1882, 488
Chinook, 365
Chippewa, 231
Choctaw, 227, 231–232, 235, 250, 355
cholera epidemics, 375, 379–381
Chou En-Lai, 811
Christian socialism, 530
Christianity, in America before Civil

8

Mohawk River Valley, commercial navigation, 289; settlement of, 263–264
Mohegan, 80
Molasses Act of 1733, 110
Molly Maguires, 518
molybdenum mining, 493
Mondale, Walter, presidential candidate 1984, 820; vice president, 817
monetary policy, 506
money wiring, 294
Mongols, 9–11
Monitor, 429
Monk, Maria, 399
Monmouth, Battle of, 170
monopolies, 487, 519, 533–534, 559, 596
Monroe, Bill, 734
Monroe Doctrine, 257–258, 579, 581; Roosevelt Corollary, 592; Roosevelt Corollary abandoned, 680
Monroe, James, congr. VA, 186; Louisiana Purchase negotiator, 234; president, 257; sec. of war, Madison, 257; ties to John Marshall, 230; Virginia dynasty of presidents, 256
Montana, dust storms 1930s, 637–638; first woman to Congress, 607; statehood, 506
Montauk, 90
Montcalm, Marquis de, 129–131
Monte Cassino, Battle of, 698
Monte Verde, Chile, prehistoric site, 8
Montes, Pedro, 280
Montgomery, AL, bus boycott, 748–749; confederate capital, 421, 423
Monticello, 223
Montreal, Battle of, 155
Montreal Protocols, 870
Moody, Anne, 745–746
Mooney, Tom, 612
moose hunters, 19–20
Moratorium (Vietnam War protest), 786
Moravian Church, 91
More, Thomas, 307
Morgan, Daniel, 171–172
Morgan, Edmund, 84
Morgan, J. P., 519, 559, 589
Morgan, John Hunt, 438
Morgan, William, 278
Mormon, Book of, 321
Mormons, 320–323, 380, 482, 500, 506
Morrill, Rep. Justin (VT), 431
Morris, Robert, 182
Morse, Samuel F.B., 293
Morton, Thomas, 73
Moses, Robert Parris, 764–765
Mossadegh, Mohammed, 738
motel growth due to auto, 628

Mother Earth, 612
Mother of Corn, 22
motherhood, 730–731
Motown Records, 735
Mott, James, 343
Mott, Lucretia, 343
Mount Holyoke Female Seminary, 343, 345
Mount Suribachi, 705
Mount Vernon, 200
Mountain Men, 372–373
Mourning Dove, 625
movies, 566–567
muckrakers, 566
Muhammad, 12
Muhammad, Elijah, 767
Muir, John, 503, 575–577, 865, 868
mulatto, 833
Muller v. *Oregon*, 588
mumps, 31
Munich Agreement, 683
Munn v. *Illinois,* 533
Murrah federal building bombed, 843–844
Murray, Charles Augustus, 262
Murray, William Vans, minister to France (Adams), 217
Murrow, Edward R., McCarthy exposé, 726; WW II radio broadcasts, 685
Museum of Modern Art, 733
Musharraf, Gen. Pervez, 852
muskets, 85
Muskogean, 23
Muslims, Kosovo, 839–840; Pres. Bush met with, 2001, 851; Spanish, 35; Yugoslavia, 836–837. *See also* Islam
Mussolini, Benito, 681–682; dismissed from Italian government, 698; hanged by partisans, 703
mutilation, 331
mutiny, Continental Army, 182; merchant ships, 304
mutual benefit societies, 523
My Lai massacre, 792–793
myths, 6–7

N

Nacht und Nebel (Watergate), 801
Na-Dene, 6
Nader Ralph, 845–847
Nagasaki (atom bomb dropped), 705–706
Nahuatl, 41
Nanking, rape of, 682
Nantucket, MA, whaling, 305
napalm, 783
Napoleon. *See* Bonaparte
narcotics trafficking, 841
Narragansett, 75–76, 78, 80, 85

Nárvaez, Pánfilo de, 46
Nashville, TN, capture by U.S. army, 426
Nasser, Gamel Abdel, 740
Nast, Thomas, 589
Nat Turner's rebellion, 334, 336
Natick, 78
Nation of Islam, 767
National Aeronautics and Space Administration, 760
National American Woman Suffrage Association, 560, 608
National Association for the Advancement of Colored People (NAACP), 546, 564–565, 568, 620, 623, 672, 715, 748, 765
National Association of Manufacturers, 632
national bank (Whig Party platform), 361, 376. *See also* Bank of the United States
National Banking Act of 1863, 432, 435
national capital for U.S., 205, 218. *See also* Washington, DC
National Congress of American Indians (NCAI), 736, 768, 770–771
National Consumers' League, 523
national debt, 835
National Defense Education Act of 1958, 741
National Endowment for the Arts, 772
National Environmental Policy Act (1970), 812
National Era, 403
National Farm Workers Association, 770
national forests, 532
National Gazette, 206
national identity, 184–185, 250, 514, 622–623, 641, 872
National Indian Youth Council, 810
National Industrial Recovery Act, 648, 663
National Labor Relations Act (NLRA), 648
National Labor Relations Board (NLRB), 818
National Labor Union, 523
National League (baseball), 504
National Organization for Women, 807
National Recovery Administration, 648
National Republicans, 277, 431
National Road, 259, 286, 289
National Security Act of 1947, 712
National Security Council, 712–713
National War Labor Board, WW I, 607; WW II, 688
National Woman Suffrage Association, 472, 501
National Youth Administration, 648, 673, 771